HISTORICAL INTRODUCTION
TO THE STUDY OF
ROMAN LAW

By

H. F. JOLOWICZ, M.A., LL.M.

Of the Inner Temple, Barrister-at-law;
Professor of Roman Law in the
University of London

1994 REPRINT

WM. W. GAUNT & SONS, INC.

WM. W. GAUNT & SONS, INC.

International Standard Book Number: 1-56169-072-4

Library of Congress Catalog Number: 93-79714

NOTICE

Printed and bound in the United States of America.

∞ The paper used in this publication meets the requirements of the American National Standard for Permanence of Paper for Printed Library Materials Z39.48-1984.

Reprint 1994

WM. W. GAUNT & SONS, INC.
Gaunt Building
3011 Gulf Drive
Holmes Beach, Florida 34217-2199
U.S.A.

HISTORICAL INTRODUCTION
TO THE STUDY OF
ROMAN LAW

LONDON
Cambridge University Press
FETTER LANE

NEW YORK · TORONTO
BOMBAY · CALCUTTA · MADRAS
Macmillan

TOKYO
Maruzen Company Ltd

HISTORICAL INTRODUCTION
TO THE STUDY OF
ROMAN LAW

By

H. F. JOLOWICZ, M.A., LL.M.

Of the Inner Temple, Barrister-at-law;
Professor of Roman Law in the
University of London

CAMBRIDGE
AT THE UNIVERSITY PRESS
1932

CONTENTS

CHAPTER I

Periods in the history of Rome and in the history of her Law

CHAPTER II

The Republican Constitution

CHAPTER III

Italy and the Provinces during the Republic

CHAPTER IV

Social conditions and the different classes of the population during the Republic

CHAPTER V

Sources of law in the Republic

CHAPTER VI

Law for foreigners, *ius gentium* and *ius naturale*

CHAPTER VII

The XII Tables

CHAPTER VIII

The law of the family and of succession at the time of the XII Tables

CHAPTER IX

Slavery and manumission at the time of the XII Tables   135

CHAPTER X

The law of property at the time of the XII Tables

CHAPTER XI

The law of obligations at the time of
the XII Tables

CHAPTER XV

Private law from the XII Tables to the Fall of the
Republic: the law of slavery and manumission

CHAPTER XVI

Private law from the XII Tables to the Fall of the
Republic: the law of property

CONTENTS

PREFACE

This book is intended, in a sense, to provide a version of *Hamlet* without the Prince of Denmark. The central subject of Roman legal studies must remain the private law of classical and later times, but an historical background has always been necessary, and is even more so now that the new problems discussed by modern authors are mainly of an historical rather than a dogmatic nature. My object has therefore been to supplement Professor Buckland's *Text-book* and *Manual* from this point of view, and to give the student what he needs to know about Roman law rather than the Roman law itself. The main emphasis is on the sources of law and the constitutional developments without which the nature of the sources cannot be understood, but I have tried in addition to explain procedure and to give an idea of the judicial structure. It seemed also that for the republican period it was possible to give some account of the state of our knowledge without explaining or presupposing the institutions of the developed law in any detail, and thus to portray the foundations on which the later edifice was built. No attempt has been made to avoid controversial topics, because in these studies controversy is the breath of life, and there is often more to be learnt from an appreciation of opposing theories than from an acknowledged fact.

The text is meant to be intelligible to any reader, even if he has no previous acquaintance with the subject, but the notes in some cases contain discussion which is not entirely self-explanatory, though it is hoped that they are not such as to make the beginner's study of the text itself any more difficult. The table of dates has purposely been kept very short. It is intended not so much to provide information as to be used for quick reference when a reader who has little historical knowledge finds difficulty in fixing the different periods in his mind.

My debt to previous literature, including general text-books, is obvious from the references, but personal assistance cannot be acknowledged in footnotes, and my warm gratitude is due to several friends. Professor Buckland read through the whole manuscript, part of it indeed twice over, and I have also to thank him for allowing me to see the proofs of the second edition of his *Text-book* for the purpose of altering my references to it. He, as well as Professor Norman Baynes and Professor de Zulueta, who each read a large part of the manuscript, made a great number of valuable suggestions and I need hardly say how much I appreciate help from scholars of their rank. My wife, though her own studies lie in a very different sphere, helped me, not only by compiling the index, but in innumerable other ways.

The kindness, competence and vigilance of the Secretary and Staff of the Cambridge University Press I now know by experience as well as by repute, and I would like to express my sincerest thanks to them.

H. F. J.

LONDON
July 1932

DATES

MONARCHY

B.C. 753   Foundation of Rome.

510   Expulsion of the Tarquins.

REPUBLIC

451–450 Compilation of Twelve Tables.

445   *Leges Canuleiae.*

367   *Leges Liciniae Sextiae.*
      Admission of Plebeians to Consulate.
      Institution of Praetorship.

338   Dissolution of Latin League.

304   *Ius Flavianum.*

300   *Lex Ogulnia.*
      Admission of Plebeians to Pontificate.

287   *Lex Hortensia.*
      Final equation of *plebiscita* with *leges.*

252   Ti. Coruncanius first plebeian *Pontifex Maximus.*

242 (about) Institution of Peregrine Praetorship.

241   First Province (Sicily).

123–122 Tribunate of C. Gracchus.

82–79   Dictatorship of Sulla.

44   Assassination of Caesar.

31   Battle of Actium.

PRINCIPATE

27   Augustus regularises his power.

A.D. 14   Death of Augustus.

Earlier Classical Period of Law

117–138 Reign of Hadrian.

138–161 Reign of Antoninus Pius.

161   Institutes of Gaius.

161–172 Reign of M. Aurelius and L. Verus (*Divi Fratres*).

172–180 Reign of M. Aurelius alone.

Later Classical Period of Law

A.D. 193–211 Reign of Septimius Severus.

211–217 Reign of Caracalla (Antoninus).

212 *Constitutio Antoniniana.*

222–235 Reign of Alexander Severus.

DOMINATE

284–305 Reign of Diocletian.

312 Conversion of Constantine the Great.

395 Death of Theodosius the Great.
Division of the Empire.

438 *Codex Theodosianus.*

476 End of Western Empire.

527–565 Reign of Justinian.

ABBREVIATIONS

B.: Basilica (*v*. Heimbach).

B.G.U.: Berliner Griechische Urkunden (Aegyptische Urkunden aus den kgl. Museen zu Berlin, Griech. Urk.), 1895- .

B.I.D.R.: Bullettino dell' Istituto di Diritto Romano.

Beseler: Beiträge zur Kritik der römischen Rechtsquellen, G. Beseler, Parts I–IV, 1910–1920.

Bethmann-Hollweg, or B.-H.: Der römische Zivilprozess, Bethmann-Hollweg, I–III, 1864–1866.

Bonfante: Histoire du Droit Romain traduite sur la 3e Éd. 1928.

St. Bonfante: Studi in Onore di Pietro Bonfante, 1930.

Boyé, Denuntiatio: La Denuntiatio Introductive d'Instance sous le Principat, A.-J. Boyé, 1922.

Bruns: Fontes Iuris Romani Antiqui, C. G. Bruns, 7th Ed. O. Gradenwitz, 1909.

Buckland: Text-book of Roman Law from Augustus to Justinian, W. W. Buckland, 2nd Ed. 1932.

—— Main Institutions: Main Institutions of Roman Private Law, W. W. Buckland, 1931.

—— Manual: Manual of Roman Private Law, W. W. Buckland, 1925.

C.: Code of Justinian.

C.I.L.: Corpus Inscriptionum Latinarum.

C. Th.: Codex Theodosianus.

Coll.: Collatio Legum Mosaicarum et Romanarum.

Collinet, Ét. Hist.: Études Historiques sur le Droit de Justinien, P. Collinet, Vol. I, 1912; Vol. II, 1925.

Mél. Cornil: Mélanges de Droit Romain dédiés à G. Cornil, 1926.

Costa, Profilo: Profilo Storico del Processo Civile Romano, E. Costa, 1918.

—— Storia: Storia del Diritto Romano Privato, E. Costa, 2nd Ed. 1925.

Cuq: Manuel des Institutions juridiques des Romains, E. Cuq, 1917.

D.: Digest of Justinian.

Fr. Vat.: Fragmenta Vaticana.

de Francisci: Storia del Diritto Romano, P. de Francisci, Vol. I, 1926; Vol. II, Parte I, 1929.

Gai.: Gaius.

Girard: Manuel Élémentaire de Droit Romain, P. F. Girard, 8ème Éd. 1929.

—— Mélanges: Mélanges de Droit Romain, P. F. Girard, Tome I, 1912; Tome II, 1923.

—— Textes: Textes de Droit Romain, P. F. Girard, 5ème Éd. 1923.

—— Organisation Judiciaire: Histoire de l'Organisation Judiciaire des Romains, P. F. Girard, 1901.

Greenidge: Roman Public Life, A. H. J. Greenidge, 1901.

H.A.: Historia Augusta.

H.-S. or Heumann-Seckel: Heumanns Handlexicon zu den Quellen des römischen Rechts, 9te Aufl. von E. Seckel, 1907.

Heimbach: Basilicorum libri LX, Ed. G. E. Heimbach, 1833–1870.

Holdsworth, H.E.L.: A History of English Law, W. S. Holdsworth, 3rd Ed. 1922–1926.

J.: Institutes of Justinian.

Jhering, Geist: Geist des römischen Rechts, R. von Jhering, Bände I, II, I, 2, 5te Aufl. 1891–1899.

Jobbé-Duval: Études sur l'histoire de la procédure civile chez les Romains, É. Jobbé-Duval, 1896.

Jörs: Geschichte und System des römischen Privatrechts (nebst Abriss des römischen Zivilprozessrechts von L. Wenger), P. Jörs, 1927.

Karlowa: Römische Rechtsgeschichte, O. Karlowa, Band I, 1885; Band II, 1901.

Kipp: Geschichte der Quellen des römischen Rechts, Th. Kipp, 4te Aufl. 1919.

Krüger: Geschichte der Quellen und Litteratur des römischen Rechts, P. Krüger, 2te Aufl. 1912.

Kübler: Geschichte des römischen Rechts, B. Kübler, 1925.

Lenel: Geschichte und Quellen des römischen Rechts, in Holtzendorffs Enzyklopädie der Rechtswissenschaft, Band I, 7te Aufl. 1915.

—— E. P.: Das Edictum Perpetuum, Otto Lenel, 3te Aufl. 1927.

Lipsius: Das attische Recht und Rechtsverfahren, J. H. Lipsius, 1915.

v. Mayr: Römische Rechtsgeschichte, R. von Mayr, 1912–1913.

Mitteis, Chrest.: Grundzüge und Chrestomathie der Papyruskunde, L. Mitteis und U. Wilcken, 2er Band (Juristischer Teil), 2te Hälfte, Chrestomathie, 1912.

—— Grundzüge: Ibid. 2er Band, 1te Hälfte.

—— Reichsr.: Reichsrecht und Volksrecht in den östlichen Provinzen des römischen Kaiserreichs, L. Mitteis, 1891.

—— R.P.R.: Römisches Privatrecht bis auf die Zeit Diokletians, L. Mitteis, Vol. I, 1908.

Mommsen, Abriss: Abriss des römischen Staatsrechts, Th. Mommsen, 2te Aufl. 1907.

—— Ges. Schr.: Gesammelte Schriften, Th. Mommsen, 8 Bände, 1905–1913.

—— Staatsr.: Römisches Staatsrecht, Th. Mommsen, 3te Aufl. 1887–1888.

—— Strafr.: Römisches Strafrecht, Th. Mommsen, 1899.

N.R.H.: Nouvelle Revue Historique de Droit français et étranger, terminating 1921, continued as Revue Historique de Droit français et étranger. (R.H.)

P. Giess.: Griechische Papyri zu Giessen, I, Ed. by E. Kornemann and P. M. Meyer, 1910–1912.

P. Hal.: Dikaiomata: Auszüge aus alexandrinischen Gesetzen und Verordnungen in einem Papyrus des philologischen Seminars der Universität Halle (Pap. Hal. 1), herausgegeben von der Graeca Halensis, Berlin, 1913.

P. Oxy.: The Oxyrrhynchos Papyri, Ed. by Grenfell and Hunt, 1898–

P.-W.: Paulys Realenzyklopädie der classischen Altertumswissenschaft, neue
Bearbeitung, Ed. G. Wissowa, 1894–   .

Pais, Ricerche: Ricerche sulla storia e sul diritto pubblico di Roma, E. Pais,
Serie I, 1915; Serie IV, 1921.

Partsch, Schriftformel: Die Schriftformel im römischen Provinzialprozess,
J. Partsch, 1905.

Pringsheim, Kauf: Der Kauf mit fremdem Geld, F. Pringsheim, 1916.

R.H.: v. N.R.H.

Rabel: Grundzüge des römischen Privatrechts, E. Rabel, in Holtzendorffs
Enzyklopädie der Rechtswissenschaft, Band I, 7te Aufl. 1915.

Riccobono, Dal d. r.: Dal diritto romano classico al diritto moderno, S. Riccobono, Annali del Sem. Giur. di Palermo, III–IV, 1917.

—— Fontes: Fontes Iuris Romani Anteiustiniani, Ed. S. Riccobono, J.
Baviera, C. Ferrini, 1909.

—— Punti: Punti di vista critici e ricostruttivi a proposito della dissertazione
di L. Mitteis, S. Riccobono, Annali del Sem. Giur. di Palermo, XII,
1928.

Rostovtzeff, or Rostovtzeff, Economic History: The Social and Economic
History of the Roman Empire, M. Rostovtzeff, 1926.

Rotondi, Scr. Giur.: Scritti Giuridici, G. Rotondi, Vols. I–III, 1922.

Siber: Römisches Recht, H. Siber, Vol. II, Römisches Privatrecht, 1928.

Sohm: Institutionen, Geschichte und System des römischen Privatrechts,
R. Sohm, 17te Aufl. 1926.

Stein, Geschichte: Geschichte des spätrömischen Reiches, E. Stein, Band I,
1928.

Strachan-Davidson: Problems of the Roman Criminal Law, J. L. Strachan-
Davidson, 1912.

Tenney Frank: Economic History of Rome, Tenney Frank, 2nd Ed. 1927.

Ulp. or Ulp. Reg.: Ulpiani liber singularis regularum.

Vinogradoff, Hist. Jurisp.: Outlines of Historical Jurisprudence, P. Vinogradoff, Vol. I, 1920; Vol. II, 1922.

Wenger: Institutionen des römischen Zivilprozessrechts, L. Wenger, 1925.

Willems: Droit Public Romain, P. Willems, 7me Éd.

Windscheid-Kipp: Lehrbuch des Pandektenrechts, B. Windscheid, 9te Aufl.
Th. Kipp, 1906.

Wlassak, Prozessformel: Die klassische Prozessformel, 1er Teil, M. Wlassak,
1924.

—— Prozessgesetze: Römische Prozessgesetze, M. Wlassak, Band I, 1888;
Band II, 1891.

Z.S.S.: Zeitschrift der Savigny-Stiftung für Rechtsgeschichte, Romanistische
Abteilung.

Chapter I

PERIODS IN THE HISTORY OF ROME AND IN THE HISTORY OF HER LAW

§ I. PERIODS IN HISTORY

The history of Rome is commonly treated in three great divisions corresponding to the different forms of government which prevailed—the Monarchy, the Republic and the Empire. These main divisions may be subdivided in different ways. Mommsen,[1] whose great history reaches only down to the fall of the republic, divides his work into five periods. Of these, the first stretches from the earliest times down to the abolition of the kingship. The ancient historians[2] have a good deal to tell us of this period, the names and characters, for instance, of the seven kings, beginning with Romulus, who is said to have founded the city in the year 753 B.C., and ending with Tarquinius Superbus, whose tyrannical conduct led to the abolition of the monarchy. In modern times, however, most of what the ancient historians have to tell us about the regal period is discredited. They all of them lived long after the events which they described, in an age when the sifting of evidence was not considered the historian's chief duty, and it is thought now that much of what they wrote down as history of the earliest times is, as regards detail, no more authentic than the story of King Alfred and the burnt cakes. The tradition on which they built is nevertheless valuable for all conjectures concerning the general conditions prevailing in the earliest days of Rome.

The next of Mommsen's periods runs from the abolition of the monarchy (traditional date 510 B.C.) until the unification of Italy. When she first appears in history, Rome is a small city-state, but already occupies a pre-eminent position in the confederation of kindred city-states known as the Latin League.[3] The relationship between Rome and her confederates was not always that of peace, but in the wars against the Latins it was Rome who was finally successful, as she was also, but only after centuries of hard fighting, against the other nations of Italy. The last great war of

---

[1] *Römische Geschichte*, 9th ed. Berlin, 1903; English translation by Dickson, 2nd ed. London, 1868.

[2] In particular Livy (59 B.C.–A.D. 17) and Dionysius of Halicarnassus (*c.* 25 B.C.).

[3] *Infra*, 56.

this period was one in which the Greek city of Tarentum in South Italy (where there were many Greek colonies) was allied with a non-Italian power in the person of Pyrrhus, king of Epirus. With the final defeat of Pyrrhus in 275 B.C., the conquest of Italy was virtually complete. Roman colonies[1] had been planted at most of the points of strategic importance, and of her late enemies, some were forced to accept direct Roman rule, while others were bound by treaties in which Rome was so much the predominant partner that they were, in fact, under her dominion. They could have no treaties with other foreign states and were bound to supply contingents to serve with the Roman armies.

The internal history of Rome during this period was hardly quieter than her external history, being taken up mainly by the "struggle between the orders", i.e. between the patricians and plebeians. The patricians were the nobility or privileged citizens, the plebeians the unprivileged citizens, and the struggle was that of the plebeians for political equality. Originally unable to intermarry with patricians and excluded from all high offices, both civil and religious, the plebeians finally succeeded in obtaining all the political privileges which they had made their object, but the last act in the drama was not played until the year 287 B.C.[2]

The third period sees Rome at grips with non-Italian powers against whom she has to fight, not only in Italy but abroad. Chief among these powers were Carthage and Macedonia, and Mommsen ends the period with the decisive victory over the Macedonian forces at Pydna in 168 B.C. The result of Rome's victories was that she now acquired territories outside Italy which came to be known as "provinces". The first province was Sicily, which fell to Rome after the first Punic war, in 241 B.C. The later wars with Carthage brought Rome the greater part of Spain and finally "Africa", i.e. the Punic possessions in North Africa which were formed into a province after the destruction of Carthage in 146 B.C. Macedonia itself had become a province in 148 B.C. This was but the logical consequence of Pydna; already at the beginning of the second century B.C. Roman influence both in the Eastern and in the Western Mediterranean had been supreme.

The fourth period Mommsen calls "the revolution". Its history is that of the breakdown of the old republican form of government, and ˙t is characterised by fierce political strife leading on several occasions

---

[1] The Roman, unlike the Greek colony, remained closely bound to the mother city, and served as a military garrison in conquered territory, cf. *infra*, 57.

[2] *Lex Hortensia, infra,* 22.

to civil war. Mommsen ends it with the temporary triumph of the conservative party under Sulla, dictator 81–79 B.C., who re-established the constitution on an entirely undemocratic basis.

The fifth period, the last in Mommsen's book, stretches from Sulla to 46 B.C., in which year the victory of C. Julius Caesar over the Pompeians at Thapsus left him master of the Roman world. This period Mommsen calls "the foundation of the military monarchy". It was one of renewed civil conflict, accompanied by expansion abroad, and in the extra-constitutional positions assumed by such leaders as Pompeius and Caesar it already foreshadows the empire. But, though Caesar was, in fact, a military autocrat for the short remainder of his life, and in a sense the founder of the Roman empire, it is not he who is usually regarded as the first emperor. There was no real revival of the republic after his assassination in 44 B.C., but there was a revival of civil war, ending only in 31 B.C. with the battle of Actium, won by C. Julius Caesar Octavianus, the great-nephew and adopted son of C. Julius Caesar, over his rival M. Antonius. It is this Octavian, better known by the title of "Augustus", which he received in 27 B.C., who is generally spoken of as the first Roman emperor.

The long centuries of the empire fall naturally into two periods, which are not, however, marked off from each other by any very definite dividing line. In the earlier period, usually known as the "principate", though the emperor is in fact supreme, his power is disguised under republican forms; but the disguise becomes ever thinner, and in the third century A.D. vanishes altogether. It is common to refer to the succeeding period of undisguised autocracy as the "dominate", because the emperor is now no longer even in theory merely the *princeps*, or "first citizen", he is *dominus*—"master"—of his subjects. If we must choose a specific date for the beginning of the "dominate", we can take A.D. 284, in which year, after about half a century of confusion during which emperors followed each other in rapid succession, Diocletian ascended the throne. This emperor introduced important reforms amounting to a change in the constitution. From his time until its end, the Roman empire remained an absolute monarchy, but no simple answer can be given to the question, "when did it end?" Diocletian himself, among his reforms, instituted an administrative division between the Western and Eastern halves of the empire. This cleavage was accentuated when the Emperor Constantine transferred his residence to Constantinople, and became final in A.D. 395. But by that time already the end of the Western empire was nearing. The invasions of the barbarians could no longer be kept in check, and the last Roman emperor of the West, Romulus Augustulus, was deposed in A.D. 476.

The Eastern empire, on the other hand, had a long future still before it, which was only to end with the capture of Constantinople by the Turks in A.D. 1453. Of all the emperors who reigned during its remaining thousand years of life, there is one who is of supreme importance for lawyers, the Emperor Justinian, who came to the throne in A.D. 527 and died in 565, for it was in his time, and largely through his personal interest, that the Roman law assumed the shape in which it has come down to succeeding generations. It is consequently with the year 565 that histories of Roman law usually close, and, apart from a few isolated matters, reference will not be made in this book to later events.

§ II. PERIODS IN THE HISTORY OF THE LAW

The history of a people's law is as long as that of the people itself, for law of a sort exists in every stage of human society. In the case of Rome, the history of the law is even longer than that of the people, for even after the fall of the empire, Roman law never quite died out, and from the eleventh century A.D. onwards, through the renewed study of Justinian's compilations, it was revived as an active force, and deeply influenced the development of the law throughout Europe. But even if we go no further than the death of Justinian, the stretch of time with which we are concerned is enormous, some thirteen hundred years, counting from the traditional date of the foundation of the city.

If it is difficult to divide general history into periods without introducing a false idea that a people develops by starts rather than continuously, it is still more difficult with legal history, for there are seldom any violent breaks. In general, changes come gradually, and it is only after a long time has elapsed that we can see how great the development has been. Nevertheless, for the sake of clarity, some attempt at a division into periods must be made.

(a) *The period of conjecture.* This includes the period of the monarchy and that of the early republic, at any rate down to the drawing up of the famous code known as the "Twelve Tables" which, according to tradition, took place in the years 451–450 B.C. For the law of these early times we have no direct evidence. The statements of historians, where they incidentally mention legal matters, are not to be relied on in detail any more than their other statements, and we have no actual legal texts or inscriptions. This does not, however, mean that we have no foundation for conjectures. It is possible, by careful sifting, to get a good deal of reliable information from the traditions preserved by the historians; we can sometimes deduce an earlier state of affairs from a close inspection of the institutions of a later age,[1] and comparison with other systems of primitive law is often available to fill gaps in our information, or to explain facts which would be unintelligible by themselves.

(b) *From the XII Tables to the end of the republic.* It is impossible to find any obvious break in this long stretch of some four hundred years. Of the XII Tables themselves, although they have not survived, we have a considerable number of what are generally believed to be authentic fragments, in quotations from them made by later authors, but our information generally for the earlier centuries of the republic is meagre, and statements for these centuries too are largely conjectural. We know of some laws passed, of the existence of certain legal institutions, and the names of some great lawyers, but of the few professedly legal works written, none has survived, and there are only very few inscriptions. Only as to the constitutional law, owing to the references which the historians necessarily make to it, is our information fairly good.

For the last century and a half of the republic, matters are already different. A few quotations from legal writers of the time survive in Justinian's Digest;[2] we have Cicero's[3] works, and in all of these, not only in the speeches delivered in court, there are numerous references to legal matters, and altogether we have a good deal of literature from which, though it is not legal, information on legal matters can be deduced. We have, too, the text of a few laws in inscriptions.

But if our sources of information for the republic are still comparatively few, the importance of this period must not be overlooked. It was the period in which the foundations were laid, and it saw the beginning of that legal literature which was to bring Roman law later to so high a pitch of development.

(c) *The first century of the empire.* The change from republic to empire did not make any immediate difference to private law, except in so far as, bringing peace after about a century of turmoil, the new order was favourable to legal development. It is also perhaps true to say that now, opportunities for political distinction being necessarily few, the law

---

[1] E.g. we have no reliable statement as to the method of choosing the kings, but from the fact that during the republic the *interrex* (who held office if both consuls died) and the *dictator* (*infra*, 53) were appointed and not elected, we can deduce that appointment by a predecessor played some part, at least, in the selection of a king, and that the monarchy was not simply elective, as some historians state.

[2] *Infra*, 486.   [3] 106–43 B.C.

remained the chief avenue for men who aspired to a public career. Legal literature increased in volume and importance during this period, and a number of quotations survive in the Digest. The period indeed merges into:

(d) *The classical period.* It is in the second century and first half of the third century of the empire that Roman law reached its fullest development in the hands of great lawyers who were as a rule both practitioners and writers. The period may be divided into an earlier classical period covered by the reigns of Hadrian and the Antonine emperors, and a later classical period under the Severi.[1] Not that there is a break in the continuity of the development, but the work of the earlier age was of a more creative character, while that of the later represents rather the working out of existing principles over the whole field of law. In the Digest there are quotations from all the authors of the classical age, but those taken from two writers of the later period alone comprise about half the work.[2]

(e) *The post-classical period down to the reign of Justinian.* With the era of confusion that succeeded the death of Alexander Severus (A.D. 235) there came a rather sudden decline in the value of the legal work done. This in itself is comprehensible enough, but even the restoration of order by Diocletian did not revive legal literature. There were no writers of distinction, and such literature as there was consisted merely of collections and epitomes of previous works. But it must not be imagined that law stood still; the great social and political changes of the sinking empire, and the influx of Greek ideas, due in part to the establishment of the Eastern empire with its capital at Constantinople, found their expression in imperial legislation and, less obviously, in custom and practice.

(f) *The reign of Justinian* forms a period by itself, because of the work, which may be roughly described as codification, undertaken by that emperor. Already in the preceding generation there had been something of a revival in legal matters, and Justinian made use of it for the purpose of reducing to order the mass of existing authorities. He was also himself a legislator who enacted a number of statutes, some of which were of great importance. But Justinian's great claim to fame is not his original legislation, nor indeed was the intellectual revival of sufficient strength to enable much original work to be done. The importance of his work lies in the fact that in his "Digest" and in his "Code" he collected a great mass of excerpts from classical authors, and of imperial enactments, and that he gave to Roman law what was, in a sense, its final form.

[1] For dates, *v.* table, p. xvii.   [2] Cf. *infra,* 488.

Chapter II

THE REPUBLICAN CONSTITUTION

§ I. ELEMENTS

Already in the monarchical constitution there had been the three elements of political organisation common to the Aryan peoples, the King, the Council of Elders (*senatus*, connected with *senex*), and the Assembly of the people. Of the distribution of functions between the three we know nothing, nor is it likely that the constitution was at all definite. The king was leader in war and chief priest, and exercised some judicial functions; the senate was his council. Presumably the questions which were reserved for the assembly of the whole people varied a good deal with the character of the king; a weak king would ask the people's approval for a proposed course of action where a strong one would do without it.

In republican times two of the elements survive, the senate and the assembly, and indeed the third does not suffer as much change as would appear, for the magistrates are the successors to the royal power. When the change from monarchy to republic was made two magistrates called "consuls"[1] were elected as heads of the state in place of the king, but the royal power was not cut down. It was limited, indeed, by the fact that there were now two heads instead of one and by the fact that the consuls only held office for a year, whereas the kings had held it for life, but, apart from this, the consuls had still the great powers which the king had exercised. In course of time these powers were restricted by statute,[2] but there remained throughout a large residue undefined by strict law, though generally controlled by the conventions of the constitution. The name of this undefined power, at first given to the consuls alone but afterwards to a few other magistrates, is *imperium*.

The magistracy was originally confined to the patricians, the plebeians being ineligible, and this was one of the points round which the struggle of the orders centred. Of this struggle something must now be said.

§ II. THE STRUGGLE BETWEEN THE ORDERS

What was the origin of the plebeians is a question which has never been satisfactorily settled. According to Mommsen they were originally

---

[1] Originally "praetors", cf. *infra*, 43.
[2] E.g. the right to put citizens to death was taken away, *infra*, 320.

"clients", that is people who without being actually slaves were in a position of dependence. They might be slaves who had been set free but remained dependent on their "patrons" or former masters; they might be foreigners who had settled at Rome and placed themselves under the protection of a Roman; or, lastly, they might be members of conquered communities allowed to live in *de facto* freedom but without political rights. This hypothesis of Mommsen's is, however, not much in favour to-day. Many prefer to regard the difference between patricians and plebeians as originally one of race, the plebeians being the original inhabitants conquered by the patricians, who thus stood to them in a relationship something like that existing between the Normans and the English in the period following the conquest. According to others, the relationship was the other way about, the patricians being the original inhabitants and the plebeians foreigners whom they only admitted to the city as inferiors. More probably correct than either hypothesis is the view that there was no racial difference and that the patricians were simply the nobility. It may well be that at Rome, as in other city-states, the greater part of the land got into the hands of a minority of families. The comparative wealth of these families enabled them to live within the city and farm their lands outside through dependents, an advantage which in turn facilitated the arrogation of superior political rights to themselves. But whatever the origin of the distinction, it is one which appears as far back in Roman history as we can go, and in all times of which we know anything for certain the plebeians were citizens—unprivileged citizens, no doubt, but not mere resident foreigners. In spite of contrary views it may be said with some certainty that they not only fought in the Roman army but were members of the popular assembly.

The struggle between the plebeians and the patricians was of a twofold character, partly economic and partly political, and originally it was probably their economic grievances which the plebs found the more serious.   ·

The chief economic questions were those concerning the public land and the law of debt.

(*a*) *The public land.* Not all land was in private ownership;[1] some belonged to the state. This was increased from time to time by successful wars. It might be dealt with in any of three ways, either assigned free to private individuals, as their property (*ager assignatus*), sold to private individuals, or left open for any citizen who wished to occupy it for agricultural purposes or for use as pasture. It is likely enough that under the

---

[1] On early communal ownership of land *v. infra*, 140.

kings the plebeians had had their share in these advantages; but the revolution which put an end to the monarchy was an aristocratic revolution, and the patrician government probably never assigned land to plebeians, while the plebeians were not in general wealthy enough to buy it. The occupation system also inured mainly to the advantage of the patricians. Perhaps they alone were by law entitled to occupy, but in any case it would be they and the few rich plebeians alone who could produce the capital necessary to make occupation pay. Slaves, cattle and seed corn would all be necessary, and the expenses would be increased if, as was usual in the case of acquisition by conquest, the land to be occupied lay at some distance from the city. Strictly, the occupation of public land gave no right except at the good pleasure of the state, which exacted a rent in kind and could reclaim the land at any moment; but in fact this right to reclaim was seldom exercised and the land, though not strictly owned by the occupant, descended from father to son, while the rent, which had never been large, was often not exacted by the patrician magistrates from the members of their own order.

(b) *The law of debt.* An even more pressing evil for the poor than their practical exclusion from the advantages of the public land was the fearful stringency of the law of debt. The poor man was liable to be taken from his farm to serve in the army and had not, like the rich, slaves who could carry on the work in his absence. He might even, for Rome was not always successful in her wars, return to find that his farm had been ravaged by the enemy. The only thing to do was to apply to some wealthy person for a loan to enable him to start again. Next year the same thing might happen and the load of debt would grow. This would be serious enough in a modern state, but in ancient Rome a man who could not pay his debts could be taken by his creditors and either killed or sold abroad as a slave. Even if the creditors did not proceed to these lengths they could, by threatening to do so, keep the debtor in a condition of abject poverty dependent entirely on their will, and this in fact seems to have been the position of a large number of the plebeians.[1]

In the lands which they had helped to conquer they had no share, and they ran the risk of losing not only their own land but their life or liberty.

The chief political questions were those concerning the magistracy, the validity of resolutions passed by the plebeian assembly and intermarriage between the orders.

(a) *The magistracy.* The regular heads of the state were the consuls, and

[1] *V. infra,* 166.

from the consulship plebeians were rigidly excluded. Nor might they be appointed to the dictatorship, which was a temporary revival of the monarchy used in times of emergency when it was necessary to concentrate the whole power of the state in a single person. The only regular magistrates besides the consuls were the quaestors, who were originally simply assistants of the consuls and appointed by them. There was of course no likelihood that the patrician consuls would wish to appoint a plebeian quaestor. The priesthoods too, which were of considerable political importance, were entirely in patrician hands.

(b) *The validity of resolutions passed by the plebeian assembly.* The plebs from very early times met together in an assembly (*concilium plebis*) and passed resolutions (*plebiscita*). It was one of their objects to obtain for these resolutions the force of law.

(c) *Intermarriage.* There was no *conubium* between the orders; that is to say, a marriage between a patrician and a plebeian was not recognised as lawful, and the children of a patrician father by a plebeian mother would be plebeians. The prohibition of intermarriage was of political, not merely social importance, because it emphasised the patrician contention that the plebeians were too basely born to be admitted to the magistracies.

The struggles in connection with the economic and the political questions are closely interwoven. There were, of course, rich plebeians who did not suffer under the economic grievances of their poorer brethren, but they realised that it was only by making common cause with the rest of their order that they could obtain the political concessions in which they themselves were interested. In the end, the political equality which they sought was completely achieved, but palliatives, at best, were provided for the poverty of the lower classes, which a wise use of the public land might have effectively remedied.

The details of the struggle belong for the most part to the period of traditional history, and what is said by the historians is, at least in part, mythical. The difficulties of reconstruction are increased by a tendency to read far back into the mythical past reforms which, in fact, took place comparatively late. Thus we frequently find references to a series of laws apparently all enacting the same thing, and only two explanations seem possible; either the earlier laws were not carried into effect, or they never existed, except in imagination. For instance, the rule that no Roman citizen might be punished capitally without appeal (*provocatio*) to the assembly is referred to no less than three *leges Valeriae* of 509, 449 and 300 B.C. respectively.[1] It is, to say the least of it, strange that it should in

---

[1] To say nothing of the *leges Porciae*.

each case be a member of the same clan who secured the passing of these laws and the probability is that only the last ever really existed.[1]

In spite of these difficulties certain facts emerge. The first step taken by the plebeians was to band themselves together into a corporation, to hold meetings and to elect officers of their own, these officers being known as *tribuni*. According to tradition their institution goes back to 494 B.C. in which year is supposed to have taken place the "First Secession of the Plebs", that is, the plebs left the city in a body and only returned on being granted certain concessions. These concessions are said to have been the recognition of the plebs as a corporation and the granting of specified powers to the tribunes (originally five, and after 457 B.C. ten in number). These officers were given (*a*) the right of convening the assembly of the plebs (*concilium plebis*) and eliciting resolutions from them. These resolutions, however, were mere self-regarding ordinances and bound no one outside the corporation. (*b*) *Intercessio*, i.e. the right to veto any magisterial act, including such acts as bringing a bill before the assembly. (*c*) *Auxilium*, i.e. the right to protect the plebeians, especially against punishment by the magistrates.

The tribunes undoubtedly had these powers later; but it is more than unlikely that they possessed such weapons—in particular, the formidable *intercessio*—from the first.

Strife continued in the succeeding years which saw some plebeian successes, such e.g. as the *lex Icilia* (traditional date 456 B.C.), a law passed under tribunician pressure which distributed the land on the Aventine Hill to poor citizens; but the next important movement is that in favour of codification which resulted in the enactment of the XII Tables. The story is that as early as in 462 a tribune, C. Terentilius Arsa, proposed that five men should be elected to draw up a code of law which should bind the consuls in the exercise of their judicial powers. The patricians successfully opposed the project for eight years, but then they were forced to give way. They managed, however, to delay matters by sending an embassy to Greece to study the code of Solon, the famous Athenian lawgiver.[2] In 451, after the return of the embassy, ten men (instead of the five originally proposed) were elected as chief magistrates instead of consuls (*decemviri consulari imperio legibus scribundis*), the ordinary constitution, including the appointment of tribunes, being temporarily suspended. Although plebeians were declared eligible for this position,

[1] Laws were called after the name of the magistrate who proposed them; hence a *lex Valeria* is necessarily one passed by a member of the *gens Valeria*.

[2] The date of Solon's legislation was probably 594–593 B.C.

the influence of the aristocracy was so great that only patricians were elected to the first board. The *decemviri* drew up their code and brought it before the assembly for ratification, after which the laws were inscribed on ten bronze tablets and set up in the market-place. As, however, the work was not considered complete another board of ten was elected for the following year (450), and two further tablets of laws were drafted. On this second board there were some plebeians, who were thus the first members of their order to hold a magistracy of the Roman people. At this point history fades more and more into myth. The new *decemviri* are said to have behaved tyrannically and to have refused to lay down their office although their work was done. Popular indignation was aroused especially against one of them, Appius Claudius, who being enamoured of a certain Virginia, instigated a dependent of his own to claim her as a slave, and then, in his capacity as magistrate, gave interim possession to the claimant instead of allowing, as the law required, that a person whose liberty was questioned should remain in freedom until the case was decided. The girl's father then slew her to avoid her dishonour and led a "Second Secession of the Plebs" which resulted in the overthrow of the *decemviri* and the restoration of the constitution. The two draft tablets were, however, put before the assembly and passed, thus bringing the number up to twelve.

In spite of the obviously legendary character of much of this story, some points are fairly clear. The compilation of the XII Tables was an episode in the struggle of the orders, and constituted a victory for the plebs. Obviously the law had not only been administered by patrician magistrates but had been unknown in a large measure to the general public. The plebeians wanted a code, so that, if a plebeian were wronged by a patrician magistrate, he could point definitely to the provision in the code which the magistrate had broken. It is likely enough that the code was intended to be a substitute for the tribunician power. The main use of the tribunes lay in their function of *auxilium*, i.e. they could stop the magistrates from treating plebeians unjustly, but this method of preventing injustice is one of the clumsiest ever invented. First a magistrate is appointed and then another person—the representative of a particular class—to interfere with the magistrate in the interests of that class. The class representative is given the power of bringing the whole of the state machinery to a standstill by his veto (*intercessio*), and there is thus a constant element of anarchy in the state. That the tribunes were an anarchical institution had been shown by the fifty odd years of strife since their institution. Very probably it was intended by codification to substitute for the personal protection of the tribunes the more regular protection by definite law, with which the plebeians might be expected to content themselves, as members of their own order could be on the commission which was to draw up the code. But if this was the intention, the violent end of the decemvirate frustrated it. The restored constitution included the appointment of tribunes, and there was never another attempt to abolish them. Indeed when the struggle between the orders was over, they became, as we shall see,[1] an important instrument of senatorial government.

In addition to the restoration of the constitution, the plebs, by their secession, obtained certain concessions which were embodied in several *leges Valeriae Horatiae*, passed by the new consuls for 449. Of these the most important were one *de provocatione*[2] and another which is represented as giving to resolutions of the *concilium plebis* the force of law.[3] A few years later, in 445, by two *leges Canuleiae*, the prohibition of marriage between the orders (which had been repeated in the XII Tables) was removed and a compromise was arranged with regard to the admission of plebeians to the magistracy.

Instead of consuls there might now be elected military tribunes (who must not be confused with the tribunes of the plebs) with consular power, it being left to the senate to decide each year which form the highest office in the state should take.[4] From the consulship plebeians were still excluded, but they might be elected military tribunes. In the succeeding seventy-eight years during which the compromise lasted, military tribunes (generally six, sometimes four) were elected fifty times, consuls twenty-eight times. In addition to being a compromise on the subject of the admission of plebeians, the arrangement was probably designed to meet the need for an increased number of magistrates with *imperium*, caused by the numerous wars of this period and the increase of judicial work, all of which had previously fallen to the consuls.

The next important moment comes with the passing of the *leges Liciniae Sextiae* in 367. The intervening years were a period of continuous strife during which the richer plebeians continued to use the economic grievances of the poor as an instrument for keeping agitation for political concessions alive. The patricians, on the other hand, though the main position had been lost by the admission of plebeians to the military

---

[1] *Infra*, 53.   [2] Cf. *infra*, 320.   [3] Cf. *infra*, 22.
[4] Technically it was a matter for the magistrate who presided over the elections to decide, but we can hardly suppose that he would take such an important decision without reference to the senate.

tribunate, continued to dispute their remaining privileges inch by inch. One victory which they won (in 443) was the establishment of a new high office confined to patricians, the censorship. Two censors were henceforward elected every four or five years to take over certain duties hitherto performed by the consuls, especially the drawing up of the *census*, the official list of the Roman people for purposes of military service and taxation. On the other hand in 421 plebeians became eligible for the quaestorship. Something too, but not much, was done to alleviate the distress of the poor by laws assigning portions of conquered territory to citizens. In 377 began the agitation by the tribunes Licinius and Sextius for the enactment of a programme of reform which included both economic and political measures. It took ten years of violent unrest before they succeeded, but in 367 their proposals became law. The measures passed were as follows:

A. *Economic*

(i) No citizen to "occupy" more than 500 *jugera* of public land or keep more than 100 oxen or 500 sheep on the common pasture.

(ii) Landlords must employ a certain proportion of free labourers. The object of this provision was to provide employment for the growing number of citizens who were thrown out of work by the increase of large estates which their owners found it more economical to cultivate by means of slaves.

(iii) Debtors are relieved by subtracting interest already paid from the capital and making arrangements for balances to be paid in instalments. This was, of course, a measure which could have only a temporary effect. The *law* of debt was not altered.

B. *Political*

(iv) The military tribunate with consular power is abolished and in future ONE OF THE CONSULS MUST BE A PLEBEIAN. The election of patricians to the first decemvirate and the small number of plebeian military tribunes had shown the necessity of reserving a place in the consulate for plebeians.

(v) The keepers of the oracles, of whom there are now to be ten (x *viri sacris faciundis*), are to be half patrician and half plebeian.

This first admission of plebeians to the priestly colleges is important politically, for the interpretation of oracles might seriously influence affairs of state.

The same year in which the *leges Liciniae Sextiae* were passed saw the establishment of two new magistracies, the praetorship[1] and the curule aedileship.[2] The abolition of the military tribunate had again reduced the number of magistrates with *imperium* to two. The creation of the praetorship raised it to three. The new magistrate was intended to take over the judicial work of the consuls, and his office is therefore, for the study of Roman law, the most important magistracy of all. Livy represents the praetorship as originally confined to patricians and its institution therefore as a compromise, but, at any rate, it did not long remain a patrician preserve, for in 337 we know that a plebeian was elected to the office.[3]

With the reservation of one consulship to their order the plebeians had gained their chief point, and the opening of other offices to them followed in due course. In 351 a plebeian was first elected censor and in 339 a *lex Publilia* reserved one censorship to the plebeians. In 300, by a *lex Ogulnia*, the pontificate, the most important of the priestly colleges from a political point of view, was thrown open to the plebs, and therewith the struggle as regards offices was over. The last act of the whole struggle was the *lex Hortensia* of 287, whereby the resolutions of the *concilium plebis* were given the force of law. The details of this matter, which is of great importance, will be discussed later when we deal with the popular assemblies.[4]

The result of the plebeian victory was that the political importance of the distinction between patricians and plebeians disappeared. But Rome did not become democratic. The old aristocracy was replaced by a new one, often described as an aristocracy of office, which consisted of the patrician families, now comparatively few in number, with the addition of those plebeian families which had gained sufficient wealth and influence to be elected to the higher magistracies. A man was considered a nobleman if one of his ancestors had held a curule office.[5] But there was a great difference between the new nobility and the old; the privileges of the patricians had been secured to them by law, those of the new aristocracy were purely the result of practice. In law there was nothing to prevent the assembly from electing to office a person who could point to no curule magistrates in his family tree, and sometimes the assembly

---

[1] Perhaps this was introduced by a clause in the rogations themselves; Greenidge, 120, n. 1.

[2] *V. infra*, 48.

[3] Mommsen, *Staatsr.* II. 204, doubts whether the office was ever confined to patricians by statute as there is no mention of a statute opening it to plebeians later.

[4] *Infra*, 22.

[5] Dictatorship, consulship, praetorship, censorship, curule aedileship.

made use of this power.[1] Generally, however, only members of the old established families, patrician or plebeian, had sufficient influence to secure election, and the feeling of the assembly appears to have been that it was best to continue entrusting the government to men in whose family government had become a tradition.

The poor, it must be admitted, did not benefit much by the admission of rich plebeians to share in the political privileges of the patricians. The limits imposed by the *leges Liciniae Sextiae* on the occupation of public land were not enforced for any length of time, and the provision for free labourers remained without much effect. On the other hand, independent circumstances, especially the increase of land available for colonies and the general growth of wealth which was due to Rome's conquests, did undoubtedly tend to better the material condition of the lower classes. Of the modification of the law of debt we shall have to speak later.

§ III. THE ASSEMBLIES OF THE PEOPLE

From the very first, Roman popular assemblies appear to have had two peculiarities which remained characteristic of them so long as they continued to exist: (*a*) the voting was always by groups, and (*b*) the assembly could meet only when summoned by a magistrate, and could transact only the business put before it by the magistrate who summoned it.

The assembly did not, like the British House of Commons, vote by a simple counting of heads. First the heads were counted in each group, the majority determining the vote of the group; then the votes of the groups were counted, and the majority determined the vote of the assembly. The first group to be used for this purpose was the *curia*, and the earliest assembly was therefore known as the *comitia curiata*.[2]

The exact nature of the *curia* is a matter of some doubt. Very probably it was, like the later tribe, a territorial division, but it appears to have been used also for military purposes and perhaps for taxation, as well as for voting. We are told by the historians that there were ten *curiae* in each of the three old tribes, *Ramnes, Tities* and *Luceres*,[3] into which the Roman

---

[1] As in the case of Cicero, consul 63 B.C., who was a *novus homo*.

[2] *Comitium* was properly the place where the assembly met, but the use of the singular is rare. *Comitia* (plural) means "an assembly".

[3] The origin of these three tribes is very doubtful. According to one view, now much disputed, they represented originally independent communities by the federation of which Rome came into existence. In any case they must not be confused with the "Servian" tribes, a later institution, for which *v. infra,* 20.

people were originally divided, and that each *curia* provided ten horse-men and a hundred foot-soldiers, so that the earliest Roman army consisted of 300 cavalry and 3000 infantry. The historians also say that each *curia* was divided into ten *gentes*, but it is not possible to accept this tradition. The *gens* corresponds to the clan and was based on real or supposed relationship between its members.[1] It was a natural unit and existed before the state; not even the Roman historians with their tendency to ascribe every institution to some definite legislator ever imagined that any one of them created the *gens*. It is therefore extremely unlikely that the *gentes* could have been fitted so neatly into the artificial curiate system; there could hardly be *exactly* ten *gentes* in each *curia*.[2]

What functions, if any, were reserved for the *comitia curiata* under the monarchy we do not know. The historians do indeed say that it was for the people to decide questions of peace and war, but this is probably only a deduction from the law of a later period. We also hear of *leges* proposed by the king and carried by the *comitia*, but legislation is rare in primitive societies and it is more than doubtful whether any such laws were ever passed.[3] Nor do modern authorities believe that the Roman historians were right in thinking that the king was elected by the *comitia*. In all probability the kingship was neither hereditary nor elective, but each king nominated his successor, the function of the *comitia* being merely to acclaim the new ruler, not to choose him.

We must indeed not imagine that there was any very definite constitu-tion. Probably it would depend very much on the personality of the king what questions he decided by himself or with the advice of the senate, and what he left to be decided by the *comitia*.

In any case the *comitia curiata* did not retain any political importance in historical times; perhaps before, more probably a century or two after, the abolition of the monarchy it was replaced, for political purposes, by another *comitia*, that is, by an assembly in which the citizens were

---

[1] Some modern writers however regard it as originally a territorial unit, e.g. de Francisci, I. 110.

[2] The *gens* itself continued to be of importance. Originally in all probability only the patricians were members of *gentes*, but in later times there were certainly plebeian *gentes* as well. All members of a *gens* have a common name (e.g. in the case of Marcus *Tullius* Cicero, Tullius is the gentile name, Marcus being the *praenomen* or personal name and Cicero that of the particular family within the *gens*) and there is an organisation which conducts the common cult (*sacra gentilicia*). It seems to have been possible for the meeting of the *gens* to pass resolutions binding on its members, e.g. that they must not bear a certain *prae-nomen* which had been dishonoured.

[3] *V. infra*, 83, n. 1.

summoned according to different grouping. Before this time the plebeians, who were probably originally excluded from the *curiae*, had almost certainly attained to membership.[1]

Although politically unimportant in republican times, the *comitia curiata* continued to meet for certain purposes connected with private law, the making of wills[2] and adrogations,[3] and it had also one formal function connected with public law. When a magistrate with *imperium* had been elected in the new *comitia* his office had to be confirmed by a *lex de imperio* passed by the curiate assembly. In fact, however, for all these purposes, which become purely formal in historical times, the thirty *curiae* were represented by thirty lictors, the attendants of the magistrates.

The individual *curiae* continued to exist; they had sacred rites and apparently communal funds, but they were of no great importance.

The assembly which replaced the organisation by *curiae* for political purposes was the *comitia centuriata*, the basis of which was the *centuria*, literally "hundred". Its institution was, according to tradition, the work of Servius Tullius, the last but one of the seven kings (traditional date 578–535 B.C.), and it thus formed part of the "Servian" constitution. That it and the rest of the "Servian" constitution really go back to the time of the monarchy is unlikely. The Roman historians were fond of ascribing constitutional features for which they could not account to Servius as the great reforming king, just as they liked to credit the second king, Numa Pompilius, with all religious institutions. In fact the centuriate organisation as it appeared in historical times was probably the result of a long development, not the creation of a single mind. Some of the figures seem to point to a date about the beginning of the fourth century B.C.[4]

The chief feature of interest about the *comitia centuriata* is its timocratic basis, that is, the preponderance given in it to wealth. The citizens were divided first of all into five *classes*, according to their wealth, each class being then further subdivided into centuries. In the first (wealthiest) class there were eighty centuries, in the second, third and fourth, twenty centuries, and in the fifth, thirty centuries. Ranking above all, but without

---

[1] This point is much disputed, but it is difficult to see why the *plebs* should have cared about gaining access to the *curiae* after the political power of the curiate assembly was lost; Lenel, 313.

[2] *Infra*, 125. When it met for this purpose the assembly was called *comitia calata*.

[3] *Infra*, 119.

[4] De Francisci, I. 225.

any definite property qualification, were eighteen centuries of *equites* (cavalry), and there were also four centuries of artificers and buglers, and one consisting of all those who had not even the qualification for the lowest class (*proletarii* or *capite censi*). In all there were thus 193 centuries,[1] and, as voting was by centuries, the wealthiest class together with the *equites* (ninety-eight) could outvote all the rest.

In the historians the property qualifications for the different classes are given in money (100,000 *asses* for the first class, 75,000 *asses* for the second, etc.), but as the organisation probably goes back before the first coining of money at Rome (middle of fourth century B.C.)[2] it has been conjectured that originally only land was counted.[3] Be that as it may, in historical times this was no longer so; all forms of wealth were taken into account, and sons under the power of their fathers, who could not own any property themselves, were presumably placed in their fathers' class.[4]

That the *comitia centuriata* has some connection with the military organisation of the Roman people is clear. The arrangement into cavalry, infantry and technical troops is sufficient proof, and we hear further that in each class half the centuries consisted of *iuniores* (men under the age of forty-six), who formed the active army, half of *seniores* (men between forty-six and sixty), who formed the reserve. We also hear that the weapons and armour with which the members of the different classes had to provide themselves varied; the first class having to provide the panoply of a fully armed infantryman, the others a less expensive equipment. On these grounds Mommsen held that the *comitia centuriata* was in origin and long remained essentially the Roman people in their military array,[5] the military organisation being used for voting purposes. There are however very serious objections to this view. The centuries of the voting assembly cannot ever have been the tactical unit used in the field, because military organisation requires a unit of standard strength, whereas the number of centuries in each class was settled once and for all and their strength therefore must have varied with growth of population and the changes in wealth. Further it would be impossible in any community for the number of men between forty-six and sixty to be as large as that of

---

[1] According to Dionysius IV. 18; VII. 59; 194 according to Livy I. 43.

[2] Tenney Frank, 69.

[3] Mommsen, *Staatsr.* III. 247. Some, e.g. Greenidge, 69, believe that only *res mancipi* counted.

[4] Festus, s.v. *duicensus* (Bruns, II. 7).

[5] *Staatsr.* III. 253.

men under the age of forty-six.[1] We must thus be content to say that the centuriate assembly, though influenced by military considerations, especially in that the right to vote goes with the duty of military service, was an organisation distinct from the real army and probably from its inception based on a timocratic principle.

At some date after 241 B.C., but before 218 B.C., the influence of wealth in the *comitia centuriata* was greatly diminished by a combination with the tribal divisions of which we shall speak below. The exact nature of this "democratic reform" is doubtful, but the most commonly accepted view is that each of the thirty-five tribes was given one century of *iuniores* and one of *seniores* in each of the five classes, making thus 350 centuries to which must be added eighteen centuries of *equites* and five of technical troops and *proletarii*. Of the 373 centuries only eighty-eight would consist of the first class and the *equites*, who would therefore lose their preponderance.[2] The old system was restored temporarily (88 B.C.) by Sulla in accordance with his aristocratic policy, but abolished again almost at once by the democratic party.

The people were divided not only into *curiae* and *centuriae* but also into tribes (*tribus*), which came to form the basis of a third assembly, the *comitia tributa*. The tribal, like the centuriate, organisation is ascribed to Servius Tullius, who is said to have divided the city into four tribes, to which seventeen "rustic" tribes embracing the land outside the walls were subsequently added. Various further additions were made with the acquisition of new territory until in 241 B.C. the number reached thirty-five at which it remained, newly acquired land being thereafter incorporated in the existing tribes. The tribes were territorial divisions, which took the place of the old *curiae* for the purposes of taxation and the military levy. But they were also, like the *curiae*, divisions of persons, although, unlike the *curiae*, they had no internal self-government and no *sacra*.

Originally only landholders were enrolled in the tribes, each in that tribe in which his land lay,[3] though there must from the first have been some room for choice and magisterial discretion, for if a man owned land in several tribes, he could not be enrolled in more than

---

[1] For these and other arguments *v.* Botsford, *The Roman Assemblies* (New York, 1909), 80–82, 203–211.

[2] For serious difficulties in this explanation *v.* Fraccaro, *St. Bonfante*, I. 103–122. General discussion and literature, Botsford, *op. cit.* 211–228.

[3] Only land held *ex iure Quiritium*, in full Roman ownership and therefore *res mancipi*, counted; Cic. *pro Flacco*, XXXII. 80.

one, and it would be for the magistrate to decide in which to place him, no doubt often in accordance with his own wishes. A great change was however made in 312 B.C. when Appius Claudius used his powers as *censor* to enrol landless citizens in the tribes, and thenceforward every Roman citizen was a member of a tribe.[1] The tribal designation became almost part of the citizen's name and passed normally from father to son,[2] new citizens being enrolled in the tribe where their home was, without reference apparently to any ownership of land.[3]

At what period the tribes were first used as the basis of an assembly— the *comitia tributa*—is unknown. That it was before the passing of the XII Tables is made probable by the reference in the Tables to the *comitia centuriata* as "*comitiatus maximus*". This implies the existence of a lesser *comitia*, which can only be the *tributa*. Livy mentions the passing of a statute by the tribes in 357 B.C.[4] But the whole growth of the institution is obscured by confusion with the *concilium plebis*, the assembly of the plebs alone, which also met by tribes. As the patricians must have become in the later part of the republic a numerically insignificant body of nobles, and as the purely plebeian assembly attained in the end equal legislative capacity with the assemblies of the whole people, it was easy for anyone unacquainted with the niceties of the constitution to confuse the two bodies, and this probably accounts for the difficulties which modern historians find in interpreting the sources.[5]

Of the *concilium plebis* we have already had occasion to speak in discussing the struggle between the orders. At first, it appears, the plebeians were in the habit of meeting by *curiae* for the election of tribunes and perhaps other business. At any rate according to Livy[6] it was enacted, by a certain *lex Publilia* of 471 B.C., that henceforward the arrangement should be by tribes, and so it remained. It seems that this reform was of democratic nature because it diminished the influence of the patricians over the plebeian assembly.[7] So long as the plebs had met by *curiae* the clients of the great patrician houses had been members of the *concilium plebis* and had been able sometimes to turn matters as their patrons

---

[1] In 304, however, the censors confined landless citizens to the four city tribes.

[2] Thus Cicero's official description was M(arcus) Tullius M(arci) fi(lius) trib(u) Arn(iensi) Cicero.

[3] For the restrictions on the admission of freedmen to tribes *v. infra*, 80.

[4] Livy VII. 16. But this was anomalous as it took place *in castris*.

[5] For a summary of the reasons for distinguishing the two tribal assemblies, *v.* Greenidge, 445–446.

[6] II. 58.   [7] Livy II. 56.

desired; once the tribe was substituted for the *curiae* these landless persons were necessarily excluded and the plebs became more independent.

The history of the steps by which the *concilium plebis* attained legislative power is more than usually obscure. We hear quite definitely of three *leges*, all of which are represented as enacting, almost in identical words, that *plebiscita*, i.e. resolutions of the plebs alone, should have the force of law. The first is a *lex Valeria Horatia*, said to have been passed in 449 B.C. as a result of the fall of the decemvirs,[1] the second a *lex Publilia Philonis* of 339,[2] the third the *lex Hortensia* of 287.[3] The relation of these laws to each other has been the subject of much conjecture. Strachan Davidson, for instance, thought that the *lex Valeria Horatia* required the consul to lay resolutions of the plebs before the senate and *comitia* and that the *lex Publilia* shortened the process by making the intervening consultation of the senate unnecessary.[4]

But the evidence for these conjectures is slight, and many modern authorities think that the *lex Hortensia*, which is the only one mentioned by legal writers, alone had any real existence.[5] The idea of the two earlier statutes would then have arisen from the tendency of Roman historians, which we have already noticed, to read back comparatively recent events into the remote past. And here the legend might have arisen from the fact that both 449 and 339 were really moments at which democratic reforms were introduced.[6] In any case there is no doubt that after the passing of the *lex Hortensia*, *plebiscita*, that is enactments passed by the plebs in the *concilium plebis*, an assembly in which the patricians had no place, were equally valid with *leges*, that is enactments passed by the whole *populus*, i.e. patricians and plebeians together, in the *comitia centuriata* or *tributa*. We thus have the strange result that in the later republic there were three bodies all equally capable of passing binding statutes, three sovereign legislatures, as we should call them,[7] the *comitia centuriata* and *tributa*, consisting of the same people, though organised differently, and the *concilium plebis*, consisting almost entirely of the same

---

[1] *Ut quod tributim plebs iussisset populum teneret.* Livy III. 55.

[2] *Ut plebiscita omnes Quirites tenerent.* Livy VIII. 12.

[3] *Ut quod plebs iussisset omnes Quirites teneret.* Pliny, *Nat. Hist.* XVI. 15 (10). See also Gai. I. 3 and J. I. 2. 4.

[4] Smith's *Dictionary of Antiquities*, II. 439.

[5] Lenel, 324. Other references, Kipp, 29.

[6] For another *l. Publilia Philonis* of 339 v. *infra*, 30.

[7] For the *patrum auctoritas*, i.e. approval by the patrician members of the senate, necessary for *leges* (but not *plebiscita*), v. *infra*, 30.

people (for the patricians must by 287 have become a numerically insignificant minority), and meeting like the *comitia tributa* by tribes. We must also remember that the *comitia curiata*, an assembly of the whole *populus*, organised again on a different basis, though it had lost its political importance, still maintained a formal existence.

Which of these assemblies was summoned in any particular instance depended on the magistrate who wished to put a proposal before the people. The normal presidents of the *comitia centuriata* were the consuls, both for legislation and for elections; the *comitia tributa* could only be summoned by "patrician"[1] magistrates, usually the consuls or praetors, and the *concilium plebis* could only meet under the presidency of a magistrate of the plebs. Though the legislative competence of all the assemblies was equal, the *concilium plebis* became more and more the usual organ for the passing of laws in the later republic as its presidents, the tribunes, had more time for, and interest in, legislation than the consuls, who were frequently engaged in military duties. So far as elections were concerned the functions of the assemblies were more strictly differentiated, the magistrates with *imperium* and also the censors being elected in the *centuriata*, the lesser magistrates of the people (e.g. curule aediles and quaestors) by the *comitia tributa*, the tribunes and plebeian aediles by the *concilium plebis*.[2] The *centuriata* was thus in practice confined usually to the most important elections, one reason for the comparative rarity of its meetings being the cumbrousness of the ceremonial involved. It was (in theory) the people in arms and could only meet with full military ceremonial outside the walls, usually in the Campus Martius. When it met a watch was placed on the Janiculan Hill (on the opposite side of the Tiber from the main part of the city and the Campus Martius) and a flag hoisted, the striking of which would be the signal that the enemy was

[1] This term does not imply that the magistrate is necessarily himself a patrician; it is used to differentiate the officers who were strictly magistrates (of the *populus*), e.g. consuls, praetors and curule aediles, from those who were not strictly magistrates at all but only officers of the plebs, the tribunes and the plebeian aediles. Justinian (J. 1. 2. 4), in distinguishing between *leges* and *plebiscita*, is somewhat misleading. He says: "A *lex* is an enactment passed by the *populus* on the motion of a senatorial magistrate (*senatore magistratu interrogante*), e.g. a consul; a *plebiscitum* is an enactment passed by the *plebs* on the motion of a plebeian magistrate, e.g. a tribune". This might lead the reader to suppose that tribunes were not members of the senate, whereas in fact they were senators.

[2] Hirschfeld, *Kleine Schriften* (1913), 261–263, thinks that shortly after 57 B.C. the *tributa* took the place of the *centuriata* for *all* elections. For the criminal jurisdiction of the assemblies *v. infra*, 318–323.

approaching and that the consul should break up the meeting. This practice continued until the latest days of the republic, although the Tiber had for centuries ceased to be the boundary of Roman territory.[1]

§ IV. CHARACTERISTICS AND PROCEDURE OF ROMAN ASSEMBLIES

As already noticed, a Roman assembly can meet only when summoned by a magistrate, and it can transact only the business put before it by the magistrate. His proposal it must either accept or reject; there is no possibility of amendment, nor, in the actual assembly itself, of any discussion. When legislation was proposed, the magistrate had to draft the bill (*rogatio*) which he intended to put before the people, or cause it to be drafted for him, and this bill was, by constitutional practice, usually debated in the senate. By strict law, however, this was not necessary, and the consent or disapproval of the senate made no difference to the validity of a law once it was passed. It was the duty of the magistrate when the bill was drafted to publish it in an edict (*proponere, promulgare*) in which he also announced the date on which he would summon the assembly to vote on it. The interval between promulgation and voting had, by a *lex Caecilia Didia* (98 B.C.), to be at least twenty-four days (*trinundinum*—three Roman weeks), and this rule seems to have been followed in practice even before it was laid down by law. After promulgation the bill might be withdrawn but it could not be altered. During this interval the magistrate could, and usually did, hold informal public meetings for discussion (*contiones*) in which he spoke himself and might allow anyone else to speak for or against the bill. Sometimes the *contio* took place immediately before the assembly proper. Before the voting the bill was read out again and the presiding magistrate asked the people whether they agreed to it or not, *velitis iubeatis, Quirites?* The people then arranged themselves in their divisions (tribes or centuries) and voted separately. Originally each man gave his vote orally, but with the growth of bribery in the late republic an attempt was made to check it by introducing the secret ballot.[2] Each man was given two tablets, one marked U.R. (*uti rogas*—"as you propose") and the other A. (*antiquo*—"I vote for the old state of things"); the former he cast into the urn if he wished to vote for the proposal, the latter if he rejected it.

---

[1] Dio Cassius XXXVII. 28.

[2] Introduced for legislation by a *lex Papiria* of 131 B.C. For elections it had been already introduced eight years previously by a *lex Gabinia*.

Once accepted by the assembly a bill became law immediately, unless, of course, it contained provisions postponing its coming into force. Publication was not necessary for validity, though it was common; sometimes the law itself provided that its provisions should be put up in public "where they could be easily read from the ground" (*unde de plano recte legi possit*). Originally wooden tablets were used for this purpose, later bronze ones. An official copy of the law was in any case kept in the *aerarium* (treasury), but there appears to have been no adequate provision for filing and arrangement, for Cicero complains that only the skilled assistants could discover an enactment which it was desired to consult, and that they therefore in fact decided what was to be law.[1]

The Romans had the principle, as must all communities with legislative bodies, that a previous enactment can always be repealed by a subsequent one, and also that where a subsequent enactment conflicts with a previous one it must be taken as repealing it to the extent of the inconsistency.[2] The Roman constitution was also, like the British, a "flexible" one, that is to say there were not, as in the constitution of the United States of America, any fundamental constitutional rules which could not be abrogated by the ordinary legislature. Just as the British Parliament could repeal, if it thought fit, the most important constitutional laws, e.g. the Act of Settlement, and would use for that purpose precisely the same procedure as that which it uses for passing a Licensing Act, so the Roman *comitia* or *concilium plebis* could, by using its ordinary procedure, alter the Roman constitution, and indeed frequently did so. But this fact did not prevent assemblies from attempting to bind their successors by laying down rules as to legislation. Most famous of such rules is one contained in the XII Tables. *Privilegia ne inroganto*, "no law may be passed against an individual", i.e. laws are to lay down general rules; the procedure of legislation is not to be used to penalise a particular individual who has not broken some general rule of the community. An example of a *privilegium* would be an English "Act of Attainder", i.e. an Act of Parliament ordering a particular person to be executed, such as was used for instance by Henry VIII to get rid of his minister Thomas Cromwell.

A later enactment which similarly attempted to lay down a rule for legislation was contained in the *lex Caecilia Didia*.[3] This forbade proposals

[1] Cic. *de leg.* III. 20. 46. This is no doubt an exaggeration.
[2] This was expressly recognised by the XII Tables. Livy VII. 17: *in XII tabulis legem esse, ut, quodcumque postremum populus iussisset, id ius ratumque esset.*
[3] *Supra*, 24.

dealing with unrelated subjects to be included in the same bill (*ne quid per saturam ferretur*), the object of such "tacking" being, of course, to induce the people to accept an unpopular proposal because they could not reject it without at the same time rejecting the proposal which they welcomed.

Now it is clear that, given the principles that a later enactment repeals a former and that there is no difference between fundamental constitutional laws and others, such limitations cannot strictly bind future assemblies. If the assembly chooses to pass a bill which does contain unrelated matters, then the bill should, at any rate in strict logic, become law and the *lex Caecilia Didia* be deemed to be repealed in so far as it conflicts with the new law.[1]

But logic is not always the deciding factor in law, and though it was sometimes argued by the Romans themselves that an act of the people must necessarily be valid even if it was contrary to some previously enacted constitutional principle, because of the implied repeal,[2] the general view seems to have been that the assembly was not entirely free to enact absolutely whatever it liked. Cicero, though of course he is speaking as an advocate and his words must not therefore be construed too strictly, argues as if it were quite settled that no *lex* could take away an individual's liberty or citizenship,[3] and in any case he tells us plainly that a clause was added to every statute which expressly limited its effect to what was lawful. "*Si quid ius non esset rogarier, eius ea lege nihilum rogatum.*" "If there be anything that it would be contrary to law to enact then no such enactment is contained in this statute."

A practical instance of the importance attaching to constitutional enactments concerning legislation occurred in the year 91 B.C. when the tribune Livius Drusus brought a bill before the assembly in which were contained proposals dealing with three unrelated matters, one a corn law, another dealing with the distribution of public land and a third depriving the *equites* of their exclusive control of the criminal jury courts which were

---

[1] Some writers on Jurisprudence therefore, especially Austin (*Province of Jurisprudence Defined*, Lecture VI), say that enactments such as the prohibition of *privilegia* are not properly laws at all, because their only force can be that of recommendations by a sovereign body of one moment to its successors as to principles which should guide them in legislation.

[2] An example of this occurs in Livy VII. 17, where it is argued that an election of two patricians as consuls is valid, in spite of the *lex Licinia Sextia*, because the election itself is an act of the sovereign people. Cf. also the arguments which Cicero puts into the mouth of his opponents: *pro Caec.* XXXIII. 95; *de Domo,* XL. 106.   [3] *Pro Caec.* XXXIII. 96.

to be transferred to the senators. This last was the proposal which was politically the most important, and the others were, at any rate partly, introduced for the purpose of securing popular support for it. In spite of the opposition of the consul Philippus, who had finally to be arrested by Drusus' orders, the bill was passed and the senate at first rejected a proposal that it should declare the new law unconstitutional as being contrary to the *lex Caecilia Didia*. From that moment however the political tide turned against Drusus and, after further agitation by Philippus, the senate finally passed the resolution declaring Drusus' law invalid. Drusus himself was shortly afterwards murdered, and the *equites* remained in control of the jury courts until Sulla's legislation ten years later. The time was, of course, one of great political excitement almost amounting to revolution and cannot be taken as typical of the ordinary course of government at Rome, but the importance of enactments restricting legislation appears clearly. Had there been no provision against *leges saturae* it is certain that the senate would not have taken upon itself to declare a law passed by the people to be invalid.

Instances of this nature would of necessity be rare; during periods of settled government constitutional principles are not usually violated, and so there is no means of finding out what exactly would happen if someone violated them; in periods of political disturbance force may have more effect than law. It is thus difficult to frame any precise rule defining the effect of enactments such as the *lex Caecilia Didia*. Perhaps the rule which would have received most general assent at Rome is that such enactments can only be abrogated expressly, not by implication.[1] We shall see that the senate was in one of its aspects the guardian of the constitution, and as in the case of Drusus, the final decision would often rest with it.

§ V. THE SENATE

The senate was in strict theory of law a purely consultative body, at first of the king, later of the consuls. It could not pass laws, as could the *comitia*; it could only give advice, and that only when asked by a magistrate with whom the executive power lay.[2] In the earlier republic it is probable that the magistrates were in fact as well as in law more powerful than the senate, but in the later republic, through the growth of a constitutional convention which made the consultation of the senate by the magistrate necessary for almost all business except routine matters and

[1] Cf. Krüger, 23.
[2] The name for a decision of the senate remains throughout *consultum*, i.e. resolution; it is never *iussum* as is a decree of the people.

the conduct of operations in the field, it was the senate which became the actual governing body at Rome.

A. COMPOSITION.   Originally, then, the senate was the king's council, and there can be no doubt that he appointed the members of it. It has indeed been suggested, on account of the importance which attached to the gentile organisation in early Rome, that the senate was a representative body consisting of the heads of the *gentes*, the chief argument in favour of this view being the traditional number of senators—300—which corresponds to the number of *gentes*, if we believe the statement that there were ten of these in each of the thirty *curiae*.[1] But we have already seen reason to reject this statement, and the idea of representation is so alien from all that we know of the composition of the senate in historical times that it cannot be believed to have operated even in the earliest period, though no doubt the king, in the exercise of his choice, would be guided to some extent by a desire to hold the balance between the various *gentes*.

In any case it is clear that originally only patricians were members of the senate; they alone were originally fully privileged citizens and, as we shall see, even in late republican times certain formal functions were reserved for the patrician senators. How and when plebeians were first admitted is unknown. According to Livy[2], on the expulsion of the kings the ranks of the senators, which had been thinned by the preceding revolution, were made up again by the addition of members of the equestrian order, and this was the origin of the famous phrase *patres conscripti* which was always used by speakers addressing the senate. The phrase must be understood as equivalent to *patres et conscripti*, the *conscripti* being the newly "enrolled" members. Plutarch[3] makes these members plebeians. According to another author[4] Servius Tullius had already introduced plebeians into the senate. At any rate they were eligible as far back as recorded history goes, though it is clear that they must have been in a minority, probably a small minority, during the struggle between the orders, as Livy constantly represents the senate as the stronghold of the patrician party. There cannot indeed have been much chance for plebeians so long as the magistrates who chose the senate were necessarily patrician, and a change presumably only took place when the military tribunate with consular power first opened the supreme magistracy to the plebs. The view that the plebeian members had the right of voting but

---

[1] *Supra*, 16.
[2] II. I.
[3] *Qu. Rom.* LVIII; *Rom.* XIII.
[4] Zonaras VII. 9.

not of speaking (though held by Mommsen) does not appear to have any real foundation.[1]

In their choice of senators the consuls, like the kings, seem to have been quite free from all legal restrictions. No doubt they were more or less constrained by custom to choose men who had held high office, but, so long as the magistracies were few, there must have been a considerable field in which they could use their unfettered discretion in making up the number of 300. The same was probably true of the censors when the function of appointing senators was first transferred to them. Exactly when this happened we do not know, but it must have occurred either before the *lex Ovinia* or by that statute itself. The *lex Ovinia* enacted, according to our account of it,[2] that the censors were to "choose the best men of every order". This is generally understood as limiting their discretion by imposing on them the duty of considering before others the claims of all former curule magistrates in turn, first the ex-consuls then the ex-praetors and then the ex-curule aediles. If this is right then the *lex Ovinia* must be subsequent to the institution of the praetorship in 367, and Mommsen puts it at about 312 B.C.[3] It is however also possible that "of every order" means "without distinction between patricians and plebeians", in which case the *lex Ovinia* would be an episode in the struggle between the orders and perhaps represents a compromise. There may have been trouble between the patrician and plebeian military tribunes about the choice of the senate, and the compromise would be an agreement to transfer the duty to the new magistrates (the censors)[4] with instructions to be impartial between the two orders. In this case the *lex Ovinia* must have fallen within the period of the military tribunate and consequently be much earlier than the date to which it is assigned by Mommsen.

Be that as it may, the power of choosing senators came to be the most important of the censors' duties, though their choice was, in fact, limited by the right which former magistrates had, by constitutional practice or in some cases by law, to be chosen, unless some good reason could be assigned for excluding them. At the time of the Punic wars this right was still confined to the ex-curule magistrates (consuls, praetors and curule aediles), but it was extended first to plebeian aediles, then to tribunes and finally under Sulla to quaestors. As a result of these extensions there were always enough ex-magistrates to fill all the seats in the senate, and in practice the right of the censors was limited to the removal of a qualified

---

[1] Willems, *Le Sénat de la République romaine*, I. 140 sqq.
[2] Festus, s.v. *praeteriti* (Bruns, II. 26).   [3] *Staatsr.* II. 418.   [4] *Infra*, 50.

person from the list if they considered him to have been guilty of serious misconduct. This remained true although Sulla raised the number of senators to 600, for he also increased the number of quaestors to twenty. The result of the filling up of the senate with ex-magistrates was that it became in effect a body elected by the assemblies, the chief importance of election to the quaestorship being indeed that it carried with it a seat in the senate. But it must not be imagined from this that the senate became a democratic body. It was only seldom that the *comitia* elected men who did not belong to the aristocracy, and, once elected to office, a man held his seat in the senate for life.

B. FUNCTIONS. (i) *Functions in connection with Legislation. Auctoritas Patrum.* In spite of the admission of plebeians to the senate certain traces of its original exclusively patrician nature survived. All acts of the *comitia* (legislative, elective and judicial) needed for their validity the *auctoritas* of the *patres*, that is, no doubt, originally of the whole patrician senate, and the right of giving this approval remained with the patrician members of the senate after the introduction of plebeians.[1] For *plebiscita*, the enactments of a body with which the old constitution had had no concern, the *auctoritas* was unnecessary (and our knowledge of the *comitia tributa* indeed is so scanty that we cannot say for certain whether it was ever needed for acts of that body). As Mommsen points out, the function of the *patres* in this matter was probably not that of a second chamber to the *comitia*; they had not to consider the expediency of the course proposed, but rather whether it was in accordance with the fundamental religious basis of the state—had the people, for instance, a just cause for making war on a state with which they had treaty relations? It is this aspect of the matter which explains the sinking of the *auctoritas* to little more than a formality. Generally there was no question of the religious admissibility of a proposal, especially not in the later republic when these matters were not taken so seriously, and the giving of the *auctoritas* became a matter of course. Originally given after the voting the *auctoritas* had by the *lex Publilia Philonis* of 339 B.C. to be given before the proposal was put to the people in the case of legislation, and this principle was extended to elections by a *lex Maenia* (? 338).

In itself this change would not have made the *auctoritas* any less important than it was before, but it appears that by this time the increasing number of plebeians in the senate and the growth of the new

[1] This is Mommsen's opinion, *Römische Forschungen*, I. 218–249. *Contra* Willems, *Droit public*, 180–185; *Le Sénat de la République romaine*, I. 38, II. 52–57.

patricio-plebeian nobility had already resulted in the view that the exercise of this function by a part of the senate was an anomaly and should be regarded as a matter of form alone.

Consultation by magistrates before the submission of a bill to assembly. The real powers of the full senate, including the plebeian members, were, unlike the shadowy powers given to the patricians, not a matter of law but of constitutional convention. It was a convention of the constitution that the magistrates should not, except for routine purposes, use their powers without first consulting the senate, and it was customary therefore for the magistrate who intended proposing legislation in the assembly to bring the matter first of all before the senate. This was all the more necessary as, once the proposal had been promulgated, there was no possibility of amendment and the *contiones* afforded but little scope for real discussion. In the senate on the other hand the proposal could be properly debated, and the magistrate might alter his original. draft in accordance with amendments suggested before he finally promulgated it. The initiative remained of course with the magistrate, but in the later republic, when the number of magistrates who had a right to summon the senate was large, it was always possible for any considerable party in the senate to find a magistrate who would call a meeting at their request. Similarly, if a magistrate, in defiance of constitutional practice, wished to put a proposal before the people without first consulting the senate, it was normally possible for the senate to find a tribune who would veto his action. Instances in which magistrates successfully ignored the senate belong to the revolutionary period.

Even if the proposal was not vetoed and passed the assembly, the senate had still a weapon left, for, as we have seen, it came to be considered the guardian of the constitution and it would generally not be difficult to find some flaw in the enactment, for instance that the auspices[1] had not been properly taken, which would invalidate the proceedings. Strictly, it was for the magistrates, as executive officers, to decide whether they should ignore the questionable enactment or put it into force, but they could hardly take so serious a step as ignoring it on their own authority, and, as happened in the case of Drusus' proposal, the ultimate decision rested in fact with the senate.[2]

[1] Before every public act, such as putting a bill to the people, it must be ascertained by omens whether the gods are favourable. This is called "taking the auspices".

[2] The senate's position as guardian of the constitution really rests on the idea that it is the great council of state and as such must be the ultimate arbiter when any religious questions arise. The fundamental principles of the constitution are

Dispensing power. Strictly, as the assembly was the only body which could make law, so it alone could exempt an individual from the operation of a law. This power was, however, gradually usurped by the senate, which would grant a dispensation in urgent cases subject, at first, to ratification by the *comitia*, this ratification being subsequently reduced to a formality or omitted altogether. An attempt made in 67 B.C. to deprive the senate of the right it had usurped only resulted in its confirmation, by a *lex Cornelia* which provided that at least 200 senators must be present when a dispensing resolution was passed.[1]

One important feature of Roman rule, the government of provinces by pro-magistrates, i.e. magistrates whose term of office had expired, rested essentially on the dispensing power of the senate, which prolonged the magistrate's *imperium* by dispensing him from the original term to which he had been restricted.[2]

(ii) *Functions in relation to the Magistracy.* With regard to the actual election of magistrates the senate exercised little power. We have already mentioned the formality of the *patrum auctoritas*,[3] and there was one other function, of greater importance, which was reserved for the patrician members.[4] This was the appointment of an *interrex*. If the supreme office of the state was vacant, as might happen if both consuls died suddenly, then there was no one competent to hold the elections, and, as the technical phrase was, the "auspices returned to the *patres*". The patrician members of the senate met together and elected an *interrex* who after holding office for five days nominated his successor and so on until one of the *interreges* held the consular elections. Any *interrex* could conduct the elections except the first, presumably because his nomination was deemed irregular.[5] The *patres* in later republican times

not purely secular matters. They, and indeed the whole of Roman public life, were conceived as having divine sanction and any departure from established custom might call down divine wrath. The senate's particular connection with religion can be seen from the practice that the first business laid before it by the consuls on assuming office should be a motion concerning religious matters. See e.g. Livy XXXVI. 1; XXXVII. 1.

[1] Asconius, *in Corn.* LVI (Bruns, II. 68). Confirmation by the assembly appears to have remained necessary in theory at least. Dio Cassius XXXVI. 39 says nothing of the quorum of 200.

[2] Originally a vote of the people was needed, but the senate had become competent already by the second century B.C. Mommsen, *Staatsr.* I. 643.

[3] *Supra*, 30.   [4] This is again Mommsen's view.

[5] The name of the interim magistrate shows, of course, that the institution goes back to the monarchy, but the procedure under the monarchy is represented as much more complicated, v. e.g. Greenidge, 47.

only exercised their functions in this matter on the initiative of the senate as a whole, which suggested that they should meet for the purpose.

The senate (i.e. the whole senate) also exercised *de facto* power with reference to another extraordinary magistracy, the dictatorship. As we shall see, the power of nominating a *dictator* in an emergency belonged to the consuls, but, already early in the republic, it became customary that this power should only be exercised at the suggestion of the senate, which finally went so far as to suggest, not only that a dictator should be nominated but also who he should be. This practice of course fell into abeyance with the disuse of the dictatorship itself after 202 B.C.[1]

On the appointment of magistrates elected in the various assemblies the senate had no influence at all beyond those indirect methods of influencing votes which are known to governments of all ages, but these were usually, though by no means always, sufficient to prevent the return of candidates who were distasteful to the majority in the senate. After their election, however, the senate, by the power which it acquired of assigning their different spheres of activity to the magistrates, exercised a very important control. The consuls, for instance, were each fully competent to exercise all the powers inherent in *imperium*, but they in fact often arranged a division, each frequently taking command of one of two armies destined for different campaigns. Though strictly the division was made either by arrangement or by lot, the senate sometimes suggested that one magistrate was better fitted than another for a certain sphere, and, above all, it came to be the undisputed prerogative of the senate to mark out the spheres themselves, i.e. decide which were to be the consular "provinces". After Sulla's reforms, the consuls always remained at Rome during their time of office and only proceeded to military commands or governorships abroad as "pro-magistrates" after their year was over, so that the decision which were to be "consular" provinces[2] might make all the difference between giving a man a great command abroad or some unimportant post in which he could gain neither fame nor riches. The senate had thus in 60 B.C., foreseeing that Caesar would be elected consul for 59, and desiring to keep him quiet, assigned the internal administration of Italy, up-keep of roads, etc., as the consular "provinces" for 58[3], a decision which Caesar simply overruled by getting a plebiscite passed which gave him the governorship of Gaul for five years.

[1] *Infra*, 55.

[2] *Provincia* properly means a "sphere of action", whence "province" in our sense, i.e. the sphere of a magistrate's activity.

[3] At this period it was legally necessary that the assignment of provinces should take place before the magistrates' year of office.

But these were, of course, revolutionary times; usually the decision of the senate in this matter was one of the ways in which it controlled the consuls.

Under the heading of functions in connection with the magistracy may also be put the power, assumed by the senate during the revolutionary period of the late republic, of passing a resolution known as *senatus consultum ultimum*, the force of which was, at any rate according to the *Optimates* (the "Conservative" party), to arm the magistrates with extraordinary powers, including, so it was alleged, that of putting citizens to death without appeal to the people. In form the resolution was only advice to the consuls (sometimes with the addition of other magistrates) to "see that the commonwealth did not suffer", but its object was to proclaim something like martial law in times of crisis, and it was in part a device intended to fill the gap in the constitution made by the disuse of the dictatorship, the original constitutional provision for creating a strong executive in times of emergency. Though the Romans would probably have agreed generally that if there was actual armed force used against the state it was permissible for the consuls to go outside strict law in meeting it, and that the senate as the great Council of State might point out their duty to the consuls, the fact was that the *senatus consultum ultimum* was only used for party purposes and during the period at which the senate really represented only one party (the *Optimates*); its legality was consequently never recognised by the democratic party. In particular the execution of the Catilinarian conspirators without trial by Cicero when consul in 63 B.C., although the senate had passed the *consultum ultimum*, was generally regarded as illegal and was the chief reason for his banishment in 58 B.C.

The two spheres in which the influence of the senate made itself most strongly and most consistently felt were those of finance and foreign affairs. Here, as throughout, the action of the senate is in form advisory, but nowhere else does the form wear so thin and the fact emerge so clearly that it is the senate itself, not the magistrates whom it advises, with whom the real decision lies.

(iii) *Financial Functions*. To understand republican finance we must first rid ourselves of the modern preconception that the greatest part of a state's income must necessarily come from taxation. At Rome the principle was rather that the state should have enough income to meet all ordinary charges without taxation.[1] Nor again must we suppose that all expenditure of a public character is necessarily met by payment out of

---

[1] As the king of England was at one time expected to "live of his own".

the public treasury. The Romans so far as possible were accustomed to provide for ordinary recurring expenditure by appropriating specific sources of revenue. The expenses of religion were thus largely met by appropriating the rents of certain state lands once and for all to the service of particular temples. Even military expenditure might be dealt with in a similar way. Until a comparatively late period the payment of money to which cavalrymen had a right for their horse and its fodder was a burden on women and orphan children who owned property but could not be rated in the census because the census list contained only the names of those capable of bearing arms. That the money payable in such cases did not go through the state treasury, but direct, is clear from Gaius, who says that if the soldier was not paid he could seize a piece of property from the person liable in order to enforce payment.[1] Even the payment of the infantry appears originally to have been a matter for the tribes, if indeed they were paid at all, but was early taken over by the state (406 B.C.).

This system of permanent appropriation was one of the chief causes of senatorial control over finance; expenditure not covered by it was necessarily a non-routine matter and so, on the general constitutional principle, needed the senate's sanction.[2]

The main ordinary source of income was the revenue from public lands. To this must be added some indirect taxes, especially the *portoria*, export and import duties, and a certain amount of fines inflicted for various offences. But Roman indirect taxes differed from ours in that they were not reconsidered annually and so variable in amount from year to year, but laid down once and for all. In the later republic, when Rome had already extended her conquests widely, there was an additional source of income in the taxation of the provinces, but here too the taxes were levied under permanent schemes and according to the final theory represented rent for the land which, although left to its original owners, was held to have become the property of the Roman state.[3] Where the ordinary revenue was not sufficient for state expenses, as generally happened during the wars of the earlier republic, it was necessary to have recourse to taxation. The tax, known as *tributum*, consisted of a proportion of the citizen's property as assessed for the census list (which was also the basis of arrangement in classes for purposes of the centuriate assembly), and it was for the consuls to say when it should be levied and what the

---

[1] Gai. IV. 27. How it was decided which person was to pay which soldier we do not know. Cf. *infra*, 191.

[2] Cf. *supra*, 27. [3] Cf. *infra*, 276.

proportion was to be,[1] but here the consuls probably never acted without senatorial authorisation. Strictly the *tributum* was not so much a tax as a forced loan exacted to meet an emergency and repayable if circumstances permitted. There are indeed instances of repayment after a successful campaign, but such cases were rare, and *tributum* was, in fact, almost always levied, until the victory of Pydna in 168 B.C.,[2] by providing the treasury with enormous booty, made it unnecessary. Direct taxation was never again imposed on citizens during the republic.[3]

As to expenditure, the chief extraordinary outgoings besides those necessary for war were for public works, roads, buildings, etc. There was no organised civil service at Rome; the higher officials were all unpaid (though opportunities for making money were not always lacking) and though they had paid assistants this did not form a large item. Most of the innumerable burdens which a modern state takes on itself (e.g. education, relief of poverty, supervision of the conditions of employment) were lacking, a fact which to some extent explains the simplicity of Roman financial arrangements when compared with our own.

In strict theory of law the state treasury (*aerarium*) was under the control of the chief magistrates, the consuls, and they alone were entitled to take money from it; but this theory does not correspond with the facts, for the senate kept a firm hold on finance, and the main financial officers were the censors and the quaestors. The duties of these officers were however quite different and must be dealt with separately.

Censors. These magistrates are sometimes said to have been the "budget-makers" of Rome, but, from our point of view, it was a very imperfect budget that they made. They had to compile the census-list and for this purpose they appear to have had a considerable discretion in the valuation of property. We hear, for instance, that Cato in 184 B.C. assessed articles of luxury at ten times their real value, which meant of course that their owners would have to pay an increased amount of tribute. It was the censors too who made the contracts necessary for getting in the public revenue; they could for instance lease public land or such sources of wealth as mines or fisheries belonging to the state at a rental, and it was they who made the contracts with the *publicani*, the tax-farmers. Taxes such as the *portoria*, or the *vectigal* (payment for public land "occupied" by squatters),[4] and the various forms of taxation in the provinces, were not, in the republic, collected directly by state officials,

---

[1] The normal amount was one thousandth part (*tributum simplex*), but we hear also of *tributum duplex* and *triplex*.
[2] *Supra*, 2.   [3] Except perhaps in 43 B.C.   [4] *Supra*, 9.

but farmed out to speculators who paid or promised a lump sum for the right to collect the taxes, hoping, of course, to make a profit by collecting more than they had to pay. The system resulted in considerable oppression, as the *publicani* were not properly controlled, and vast profits were often made.[1] Sometimes however they overreached themselves, either when the competition in bidding between different companies of *publicani* was particularly keen, or when a harvest turned out badly,[2] and were faced with bankruptcy if held to their bid. In such cases only the senate could release them from their contract, and we know of several instances in which this was done.[3]

Besides arranging for the collection of public revenue the censors were also to some extent spending officers; they, for instance, often arranged contracts for public buildings, roads, etc., in which the state was the paying, not the receiving, party. In these matters, however, they had less discretion, being only allowed to draw from the *aerarium* up to a definite amount placed to their credit by order of the consuls and senate. They were thus in this respect in a position similar to that of other magistrates who had similar credits opened for them for their expenses, for instance in the payment of their subordinates.[4]

The registers of the censors (*tabulae*), showing as they did a large proportion of the income which the state might expect, were the nearest thing which the Romans had to a budget and were no doubt largely used in estimating the amount of money which might be spent, but they were necessarily incomplete, for censors were only elected every five years and held office for not longer than eighteen months,[5] and in the intervals business which could not wait was transacted by the other magistrates. Also extraordinary income, such as that derived from booty, would find no place in the censorial accounts.

The Quaestors. The *aerarium* itself was under the supervision of the quaestors. Originally there was but this one treasury administered by the

---

[1] The contracts were not given to individuals but to companies, and it appears that it was possible to take a share in such a company by investing capital, without doing any work, in much the same way as one takes a share in a limited company to-day.

[2] Many taxes being calculated by taking a percentage of the crops.

[3] One famous case occurred in 59 B.C. when the question whether the *publicani* of Asia should be released or not was one of the most important issues between the political parties.

[4] Our system of appropriation of moneys to particular expenses, so that money allowed to an official for one purpose cannot be used for another, was unknown.

[5] Five years were thus the normal term for censorial contracts.

two quaestors as assistants to the consuls, the consuls having control of the treasury as of all other departments of state. In 421,[1] however, the number of quaestors was raised to four. Two (*quaestores urbani*) were to remain in charge of the *aerarium* at Rome and each consul was to have one of the others as a separate assistant when he took the field. A separate treasury was then established for him and similar separate treasuries were established later for provincial governors. These, though under the control of the governor, remained in relation with the central treasury at Rome, the provincial quaestors being given money or credits on the central treasury for the expenses of government and being bound to render account on their return. Meanwhile the governor had, however, full discretion as to the use to which he would put moneys which flowed into his treasury. By no means all moneys went through the central treasury.

Besides their duty of keeping the accounts of the *aerarium*, the two *quaestores urbani* had other duties, such as sale of property (e.g. slaves and booty) which fell into the hands of the state. They also sometimes made financial statements in the senate.

The key to the understanding of Roman finance lies in the principle that every holder of *imperium* was bound to delegate the keeping of the account of moneys which came under his control. For the consuls and most pro-magistrates these delegates were provided in the elected quaestors and ex-quaestors, who, like their superiors, usually went to a province after their year of office; but where there was no such delegate provided, it was the duty of the holder of *imperium* to choose one himself. The object of this rule was clearly that there should be a record of every payment made by order of a magistrate with *imperium* which would make it possible to call him to account for moneys spent improperly, without limiting his discretion in the spending of them. The urban quaestors had a more independent position than any others because their superiors (the consuls) were constantly away from Rome. This meant that in fact they laid out moneys only on the authorisation of the senate. They were entitled to pay on the command of the consuls alone, but in the later republic even the consuls never gave such orders without previously consulting the senate.

We thus get the position that the quaestors are the people who hold the keys of the treasury; they pay out moneys at a consul's order either to him or to other magistrates, but owing to the convention that the consul must consult the senate, it is the senate which has the real control.

[1] When the office was opened to plebeians, *supra*, 14.

(iv) *Functions in connection with Foreign Affairs*. That the declaration of war was a function reserved for the people has already been mentioned,[1] though in this most vital matter the magistrate was of course bound in practice to consult the senate before bringing a proposal before the assembly. It is not so easy to answer the question where, according to the Roman constitution, lay the power of making peace, or, what is in effect the same,[2] the treaty-making power. It is likely enough that the power of binding the Roman state by treaty was originally regarded as inherent in the *imperium* of the magistrate as the representative of the commonwealth, but in historical times this was no longer true.

Treaties cannot be deemed binding unless the magistrate's act is either authorised beforehand by the community or subsequently ratified. On more than one occasion a deluded enemy learnt, to his cost, that the Romans would refuse to acknowledge the most solemn oath taken on their behalf by a magistrate, and consider their consciences satisfied by delivering him and all who had taken part in the ceremony naked and bound to the people with whom they had contracted.[3]

For purposes of the authorisation or ratification of treaties the community meant the "Senate and People of Rome", the style of the Roman state used particularly for international relationships, in which, be it noticed, the senate comes first. In fact the decision lay from early republican times with the senate, and the ratification of the senate's decision by the people was a formality. Towards the end of the republic it was occasionally omitted, though Cicero could still argue that it was legally necessary.[4] The treaty once authorised was usually concluded by sending a mission consisting of two or three *Fetiales*, members of the priestly college specially charged with international ritual, who took an oath on behalf of the senate and people.

The concentration of all international matters in the hands of the

---

[1] *Supra*, 17.

[2] For, in theory, any state not bound to Rome by treaty is an enemy.

[3] The most famous instance is that of the "Caudine Forks" in 321. The Roman army under the consuls T. Veturius Calvinus and Sp. Postumius was trapped in a defile by the Samnites. As escape was impossible, the consuls concluded a treaty by which they agreed to make peace if the lives of the Romans were spared. This was done, and the army, after being stripped of its arms and made to pass under a yoke (the symbol of defeat), returned home. The senate, however, on the advice of Postumius himself, repudiated the agreement, the argument being that the people could not be bound by a treaty made without their consent and that all that law demanded was the delivery of the actual contracting parties to the enemy.

[4] *Pro Balbo*, xv. 34.

senate was the natural outcome of its permanence when contrasted with the ever-changing individual magistrates, and one result of this concentration was that a general in the field, once peace was in sight, directed the ambassadors of the other state straight to the senate at Rome before which all but the preliminary negotiations took place. Also, after an enemy had been so completely conquered that there was no question of a treaty, but only of complete surrender (*deditio*), it was the senate which sent out commissioners to assist the commander in settling the organisation of the conquered territory. This organisation was generally laid down in a *lex*, a sort of charter, which however did not receive the sanction of the *comitia*. During the period when provinces were being added to the Roman empire the senate's supremacy was so clearly recognised that its authority was sufficient.

In speaking of the "foreign affairs" of Rome one must of course remember that in the later republic Rome was already supreme in the Mediterranean and indeed over most of the known world, so that there was no international intercourse such as exists to-day between independent states, the only power which could at all measure itself with Rome being the distant kingdom of Parthia. But it must also be remembered that the vast majority of the inhabitants of the lands ruled by Rome were not citizens, but foreigners (*peregrini*), so that the government of the provinces outside Italy was also in a sense part of "foreign affairs". Here too the senate, as the permanent government, exercised what supervision was exercised at all over the provincial governors. Permanent representation either of subject communities or of independent powers at Rome, such as exists in our modern embassies, was unknown, all business being transacted by delegates appointed for the particular occasion. Roman history records many instances of these and of the impression made on the delegates by the assembled senate, a body which must have seemed to many of them, as it certainly did to one, "an assembly of kings".[1]

(v) *Functions in connection with Religion.* As the great Council of State, the senate was, of necessity, often concerned with matters affecting the state religion, and it is difficult to say that any part of Roman religion was quite independent of the senate. Not only was the first sitting of each year devoted to the presentation of a report by the consuls on sacred matters,[2] but at every meeting religious affairs took precedence of all others.

---

[1] These words were used by Cineas, ambassador of Pyrrhus, king of Epirus, when in spite of Pyrrhus's victory at Heraclea in 280 B.C. the senate refused to discuss terms so long as foreign troops remained on Italian soil.
[2] *Supra*, 31 n. 2.

To some extent the most important sacred "colleges", such as the pontiffs and augurs, whose members would generally, though by no means necessarily, be members of the senate, acted as standing committees for matters falling within their province; but these bodies possessed little initiative, and senatorial authority was needed to carry out their proposals. Thus the senate might order ceremonies of purification to be undertaken if the priestly college announced the appearance of some "prodigy" which was taken as indicating divine wrath; it might also order the consultation of the Sibylline books,[1] a matter sometimes of very great political importance. The senate's approval was of course necessary, on general principles, if money was to be spent on any religious ceremonies or festivals out of the ordinary course of events, and it could decree extraordinary festivals, a power which was sometimes used for the purpose of obstructing undesirable public activities. The reception of a new deity into the public worship of Rome, though strictly perhaps a matter for the people, was generally decreed by senate, sometimes as a result of consulting the Sibylline books.

C. PROCEDURE. To understand the procedure of the senate it is necessary to remember throughout that the senate is a council whose business it is to give advice to the magistrate, and that it has no independent executive authority of its own. This appears first from the fact that the senate can only meet when summoned by a magistrate, originally only a magistrate of the *populus* with *imperium*,[2] who consults it previously to acting himself. In the later republic[3] however, owing probably to the growth of the legislative power of the *concilium plebis*, and the consequent necessity that its presidents should be able to consult the senate before proposing *plebiscita*, the tribunes obtained the right of convening the magistrates' council. This multiplication of possible conveners of the senate is important, for it meant that any considerable section of opinion could normally secure the holding of a meeting in order to express its views even if all the magistrates with *imperium* were desirous of preventing such expression. In this way, as well as by the use of their veto in accordance with the senate's wishes, the tribunes

---

[1] A collection of oracular utterances in Greek, said to have been bought by the last king of Rome, Tarquinius Superbus, from the Sibyl at Cumae. They were under the custody of a special college, x *viri*, later xv *viri sacris faciundis*. Cf. *supra*, 14.

[2] Dictator, consuls, praetors, interrex and necessarily the military tribunes with consular power when these existed, *supra*, 13.

[3] At any rate not before 304 B.C. (Greenidge, 127).

became, in the later republic, an important instrument of senatorial rule.

As the senate could only be summoned by a magistrate, so it could only discuss business put before it by a magistrate; there were no "private members' bills", though as we shall see it was possible for the motion on which the House voted to be framed by a non-magisterial member.

The normal conveners were the consuls, but once the senate was convened it was not the convener alone who could put business before the House. The consul's business comes first,[1] then the praetor's and then the tribune's. The proceedings on each question began with a statement by the magistrate who brought forward the business, and it was also permissible for any magistrate to speak, without invitation, at any moment during the debate. After the opening statement the House might proceed immediately to a vote, but more usually a debate followed. In the form of debate, however, the theory of consultation by the magistrate appears again clearly. It was not for any member wishing to speak to "catch the Speaker's eye", it was for the presiding magistrate to call upon the member to deliver his opinion (e.g. *Marce Tulli, quid censes?*). In this duty, however, the magistrate was more or less constrained by custom to follow a prescribed order of seniority. When the censorship was still a living force, it had been customary for the censors to choose some particularly distinguished man to head the list of the senate and he, as *princeps senatus*, would always be asked first. After Sulla's reforms had reduced the importance of the censorship this was no longer done, and the president could choose any person of consular rank (i.e. an ex-consul) to speak first. After the consulars came the praetorians, then the ex-aediles, the ex-tribunes and finally the ex-quaestors.[2] When asked his opinion, the senator need not make a speech, he might simply express his agreement with the view already stated by some previous speaker, and it was also possible for him to make such agreement clear before he was asked by moving and taking his seat near the person whom he supported. On the other hand, when once a senator was on his feet the presiding magistrate had no power to restrict him to relevant matters; he could

---

[1] "Business", not "motion", for, strictly, the magistrate asks for advice and does not propose anything himself. In fact of course his statement might contain a proposal.

[2] Those who had not held curule office would thus seldom have a chance of speaking. They were called *pedarii*, a name which is said by Festus (Bruns, II. 23) to come from the fact that they used their feet (i.e. in a division), but not their voices. See, however, Gell. III. 18.

express his opinion on anything he considered of public importance.[1] Nor was there any time limit to speeches except that the sitting had to be suspended at sunset, and obstruction by interminable oratory was by no means unknown.

When the debate was over it was for the presiding magistrate to choose the order in which the opinions expressed by members should be put to the vote, and the voting took place by those in favour moving to one side of the House, those against to the other. If one motion on a subject was passed, the remainder were automatically dropped.

Once passed, a motion became a *senatus consultum* provided no tribune or other magistrate with the right of *intercessio* vetoed it. It was open to veto because, in strict theory of law, it was only advice by the senate to the magistrate who had elicited it and took its binding force from his authority, and an act of a magistrate was open to veto by a tribune or colleague of equal or higher rank. If vetoed, the motion which the senate had passed became not a *senatus consultum*, but merely an *auctoritas*, an expression of opinion which bound nobody but might command the respect of magistrates or others concerned. All resolutions were committed to writing under the supervision of a small committee chosen for each case by the presiding magistrate, and were deposited in the *aerarium* under the supervision of the quaestors. To prevent forgery the plebeian aediles were, during the time of the struggle between the orders, given a share in the control—we hear of the deposit of *senatus consulta* under their care in the temple of Ceres—but the exact way in which responsibility was shared is unknown.

As to publication, there was no general system by which the senate's resolutions were made public; sometimes they were announced in a *contio*, sometimes put up in a public place to be read, and sometimes copies might be sent to interested parties, such as the ambassadors of allied states.

§ VI. THE MAGISTRACIES

A. THE CONSULATE. We have seen that on the downfall of the monarchy the kingly power was limited by being transferred to two annually elected officers, known in historic times as consuls,[2] and that

---

[1] This was known as *egredi relationem*. The most famous case is that of Cato (censor 184 B.C.), who tacked on to every speech the remark "Carthage should be destroyed", a piece of advice which the Romans finally took.

[2] The earliest title is said to have been *praetores*, literally "leaders" (*prae-ire*). *Consul* may, as Mommsen thought, be derived from con (*cum*) and *salire*, hence "those who leap together", a reference to ritual dancing. (*Staatsr.* II. 77.)

the struggle between the orders turned largely on the question of the eligibility of plebeians to this office, which continued throughout the republic to be the highest in the state. Like the royal power of which it was the successor, the consular *imperium* was, strictly, unlimited, extending to all departments of government, and including leadership of the army, jurisdiction and the right of putting business before the assembly as well as, of course, before the senate, the advisory body originally of the kings, now of the consuls. The only sphere in which the consuls did not succeed fully to the kingly power appears to have been that of religion. The position of head to the priestly college of *pontifices* passed to a separate official, the *pontifex maximus*, and for certain minor religious purposes the name of "king" was retained by a priest known as the *rex sacrorum*.

The election of the consuls took place in the *comitia centuriata*,[1] which was summoned for this purpose normally by a consul, exceptionally by a dictator, an *interrex* or a military tribune with consular power. For a praetor to hold the consular election was quite irregular. The date of the elections, the most important regular political event in the year, which drew numbers of citizens from all parts of Italy to Rome, varied considerably from year to year until settled by Sulla, after whose time they were held in July. The consular year however (since a law of 153 B.C.) always began on January 1st, so that there was a considerable interval during which the successful candidates were *consules designati* before entering on their office. Once elected, a consul could not legally be removed from office, except perhaps by a dictator, but removal of a consul did occur in a few cases during the revolutionary period. If a consul died or resigned it was for his colleague to hold an election to fill his place for the remainder of the year. If both consuls died, an *interrex* had to be appointed.[2]

The consul's *imperium* is in effect the royal power, limited by the principle of colleagueship and the annual tenure of office. It is thus a general authority, military and civil, and undefined except in so far as special limitations are put upon it by specific statutes or by the assignment of special functions to other magistrates. These limitations apply however almost exclusively within the city or the first milestone therefrom (*domi*); outside (*militiae*) the holder of *imperium* is untrammelled. The most important restriction based on statute was that concerning *pro-*

---

[1] The formal confirmation of the *imperium* by the *comitia curiata* (cf. *supra*, 18) took place at the beginning of the year of office.

[2] *Supra*, 32.

vocatio.[1] The right of choosing the senate given to the censors,[2] and the jurisdiction in civil matters assigned to the *praetor urbanus* are examples of powers originally belonging to the consuls and subsequently transferred to other magistrates. But apart from these legal restrictions and much more important is the all-pervading power of the senate of which the consuls came in effect to be merely the chief executive officers. Indeed, after Sulla's reorganisation of the constitution, the consuls are during their year of office no more than the chief executive officers in Rome and Italy; previously, although special praetors or ex-magistrates had been appointed as occasion required to be provincial governors, the consuls themselves had frequently commanded the armies of the republic outside as well as in Italy; according to the system introduced by Sulla, governorships of the provinces, and therefore the command of the troops stationed there, were regularly held by magistrates (consuls and praetors) whose year of office had come to an end. During their year of office the consuls and praetors did not leave Italy, and the importance of this principle politically was that it meant separation of military from civil power, for Italy, all the inhabitants of which were now citizens, was regarded as permanently pacified, and it became a constitutional principle that there should be no troops stationed within its boundaries.

The inconvenience of the principle of colleagueship, which meant that there were two officials whose functions and competence were precisely the same, was surmounted by a number of different expedients. In the last resort there was always the principle of *intercessio* to decide in case of disagreement, i.e. either consul could veto any act of his colleague, so that matters remained as they were. But of course government would have been impossible if it had been necessary to have recourse to this expedient often. To some extent the consuls divided their spheres of action by agreement; more commonly they acted together. They could, for instance, convene the senate together, or the assembly, and that they did so is witnessed by a number of laws bearing the names of consular colleagues. Where the business was such that only one man could do it, the matter might be arranged either by agreement or by lot, but there was also an old practice by which the consuls took turns of such duty. At home they changed every month, the older magistrate generally taking the first turn; only the consul whose turn it was had the *fasces* borne before him. In the field the more questionable practice of taking daily turns of supreme command prevailed.

Jurisdiction was always in theory a function of that *imperium* of which

[1] Cf. *infra*, 320.   [2] *Supra*, 29.

the consuls were the chief holders, but in fact, when a special jurisdictional magistracy, the praetorship, had been established, the consuls ceased to have any concern with civil litigation,[1] and their criminal jurisdiction was, as we shall see, exercised on their behalf by the quaestors.

Of outward signs of rank the consuls had many. The magisterial *toga praetexta* (purple-edged toga) and the curule chair they shared with some other magistrates, but they alone were preceded by the full number of twelve lictors, bearing the *fasces*, or bundles of rods, the symbol of coercive authority, to which, as soon as the consul quitted the precincts of the city, the axe was added to show that he had exchanged the limited authority which he exercised *domi* for the unrestricted powers of the magistrate with *imperium militiae*. Most notable privilege of all was that by which the names of the consuls formed the official designation in the calendar of the year in which they had held office.

B. THE PRAETORSHIP. The events which led up to the creation of the first praetorship in 367 B.C. have already been described.[2] The new magistrate was to take over the duties hitherto performed by the consuls with respect to civil jurisdiction. This, it may as well be noted at once, does not mean that the praetor was a judge in our sense of the word. A Roman civil trial, until well on into the empire, always took place in two stages, the first of which alone was the concern of the jurisdictional magistrate. This was the stage *in iure*, in which only the preliminaries and especially the issue[3] between the parties was settled. It was in the second stage, *apud iudicem*,[4] that the actual trial took place and the issue raised was decided, the judge (*iudex*) in this stage being, not a magistrate, but a private person appointed for that purpose.

It is this division of functions between the magistrate and the *iudex* which alone makes it possible to understand how the Romans were able to manage for so long with a single jurisdictional magistrate, for it was not until about 242 B.C. that a second praetor was appointed and a division of duties made, one praetor superintending the jurisdiction between citizens (*praetor urbanus*) and the other that between foreigners or between

---

[1] Though transfers of property by *in iure cessio* and manumissions *vindicta*, which were actions in form, could take place before them.

[2] *Supra*, 15.

[3] Settling the issue means settling exactly what is the question, whether of law or fact, between the parties which the trial is to decide.

[4] *V. infra*, 186.

citizens and foreigners and hence known as *praetor qui inter peregrinos ius dicit*, or more shortly *praetor peregrinus* ("foreign" praetor).

The number of praetors did not remain at two for long. The first provision which Rome made for the government of provinces which she acquired beyond the seas was by the appointment of new praetors, two being added about 227 B.C. for Sicily and Sardinia, acquired by Rome as a result of the first Punic war, a further two in 197 B.C. for the two new Spanish provinces. At this number of six the praetorship remained until Sulla, for although new provinces were created they were governed more and more under the new principle of pro-magistracies.[1]

The position of the praetor is best understood by thinking of him, in the Roman phrase, as a minor colleague of the consul. He, like the consul, is elected by the *comitia centuriata* and he has full *imperium*, which means that he is potentially capable of all the duties which the consul performs, military and administrative as well as judicial. But he is subordinate to the consul; the consul's *intercessio* prevails against his act, whereas he cannot veto an act of the consul, and his inferiority is made outwardly manifest by the lesser number of lictors, six, by whom he has a right to be accompanied. Above all he differs from the consul in that he is always given a definite sphere (*provincia*) in which to exercise his *imperium*, while that of the consul is not so limited. But, although each praetor has a *provincia*, he is not elected to it in the first instance by the people. They only elect six praetors and the *provinciae* are afterwards distributed among the successful candidates by lot. The normal *provinciae* are the two jurisdictional spheres of the city and the four oversea governorships, but it was possible for this arrangement to be varied at times; two spheres, e.g. those of the *praetor urbanus* and *praetor peregrinus*, might be combined, in order to leave a magistrate free for some particular duty outside the usual six spheres; or the same purpose might be achieved by continuing the existing governor of a province for a year beyond his original term of office. The decision in such matters rested with the senate. After Sulla's reconstruction of the constitution the position was somewhat different. There were eight praetors elected annually, and they all remained at Rome during their year of office, two, as before, taking the civil jurisdiction and the remaining six being used as presidents of the *quaestiones perpetuae*, or standing criminal courts which had been made a permanent feature of Roman public life by Sulla. Only after the year did the praetors, like the consuls, proceed to governorships of provinces abroad.

[1] *Infra,* 67.

Though primarily confined to his allotted *provincia*, each praetor, being endowed with *imperium*, could also act outside it if necessary. Thus we find the praetors summoning the senate or the people or undertaking the levy, but only (in normal cases) in the absence of the consuls. In such cases it was the *praetor urbanus* who was expected to take the lead, his office ranking highest. He would also almost necessarily be present in Rome, for we hear that he was forbidden by statute to leave the city for more than ten days during his year of office.[1] The special functions of the urban and peregrine praetors with respect to jurisdiction, especially their edicts, which were of the very greatest importance in the development of the law, must be left for separate discussion.[2]

C. THE AEDILESHIP. The aediles were originally purely plebeian officers, assistants of the tribunes, as the quaestors were assistants of the consuls, and were elected, like the tribunes themselves, in the *concilium plebis*. A complete change, however, came over the office as a result of the creation in 367 of two new officers with the same title who were true magistrates of the whole people and as such were elected by the *comitia tributa*. Henceforward the connection with the tribunate is forgotten[3] and the four aediles act largely together as a single "college". Some differences between the plebeian and "curule" aediles remain; the former must always be plebeians, the latter are elected in alternate years from the two orders; the curule aediles have not only the curule chair from which they derive their name but also the magisterial *praetexta*, whereas the plebeian aediles, like the tribunes, have no outward sign of their office, and are in general considered to hold a lower rank.

The duties of the office, though rather heterogeneous, can be described as in the main municipal. The aediles were responsible for the *cura urbis*, which included the supervision of cleanliness in the city, the repair of roadways, public places and public buildings, and the water supply. They were also in charge of the corn supply and of some of the public games, and had some share in the control of the state archives.[4] In connection with their general *cura urbis* they exercised a certain amount of minor criminal jurisdiction, for they had *coercitio* (the general magisterial right of enforcing order and obedience to their commands by imprisonment, seizure of pledges and money fines), but had to bring their sentences before the people for review when they inflicted fines beyond a certain

---

[1] Cic. *Phil.* II. 13. 31.   [2] *Infra*, 95–99.
[3] So much so that the aedileship ranks higher than the tribunate.
[4] *Supra*, 43.

maximum. This is an anomaly of which the explanation is uncertain; the aediles had no *imperium* and could not summon the assembly for any other purpose.

Their most interesting function from the point of view of legal history is the control of the market-place, for in connection with it the curule aediles[1] exercised a certain amount of civil jurisdiction for the purpose of which they issued edicts corresponding to those of the praetors; these edicts were of great importance in the development of the law of sale.[2]

D. THE QUAESTORSHIP. The quaestors were originally assistants of the consuls and, as such, chosen, in all probability, by the consuls themselves. In historical times, however, they are elected in the *comitia tributa* and count as magistrates of the Roman people. The number, originally two, was raised in 421 to four,[3] and about 267 another four were appointed to assist the consuls in the administration of Italy. Sulla, as we have seen, raised the number to twenty.[4]

The duties of the quaestors are partly the result of their originally subordinate position and partly indicative of the independent status they afterwards attained. The two urban quaestors are, in essentials, independent magistrates. With their financial functions, which are the most important, we have already dealt,[5] but they also had duties in connection with criminal justice. It had become a principle that the consul must not himself defend a sentence before the people on appeal, the reason being, no doubt, that it would be inconsistent with his dignity if the people reversed his decision. In criminal jurisdiction the consuls were therefore always represented by the quaestors, or in cases of treason by the *duoviri perduellionis*. These representatives both issue the sentence and conduct the appeal before the people.[6]

Those quaestors, on the other hand, who are attached to magistrates with *imperium* outside the city are in a more dependent position. Though their chief duties were financial, they were used by their superiors as delegates in all types of duty, military, administrative and even judicial. The relationship between the higher magistrate and his quaestor was considered to be a personal one, and when the superior's office was prolonged, that of his subordinate was regularly prolonged also. Those quaestors, however, who were concerned with the administration of

---

[1] This jurisdiction was not shared by their plebeian colleagues, probably because at the time when it was instituted the plebeian aediles had not yet acquired the character of magistrates of the people. Mommsen, *Staatsr.* II. 501.
[2] *Infra*, 303.　　　[3] *Supra*, 38.　　　[4] *Supra*, 30.
[5] *Supra*, 37.　　　[6] Cf. *infra*, 319.

Italy, though strictly subordinate to the consuls, had in fact definite posts allotted to them which they administered with considerable independence. Not all these positions are known, but there was one at Ostia, concerned with the corn supply, and another appears to have been concerned with the department of "woods and forests" (calles).

E. THE CENSORSHIP. We have already spoken of the institution of the censorship (in 443 B.C.) as an incident in the struggle between the orders,[1] which constituted a patrician victory in so far as the new office was confined originally to patricians. When the office became open to plebeians is uncertain, but we hear of a plebeian censor for the first time in 351 B.C. and soon afterwards, the same rule applied as to the consulship, that one of the two colleagues must be a plebeian.

The original purpose of the new magistracy was clearly to relieve the supreme magistrates of one of the duties that they had previously performed, that of taking the census, and at first the censorship appears to have been comparatively unimportant. But the control which it gave over the whole moral life of the people, and especially the power of appointing senators,[2] made it, in the end, an office of even greater dignity than the consulship itself, and it was, with hardly an exception, held only by men of consular rank. The election was held in the comitia centuriata under the presidency of a consul, but the censor had no imperium, and, though he sat on the curule chair, he did not have the fasces borne before him. On the other hand the eminence of his office became apparent when he died, for he alone of all magistrates was buried in the full purple toga which had been the emblem of royalty. The censors also differed from other magistrates in that they were not elected annually; they were only elected for the purpose of taking the census, a duty which ended with the lustrum, or ceremonial purification of the people, and they had to lay down their office when this was completed, or at the latest eighteen months after their election. Then no others were appointed until a new census was to be taken, the usual interval being four or, later, five years. Re-election was forbidden.

The census was far from being a mere numbering; it was the registration of the whole people in their divisions of tribes and centuries, and its purpose was chiefly military and financial. Incidentally it was also political, for the centuries and the tribes were both voting units. For the purpose of registration the censors summoned the members of the centuriate assembly, that is the arm-bearing citizens, to meet them in the

---

[1] Supra, 14.   [2] Supra, 29.

Campus Martius, and each citizen, or at least each head of a family, had to make a return of the members of his family and his property; this latter return was needed partly for the purposes of assessing the *tributum*, and partly because the divisions in the centuriate assembly depended upon wealth. In addition the censors held a separate review of the eighteen centuries of *equites* in the *forum*. The supervision over the morals of the community, the famous *regimen morum*, was an outcome of the census. In the lists which they made up the censors could affix a *nota* or mark of censure against a man's name if they disapproved of his conduct, and there was no restriction as to the reasons for which they might express this disapproval. It might be some action in his private life, such as luxurious living, or divorcing a wife without taking the opinion of a family council; it might be the following of a disgraceful trade; it might be the commission of some disgraceful wrong, such as theft, against another person, or again some act in connection with public life, desertion or cowardice in the army, or what the censors considered improper conduct as a magistrate. The censors appear to have published the principles on which they would act in an edict and, no doubt, the views of different individuals varied, although the general attitude was that the censors were there to uphold the ancient simplicity and sternness of Roman manners. The only safeguards against abuse of these great powers were that the reason for the *nota* must always be given and that the two colleagues must concur in affixing it. It was also usual to summon the person affected to defend himself, but there was no formal trial.

The effect of the *nota* was to remove the censured person from the tribe to which he belonged, usually to remove him altogether from the tribes, so that he became an *aerarius*, or citizen without the right of voting and subject to a poll-tax, but apparently the result might sometimes only be to degrade the citizen from a "rustic" to one of the four "urban" tribes, which were less honourable, partly because they contained all the freedmen. In the case of *equites* the censure was expressed by the command "sell your horse", which implied dismissal.

The revision of the list of senators was no part of the *census*, but perhaps the most important power of all, and here the censorial *nota* meant the exclusion of a person otherwise entitled to a seat. In addition to affixing the *nota* the censors might punish conduct they considered reprehensible by increasing the amount of *tributum* a man had to pay, either directly by multiplying the usual thousandth or indirectly by valuing certain property, especially objects of luxury, at a much higher figure than their real value.

Of the financial duties of the censors, especially the giving of public contracts, we have already spoken.[1] In connection with these functions they had, no doubt, incidentally to decide disputes, for the Roman principle was that where the state was concerned the magistrate decided, not the courts. But it appears that, in the late republic at any rate, if a dispute occurred between individuals, the censors could appoint a *iudex* or *recuperatores*.[2]

As to criminal jurisdiction, the censors did, it seems, sometimes levy fines in connection with their various duties—the idea that a magistrate should not be able to do so was repugnant to the Roman conceptions of magisterial dignity—but as they could not summon the people it is probable that their fines were always below the amount at which *provocatio* became possible.[3]

The regular interval between censorships was, as we have said, four or five years, but there were many cases in which longer periods were allowed to elapse, and appointment became very irregular after Sulla. After 22 B.C. censors were never again appointed, though the emperors continued the supervision of morals and occasionally took the title of censor. The fact was that the census had become unwieldy in the late republic when the number of citizens had greatly increased, and, in effect, it was only a compilation taken from individual lists made in the various municipalities. It was also unnecessary either for taxation, as tribute was no longer imposed on citizens,[4] or for military purposes, now that the old citizen army had been replaced by a professional force voluntarily recruited.

The powers of the censorship were also disliked by the senate as a check on the power of the nobility and were no longer necessary to fill up the senate as, under Sulla's scheme, there were always sufficient ex-quaestors to take the vacant places.

F. THE TRIBUNATE.   The institution of the tribunate as a measure of defence by the plebeians, the raising of the numbers from five to ten and the chief powers of the office have already been described. By the time that the struggle between the orders was over the tribunes had been for so long part of Roman public life that there was no attempt to abolish them and they continued to exist throughout the republic and well into the empire. Strictly, they remained magistrates not of the whole *populus*, but of the *plebs* only; they continued to be elected in the *concilium plebis*;

---

[1] *Supra*, 36.
[2] *Lex agraria*, l. 35 (Bruns, I. 80).
[3] Strachan-Davidson, I. 177.
[4] *Supra*, 36.

they must be plebeians, and they bore no outward sign of rank whatever; in effect however they ranked as magistrates and the office was one regularly held by plebeians in the *cursus honorum*[1] or magisterial career. They also obtained the right not only of sitting in but also of convening the senate.[2]

The three powers which gave to the tribunate its greatest political importance were the *intercessio* by which they continued to be able to bring the whole business of the state to a standstill, their legislative power as presidents of the *concilium plebis* and their general power of *coercitio* which continued to be used chiefly for dealing with political offences, and especially for the prosecution of magistrates after the expiration of their term of office. Where the punishment which the tribunes desired to inflict was so severe as to be beyond the jurisdiction of the *concilium plebis*, the consul was bound to summon the centuries[3] for the tribune, so as to enable him to defend the sentence before them.

Although it had become an integral part of the Roman constitution, the tribunate retained its anarchical possibilities, and it was constantly used as an instrument of party strife, now by one side and now by the other. Frequently its great negative powers[4] made it an instrument by which the senatorial party kept control over magistrates who might wish to use their theoretically enormous powers without sufficient respect for the senate's wishes, but the tribunate was also the office chosen by reformers, such as the Gracchi, and demagogues, such as Saturninus, and its powers remained a danger to senatorial supremacy. For this reason they were drastically curtailed by Sulla when he re-established the constitution on an aristocratic basis, but the original position was shortly afterwards restored, and the tribunate remained important down to the end of the republic. Its powers and also the *sacrosanctitas*, or inviolability, which still attached to it, made it one of the two chief bases on which Augustus constructed the legal justification of his autocracy.

G. THE DICTATORSHIP. The republican constitution made provision from the first for a temporary return to monarchy in times of crisis when the principle of colleagueship was likely to cripple the efficiency of the state. Nor was it, as we might have expected, for the people to decide

---

[1] *Infra*, 76. [2] *Supra*, 41.

[3] Which alone were competent to deal with capital charges in accordance with the law of the XII Tables.

[4] It is generally said that the tribunes had no positive powers, or only very few, such as those in connection with guardianship under the *lex Atilia* (Gai. I. 185). But *v.* Karlowa, I. 224–225.

when this was necessary, but for the consuls themselves. In an emergency either consul could nominate a dictator who then became superior to himself, his colleague and all other magistrates. Which consul was to exercise the power was decided either by the possession of the *fasces*,[1] or in default of agreement by lot, and, in any case, during the long period of senatorial government the power was only exercised on the authority of the senate. The emergency for which the dictator was appointed was usually military, but by no means necessarily; a dictator might be appointed, e.g., to hold the elections when both consuls were ill, or for some purely ceremonial function such as holding certain games. Though he was appointed without reference to the people, the dictator's *imperium*, like that of the consuls and praetors, had to be confirmed by a *lex curiata*. When a dictator was appointed for a special purpose he was expected to retire as soon as that purpose was fulfilled, but in any case he could not hold office for longer than six months, and apparently his powers also came to an end when the term of office of the consul who had appointed him expired. The persons appointed were nearly always men who had held the consulate and the office, originally confined to patricians, probably became open to the plebs at the same time as the consulate. During his tenure of the office the dictator was supreme; his superiority over the consuls was shown by his right to twenty-four lictors, a greater number than even the kings had had, and the axes appeared in the *fasces* even within the city. He was not, until comparatively late, subject to the rules of *provocatio*,[2] and originally he was apparently also free from tribunician *intercessio*; even after this had been changed (perhaps about the beginning of the third century B.C.) the tribunes appear to have used their rights very rarely, if ever. As bearer of *imperium* the dictator was entitled to do all the acts that a consul could do and he could further do one thing that no other magistrate could do, namely, give *imperium* to his own delegate, for every dictator nominated a *magister equitum*, who, though primarily, as the name implies, appointed to command the cavalry, was a general assistant and might have various duties delegated to him, e.g. full command at Rome while his superior was in command of the army in the field. The *magister equitum* had the right to six lictors and ranked equally with a praetor.

The dictatorship as part of the regular constitutional machinery did not last as long as the republic. Already in 217 B.C. there was a departure from the established practice when the dictatorship was conferred by *election* on Q. Fabius Maximus, and the original character of the office

---

[1] *Supra*, 45.   [2] Perhaps he was subjected to them by the *l. Valeria* of 300 B.C.

was further weakened when, in the same year, the *comitia* conferred equal power on the *magister equitum*. After 202 B.C. no dictator in the old sense was ever appointed. The title, it is true, was taken both by Sulla and by Caesar as the basis of their arbitrary powers, but in neither case was the nomination regular, and, in fact, both were successful party leaders able to impose their wills on the community in the revolutionary period because of their command of military force. The old dictatorship had disappeared because it was incompatible with complete senatorial supremacy.

H. THE MINOR MAGISTRATES. First among these must be reckoned the military tribunes, of whom there were normally six to each legion. Originally they were appointed by the consuls, but in 362 B.C. the election of six out of the regular number of twenty-four needed for the regular four legions was entrusted to the *comitia tributa*, and later others were similarly elected. The number however varied with the number of the legions and it was always for the consuls to fill up vacancies.

Minor civil magistracies were: (*a*) the *tresviri capitales* who exercised subordinate functions in connection with criminal jurisdiction, providing for the imprisonment of accused persons pending trial, arranging for executions and probably dealing on their own authority with slaves and foreigners. From their responsibility for the prevention of nocturnal disorder they were commonly known as *tresviri nocturni*. (*b*) The *tresviri monetales*, or masters of the mint, whose office, originally occasional, had become permanent by the end of the republic. (*c*) Six commissioners for the upkeep of roads, of whom four were responsible for the streets of Rome itself, two for those in the immediate neighbourhood. They worked under the control of the aediles. More important for the lawyer are the judicial magistrates, (*d*) four *praefecti Capuam Cumas*, praetorian delegates for jurisdiction in these cities,[1] and (*e*) x *viri stlitibus iudicandis*.[2] These were associated with lawsuits involving freedom, and though they acted, during the republic, only as jurymen, were elected, and counted as magistrates. The reason is perhaps to be found precisely in the great importance, especially to the lower classes whose family tree might be hazy, of these trials for liberty.

The electing assembly was in all cases the *comitia tributa*, and by the end of the republic, all the minor civil officers were spoken of collectively as the *viginti sex viri*; it was usual, perhaps necessary, to have served in one of these offices before holding the quaestorship.

---

[1] Cf. *infra*, 62.   [2] *Infra*, 200.

Chapter III

ITALY AND THE PROVINCES DURING THE REPUBLIC

By the end of the republic the extent of Rome's dominions was very nearly as great as it ever became, and included already the greater part of the known world. This great empire was not, like that of Alexander, the work of a single conqueror, but the result of centuries of warfare and expansion, and its government was therefore not a coherent scheme imposed by a single mind, but an intricate structure embodying the expedients of many successive generations of rulers. Nor can it be said that the political institutions of Rome, though no doubt they helped her to acquire her empire, proved a success as a means of governing it. The city-state constitution broke under the strain imposed on it and had to be replaced by a military monarchy, for it must be remembered that, at the end of the republic, the constitution of Rome was still that of a city-state. If the territories which we call the "Roman Empire" can be said to have a constitution at all, it must be described as a kind of federation of city-states of which the sole bond is their common subjection, though in varying degrees, to the supreme city, whose governing organs have to serve the purpose of governing also the whole federation.

In tracing the development of this federation it is best to distinguish three stages, those of the Latin league, the conquest of Italy, and the acquisition of the provinces beyond the seas and beyond the Alps. Not that these stages represent distinct periods; Rome had already conquered several Italian states before she finally suppressed the last revolt of the Latins, and she had acquired provinces overseas before she had finished with Italy, but it was only through her leadership in Latium that she was able to achieve her supremacy over Italy, and at the end of the republic, as well as during the early empire, Italy represented a privileged part of the Roman dominions contrasted with the subject territories beyond her borders.

§ I. ITALY

A. THE LATIN LEAGUE. The early history of federation among the Latin cities is shrouded in mystery. According to tradition there existed from the earliest times a league, both religious and political, with its centre at Alba Longa, and the headship of this league was wrested from Alba by the Romans under the third king, Tullus Hostilius. It seems however that the Alban league was but one of a number of shifting combinations and that, though Rome under the later monarchy exercised a clear hegemony in Latium, this was not due to her succession to the position of Alba.[1] After the fall of the monarchy there followed a period of weakness in which the Latin cities combined against Rome. What were the headquarters of this combination cannot be determined, but the tradition of a treaty made after fighting with a Latin league in the early years of the republic is probably to be accepted,[2] and in this treaty Rome appears, not as a member of the league, but as an equal. The league appears to have had some form of government for federal purposes, separate from the governments of the individual cities, but in this Rome had no part, and the treaty provided for an equal division of booty between Rome on the one side and the league as a whole on the other. The command of the joint army was, it is said, to be held alternately by the Roman general and the commander of the federal forces.

One important joint activity of Rome and the league was the foundation of colonies. A colony in the Roman sense is primarily a military settlement planted on conquered land with the object of holding down the surrounding territory, though of course it served also the purpose of providing for surplus population, for the colonists were always given parcels of land in the new cities. The Roman or citizen of any Latin state who became a member of a Latin colony lost his original citizenship, for the colony was a separate state, and the rule was that no one could be a citizen of two states at the same time. At first the colonies became members of the league on the same footing as the original cities, but this appears to have changed even before the dissolution of the league, the newer colonies being allies, not members. Their citizens, however, like those of the older colonies, shared those rights in private law which were characteristic of "Latinity" and are of greater importance than the constitution of the league for the understanding of subsequent legal developments.

Chief of the private rights was *commercium*, which the Latin cities had originally not only with Rome but with each other. The general rule of antiquity was that the law of a community was for the members of that community only, and that the stranger was without rights. If there was no treaty to the contrary with his state the foreigner could be seized as a

---

[1] Last, *Cambridge Ancient History*, VII. 404.
[2] Last, *loc. cit.* 489. The traditional date of this *foedus Cassianum* is 493 B.C.

slave and his property taken by the first comer as goods without an owner. Where there was a treaty protection of the citizens of the contracting states could be arranged, and the development of the *ius gentium* secured protection even for those without a treaty.[1] But the bond of *commercium* meant more than this. It meant that the Latin was admitted to the Roman methods of acquiring property and of contracting obligations, including not only mancipation, but probably also *nexum* and the literal contract.[2] Latins could also, unlike other aliens, benefit under a Roman will, but this was probably not a result of their *commercium*. Similarly, no doubt, though we hear little about it from the other side, the Romans enjoyed the same privileges in the Latin cities.

The right to use mancipation for the acquisition of property did not mean that the Latin, when he acquired property, owned it *ex iure Quiritium* (by Roman right), or that he could use the *legis actio* (the old Roman method of procedure) to assert his ownership in a Roman court, for no one who is not one of the *Quirites* can own *ex iure Quiritium*.[3] He was consequently debarred also from acquiring property by *in iure cessio*, which involved the use of the *legis actio* in a collusive manner. The difficulty that mancipation, as described by Gaius, also involves the assertion of ownership *ex iure Quiritium* is best met by assuming that there were two forms, one, that described by Gaius, for use between citizens, another, in which the words *ex iure Quiritium* did not occur, which was used when one of the parties was not a Roman.[4]

Where *conubium* existed in addition to *commercium* this meant that if a Latin married a Roman woman the union was recognised by Roman law, with the result that the children followed the status of the father,[5] whereas in unrecognised unions they followed the mother, and on the other hand if a Roman married a Latin woman with *conubium* the children were Roman citizens and in the power (*patria potestas*) of their father.[6]

[1] *Infra*, 100–105.

[2] Mitteis, *R.P.R.* 117–119. Ulpian's words (Reg. XIX. 5), *Commercium est emendi vendendique invicem ius*, must be taken as giving only a rough description, *ibid.* p. 119.

[3] This is much disputed, e.g. by Girard, *Organisation Judiciaire*, 206, n. 2. But see Mitteis, *R.P.R.* 123–124; Wlassak, *Prozessgesetze*, II. 138, n. 28, 184–188; *Z.S.S.* XXVIII. 114–129.

[4] Mitteis, *R.P.R.* 120, n. 28; Wlassak, *Z.S.S.* XXVIII. 124.

[5] Gai. I. 77.

[6] Gai. I. 56, 76. The extent to which *conubium* existed is very doubtful. Ulpian (Reg. V. 4) says that Latins did not have it unless it was specially granted and Gaius (I. 79) implies that a marriage between a Roman and a Latin was one

In addition to *commercium* and perhaps *conubium* there were also some minor political rights; the Latins resident in Rome were permitted to vote in a tribe chosen by lot on each occasion, and there was also probably the right, which became very important later, by which Latins taking up their permanent residence in Rome and abjuring the citizenship of their homes could become Roman citizens. The Romans no doubt had corresponding rights in the Latin cities.

After the revolt of the Latins and Rome's victory in 338 B.C. there was a radical change in the situation. The league was dissolved and the federal government was abolished. Some of the cities were deprived altogether of their constitutions and given either full Roman citizenship or *civitas sine suffragio* (i.e. citizenship without the right to vote or to be elected to a magistracy), which meant that they had full rights in private law and bore all the burdens, especially military service and *tributum*,[1] which fell on Romans, but could take no part in the government and were themselves subject to the Roman magistrates. In more favoured cases the local constitution and local citizenship were left intact, but the city was forced to conclude a separate treaty with Rome by which she surrendered her power both of making war against, and of concluding treaties with other states, whether Latin or not, and agreed to furnish contingents to serve with the Roman armies.

All *commercium* and *conubium* between Latin states was forbidden, but the Latins retained their right of *commercium* (and perhaps in some cases *conubium*) with Rome herself, together with the restricted voting rights and probably the right of exchanging their own for the Roman citizenship by taking up permanent residence at Rome.

The subsequent history of Latin rights is that of the Latin colonies. Settlements with rights similar to those of Latin cities continued to be made, and were among the chief methods adopted for securing Rome's hold on Italy, but it was, of course, now Rome alone which decided when and where they were to be sent, and who chose the colonists. These might be Romans or be taken from any of the allied states, but every colonist who was enrolled, the Roman included, lost his original citizenship on receiving that of the new city.[2]

---

without *conubium*. Both authors are thinking of *Latini coloniarii*, i.e. the members of the later Latin colonies and the non-Latin communities to which Latin rights were extended (*infra*, 60). The *Latini prisci*, i.e. the original members of the league and the early colonies, clearly had some advantages over the *coloniarii*, and *conubium* may well have been one of them.

[1] *Supra*, 35. [2] Gai. I. 131.

For colonies founded after 268 B.C.[1] the privileges of Latinity were somewhat curtailed, though it is not clear in precisely what respect.[2] There were also restrictions on the right of the Latins (if indeed it had ever been unrestricted) to become Roman citizens by transferring their residence to Rome. A law of unknown[3] date is said to have enacted that this should only be allowed provided the Latin left a son in his own city, and we find for the first time in 123 B.C.[4] (though it may have existed earlier) a rule that only those who are elected to a magistracy in a Latin city have the right to become Roman citizens. It may be, however, as Mommsen thinks, that this restriction only applied to colonies founded after 268 B.C.[5]

In the course of republican history "Latinity" thus became a recognised status, privileged in comparison with that of the other allies by reason of the private rights and the chances of obtaining Roman citizenship, and this status could be granted not only to colonies in the original sense of the word but also to cities which were neither colonies nor had any connection with the Latin race.

It was thus granted in 89 B.C. to the inhabitants of Italy north of the Po (*Gallia Cisalpina*) who were not yet considered ripe for the citizenship which was then extended to the rest of Italy,[6] and it continued to be granted in the remainder of the republican period, especially by Caesar, and in the early empire to communities in the provinces as a kind of half-way house to citizenship. Latin rights were even, under the empire, taken as a model for the status granted to certain freedmen who did not become citizens on manumission, the "Junian" Latins; but this "Latinity", which did not imply membership of any community with Latin rights, is a mere anomaly from the point of view of republican law.[7]

B. THE REMAINDER OF ITALY. Towards the rest of Italy Rome pursues a policy similar to that adopted towards the Latins after the dissolution of the league. Some of the states over which she gains supremacy she dissolves and incorporates, others she binds to herself by treaties which, though leaving them technically autonomous, embody such restrictions on that autonomy that they become in fact dependent. Confederations are everywhere broken up and the allies of Rome are forbidden to conclude treaties with other powers.

---

[1] The date of the foundation of Ariminum, *v.* Mommsen, *Staatsr.* III. 624.
[2] Cf. *supra*, 58 n. 6.
[3] Mommsen dates this law about 268 B.C.
[4] *Lex Acilia*, 78 (Bruns, I. 72).   [5] *Staatsr.* III. 640.
[6] *Infra*, 66.   [7] *V.* e.g. Gai. I. 22.

If we look at the position in 266 B.C., when her victory over Pyrrhus in 275 and subsequent victories over her Italian enemies have made Rome supreme in Italy south of the Apennines, we find that the inhabitants fall already into four classes:

(i) Roman citizens with full rights. These include not only the inhabitants of Rome itself, but also those of the communities incorporated with the full citizenship and the members of the Roman colonies, for Rome used settlements of citizens with full rights as well as those with Latin rights for securing her hold on conquered territory. As the colonists in these cases remained Romans, the foundation of such a colony was not, as in the case of a Latin colony, the creation of a new state, for citizenship of such a new state would have been incompatible with Roman citizenship. The land given to the colonists became theirs fully *ex iure Quiritium* and was incorporated into one of the Roman "tribes",[1] just as the owners themselves remained on the census lists, lived under Roman law and were subject to the jurisdiction of the praetor. A minor degree of self-government was, however, given to the colony as to the *municipium* of *cives sine suffragio*,[2] and the colonists were frequently dispensed from military service with the Roman armies because they were in fact intended to act as a standing garrison where they lived.[3]

(ii) *Cives sine suffragio.* Citizenship without the right of voting, such as had been forced on some of the Latin cities, continued to be given to conquered communities which were too dangerous to be left independent even under a treaty of alliance, and the penal nature of this grant was usually made clearer by the confiscation of a considerable proportion of the conquered land. Incorporation of this sort, as indeed incorporation with full citizenship, necessarily implied the destruction of

---

[1] *Supra*, 20.

[2] *Infra*, 63.

[3] The foundation of a colony, whether Roman or Latin, was always preceded by a *senatus consultum* and a *lex* or *plebiscitum* which laid down the place to which it was to be sent, the number of colonists, the amount of land to be assigned to each and the names of the leaders. Citizens were then called upon to give in their names and, if sufficient volunteers were not forthcoming, compulsion could be used, for the foundation of a colony was, in a sense, a military expedition. When the enrolment was complete the colonists marched out under their leaders in military order and when they arrived at their destination the limits of the new city were marked out with full ceremony. A plough was drawn round the circuit where the wall was to be built, the share being raised at the places appointed for the gates, and the plan of the city, with streets at right angles to each other, as can be seen in several excavated cities to-day, was drawn out by the expert surveyors (*agri mensores*) who formed one of the chief Roman professions.

the conquered city as a separate state, the enrolment of the inhabitants in the Roman census list and their liability to tribute and military service in the legions. But these facts did not necessarily prevent a considerable amount of local self-government from being left in the hands of the local authorities, and the position of different communities varied very greatly. In some the full logical consequences of incorporation were drawn; the existing constitution was abolished and the city placed directly under the Roman authorities. Such, for instance, was the position of Anagnia, where, we are told, no magistrate with secular functions was left at all. In other cases, as with Capua (the second largest city of Italy), in spite of the grant of citizenship, powers almost equal to those of independent federated states were left to the local magistrates, such, for instance, as the right of assessment for taxation and the raising of troops required for the levy. With the grant of Roman citizenship went logically, according to Roman ideas, also the use of the Roman law and subjection to the jurisdiction of the *praetor urbanus*, but with the increase in the number of citizens it was obviously impossible to send every case to Rome for trial; nor could the praetor go on circuit, for he might not be absent from Rome for more than ten days during his year of office. The device of delegation was therefore adopted and *praefecti iure dicundo* were appointed by the praetor to take the civil cases in outlying communities. It is probable that these delegates also exercised general functions of government in those cities which were allowed no local magistrates. In cities with local self-government they exercised some supervision over the local administration, but their main task was jurisdiction, and for this therefore they were sent to cities whose inhabitants had the full citizenship as well as to these *sine suffragio*, at any rate where the city was so far from Rome that to send every case before the praetor would have been an intolerable hardship.

Originally all prefects were nominated by the praetor whose delegates they were, but, as we have already seen, four were in later times elected in the *comitia tributa* and counted as minor magistrates of the Roman people.[1]

The growth of local self-government among communities of citizens implies a departure from the general principle, which applied in Italy as well as in Greece, that state and city are convertible terms, for it means that a man may be a citizen of Rome and also have rights as a member of a subordinate community. This double citizenship is at the bottom of the

---

[1] *Supra,* 55.

Roman conception of *municipium*[1] in the later sense of the term, i.e. a township of citizens with minor rights of self-government. In the period of which we are speaking the word had not yet this technical meaning, but the fact was there and was to be of the greatest importance in the history of Roman, and indeed European, governmental institutions.

(iii) *Latins.* This term now means almost exclusively the inhabitants of the Latin colonies, for the original Latin cities had nearly all obtained Roman citizenship. The Latins were, strictly, like other "allies", members of autonomous states bound to Rome by treaty; they were free from *tributum*, sent separate contingents to the army which served under their own officers, and owned their own land according to their own law, but their position was more favourable than that of the other allies on account of their privileged position in private law and their tie with Rome closer in other ways also. The newer colonies had been planted by Rome alone; their legal[2] and social system was modelled on the Roman, and they looked upon Rome as their mother city and their support against the frequently hostile populations of alien race among whom they were settled.

(iv) *Socii* (allies). The position of the "allied" states, though less favourable than that of the Latins, was in this period better than that of *cives sine suffragio*. The provisions of the treaty which bound them to Rome no doubt varied in the different cases,[3] but in general the allied state gave up her right of concluding treaties or making war separately from Rome and agreed to send troops, the number of which was probably fixed by the treaty, to serve with the Roman forces. The coinage of silver (first undertaken at Rome in 269 B.C.)[4] was also reserved to Rome, but for the rest the states were independent. They retained their own constitutions (though these might be remodelled to suit Rome), their own systems of law, their own finance and administration (except that Romans were dispensed from paying import and export duties), and their ownership of their territory was recognised by Rome. They need not admit

[1] The word *municipium* was derived by the ancients (Festus, s.v. *municipium*, Bruns, II. 15) from *munus capere* and thought to refer to the position of *cives sine suffragio* who "took the burdens" of Roman citizenship but did not share in its privileges. More probably it meant originally something quite different and *munus* signified not "burden" but "gift", *municipes* being thus originally "gift takers", i.e. members of states allied to Rome by a treaty of friendship which was symbolised by the interchange of gifts.

[2] Cicero speaks (*pro Balbo*, VIII. 21) of the voluntary acceptance by the Latins of several Roman *leges*.

[3] The later technical distinction between *foedus aequum* and *foedus iniquum* (*infra*, 68) is not attested in Italy.

[4] See Tenney Frank, 77.

Roman garrisons and were free from Roman taxation except in so far as the provision and payment of troops necessarily involved expense.

A century after the defeat of Pyrrhus, when the third period into which Mommsen divides his History comes to an end with the battle of Pydna[1] (168 B.C.), the condition of the Italians has changed considerably for the worse. This is due, in the main, to the great struggle with Carthage in which Rome had been forced to employ ruthlessly all the resources at her disposal and particularly to the measures of punishment meted out to those of her allies who had made common cause with the enemy. Most severe of all was the treatment of Capua[2] and of the rest of Campania with the exception of a few faithful cities. The Capuan constitution was entirely destroyed and nearly all her territory confiscated and made *ager publicus*. Many of the Campanians themselves and others in the south of Italy, the Bruttii for instance, did not even obtain the citizenship *sine suffragio*, but remained *dediticii*. This meant that the condition of surrender (*deditio*) into which they had fallen when subdued by the Romans, instead of being exchanged for incorporation or alliance, was perpetuated. They were not rightless in private law, for they remained free, and all free persons were regarded as having rights under the *ius gentium*,[3] but they had no status in public law at all, and were simply subjects with whom the Roman government could do what it liked.[4]

But even apart from these cases of exceptionally harsh treatment the Roman yoke began to bear more heavily on the Italian "allies" and even on the Latins. Many cities had to submit to an unfavourable revision of the treaties which bound them to Rome; military burdens were imposed on Latins and allies more heavily than on Romans, and they were not given a fair share of the spoils of war. Roman legislation[5] and Roman administrative measures[6] were sometimes extended without legal justification to both classes, and Roman magistrates, knowing that there could

[1] *Supra*, 2.

[2] Previously in an exceptionally favourable position, *supra*, 62.

[3] *Infra*, 100–105.

[4] Strictly *deditio* is the agreement by which the enemy surrenders completely to Rome on the promise of mercy (*fides*), and the word does not apply to the conquest of a people whose city is taken by storm, but the position of the conquered is similar to the two cases. The exact meaning of *dediticii* under the empire is still uncertain, v. *infra*, 353.

[5] E.g. in 193 B.C. when usury laws were extended both to Latins and other Italians.

[6] The *S.C. de Bacchanalibus*, a measure directed against the excesses involved by the foreign cult of Bacchus and resulting in the execution of many thousands of persons, was applied all over Italy, cf. *infra*, 323.

be no effective resistance, did not scruple to behave like foreign conquerors in "federated" cities.

One symptom of the changed attitude of the Romans was that they became much less generous with the grant of their citizenship. They were now definitely the masters in Italy, not merely the leading state, and they did not want to diminish the value of their privileges by sharing them with too many others.[1] At the same time the citizenship which had, in earlier days, often been imposed as a measure of punishment on communities whose constitutions were destroyed, came to be the chief object of ambition to the Italian peoples who could now no longer hope for any real independence.[2]

The claim of the allies to the citizenship was favourably viewed by the leaders of the democratic party at the beginning of the revolutionary period (in particular C. Gracchus) and from 125 B.C. onwards proposals were brought forward for granting it. All, however, failed because of the united opposition of the senatorial party and the city mob who were jealous of their privileges and in this matter refused to follow their usual leaders.

The climax was reached in 95 B.C. when the reactionary consuls of the year carried a proposal (*lex Licinia et Mucia*) which, so far from granting the citizenship to the Italians, curtailed the existing privileges of the Latins, apparently by taking away their right (in so far as it existed) of acquiring the citizenship by settling at Rome, and resulted in wholesale expulsions from the city. This measure and the failure of a proposal of Drusus in 91 to extend the citizenship to the allies resulted in the Social war (91–88 B.C.). Though the Romans succeeded, after more than two years' hard fighting, in suppressing this revolt, in which the greater part of Italy took up arms against them, it was only at the cost of relinquishing the principle for which the struggle had been begun.

Two laws were proposed and passed before the war was over, one a *lex Iulia* by the consul L. Caesar in 90 B.C. which gave the citizenship to all allies who had not yet revolted, the other, a *lex Plautia Papiria* in 89 B.C. by two tribunes allowing two months to any person domiciled in Italy during which he could obtain the citizenship by giving in his name to a Roman magistrate. These measures clearly did not include Italians still in revolt, but in fact citizenship was extended shortly after their

[1] Cf. the restrictions on the acquisition of citizenship by Latins, *supra*, 60.
[2] One of the chief reasons was the protection which the right of *provocatio* gave to a citizen, but to no one else, against arbitrary punishment by a Roman magistrate.

submission to all cities in Italy south of the Po,[1] and this extension remained the solid achievement of the Social war. As a result double citizenship, Roman and local, became the rule in Italy. The Latin or Italian city which had previously been, at least in theory, a sovereign state in alliance with Rome, became what *municipia* in the strict sense had long been, merely a community for the purposes of local government, and the difference between *coloniae*, *municipia* and *praefecturae* became one of name only. The acquisition of the Roman citizenship by the Italians also brought with it, of necessity, the application of Roman law, and the new citizens, like the old, were subject to the jurisdiction of the praetor or his delegates. But the powers of local self-government remaining to the cities, or newly bestowed on them, are considerable. Local assemblies elect magistrates, local senates deal independently with their own finances; criminal jurisdiction is largely local, and there comes into existence a civil jurisdiction under Roman law exercised by local magistrates in subordination to the praetor at Rome.

§ II. THE PROVINCES

Provincia literally means simply "sphere of action of a magistrate", and the sense from which our word province is derived is simply the result of the territorial application of the same idea. A "province" is a sphere of action with territorial limits assigned to a magistrate with *imperium*, and, as such, is outside Italy, for within Italy there were no such geographical limits on the *imperium*. It is the unity of command given to the governor within these limits which really constitutes the unity of the province within which may live people actually governed in different ways and standing in varying relationships to Rome. For all of them the governor represents the authority of the Roman state, whether they are Roman citizens resident in the province, members of Roman or Latin colonies or other inhabitants living in their original communities which might or might not have a considerable measure of self-government. It is this fact which explains how the Romans managed to govern their great empire with so few officials. When they acquired territory they did not incorporate it into a coherent administrative system of their own; they left it as a rule in much the same condition as that in which they found it, but subjected great areas of it to the general supervision of a magistrate

---

[1] Italy north of the Po, the "Cisalpine Gaul" of the Romans, was given *latinitas* in 89 B.C.; the further step to citizenship was only finally taken under the supremacy of C. Iulius Caesar in 49 B.C.

holding *imperium* and thus vested with the supreme authority which *imperium* gave outside the city. The governorship was, in fact, the military command of the Roman general perpetuated as a system of control in times of peace, and the chief limit on the governor's power was not any legal restriction but the physical impossibility of attention to detail with the very small staff which the state put at his disposal.

The first method by which the Romans provided for magistrates with *imperium* to govern their provinces was an increase in the number of praetorships, but with the growth of the empire this measure proved insufficient, and resort was had to the prolongation of the power of magistrates after their year of office had elapsed. This was never deemed permissible within the city, but elsewhere the senate frequently used its dispensing power for this purpose. It was also the rule that a military commander outside the city retained his command until relieved by his successor. Prolongation however was of magisterial power, not of the office itself, and the ex-magistrate exercised his *imperium pro consule* or *pro praetore*, "in place of the consul or praetor", according to the rank he had held. It must be remembered that, in the period before Sulla, consuls frequently undertook commands overseas and these commands were often prolonged in this way, as were those of praetors whose successors were needed for other purposes. It was thus already common for provinces to be administered by pro-magistrates before the time of Sulla, and Sulla fixed the practice by providing that both consuls and all the praetors should remain in Italy during their year of office and proceed to a province only afterwards. By a law of Pompey's, passed in 52 B.C., this was again altered, and five years were to elapse between the tenure of office at Rome and the provincial governorship, a rule which, though it fell into abeyance during the civil wars, was revived by Augustus.

The governor's staff included only one actual magistrate, the quaestor, of whose duties we have already spoken; there were *legati*, i.e. senators without office (one usually in a praetorian, three in a consular province), whom he could employ as his delegates in any type of duty, military, administrative or judicial. These men were originally appointed by the senate, but in later times chosen by the governor himself. The governor had also a number of *comites* (literally "companions") with him, i.e. usually younger men who were being initiated into public life, whom he could use for any purpose he thought fit. Both the *legati* and the *comites* have an important later history under the empire.

Rome's first provinces came to her as a result of her struggle with

Carthage; Sicily, the first, was created in 241 B.C. after the end of the first Punic war, and Sardinia ten years later; the two Spanish provinces were kept at the end of the second war in 201, and Africa was added after the destruction of Carthage had ended the third in 146. Meanwhile, Rome had become involved in the affairs of the Eastern Mediterranean. Macedonia became a province in 148, Asia in 129, and the expansion did not cease during the period of the revolution. By the end of the republic there were in all fifteen provinces: Sicily, Sardinia, Hither and Further Spain, Illyricum, Macedonia, Achaea, Africa, Asia, Gallia Narbonensis, Gallia Cisalpina, Bithynia, Cyrene with Crete, Cilicia and Syria.

In these extra-Italian dominions Rome's policy was partly similar to that adopted in Italy, partly different. Incorporation of provincials as citizens either with or without voting rights, such as had been common in the earlier phases of the conquest of Italy, was unknown, but the policy of alliance by treaties which, in fact, left the other party dependent on Rome was widely adopted. Federations were, as in Italy, usually broken up, though, where they were not considered dangerous, they might be left as religious institutions, or even occasionally created. The treaties which Rome made with her dependent states fell into two classes; either they were "equal", i.e. in form treaties made between two sovereign communities, or they were "unequal", in which case they contained a clause by which the other party acknowledged its inferiority by agreeing, "courteously to respect the dignity of the Roman people" (*maiestatem populi Romani comiter conservare*). Whichever form was adopted the state was "free and federated". In some cases, as in that of Marseilles, these treaties represented older agreements which had been concluded when the parties were really on an equal footing, and many states retained real self-government in so far as all internal affairs were concerned, including even criminal jurisdiction over Roman citizens within their territory.[1] External relations were, of course, strictly controlled by Rome, or, rather, no external relations were, as a rule, allowed except with Rome herself.

Next in rank to the "free and federated" states come those which are "free" but not "federated", i.e. those whose freedom is guaranteed, not

---

[1] Treaties with kings, though unknown in Italy, occur frequently elsewhere. Rome's sphere of influence, like that of modern imperial states, was not bounded by the territory which she ruled directly, and a common preliminary to incorporation in the empire and method of government adapted to less civilised peoples was the recognition and support of a native king, who in return took his orders from Rome and had to protect her frontiers.

by a treaty but by a unilateral act of Rome herself, which, unlike a treaty sworn to by both parties, could legally be revoked at any moment. One document of this nature, or rather a considerable fragment of it, has survived in an inscription.[1] It is a plebiscite of 71 B.C. and enacts, among other things, that the citizens of Termessus (in Pisidia) are to be "free friends and allies of the Roman people and enjoy their own laws in so far as they are not incompatible with this statute". There is a significant absence of any statement that the Termessians have consented to this arrangement.

The rest of the provincials who did not belong to either class of favoured state were mere subjects, and, although they are included in the general term *socii* (allies), it is difficult to find any legal formula which will distinguish them from the *dediticii*.[2] There were, however, important variations in the actual treatment of different classes. Where, as in Sicily and the Hellenised East, there were city-states and a high standard of civilisation in existence before the coming of the Romans, these city-states were left with a considerable amount of local self-government and the use of their own law, but it must be remembered that, even in these countries, there were large numbers of people who were not citizens of the city-states but subject to them, as well as others who had no connection with any city-state at all but lived in villages and cultivated the soil. In the East, especially in the province of Asia, these last had in many cases been serfs attached to royal estates, and though Roman law itself did not at this time[3] recognise serfdom (as opposed to slavery) their position does not appear to have been bettered by the Roman occupation. Nor, indeed, was that of the subjects of the cities who continued, in the Roman phrase, to be "attributed" to those cities. It is difficult however, with the small amount of evidence we have, to know how far the depressed condition of these classes was due to burdens imposed on them by general rules of law, and how far it was due simply to their poverty in comparison with the wealthier city-dwellers and Roman landowners whose tenants they became.

The organisation of a province, once it was acquired, was usually laid down in a *lex data* or charter, generally the work of the conquering general himself with the assistance of a senatorial commission of ten *legati*, or at least submitted to the senate for ratification. Of this nature was the *lex Rupilia* governing conditions in Sicily, of which we know a good deal

[1] *Lex Antonia de Termessibus* (Bruns, I. 92).
[2] *Supra*, 64.
[3] For the "colonate" of the later empire *v. infra*, 448.

from Cicero's Verrine orations. Such a *lex data* would, among other things, define the status of the different classes of inhabitants, establish principles of taxation, regulate local government and lay down rules for the administration of justice. Of the *lex Rupilia*, for instance, we know that it provided that where one member of a state had a dispute with another member the matter was to be decided in the court of that state and by the law of that state; only where members of different states were concerned did the case come into the governor's court.[1] Similar rules no doubt applied elsewhere. Much, however, was left undetermined by the "law" of the province and had to be supplied by the edict of the governor. These edicts which the governor, like every other Roman magistrate, was empowered to make at the beginning of his term of office, laid down the principles which he intended to apply during his tenure of power. As happened with other magistrates, especially the two urban praetors, each governor usually took over the bulk of his predecessor's edict and added only a comparatively small amount of his own, with the result that these provincial edicts, like the urban edicts, grew into an important and permanent body of law. The power of issuing edicts, which no court or other body could disallow, is in itself sufficient to show how little the powers of the governor were fettered even by the law of the province. It was, in fact, the great weakness of Roman provincial government under the republic that there was no one to control the governor, the only check provided being under the laws against extortion, which enabled him to be prosecuted after his term of office had come to an end. This was a safeguard which the corruption of the criminal courts at the end of the republic often made illusory.[2]

The fact is that the Romans of republican times regarded the provinces from a purely selfish point of view and chiefly as sources of income. The "federated" cities and some others were immune from taxation, but on the bulk of the provincials the burden was very heavy. Not only had they to pay taxes to the Roman state, but these taxes were generally farmed out. Roman companies paid an agreed sum for the right to collect them during a specified period, with the result that a great number of Roman private citizens were able to enrich themselves at the expense of the provincials. The governor too and his staff, it must be remembered, received no salary and expected to find opportunities of making money out of their position.

[1] Cic. *in Verr.* II. 13. 32.
[2] The first law against extortion by provincial governors was the *lex Calpurnia repetundarum* of 149 B.C.; cf. *infra*, 325.

So far as military service was concerned the position of the provincials differed radically from that of the Italians. The treaties with the "federated" states stipulated for military support and the maritime Greeks had from time to time to furnish ships, but the mass of the population was not called upon, and this policy shows clearly the difference between Italy, which the Romans regarded as a military confederacy under their leadership, and the subject world whose business it was to pay taxes.

The leading ideas of Roman provincial government in the republic are thus: (1) The subjection of great areas to the autocratic authority of a single magistrate whose duties are military, administrative and judicial. Individual states of the "free and federated" or "free" class, where geographically within the province, are not strictly subject to the governor, but his influence in fact extends to them. Where, as often happens, such a city is the chief one in a province he may make it his residence and the local authorities will have to let him have his way. (2) Retention in a large measure of the existing territorial organisation, especially when this is of the city-state type. (3) Exclusion of the provincials from the citizenship (and from Latinity) as well as from the military burdens which fall on the Italian allies, in place of which they have to pay heavy taxation. The vast majority of Roman subjects are, so far as her law is concerned, *peregrini*, "foreigners", outside the pale of the strict Roman law and only entitled to such rights as all free persons have under the *ius gentium*. The word *peregrinus* in fact comes to mean, not a foreigner who belongs to an independent state, for of such, by the end of the republic, there were few in the known world, but a subject of Rome who is not a Roman because he is not a citizen.

Chapter IV

SOCIAL CONDITIONS AND THE DIFFERENT CLASSES OF THE POPULATION DURING THE REPUBLIC

Rome owed her rise to the fighting qualities of her peasant-proprietors. The traditional picture of the earliest republic and the struggle between the orders clearly show that then already the normal Roman was a landowner. It is true that the distress of the plebeians indicates that their plots must often have been very small, and it is also true that, according to modern archaeological theories, there had probably existed, before recorded history begins, in Latium generally, as in Etruria, a system of villeinage, i.e. that the bulk of the population had been semi-free tenants working on large estates owned by great landlords.[1] But what we know of the economic side of the struggle between the orders is sufficient to show that this state of affairs was over when that struggle took place. One of the chief complaints of the plebeians is that they are forced to serve as soldiers and that on their return from a campaign they find their land ruined through lack of attention, or worse still actually devastated by the enemy, and that they are thus forced to borrow from the larger landowners in order to begin again. This is not the sort of complaint which would be made by a semi-free tenant, whose lord would have the responsibility for setting him up again. The cry too is that the patricians monopolise the advantages of the public lands instead of dividing them up among the poor plebeians, which again shows that the plebeian is capable of holding land and regards such ownership as his normal condition. The "Servian" constitution (whatever be the date that should be assigned to it) also indicates that the normal Roman is a landowner, for its "tribes" are divisions of the land, and probably only landowners are originally enrolled—a procedure which would not have been accepted had there been a great number of landless men, for the arrangement is clearly intended to include the bulk of the population.

If the normal citizen was a small landowner we must not imagine that the estates of the aristocracy were very great either. The tradition of the patricians who had to be called from the plough to lead the armies of the republic probably represents the truth. Rome was a poor and weak state from the expulsion of the kings until at least the time of the capture of

[1] Tenney Frank, 12.

Veii (traditional date 396 B.C.), her first great conquest of a foreign people. The earlier part of the struggle between the orders took place during this period of weakness and the main plebeian victory (the Licinio-Sextian laws of 367) was won very early in the period of expansion. The economic provisions among these laws show that Rome was already beginning to go along the disastrous path of large estates and slave labour. One law limited the amount of public land which could be occupied by any individual to 500 *iugera*,[1] and another laid down that landlords must employ a certain proportion of free labourers. But these measures themselves, though they were not strictly enforced, at any rate after the first few years, must have done something towards remedying the evils at which they were aimed, and still more was done to help the peasants by the use which Rome made of her conquests. After the capture of Veii the city was razed to the ground and her territory divided among the citizens of Rome in equal lots, the plebeians having their fair share, and subsequently Rome made many "assignations" of conquered territory to individuals in addition to sending out colonies, which, besides their military function, served the purpose of providing land (in very small lots generally) for her increasing body of citizens.

The result of this policy was a population consisting chiefly of a homogeneous race of peasant-proprietors, men "with a stake in the country", who were patriotic enough, hardy enough and numerous enough to provide the relatively very large armies which enabled Rome to continue her career of conquest once it was begun. These peasants tilled their land themselves with the help of their families and in some cases of one or two slaves or persons *in mancipio*.[2] Commerce and industry seem to have played a comparatively small part in the early development of Rome, and the government was, as we have seen, aristocratic. The success of the plebeians in their contest with the patricians did not change matters; it merely replaced the ancient aristocracy, which had a legal monopoly of office, by a new one in which, though every citizen had equal rights before the law, a comparatively few families, plebeian now as well as patrician, in fact furnished nearly all the magistrates and retained its power through the senate. The aristocracy thus evolved was probably the most successful the world has ever seen. It was not brilliant, and great statesmen were rare, but, like the rest of the Roman people, it was characterised by deep devotion to the state, a steadiness which never failed in the face of the most desperate situations, and a readiness to accept responsibility which made it possible to entrust the

[1] A *iugerum* is about three-fifths of an acre.   [2] *Infra*, 112, n. 3.

great powers of the curule magistracies to a succession of ordinary aristocrats, and thus build up a governing body of men with wide experience of public functions. The Romans had the same fondness for entrusting great powers to individuals which is shown by the English and, like the English, they took a sort of pride in the eccentric use of power; M. Livius, who when censor in 204 B.C. disfranchised thirty-four out of the thirty-five tribes because they had first condemned him in spite of his innocence and then elected him consul and censor, would have precipitated a revolution in most countries.

A great change, both in the external conditions of life and in the spirit of the country, began with the ending of the second Punic war. In seventeen years of continuous warfare the fairest districts had been ravaged, enormous numbers of men had fallen and the whole manhood of the country had been demoralised by continued military life. Agriculture suffered, not only from devastation and lack of the cultivators who were called away on military service, but from competition with the corn which was now imported in great masses from Sicily. Worst of all, the peasant-proprietor was gradually giving way to the great landlord who cultivated his estate mainly by slave labour. The wars enriched the aristocracy who were able to make great sums out of booty and out of the government of the conquered peoples and they also enriched tax-farmers and business men who found new fields for their enterprise. In Italy, as a result of war and confiscation, large tracts of country were acquired by the Roman state, and now that the number of citizens no longer sufficed to cover them with peasant settlements, the only profitable method of exploitation was to let the land in large blocks to people with money, or to continue the old Roman custom of allowing them to "occupy" it, i.e. simply take it informally and thus come under an obligation to pay the state a proportion of the produce. Everything favoured the capitalist. The successful wars made it possible for him to get as many slaves as he liked, and slaves were not only cheaper than free labour but there was no danger of their being called away for military service. Much land was suitable only for use as pasture, and pasture does not pay unless it is managed on a large scale, for a few herdsmen can look after a great number of cattle. On the other hand, competition with the corn-growing provinces was making the fertile parts of Italy turn more and more to wine and olive growing, both of which need capital, for the small man cannot afford to wait the five years before vines or the fifteen years before olive trees will bear. The capitalist therefore tended to absorb the new land and to buy up the peasant-proprietor, who might of course settle in a colony, or go abroad to the provinces as a business man, but who might also drift to Rome and become a more or less idle proletarian living largely on the corn imported from the provinces which the government now already began to distribute, not yet for nothing, but at very low prices. In the second century B.C. there were, no doubt, still large numbers of peasant-proprietors, and it was these men who conquered the East as they had conquered Hannibal, but the process of concentration of the land in fewer hands was going on all the time and was to be largely instrumental in bringing about the revolution. *Latifundia perdidere Italiam*—"The great estates ruined Italy".

That the wealth which flowed to Rome from her conquest of the East had the effect of corrupting her population is an old and true story. Contact with the East meant contact with decadent Hellenism, and wealth gave the opportunity of copying Hellenistic vices. But with wealth and vice come more desirable things—literature, art and philosophy. The state, the family and the farm had been the only things that mattered to the old-fashioned Roman; now he saw that there might be more in life. In the third and second centuries B.C. the upper classes became permeated by Greek culture; Greek literature became the basis of education and Greek rhetoric already began to exercise its dangerous fascination over Roman minds. For speculative philosophy the practical Roman had little taste, but the great days of Greek speculation were over and emphasis was already laid rather on the ethical than on the metaphysical side of philosophical teaching. This was true of all the three chief systems, the "new Academy" and Epicureanism as well as Stoicism, but it was Stoicism which found the most favour at Rome. In the first place its speculative system left a place for the gods and their worship, whereas the Epicureans taught that the gods, if they existed at all, had no concern with the lives of men, and it thus did not come into conflict with that religion of the state which the Romans cherished from patriotic motives, even when they did not believe in it. But above all the Stoic ethic, with its ideal of the perfectly wise man who masters his passions in order to live the "life in accordance with nature", appealed to the Roman sense of duty and gave a theoretical justification for that service of the state which had been the guiding principle in the city's life.

The decay of agriculture in Italy and the consequent growth of a landless proletariate, together with the increasing differences in wealth brought about by the new opportunities of acquiring a fortune, of which naturally only a minority were able to avail themselves, were the causes which led to the attempted reforms of the Gracchi (133–121 B.C.) and to the revolutionary period which was to last a century, and then only end in the establishment of the empire. This period presents a number of the most astonishing contrasts. From the point of view of the governmental system it was a time of breakdown, occasionally anarchy, and from that of the governing class of moral decay, and yet it was the most brilliant epoch of Roman history. Foreign conquest did not cease, literature reached a standard never approached before and equalled only by the immediately succeeding period under Augustus, a series of brilliant personalities from Gaius Gracchus to Augustus himself passes across the stage of history, and in the latter years, when civil war was imminent or actually raging, the whole scene is lit up for us, not merely by professional historians, but by the literary genius of two men who were themselves among the chief actors in the drama—Caesar and Cicero. Though the lawyer finds his "classical age" in the more orderly, if duller, times of the early empire, it is the last century of the republic which is "classical" for the student of language and literature.

It is, of course, impossible to classify exhaustively all the different orders of men who went to make up what had become a vast and highly civilised state, almost as complex in its social and economic structure as those of modern Europe. We can, however, roughly classify as follows:

(a) *The senatorial nobility*. Office was almost exclusively confined to the nobility, that is to say to members of families who could count curule magistrates among their ancestors, though from time to time a *novus homo* might, by his ability, force his way into the privileged circle. A young man of this class who, as was nearly always the case, was destined for a public career, would as a rule spend some years in military service, though this was apparently no longer legally necessary at the end of the republic. He would then start on his *cursus honorum* (career of office) by holding one of the magistracies which formed the XXVI virate and, on election to the quaestorship, would become a member of the senate for life. The offices had to be held in order; the praetorship might not be held before the quaestorship, nor the consulship before the praetorship, and a minimum age was laid down for each. For the quaestorship this had been twenty-eight; in Cicero's time it was thirty; for the consulship it was forty-three. Between these two offices there were not only the other offices—aedileship, praetorship, and, for plebeians, tribunate—but service in the provinces, and the rule was that two years must elapse between the tenure of two "patrician" offices. Not before the lapse of ten years might the same office be held again.

The exercise of any trade or profession was a disqualification for office and the senators had thus necessarily to be men of wealth. They were, in fact, all large landowners, often owning several estates in Italy and in the provinces. From direct participation in business, senators had long been excluded by a *lex Claudia* of 218 B.C., which prevented them and their sons from owning a sea-going ship except for the transport of the produce of their own lands, and probably also forbade them to participate in the acceptance of contracts for the farming of state revenues. In any case, all types of speculative business were regarded as unbecoming to a senator and could only be indulged in secretly, if at all.

By the end of the republic the senatorial nobility was unworthy of the position it held in the state. Cicero, champion of the "order" though he is, inveighs against the degenerates who loll at ease in their villas and care more for their fishponds than for their public duties. The craze for luxury caused many of the aristocracy to run into debt, and the unfortunate provincials had to find enough money, not only to repair the shattered fortunes of their governors, but also to bribe the juries when the governor was prosecuted for extortion on his return. At the height of her power Rome was, in fact, the prey of a degenerate governing class and it needed the strong hand of a monarch to reduce the turbulent nobles to order.

(b) *Equites*. The "knights" had become by the end of the republic a second order in the state consisting of wealthy persons, especially *publicani*. The exact history of their rise is a matter of dispute, but the main facts are these. According to the "Servian" constitution there were eighteen centuries of *equites* who formed the cavalry of the army, as the remainder of the centuries were the infantry. For these equestrian centuries there was probably no fixed property qualification, but they no doubt consisted of well-to-do people in the first class, for they took precedence in voting over the other centuries. They were known as *equites equo publico*, because the money for the purchase and upkeep of their horses was provided out of public funds, in fact by unmarried women and orphans with property, who could not appear in the census-list, and made this contribution to the public need instead.[1] Possession of a "public horse" was not originally incompatible with a seat in the senate, and in the earlier republic many senators no doubt remained in the cavalry as long as their age permitted.

In the later republic, however, a knight was bound to give up his horse on entering the senate, and the ranks of the *equites* appear to have been filled mainly with young men of good family. They did not at this time serve as a corps, the cavalry of the army being drawn mostly from the

[1] Cic. *de Rep.* II. 20. 36; cf. Gai. IV. 27.

"allies", but were used as officers on the staff of generals and in other positions of trust. In any case these *equites* did not form a separate order of society.

As early, however, as the siege of Veii (captured 396), we hear of *equites equo privato*, i.e. those who provided their horses at their own expense. Such people would, of course, have to be comparatively wealthy, but we know of no definite qualification.

The important step of making the *equites* a separate order was taken when C. Gracchus transferred to them from the senators the duty of sitting as jurymen in the courts, especially in that which tried cases of extortion. Mommsen was of opinion that the *equites* concerned were only the 1800 who had the "public horse",[1] but it is considered more probable by most authorities that other *equites* were included.[2] Very likely it was Gracchus who first laid down the equestrian census of 400,000 sesterces which we find in existence at the beginning of the empire, but, in any case, from his time onwards, the knights became a class of wealthy business men, and seeing that the chief activity of great capitalists at Rome was the undertaking of state contracts, their interests were largely identified with those of the *publicani*. In many respects their *ordo* had interests divergent from those of the senatorial nobility who were debarred from participation in business,[3] and it was the object of Gracchus to enhance the antagonism between the two classes in order to further his attack upon senatorial privilege.[4]

The *equites*, like the senators, had certain outward signs of rank; they wore the *angustus clavus*, i.e. narrow purple stripes on the tunic (whereas senators wore broad stripes); they obtained the right to the gold ring, which in earlier times had been a senatorial privilege, and they also had special seats allotted to them in the theatre.

Under the empire the equestrian nobility became even more important; admission to it was a necessary first step to any public career, civil or military, for others than the sons of senators, and many very important posts were confined to men of equestrian rank, to the exclusion of senators.

(c) *The middle and lower classes.* Among these we must reckon all free persons who did not belong either to the senatorial or equestrian orders.

---

[1] *Staatsr.* III. 530; *Strafr.* 209.
[2] Strachan-Davidson, II. 85 *sqq.*   [3] Cf. *supra*, 77.
[4] In the provinces especially the two might come into collision; if a governor was strict in his supervision of the tax-farmers he would find a jury of *equites* unsympathetic if he had to stand his trial for extortion afterwards at Rome.

In the last centuries of the republic, in spite of the anarchical state of the government, Italy appears to have been prosperous. In the growing cities there were business men wealthy enough to build themselves elegant houses, and many others living on the income brought them by estates of moderate size, worked, like the great ones of the senators, mainly by slave labour. Among this well-to-do municipal aristocracy, from which the local magistracies were filled, must also be reckoned some of the ex-soldiers who were given plots of land on their discharge. We know, for instance, that a number of Sulla's veterans were settled at Pompeii and became the leading element in the population.

In the country the free peasantry was certainly not extinct, and though many suffered from the loss of their holdings as a result of confiscation in the civil wars, their places were taken by the veterans settled on the land by the military leaders. There must also have been considerable numbers of free tenants of the landlords, though in the main cultivation was done by slaves. These tenants were not independent people like the English tenant-farmer, working lands in much the same way as an owner and finding their own markets for their produce, but quite small men forming part of the larger economic unit constituted by the estate as a whole, and very closely dependent on the landlord.

In the cities there was no great class to correspond with the mass of working-men in a modern industrial state, first because most of the corresponding work was done by slaves, and secondly because industry in the ancient world never developed to the extent to which it has grown in the modern. But there were, of course, numbers of artisans, some working in small shops, which made goods to order for customers, and others making standard articles for an indefinite market. The factory system, however, did not prevail to any great extent; most of the articles appear to have been made in small shops and distributed through business men who bought them from the makers; Roman industry never played such a large part in producing great fortunes as did commerce.

The greater part of the working-classes were, however, not free men but slaves, of whom great masses worked on the estates, great and small, and in the workshops of the cities. The status of all these men was legally identical; they were owned like any other piece of property by their masters, but in practice their positions varied very greatly, from the farm-labourer who was often forced to work in chains, who slept in a sort of barracks and was excluded from all possibility of family life, to the slave-bailiff in charge of a great estate owned by an absentee landlord, or the confidential secretary of a Roman of high rank who might, like Cicero's slave, Tiro, become a "humble friend" of the family. Often, too, a wealthy man might set up a slave of his to manage a business on his own account with a *peculium*, i.e. an amount of money or property which, though it remained legally in the ownership of the master, the slave was permitted to administer for himself. The master might, of course, reserve to himself a certain amount of the profits of the business, and in any case he could not lose more than the amount of the *peculium*, so that this was a useful kind of "limited liability" trading.

These better-placed slaves were often allowed by their masters to accumulate money in their *peculia* and purchase their own freedom with their savings, that is to say the master would agree (though such an agreement would not be enforceable at law) that if the slave saved a certain sum he would take that sum and manumit the slave. Such an arrangement naturally acted as a powerful inducement to the slave to work hard. Many slaves were also manumitted from motives of liberality, or indeed of ostentation. This last motive applied particularly to manumissions by will, for the Romans were much addicted to funereal pomp, and it made a good impression if a large number of grateful freedmen followed a man in his last procession.

The social and political importance of this practice of manumission was very great indeed, especially as Roman law, more generous in this respect than the Greek systems, gave to the manumitted slave (provided the proper formalities were fulfilled) not only complete freedom but citizenship. The result was that from the time when slaves began to be numerous a great part of the citizen population was of servile birth, and, what is still more important, of foreign race, for most of the slaves were prisoners captured in war. Greeks and other races of the Eastern Mediterranean especially mingled their stock with that of Italy in this way, for they had the civilisation which fitted them for the better positions, while the Gauls, for instance, were mostly used for hard physical labour in the fields or mines and had little chance of manumission.

The freedman (*libertinus*),[1] although a citizen, was not on an entire equality with the free-born man as regards political rights. He had a vote, but as all freedmen were confined (except for short periods when democratic leaders succeeded in passing laws removing the restriction) to the four "city" tribes, there were thirty-one out of the thirty-five tribes which he could not influence. From voting in the centuriate assembly he was no

---

[1] *Libertinus* is the general word, including "Latin" freedmen; *libertus* implies citizenship. Buckland, *R.H.* II. (1923), 293–296.

doubt originally excluded, for, throughout the republic, freedmen might not serve in the legions (though regularly used for the less honourable service in the fleet), but when the *comitia centuriata* ceased to have any close connection with the army and was based to some extent on tribal divisions[1] freedmen were probably included. For magistracies and the senate freedmen were not eligible.[2]

In spite of their political disabilities freedmen formed a very important class of the population. Most of them came of quick-witted races and it was naturally the most intelligent that secured their freedom, though a youth passed in the abominable condition of slavery did not tend to make them too scrupulous.[3] They congregated mostly in the towns, where they probably made up the larger part of the free working population. Some, no doubt, became rich, though we do not yet hear of the colossal fortunes which became proverbial in the early empire.

Particular importance attaches to the proletariate in Rome itself. Now that the citizen body was spread all over Italy it was, of course, impossible for the great majority of voters to attend the assembly except very occasionally. Numbers of out-voters came for the consular elections in the summer, but legislation was practically in the hands of those who happened to reside in Rome. It must be remembered that the *comitia* remained throughout a primary assembly; the device of representative government was never adopted. Anyone therefore who could keep the populace in the city in a good temper had in his hands the legislative organ of the Roman state. The chief means adopted for this purpose was the distribution of corn by the state at very low prices, a practice which had begun under C. Gracchus. In Cicero's time every citizen who applied received a ration equal to that of the soldier for about one-third of the market price. These distributions were made at the expense of the state, but there were other advantages which came out of private pockets, especially the costly games which an aspirant to the higher magistracies was almost forced to provide if he did not want to receive an unpleasant check to his career.

The result was naturally that the *plebs urbana* degenerated and that the *comitia* became merely a machine for registering the wishes of the man

---

[1] *Supra*, 20.

[2] *Libertinus* originally included the children of freed slaves and *ingenuus* consequently meant a person whose grandfather had been free, but by the end of the republic anyone who was born in a state of freedom was *ingenuus*, *v.* Gai. I. 11: *Ingenui sunt qui liberi nati sunt.*

[3] *Nec turpe est quod dominus iubet*, Petronius, *Cena Trimalchionis*, 75.

who could obtain the greatest popularity at the moment or could bring an army to overawe the population.

This last proceeding would, of course, have been quite inconceivable in the earlier republic when the army was almost identical with the population, but a momentous change had taken place. Under the older system military service was compulsory and based on a property qualification: the *capite censi*[1] had not been liable. In the third and second centuries B.C. owing to wars, and emigration to the provinces, the number of citizens and especially (owing to the growth of *latifundia*) of citizens with the requisite amount of property decreased, and military service also became unpopular with the well-to-do classes. On the other hand there were a number of unpropertied citizens who were only too glad to have a livelihood provided for them in the army and resented their discharge at the end of a campaign. Successive lowering of the census required for enrolment did not meet the case and the final step had to be taken in 107 B.C. after a crushing defeat by the Gauls had annihilated a whole army. Marius, then consul, and one of the greatest of Roman soldiers, opened the ranks to all citizens who cared to enlist, irrespective of any property qualification. The result was that the Roman army became a mercenary one. The soldier was a professional; his interests lay with the army and not with the state as a whole, and his loyalty was for the general who led him and on whose good offices he depended for an allotment of land when his time of service was over. It thus became possible for Roman generals to use their armies as instruments for working their will upon the state, and this power, once realised, led through the long agony of the civil war to the establishment of the military autocracy that we call the empire.

[1] *Supra*, 19.

Chapter V

SOURCES OF LAW IN THE REPUBLIC

The phrase "source of law" is used in a number of different senses which will be found discussed in works on Jurisprudence. In the sense in which it is used here it means a method by which new rules of law can come into existence. In England to-day there are two chief sources of this nature, Statute and Precedent; if a rule is laid down in an Act of Parliament it becomes a rule of law; if in deciding a case which raises a new point of law a judge applies a certain principle the decision is a precedent and the principle becomes (subject to certain limitations) a rule of law. The corresponding sources at Rome during the republic were:

§ 1. *LEX AND PLEBISCITUM*

Lex was strictly an enactment of the *comitia*,[1] either the *centuriata* or the

---

[1] This refers only to republican times. The historians indeed represent the kings as authors of various *leges* (*v.* collection, Bruns, I. 1–15), and Pomponius even supposes that the kings, like the republican magistrates, put proposals for laws before the assembly (D. 1. 2. 2. 2). It is, however, unlikely that there was any real legislation at so early a date. The rules mentioned may be old, but their ascription to *leges* is a result of the common error that there can be no law without legislation. A book purporting to contain a collection of *leges regiae* is said by Pomponius (*loc. cit.*) to have existed in his day and to have been called *ius Papirianum* because it was compiled by a certain Sextus Papirius in the time of the last king, Tarquinius Superbus. Further on, however (§ 36), he speaks of Publius Papirius as the man who made a collection of royal laws, and Dionysius (III. 36) says that Gaius Papirius, the first *pontifex maximus*, restored a collection made by the fourth king, Ancus Martius, of a number of ordinances of the second king, Numa, which had been put up in the forum on tablets and had gradually become illegible. These stories are mere legends, and the collection was certainly made much later than they suggest. In D. 50. 16. 144 there is a reference to a commentary on the *ius Papirianum* by a certain Granius Flaccus, and as the only man of that name known is one to whom Caesar dedicated a work on religious formulae (*de indigitamentis*), it has been held that the work existed at the end of the republic. The identification is, however, quite uncertain, and Hirschfeld (*Kleine Schriften*, 239–245) holds that the *ius Papirianum* was unknown in Cicero's time (for Cicero does not mention it, *ad Fam.* IX. 21, where one would certainly expect him to do so if he knew of it), and that it was fathered on a Papirius in order to exalt the lineage of the Papirian *gens*. Pais, however (*Ricerche*, I, 243–270, summarised *Z.S.S.* XLV. 587–589), considers it much older, dating from the middle of the second or early first century B.C., really made by a

tributa,[1] while *plebiscitum* was one passed by the *concilium plebis*. As soon, however, as its enactments had been put on a level with those of the *comitia*,[2] the *concilium plebis* became the usual organ of legislation, and laws passed by it were frequently called *leges*. This practice indeed was so common, even among lawyers, that it can hardly be called incorrect.[3]

Apart from the XII Tables themselves, which were of course a *lex*, statute was not a very fruitful source of law during the republic. Roman legislation, like our own, was usually of a political character and the development of private law was, in the main, left to the other sources, especially interpretation and magisterial edict. There were, however, a number of *leges* (or *plebiscita*) of constitutional importance which affected private law and some which, so far as we know, had no political significance. Chief among the latter class is the *lex Aquilia*,[4] which recast the whole law of damage to property, and was the basis of all subsequent law on this subject. Among laws which were the result of political struggles we can mention the *lex Canuleia* of 445 B.C., which removed the prohibition of intermarriage between patricians and plebeians that had still been kept in the XII Tables, and the *lex Poetilia* (? 326 B.C.), which mitigated the severity of the law of debt. A political character also probably attached to the various statutes dealing with suretyship discussed by Gaius III. 121–123.[5]

A distinction is drawn by Ulpian[6] between three different degrees of "perfection" which may attach to a law.

member of the Papirian *gens*, and based on a publication of the sacred law which he supposes to have taken place after the opening of the pontificate to the plebeians. Or, in his view, it may possibly have been a collection made by the pontiffs themselves at a time when a Papirius was *rex sacrorum*. Whatever its date there can be little doubt that the work really represented, in part at least, genuine pontifical tradition. Its actual title appears to have been *de ritu sacrorum* (Servius, *in Aen.* XII. 836, Bruns, II. 78), and this fits well with the nature of most of the rules attributed to regal laws of which we hear, for they all belong to the borderland between law and religion.

[1] The *curiata* had ceased to have any political importance in republican times. *Supra*, 17.

[2] *Supra*, 22.

[3] Ulpian, e.g. in D. 9. 2. 1. 1, says *Quae lex Aquilia plebiscitum est, cum eam Aquilius tribunus plebis a plebe rogaverit.*

[4] *Infra*, 285.

[5] Other important *leges* are the *lex Aebutia* introducing the formulary procedure, the *lex Plaetoria* protecting minors against fraud, *leges Atilia* and *Iulia et Titia* concerning *tutela*, and *leges Furia, Voconia, Falcidia* dealing with legacies, and *lex Cincia* restricting gifts.

[6] *Reg.* I. 2.

A *lex perfecta* is one which forbids an act and declares the act invalid if done; a *lex minus quam perfecta* is one which does not declare the forbidden act invalid but imposes a penalty on the person doing the act; a *lex imperfecta* is one which forbids an act but neither declares it invalid if done nor imposes a penalty.

An example of the last class is the *lex Cincia* (204 B.C.), which forbade gifts above a certain amount except among near relatives, but neither invalidated them nor punished the offender.[1]

The *lex Furia testamentaria*, on the other hand, is a *lex minus quam perfecta*. It forbade legacies of more than 1000 *asses* except to certain persons, but did not invalidate them; instead it gave an action for a fourfold penalty against the person who had received such a legacy.[2]

What reason there can have been for passing *leges imperfectae* is unknown; it is suggested that the form comes from that adopted for *plebiscita* at a time when these had not yet obtained the force of law, and consequently could not either invalidate a transaction which was otherwise valid or impose penalties, but there is no evidence to show that this conjecture is right.[3]

At the end of some *leges* there was a paragraph called *sanctio*, which laid down penalties for contravention of the law, but whether we are to imagine that all laws normally contained such a paragraph and that *leges imperfectae* were characterised by its absence is unknown.[4]

§ II. *INTERPRETATIO*

The history of Roman law, so far as we really know anything about it, begins with a code, the XII Tables. No doubt much of the contents of the code was taken from existing customary law, but custom played on the whole a subordinate part in subsequent development. Law was

---

[1] It must not, however, be supposed that the law was without effect; the praetor enforced it, within limits, by *exceptio* and *replicatio*. Cf. *infra*, 210; Buckland, 254–255.

[2] Gai. II. 225; IV. 23.

[3] Cf. *infra*, 224, n. 7.

[4] Cf. J. 2. 1. 10: *Legum eas partes quibus poenas constituimus adversus eos qui contra leges fecerint sanctiones vocamus.* The last paragraph of the *lex de imperio Vespasiani* (Bruns, I. 202) is also headed *sanctio*. It does not threaten any penalties, but on the contrary relieves any person acting in accordance with the law from any penalty he might incur under previous enactments. In late Latin, *sanctio* sometimes means "law" in general, e.g. Const. *Deo Auctore*, 2, where Justinian orders the compilers of the Digest to "collect and amend the whole law of Rome"—*omnem Romanam sanctionem.*

primarily for the Romans statute law, and it was developed (apart from the edict) mainly by what was known as "interpretation" of the statutes.

According to a unanimous and entirely credible tradition this function was, in early times, exercised by the *pontifices*, a small "college" of men who, though they may be described as priests of a sort, did not have to belong to any special caste, except that until 300 B.C.[1] they had to be patricians. Membership of the college was in no way incompatible with other offices; on the contrary, it was an added distinction to the public career of a member of the aristocracy. Nor must we imagine, on the other hand, that the pontifices were judges; their business was, almost certainly, like that of the later *prudentes*, advisory. They advised the magistrate as to the law, and they also apparently advised individuals; at least, this is very probably what is meant by Pomponius' enigmatic statement that one of the *pontifices* was appointed every year "to be in charge of private matters".[2] It is not difficult to understand why it should have been the pontiffs who were the earliest legal authorities. It is true that Roman law took on a secular character at a comparatively early stage in its history, but with the Romans, as with all peoples, law and religion were not originally differentiated, and there were many spheres, even after the XII Tables, and in later times, where the *ius sacrum*, the religious law strictly so called, touched the ordinary civil law. The pontiffs were the guardians of religious tradition, and, as such, would naturally be the authorities to be consulted in purely legal matters as well. Thus, for instance, the calendar was primarily a religious matter and, as such, regulated to a large extent by the pontiffs; but it was also of great legal importance, as on very many days there were religious reasons why the magistrate might not sit in his court.[3] Again, much of the law relating to the family was of a religious character. Adrogations and, originally, will-making could only take place in the *comitia curiata* meeting under the presidency of the *pontifex maximus*, who was especially interested in the preservation of *sacra*, i.e. the family religious rites, which might be adversely affected by the changes in the natural order of descent which these acts involved.

By their different kinds of advice, the pontiffs were able to influence

[1] *Supra*, 15. But the first plebeian, *pontifex maximus*, was not created until 253 B.C.

[2] D. 1. 2. 2. 6: *qui praeesset privatis*, i.e. probably *rebus*—private law matters as opposed to sacred law matters. Wlassak, *Prozessformel*, 103.

[3] It must be remembered that the Roman calendar was a complicated matter, being an adaptation of an original lunar year, which was brought into harmony with the solar year by the occasional intercalation of an additional month, until Caesar's reform introduced the system of leap-years.

the development of the law very considerably. They might even, under the cover of "interpretation", create an entirely new institution, as they did in emancipation. The XII Tables apparently provided no method by which a father could voluntarily set his son free from his power, but there was a clause, intended clearly to punish cruel misuse of his rights by the father, which enacted that if the father sold the son three times the son was to be free from his power.[1] A triple sale of this sort was possible because if the buyer of the son manumitted him (which he might do just as he could manumit a slave), the son fell back into the power of the father. By "interpretation" this clause was used for the purpose of emancipating the son from the father's power. The father made a pretended sale[2] of the son to a friend three times; after each sale the son was manumitted by the friend; after the first two manumissions he reverted to the power of his father, but after the third he was *sui iuris*.

Here we find, as in several other cases in ancient Roman law, the use of a recognised legal proceeding for purposes for which it was never intended; a pretence of a sale is made in order to achieve objects which have nothing to do with ordinary real sales. But when we come to the emancipation of daughters or grandchildren, there is something further, a definite twisting of the clause in the XII Tables to mean what it almost certainly did not mean. The clause mentioned only *sons*; it was probably only with reference to them that there was this limit on the father's power; it was intended that the head of the family should be able to sell the less important members of the family as often as they were manumitted by a buyer. But once the clause had come to be used to permit of the emancipation of sons, it was interpreted to mean that only in their case were three sales necessary; in the case of daughters or grandchildren one was allowed to suffice; the daughter or grandchild was therefore emancipated by being "sold" once, and once manumitted.

Equally important with this interpretation was the work of the pontiffs in shaping the *legis actiones*, or forms of words used to bring a claim before the court. Such claims had to follow closely the text of the law on which they were based, and they had to be exactly correct in every word. Gaius tells us that anyone who made the slightest mistake lost his case,[3] and he gives an instance[4] of a person who was non-suited because,

---

[1] Tab. IV. 2: *Si pater filium ter venum duit, filius a patre liber esto.*

[2] Cf. *infra*, 118. "Emancipation", the freeing of a child from the power of his father, must be carefully distinguished from "manumission", the freeing of a slave or person *in mancipio* by his master.

[3] Gai. IV. 30.   [4] Gai. IV. 11.

wishing to bring an action under the clause of the XII Tables dealing with "cutting down of trees" against someone who had cut down his vines he spoke of "vines" instead of "trees" in his claim. It is clear that the people who could ultimately decide what forms were correct had very great power and that litigation was a very perilous thing for the layman who thought that the justice of his claim was sufficient guarantee of success.

The pontifical monopoly of law, for as such it is represented, was one of the great strongholds of the patricians, from whose ranks the *pontifices* were originally exclusively drawn. One successful attack on it had, of course, been made when the XII Tables laid down a written text, but much remained to be done.

Tradition ascribes the breakdown of the monopoly to the action of a certain Gn. Flavius,[1] secretary to Appius Claudius Caecus (censor 312 B.C.), and son of one of his freedmen, who is said to have stolen and published a collection of *legis actiones* made by his master. It became known as the *ius Flavianum*; and Flavius' act was so much appreciated by the people that they elected him tribune and then curule aedile (304 B.C.), in which latter capacity he put up a copy of the calendar in the forum, so that anyone could see for himself on what days an action might be brought. As Appius Claudius, though belonging to a great patrician house,[2] was himself a democratic innovator, and is mentioned as a jurist of note, it is likely enough that Flavius' publications were really made at his instigation. It is also highly probable that we should connect the popularisation of law with the opening of the pontificate to the plebeians by the *lex Ogulnia* of 300 B.C.; at any rate it was the first plebeian *pontifex maximus*, Tiberius Coruncanius (253 B.C.), who, according to Pomponius, *primus profiteri coepit*.[3] Exactly what these words mean we do not know, but they clearly refer to some sort of public activity, perhaps to the admission of members of the public generally, and especially of students desirous of learning the law, to his consultations. At any rate, there now came into existence a class of men known as *iuris consulti* or *iuris prudentes*, persons "learned in the law", who made law their speciality.

For the jurists of the earlier republic almost our only source of information is the long fragment from Pomponius' *liber singularis enchiridii*

---

[1] On Flavius *v.* Pais, *Ricerche*, I. 217–240, summarised with reference to other literature by Kreller, *Z.S.S.* XLV. 600–605.

[2] He was a great-grandson of the decemvir.

[3] D. I. 2. 2. 38. Cf. *ibid.* 35: *Ex omnibus qui scientiam nancti sunt ante Ti. Coruncanium publice professum neminem traditur.*

(single volume handbook) preserved in Digest 1. 2. 2. The fragment is probably the whole of the "historical introduction" to the handbook and falls into three parts, the first[1] dealing with the origin of the law, the second[2] with the different magistracies, and the third[3] with the *prudentes*. The text is unfortunately very bad; some of the authorities, especially for the most ancient period, that Pomponius used were unreliable, and, like other Roman historians, he is fonder of picturesque anecdote than accurate detail, but the value of the fragment is still very great. For the later republic we have, in addition to Pomponius, a number of references in Cicero's philosophical works as well as allusions to his contemporaries in the letters and speeches, and there are references in the legal writers of the imperial age.

After *Papirius*[4] Pomponius first mentions *Appius Claudius* the decemvir and then passes immediately to his great-grandson *Appius Claudius Caecus*,[5] who, he says, was the author of a lost treatise *de usurpationibus* (the interruption of prescription). Next come *P. Sempronius* (consul 304), called "the wise";[6] *C. Scipio Nasica*, who received the surname *Optimus* and was given a house in the *via sacra* at the public expense so that it should be easier to consult him; and *Q. Maximus*, of whose legal work nothing is said. Of *Tiberius Coruncanius*[7] Pomponius says that none of his writings had survived, but that his *responsa* were "numerous and memorable". *Sextus Aelius Paetus*[8] (consul 198) is next mentioned. He was the author of the *tripertita*, so called because "the law of the XII Tables came first, then followed the *interpretatio* and finally the *legis actio*". This may mean that each clause of the XII Tables was given separately and followed immediately by its juristic developments and the appropriate *legis actio*, or that the three parts were separate; we have no means of judging. Sextus Aelius is also said[9] to have compiled the *ius Aelianum*, a collection of *legis actiones* which superseded the *ius Flavianum*, but whether this was identical with the *tripertita* or not is unknown.[10] The *tripertita* still existed in Pomponius' time and were, he says, called "the cradle of the law". With Sextus Aelius are mentioned his brother, *P. Aelius* (consul 201), and *P. Atilius*, who was surnamed *sapiens*. After

---

[1] *Pr.* –12. [2] 13–34. [3] 35–53.

[4] *Supra*, 83, n. 1. [5] *Supra*, 88.

[6] Pomponius says that the people called him σοφός, but the people would hardly choose a Greek name. Pomponius is simply copying a Greek source, *v.* Kipp, 98.

[7] *Supra*, 88. [8] Surnamed *catus* (sagacious).

[9] D. 1. 2. 2. 7.

[10] If the three parts were separate it might be identical with the third.

the Aelii come *M. Porcius Cato* (censor 184) and his son who bore the same name (died 152). The elder Cato is the famous statesman, but the younger was the more important as a lawyer, and more books of his than of his father's survived. There follow three men of whom Pomponius says that they "laid the foundations of the civil law", which probably means that they were the first to write books which were not mere collections of forms, but contained independent discussions. The three were *P. Mucius Scaevola* (consul 133 and later *pontifex maximus*), *M. Iunius Brutus* (praetor, but not consul) and *M. Manilius* (consul 149). Brutus' work, which was called *de iure civili*,[1] was in the form of a dialogue with his son. Manilius' *monumenta* are said by Pomponius to have survived in his time and it was probably the same man who was also author of a collection of forms for contracts of sale (*Manilianae venalium vendendorum leges*) mentioned by Cicero.[2]

After the three "founders of the civil law" came *P. Rutilius Rufus* (consul 105), a disciple of the Stoic philosopher Panaetius, and probably the originator of the Rutilian type of action;[3] *P. Verginius*, of whom nothing is known; *Q. Aelius Tubero* (consul 118), like Rutilius, a disciple of Panaetius; *Sextus Pompeius*, uncle of Pompey "the Great", and *Caelius Antipater*, who, Pomponius says, wrote histories and gave more attention to oratory than to law.

With the next name, that of *Q. Mucius Scaevola* (son of P. Mucius), we enter a new period, and one of which more is known. The writings of the earlier jurists (though copies of some of their works survived) were known in the classical age almost exclusively through quotations, but those of Q. Mucius were clearly read in the original, and even in the Digest there were some excerpts taken directly from his works, while citations from him in the excerpts taken from other writers are innumerable. He was an active statesman, consul in 95 and, like his father, *pontifex maximus*, and he met his death at the hands of the Marian party in 82. Pomponius says of him that he was the first to "arrange the *ius civile* in *genera*", and we can obtain some notion of what this means from Gaius' statement that he distinguished five kinds of *tutela*.[4] His chief work, eighteen books *iuris civilis*, was the first systematic legal treatise ever produced and became the basis of most of the later works on the *ius civile*. In addition he wrote a *liber singularis* ὅρων, i.e. of definitions, but

---

[1] Cic. *pro Cluent.* LI. 141; *de Or.* II. 55. 223.
[2] *De Or.* I. 58. 246. Some are preserved in Varro, *de Re rust.* II. 5. 11 (Bruns, II. 63). They may have formed part of the *monumenta*.
[3] Gai. IV. 35. *Infra*, 212, n. 2.   [4] I. 188.

containing rules as well, which is used in the Digest. Some modern scholars would make him the founder of a school of jurists, subsequently continued by Labeo and the Proculians.[1] In any case he had many pupils, chief of whom was *C. Aquilius Gallus*, a colleague of Cicero's in the praetorship (66 B.C.)[2] and originator of the *formulae de dolo*[3] as well as of the Aquilian stipulation.[4] A pupil of Gallus was *Servius Sulpicius Rufus* (consul 51), whose influence on the development of the law was as great as that of Q. Mucius.[5] He was a friend and rival of Cicero's in the courts, and, it is said, only took up the study of the law on account of a reproach levelled at him for his ignorance by Q. Mucius.[6] According to Pomponius, he left "nearly 180 books", several of which were still extant. His works included *reprehensa Scaevolae capita*, i.e. corrections of Q. Mucius' views, a book on dowries, and the first commentary on the edict in "two very short books". His pupils were many, among them *A. Ofilius*, who was a friend of Caesar and survived into Augustus' time. He remained a member of the equestrian order and is especially noteworthy as having written the first full commentary on the edict. Another pupil of Servius' was *P. Alfenus Varus*, said to have begun life as a bootmaker, who became consul in 39 and attained the honour of a funeral at the public expense. His works included *Digesta* in forty books, two epitomes of which are used in Justinian's Digest. A number of other pupils of Servius are mentioned by Pomponius, of whom scarcely anything is known except that the works of some of them were collected by a certain Aufidius Namusa. More important were *A. Cascellius*, who was still alive in the time of Augustus, and may have been the creator of the *iudicium Cascellianum*,[7] *C. Trebatius Testa*, a friend of Cicero's who enjoyed a great reputation as a jurist and was consulted by Augustus as to the advisability of enforcing codicils,[8] and *Q. Aelius Tubero*, who is said to have become a jurist only after defending Q. Ligarius before Caesar and failing to secure his acquittal. He achieved a reputation for learning in both private and public law and left books in both branches.

That these *iurisprudentes* were not professional lawyers in our sense is clear; not only did they not receive any remuneration for their services, but they were public men who devoted only some of their time to law,

---

[1] *Infra*, 384.
[2] He was president of the *quaestio de ambitu* (bribery court). Cic. *pro Cluent.* LIII. 147.
[3] Cic. *de Off.* III. 14. 60; *de Nat. deor.* III. 30. 74.
[4] J. 3. 29. 2.   [5] Cf. *infra*, 386, n. 4.   [6] *Infra*, 94, n. 2.
[7] Gai. IV. 166, 169.   [8] J. 2. 25. pr.

and indeed did so as part of their public career. As we have seen, many of them were consuls, which means that they had gone through the whole *cursus honorum*, and some were distinguished as generals and as provincial governors. Tiberius Coruncanius was the leader of an army which withstood Pyrrhus in 280; Sextus Aelius was in command of an army in the first Macedonian war, and Q. Mucius' tenure of the proconsulate of Asia was regarded as a model of what a governor should do.[1] In some cases, no doubt, the chief stimulus to learning was the hope that, by giving legal aid to citizens, the jurist might gain the popularity needed for success at the polls.[2] Towards the end of the republic the legal career was apparently becoming slightly more specialised, though the chief lawyers were still men who held high office, for we hear that Aquilius Gallus refused to stand for the consulship in order to devote himself more intensely to law,[3] and that he retired at times to the island of Cercina where he wrote several of his books.[4] Cicero,[5] discussing what qualities are needed for an ideal jurisconsult, says that he must be one who is skilled " *ad respondendum et ad agendum et ad cavendum* in all matters of law and custom that can be needed by private people in the state". Of these activities, *respondere* is the most important. It means giving advice in the sense in which lawyers use that word, i.e. especially advice as to what the law is, and such advice might be given either to a private individual, as with our "opinions" of counsel, or to a judge who was trying a case, for it must be remembered that the judges (*iudices*) at Rome were not, like our judges, professional lawyers, but laymen, more like our jurymen, except that they generally sat singly and belonged to the wealthier classes of the community. Such a judge, if in doubt as to a point of law, might very well wish to ask the opinion of a jurisconsult, and would be almost certain to follow the opinion when he got it, though, during the republic, there was no compulsion to do so. It might also happen that a litigant had taken the opinion of a jurisconsult and gave evidence of this opinion before the judge who was trying his case.[6] The result was that these opinions were,

[1] He was also one of the proposers of the unfortunate *lex Licinia Mucia* which precipitated the Social war, *supra*, 65.

[2] Witness the story of C. Figulus, who, being disappointed at a consular election, afterwards refused to give legal advice, sending clients away with the pun, *An vos consulere scitis, consulem facere nescitis?* (Val. Max. IX. 3. 2).

[3] Cic. *ad Att.* I. I. I.

[4] Pomponius, D. I. 2. 2. 43.   [5] *De Or.* I. 48. 212.

[6] Pomponius, D. I. 2. 2. 49: *Ante tempora Augusti...(prudentes)...plerumque iudicibus ipsi scribebant, aut testabantur qui illos consulebant.* But *v.* also *infra*, 366, n. I.

in effect, very much like decisions, and, though Roman law did not attach any binding force to precedent, the opinions of the jurists helped to mould the law in a manner not entirely different from that in which judgments mould English law. From the beginning of the empire the importance of *responsa* as a source of law was to become much greater, but they were already among the sources during the republic. As a rule, no doubt, *responsa* were given for an actual case, whether one which led to litigation or not, but this was not necessary. A purely hypothetical case might be raised, for instance, by a pupil, discussed and decided by the jurist, and, since there was in any event no formality, the influence of the decision might be equal to that of one given on real facts. That discussions in the circle of a jurist did take place is evidenced by Cicero,[1] but whether the curious phrase *disputatio fori* used as a synonym for *interpretatio*,[2] i.e. for the law created in this way, has any connection with this practice is uncertain.

Under *respondere* in its widest sense can also be included advice given to magistrates in connection with their legal duties, for the magistrates, though as public men they would have some knowledge of law, were only exceptionally experts. Especially in the highly important work of drawing up their edicts they must have been assisted by jurists, so that the edictal law, as well as the civil law proper, is in fact largely the work of the *prudentes*.

Of the other jurisprudential activities mentioned by Cicero, *cavere* means the drafting of legal forms for contracts, wills and other transactions where expert help was needed.[3] Perhaps we should include under it what Cicero elsewhere[4] calls *scribere*, the formulation of written documents, but it must be remembered that many important transactions, which would with us be embodied in written documents and merely signed by the parties, had in Roman law to be concluded by the spoken word

---

[1] *Top.* XIV. 56: *Vestras in respondendo disputationes.*

[2] Pomponius, D. 1. 2. 2. 5, where it is also said that *ius civile* was sometimes used in this restricted sense, just as we speak of "common law" sometimes as opposed to statute law, and sometimes including it as opposed to equity.

[3] *Cavere* literally means "to take precautions", hence to draft a form of words which seeks to take precautions against various eventualities, as legal documents do. N.B. especially the use of the word as a synonym for *stipulari*, because stipulation, being (unlike the informal contracts) capable of giving binding force to any sort of engagement into which the parties might wish to enter, was always used where elaborate provisions had to be made. The noun *cautio* very frequently means the written document which is evidence of the stipulation, cf. *infra*, 428.

[4] *Pro Mur.* IX. 19.

(stipulation), even if a document was also prepared as evidence of what had been said.

Agere refers to assistance in litigation—help on points of procedure, the drafting of forms to be used by the parties to a lawsuit especially, if modern authorities are right,[1] the drafting of the *formula* (in the technical sense), which under the "formulary" system of procedure formed the basis for the trial of the action by the *iudex*.[1]

Advocacy proper was not the business of the jurisconsult but of the orator, who, though of course he might also be a jurist, was much more often not legally trained. According to ancient ideas, the training needed was one in oratory itself, and many young Romans went to the Greek schools for the purpose of receiving this sort of education; the strictly legal knowledge necessary for arguing points of law involved in his case the orator was expected to get from an expert on each occasion, though in course of time he would naturally pick up a fair amount for himself. Cicero, for instance, though he did not in the least consider himself a lawyer, obviously knew a great deal of law.[2]

In addition to his immediate practical activities of *respondere, cavere* and *agere*, the jurist, as we have seen, sometimes spent part of his time in writing books on legal subjects. This was the only type of literature in which the Romans were completely independent of Greek models. In Greece there was nothing between the generalities of philosophers who were not interested in the detailed system of any one state and mechanical collections made by attorneys.[3] The Romans, it is true, borrowed some of the generalities, but these remained without much effect in practice, and Roman legal literature was above all practical; the jurist never loses sight of the facts of Roman life and the way in which they had to be treated in the forum. Of republican literature, indeed, nothing has survived except a few isolated fragments from Q. Mucius, but it is clear from

---

[1] *Infra*, 202, n. 2.

[2] The relations between the orator and the jurist are well illustrated by the story which Pomponius tells (D. 1. 2. 2. 43) of Ser. Sulpicius, who "having obtained the chief position as a pleader of causes, or at least the second after M. Tullius (Cicero), is said to have gone to Q. Mucius to consult him about the affairs of a friend of his. Q. Mucius gave him an answer on the law, but Servius did not understand and asked again. Again Mucius answered him and again he did not understand. Then Mucius broke out at him and said that it was disgraceful that a patrician, a nobleman and an advocate should be ignorant of the law with which his business lay. Servius was so stung by this reproach that he devoted himself to the study of the law". In this study, as we have seen, he attained great eminence.

[3] *P. Hal.* 1 is believed to be such a collection, *v.* p. 26 of the edition.

the great period which begins with the empire that a solid foundation must have been laid during the republic. The days of mere collections of forms like the *ius Flavianum* and the *ius Aelianum* were over long before it ended. Detailed and systematic works of an original character were written, though these too, no doubt, were constructed largely on the "casuist" principle, i.e. on the discussion of individual cases (actual or hypothetical) which continued to characterise Roman legal literature throughout, except in those works which were intended as handbooks for students. Such handbooks did not, so far as we know, come into existence during the republic.

That some jurists were also active as teachers has already been mentioned incidentally. Generally this teaching was confined, in republican times, to the admission of young men to consultations and to the discussions which accompanied them,[1] and some preparation was provided by a knowledge of the XII Tables, which in Cicero's boyhood were still regularly taught at school.[2] It is presumably to the presence at consultations that Pomponius is referring when he speaks of one jurist as having been the *auditor*[3] of another. Towards the end of the republic, however, there appears to have developed a rather more systematic type of instruction which fell into two stages, one more advanced than the other,[4] but regular lecturing by professional teachers did not exist until the empire.

§ III. EDICTA MAGISTRATUUM

All the higher magistrates had the right to issue edicts, i.e. proclamations in which they notified the people of their orders and of their intentions, each naturally within his own sphere.[5] From the edicts of those whose duty included jurisdiction, especially from that of the

---

[1] *Supra*, 93.

[2] *De Leg.* II. 23. 59: *Discebamus enim pueri* XII *ut carmen necessarium, quas iam nemo discit.*

[3] E.g. D. I. 2. 2. 42: *Mucii auditores fuerunt complures, sed praecipue auctoritatis Aquilius Gallus, Balbus Lucilius etc.*

[4] Of Ser. Sulpicius Pomponius says (§ 43) that he "heard" several jurists but was *institutus a Balbo Lucilio instructus autem maxime a Gallo Aquilio—instituere* referring presumably to the more elementary, *instruere* to the more advanced instruction. But this is perhaps the result of subsequent editing of the fragment, v. Ebrard, *Z.S.S.* XLV. 127.

[5] We know, e.g., of an edict issued by the censors of 92 B.C. in which they denounced the growing practice of attending schools of rhetoric as contrary to *mos maiorum* (ancestral custom).

praetor urbanus,[1] there arose the *ius honorarium*[2] or magisterial law, which came to be placed side by side with the *ius civile* arising from statute and interpretation, and was interwoven with it in a way which, in spite of important differences, may be compared with the manner in which the common law and equity have combined to make up the English legal system. In the case of the praetor and the other jurisdictional magistrates, it was the practice that the edict should be published each year when they entered upon their office and put up in a conspicuous place in the forum.[3] As it was intended that it should be valid throughout the year, it was called *perpetuum* (continuous).[4] Each praetor had, in theory, a perfectly free hand in the matter of his edict, but it became customary for him to take over and republish as his own the bulk of his predecessor's edict, making only such erasures or additions as he or his technical advisers saw fit, and there thus grew up a document of considerable size, known as the *edictum tralaticium*, because it was thus "carried on" from year to year; it was this document on which the jurists wrote commentaries.[5] There was originally no compulsion on the magistrate to adhere to the intentions he had expressed in his edict;[6] presumably the pressure of public opinion was enough, but towards the end of the republic, when, as we know from Cicero's account of Verres' misdeeds, unscrupulous magistrates did not hesitate to misuse their powers in their own or their friends' interest, a *lex Cornelia* of 67 B.C. was passed forbidding praetors to depart from their *edicta perpetua*.

The praetor was entitled to issue edicts and, in fact, these edicts were a very important source of law, but the praetor was not a legislator; he could not alter the law directly and openly as could the sovereign assembly by a *lex* or a *plebiscitum*, and his edict consequently did not take the same form as a statute. It consisted, on the contrary, chiefly of statements by the praetor of what he would do in certain circumstances, of the way in which he would carry out his duty of jurisdiction, and it was the great

[1] But also that of the *praetor peregrinus*, the provincial governors, the curule aediles (cf. *supra*, 49) and the quaestors, whose position in the senatorial provinces was analogous to that of the aediles at Rome. Gai. I. 6.

[2] From *honor* = magistracy.

[3] It was written on white boards, hence *album*.

[4] It was also open to the praetor to issue further edicts during the year if occasion arose. Cicero once speaks of such an edict as *repentinum* (*in Verr.* III. 14. 36) but this was not a technical term.

[5] *Supra*, 91.

[6] Except the *intercessio* of a colleague or a tribune, which was always possible. Cicero relates that it was constantly used when Verres was praetor (*in Verr.* II. 1. 46).

freedom he had in this respect that made it possible for him to influence the law to such an enormous extent. He would thus say that in such and such a case he would give an action (*iudicium dabo*), i.e. if a man came to him with a complaint against another which did not, at civil law, give him any claim against that other for redress, the praetor might nevertheless allow him an action. Or the praetor might say that in certain circumstances he would put a man into possession of property (*possidere iubebo, bonorum possessionem dabo*), or that he would put a man back in his original position (*in integrum restituam*), i.e. account some transaction, e.g. a contract into which the complainant had been induced to enter by fraud, as never having taken place, and so on. The praetor could also refuse to allow a plaintiff to proceed with his claim, though he did not as a rule announce his intention in exactly this way in the edict.[1] The essence of the praetor's power lies in fact in his control over remedies. He does not give a right (as a law can), he promises a remedy, and once there is a remedy there is, by implication, a right also. This is perhaps most clearly seen from an example taken from the law of inheritance. If a man died intestate leaving no children and no relations,[2] then there was, at civil law, no heir to his estate and it was open to anyone to seize the property without any fear, so far as the civil law was concerned, that any other person would be able to bring an action to get it away from him. The praetor was of opinion that in these circumstances the widow of the deceased[3] should have a claim. He could not however assert that she was heir; at civil law she was not, and he could not alter the civil law, but he could, and did, say in his edict that he would "give her possession of the goods", i.e. that he would give her a remedy[4] by which she could get the property of the deceased from anyone who had taken possession of it, and since there was no one who could show a better title she would be able to keep what she had got. We can thus say that by the *ius honorarium* the widow had a *right*, although she had none at civil law, and though the praetor did not, in so many words, say that she had one at all. This is, of course, but one example of a whole complex system of *bonorum possessiones*, all of which taken together form the praetorian

---

[1] See however D. 12. 2. 9. 5 (Lenel, *E.P.* 430) and D. 25. 4. 1. 10 *sub fin.* (Lenel, *E.P.* 313).

[2] Apart from the *gens*; not everyone belonged to a *gens* and in any case the right of the *gens* to inheritance on intestacy disappeared at the end of the republic or beginning of the empire, *v.* Gai. III. 17 and *infra*, 124.

[3] The civil law took no account of the widow unless she had been married with *manus*, cf. *infra*, 123.

[4] *Infra*, 260.

law of succession which became engrafted on the civil law rules of *hereditas*. In a similar way, as we shall see, it becomes possible to speak of praetorian ("bonitary") ownership, i.e. ownership protected by praetorian remedies in opposition to ownership strictly according to the civil law (*dominium ex iure Quiritium*), and the parallelism extended throughout the whole legal system. How the civil and praetorian rules worked in with each other in practice is of course a matter for detailed study in each instance, but one famous remark on their relationship may be explained here. Papinian says that the function of the *ius honorarium* is to "aid, supplement or correct" the civil law.[1] Again the system of inheritance, of which Papinian is probably thinking, helps us to see best what is meant. "Aiding" refers to the provision of praetorian remedies in addition to those of the civil law for the use of a person who has a civil law right; thus the interdict *quorum bonorum* (like all interdicts a praetorian remedy) was in many cases available for the person who was civil law heir. "Supplementing", though it is not possible to draw a hard and fast line between it and "aiding", refers especially to the granting of remedies to persons chosen according to the praetorian system in default of any who had rights at civil law, as in the case of the widow mentioned above. "Correcting" occurs when the praetor gives remedies to a person who is not entitled at civil law although there does exist someone who is so entitled, e.g. a person nominated heir in a will which satisfies praetorian but not civil law requirements will be preferred to the intestate heir, who, since the will is invalid at civil law, is by the civil law entitled to succeed.[2]

The right to issue edicts is no doubt in a sense immemorial, but it does not follow that the praetor had from the beginning of things the great powers which we have just outlined.[3] It may indeed be regarded as certain that in very early times the primitive system of *legis actiones* had to suffice for all purposes without modification; in other words that the civil law alone prevailed. It is also certain that the praetor's power must have received a considerable addition when the *lex Aebutia*[4] introduced the formulary system of procedure, for that system substituted for the rigid and unalterable *legis actiones* a method of trying cases by a

[1] D. 1. 1. 7. 1: *Ius praetorium est quod praetores introduxerunt adiuvandi vel supplendi vel corrigendi iuris civilis gratia.*

[2] But the praetorian successor will not always keep what he has got by these remedies, *v. infra*, 260.

[3] Gai. IV. 11.

[4] Date unknown, probably latter half of second century B.C. Cf. *infra*, 222–229.

form of words which depended on the praetor. What scholars are not agreed about is the amount of power which the praetor had in the later stages of the *legis actio* period, some believing that he was then still something of an automaton, so that if the proper words were spoken by the plaintiff he had to let the case go on and could neither stop it nor influence it, others that even before the *lex Aebutia* the praetor had a very free hand. This question however must be deferred for later consideration.

Of the edicts other than that of the *praetor urbanus* and the curule aediles we know little. The *praetor peregrinus*, seeing that he dealt with foreigners to whom the *ius civile* and the *legis actio* system did not in any case apply, must have had a very free hand from the beginning, and it is probable that many innovations were first made in his edict and only subsequently taken over into that of the urban praetor. At any rate the two seem to have corresponded to a great extent by the time of Cicero, who says that he intends to model a part of his own edict as proconsul of Cilicia on those of the praetors at Rome,[1] which would only be possible if they were similar to each other. Most of our knowledge about the provincial edicts comes from what Cicero says in this connection and from references to the Sicilian edict in the speeches against Verres. His remarks on his own intentions with regard to Cilicia show us what an enormous amount was left to the discretion of the individual governor. He says, for instance, that he will follow the example set by Q. Mucius Scaevola in the edict he promulgated as proconsul of Asia, and allow the Greek cities to live according to their own law[2]—which shows that, if he had wished, he might have substituted some entirely different system during his term of office.

§ IV. CUSTOM

Roman law, like that of other nations, of course originated in custom, but the part played by custom as a source of law in historical times is comparatively small. For the Romans law was primarily statute law, as is shown by their tendency to ascribe all ancient rules to laws enacted by one or other of the kings, and the basic law of Rome, the XII Tables, was, in fact, statutory. Nevertheless, custom was responsible for the introduction of some rules—Gaius, for instance, tells us that the *legis actio per pignoris capionem* was used for the enforcement of some claims in accordance with statute, in others by custom,[3] and Cicero enumerated *mos*[4] among the sources of law. But the republic had no definite theory in the matter, and the discussion of imperial views must be postponed.[5]

[1] *Ad Att.* VI. I. 15.   [2] *Ad Att.* VI. I. 15.   [3] Gai. IV. 26.
[4] *Top.* V. 28.   [5] *Infra*, 359.

Chapter VI

LAW FOR FOREIGNERS, *IUS GENTIUM* AND *IUS NATURALE*

The strict theory of Roman law which remained throughout its history was that the *ius civile* was only for citizens, and, as there was originally no other law than the *ius civile*, the foreigner was both rightless and dutiless. It was open to any Roman to seize him and his property as things without an owner, and, on the other hand, there was no court in which he could be sued. Whether there was ever a time at which practice was entirely in consonance with this theory may be doubted, but at any rate as soon as intercourse with other states became at all common and civilisation advanced, such a barbarous system could no longer be maintained. We have seen that an exception was made in the case of members of the Latin league, whose admission to *commercium* means that their rights were protected at Rome, and very early history already provides an example of a treaty with a foreign state which guarantees mutual protection of legal rights, at least so far as they arise out of commerce. This is the treaty said to have been concluded in the first year of the republic[1] (509 B.C.) between Rome and Carthage. Unfortunately we have no record of the nature of the protection granted in this treaty, but other treaties appear to have made provision for *reciperatio*,[2] i.e. the appointment of a court of several jurymen (*recuperatores*), perhaps taken from nationals of both the states concerned. Finally, quite apart from special treaties, the foreigner was no longer in fact treated as rightless; to treat him so would have been to put a stop to the possibility of commerce, and the commercial interests of Rome were growing. We have seen[3] that about 242 B.C. a special praetor was appointed to deal with disputes in which foreigners were concerned, and from our accounts there can be no doubt that the single praetor had been dealing with such cases, as well as those in which citizens alone were involved, for some time previously. About the

---

[1] This is the date given by Polybius (III. 22). Reasons for accepting it rather than a date in the fourth century are given by Last, *Cambridge Ancient History*, VII. 859–862.

[2] *Reciperatio est...cum inter populum et reges nationesque et civitates peregrinas lex convenit, quomodo per reciperatores reddantur res reciperenturque, resque privatas inter se persequantur.* (Festus, s.v. *reciperatio*, Bruns, II. 30.)

[3] *Supra,* 46.

same time, it must be remembered, Rome also acquired her first provinces,[1] which meant that her governors would have to concern themselves with jurisdiction abroad in which foreigners would necessarily be involved.[2]

Two questions arise in connection with the courts in which a Roman magistrate exercised jurisdiction over foreigners; first as to the procedure used and secondly as to the law applied. The strictly Roman *legis actio* procedure was not available,[3] and the magistrate would have to find some method for himself. Very probably the comparatively flexible formulary procedure, which appears to have been based on Greek precedents, was first introduced in these courts, but its origin is too uncertain for us to speak with any confidence.[4] The law of course could not be the *ius civile* pure and simple because that applied to citizens only, and probably the foreigners concerned were far from eager that it should be extended to them in its entirety; its cumbrous formalities, in which a single slip might mean disaster, would be particularly unattractive to those who came from Greek states and were used to a more developed and freer system. The problem might have been solved by applying the principle of personality, i.e. of judging a man according to the law of his own state,[5] and to some extent this was done. Foreigners belonging to the same state were, we know,[6] generally allowed to settle their disputes according to the law of that state when they came before the local courts, and it is probable that the same principle applied if the matter was litigated before the Roman governor's tribunal.[7] But if this principle had been consistently carried through it would have been necessary to develop rules of "private international law" in order to decide in doubtful cases, where a Roman and a peregrine or peregrines of different states were concerned, which system was to be applied. Such rules did not come into existence,[8]

---

[1] *Supra*, 68.

[2] The principle that magisterial *imperium* is unlimited where foreigners are concerned permits its use for administering justice to them in spite of the rule that law affects citizens only. Cf. Weiss, s.v. *ius gentium*, P.-W. x (1) at column 1220.

[3] *Contra*, Girard, but see references *supra*, 58, n. 3. The arguments applying to Latins apply *a fortiori* to other foreigners.   [4] *Infra*, 223.

[5] Schönbauer ("Studien zum Personalitätsprinzip im antiken Rechte", Z.S.S. XLIX. 345–403) admits the application of the principle of personality, in a sense, but protests against the introduction of the modern implications of the phrase. There was no conception of any comity between independent states which could imply reciprocal recognition of each other's law. The application to each man of his own law was simply a rule adopted for convenience within the sphere of Roman power and, of course, capable of being overridden whenever the Roman government saw fit.

[6] *Supra*, 70 and 99.   [7] Mitteis, *Reichsr.* 125.   [8] Mitteis, *op. cit.* 123.

partly perhaps because of the multitude of states whose systems the Roman courts would have had to notice, but more especially because, as the Roman power grew, so the "foreigners" concerned were more and more generally, in fact, subjects of Rome, with the niceties of whose law the Roman magistrate might get a little impatient. In any case there did grow up, through the edicts of the *praetor peregrinus* and the provincial governors, a system which was neither the Roman *ius civile* nor a code of "private international law", but a general system of rules governing relations between free men as such, without reference to their nationality. Much of this system of law, seeing that it was based on the edicts of Roman magistrates, was Roman in origin, but it was Roman law stripped to a great extent of its formal elements, and influenced by other, especially Greek, ideas. Thus the Roman contract of stipulation was one of the institutions extended in this way to foreigners, i.e. a foreigner can be bound and entitled under it,[1] and it is not difficult to see why, for although the stipulation is what we call a formal contract,[2] the forms required are the simplest imaginable, and the contract is useful for all manner of purposes. Mancipation,[3] on the other hand, with its elaborate ceremony, involving the use of scales and copper and the speaking of set words, remains exclusively a transaction of the *ius civile*. It must also be noticed that the rules of which we are speaking refer almost exclusively to transactions *inter vivos*;[4] matters of family law and of succession remain under the personal law of each particular man.[5]

That the phrase *ius gentium* was ever applied to these rules developed in the peregrine and provincial edicts cannot be shown,[6] but it is clear that they were of great importance in leading up to the conception of

---

[1] Provided he did not use the word *spondeo*, which was reserved for citizens; Gai. III. 93.

[2] I.e. a particular form, in this case an oral question and answer concluded in corresponding terms, is necessary for its validity.

[3] *Infra*, 145.   [4] Mitteis, *R.P.R.* 64.

[5] E.g. the question of *patria potestas* can only arise if both father and child are Roman citizens. No foreigner can take under a Roman will; whether a Roman can take under a foreign will is a question for the foreign law.

[6] Schönbauer, *Z.S.S.* XLIX. 383–396, puts forward the view that the phrase *ius gentium* was first used in the earlier period of Roman expansion, about 200 B.C., and thus before the influence of Greek philosophy made itself felt (about 150 B.C.). It meant the new system which grew up by custom, not among foreigners, but in the great community centring at Rome which then came into existence, and was the "law of the world", i.e. of this community as opposed to the old law of the city-state. In support of his contention, Schönbauer cites several passages from Plautus in which the word *gentium* appears to have a similar sense, e.g. *ubi gentium?* "where in the world?" (Cf. Nettleship, *Journal*

the *ius gentium*, for, once established, they in their turn influenced the development of the law as applied between citizens, especially in the direction of making it less formal, and thus there came into existence the *ius gentium*, in its practical sense, i.e. "that part of the law which we apply both to ourselves and to foreigners". In this sense there is a great deal of law which is *iuris gentium*, e.g. not only the stipulation among contracts, but all the informal contracts, both "real" and "consensual"[1] (the consensual at least being probably importations from the rules developed for foreigners), and much of the law of delict, which is extended from the civil law to apply where foreigners are concerned by the "fiction" that the foreigner is a citizen.[2]

In the sources this "practical" sense of the phrase *ius gentium* is not always clear, because the Roman writers themselves do not distinguish it from a rather different sense which is not practical but derived from Greek philosophical theories. Aristotle, speaking of law in general, had divided it into two parts, that which was "natural" ($\phi\upsilon\sigma\iota\kappa\acute{o}\nu$) and that which was man-made ($\nu o\mu\iota\kappa\acute{o}\nu$),[3] and he asserted that natural law was the same everywhere and had equal validity everywhere; as well as being "natural" it was "common" ($\kappa o\iota\nu\acute{o}\nu$).[4] This idea became a commonplace, especially among the Stoics, with whose ideal of a "life according to Nature" it of course fitted admirably. Cicero repeats lofty sentiments about the law of Nature in a similar strain; he does not, any more than the Greeks, get beyond elementary moral rules when he gives instances of the precepts of this law,[5] but it is clear that for him, as for Aristotle, the universality of a principle is a proof of its naturalness and hence of its validity, for the law of Nature is no mere ideal, it is a binding law and no enactment of the people or senatus-consult can prevail against it.[6] The argument, though not put in these words, is obvious: if all races of mankind acknowledge a practice it must be because it has been taught them by their universal mother, Nature. Cicero thus identifies

---

of Philology, XIII. 169–181). Even if this conception of *gentes* as including the Romans (*contra*, Mommsen, *Staatsr.* III. 9, n. 2, *v.* Mitteis, *R.P.R.* 62, n. 3) is right, it is still true to say that much of the freer law which went by the name of *ius gentium* resulted from contact with foreign peoples whose system was already less formal than that of the Romans themselves.

[1] *Infra*, 293 and 297. [2] Gai. IV. 37. [3] *Eth. Nicom.* V. 7. I.
[4] *Rhet.* I. 13. 2. [5] E.g. *de inv.* II. 22. 65 *sqq.*; II. 53. 161.
[6] *De Rep.* III. 22. 33. Cf. Blackstone, *Commentaries*, I. 41: "This law of nature, being coeval with mankind, and dictated by God himself, is of course superior in obligation to any other...no human laws are of any validity if contrary to this".

the law of Nature with the *ius gentium*[1] in the sense of law common to all peoples, and draws the inference that what is part of the *ius gentium* should also be part of the *ius civile*,[2] i.e. of the law of each particular state, although what is *ius civile* is not necessarily *ius gentium*, for, as in Aristotle's view, there are matters on which Nature is indifferent and each community can lay down rules for itself. This theoretical view of the *ius gentium* as law common to all mankind became current coin among the jurists. Gaius begins his Institutes almost in the words of Aristotle, "All peoples who are governed by laws and customs apply partly their own law, partly law which is common to all mankind; for the law which each people has made for itself is peculiar to that people and is called its *ius civile*, the special law of the state; but that which natural reason has appointed for all men is in force equally among all peoples, and is called *ius gentium*, being the law applied by all races. Thus the Roman people applies partly its own law, partly that common to all men".

The difference between this "theoretical" meaning and the "practical" meaning of which we spoke above, is best seen when we consider the correlative term to *ius gentium*. In each case it is *ius civile*, but in translating this phrase into English we have to differentiate. Where the "practical" meaning is in question, we say "civil law", meaning "Roman law", e.g. the answer to the question whether *mancipatio* is an institution of the *ius gentium* is "No; it is an institution of the civil law". But where the theoretical meaning is in question, as in the passage from Gaius above, we have to refer to the particular state in question, e.g. if we ask, "Is the rule that a husband or son must authorise a woman's contract[3] part of the *ius gentium*?" the answer would have to be: "No; it is a rule of Bithynian civil law". Justinian makes this quite clear. "If", he says, "a man wishes to call the laws of Solon or Draco Athenian civil law, he will not be wrong."[4]

It is true that this distinction is not made by the Romans themselves—they did not in fact succeed in distinguishing morals from law in theory—but it is there all the same and must be grasped if we are to understand the different senses in which an institution can be said to be part of the *ius gentium*. The sense in which the stipulation, for instance, can be so classified has been explained; it is part of the *ius gentium* because an Athenian or a Gaul or a Junian Latin, who has no state, may be bound or entitled under it. But when the Romans say that slavery and manu-

---

[1] *De Off.* III. 5. 23. *De Har. Resp.* 14. 32. Some however hold that Cicero also distinguished between *ius gentium* and *ius naturale*. V. Costa, *Cicerone Giureconsulto*, I. 26–27.

[2] *De Off.* III. 17. 69.   [3] Gai. I. 193.   [4] J. I. 2. 2.

mission[1] or the right of capturing things in war (*occupatio bellica*)[2] is part of the *ius gentium* they mean something different. They mean that these institutions are common to all systems of law which they know, not that they will be recognised in a Roman court. A person who alleges that he has been manumitted by a foreigner cannot claim to be free by Roman law;[3] whether he is free or not will depend on the law of his manumitter's state. It is true that all states know manumission, but the rules on the subject differ greatly from state to state; whereas when a stipulation is mentioned the Roman institution of that name is meant, and any rules there may be in the systems of other states with regard to some similar contract do not matter in the least. It is this latter sort of *ius gentium* alone which really concerns the practical lawyer; the rest is philosophical ornament.

As appears from what has already been said the law of Nature is only another name for the (theoretical) *ius gentium*. Not only does Cicero identify them,[4] but the lawyers generally use the two phrases indiscriminately.[5] Only one refinement which occasionally appears needs mention. If there was one institution which was really common to all peoples of antiquity it was slavery, which consequently is always reckoned as *iuris gentium*. According to Aristotle it was also natural, for some men were slaves by nature,[6] but other Greek philosophers had different views; man was by nature free, and we thus find slavery defined occasionally as an institution of the *ius gentium* contrary to Nature and resulting from war.[7] But this is the only case in which a discrepancy between the two systems can be found. An identification, ascribed to Ulpian, of the law of Nature with the instincts which men share with animals is unfortunately given prominence by appearing in Justinian's Institutes,[8] but it is an isolated opinion in legal literature and was never made the basis of any consistent theory.[9]

---

[1] D. 1. 1. 4.   [2] D. 41. 1. 5. 7.

[3] *Qui enim potest iure Quiritium liber esse is, qui in numero Quiritium non est?* Cic. *pro Caec.* XXXIII. 96.

[4] *Supra*, 104.   [5] Compare e.g. Gai. I. 86 with I. 89.

[6] *Pol.* I. 5. 8.   [7] E.g. J. I. 2. 2.

[8] J. I. 2. pr. = D. I. 1. 3.

[9] The idea appears to have been developed in the Greek schools of rhetoric, *v.* Pollock, Note E, on Maine's *Ancient Law*, and Castelli, *St. Perozzi* (1925), 52–57. Its basis was Pythagorean, *v.* Cic. *De Rep.* III. 11. 19 and Vinogradoff, *Common Sense in Law*, 236. Some scholars hold that the trichotomy, *ius civile, ius gentium, ius naturale*, as opposed to the dichotomy *ius civile, ius gentium* (=*ius naturale*), is post-classical, *v.* Mitteis, *R.P.R.* 62, n. 3 b, and other literature cited de Francisci, II. 229, n. 25. Koschembahr-Lyskowski, *St. Bonfante*, III. 467–498, on the other hand, thinks that it is the identification of *ius naturale* with *ius gentium* which is due to Justinian.

Chapter VII

THE XII TABLES

We have already described how, according to the story, the XII Tables came to be compiled and enacted;[1] now something must be said of their contents, so far as they can be ascertained from the surviving fragments, and of the stage in legal development to which these fragments point. The greater part of the text has perished completely; the original bronze[2] tablets are said to have been destroyed when the Gauls burnt Rome in 390 B.C. It may be that substitutes were afterwards made and put up in the forum,[3] but no such authoritative text was in existence at the end of the republic. On the other hand private copies must have been very numerous, as is shown by frequent quotations and by Cicero's statement that in his youth the XII Tables had been learnt by boys at school. The lack of an official text however had as a result that the language gradually became modernised. Though the fragments that we have look archaic it is known that their language, except in a few instances, is nearer to the Latin of classical times than to that of the fifth century B.C. The surviving fragments come from quotations in authors of the last century of the republic or later times, who sometimes give the text of the law in what purports to be the original words, sometimes merely state its provisions in their own language. A good deal is to be got from Cicero, something from the jurists, especially Gaius, a fair amount from grammarians and antiquarians who were interested especially in curiosities and obsolete words, and the remainder is gathered at large from Roman literature. Of the arrangement very little is ascertainable; in a few cases the number of the tablet on which a provision appeared is known; Cicero, e.g., says[4] "we learnt the *si in ius vocat* when we were children", which seems to show that these words (concerning the summons of the defendant by the plaintiff) stood at the beginning of the whole text, and

---

[1] *Supra*, 11.

[2] That this was the material used is stated by the historians. Some modern writers think that at so early a date wood would have been used. The text of Pomponius (D. 1. 2. 2. 4) gives *eboreas* (ivory), but that has been conjectured to be a MS. error for *roboreas* (wooden).

[3] Livy (VI. 1) says that a collection of treaties and laws, including the XII Tables and some *leges regiae,* was made and that *some* of it was "published to the people".

[4] *De Leg.* II. 4. 9.

consequently that the code began with the provisions relating to procedure, which is likely enough in any case, as these were probably considered the most important of all. The prohibition of *conubium* between patricians and plebeians was, we know, in one of the last two tablets (those supposed to have been drawn up by the second "college" of *decemviri*) which, Cicero says[1] (perhaps for that reason), contained "unfair" laws, and it is interesting to hear that testamentary succession was dealt with before intestacy.[2] Modern editions all follow more or less the order adopted by Dirksen (1824), but rather for convenience of citation than for any other reason.[3] What portion of the original bulk appears in these works it is of course impossible to say, but, seeing that the Romans were fond of referring to their great code where possible, it is likely enough that we have at least a reference to most of the more important provisions.

The style is characterised by extreme brevity and simplicity, the whole code being, so far as we can tell, a series of staccato imperatives, but the language is always careful and exact. The amount of detail varies naturally with the importance of the matter; procedure for instance being dealt with very carefully, presumably because most of the difficulties had arisen in connection with it, whereas mancipation, which was no doubt well known long before, is dismissed with a simple confirmation of its validity.[4] A peculiarity is the frequent change of subject without any indication except the context to show to whom the imperative is addressed.[5]

A question which has always been much discussed is that of possible Greek influence.[6] The traditional story includes an embassy to Greece to study the laws of Solon,[7] and an Ephesian named Hermodorus is said to

[1] *De Rep.* II. 37. 63.

[2] D. 38. 6. 1. pr. Other scraps of information are that the rule by which a father who sold his son three times lost *patria potestas* (*supra*, 87) was in the fourth table (Dionys. II. 27), and that restricting funeral expenses in the tenth (Cic. *de Leg.* II. 25. 64). Attempts have also been made since the time of J. Gothofredus (1587–1652) to utilise the numbers of the books from which the excerpts in the Digest from Gaius' commentary on the XII Tables are taken, on the assumption that, as there were six books in this work, each was devoted to two tables. But there is nothing to show that Gaius adopted this arrangement and there are some special difficulties.

[3] *V.* Bruns, I. 15–40; Riccobono, *Fontes*, I. 21–63; Girard, *Textes*, 9–23.

[4] Tab. VI. 1: *Cum nexum faciet mancipiumque, uti lingua nuncupassit, ita ius esto.*

[5] E.g. Tab. I. 1: *Si in ius vocat* (i.e. the plaintiff) *ito* (the defendant). *Ni it* (the defendant), *antestamino* (the plaintiff). *Igitur em* (the defendant) *capito* (the plaintiff).

[6] *V.* especially Pais, *Ricerche*, I. 147–179.

[7] *Supra*, 11.

have assisted the decemvirs.[1] No more authority attaches to these tales than to the rest of the legends which gathered round the XII Tables, but Greek influence cannot for that reason be ruled out of account. The ancients themselves certainly believed in it. Two passages from Gaius' commentary preserved in the Digest allege identity between rules of the XII Tables and those of Solon;[2] Cicero speaks of restrictions on display at funerals as having been taken from Solon's legislation,[3] and Dionysius goes so far as to say that the decemvirs compiled their code from the (written) laws of the Greeks and unwritten Roman customs.[4] Other instances of similarity with Greek rules have been collected by modern authors,[5] and some borrowing is *a priori* not unlikely, for Hellenic influence exercised through the Greek colonies in Southern Italy and Sicily appears, especially in religious matters, at an early date and may well have extended to law as well.[6] When all has been said, however, the evidence covers but a small part of the code and almost exclusively matters of detail. The great majority of the surviving fragments appear to have a purely native origin and this view of them fits well with the tradition that what the plebeians wanted was not so much reform as certainty. No doubt some disputed points were settled and some innovations were introduced, of which a few may well have been copied from Greek originals, but as a whole the XII Tables are based on the customary law of Rome herself.

More vital than the question of Greek influence is that of authenticity.

[1] Pomponius (D. 1. 2. 2. 4) says that Hermodorus suggested (*auctor fuit*) some laws to the x viri, Pliny, *H.N.* XXXIV. 11 (5), that he was "interpreter". Pais, *op. cit.* 156, puts the date at which the legend first became current between 228 and 146 B.C.

[2] D. 47. 22. 4 (= Tab. VIII. 27), allowing *sodales* (members of societies) to make their own rules provided they do not contravene "public law", and D. 10. 1. 13 (= Tab. VII. 2), concerning the space to be left between buildings erected by adjoining landowners. The Solonian rules on the latter point were in force at Alexandria in the third century B.C., v. P. Hal. cols. IV and V. Bonfante, I. 135, points out that Gaius himself is really dealing with a different matter—the principles which are to guide a *iudex* in the *actio finium regundorum*.

[3] *De Leg.* II. 23, 59; 25, 64 (= Tab. X. 2, 3, 4). The details in connection with funerals correspond too closely with what we know from elsewhere of Greek rules to be the result of chance, v. Mitteis, *R.P.R.* 14, n. 35.   [4] X. 57.

[5] Pais, *op. cit.* I. 147–179; Mitteis, *R.P.R.* 12–16. Most interesting is the correspondence of *privilegia ne inroganto* (Tab. IX. 1) with the Athenian rule quoted by Demosthenes, *c. Aristocr.* 86. 649: μηδὲ νόμον ἐπ' ἀνδρὶ ἐξεῖναι θεῖναι, ἐὰν μὴ τὸν αὐτὸν ἐπὶ πᾶσιν Ἀθηναίοις.

[6] Mitteis, *R.P.R.* 15, emphasises the evidence of Greek loan-words, one of which, *poena*, actually occurs in the XII Tables (VIII. 3).

In recent times doubt has been cast not merely on details of the tradition, but on the central story of a codification dating from the fifth century B.C., and on the identity of the document known to the later Romans as the XII Tables with that codification. The leader of the attack is Pais,[1] who holds that the legislative decemvirate of the fifth century is a myth based on the existence of the later X *viri stlitibus iudicandis*, and that Appius Claudius the decemvir is a legendary double of Appius Claudius the censor of 312 B.C. He does not deny that there were tablets "resulting from one or more legislative acts" promulgated officially and put up in the forum, but the legislation as a whole cannot, in his view, go back to the fifth century. The document known to the later Romans as the XII Tables he regards as one which grew up through several generations and did not receive its final form until the end of the fourth century, the time of Appius Claudius the censor, and Gn. Flavius. Then, and then only, did the secularisation of law take place and the pontifical monopoly break down. Pais does not actually affirm the identity of the final form which the XII Tables assumed with the *ius Flavianum*,[2] but the two are, in his view, closely connected. Among the chief reasons given by Pais are the totally unreliable character of the whole of early Roman history down to the burning of Rome by the Gauls (390 B.C.) and the divergent character of the actual provisions, some of which are ancient and barbaric, others indicative of a far more advanced civilisation in which Greek influence is already strong. He points out also that the traditions concerning the *decemviri* are contradictory, not only in detail, but in fundamental points. The last two tablets, for instance, are said to have been drafted by the second college and to have contained "unfair laws", in particular that forbidding *conubium* between the orders. In that case why did not Valerius and Horatius, the consuls of 449, who were favourable to the plebeians, repeal them after the fall of the decemvirate, and why was *conubium* not allowed until the passing of the *lex Canuleia* some years later (445)?

Even more radical than Pais is Lambert,[3] who entirely denies the

[1] *Storia di Roma*, I. 1 (1898), 550–605; I. 2 (1899), 546–573, 631 *sqq.*; II (2nd ed. 1915), 217–301; *Ricerche*, I, Arts. I–VII, of which the first is a re-publication with slight alterations of that printed in *Studi storici per l'antichita classica*, II (1909), 1–51. An account and review of Pais' later work is given by Kreller, *Z.S.S.* XLV. 589–605. For the literature on the subject generally *v.* Bonfante, II. 77–78; de Francisci, I. 208, n. 19.   [2] *Supra*, 88.

[3] "La Question de l'authenticité des XII Tables et les annales maximi" (*N.R.H.* XXVI (1902), 149–200); "Le problème de l'origine des XII Tables"

legislative character of the XII Tables. In his view they were in fact a collection made, partly of very old materials, in the first half of the second century B.C., very probably by Sextus Aelius, from whose *tripertita* all subsequent writers derived their knowledge of the so-called code. He compares the *ius Papirianum*, which was also (according to the common view) a private collection to which legislative character was mistakenly attached, and cites as parallels other "codes", Western as well as Eastern, which were, in fact, collections of earlier material derived from a sacred source.

Neither Pais nor Lambert has succeeded in convincing the majority of competent scholars.[1] It is generally agreed that there were interpolations, and that these were facilitated by the absence of an authoritative text, but that the Romans of the first century B.C. should have been so entirely mistaken about an event which, on Pais' and on Lambert's theories, was then comparatively recent, is really inconceivable. The time of Sextus Aelius lies in the full light of history, and even that of Flavius is, and was, quite well known. The case of the *ius Papirianum* is not really parallel. There was no pretence that it had ever been issued as a single piece of legislation. The XII Tables, on the other hand, were regarded as a coherent whole, and, indeed, the whole attitude of the Roman jurists would have been different if they had not believed in the existence of a fundamental code. Above all, the state of the law shown by the surviving fragments is much too archaic for 200 B.C. or even for 300, and neither date would leave enough time for the development of the law as shown by the XII Tables into the already complex system of Cicero's time. In spite of all possible scepticism as to the details of the story of their compilation, it remains as certain as it can well be that the XII Tables are really an enacted code of law and that tradition is not far wrong in assigning them to the middle of the fifth century B.C.

Not only did the Romans regard the XII Tables as a code, but they put the value of this code very high. Livy, who shares the general enthusiasm, describes them as "the source of all public and private law";[2]

(*Revue générale de droit*, XXVI (1902), 385–421, 480–497; XXVII. 15–22); "L'histoire traditionnelle des XII Tables et les critères d'inauthenticité des traditions en usage dans l'école de Mommsen" (*Mélanges*, Appleton, 1903); *La fonction du droit civil comparé*, I (1903), 398 *sqq.*

[1] See especially Girard, *Mél.* I. 1–64 (=*N.R.H.* XXVI (1902), 381–436); Lenel, *Z.S.S.* XXVI. 498–524; Bonfante, II. 77–103; Greenidge, *English Historical Review*, XX (1905), 1–21; and against Lambert, Pais, *Ricerche*, I. 49–72. Baviera, however, *St. Perozzi*, 1–51, reinforces Pais with some notable arguments and de Francisci, I. 193–207, adopts an intermediate position.   [2] III. 34.

Ausonius, in the fourth century A.D., goes even further and adds "sacred law".[1] These statements are exaggerations. Though a few rules which belong to the *ius sacrum* are incorporated,[2] the code as a whole is secular in character and it is an indication of the legal genius of the Romans that they were able, at so early a stage in their development, to separate law so completely from religion. Public law, in the sense of constitutional law, is represented in our fragments only by two provisions, that forbidding *privilegia*[3] and that forbidding the trial of a citizen on a capital charge by any assembly except the *comitia centuriata*.[4] Both of these are of great importance from the point of view of "the liberty of the subject", and, if genuine, were no doubt included for that reason. Had there been any general codification of constitutional law the old constitution could hardly have been restored so easily on the fall of the decemvirate. Almost the whole of the code, then, was devoted to private law, and the stage of development which it indicated is that of a community of peasant-proprietors, in which there is as yet very little commerce and writing is still uncommon.

---

[1] *Idyll*, XI. 61–62: *Ius triplex tabulae quod ter sanxere quaternae: sacrum privatum populi commune quod usquam est.*

[2] Especially the regulations for burial collected in Tab. X, though even these are chiefly dictated by a desire to avoid lavish expenditure and unseemly expressions of grief. *V.* also VIII. 21: *Patronus si clienti fraudem fecerit sacer esto.*

[3] Tab. IX. 1: *Privilegia ne inroganto*; cf. *supra*, 25.

[4] Tab. IX. 2: *De capite civis nisi per maximum comitiatum ne ferunto*; cf. *infra*, 320.

Chapter VIII

THE LAW OF THE FAMILY AND OF SUCCESSION AT THE TIME OF THE XII TABLES

The Roman family is purely patriarchal; if there ever was a time when the more primitive matrilinear system prevailed among any part of the population[1] it has left no traces in the legal system, and Roman law is indeed characterised by the exceptionally great power which it allows to the father as head of the family. Originally, no doubt, this power was a general, rather vaguely conceived, supremacy, but by the time of the XII Tables it has crystallised and become differentiated, so that its name varies according to the persons over whom it is exercised.[2] Over the wife and the sons' wives it is *manus*, over the children and slaves *potestas*, *patria potestas* in the former, *dominica potestas* in the latter case, while the bondsmen are said to be *in mancipio*.[3]

§ I. MARRIAGE

The normal marriage at this period is accompanied by *manus*, i.e. the woman passes out of her father's family and comes under the despotic rule of her husband. It appears, however, that already by the time of

---

[1] It has been conjectured that the plebeians were of Etruscan origin and that the Etruscan system was matrilinear. In support of this view are cited the taunts which the patricians levelled at the plebeians on account of the irregularity of their unions. Cf. Livy IV. 2 (speech of the consuls against the proposal to grant *conubium* between the orders): *Quam enim aliam vim conubia promiscua habere, nisi ut ferarum prope ritu vulgentur concubitus plebis patrumque? V.* also R. von Mayr, *Römische Rechtsgeschichte*, I. I. 38; Muirhead, *Historical Introduction to the Private Law of Rome* (3rd ed.), 32.

[2] The word originally used for the undifferentiated power seems to have been *manus* (cf. Old English *mund*), which still appears in compounds, e.g. *manumissio, emancipare*, without reference to power over a wife. Cf. Jhering, *Geist des römischen Rechts*, II. 162; Mitteis, *R.P.R.* 75.

[3] This status is the result of the power possessed by the Roman father to sell his children. If the child was sold abroad he became a slave among the foreign people, but if he was sold to a Roman he was held *in mancipio*. He was subject to the buyer and, so far as his private life was concerned, no doubt in much the same position as a slave, but he remained legally a free man and a citizen, though his political rights were perhaps in abeyance. On manumission he fell back into the *potestas* of his father, unless there had already been three sales, in which case, by a rule of the XII Tables, the *patria potestas* was finally broken. Cf. *infra*, 118.

the XII Tables this was not necessarily the case. Apart from the question of *manus*,[1] marriage was to the Romans, as to the other peoples of antiquity, a *de facto* rather than a *de jure* matter, in the sense that two people were held to be married, not because they had gone through any particular ceremony, but because they in fact lived together as man and wife.[2] This state of affairs begins ordinarily with the bringing of the bride to the house of the bridegroom (*domum deductio*), but no special legal significance attaches to this proceeding, except in so far as it is in fact the beginning of conjugal life. As we shall see, however, *manus* would in early times normally result if such conjugal life were continued for a period, and thus it may properly be said that marriage with *manus* was the rule at the time of the XII Tables. *Manus* may arise in any one of three ways, by *confarreatio*, *coemptio*, or *usus*.[3]

Confarreatio was a religious ceremony in which the essential point was the transfer of the woman from the domestic cult of her father's family to that of her husband's. It was almost certainly confined to patricians. Gaius says that the name comes from the use of a cake of spelt[4] (*far*) in the sacrifice made to Jupiter Farreus, that there must be ten witnesses[5] and that certain solemn words had to be spoken. From another source[6] we know that the *pontifex maximus* and the *flamen Dialis* (priest of Jupiter) were also present. In Gaius' time it was still necessary that the *rex sacrorum* and the greater priests should be born of confarreate marriages and themselves be married in this way.

---

[1] And apart from the sacred relationships produced by *confarreatio*. The idealistic definitions of marriage found in the later jurists, e.g. Modestinus, D. XXIII. 2. 1: *Nuptiae sunt coniunctio maris et feminae et consortium omnis vitae, divini et humani iuris communicatio*, appear to be derived from confarreate marriage, *v.* Jörs, 196, n. 3, quoting Dionys. II. 25.

[2] The Latin phrase which most clearly corresponds to our "to get married" is (of the husband) *uxorem ducere*, to take as wife, but it retains throughout the original sense of an actual taking into the house, *v.* Levy, *Ehescheidung*, 69. So, in Attic law, though a formal betrothal (ἐγγύησις) is a necessary preliminary to a lawful marriage, no further ceremony was legally required (Lipsius, 469).

[3] Gai. I. 110–113. As to the relative antiquity of these three forms of marriage with *manus* there is much difference of opinion, but that they all existed already by the time of the XII Tables is generally agreed. That *usus* did is clear from the provision that it might be prevented by the *usurpatio trinoctii*; *v. infra*, 115.

[4] Spelt is a kind of coarse wheat.

[5] Thought by some (but without cogent reasons) to be representative of the ten *curiae* of the bridegroom's tribe.

[6] Servius, *in Georg.* I. 31, Bruns, II. 78. A few more details are mentioned in *in Aen.* IV. 374, Bruns, II. 76.

Coemptio, as opposed to *confarreatio*, is a secular form of marriage and is open to plebeians; the husband acquires *manus* over the wife by mancipation, i.e. by the formal act of purchase with the scales and copper in the presence of five citizen witnesses of full age, in the same way as a man acquires ownership over certain kinds of property,[1] but the words used differ from those of an ordinary mancipation.[2]

There are two main views as to the original nature of this institution: (i) Some scholars hold that it never was a real purchase but only came into existence after mancipation had become a "fictitious sale", and was introduced by the plebeians in order that they might acquire rights over their wives similar to those which *confarreatio* gave the patricians.[3] According to this view the marriages of plebeians had hitherto been unrecognised by the civil law and the object for which the plebeians introduced *coemptio* was to obtain such recognition, and thus counter the patrician argument that persons born of unrecognised unions were not fit for the high offices of state. In support of this view it is urged that *coemptio* is too purely secular an institution to belong to the earliest stratum of Roman law. (ii) The second view[4] is that *coemptio* is simply the Roman form of the widely spread institution of marriage by purchase, and that originally some real consideration was given to her father or guardian in exchange for the bride, or more probably, as the analogy of Germanic law suggests, for the power[5] (*manus*) over her. It is true that in historical times the bride regularly appears as a party to the transaction herself—it is she who "makes the *coemptio*"[6], i.e. "sells" herself—but this is presumably a later development. On the face of it, this second view

---

[1] For mancipation *v. infra*, 145.

[2] Gai. I. 123. According to Boethius, *in Cic. Top.* III. 14, *v.* Bruns, II. 73, the man asked the woman whether she would be his *materfamilias* and she asked him whether he would be her *paterfamilias*. Presumably this happened before the *coemptio* proper. As to the words which Plutarch (*Qu. Rom.* 30) says were addressed by the bride to the bridegroom, *ubi tu Gaius ego Gaia*, they certainly could occur in connection with marriage by *coemptio* (*v.* Cic. *pro Mur.* XII. 27), but can hardly have been part of the *coemptio* itself. The ridiculous idea found in some late authors (Servius, *in Georg.* I. 31, Bruns, II. 78; Isidor. *Or.* V. 24–26, Bruns, II. 81) that the *coemptio* was a reciprocal sale, the wife buying the husband and the husband buying the wife, is due to their misunderstanding something that Ulpian evidently said in a passage now lost. Boethius, who refers to Ulpian, no doubt reproduces him correctly when he speaks of reciprocal *questions*. Cf. Girard, 165, n. 3.

[3] Karlowa, II. 166; Muirhead, *op. cit.* 60.

[4] Vinogradoff, *Historical Jurisprudence*, I. 248.

[5] *Supra*, 112.

[6] Gai. I. 115, 195 a. See however Corbett, *Roman Law of Marriage*, 80–83.

seems preferable; marriage by purchase is so common among other races that it would be almost surprising if the Romans had not known it, and, above all, the hypothesis of a deliberate introduction of a new form of marriage for a political purpose is contrary to all that we know of primitive legal conservatism; there is no branch of the law in which deliberate innovation is less likely to take place than in that of the family.

Usus. Gaius[1] says that if a woman "remained married" (*nupta perseverabat*—it is important to notice the words) to a man for an unbroken year she came under his *manus* and that it was provided by the XII Tables that if she did not wish this to happen, she could prevent *manus* from arising by absenting herself for three nights in each year. This, then, was a third method of contracting marriage with *manus*—uninterrupted cohabitation as man and wife for a year. The details and history of the institution present considerable difficulty, and we can again say that the views of scholars fall into two main groups:

(i) According to the first opinion[2] *usus* was not originally a separate form of contracting marriage at all, but arose simply from the principle that any defect in either of the other forms would be cured provided that the *de facto* relationship of man and wife continued for a certain time. *Confarreatio* and *coemptio* were both complicated ceremonies in which a slip might easily occur; such a slip would invalidate the ceremony, but if the parties lived together for a year the defect would be cured and the *manus* which the ceremony had been intended to create would arise, just as in an ordinary mancipation of property, if there were a slip in the ritual, ownership would not pass at once, but would arise after a year (in the case of movables) by usucapion[3] if the transferee remained in possession for that period. Now between a defective ceremony and no ceremony at all it is impossible to draw any hard and fast line, so that, as a further step, it perhaps became the rule that if two people lived together with the intention of being married they would, even without any ceremony at all, become married with *manus* after the end of a year. Once this was recognised there had come into existence a new and informal method of contracting marriage with *manus*. But what was the position before the year was out? It is clear that *manus* did not arise, but was not the woman considered to be already married nevertheless? Gaius, it must be remembered, speaks of her "remaining married" (not merely cohabiting) for a year before *manus* arises, so that it is clear that he at least

---

[1] I. 111.
[2] *V.* especially Mitteis, *R.P.R.* 252.
[3] For *usucapio v. infra*, 152.

considered that she was already married before the year was up. If we suppose that he is correctly reproducing the law as it stood at the time of the XII Tables, then we have here the beginnings of marriage without *manus* such as became common in the later republic.[1] Presumably the position of the woman who availed herself of the rule about the three nights' absence was similar; Gaius speaks as if this prevented her from falling under *manus* but did not affect the existence of the marriage. Indeed, as Karlowa[2] points out, the provision in the XII Tables was probably intended to have precisely this effect, i.e. that by the mere formality of absenting herself the wife could prevent *manus*, although she had every intention of returning. No doubt previously wives had often been away from their husbands for longer periods than three nights, but if they intended to return, this was no interruption of the time of prescription; the novelty was that an absence which did not affect the existence of the marriage should interrupt the prescription and save the woman from falling into *manus*.

(ii) The other main view is that *usus* was already in its origin a separate method of contracting marriage, a kind of marriage on approval, comparable to the "handfast" marriages found at one time in the north of England and in Scotland, which became permanent if the woman bore a child or became pregnant within a year and a day, but might be dissolved if she did not.[3] It is also suggested that *usus* may be connected with marriage by capture, the idea being that if the union lasted for a year the father lost his right to the woman.[4] There is, to a modern mind, the apparent difficulty about this second view, that there would be no clear line between marriage and concubinage, and that a man's concubine might become his wife without his desire, if the cohabitation lasted for a year. But this objection would not have the same force to a Roman who was used to regarding marriage as a *de facto* relationship distinguishable from concubinage, not by legal ceremonies, but by the attendant circumstances, such as preceding betrothal and the customary festivities. There would be no more difficulty in early times than there was under the later system, when free marriage had become the rule, in ascertaining the intentions of the parties, and of course only where marriage was intended would *usus* operate to produce *manus*.

[1] *Infra*, 239.
[2] II. 163.
[3] Cf. Vinogradoff, *Hist. Jurisp.* I. 246.
[4] Cf. Kübler, 33. The legend of the Rape of the Sabine women suggests that marriage by capture was known in early Rome.

Divorce. Whether confarreate marriage was dissoluble at all in the earliest times is a matter of doubt. In historical times, the marriage of the *flamen Dialis* alone was indissoluble,[1] while for other cases a reverse ceremony with the cake of spelt, called *diffarreatio*,[2] was available. It may well be that this ceremony was a comparatively late invention of priestly jurists,[3] and that originally no divorce at all was possible in this sacred form of marriage.

For the purposes of the other types of marriage with *manus*, it is as well to distinguish, even in this early period, between the ending of the *manus* and the ending of the marriage itself, though the two, no doubt, would almost always terminate together. The marriage itself, being a *de facto* relationship, would terminate by the actual breach of conjugal life—the parting between husband and wife in such a manner that they did not intend to come together again. So long, of course, as *manus* exists, such a parting is only possible at the instance of the husband, because the *manus* gives him control over the wife. She cannot go unless he sends her away, and for this sending away there appear to have been traditional formulae, mentioned even in the XII Tables,[4] though it can hardly be that the use of these formulae was ever legally necessary. The *manus*, on the other hand, could only be broken by a legal act, a re-mancipation of the wife to her father, or to some other person who could then set her free, with the result that she became *sui iuris*. In the comparatively rare cases where there was no *manus*, such re-mancipation would, of course, be unnecessary. The Roman husband was, however, not able to use his powers of divorce lightly. Custom required that, before sending his wife away, he should summon a family council on which the wife's relatives must be represented, and a good cause for his action shown.[5] The reasons which would justify divorce are said to have been adultery, wine drinking, tampering with keys and witchcraft.[6] Divorce on insufficient grounds might involve punishment by the censors[7] or possibly something more

---

[1] Festus, s.v. *flammeo*, Bruns, II. 16, and Gell. x. 15. 23.

[2] Festus, s.v. *diffarreatio*, Bruns, II. 7; Plutarch, *Qu. Rom.* L, says that it included many strange and terrible rites.

[3] Karlowa, II. 186. *Contra*, Brassloff, *St. Bonfante*, II. 368–369.

[4] Cf. D. 48. 5. 43 from Gaius' commentary on the XII Tables (*Si ex lege repudium missum non sit etc.*). The oldest known phrase appears to be *baete foras*, *v.* Bruns, I. 22, n. 3.

[5] Val. Max. II. 9. 2.

[6] Dionys. II. 25; Plutarch, *Qu. Rom.* XXII. For discussion see Karlowa, II. 187.

[7] Val. Max. II. 9. 2 relates that in 307 B.C. the censors expelled L. Antonius from the senate for putting away his wife without the consent of a family council.

severe in very early times,[1] but it would be contrary to the whole trend of Roman thought to suppose that it would be invalid.[2]

§ II. PATRIA POTESTAS

The complete power of the Roman father over his children has become proverbial, and the Romans knew that it was an institution peculiar to themselves. It extended not only over all sons and daughters (so long as they had not passed into the *manus* of a husband), but also over the children of the sons and more remote descendants through males, without any limit other than that imposed by the span of human life.

The oldest male ancestor not only has complete control over the persons of his descendants, even to the extent of inflicting the death penalty on them in the exercise of his domestic jurisdiction,[3] but he alone has any rights in private law. No subordinate member of the family can own any property, and any acquisitions that they make go straight to their *pater*, just as the acquisitions of a slave become the property of his master. No person, male or female, *in potestate* can marry without the consent of the *pater*, and if the sons or grandsons marry, it is the *pater* who obtains the *manus* over their wives. One limitation there was, presumably from the earliest times: *patria potestas* has no concern with public law, and a son under power could vote and hold a magistracy just as freely as a *paterfamilias*.[4] In private law the only limitation, if it can be called one, which we know to have existed at the time of the XII Tables, was the rule that if a father sold his son three times the son was to be free from the father. This rule, as we have seen,[5] was used to make emancipation possible, but it is not known whether emancipation existed already at the time of the XII Tables. It could, clearly, only have existed if the provision concerning the three sales was a restatement of a customary rule.

If the tie between father and child can be artificially broken by eman-

---

[1] According to Plutarch, *Qu. Rom.* XXII, a law of Romulus laid down that a man who divorced his wife, except on one of the permitted grounds, should forfeit half his fortune to the wife, and half to Ceres; whereas one who sold his wife should be sacrificed to the gods of the underworld. This, as Mommsen says (*Strafrecht*, 689), represents, at most, a pious wish of the priests.

[2] Cf. Mitteis, *R.P.R.* 252.

[3] He could also sell the child, cf. *supra*, 112, n. 3. It was customary that no serious exercise of domestic jurisdiction should take place without the summoning of a council of friends and relations.

[4] Pomponius, D. 1. 6. 9: *Filius familias in publicis causis loco patris familias habetur, veluti ut magistratum gerat, ut tutor detur.*   [5] *Supra*, 87.

cipation it can also be artificially created by adoption. Desire for continuity of the family was always strong at Rome, and it was of especial importance that there should be a son to carry on the *sacra* or religious cult of the family. In republican law as we know it there were two entirely different forms of adoption, according as the person to be adopted was one under *potestas* (i.e. *alieni iuris*), who was merely to be transferred to another *potestas*, or a *paterfamilias* (i.e. a male *sui iuris*), who was to give up his independence and come under the *patria potestas* of someone else.[1] In the former case the process was *adoptio* (in the strict sense) and the rule about the three sales was again pressed into service to break the *potestas* of the real father. The child (or rather "person to be adopted"—for he might be of any age) is twice sold to a third party and after each sale manumitted; then he is sold a third time, so that the *patria potestas* has gone irretrievably. The next step is that the adopting father should bring an action against the third party who now holds the child *in mancipio*, claiming that he is his son. The action is of course collusive, so that the third party makes no defence and the magistrate adjudges the child to the adopter, into whose *patria potestas* he thus passes. This is one of a number of cases where the Roman jurists used a collusive action to bring about results for which no direct method was provided by law.

Adrogatio was a more important affair; first there was an investigation by the pontiffs into the desirability of the transaction and then, if they had no objection, the *comitia curiata*, meeting probably under the presidency of a pontiff, had to give their approval, the institution taking its name from the *rogatio* or bill which was submitted to them.[2] The reason why there was need here of approval by the religious authorities and by the assembly, whereas none was needed for *adoptio*, is not difficult to see. *Adrogatio*, being the adoption of a person *sui iuris*, meant that a family was extinguished and merged into another. The family might consist only of the person adrogated himself, or of him together with those whom

---

[1] A person is *alieni iuris* if he or she is *in manu*, *in mancipio*, or *in potestate* (*patria* or *dominica*) to another. All other persons are *sui iuris*, and if male are *patresfamilias*, which is simply another way of saying the same thing in their case, for the word has nothing to do with being married or having children; the new-born infant, if he is not in *potestas* (e.g. if he is illegitimate), is a *paterfamilias*. The word *materfamilias* is occasionally used in a corresponding sense as the opposite of *filiafamilias* (e.g. D. 1. 7. 25), but its older meaning appears to be "wife" and indeed especially one married with *manus*; cf. the formula used in *coemptio*, *supra*, 114, n. 2.

[2] Gai. 1. 99.

he held in his *potestas* (who would follow him into the *potestas* of the *adrogator*), but in either case it was extinguished, and provision might have to be made for the continuation of its domestic cult. This no doubt was the special interest of the pontiffs.[1]

That *adrogatio* existed already at the time of the XII Tables is generally assumed, though there is no actual proof; the institution has an archaic flavour about it, and, above all, the use of the *comitia curiata*, the earliest form of assembly, which ceased to function as a political institution from early republican times,[2] points to the origin of *adrogatio* at a period before that of the XII Tables. In historical times the *comitia curiata* was for the purposes of adrogations represented by thirty lictors, one for each of the thirty *curiae*, so that its approval was a mere matter of form. The preliminary investigation of the pontiffs however remained a reality.

§ III. GUARDIANSHIP

Throughout the history of Roman law a child under the age of puberty[3] needed a guardian and so also at the time of the XII Tables (and for long afterwards) did a woman of any age who was *sui iuris*. In these cases the guardian was called *tutor*. Beyond incapacity due to youth or sex Roman law also recognised two other cases, that of the lunatic (*furiosus*) and the spendthrift (*prodigus*), but in these cases the guardian was called by a different name—*curator*. It must however be understood that there is never any question of guardianship of either sort except where the person concerned is *sui iuris*; a person who is *in potestate, in manu* or *in mancipio* can have no guardian, because the chief function (and in later law the only function) of the guardian is to administer the property of the incapable person, and a person *alieni iuris* can have no property to be administered.

At the time of the XII Tables the rules for the appointment of *tutores* were simple in the extreme. A man might in his will appoint a *tutor* for any person in his *manu* or *potestas* who would become *sui iuris* at his death.[4]

---

[1] It is probable that there was a second vote of the assembly declaring that the *adrogatus* had no longer any part in his family *sacra* (*detestatio sacrorum*).

[2] *Supra*, 17.

[3] Fixed at twelve for girls and later at fourteen for boys; *v.* Gai. 1. 196; J. 1.22 pr.

[4] Provided, of course, that the person in question would need a *tutor*. Thus he could appoint for his wife (*in manu*), and for his daughter (unless she were married with *manus*), at any age, and for his son or grandson by a deceased son in case they were under puberty at his death. He could not, on the other hand, appoint a *tutor* for a living son's wife, for she would come under the *manus* of her husband when he (the father-in-law) died, or for his grandson by a living son, for that grandson would come under the *potestas* of his own father. *V.* Gai. 1. 144–148.

Failing a *tutor* appointed by will, the *tutela* went, in the case of free-born persons, to the nearest male agnate (i.e. to the person most closely related, relationship being reckoned through males exclusively),[1] or nearest agnates jointly, if there were several related in the same degree;[2] failing agnates it went to the *gentiles*.[3] In the case of freed persons (who could have no agnates) the *tutela* went to the patron (i.e. the person who had manumitted them) or his children. This was not definitely laid down by the XII Tables, but was inferred from the rule that the patron or his children were to take the succession to freed persons if they died intestate.[4]

The *cura* of lunatics went first to the agnates, failing them to the *gentiles*;[5] there was no provision for the appointment of *curatores* by will. Spendthrifts similarly were under the *cura* of their agnates,[6] at any rate if they had received the property which they were wasting by succession on intestacy. In later times restraint could be imposed on all property, however acquired, and the interdiction which made a man legally a *prodigus* was pronounced by a magistrate, but it may be that, at the time of the XII Tables (when only property received on intestacy was concerned), the agnates themselves, or the *gens*, had power to issue the decree.[7]

Guardianship (both *tutela* and *cura*) became in the developed law an institution intended, as it is with us, to shield the incapable person from the consequences of his own inexperience, disease or folly, but at the time of the XII Tables this was clearly not its main purpose. It was then

---

[1] *Infra*, 122.   [2] Gai. I. 155.
[3] I.e. the members of his *gens*; it may be that originally the *gens* exercised their rights as a corporation, but in the later law the members of the *gens* appear to have acted as individuals.
[4] Gai. I. 165.   [5] Tab. V. 7.
[6] Ulpian, Reg. XII. 2. Presumably on the failure of agnates *cura* went here too to the *gentiles*, but there appears to be no legal text which states this definitely.
[7] The whole question of the treatment of *prodigi* at the time of the XII Tables is much disputed. For the view adopted here see de Visscher, *Études de droit romain* (1931), 20–107 = *Mél. Cornil*, II (1926), 539–611, and Collinet, *ibid*. I. 147 *sqq*. The form of magisterial interdiction is preserved by Paulus (*Sent*. III. 4A. 7): *quando tibi bona paterna avitaque nequitia tua disperdis liberosque tuos ad egestatem perducis, ob eam rem tibi ea re commercioque interdico*. De Visscher takes *bona paterna avitaque* to refer to property left to the spendthrift in his father's *will*, and supposes that the form of the interdiction only came in after the XII Tables, when the magistrate found it advisable to prohibit spendthrifts from dealing with such property, which could not be touched by the agnates because the agnates were confined to property inherited on intestacy. Others (e.g. Girard, 244), who suppose a magisterial decree to have been necessary from the first, take these words as referring precisely to property inherited *ab intestato*.

assigned[1] to the successors on intestacy, the very people who would benefit if the ward died without attaining testamentary capacity,[2] for their own, or at any rate the family's advantage. This is particularly clear with respect to the *tutela* of women; the agnates were given power over them to prevent their losing the family property or taking it with them in an undesirable marriage.[3] Marriage with *manus* needed the consent of the guardians, who could thus prevent a match of which they disapproved. The whole institution is in fact one intended to keep the property in the agnatic family.

§ IV. THE AGNATIC FAMILY

Outside the immediate circle of persons subject to the same *paterfamilias* relationship was still traced exclusively on the agnatic principle, i.e. only relationship through males was recognised. Two people are related agnatically if they are in the *patria potestas* of the same man, or if there is some common ancestor in whose power they would both be if he were alive.[4] Two brothers or a brother and a sister are thus agnates, and so are a man and his brother's son or daughter, because they are both in the *potestas* of the same man, i.e. the father of the one and the grandfather of the other (or would be if he were alive), but a man and his sister's son are not related agnatically because they could never be in the same *potestas*—they are mere cognates, cognates being all relatives whether the relationship be traced through males or females. The bond of *patria potestas* can, as we have seen, be created artificially by adoption, which gives to the adopted child all the rights he would have had if he had been born in *potestas*; he becomes by the adoption the agnate of all his adopting father's agnates. On the other hand he loses all agnatic connection with his previous family, as does also the person who is emancipated. *Manus* has the same effect as *patria potestas*; on marriage with *manus* the woman passes out of the agnatic family of her father into that of her husband, in which she occupies a position similar to that of her husband's daughter.

The working of the agnatic principle has already been seen in relation to guardianship; still more important is its operation in relation to intestate succession, to which we now pass.

---

[1] Apart from testamentary appointment of tutors.

[2] By reaching puberty in the case of a boy, by recovering his senses or having the interdiction removed in the cases of the lunatic and the *prodigus* respectively.

[3] If a woman who is *sui iuris*, and consequently able to own property, marries with *manus*, all her property passes to her husband.

[4] Or, of course, if they are father and child.

§ V. INTESTATE SUCCESSION

By the XII Tables, if a man dies intestate the first people entitled to succeed to his estate are his *sui heredes*, i.e. all those in his *patria potestas* or *manus* who become *sui iuris* at his death. Thus if he leaves a widow *in manu*, a son who has himself a son, a grandson by a predeceased son, a married daughter and an unmarried daughter, his estate will be divided into four parts of which the widow, the son, the grandson by the pre-deceased son[1] and the unmarried daughter will each get one. The grandson by the living son gets nothing; he is not a *suus heres* because he does not become *sui iuris* by the death of his grandfather but comes under the *potestas* of his own father. The married daughter also gets nothing, because, provided she was married with *manus*, she has passed out of her father's power.

The form in which the rights of the *sui heredes* are mentioned in the XII Tables is worthy of notice. They are not so much given the in-heritance as assumed to take it, for the statute simply says "if a man dies intestate without having a *suus heres*, the nearest agnate is to take".[2] The reason for this is to be found in the original co-ownership of all the members of the family in the family property, of which the father in primitive times appears to have been regarded rather as the administrator than the owner. The original vague administrative supremacy of the head of the family had crystallised into ownership over the property as it had crystallised into *potestas*, *manus* and *mancipium* over the persons, but a trace of the older conception remained throughout in the manner in which *sui heredes* succeeded on the death of a *paterfamilias*. Whereas any other successor only assumed the rights and duties of an heir after signifying his acceptance of the succession (*aditio hereditatis*), the *suus heres* assumed them at once on the death of the *paterfamilias* without any act on his part and even without his knowledge or desire. His succession was in fact not so much a succession as a coming into the enjoyment of what, in a sense, had already partly belonged to him.[3] Failing *sui heredes* the succession goes to the nearest agnate or agnates, if there are several in the

---

[1] If there are several children by a predeceased son they share the part which would have gone to their father—i.e. the succession is *per stirpes*, not *per capita*; v. Gai. III. 8.

[2] Tab. v. 4: *Si intestato moritur cui suus heres nec escit, adgnatus proximus familiam habeto.*

[3] D. 28. 2. 11 (Paulus): *Post mortem patris non hereditatem percipere videntur, sed magis liberam bonorum administrationem consequuntur.* Cf. Gai. II. 157: *Vivo quoque parente quodammodo domini existimantur.*

same degree.[1] In the case of women and children this is necessarily the first class because, since a woman cannot have *patria potestas*, she cannot have any *sui heredes*, and a child cannot have any children. No distinction is made in agnatic succession any more than in that of *sui heredes* between male and female agnates.[2] Thus a sister of the deceased (by the same father) will share equally with a brother and will exclude an uncle; an aunt similarly (if the father's sister) will share with a father's brother and exclude a first cousin (the son of a brother of the deceased's father).

It is to be noted that the XII Tables do not say of the agnates that they are to be *heredes*, but that they are "to take the *familia*". From this it has been conjectured that they did not originally count fully as *heredes*, as did the *sui* and perhaps also the heirs appointed in a will, but in historical times the agnate certainly does count as an heir in the full sense.[3]

In default of agnates the succession went to the *gentiles*.[4] It has been suggested, on the analogy of Germanic law,[5] that the rights of the *gens* were anterior to those of the agnates, i.e. that originally, if there were no *sui*, the property reverted to the clan, perhaps the original owner of the land. On this view the preferential right of the agnates, members of the *gens* who can actually show their relationship to the deceased and do not merely bear the same name, is a later development. We do not know whether the *gens* took as a corporation or whether, as the use of the word *gentiles* suggests, they took as individuals. It seems that, at any rate in the latest period in which gentile rights survived, the succession was taken by individuals, for we read that Caesar was "deprived of his gentilician successions",[6] but this may well have been different at the time of the XII Tables.

In the case of freed persons, who could have no agnates, the succession went, in default of *sui heredes*, to the patron, or, if he were no longer living, to his children. These rules applied, not only to those manumitted from servitude, but also to those manumitted from *mancipium*; thus when

---

[1] Degrees are reckoned by the number of steps to be taken in the family tree from one person to the other; thus a grandfather and grandchild are related in the second degree, and an uncle and nephew in the third, two steps up from the nephew to the common ancestor and one down again to the uncle.

[2] See, however, *infra*, 256, n. 7.

[3] Cf. Buckland, *Textbook*, 368; *Manual*, 228.

[4] Tab. v. 5: *Si adgnatus nec escit, gentiles familiam habento.*

[5] Karlowa, II. 881.

[6] Suetonius, *Caesar*, I. 7. The latest evidence for survival is the *Laudatio Turiae* (B.C. 8–2, Bruns, I. 321) which presupposes gentilician *tutela*. Gaius, III. 17, says *totum gentilicium ius in desuetudinem abisse.*

a child was emancipated, if the father had taken care to have the child re-mancipated to him after the third sale, so that he undertook the last manumission himself, he, as quasi-patron, was successor on intestacy to his child; if the last manumission was carried out by the *extraneus* such rights went to him.[1]

§ VI. TESTAMENTARY SUCCESSION

When we pass from intestate to testamentary succession our difficulties in ascertaining the state of the law at the time of the XII Tables become much greater. We know that a will of some sort existed,[2] and this is in itself a noteworthy fact, for most peoples have not yet invented a will at a parallel stage in their legal development. The existence of a will means that a man's power over his property extends beyond his lifetime, that he can take it away from those to whom the law would give it at his death and say that someone else is to have it. We are so accustomed to this extreme development of the right of property that it seems natural to us, but it is in fact a development which comes as a rule only late in a people's legal history.[3] We know also that the XII Tables dealt with testamentary before intestate succession,[4] and that throughout their history the Romans continued to regard testamentary succession as normal. Beyond these facts however all is more or less plausible conjecture. We can tabulate the chief points on which there is difference of opinion as follows:

(i) To what type of will did the words in the XII Tables refer?

We know from Gaius[5] that "in the beginning there were two kinds of will, one made *comitiis calatis*, the other *in procinctu*". The former was made in the *comitia curiata*, summoned twice a year for the purpose[6] probably under the presidency of the *pontifex maximus* and known as the *comitia calata*.[7] The *testamentum in procinctu* was made when the citizens were met, not in the assembly, but in military array, "for", says Gaius, "*procinctus* is the host ready and armed". "Thus", he continues, "they

---

[1] And rights of guardianship if the child were female or under the age of puberty; cf. *supra*, 121.

[2] Tab. v. 3: *Uti legassit super pecunia tutelave rei suae ita ius esto* (but there are varying versions of this text, *v. infra*, 141, n. 4). Also the rules of intestate succession presuppose the possibility of a will: *si intestato moritur....*

[3] Cf. Maine, *Ancient Law*, 157.   [4] *Supra*, 107.   [5] II. 101.

[6] The dates were, according to Mommsen (*Staatsr.* II. 38, *Römische Chronologie*, 242–243), March 24th and May 24th.

[7] The word was apparently applied to the *comitia* only when meeting under religious authority; *v.* Labeo, quoted by Gell. XV. 27.

made the one sort of will in peace and ease and the other when they were about to proceed to battle." It appears from other sources[1] that the moment for making the will *in procinctu* was between the two takings of the auspices, and that the citizen-soldier made it in the hearing of three or four comrades. To these two public forms of will[2] was afterwards added a private form, that *per aes et libram* (mancipatory will) which consisted of the mancipation of the whole of the testator's fortune at a nominal price to a friend (hence called *familiae emptor*) who was asked to dispose of the property after the testator's death in accordance with his instructions. At first an expedient adopted in cases of emergency when there was no time to wait for the next meeting of the *comitia calata*, the mancipatory will developed into a true will and was in the later republic, and still in classical times, the usual form.[3]

In all probability, though we cannot be certain, the mancipatory will was not yet in existence at the time of the XII Tables and the famous words about wills referred to the public forms alone. The chief reasons on which this now generally accepted view is based are:[4] (i) Gaius says of the mancipatory will that "it was added to the earlier forms". As the Romans always regard the law of the XII Tables as fundamental, this way of speaking indicates that the mancipatory will is a subsequent introduction. (ii) The better versions of the XII Tables speak only of dispositions over the *pecunia*, not the *familia*,[5] so that it is unlikely that they can have referred to a proceeding in which the central point was the mancipation of the *familia*. (iii) In the formula of the mancipatory will occur the words *secundum legem publicam*;[6] these are almost certainly a reference to the XII Tables, which must consequently have been in existence already when the mancipatory will was invented. (iv) If it had been referred to in the XII Tables it would have been the first will free from pontifical interference, but Gaius does not mention this advantage.[7]

(ii) Was the part played by the people in the comitial will that of legislators or merely that of witnesses?

At first sight it would seem obvious that their part was that of legislators, i.e. that they had to ratify by their votes the will which the testator proposed to make. A will generally means an interference with the legal rights of a man's family, or *gens*, to his property after his death,

[1] Schol. ad Verg. *Aen.* x. 241, Bruns, II. 77; Plutarch, *Coriolanus*, IX.
[2] Both were obsolete before the end of the republic.
[3] *Infra*, 249.   [4] See v. Mayr, I. 2. 102.
[5] *Supra*, 125, n. 2.   [6] *Infra*, 249, n. 5.
[7] *V.* Girard, 854.

and it seems natural enough that such an interference should first of all have been allowed only if sanctioned by the sovereign people itself in a sort of private Act of Parliament, just as was an adrogation, where voting certainly took place. Many scholars are however of the opposite opinion and think that there was no voting and that the people were summoned only to witness the testator's declaration. The chief arguments for this view are: (i) The word *testamentum* itself is connected with *testis*, a witness, and the formula of the later mancipatory will, which is in all probability taken from the comitial will, includes an appeal to witnesses—*ita do ita lego ita testor, itaque vos, Quirites, testimonium mihi perhibetote.*[1] (ii) According to Labeo[2] the comitial will was made *in populi contione*, and there was never any voting in a *contio*.[3]

Two intermediate opinions are also possible. One is that the function of the people was originally legislative but degenerated later into that of witnessing merely,[4] the other that the words of the XII Tables dispense the testator from the necessity of securing the people's consent to mere particular gifts to individuals (legacies), while leaving him still bound to obtain it if he wished anyone other than his natural successor to succeed him as *heres*.[5]

(iii) Was the comitial will one in which, as in the will of the developed law, a universal successor (*heres*) was appointed, or did it merely contain legacies, i.e. particular dispositions?

To make this question clear it is necessary to say something of the highly important distinction which exists in the Roman law of historical times between the heir (or "universal successor") and the legatee.[6] In historical

---

[1] "Thus I give, bequeath and make my will, and so do you, citizens, bear me witness." *V.* Gai. II. 104 and *infra*, 249.

[2] As reported by Laelius Felix, quoted by Gell. xv. 27. 1-3.

[3] *Contio* is an informal gathering of the people on the summons of a magistrate to listen to speeches, such as preceded the voting on any legislative proposal. There seems to be no reason why the proposed will should not similarly have been read first in a *contio* before the people proceeded to vote on it.

[4] Thus Girard, 853, who supposes that the change was definitely made by the XII Tables. He points out, 855, that the will *in procinctu* must have been introduced subsequently to this change, for the citizen-soldiers can never have had any function but that of witnessing in this form of will, and it is improbable that the *iuniores* (men under forty-six), who alone formed the active army, should have had a freedom of testation denied to their elders.

[5] Thus Mitteis, *R.P.R.* I. 82, n. 24, followed by Wlassak, *Z.S.S.* xxxi. 204.

[6] It may be that the expressions *successio in universum ius* (D. 50. 17. 62), etc. are interpolated, as some authorities now hold (e.g. Bonfante, *Scritti Giuridici*, I. 250 *sqq.*; Longo, *B.I.D.R.* xiv. 127 *sqq.* and 224 *sqq.*; xv. 283 *sqq.*), and it seems clear that the classical writers had not any general idea of "particular" or

times, when a man dies intestate his successor according to the rules of intestacy becomes his *heres*, that is to say he takes over the legal position of the deceased, all his rights and duties (so far as they are transmissible at all)[1] as a single whole; the *heres* becomes owner of the things which the deceased owned, he becomes creditor where the deceased was creditor and debtor where the deceased was debtor. The position is similar where there are several *heredes*, except that in each case the right or the duty is necessarily divided between them. Thus if *A* dies intestate leaving two sons (*sui heredes*) *B* and *C*, *B* and *C* will not get each of them certain particular things that belonged to *A* but will be co-owners of every single thing that he owned; they will each be entitled to receive a fraction of every debt owed to the deceased, and each be liable for a fraction of every debt, and liability for debts, it must be understood, is not limited to the value of the assets. If the deceased did not leave enough property to pay his debts, the heirs must pay them out of their own pockets. Now when a man makes a will he *must* nominate one or more *heredes*, people who will be universal successors in exactly the same way as the intestate heirs; unless it contains such an "institution" of heirs the will is utterly void;[2] but he *may*, if he wishes, also make specific gifts called "legacies" (*legata*) to particular individuals, who take only the specific thing or right bequeathed to them, having no share in the other rights or liabilities of the deceased. Such a legacy is always the taking away from the *heres* of something which would otherwise go to him. A testator may also appoint a guardian (*tutor*) for his wife (if in *manu*) and his children, and may manumit his slaves.

Our question is whether the comitial will was already of the same nature as the will of historical times in that it necessarily included the institution of an heir, or merely consisted of legacies.[3]

In the opinion of the last generation of scholars, represented, for instance, by Maine, there was (in spite of important differences in detail)

"singular" as opposed to "universal" succession (*v.* Mitteis, *R.P.R.* 112), but it remains true that the distinction subsequently formulated by means of these expressions existed in classical times.

[1] Some rights and duties, e.g. those of a husband in relation to his wife, are not transmissible.

[2] Cf. Gai. II. 229: *Testamenta vim ex institutione heredis accipiunt, et ob id velut caput et fundamentum intellegitur totius testamenti heredis institutio.* Cf. also *ibid.* 248.

[3] Together with the appointment of tutors which appears to be vouched for by the words of the XII Tables as reported by Ulpian, Reg. XI. 14: *Uti legassit super pecunia tutelave suae rei, ita ius esto.*

no doubt but that the Roman will was from the beginning the appointment of a universal successor. Maine starts from the point of view that in primitive law the individual counts for nothing, that the unit in the state is not, as in more advanced systems, the individual, but the family. The family is a corporation resting on the religious basis of a common cult of which the *paterfamilias* is chief priest. All property is family property and, though it may be at the disposal of the *paterfamilias*, he is not owner of it but trustee or administrator on behalf of all the members. It is the *paterfamilias* too who represents the family in all its dealings with the state and with other families, being responsible, for instance if a member of the family wrongs a member of another family. When he dies, there is no succession to him in the modern sense; the corporation continues; it merely has a new head. Maine thus sees the origin of the will in the appointment of a new head when there is no one to succeed by right of blood,[1] and the will is thus, like the artificial creation of blood-relationship by adoption, an institution for perpetuating the family corporation and necessarily, from its inception, a method of universal succession.

In its main conclusion (though not in its detail[2]) Maine's view is still the prevailing one, but mention must be made of an entirely different opinion which is held by some modern scholars, and especially by Lenel.[3] According to Lenel the comitial will had no connection with universal succession but was merely a collection of particular dispositions or legacies. At the time of the XII Tables, he thinks, the only true *heres* was the successor on intestacy;[4] and the possibility of creating a similar

[1] "It (the will) was at first, not a mode of distributing a dead man's goods, but one among several ways of transferring the representation of the household to a new chief. The goods descend no doubt to the Heir, but that is only because the government of the family carries with it in its devolution the power of disposing of the common stock", *Ancient Law*, 172.

[2] Maine thought e.g. that the will referred to in the XII Tables was the mancipatory will (*Ancient Law*, 179). On this point *v. supra*, 126.

[3] "Zur Geschichte der heredis institutio" in *Essays in Legal History*, edited by Vinogradoff, Oxford, 1913, 120–142. *V.* also *Z.S.S.* XXXVII. 129–135.

[4] Lenel points out that in the fragments of the XII Tables the word *heres* only occurs with reference to the *suus heres*. Of the agnate it is said (*v. supra*, 123, n. 2) not *heres esto* but *familiam habeto*. The reason for this is not (as some have thought) that the agnate was not looked upon as *heres*, but that whereas the *suus* becomes heir immediately by operation of law on the death of the deceased, the agnate does not do so until he has actually taken possession of the things left by the deceased; that is the point of the words *familiam habeto*—they authorise the taking of possession. Lenel says that we must not import into so primitive an age as the fifth century B.C. the abstract conception of "an inheritance", the complex

universal successor by will did not come until a late stage in the development of the mancipatory will, when the *familiae emptor* ceased to have any real importance as executor of the wishes of the deceased and the mancipation to him became a mere piece of ceremonial necessary for passing the rights and duties under the will to the heir mentioned in the written tablets.[1] This change, Lenel thinks, had not yet taken place in the time of Plautus,[2] in whose plays there is, according to his view, no trace of the appointment of an heir by will (*heredis institutio*). Among the chief arguments in favour of Lenel's view are the following: (i) The fragment of the XII Tables dealing with wills uses the word *legare*, which of course means, at any rate in later Latin, "to give a legacy"; had the institution of an heir been essential this word could not have been chosen. (ii) The words of the "nuncupation" used in the mancipatory will are, as is agreed, probably copied from those of the comitial will, but they too are appropriate only to the giving of legacies, not to the institution of an heir.[3] (iii) The solution which supposes that the words *uti legassit* etc. are merely intended to grant freedom from comitial control in the matter of legacies, while the institution of an heir is still subject to the consent of the assembly,[4] is impossible because this would have meant that a testator might in fact have made the control of the assembly nugatory by giving away all or nearly all his property in legacies. (iv) On the usual theory that institution of an heir was a necessary part of the will from its inception, Roman law is unique; no other early system of law knows of a universal succession independent of blood relationship both real and

of rights and duties treated as a whole, which is familiar to the developed law. To men of the fifth century what a dead man left behind him was not "an inheritance", but a number of concrete things, his house, land, cattle, etc. In the case of the *suus*, who is already living in the house and already a kind of co-owner, it is simple enough that he should become *heres* on the death of his parent by direct operation of law, but the statute cannot conceive this in the case of a stranger (*extraneus*—anyone not a *suus*); there must first be an actual taking of possession which will put him into the position which the *suus* already occupies. If then the statute does not dare say even of the agnate succeeding on intestacy *heres esto*, still less is it possible that a testator should have had the power to say so in a will and that his creating an heir should have been necessary for its validity. All the comitial will did (according to Lenel) was to authorise the taking of physical possession by the various legatees of the various things left to them, in the same way as the law authorises the taking of physical possession of all the property by the nearest agnate in case of intestacy.

[1] *Infra*, 249. [2] Died 184 B.C.
[3] *Haec ita ut in his tabulis cerisque scripta sunt ita do ita lego ita testor, itaque vos, Quirites, testimonium mihi perhibetote*, Gai. II. 104.
[4] Cf. *supra*, 127.

fictitious (i.e. by adoption). What is found both in Greek and in early Germanic law is that testamentary dispositions begin by being of two kinds. On the one hand there is adoption which enables a childless man to provide himself with an heir who will take the position of a natural son, and on the other individual gifts of particular things made during a man's lifetime but taking effect only at his death.[1] If we suppose the comitial will of Roman law to have consisted only of legacies we have in it a parallel to the individual gifts of Greek and Germanic law, whereas the parallel to the adoptions of those systems is to be found in the Roman *adrogatio*,[2] the method by which a man could, with the consent of the pontiffs and the *comitia curiata*, take another person into his family as his son and so make him his heir.

In spite of the eminence of its author, Lenel's thesis has not found general acceptance.[3] The great difficulty is to see how, on his assumption

---

[1] The Athenian form of adoption (εἰσποίησις), which was open only to those who had no natural sons, might take place either during the lifetime of the adopting father or after his death in accordance with instructions left by him in a will. In both cases it needs the concurrence of the φρατρία (clan) and like the Roman *adrogatio* it is primarily intended to perpetuate the family as a religious entity and to secure the performance of the proper rites after the death of the adopter. The will without εἰσποίησις is a development of gifts to take effect at death (cf. the Roman *donationes mortis causa*) and finally superseded the will with εἰσποίησις which had disappeared in the Hellenistic period (*v.* Bruck, *Schenkung auf den Todesfall,* I (1909), 97 *sqq.* and *Totenteil und Seelgerät* (1926), 271). In Germanic law there was originally no possibility of testamentary dispositions (*nullum testamentum,* Tacitus, *Germ.* 20) but a childless person might secure the passing of his property to another by a form of adoption, known by the Lombards as *thinx* or *gairethinx* and by the Franks as *adfatimus*, both of which were, like *adrogatio*, public acts, though otherwise very different from the Roman institution. In the seventh and eighth centuries *donationes post obitum* became common, especially in favour of the Church, by which property was transferred in individual things subject to a right remaining for life with the giver (*v.* Brunner in Holtzendorff's *Enzyklopädie der Rechtswissenschaft* I (7th ed. 1915), 149). It appears from the study of comparative law that it is a general rule that the earliest forms of disposition intended to take effect at death are bilateral, i.e. both the giver and the recipient have to signify their agreement (as with adoption); the idea that the unilateral expression of a man's intention can take effect after his death is only of later growth. Cf. Bruck, *Schenkung auf den Todesfall,* 13.

[2] *Supra,* 119.

[3] *V.* especially Girard, 850, n. 3, and Buckland, *L.Q.R.* XXXII (1916), 97–116. On the other hand Korošec (*Die Erbenhaftung nach römischem Recht,* 1927) holds that originally all obligations were intransmissible both actively and passively and consequently that Lenel is right in his view of the material character of *hereditas* but wrong in thinking that there was any liability for debts imposed on the *familiae emptor* or the legatees.

as to its origin, the Roman will ever developed the characteristics which we know it to have possessed in the late law, in particular how the rule that the validity of the whole depends on that of the nomination of the heir came to be regarded as so fundamental. In later law too it is a fundamental rule that the heir alone is liable for debts and that his liability is unlimited, whereas in Lenel's view originally all legatees were liable but only up to the value of what they received; there must thus, according to him, have been a complete change in two essential points between the earlier and later periods, and yet it is extraordinarily difficult to believe that any system, once having the principle of liability limited to the assets, should have thereafter adopted the highly inconvenient one of unlimited liability; one of the most important of the innovations in the latest stage of Roman law under Justinian consisted precisely in the possibility of limiting the liability of the heir to the value of the assets he received, and was introduced because of the inconvenience of the other system.[1] It is also very difficult to believe that the peremptory *heres esto* (the words by which the heir is appointed) originated, as Lenel thinks, in the mancipatory will, which was an expedient invented by practitioners for cases in which it was not possible to use the comitial form, and not in the original comitial form itself, where in a quasi-legislative act such a form appears quite natural.[2] To Lenel's argument, that freedom to give legacies would have made nugatory any limitation of the testator's right to choose his heir as he wished,[3] it may be answered that the same difficulty must have occurred in Athenian law, where a man with children could not disinherit them, but could make a "legacy will"; it was presumably a matter for judicial discretion in each case to decide whether the amount given away in legacies was so great as to amount to a disinheritance of the children.[4]

Very different from Lenel's view is that of Bonfante.[5] For Bonfante the appointment of an heir is, in accordance with the usual view, an integral part of the original will, and for him, as for Maine, the function of the will was not to provide for the distribution of property (except incidentally) but to appoint a new chief who should succeed to the

---

[1] The *beneficium inventarii*, J. 2. 19. 6.

[2] Girard (*loc. cit.*) also points out that on Lenel's view it was apparently impossible, if one wanted to give any legacies at all, to arrange for one's son to be heir.

[3] *Supra*, 130.

[4] V. Bruck, *Schenkung auf den Todesfall*, 149.

[5] *Histoire*, I. 186–194; *Scritti Giuridici*, I. Nos. v–xix; *Corso di diritto Romano*, vi; cf. also Lévy-Bruhl, *N.R.H.* xlv (1921), 634–669.

"sovereignty" of the testator.[1] Maine, however, thought that the will was not, even at Rome, a primitive institution, and that it originated in the appointment of a stranger where there was no son who would succeed by right of blood, whereas Bonfante regards the will as extremely ancient,[2] and as having for its original purpose the designation of one son out of several as the successor. It thus took the place which in some other systems is taken by the principle of primogeniture. Designation by a predecessor always played an important part in the succession to public office at Rome,[3] and since the chieftainship was analogous to a public office, it is natural to suppose that the Romans, among whom primogeniture was quite unknown, used designation to provide for this case too. Only thus, in Bonfante's opinion, can we account for the predominance of testamentary over intestate succession even in the earliest times, and only on the supposition that the heir succeeds to a type of sovereignty can we explain the rule *nemo pro parte testatus, pro parte intestatus decedere potest*.[4] This maxim has no justification in a system which looks at succession merely from the point of view of property, but it is perfectly intelligible that a family cannot have two heads, one appointed by will and the other by direct operation of law. Legacies are quite a different matter; they are a development of *donationes mortis causa* and it is to them that the words of the XII Tables, *uti legassit* etc., are to be applied. Not until long afterwards did it become possible to appoint an heir who was not a member of the family.

Bonfante's theory has the great merit of accounting for the will as an immemorial institution without the assumption that there could be, even in primitive times, a "universal successor" unconnected with the deceased by blood or adoption, but it raises as many difficulties as it solves. It cannot, for instance, explain the rule that *sui* must be disinherited expressly if they are not to succeed.[5] This rule must in fact rest on an

---

[1] The sovereignty as it appears in historical times is exercised only over a man's agnatic descendants; on the death of the *paterfamilias*, the group over which he reigns breaks up into as many smaller groups as there are lines of descendants. Bonfante's theory presupposes a time when this was different and the successor ruled over the whole group.

[2] For linguistic arguments in favour of an early Roman origin *v.* Goldmann, *Z.S.S.* LI. 223–228.

[3] Cf. *supra*, 5, n. 1, *infra*, 348.

[4] "No one can die partly testate, partly intestate", i.e. if a man leaves a valid will at all, it must regulate the whole of his succession. Hence, if *X* was appointed heir to an individual thing, even though the testator intended the rest of his property to devolve as an intestacy, *X* took the whole. *V.* Buckland, 296.

[5] Gai. II. 123–129.

original right to succession vested in all *sui*, which could only be defeated by a direct exercise of despotic power by the head of the family. On Bonfante's theory that succession of one son under a will was normal, there can have been no such right, and the further rule that the birth of a *suus* (*postumus*)[1] after the making of a will, upset it, becomes quite incomprehensible.[2] If a man had made a will appointing one son, it would have been nonsensical to invalidate that will because a child was born whom no one would certainly think of appointing to "sovereignty" at least if others were available, until he had grown up. The successoral rights of woman are also difficult, if not impossible, to explain on Bonfante's theory.[3] The riddle is unsolved, but it still seems more probable that with the Romans, as with other peoples, the will, in so far as it appoints a "universal successor", could only be made originally where there was no natural descendant to succeed as of course.

[1] Gai. II. 130–143.
[2] Rabel, "Die Erbrechtstheorie Bonfantes", *Z.S.S.* L. 295–332, at p. 330.
[3] *V.* Rabel, *op. cit.* 321.

Chapter IX

SLAVERY AND MANUMISSION AT THE TIME OF THE XII TABLES

Slavery is an institution common to all the races, whether civilised or barbarian, of the ancient world and it was certainly recognised from the earliest times at Rome. Its chief source was then, as at all times, capture in war, and there is no doubt that the rule which makes a child the slave of the person who owns his mother goes back to remote antiquity. Such minor modifications of this rule as exist in classical times are due to a late principle of favouring liberty wherever possible and were no doubt absent from the earliest law. The slave was always at Rome, so far as the law was concerned, a piece of property and any limitations on the power of the master to do as he liked with him were, at the times of which we are speaking, still in the distant future. In two respects only can we say that the civil law recognised the humanity of the slave, (*a*) in the possibility that the master might acquire rights through him and (*b*) in his capacity to become a free man, incapable of being owned, on manumission.

(*a*) The civil law rule was that an act-in-the-law carried out by the slave enured to the benefit of the master, but could not place the master under any liability. A slave could thus, in the later law, make a stipulation for his master, because stipulation is a unilateral contract out of which duties arise only on the side of the promissor. If then *A*'s slave says to *B*: "Will you pay my master 10?" and *B* replies "I will", *B* thereupon owes *A* 10. Not so with a sale, because a sale is bilateral, and the seller only acquires a right to the payment of the price in return for placing himself under the duty of delivering the thing sold. If therefore *A*'s slave purports to sell *A*'s property to *B*, *B* cannot force *A* to do anything, but *A* can enforce the contract against *B* if he likes, provided, of course, that he is willing to do his part. These examples belong to a period later than the XII Tables, but there is no reason to doubt that the principle is ancient. A slave could, in classical times, receive a thing by mancipation on behalf of his master,[1] and so presumably could he as soon as mancipation had become a mere conveyance, not necessitating the real

---

[1] For discussion *v.* Buckland, *Slavery*, 712 *sqq.*

payment of any price.[1] *In iure cessio* to a slave was however not possible because, as Gaius says,[2] he could not claim anything as his own.

The only way in which a man's legal rights could be adversely affected by his slave's act was by delict on the part of the slave, for if the slave committed a delict the master must either pay damages, or lose his slave. But this cannot be regarded as an admission of the slave's humanity because very similar rules applied in the case of damage inflicted by animals.[3]

(*b*) Manumission. The developed civil law knew of three methods of manumission, all of which had the effect, provided they were correctly carried out, of making the slave not only free but a citizen.

(i) *Censu.* This consisted in the enrolment of the slave with his master's consent in the list of citizens drawn up at the *census*.[4] It was the slave who actually gave his name to the magistrate charged with the *census*, but the authorisation of the master was of course necessary, and if it were not given the magistrate would refuse to accept the name, as, no doubt, he might also refuse if he himself considered the man unfit for citizenship.

(ii) *Vindicta.* A more common method was that which consisted in the use for the purpose of manumission of the form appropriate to an action in which liberty was claimed (*causa liberalis*). It might, of course, happen that a person held as a slave wished to claim that he was really free. In such a case it was not open to him to bring the necessary action himself; he had to get some citizen to act as claimant (*adsertor libertatis*) and the proceedings took the form (so long as the *legis actiones* were in use) of a *legis actio sacramento*.[5] The parties came before the magistrate and the *adsertor*, touching the man with the wand (*vindicta* or *festuca*), asserted his freedom; then the defendant also touched the man and asserted that he was his owner, and finally after further formalities,[6] the matter was sent for trial by a *iudex* in the ordinary way.

When a master wants to use this process for the purpose of freeing his slave, he gets some citizen (in fact one of the magistrate's lictors was commonly used) to act as *adsertor* and make a claim that the man is free; then, instead of contesting the claim (as he would do if involved in a real *causa liberalis*), he remains silent, and so admits the claim. He does, however, here too place his wand on the man, and it appears indeed that

---

[1] Cf. *infra*, 146.   [2] II. 96.   [3] *Infra*, 174.
[4] *Supra*, 50.   [5] *Infra*, 182.
[6] As in any other action tried by *sacramentum*, but there was a special provision that the amount of the stake must never exceed fifty *asses*, so that people should not be discouraged from acting as *adsertores*; v. Gai. IV. 14.

it is from this act of his rather than from that of the lictor that the proceeding takes its name.[1] The process then ends with the declaration (*addictio*) by the magistrate that the man is free.[2]

This form of manumission is usually referred to as a fictitious or collusive action, but these expressions are a little misleading. The magistrate[3] knows all about the purpose of the transaction and can, if he disapproves, refuse his *addictio*.[4] Further, the effects are not the same as they would be in the case of an ordinary action, for the manumission has not, like a decision in an ordinary action, merely an effect between the parties; the man becomes free for all purposes. Also he becomes free only from the moment of manumission, whereas the decision of a *causa liberalis* in favour of liberty would necessarily imply that the man had been free before the action was begun. He becomes, too, the freedman of his former master, whereas if he had been free all along he might not be a freedman at all but free born. Manumission *vindicta* is in fact a form of *cessio in iure*, and here too we have to deal with a hybrid institution, beginning perhaps as a sort of collusive action, but coming to be recognised as something quite different.[5]

(iii) *Testamento.* Manumission by will was the most common of the three forms, for a man who dislikes parting with his property during his lifetime, may have no objection to being generous at the expense of his heirs. The gift of liberty must, like a legacy, be in authoritative words, the usual form being *Stichus liber esto* or *Stichum liberum esse iubeo*; like a legacy, too, it is dependent on the validity of the will as a whole, and where the heir is an *extraneus* takes effect only from the moment of his entry.

Of the relative antiquity of the three forms we can say little. Manumission by will certainly existed as early as the XII Tables, for we find a reference to conditional gifts of liberty,[6] and a condition could not be

[1] Karlowa, II. 133, n. 3.

[2] It appears from certain non-legal texts (*v.* Karlowa, II. 133, n. 4) that the master also gave the slave a box on the ear and turned him round, but it is probable that these acts had no legal significance and were not confined to manumission *vindicta* (*v.* Wlassak, *Z.S.S.* XXVIII. 2–3). It is suggested that the box on the ear was a last assertion of ownership and that the turning round indicated the change in the man's position.

[3] Not necessarily the praetor or proconsul; any magistrate with *imperium* could exercise this "voluntary jurisdiction".

[4] Wlassak, *Z.S.S.* XXVIII. 97–114. The matter is disputed, cf. *infra*, 225, n. 2.

[5] Cf. *infra*, 151. It is noticeable that the Romans never themselves speak of either *manumissio vindicta* or *in iure cessio* as fictitious whereas Gaius (I. 113, 119) does call mancipation *imaginaria venditio*, Wlassak, *loc. cit.* 76.

[6] Tab. VII. 12.

attached to either of the other forms. Very probably the code did nothing more than confirm an existing institution.[1]

Manumission *vindicta* is said by Livy[2] to have been used first to liberate a slave who had given information of a monarchist plot in the first year of the republic, and this would of course mean that it existed at the time of the XII Tables if any particular credence could be given to the story. For manumission *censu* there is no evidence. It is sometimes said that both *vindicta* and *censu* being fictitious processes, in which there is a pretence that the slave is already free, must be older than *testamento* which is a direct gift of liberty, the idea being that original Roman law knew of no manumission at all.[3] If we deny the fictitious nature of *vindicta* this argument falls to the ground and we are left without any information as to the relative age of the three forms. One thing however is clear and important; all forms require the co-operation of a public authority, that of the magistrate in the case of *vindicta* and *censu*, that of the *comitia* in the case of *testamento*, for at the time of the XII Tables wills still have to be made in the assembly. The reason for this is also clear; manumission results in the creation of a new citizen and that is an important matter for the state.

[1] Ulp. 1. 9; *v*. Buckland, *Slavery*, 443.

[2] II. 5.

[3] Buckland (*Slavery*, 443) does not press this theory but thinks it more reasonable than the reverse theory, i.e. that the direct form must be the older, which is also sometimes advanced.

Chapter X

THE LAW OF PROPERTY AT THE TIME OF
THE XII TABLES

§ I. *RES MANCIPI AND NEC MANCIPI*

Most, if not all, systems of law are compelled by the very nature of things to distinguish landed from all other types of property, for land is necessary for the production of food and the erection of dwelling-places, and, unlike other things, it cannot be moved. In English law, in the guise of the distinction between "real" and "personal" property, this contrast is particularly marked; in Roman law, though it existed as early as the XII Tables,[1] its importance is overshadowed by a different and purely Roman distinction, that between *res mancipi* and *res nec mancipi*. *Res mancipi* were land subject to Roman ownership,[2] slaves, beasts of draft and burden, including cattle, and rustic servitudes[3] belonging to land subject to Roman ownership; *res nec mancipi* were all other things. In the developed law the point of the distinction is that full Quiritarian ownership in *res mancipi* can only be transferred by the solemn method of conveyance known as *mancipatio* or the equivalent ceremony of *in iure cessio*, whereas the ownership of *res nec mancipi* can be transferred by mere delivery (*traditio*). Thus if *A* wants to make *B* the gift of a sheep and delivers it to him for that purpose the sheep becomes immediately the full Quiritarian property of *B*, but if he wants to give him an ox and does the same the ox remains the property *ex iure Quiritium* of *A*, because an ox is a *res mancipi* whereas a sheep is not.

The reason why the particular classes of things known as *res mancipi* were singled out for special treatment is not difficult to see; they are the things which are most important for the peasant proprietor, the land, the slaves and beasts with which it is worked, and the rights of way and water without which an estate, if it is away from the public road or has no water on it, cannot well be farmed. Such things must not pass from hand

[1] The times for usucapion are different according as the thing in question is *mobilis* or *immobilis*, *v. infra*, 152.

[2] After the extension of citizenship to the whole of Italy (*v. supra*, 66) this meant all land in Italy, but when the citizenship was further extended the deduction that the land of the new citizens was capable of Quiritarian ownership was not drawn. Occasionally however land in the provinces might be assimilated legally to land in Italy by grant of the *ius Italicum*, *infra*, 352, n. 4.

[3] *Infra*, 159.

to hand as less important things may; if the ownership in them is to change there must be a public act of transfer of which witness can afterwards be given in case of any dispute.[1] Nevertheless it is probable that the category of *res mancipi* as it appears in the developed law is not exactly the same as it had been in some earlier period. It has been pointed out that the ceremonial of mancipation is not at all appropriate to a conveyance of land, because it includes the grasping of the thing to be acquired by the transferee[2] and the grasping of land is an impossible, or at least an undignified, gesture.[3] And it may well be that the reason why land was not originally included among the *res mancipi* was that it was not capable of private ownership, or if capable of ownership, was not alienable but had to descend from father to son. We know that very early law does not as a rule recognise private property in land; among the Germanic tribes, for instance, it was unknown in Caesar's day,[4] and even in the time of Tacitus it existed only for the homestead, the remainder of the land being owned by the village community as a whole and redistributed to individuals for cultivation every year.[5] Traces of original clan or tribal ownership are also to be found in Greek law,[6] and indeed, so long as there is plenty of land for everyone who can till it, and a great part of the available land is necessarily left fallow each year because the proper use of manure is unknown, the desire for individual ownership will hardly make itself felt. It is then likely enough on *a priori* grounds that there was a time at Rome also when land, or the greater part of it, was not owned privately, and this probability is supported by the tradition that at the foundation of the city Romulus distributed a "lot" (*heredium*) of two *iugera* to each citizen.[7] As this would not be nearly enough to support a family the distribution would imply that there existed also some form of communal cultivation, the *heredium* being the homestead merely, and very probably, as its name seems to imply, inalienable. But this tradition

---

[1] *Infra*, 148. Perhaps *res mancipi* were originally the only things which counted for assessment to the *census*, *v. supra*, 19, n. 3.

[2] *Infra*, 145.

[3] There is no reason to think that the land was symbolised by a clod of earth in the case of mancipation (though it was in a *legis actio per sacramentum*, *v.* Gai. IV. 17); Gaius could not have omitted to refer to such a practice, had it existed, in his description of the mancipation of land in I. 121. In the case of servitudes grasping was of course completely impossible.

[4] *B.G.* VI. 22.

[5] *Germ.* c. 26. See however Dopsch, Appendix III to Reeb's edition (1930), 152 *sqq.*

[6] Vinogradoff, *Hist. Jurisp.* II. 206.

[7] Varro, *R.R.* I. 10. 2, Bruns, II. 62; Pliny *H.N.* XVIII. 2 (2).

is not particularly trustworthy,[1] and in any case we do not know what form the communal ownership of the remaining land took, whether it was distributed among the different *gentes*, as is most probable, or among some other subdivisions of the state. At the time of the XII Tables at any rate, it is clear that private property in land already existed and was not confined to the *heredium*; the definite rule for the usucapion of land[2] is sufficient evidence, and indeed the early history of the struggle between the orders[3] is incomprehensible without this assumption.[4]

---

[1] It may be a dating back of what occurred in quite different circumstances when colonies were founded; *v.* Lenel, I. 311.

[2] *Infra*, 152.

[3] The struggle was to a certain extent one between rich and poor (*supra*, 8) and in early times this can only mean those who are rich or poor in land. It is however possible that land remained inalienable even though privately owned.

[4] Another difficult question with respect to the division between *res mancipi* and *res nec mancipi* is its connection, if any, with what was apparently a still older division of property, that into *familia* and *pecunia*. These two words appear, sometimes together, sometimes separately in a number of ancient legal phrases. They appear together in the formula spoken by the *familiae emptor* in the mancipatory will (*familiam pecuniamque tuam* etc., Gai. II. 104); *familia* appears alone in the rules of the XII Tables concerning intestate succession (*supra*, 123) and in the phrases *familiae emptor* and *actio familiae erciscundae*; *pecunia* appears alone in the words quoted by Cicero from the XII Tables concerning the *curator* of a lunatic (Tab. V. 7): *si furiosus escit adgnatum gentiliumque in eo pecuniaque eius potestas esto*. What the precise form of the rule in the XII Tables concerning testamentary succession (*supra*, 125) was is uncertain as our authorities give different accounts. Gaius (II. 224) and Pomponius (D. 50. 16. 120) give *uti legassit suae rei, ita ius esto*, Ulpian (Reg. XI. 14) gives *uti legassit super pecunia tutelave rei suae* and Paulus (D. 50. 16. 53 pr.) similarly speaks of *pecunia* and *tutela* (though the passage is corrupt). Cicero on the other hand (*de Inv.* II. 50. 148) gives *uti super familia pecuniaque sua*. This confusion goes to show that later writers did not attach any very definite meaning to the words, and that *familia* at any rate could include all property seems clear from the phrases *familiae emptor* and *actio familiae erciscundae*, for neither the mancipatory will nor the action were confined to one sort of property. But at some time or other the words must have had distinct meanings and it is very possible, as many scholars have thought (e.g. Mitteis, *R.P.R.* 81; Karlowa, II. 73; *v.* also Girard, 272) that *familia* was the earlier equivalent of *res mancipi* (before the inclusion of land), *pecunia* of *res nec mancipi*. *Familia*, which is probably connected etymologically with *domus*, appears to have meant originally "household property", whereas *pecunia*, derived from *pecus* (animals that graze in herds), would include the lesser domestic animals (sheep, goats, etc.) and indeed may at one time have included cattle, for it is not certain that these were always *res mancipi*. According to this *familia* would have referred originally especially to the slaves, in which sense it is also commonly used in classical Latin.

§ II. OWNERSHIP

We have spoken so far of ownership as something which explains itself,
but in order to understand the next point it is necessary to enquire a little
more closely into its nature. The Roman law of classical times is dominated by the *absolute* conception of ownership which it has evolved and
by the action through which this right is asserted, the *vindicatio*. Ownership, in the developed law, may be defined as the unrestricted right of
control over a physical thing, and whosoever has this right can claim the
thing he owns wherever it is and no matter who possesses it.[1] If I
possess a thing and you own it, then all you have to do is to prove your
ownership and I must give it up; it is not necessary for you to allege that
I have done you any wrong. I, on the other hand, the possessor, have
nothing to do but to sit tight and wait for you to prove your right; if you
do not succeed in proving that you are owner, I remain in possession.
Now this very clear-cut conception is not to be found in all, or even most
systems of law. English law, for instance, has never known an action
corresponding to the *vindicatio*, at any rate with respect to movables.
The actions by which an owner recovers his thing which has got out of
his possession all allege that the defendant has done some wrong to the
plaintiff, that, for instance, the defendant "unjustly detains" the thing[2] or
that the plaintiff lost it, that it came into the hands of the defendant and
that the defendant has converted it to his own use;[3] to use technical
language, the actions for the recovery of movables all "sound in tort".
Further, the wrong alleged is, strictly, not one to ownership, but to
possession, for, if the thing be "bailed", e.g. lent, by the owner to another,
it is the bailee who can bring the action against the third party in whose
hands the thing is found, the bailor being originally confined to his rights
against the bailee. Hence it can be said that "although the bailor was the
owner, the sum of his rights as owner was originally his better right as
against the bailee to get possession; for this better right to get possession
was the only form of ownership which the mediaeval common law
recognised".[4] This idea of a *relative* right to possession as contrasted
with the *absolute* Roman *dominium*, is common to other Germanic

---

[1] Subject, of course, to any special right the possessor may have and subject
to the rules of "bonitary" ownership, *infra*, 273.

[2] "Detinue".

[3] "Conversion".

[4] Holdsworth, *H.E.L.* III. 337.

systems of law besides the English, and it indeed appears that the Greeks also knew only of a similar relative right.[1]

It must however be emphasised that the Roman conception, which simplifies matters very considerably, is an achievement of the developed law; in its origin Roman law was, in all probability, similar to other systems. In the developed law, as we have seen, the conception of absolute ownership applies to all sorts of things, *res nec mancipi* as well as *res mancipi*, the only difference being that *res mancipi* need mancipation (or *in iure cessio*) if they are to be transferred, whereas *res nec mancipi* do not, but it may well be that the original distinction went further, and that *res nec mancipi* did not need mancipation, and indeed could not be mancipated, for the simple reason that they were not capable of being fully owned, and that therefore the assertion of full ownership ("I say that this thing is mine by Quiritarian right") which is a necessary part of both mancipation[2] and *in iure cessio*[3] would have been inapplicable to them. This conjecture would explain what is otherwise puzzling, namely the possibility, apparently from the earliest times, of transferring *res nec mancipi* by mere informal delivery of possession (*traditio*), the explanation being that it was originally not strictly ownership that passed at all in the case of such things. This, of course, does not mean that the recipient of a *res nec mancipi* was not originally protected in his possession; he would not be able to bring a *vindicatio*, but he could bring an action for theft if the thing got out of his hands without his consent.[4] If the thing got out of his hands with his consent by what English law calls a "bailment", we cannot say for certain what the position was in general, but very possibly the bailee who refused or was unable to return the thing was treated as a thief:[5] at any rate we know that the XII Tables gave an action for double value against the depositee who failed to return the thing deposited and this is the same penalty as was usually inflicted for theft.[6]

Even with *res mancipi* the evolution of the absolute right of ownership was no doubt gradual; we have seen that one of its characteristic features

[1] Vinogradoff, *Hist. Jurisp.* II. 198. The French law of movables is based on similar ideas.

[2] *Infra*, 145.   [3] *Infra*, 150.

[4] It was not necessary to show that the person in whose possession the thing was found was the actual thief; if it was in his house that was enough to found the *actio furti concepti*, *infra*, 171.

[5] Cf. Beseler, IV. 105: "Non-fulfilment of a real contract is originally embezzlement".

[6] Tab. VIII. 19; cf. *infra*, 175.

is the position of the defendant in a *vindicatio*; he himself need not show how he came to be in possession, need not, in technical language, show title; so long as the plaintiff does not prove title he can keep the thing. But in the earliest form of *vindicatio* known to us this is not yet the case. If we look at the form of the *legis actio per sacramentum in rem* as given by Gaius[1] we see that not only the plaintiff asserts that the thing in question is his, but the defendant makes a similar assertion; then the plaintiff asks the defendant on what grounds he makes the claim. It is clear therefore that the defendant could not simply rely on his possession, but had to show some title, and it is further clear from what Gaius goes on to say that the defendant could not even rely on retaining the interim possession of the thing, i.e. until the action was decided, for the praetor gave this to "one or other of the parties", i.e. might give it to him or to the plaintiff. All this is quite different when we come to the procedure of classical times.

§ III. METHODS OF ACQUIRING OWNERSHIP

The Romans themselves did not devote much discussion to the abstract questions considered in the preceding paragraph; the main topic which they consider under the heading of ownership is that of the methods by which it is acquired. These methods they divide into civil law methods and natural law methods.[2] The civil law methods discussed are *mancipatio*, *in iure cessio* and *usucapio*, those of the natural law include *occupatio* (i.e. the right of a man who has been the first to take possession of an ownerless thing such as a wild beast), *specificatio* (the right obtained in some cases by the maker of a new thing out of existing materials), *traditio* (informal delivery of possession) and others. The civil law methods are open only to citizens (or those with *commercium*), the natural law methods, being part of the *ius gentium*, are open to foreigners as well. In this connection Justinian[3] ventures a historical conjecture. "It is more convenient", he says, "to begin with the older law, and it is clear that the natural law is the older, seeing that it is the product of Nature herself and so coeval with the human race; for civil rights only came into existence when states were first founded, magistrates appointed and laws written down." Now, in a sense, as applied to methods of acquiring ownership this is true; no doubt grabbing came before mancipation, but in another sense it is the reverse of what we know now to be the general truth with regard to the historical evolution of law, namely that formality (and the

---

[1] IV. 16.   [2] Gai. II. 65; J. 2. 1. 11.
[3] Perhaps following Gaius, but D. 41. 1. 1 pr. may be interpolated.

civil law methods are characterised by formality) comes before informality. The recognition that mancipation gave title and the working out of legal rules on the subject certainly preceded the recognition in legal theory of the rules of *occupatio*. *Traditio* similarly, as we have seen, originally escapes notice as a means of acquiring ownership because full ownership is not recognised in those things which pass from hand to hand in this informal way. In speaking of the law of the XII Tables we can thus confine ourselves to the civil law methods.

A. MANCIPATIO. "*Mancipatio*", says Gaius,[1] "is a sort of symbolical sale" (*imaginaria venditio*). For its accomplishment are needed the two parties to the transaction (the transferor and transferee), at least five witnesses, who must be Roman citizens above the age of puberty, a pair of scales and another citizen of full age to hold them (*libripens*), and a piece of copper (*aes*, also called *raudusculum*). The ceremony consists in the transferee's grasping the thing to be transferred, if it is a movable,[2] and saying, e.g. if it is a slave that is being transferred, "I assert that this man is mine according to Quiritarian right, and be he bought to me with this piece of copper and these copper scales" (*Hunc ego hominem ex iure Quiritium meum esse aio, isque mihi emptus esto hoc aere aeneaque libra*). Then he strikes the scales with the piece of copper and gives it to the transferor "by way of price" (*quasi pretii loco*). It was also usual and perhaps necessary, though Gaius does not mention it, to add to the words spoken "at the price of—*pretio*—").

Such was the ceremony in the classical age, and at that time mancipation was a mere conveyance, i.e. whatever the reason for which one man wanted to transfer the ownership of a *res mancipi* to another, mancipation was open to him as a means of so doing. It might be that the reason was a sale, i.e. that he wanted to convey the ownership in the thing because he was under an obligation to do so arising out of a contract of sale, but it might also be any other reason, because e.g. he wanted to make a gift or to fulfil a promise he had made by stipulation, and even where the reason was a sale, the sale is quite distinct from the mancipation; the sale is the contract out of which arises the obligation to convey, the mancipation is the conveyance by which that obligation is fulfilled. The piece of copper given by the transferee to the transferor has no connection with the real price even if there has been a preceding sale and it is given equally when there is no sale at all.

But at one time, clearly, mancipation had not been a symbolical sale

[1] I. 119.   [2] *Supra*, 140.

but a real one. At a time when coined money was not in existence its place as a medium of exchange was, to a certain extent, taken by uncoined copper, which naturally had to be weighed in order that the recipient might know that he was getting the amount for which he had bargained. The primitive "sale" by mancipation was however quite different from the sale (*emptio venditio*) of the developed law. Whereas *emptio venditio* was a mere contract, i.e. an agreement giving rise to obligations (on the part of the seller to transfer the thing sold and on the part of the buyer to pay the price for it) and quite separate from the subsequent conveyance and payment by which these obligations were fulfilled, the primitive mancipation was a sale and a conveyance in one, for there is no previous contract and the payment of the price (i.e. the weighing out of the metal) is part of the form necessary for the conveyance. This "sale for ready money" (or rather for ready copper) is in fact the only sort of sale known to primitive law. It used to be generally assumed that the occasion of the change from sale (of a sort) to conveyance pure and simple by the substitution of a pretended weighing out of copper for a real one must have been the introduction of coined money, for, of course, once this existed it could be counted instead of weighed, and the payment of the price necessarily became something separate from the mancipation itself. We know now, however, that money was only coined at Rome at a comparatively late date, about the middle of the fourth century B.C. or a hundred years after the XII Tables, and the XII Tables seem to have recognised mancipation already in its symbolical form. At least Paulus[1] says that they "confirmed" both mancipation and *in iure cessio*, and we have preserved elsewhere the sentence to which he was probably referring—"When he makes a *nexum* or a *mancipium*, as his tongue speaks, so let the right be" (*Cum nexum faciet mancipiumque, uti lingua nuncupassit, ita ius esto*).[2] It may very well be, as Girard thinks,[3] that these words are intended to confirm the efficiency of the symbolical weighing, i.e. when the transferee asserts that the thing is his, this is to be so, even though the weighing was a mere pretence. But even if this was not the point of the words, it is probable that the need for a form by which it was possible to convey a thing without receiving immediately the consideration for it would have been felt before the middle of the fifth century B.C.[4] Men

[1] Fr. Vat. 50.   [2] Tab. VI. I.   [3] *Manuel*, 310.
[4] Cuq however holds (*Manuel*, 271) that the weighing continued to be real even after copper coinage had been introduced (i.e. the coins were weighed) because the unit of weight used for coinage did not correspond to the unit of weight by which prices were reckoned. According to him the weighing only became superfluous with the introduction of silver coinage in 269 B.C. It

must presumably at a fairly early date have wanted to make gifts, to give dowries to the intended husbands of their daughters, and also to sell on credit.[1]

The witnesses, who were the chief element in the ceremony besides the weighing out of the copper, are there to ensure the publicity of the act and to prevent future disputes. The transfer of a *res mancipi* was, no doubt, an important matter in early Rome and the man found to be in possession of a slave or of cattle which the whole district probably knew to have belonged previously to someone else must be able to justify the fact. The obvious thing therefore, at a time when writing was little used, was to summon witnesses who would be able to testify afterwards that all was in order. The presence of the witnesses, who would of course normally be neighbours, is also a certain guarantee to the transferee that the transferor has the right to convey the thing in question, for they would usually know

is possible (cf. Buckland, 238) that the words of the XII Tables mean no more than that servitudes could be created by mentioning them in the form of words spoken, e.g. if *A* wanted to transfer the ownership in a thing to *B* but reserve a right of way himself he could get *B* to say "I assert that this thing, subject to a right of way, is mine", etc.

[1] It is much disputed whether the XII Tables contained a rule that where the reason for the mancipation was a sale, the price must be paid before the property passed, i.e. that until this was done, even after the mancipation, the thing remained the property of the vendor. Such a rule (with the addition that the property also passes at once if security is given) is stated by Justinian (Inst. 2. 1. 41) for *traditio*, and referred to the XII Tables. But it is unlikely that the XII Tables dealt with *traditio* at all, and the rule itself probably did not exist even in classical law, but was introduced in post-classical times under Greek influence (*v. infra*, 521). It has however often been conjectured that the rule of the XII Tables to which Justinian refers was one dealing with *mancipatio*. Girard, 312, who thinks that the XII Tables confirmed the efficacy of the purely symbolical weighing (*supra*, 146), supposes that the rule concerning the payment of the price was introduced at the same time in order to give the same protection to the seller under the new system as he had had under the old, i.e. under the old system the property had not passed unless the copper was really weighed out, under the new it should not pass (in case of sale) unless the price (now separate from the merely pretended weighing) were paid. There are however several other views; one (accepted by Mitteis, *R.P.R.* 186, n. 73, as possible) is that the rule existed but was made ineffective by the addition of the words *isque mihi emptus esto hoc aere aeneaque libra* to the original form of words spoken by the transferee, i.e. this statement that the price had been paid was (according to the formalist principles of early law) taken as equivalent to the real payment. Another view (*v.* Buckland, 240, n. 2) is that the XII Tables rule meant that the *actio auctoritatis* (*infra*, 149) did not lie unless the price had been paid. Pringsheim, *Z.S.S.* L. 391, holds that it merely confirmed the requirement, already inherent in the ritual of mancipation, that payment of price and passing of ownership were concurrent.

what *res mancipi* the people in the district owned.[1] The reason why the number of five was chosen is sometimes said to be that the witnesses were intended to represent the people according to the five classes in which they were grouped under the "Servian" constitution, but the evidence for this view is very slight.[2] The form of words spoken by the transferee causes some difficulty; its two parts appear to be in an illogical order; we should expect the statement "I say that this thing is mine" to come after, not before, the words "let it be bought to me", and in any case the assertion of ownership is untrue until the ceremony is completed by the handing over of the piece of copper. A possible explanation is that the assertion of ownership is a later addition to the formula, put in to make it clear that the transferor was making himself responsible in case, owing to his defective title, ownership did not pass to the transferee and the transferee was subsequently evicted.[3] It is also noticeable that in the form of mancipation, as Gaius gives it, the transferor says nothing, but apparently acquiesces silently in the whole transaction by receiving the piece of copper. There is a little evidence in literary sources from which it has been inferred by some scholars that he did say something, but this inference should probably not be drawn. It is very unlikely that Gaius should have omitted to refer to so important a part of the ceremony, had it existed, and we know that it was usual in Roman formal transactions for the person who benefited to take the leading part.[4]

The effect of mancipation, when it is completed,[5] is, of course, normally to transfer ownership; but ownership can only be transferred by one who has it; if the transferor was not the owner the transferee could

---

[1] For similar provisions in Anglo-Saxon laws see Holdsworth, *H.E.L.* II. 81: "A person who bought secretly ran great risks. Not only might the real owner of the property claim his own, but he might also make a charge of theft against the purchaser. A purchaser who had bought secretly...might find it hard to disprove this charge".

[2] The chief piece of evidence is that Festus (s.v. *classici*, Bruns, II. 5) says that the witnesses to the mancipatory will were called *classici testes*; they were also addressed by the testator as *Quirites* (*infra*, 249, n. 7); *v.* Buckland, 238.

[3] *Infra*, 149. It is also possible that the assertion of ownership was the original part of the formula and that the words "let it be bought to me etc." were added later to comply with a rule of the XII Tables that the price must be paid before ownership passes. Cf. *supra*, 147, n. 1. Eisele, *Beiträge* (1896), 260 and Schlossman, *In iure cessio und mancipatio, Kieler Programm*, 1904 (quoted by Beseler, *Beiträge*, IV. 100) regard the classical mancipation as a "contamination of a sale ritual with elements of *in iure cessio*".

[4] *V.* Buckland, 236.

[5] Provided (in case of sale) that the price has been paid, if there really was a rule to this effect.

not become owner either. In such case however the transferor was responsible, if eviction took place, that is to say in case the real owner brought an action against the transferee and was able, by proving his title, to get the thing away from the transferee. When such an action was threatened it was the business of the transferee to inform the transferor and call upon him to support the title he had transferred (*laudare auctorem*, i.e. to call upon him as author of the title), and if the transferor failed to defend the action so that eviction followed, the transferee could bring another action against him for double the purchase price. This action was almost certainly called the *actio auctoritatis*, and is of great importance as the starting-point for the liability of the seller for title as developed in the later law. Apparently the liability to the action arose necessarily, without any special agreement, from the mancipation itself, and could not even be avoided by a special agreement excluding it, for when it was desired to exclude it the practice was, at any rate in the later law, to mention a single *sestertius* (*nummus unus*) as the purchase price, so that the *actio auctoritatis* would be only for the nominal sum of two *sestertii* and not be worth bringing. This was done, for instance, when the mancipation was used to transfer property by way of gift.[1] The liability however only lasted until the period of usucapion had elapsed. If two years in the case of land or one year in the case of movables had passed and the transferee had remained in undisturbed possession, then there would be no need for any *actio auctoritatis* because by that time the thing, even if it had not originally belonged to the transferor, would in the normal course of events have become the property of the transferee by usucapion.[2]

Another action which might arise by reason of the mancipation was that *de modo agri*. Where a piece of land which was mancipated was stated to be of a certain area and was found afterwards, on measurement, to be smaller, this action lay for double the proportionate part of the price. This liability of the transferor by mancipation is certainly very old and probably as old as the XII Tables, for there are

---

[1] *V.* Bruns, I. 335.

[2] *Infra*, 152; Tab. VI. 3: *Usus auctoritas fundi biennium est, ceterarum rerum omnium annuus est usus*. Here *auctoritas* refers to the liability to *actio auctoritatis*; *usus* is probably also nominative, *et* being omitted, so that the whole means "the time for usucapion and the time during which *actio auctoritatis* can be brought is two years in the case of land etc.". There is a further reference to *auctoritas* in Tab. III. 7: *Adversus hostem aeterna auctoritas* (*esto*), but what this means is much disputed. For various explanations, none very convincing, see Karlowa, II. 406; Kübler, 41; Cuq, *Manuel*, 273; Schönbauer, *Z.S.S.* XLIX. 379.

some words of Cicero quoting the XII Tables which almost certainly refer to it.[1]

B. IN IURE CESSIO. This, like *mancipatio* (to which it was frequently an alternative), was a form of conveyance, and, as its name implies, took place before the magistrate. In classical times, according to Gaius' description,[2] the parties go before a magistrate of the people, the urban or peregrine praetor at Rome, or the governor in the provinces, and the intended transferee, grasping the thing to be conveyed, says (if e.g. it is a slave) "I assert that this man is mine by Quiritarian right" (*Hunc ego hominem ex iure Quiritium meum esse aio*). The magistrate then asks the transferor whether he makes a similar claim (*an contra vindicet*); the transferor either remains silent or says "no"; and the magistrate then "adjudges" (*addicit*) the thing to the transferee.

This process is usually, and probably rightly, described as a sort of collusive action; in order to achieve the desired result of transferring the ownership in a thing, the parties pretend that it already belongs to the transferee, who claims that it is his; his claim is then admitted by the transferor and confirmed by a judgment of the court. The process begins in exactly the same way as does a disputed action under the old system of procedure by *legis actio*,[3] where also the plaintiff has to make this *vindicatio* or assertion of ownership, and the language of Gaius corresponds to this idea, for he speaks of the claim as a *vindicatio* and says that the process was called *legis actio*. There are however some important features which distinguish *in iure cessio* from an ordinary action. In the first place the *addictio* did not, it seems, take place in an ordinary action; if the defendant made no answer the plaintiff would simply take the thing with him.[4] Secondly the *addictio* cannot merely be construed as a judg-

---

[1] Cic. *de Off.* III. 16. 65 (Tab. VI. 2): *Cum ex XII tabulis satis esset ea praestari, quae essent lingua nuncupata, quae qui infitiatus esset dupli poenam subiret, a iuris consultis etiam reticentiae poena est constituta.* Karlowa, II. 372, uses this quotation as an argument in favour of his view that the transferor in a mancipation also had to say certain words—*nuncupatio* (cf. *supra*, 148), but this is not a necessary inference. The transferor would of course have to tell the transferee what exactly it was that he was transferring—whether e.g. the land was free from servitudes—and the transferee would embody these statements in his ceremonial assertion of ownership. There is no difficulty in making the transferor responsible for what is so said for he acquiesces in it when he receives the *raudusculum*.

[2] II. 24.

[3] I.e. a *legis actio per sacramentum in rem*; v. *infra*, 182. The forms given for this process by Gaius (IV. 16) should be compared with what he says of *in iure cessio*.   [4] Buckland, 233. See however, *infra*, 183, n. 2.

ment by consent, for a judgment is only effective between the parties to the action,[1] whereas *in iure cessio* has an effect as regards third parties also. Suppose for instance that *A* is in possession of a thing and *B* claims that it is his, brings a *vindicatio* and gets judgment, that judgment settles the matter between *A* and *B*, so that if *A* claims the thing again *B* can simply answer that the matter has been decided; but if a third party, *C*, claims the thing from *B*, the judgment in the action *B v. A* is no answer to him. Similarly if *C* has got possession of the thing and *B* wants to claim it, he cannot allege the judgment in support of his claim. But if *A* had ceded the thing *in iure* to *B* and *C* got into possession of it, then *B* can use this to support his claim and he will succeed if he can show that *A* owned it and then ceded it to him just as he would if he could show that *A* owned it and then mancipated it to him.

For these and other reasons it has been held that *in iure cessio* was not a collusive or "fictitious" action at all but from the beginning a convey-ance in which the machinery of the court was used to give expression and effect to the will of the parties.[2] The chief objection to this view is that the Roman law never seems to have known any such principle as that the magistrate can give effect by his authority to the will of the parties to a transaction, and in fact *in iure cessio* is especially used to bring about results which the will of the parties was originally incapable of producing.[3] Further, there are some rules which can only be explained on the view that *in iure cessio* is a form of litigation, especially the rule that persons *in potestate* cannot take part in one any more than in a *legis actio*.[4] The truth is that neither explanation alone suffices to account for all the facts and the institution must therefore be assumed to have a hybrid character. It began, in all probability, as a collusive action, an expedient invented by practitioners, but it became subsequently so common that it was recognised as a conveyance and emancipated from some of the rules which would have attached to an action pure and simple.

Whether *in iure cessio* is of earlier or later origin than mancipation is not certainly known, for both go back beyond our records, but the probability is that mancipation is the older. Mancipation belongs to a group of transactions "by copper and scales" (*per aes et libram*) including a form of loan[5] and a method of discharging debts,[6] and both of these,

---

[1] And those deriving title through them.
[2] See esp. Wlassak, *Z.S.S.* xxv. 102.
[3] Mitteis, *R.P.R.* 278; cf. *infra*, 152, n. 1.
[4] Gai. ii. 96; *Schol. Sin.* 49.
[5] *Infra*, 166.   [6] *Infra*, 163.

like mancipation itself in its original form of sale, are institutions such as even the most primitive legal system needs. Those transactions, on the other hand, for which *in iure cessio* is necessary (and not merely alternative to mancipation) belong in no case, so far as we can see, to the oldest stratum; it is, for instance, the only way of creating urban and personal servitudes *inter vivos*, and both these types are known to be of later origin than the rustic servitudes, which can be mancipated.[1] But in any case it is fairly certain that *in iure cessio* existed already at the time of the XII Tables, for Paulus says that the XII Tables "confirmed" it, as well as mancipation.[2] In the later law it was an alternative to *mancipatio* as a conveyance of *res mancipi* and to *traditio* as a conveyance of *res nec mancipi*, but it was little used owing to the greater convenience of the other methods, and its chief sphere of application was to those "incorporeal things" to which mancipation was inapplicable. As it was a civil law method of acquiring ownership it could only be used by citizens and it was not applicable to provincial land, because, like mancipation, it involved the assertion of Quiritarian ownership of which provincial land was not capable. Its effect was also, naturally, to transfer Quiritarian property, provided the transferor was Quiritarian owner, but there was nothing to correspond with the *actio auctoritatis*, because, seeing that the process was in form a claim that the property already belonged to the transferee, the transferor could not logically be made liable for defective title. Nor, for similar reasons, could there be any question of making the passing of ownership dependent on the payment of the price where the ground of the conveyance was a sale.

C. USUCAPIO. By *usucapio* is meant the acquisition of ownership by continued possession for a certain time. The requisite periods were already laid down in the XII Tables as two years for land, one year for all

---

[1] Gai. II. 29, 30. Other cases are the transfer of an inheritance before acceptance by the intestate heir (Gai. II. 35), the transfer of the *tutela* of women by their *tutor legitimus* (Gai. I. 168–172), and the claim made by the adopting father with which the ceremony of *adoptio* ends. Manumission *vindicta* is also a kind of *in iure cessio*, though the action which was brought collusively was not a *vindicatio* but a *causa liberalis*. It is possible that the use of *in iure cessio* as a conveyance of property originated at a time when *mancipatio* did not apply to land (*supra*, 140) and was originally a device to overcome the rule that land was inalienable. It is highly probable that the other cases too were designed to obtain results for the achievement of which the earliest Roman law provided no method at all. *Adoptio* is only made possible by a twisting of a rule in the XII Tables and manumission *vindicta* is represented by Livy (II. 5) as having been invented in the first year of the republic.

[2] Fr. Vat. 50 = Tab. VI. 5 b.

other things.[1] In the classical law there was much elaboration of the conditions in which possession would lead to ownership in this way; in particular it was necessary that the possession should have begun in good faith and that there should have been a *iustus titulus* for its inception. This is not the place for a detailed discussion of these requirements, but their nature can be understood to some extent by taking the simplest and commonest case of usucapion, that is when a man buys and has delivered to him a thing which does not belong to the seller. In such case he will not become owner of it immediately, but provided he was in good faith (and provided the thing was not a stolen thing) he will become owner after his possession has continued for the requisite year or two years. Here the "good faith" (*bona fides*) required is the belief that the seller was qualified to transfer ownership in the thing; the *iustus titulus* is the sale, "an event or dealing which is normally the basis of acquisition".[2] Other such *iusti tituli* are gift, legacy and dowry. It is at least highly probable that at the time of the XII Tables neither *bona fides* nor *iustus titulus* were required, that they are in fact refinements of which a comparatively primitive legal system is incapable. What, however, the XII Tables certainly did lay down was that a thing which had been stolen (*res furtiva*) could not be usucaped.[3] This, as Gaius is careful to point out,[4] does not merely mean that the thief cannot usucape the thing which he has stolen, but that no one else can either, not, for instance a man who has bought it from the thief, however innocent he may be. This rule is much more in consonance with what we know of early law than any rule requiring good faith would be, for early law tends to fix its attention on outward and easily provable facts, not on states of mind which it has no means of investigating; whether a thing has been stolen or not is generally a matter which is easily ascertainable, but whether a man was in good faith or not is a question which can only be solved by

---

[1] Tab. VI. 3 (*supra*, 149, n. 2); Gai. II. 42. The exact sense of the word *usus* employed by the XII Tables is not known, or rather it is not probable that it had a very exact sense beyond that of "having and using"; as soon as the lawyers came to give it an exact sense it comes to mean "possession", and the possession required for usucapion is, in general, the same as that required for the possessory interdicts (*infra*, 268). If, as is probable (*supra*, 143), full ownership *ex iure Quiritium* was at the time of the XII Tables not yet recognised in *res nec mancipi*, then the words quoted would necessarily only refer to *res mancipi*, a view which is supported by the juxtaposition of *auctoritas* which only results on mancipation (cf. Cuq, 280, n. 8).

[2] Buckland, *Manual*, 129.

[3] Gai. II. 45.   [4] II. 49.

comparatively modern methods of eliciting and weighing evidence.[1] Furthermore, if the rule requiring good faith had existed from the earliest times it is highly improbable that the much clumsier requirement that the thing must not be stolen should ever have come into existence, whereas the reverse process is easily conceivable with the advance of legal science and explains the co-existence of both rules in the developed law.[2]

The combined effect of the rule forbidding the usucapion of stolen things and the wide definition of theft in Roman law[3] was to make the usucapion of movables comparatively rare. Generally, when a man got into possession of something belonging to another, theft would have taken place at some time. Thus if *A* has obtained possession, even quite innocently, of a thing belonging to *B* and sells it to *C*, knowing that he has no right to do so, then *C* can never usucape because in the very act of selling a thing which he had no right to sell *A* committed theft and so made the thing a *res furtiva*. With immovables the case was different for, in the opinion which prevailed, land could not be stolen, so that in the case supposed above, if land were in question, *C* would be able to usu-

---

[1] Foreign writers usually speak in this connection of the "objective" standards of primitive law as opposed to the "subjective" standards applied by more advanced systems.

[2] Another important ground for believing that good faith was not originally necessary for usucapion is the existence, even in the developed law, of a number of cases (described by Gai. II. 52–61) in which it was not required. These are most easily explained as survivals from an older state of the law. The chief case is *usucapio pro herede*. If a person took possession of a piece of property belonging to a vacant inheritance (i.e. between the death of a deceased person and the acceptance of the inheritance by a *heres extraneus*) he could usucape it even though he knew well that he had no right to take it. The rule about theft did not prevent him, for it was a principle that there could be no theft of a thing forming part of a vacant inheritance, seeing that such a thing had no owner. It is held however by some writers (e.g. Cuq, 281) that the rule forbidding usucapion of stolen things meant originally only that the thief could not usucape and that subsequently, when *bona fides* was made a requisite, the thief's disability was referred to his lack of good faith and the rule of the XII Tables was then applied to those who acquired in good faith from the thief. A rather different possibility is that the XII Tables referred only to the thief and that the extension of the prohibition to those acquiring in good faith from him was due to the *lex Atinia*. This law (dating probably from about the middle of the second century B.C.) is quoted together with the XII Tables as authority for the rule against the usucapion of *res furtivae* by Justinian (Inst. 2. 6. 2) and Julian (D. 41. 3. 33 pr.). The *lex Atinia* also provided that the thing once stolen should cease to be so regarded after it had returned to the hands of the owner.

[3] *Infra*, 172.

cape.[1] Such was the position in the developed law, but it may well be that at the time of the XII Tables it was different, in that the definition of theft was probably not yet as wide as it subsequently became, but included only actual dishonest taking (not all dishonest handling) of someone else's property. If so, usucapion of movables would at that time have been commoner than it was at a later period.[2]

The purpose of usucapion, as is explained by Gaius,[3] was that "ownership of things should not remain uncertain for too long a time", in other words that where a man has failed to take steps to recover his property he should, after a certain time, be deprived of it in favour of the possessor; people who have been in possession of a thing without disturbance for some time must not suddenly be confronted with claims founded on titles which the claimant has not hitherto troubled to enforce. It must however be noticed that the periods in Roman law are short, and, though no doubt suitable at a time when the city was small and people could find their property with comparative ease, they were found inconvenient in later times when the empire expanded.[4] Another use of the institution was

[1] Though land could not be stolen it could be occupied by violence and land so occupied was incapable of usucapion by a *lex Plautia* (probably about 77 B.C.) and a *lex Iulia* (probably of Augustus); *v.* Gai. II. 45.

[2] The XII Tables forbade the usucapion of other things besides *res furtivae*. These were (*a*) the five feet between estates belonging to different owners (Tab. VII. 1). Each owner was bound to leave uncultivated and unbuilt 2½ feet at the edge of his land so that there was always a passage five feet in breadth. According to some authors (e.g. Karlowa, II. 518 *sqq.*) the passage between buildings had only to be 2½ feet wide in all. Why the usucapion of this passage should be expressly forbidden is not quite clear, for it would appear that as it had to be left free and was clearly used by both neighbours, neither could legally exercise such effective possession as would in any case result in usucapion. Presumably the express prohibition is due to a failure to recognise this logical consequence. (*b*) the *forum sepulchri*, explained as the entrance to a tomb, and the *bustum*, the place where a corpse was burnt, and the ashes interred (Tab. X. 10). In the developed law all places where bodies were buried were "religious" and incapable of private ownership and hence naturally of usucapion, but this would not apply to the entrance to a tomb. It is however useless to try to fit in the rules of the XII Tables with the later scheme; they are clearly particular expressions of a principle which was not yet formulated in an abstract way and do not exactly correspond to the later formulation. (*c*) a *res mancipi* belonging to a woman in the *tutela* of her agnates unless it had been delivered with the *auctoritas* of her tutor (Tab. V. 2, Gai. II. 47). The rule was subsequently altered by a *constitutio Rutiliana* of uncertain date.

[3] II. 44.

[4] Longer periods were adopted for the provincial institution of *longi temporis praescriptio*, and Justinian prolonged the period of usucapion for movables to three years (Inst. 2. 6. pr.).

that it cured defective conveyances. If a *res mancipi* were transferred by delivery (*traditio*) only, or if there had been an attempt at mancipation but some mistake had occurred in the ceremony, ownership *ex iure Quiritium* did not pass, but, provided that the transferee remained in possession for the requisite period, he would subsequently become full owner in spite of the defect in the original conveyance. *Usucapio*, as foreign writers sometimes put it, cured defects both of substance and of form; when an attempted conveyance has been ineffective, either because the transferor had no title to convey (acquisition *a non domino*) or because the form of conveyance adopted was inadequate (acquisition *a domino*), the transferee nevertheless becomes owner after a certain period has elapsed. As a result of this dual capacity *usucapio* was very important in facilitating proof of title. Where a man has received a thing from another he can (apart from rules of usucapion) only prove his title by proving the conveyance and the title of his predecessor, who will only have title if he can prove that of his predecessor and so on *ad infinitum*, until one comes to a title which is not derived at all but original, as for instance that by *occupatio*.[1] Given the rules of *usucapio* however it is only necessary for a man to show that his possession has lasted for the requisite time, and, in the developed law, that there was some *iustus titulus* for his acquisition; his ownership is then proved,[2] and it is immaterial whether he acquired from an owner or a non-owner, and whether the conveyance was adequate or not. This point is very important, for it was probably one of the factors which helped the Romans to develop their conception of absolute ownership;[3] they could require that a man who wanted to claim a thing as his should show a title not only as against the defendant but as against everyone because, whereas the proof of ownership is often very difficult in other systems and has received the name of *probatio diabolica*, in Roman law, by reason of the rules of usucapion, it would often not be diabolical at all.

D. THE REMAINING CIVIL LAW METHODS OF ACQUISITION. These can be dealt with shortly. First come the methods of acquisition from the state. It was the custom, no doubt from the earliest times, for booty taken in war to be sold by the magistrates, usually the quaestors, at a public auction. At such auctions a spear was set up, perhaps as a symbol that the right acquired would be under the protection of the state forces,[4] and the sale consequently known as *venditio sub hasta*. The ownership in

---

[1] *Supra*, 144.

[2] Good faith does not have to be proved; it is assumed until the contrary is shown.

[3] *Supra*, 142.   [4] *V.* Cuq, 258.

property bought in this way passed to the purchaser, apparently even before delivery;[1] at any rate there was no need for any mancipation in the case of *res mancipi* (and slaves would often be amongst the things sold). This is indeed according to the general principle of Roman law that the state is not bound by the rules that apply to individuals. Not only movable booty but land which belonged to the state (whether by reason of capture from an enemy or for any other reason) might be sold or, as we have seen,[2] assigned to individuals without payment, as was frequently done on the foundation of a colony. Here too the property passed without any form such as would have been needed in private law.

The only other method of acquisition which needs mention here is *adiudicatio*. In partition actions the *iudex* of classical times can not only, as in other actions, condemn one party to pay the other a sum of money, but can also assign sole ownership in the whole or part of the property concerned. If, for instance, *A* is co-owner of a piece of land with *B* and wishes to end the co-ownership, he can bring an action against *B* for division. The *iudex* can then either assign part to *A* and part to *B* or he can assign the whole to one and condemn that one to pay the other compensation.[3] In either case the judgment acts as a method of vesting ownership, *dominium ex iure Quiritium* if the trial is a *iudicium legitimum*,[4] otherwise only praetorian ownership which will ripen into *dominium ex i. Q.* after the period for usucapion has elapsed. In classical law there were three actions in which the *iudex* had this peculiar power, the *actio familiae erciscundae* for the division of property which was held jointly because it had been jointly inherited, the *actio communi dividundo* where it was held jointly for any other reason, and the *actio finium regundorum* for regulating boundary disputes.[5] Of these actions the first[6] and the last[7] certainly go back as far as the XII Tables.[8]

---

[1] At least this is so in classical times for fiscal property sold by an agent; D. 49. 14. 5. 1.   [2] *Supra*, 8.

[3] Audibert, *Mél. Appleton*, 1–37, *N.R.H.* XXVIII. (1904), 273–305, 401–439, 649–697, holds that originally only *adiudicatio* was possible and that *condemnatio* is a later addition. *Contra*, Berger, *Teilungsklagen*, 93 *sqq.*

[4] I.e. tried within a mile of Rome before a single *iudex*, all parties being citizens; Gai. IV. 104.

[5] The nature of this action is much disputed, *v.* Girard, 670–673. On the effect of *adiudicatio v.* especially Arangio-Ruiz, *B.I.D.R.* XXXII. 5–60.

[6] Tab. v. 10; D. 10. 2. 1 pr.   [7] Tab. VII. 5.

[8] It must be remembered that the "natural law" methods of acquiring ownership are omitted here, not because they did not exist at the time of the XII Tables, but because there is no evidence of their regulation by law. Anything that could be said about them would be merely a statement of the rules as worked out by the later jurists.

§ IV. RESTRICTIONS ON OWNERSHIP

Restrictions on the general right which an owner has of doing what he likes with his thing are of two kinds. They may be such as are imposed on all owners of a particular kind of property in the interest of the public generally or of the neighbours, or they may be merely imposed in a particular case by reason of a right in the thing which happens to be vested in a particular person other than the owner. Restrictions of both sorts existed already at the time of the XII Tables.

A. RESTRICTIONS IMPOSED ON ALL OWNERS OF A PARTICULAR SORT OF PROPERTY. In practice this means restrictions on owners of land. (i) As we have seen already, an owner may not cultivate or build up to the extreme limit of his property.[1] (ii) He must allow the branches of his neighbour's tree to overhang his land provided they are at least fifteen feet from the ground; branches lower than fifteen feet he can insist on having cut off. Where the tree itself overhangs there is a similar right, or perhaps even the whole tree has to be cut down.[2] (ii) Where fruit from his neighbour's tree has fallen on his land he must allow the neighbour to come upon the land to collect it.[3] (iv) He must not make such alterations on his land as will interfere with the natural flow of water from his neighbour's land to his.[4]

B. RESTRICTIONS BY REASON OF RIGHTS VESTED IN A PERSON OTHER THAN THE OWNER. In the developed law there were several kinds of these *iura in re aliena*, rights in property of which the ownership is with someone else,[5] but at the time of the XII Tables there existed only the most ancient of what came to be known as "rustic praedial servitudes". A praedial servitude is a right vested in the owner of one piece of land (the "dominant estate") to do something on a neighbouring piece of land (the "servient estate") or to prevent the owner of that estate from doing something which he would otherwise be at liberty to do; the right must "run with the land", that is to say it must be such that if the dominant estate passes into other hands, the right goes with it, and

---

[1] *Supra*, 108, n. 2.

[2] Tab. VII. 9. In the later law these rights were sanctioned by interdicts (*infra*, 235); the XII Tables apparently gave actions; D. 43. 27. 1. 8; 2.

[3] Tab. VII. 10. In the later law there was an interdict *de glande legenda* for the enforcement of this right. "*Glans*" properly means "acorn", but was used to include the fruit of all trees.

[4] Tab. VII. 8. The action was *aquae pluviae arcendae*.

[5] *Infra*, 277.

similarly, if the servient estate passes into other hands, the liability goes with it. Praedial servitudes in the developed law are either "rustic" or "urban" according, generally, as they serve the needs of agricultural land or of buildings, and thus we find that rights of way, rights of drawing water or taking it across the lands of another and rights of pasturage are classed as rustic, while the right of preventing a neighbour from increasing the height of his house or obstructing the access of light, and the right to support, are said to be urban.[1] As a class the urban servitudes are unquestionably later in origin than the rustic, because the need for them only arose when building space in the city became valuable and the old-fashioned Roman house, built round a courtyard with its windows looking inwards, began to be superseded by structures more like our blocks of flats, and when, in spite of the rule in the XII Tables providing for passage ways, the detached house was superseded by the "semi-detached" or "terrace" house.[2] All rustic servitudes however, are not equally old; the only one which is actually mentioned in the extant fragments of the XII Tables[3] is that of *via* (the right to use a prepared roadway across another's land[4]), though it is highly probable that the other rights of way (*iter*, right to walk or ride, and *actus*, right to drive cattle) and the right to take water across another's land (*aquaeductus*) are equally old,[5] for they are all necessary to agriculture as soon as private

[1] There is great difficulty in establishing the exact principle on which the distinction between urban and rustic servitudes was drawn. Some texts (e.g. J. 2. 3; D. 8. 2. 2; 8. 3. 1) give lists of each kind of servitude from which it would appear that the same servitude was always either rustic or urban, but sometimes a servitude generally appearing as urban is classed as rustic (D. 8. 3. 2 pr.) and *vice versa* (6. 2. 11. 1), and this fact has led to the view that the same servitude might be urban or rustic according to the nature of the dominant tenement, i.e. according as it was built upon or not; *v.* Girard, 387; Buckland, 262. The practical results would in most cases be the same, for a right of support (e.g.) cannot be wanted unless there is a building on the dominant tenement, and rights of way and water are usually only wanted in the country, not in the town where everyone has access as a rule to a public way and a public water supply.

[2] The oldest urban servitude is very probably that of drainage (*cloacae immittendae*), which may have arisen when Rome was hastily rebuilt after its destruction by the Gauls in 390 B.C. If, as Livy says (v. 55), it was built in such a haphazard way that the public drains, originally made under the public streets, passed under private houses, it may also have happened that the drains of one man's house passed under that of another man and that the right to keep them there had to be secured.

[3] Tab. VII. 7.

[4] This is the usual explanation, but *v.* Lenel, *E.P.* 192.

[5] The other important water servitude, *aquae haustus*, the right of drawing water, appears to be of later origin.

property in land exists. With regard to *via*, the XII Tables laid down a fixed width for the roadway (eight feet, sixteen at the bends)[1], and also provided that if the road were not kept in repair the person entitled "might drive his beast where he would",[2] i.e. go off the road. It must be remembered that the rustic servitudes (and perhaps only the oldest of them) alone are *res mancipi* and can be created by mancipation; the reason for this is not difficult to understand if we consider that a primitive mind would see in a "right of way" not an abstract limitation on an abstract right of ownership but a very concrete path, part of a concrete field and so transferable by the same methods as was the field. When servitudes of the type of "ancient lights" (*ne luminibus officiatur*) come to be recognised it is impossible to regard them as a part of the neighbour's land, and the later servitudes are therefore not *res mancipi*. There is however no reason to suppose that *in iure cessio* could not be used as an alternative to mancipation for those servitudes which were *res mancipi* as well as being the only method applicable to the others. The form of an *in iure cessio* in the case of a servitude would be a claim by the owner of the estate which was to become dominant that he already had the right and an admission by the owner of the intended servient estate that this was so.[3]

---

[1] Tab. VII. 6.

[2] Tab. VII. 7.

[3] No mention is made above of the "personal" servitudes of usufruct and *usus*, because, in spite of their great importance in the developed law, they certainly did not exist at the time of the XII Tables.

Chapter XI

THE LAW OF OBLIGATIONS AT THE TIME OF THE XII TABLES

§ I. INTRODUCTION

Justinian defines an obligation as "a legal bond by which we are placed under the necessity of performing some duty in accordance with the laws of our state",[1] and this definition describes with considerable accuracy the developed Roman and the modern conception of an obligation. But it must be realised that this apparently simple conception is by no means primitive, and that its elaboration by the Roman jurists was an achievement not less difficult and not less important than the development of the absolute conception of ownership. When we say to-day that *A* is under an obligation to *B*, we imply that, if *A* does not voluntarily perform his duty in accordance with that obligation, *B* can bring an action[2] in the courts against him and, after getting judgment, have *A* forced by state authorities either to do what he should have done originally, or, if that is impossible or undesirable, to do something else instead, generally to pay him money. Thus if *A* is under an obligation to pay *B* £100 or to convey Blackacre to *B*, the state will, in the end, sell sufficient of *A*'s goods to bring in the necessary £100 or take away Blackacre from *A* and give it to *B*. If *A*'s obligation be to act as secretary to *B* the state will not force him to act in that capacity, but it will make him pay money instead. The duty to do something for *B* is always coupled with the liability to be forced to do that thing or to have the next best thing done at one's expense.

In the early stages of law, on the other hand, these two things, duty and liability, are by no means necessarily combined. At a time when the state has not yet undertaken generally the enforcement of duties between private persons, it by no means follows that because a duty is recognised, therefore it will be enforced, and the primitive creditor consequently asks for something tangible which will serve as security for the per-

---

[1] J. 3. 13 pr.
[2] There are, even in modern law, some cases in which an obligation, though recognised by law, is not enforceable by action; *v*. e.g. Salmond, *Jurisprudence*, 253 *sqq*., and cf. the "natural obligations" of the late Roman law.

formance of the duty by the debtor; he wants to have in his power some person or some thing which will be liable; in other words, he wants a hostage or a pledge with whom or with which he can do what he likes if he does not get his rights. It must be noted especially that it is not a question (originally) of getting the hostage to do what the debtor ought to do, or of selling the pledge and paying oneself out of the proceeds; it is a question of having the hostage or pledge in one's power, and, in the case of the hostage, of being able to wreak vengeance on him.

A further difference between developed and primitive law is that primitive systems have not yet made the distinction, common to advanced systems, between delict and contract as sources of obligation. In the developed Roman and in modern law we can say that if *A* is under an obligation to *B* it is usually (by no means always) either because *A* has agreed to perform the act which forms the content of the obligation (contract), or because he has committed some wrong (delict) against *B* for which he must pay *B* damages. In early law, on the other hand, the idea of wrong is still undifferentiated, and it is only very gradually that the particular sort of wrong which consists in not doing what one has agreed to do is separated from other wrongs. Further, the natural reaction against wrong is a desire to take vengeance on the wrongdoer, and the recognition that such vengeance is permissible and not itself a wrong is the beginning of the law of obligations. The next step is that the person wronged may agree to forgo his vengeance if the wrongdoer will pay him composition, and it is precisely in these agreements for composition that we find the clearest example of the distinction between duty and liability, as well as, obviously, the germ of contract. Suppose that *A* has committed a delict against *B*—has stolen his property—*B* is justified in avenging himself on *A*, and if he is strong enough, will capture *A* for the purpose. *A* may then promise to pay composition and *B* may agree to accept it, but it may easily happen that *A* will be unable to collect the money so long as he remains in custody, whereas *B*, having once got hold of him, does not want to let him go. *A* therefore gets a child or kinsman to be hostage for him in the meanwhile. The result of this is that although *A* *owes* the money, he is no longer *liable*, whereas the hostage, who does not *owe* the money, is *liable*, because liability is something quite physical; it means being in the power of the creditor. Then, in some systems, at any rate, comes a stage when *A* can become hostage for himself, or, rather, as one can now say, surety. That is to say *B* lets him go on his undertaking to be liable, which means that *B* shall be allowed to take him again if he does not pay. The physical binding is replaced, for the time being, by a metaphorical bond, which may in certain circumstances be converted into a real one again.

The distinction here drawn between duty and liability was first discovered by modern scholars in their investigations into ancient Germanic law, and it is in Germanic law only that its existence can be proved to demonstration.[1] None the less it is now widely held that somewhat similar ideas formed the foundation of the Roman law,[2] and the chief evidence for this view comes from the Roman terminology itself. *Obligatio* means literally a "binding", and there can be little doubt that originally it was no mere metaphor; the same idea is to be seen in the word *nexum*, which, as we shall see, refers to the earliest known contract.[3] More significant still is the word *solutio*, which in the developed law means payment, or rather fulfilment of an obligation. Literally it means "loosening", and that this was originally no mere metaphorical loosening of a metaphorical "bond" appears clearly enough in the formula of the solemn payment *per aes et libram*, where the debtor who is to be discharged says, "I free and release *myself* from you"—*me a te solvo liberoque*.[4]

Now, at the time of the XII Tables the law was no longer in its most primitive condition. The state had already restricted self-help very considerably, but the time when it would take upon itself the task of seeing that people carried out their duties to each other was still in the far distant future; the most it could do was to say when one man was liable to another, to decide in some, indeed in most, cases how that liability could be redeemed, and to provide methods for preventing unauthorised enforcement of liability. Thus, so far as what is later called delict is concerned, it already provides generally that a certain penalty is to be paid by the wrongdoer to the person wronged, in other words, that the person wronged must forgo his right to vengeance if he receives

---

[1] Brunner, in Holtzendorff's *Enzyklopädie der Rechtswissenschaft*, I (7th ed. 1915), 65. For similar ideas cf. Pollock and Maitland, *History of English Law*, II. 185 *sqq*. The words "duty" and "liability" are here used as (not very exact) equivalents of the German words "Schuld" and "Haftung". For Greek law *v.* Partsch, *Griechisches Bürgschaftsrecht*, 13 *sqq*.

[2] Rabel, I. 453; v. Mayr, *Röm. Rechtsgeschichte*, I. 2. 57; Cornil, *Mél. Girard*, I. 199–263. It has been asserted that *debitum* = "Schuld", *obligatio* = "Haftung", but for difficulties, especially with regard to *debitum*, *v.* review of Steiner, *Datio in solutum*, by Koschaker, *Z.S.S.* XXXVII. 348 *sqq*.

[3] It is suggested by Beseler, *Beiträge*, IV. 96, that *noxa* comes from the same root and that *noxae dare* consequently means "to hand over to be bound".

[4] Gai. III. 174.

a certain sum by way of composition, but in other cases the right to take vengeance (though in a restricted form) is expressly preserved, and it is for the person wronged to consider whether he will accept composition instead, and, if so, at what rate.[1] Contract is still in its infancy. The agreement to pay and accept composition for delict is of course recognised, and so probably are forms by which suretyship can be undertaken. We know of two old kinds of surety at Rome—*vas* and *praes*— of which the former was certainly mentioned in the XII Tables.[2] The chief method however of creating liability (other than delict) appears to have been that which usually goes by the name of *nexum*. Something will have to be said later of this much disputed institution, but for the moment it will be enough to say that it was a form of loan of money or uncoined metal, and, as its name indicates, one which "bound" the debtor.

It seems at first sight inconceivable that a society could exist at all in which the idea of contract was as little developed as this. How, it may be asked, could men do without at least sale and hire, loan of chattels and deposit? The answer is twofold. First one must distinguish the question of the existence of the economic relationship covered by each of these contracts of the later law from the question whether there arose as yet any liability from promises made or implied in such relationships, and secondly one must realise that many of the results achieved later by the idea of contract can be, and were, achieved by that of delict. Thus it is quite clear that the economic relationship of sale or barter existed, that people in fact exchanged goods for the primitive equivalent of money (especially uncoined metal), or for other goods, but this proceeding did not result in any obligations and was not a contract because the two parties almost always carried out their respective parts of the bargain simultaneously. Thus mancipation, before the weighing out of the copper became purely symbolical, was clearly, from the economic point of view, a sale—the exchange of a thing for money of a sort—but it was no sale in the sense of the later contract, for in that sense a sale means an agreement to transfer a thing in return for a money payment, and when the agreement is once reached the seller is under an obligation to do what he has promised to do, as the buyer on the other hand is under an obligation to pay the price that he has promised. In the mancipation there was no scope for these obligations because the transfer of the thing and the weighing out of the copper were both parts of the same transaction; the property in the thing passed only when the copper was given, and the

---

[1] Cf. *infra*, 176.
[2] Tab. I. 10.

copper was only given when the property in the thing passed. Once the mancipation is complete there is nothing left for either party to do, and before it is complete no legal effect is produced.[1] When the weighing out became symbolical it did become possible to mancipate property without receiving an equivalent at once; in other words it became possible to give credit, but there is no reason to think that, at the time of the XII Tables, a seller who had thus given credit had an action for the price. It may well be that he could secure himself by making a *nexum* whereby the price was treated as a loan from him to the buyer, though there is no direct evidence of this practice.[2] Further, if there was a rule that property did not pass until the price was paid, the seller was protected by his ability to vindicate the property.[3] The converse case—that the buyer should pay the price before the transfer of the thing—would presumably be very rare indeed. If a mancipation had taken place, but the thing had remained in the possession of the seller, it would none the less belong to the buyer, who would thus be protected by his power to vindicate.[4] Where it was a *res nec mancipi* that was sold we cannot say what rules there were, but there can be no doubt that such sales were almost invariably for ready money and that there was no general principle that an unpaid seller was entitled to recover the price or a buyer who had paid to sue for the thing.[5]

Of the relationships covered by the later contract of "hire" (*locatio conductio*), which included the renting of land and chattels, contracts of service and contracts to do jobs, we know even less. That they all existed cannot be doubted, though none of them can have been as common as they subsequently became. The renting of land and houses was necessarily rare in a community which consisted chiefly of peasant-

---

[1] If after mancipation the buyer is evicted, the seller is, it is true, under an obligation to pay double the price (*supra*, 149), but, as the double liability shows, this is regarded as a delictal obligation, a punishment for lying about his ownership.

[2] For the suggestion *v.* Cuq, 271, n. 3.   [3] *Supra*, 147, n. 1.

[4] Unless indeed transfer of possession was at this time necessary in addition to the ceremony of mancipation for the transfer of ownership; *v.* Riccobono, *Z.S.S.* XXXIV. 178.

[5] That sales were usually for ready money and that the occasional seller who did not insist on immediate payment had no action as a rule to enforce it afterwards is best shown by the particular case mentioned in Gai. IV. 28. The XII Tables, he says, allowed *pignoris capio* (one of the forms of action) against a man who had bought an animal for sacrificial purposes and did not pay for it. Had there been any general rule allowing an action for the price such special provision would not have been necessary.

proprietors;[1] the occasions for the hiring of movables would be few; the trades which undertake "jobs" were hardly developed, and, though there were, no doubt, some free labourers, the work of tilling the soil must have been done mainly by the owners, their families and their slaves. There was certainly no general principle that money promised in payment for the use of a thing or services was recoverable,[2] but the law of property and the law of delict would prevent some kinds of injustice. The man who refused to return a thing he had hired would have to give it up on vindication by the owner and could very possibly be treated as a thief; and the same reasoning applies to the case of the man who had received a thing in order to do some work on it—a piece of cloth, for instance, to make up into a garment.

So too with the relations later covered by the "real" contracts of loan (of chattels) and deposit. The borrower and the depositee who attempted to retain things which did not belong to them would be in the same position, and in the case of deposit there is the definite evidence that the XII Tables allowed an action *in duplum*—an action that is for a penalty exactly the same as that for theft.[3] That some form of pledge too had at least a *de facto* existence we cannot doubt, but the early law on this subject is wrapped in mystery.[4]

With this much by way of introduction it remains to say something in greater detail of the contract—if it can be so called—of *nexum*, and of the law of delict.

§ II. NEXUM

In the accounts of early Roman history considerable prominence is given to the sufferings of certain people called *nexi* (literally "bound"), who, it is clear, were debtors (generally plebeians) who had borrowed money under such severe conditions that they might, if unable to pay, become the bondsmen of their creditors, liable to work for them, to be chastised by them and in a very literal sense "bound". It is further clear that the transaction on which the position of these *nexi* rested was, like mancipation, one "by the scales and copper". The possibility of this bondage resulting from debt came to an end by the passing of a certain

---

[1] The small farmer sometimes, no doubt, held the land he tilled *precario*. This form of "tenancy at will", in which no rent was paid but the grant was revocable at will by the landlord, appears to have originated in the relation between patron and client.

[2] Again we have one special case where *pignoris capio* is allowed; Gai. IV. 28.

[3] Cf. *infra*, 175, n. 3.   [4] Cf. *infra*, 312.

lex Poetilia, probably of 326 B.C.[1] This is about all that can be said with certainty, for naturally enough no classical legal writer deals with an institution which was obsolete some five centuries before the classical period, and the historians are not concerned to give an exact legal account of the position which gave rise to the sufferings they describe. The best evidence we have consists of a few passages from the lexicographers (the chief one of which is however badly mutilated)[2] and a passage of Gaius which describes, not *nexum*, but the method of releasing a debt contracted "by the scales and copper".[3] The result is that scholars differ very considerably in their interpretation of the evidence, and the opinions which have been held as to the nature of *nexum* are innumerable.

The theory which was dominant in the second half of the nineteenth century, and which still, with modifications, counts some notable adherents, is that of Huschke.[4] According to his view *nexum* was a form of loan, contracted with the ceremonial of the scales and copper, the *libripens* and the five witnesses, and thus was the counterpart, in the law of obligations, to mancipation in the law of property. The lender originally really weighed out the copper to the borrower; later, by a development analogous to that which took place for mancipation,[5] the weighing became symbolical, and the actual payment of the money lent was separated from the ceremony. The XII Tables confirmed this transaction in the same way as they confirmed mancipation itself, by the words *cum*

---

[1] *V. infra*, 190, n. 4.

[2] Varro, *L. L.* VII. 105 (Bruns, II. 60): *Nexum Manilius scribit omne quod per libram et aes geritur, in quo sint mancipia; Mucius quae per aes et libram fiant ut obligentur, praeter quae mancipio dentur. Hoc verius esse ipsum verbum ostendit, de quo quaerit; nam id est, quod obligatur per libram "neque suum" fit, inde "nexum" dictum. Liber, qui suas operas in servitutem pro pecunia quam debebat* (*debet dat—* Schwegler) *dum solveret, nexus vocatur, ut ab "aere" "obaeratus". Hoc C. Poetilio Libone Visolo dictatore sublatum ne fieret; et omnes qui bonam copiam iurarunt, ne essent nexi, dissoluti.* For the numerous difficulties in the text *v.* Bruns, *loc. cit.* The passage is particularly important as it cites the opinions of two lawyers, Manilius and Mucius (*v. supra*, 90), but even they lived a long time after the *lex Poetilia*. If the statement in Varro's text that the passing of the law was due to the dictator Poetilius is right, then its date would be 313 B.C., but Livy (VIII. 28) refers it to the consuls of 326, one of whom was a Poetilius.

[3] III. 173–175.

[4] *Ueber das Recht des Nexum*, Leipzig, 1846. For the modern modifications of Huschke's theory *v.* especially Girard, 508 *sqq.* De Zulueta, who himself regards this theory, though not proved, as the most probably correct, gives a full summary of the different views in *L.Q.R.* XXIX (1913), 137–153, as well as references to all the relevant literature.

[5] *Supra*, 146.

nexum faciet mancipiumque, etc.[1] So far the transaction is precisely similar to mancipation, but the words spoken in the case of a loan necessarily differed from those used in a conveyance, and Huschke conjectured that they were spoken by the lender (as the person acquiring rights under the transaction), and consisted of a form in which he declared that the borrower was *damnas* (condemned) to repay him the money, the importance of this word lying in the fact that it gave rise to an obligation which could be enforced, like a judgment, by immediate execution against the person. This means that if the debtor did not repay at the due date, the creditor could seize him without first getting judgment, by the process known as *manus iniectio*, and, after certain delays,[2] either kill him or sell him as a slave. The creditor might, of course, not proceed to these extremities at once, but keep the debtor in dependence on him by threatening to exercise his rights.

The liability to execution without judgment was, in Huschke's view, a direct consequence of the use of the word *damnas*, to which he attributed this special efficacy.

The attack on this previously dominant theory was opened by Mitteis in 1901.[3] Mitteis had little difficulty in showing that there was no magic in the word *damnas*, which is connected with *damnum* in the sense of penalty and consequently only means "liable". He also urged that Huschke's theory was inconsistent with the picture of *nexum* given by the historians, from which it appears that the entering into the state of bondage was not the result of the loan itself, but was the last desperate act of insolvent borrowers when faced with an action which would inevitably lead to judgment, *manus iniectio*, and either death or slavery. Huschke is bound to explain phrases like "they entered into *nexum*"[4] as merely

---

[1] *Supra*, 146. There is no direct evidence that these words come from the XII Tables, but the way in which Festus quotes them (s.v. *Nuncupata pecunia*, Bruns, II. 18) leaves little doubt about the mattter. If they do come from the XII Tables, then they prove that *nexum* existed at that time, but in any case the institution is so primitive that there can be no question as to its existence at the time of the codification.

[2] *Infra*, 189.   [3] *Z.S.S.* XXII. 96 *sqq.*; XXV. 282; *R.P.R.* 136 *sqq.*

[4] Livy VII. 19: *nam etsi, unciario foenore facto, levata usura erat, sorte ipsa obruebantur inopes, nexumque inibant.* Another very serious objection of Mitteis' is that the historians several times (e.g. Livy VIII. 28) speak of sons entering into *nexa* on account of debts which they had inherited from their fathers. How, he asks, is this possible if, as Huschke supposes, the son was already *nexus*, in the sense that he was liable to *manus iniectio* if he did not pay? De Zulueta (*op. cit.* 144) supposes that the *nexum* debt did not descend, at least with full force, upon the heir, but then we must presumably imagine that the heir entered into the *nexum* again of his own free will from considerations of family honour.

referring to the *de facto* beginning of the state of bondage which had been hanging over the debtor in case of failure to repay ever since the loan was received. Mitteis holds that in fact these phrases must refer to a new transaction. This transaction was, in his view, a mancipation of himself by the debtor to the creditor, whose bondsman he thus became by a sort of self-sale, or rather self-pledge, for he would be released if the debt were subsequently paid. The original debt, Mitteis holds, was incurred by a separate transaction, also called *nexum*, which would have been enforceable by *legis actio per sacramentum*, and the self-mancipation was made in order to escape, by voluntary entry into bondage, the execution which would otherwise have followed on judgment. This theory explains the constant use, especially by Cicero, of *nexum* as the equivalent of mancipation; it explains Varro's statement that a *nexus* was a "free man who gave his services into slavery, for money which he owed until he should pay it",[1] and it is in accordance with developments in other systems in which self-sale or self-pledge is frequently found, but the difficulties are at least as great as those which stand in the way of Huschke's conception. If we assume that copper was weighed out on the first *nexum*, there would be none left to weigh out on the second, the self-mancipation,[2] and further, however common self-sale may be in other systems, it is otherwise unknown in Roman law and appears to be contrary to principle. In fact, though much of the argument on which Huschke based his opinion has been shown to be erroneous, his hypothesis is still, in the main, probably the most acceptable. *Nexum*, so we can still believe, was a transaction carried out by the scales and copper whereby the debtor made himself liable to *manus iniectio* without judgment if he failed to pay on the appointed date. It had thus a "real" element because it gave the lender a right (eventually) against the body of the borrower,[3] but that is not the same thing as saying that it was a form of self-sale. It gave rise to *manus iniectio* because that was originally the only form of liability known; it was in fact a form of legalised self-help. Only subsequently, when other *legis actiones* necessitating a trial were introduced, did the treatment of debtors so liable come to be regarded as particularly harsh. Indeed as a positive argument in favour of this view there still remains the passage in Gaius[4] where we are told that a judgment debt and one contracted *per aes et libram* both had to be released by the form *per*

---

[1] *Supra*, 167, n. 2.   [2] *Z.S.S.* XXIII. 350.

[3] It was thus a transaction directed towards the creation of "liability", in the sense explained above, 161.

[4] III. 173–175.

aes et libram. Why should this have been so if there was not something common about the consequences of these two forms of debt?[1]

III. DELICT

Of the four[2] chief delicts of the developed law two were already recognised under the names which still attached to them later, *furtum* (theft) and *iniuria* (later including all offences against a person's dignity and a good deal more, but at this early date going, in all probability, no further than actual assault).

A. FURTUM.[3]   A distinction was drawn between *furtum manifestum,*[4] when the thief was caught in the act, and *furtum nec manifestum,* when he was not. In the former case the thief, if a free man, was scourged and "adjudged" (*addictus*) to the person from whom he had stolen. It was doubtful, says Gaius,[5] whether he thereby became a slave or was in the position of an *adiudicatus* (i.e. one who was seized by his creditor after judgment by *manus iniectio*).[6] If the thief was a slave he was scourged and then thrown from the Tarpeian rock. In the case of *furtum nec manifestum* the penalty was already pecuniary, double the value of the thing

---

[1] Even in this brief account it is necessary to mention the opinion held by Lenel (*Z.S.S.* XXIII. 84 *sqq.*), who agrees with Mitteis' view that there were two stages and that the second stage was a self-mancipation. The first stage however, he holds, was not a proceeding *per aes et libram* at all, but quite a different sort of transaction, probably a kind of *vadimonium,* i.e. a contract derived from one of the earliest types of suretyship. Originally a man who had committed a delict had to find someone else as surety, later he was allowed to be his own surety and hence arose a general method of contracting. Lenel then has to say that *nexum mancipiumque* in the XII Tables refers to one transaction only, not two, and has to explain the opinion of Mucius recorded by Varro (*supra,* 167, n. 2) as meaning, not that *nexum* includes "all transactions *per aes et libram* except conveyance by mancipation", but as meaning that it includes all the obligation side of mancipation (i.e. the *actiones auctoritatis* and *de modo agri*), whereas *mancipium* refers to the conveyance itself. There are many difficulties in the way of this interpretation, but the greatest is, that there is no real evidence for the existence of such a contract as Lenel postulates until we come to the stipulation (*infra,* 289) which very probably did arise in the way in which Lenel supposes his *vadimonium* to have arisen.

[2] *Furtum, rapina* (robbery), *damnum iniuria datum* (unlawful damage to property) and *iniuria.*

[3] Tab. VIII. 12–16; Gai. III. 183–208.

[4] In later times there were differences of opinion as to the exact definition of *furtum manifestum*; Gai. III. 184; J. 4. 1. 3. On the subject in general *v.* de Visscher, *R.H.* I (1922), 442–512 = *Études de droit romain,* 135–214.

[5] III. 189.

[6] And so eventually liable to death or slavery abroad; *v. infra,* 189.

stolen having to be paid.[1] It was further provided that if a man suspected that goods which had been stolen from him were in someone else's house, he could search that house, but must do so naked except for a loin-cloth (*licium*), and holding a platter (*lanx*) in his hand. If after search made in this way the property was found, then the person in whose house it was found was held guilty of *furtum manifestum*. Where goods were found after a search made without these solemnities, but in the presence of witnesses,[2] there was an action *furti concepti*, for three times their value, but, as a rather rough and ready method of putting right the injustice to which this might obviously lead, if the householder could show that someone else had put the stolen goods in his house, then he had an action, also for three times the value, against that person (*actio furti oblati*). The search with the loin-cloth and platter appears to be a very ancient institution, dating back to a time before the separation of the Indo-Germanic peoples, for so many parallels are found that direct borrowing is most unlikely.[3] The reason why the searcher should be naked (or nearly so) is fairly clear—he should not conceal anything about

---

[1] According to the usual view, but *v. infra*, 177, n. 5.

[2] Mommsen, *Strafrecht*, 748, thinks that there was only one type of search, that *lance et licio*; and that the XII Tables treated the person on whose premises stolen goods were found as *fur manifestus*. The action for threefold damages was, in his view, like that for fourfold in case of manifest theft, a praetorian innovation, the reason for difference in treatment being that in the case of *furtum conceptum* the owner was certain to get the goods back, which he would not always do in that of *furtum manifestum* (753). But this view is contrary to the plain statement in Gai. III. 191 that the threefold actions date from the XII Tables, and if by search "with witnesses" (III. 186) Gaius meant search *l. et l.* it is strange that he should say nothing of the witnesses where he expressly describes the solemn search in III. 192–193. The testimony of Gell. 11. 18. 12 and Paul. *Sent.* II. 31. 14, even if it were clearer than it is, could hardly stand against that of Gaius. De Visscher (*Revue d'histoire du droit*, VI (1925), 249–277 = *Études de droit romain* (1931), 215–253), like Mommsen, thinks that only the search *l. et l.* existed, but in his view the householder was not treated as *fur manifestus* unless actually guilty, or rather unless there were circumstances, e.g. the trail of a stolen animal leading to his house, which sufficed for the presumption of guilt. If there were no such circumstances the *actio furti concepti* lay. Had guilt been presumed merely from the finding of stolen goods, Roman law would have been more barbarous than other primitive systems. Again the objection is that Gaius does appear to distinguish two kinds of search, and perhaps the system is not so unjust as it would seem. A man who is conscious of his innocence ought to allow ordinary search, and then he will suffer only the threefold penalty of the *actio concepti*, if the goods are found.

[3] Similar searches are found among the Greeks, the Germans and the Slavs. For references *v.* Egon Weiss, "Lance et licio", *Z.S.S.* XLIII. 455–465 at p. 457.

his person and then pretend to have found it in the house. The platter is less easily explained; Gaius quotes, without accepting, two explanations, one that it is to put the stolen thing on, if found, and the other that it is to keep his hands occupied and prevent his smuggling anything in.[1] Gaius, in whose days the whole process had long been obsolete, says that the law prescribing it is ridiculous because it did not give any means of forcing the householder to submit to such a search, and, he says, a man who objected to a search without ceremonial would object still more strongly to one with it, because the penalty would be greater if the thing were found (i.e. it would count as *furtum manifestum* whereas in case of unceremonial searching there was only the threefold penalty of *furtum conceptum*). One way out of the difficulty is to suppose that the householder who refused to allow a search "with the loin-cloth and platter" was deemed guilty of the "manifest" theft of the goods claimed,[2] but if so it is strange that the XII Tables said nothing about it,[3] and a more probable explanation is that the claimant was expected, if opposed, to use force, that this was, in fact, one of the cases in which the primitive law left a man to enforce his rights himself.[4] If the thief came by night or if in the daytime he defended himself with a weapon the XII Tables allowed him to be killed without trial; in the latter case however the slayer must cry aloud in order to prevent any suspicion that he was a murderer attempting to hide his act.[5]

In the classical law the definition of theft was a very wide one, for it included not only taking a thing away, but all "fraudulent handling" (*contrectatio fraudulosa*); it is theft, for instance, to take into battle a horse which has been lent for riding, or to sell a thing belonging to someone else knowing that one has no right to do so, even though one came into possession of it quite innocently. It is likely enough, however, that this very elastic definition is a later refinement and that, as the etymology suggests,[6] *furtum* implied originally an actual removal of the thing. At

---

[1] The former is the more probable, for the nakedness is sufficient to guard against his hiding anything; *v.* Weiss, *op. cit.* 459.

[2] So e.g. Girard, 436.

[3] Gaius says (III. 192) "the law laid down no penalty", and he is not likely to be mistaken, for he was the author of a commentary on the XII Tables.

[4] Weiss, *op. cit.* 464. The modern rule is that where the law gives a right to a man it also provides him with the means of enforcing it, but it is a mistake to imagine that this rule holds for primitive law as well. For other explanations *v.* Hitzig, *Z.S.S.* XXIII. 329, and Mommsen, *Strafrecht*, 748, n. 2.

[5] Tab. VIII. 12 and 13. According to Gaius (D. 9. 2. 4. 1) he must cry out if he kills a thief by night too.

[6] The word *fur* (Greek φώρ) is connected with *ferre* and so means "one who carries away". This derivation is already given by some ancient writers, e.g.

any rate it seems clear that originally, as in the classical law,[1] theft was only possible in the case of things that could be removed and not in the case of land.[2]

B. DAMAGE TO PROPERTY. The later law on this subject is based so completely on a statute (the *lex Aquilia*, of uncertain date, but certainly later than the XII Tables) that it is difficult to discover what were the earlier provisions which were superseded.[3] We do not even know whether the XII Tables contained any general rule on the subject,[4] or whether there were a number of special cases which it dealt with separately, either by fixing a definite penalty, as in the case of *iniuria*, or in some other way. If there was any general provision it is highly probable that it covered only damage to movable property, for there are a number of fragments which mention particular cases of damage to immovable property; had the general rule covered land also these provisions would not have been necessary. The offences dealt with are those which would specially concern an agricultural population; the nocturnal cutting of another's crops or letting animals graze on them was punished capitally,[5]

J. 4. 1. 2, where it is mentioned as an alternative to fanciful suggestions that the word is connected with *furvum* (black) or with *fraus*.

[1] Gai. II. 51. At one time there had been a number of jurists who were of opinion that even land might be stolen.

[2] The suggestion that "carrying away" formed part of the original conception of theft may seem at variance with the opinion expressed above (166) that the bailee who refused to return the thing bailed to him was treated as a thief. Both views may however be correct. Primitive law has "objective" standards, i.e. it lets certain consequences follow from certain outward facts because it regards those facts as proof of the other facts with which it seeks to deal. If a man refuses to give up a thing lent to him it is generally because he has taken the thing away or at least hidden it with the intention of keeping it to himself; that is enough to make the law say that everyone who acts similarly is a thief. In any case it is not suggested that there was any statutory rule needing strict construction. The fact that the XII Tables dealt with the cases of deposit (*supra*, 166) and of the dishonest tutor (*infra*, 175) by punishing them in the same way as they punished thieves, can be used as an argument either way, for, as Mommsen says (*Strafrecht*, 738, n. 2), it is uncertain whether these cases are to be regarded as particular cases of theft, or as analogues of theft.

[3] Cf. *infra*, 285. Ulpian says (D. 9. 2. 1) that the *lex Aquilia* "derogated from" previous rules on the subject contained in the XII Tables and in other statutes.

[4] Tab. VIII. 5. We have only two fragments of Festus, one saying that the word *rupitias* (?*rupit*) in the XII Tables meant *damnum dederit*, the other saying that *sarcito* means *damnum solvito* or *praestato*. Many scholars put these fragments together (though there is nothing in Festus to connect them) and deduce a rule that if a person damaged property belonging to another he had to make compensation.

[5] Tab. VIII. 9. The punishment was "suspension" (i.e. crucifixion) on a tree as a sacrifice to Ceres, the goddess of corn.

unless the offender was under the age of puberty, in which case he was flogged or had to make good the damage twice over.[1] The person who set fire to a dwelling-house, or a heap of corn near such a house, was burnt if he had done so intentionally; if by accident, he had to make good the damage and, if too poor, was "lightly chastised".[2] For the unlawful cutting down of another's trees a penalty of 25 *asses* for each tree was laid down,[3] and there were also provisions, details of which are lost, against the use of magical incantations to destroy or get for oneself another's crops.[4]

Damage done by quadrupeds (*pauperies*) was specially regulated, the rule being that the owner had either to make compensation or give up the animal,[5] a rule which, as we shall see,[6] also applied in the case of delicts by slaves and children under power.

C. INIURIA.[7] The XII Tables punished the "breaking of a limb" (*membrum ruptum*)[8] by talion, that is by allowing the infliction of a similar injury on the wrongdoer, but, as is expressly stated in a fragment which is preserved, only "if no agreement for composition be made". The fracture of a bone (*os fractum*) was dealt with by a fixed pecuniary penalty of 300 *asses* where the victim was a free man, 150 *asses* where he was a slave. "For all other *iniuriae*", says Gaius, "the penalty laid down

---

[1] The words are obscure; possibly, as Mommsen suggests (v. Bruns, I. 31), the flogging was inflicted on an *impubes sui iuris*, while in the case of one *in potestate* the father had either to pay double damages or surrender the boy (*noxae deditio*).

[2] Tab. VIII. 10.   [3] Tab. VIII. 11.
[4] Tab. VIII. 8.   [5] Tab. VIII. 6.
[6] V. infra, 176.   [7] Tab. VIII. 2; Gai. III. 223.
[8] This is usually understood to include all injuries which result in the complete loss or disablement of one of the limbs, including eyes, ears and nose; v. Girard, 429, n. 2. If this was so, then, as has been pointed out, there seems to be no provision for such wounds, whether more or less serious than the breaking of a bone, which do not result in the loss of a limb. Binding (Z.S.S. XL. 106–112) therefore suggested that some provision dealing with them had been lost. Appleton (Mél. Cornil, I. 51–79) supposes that *membrum ruptum* included all these injuries (especially, e.g., those inflicted with sharp weapons), and that the XII Tables allowed talion in these cases precisely because it was impossible to fix a tariff which would meet the infinitely varying degrees of seriousness, whereas the fracture of a bone was a relatively easily ascertainable and stable injury for which a price could be laid down. Girard (loc. cit.) points out that it is difficult to believe that, once a fixed penalty had been introduced for *os fractum*, talion could have survived for less serious injuries. I doubt whether this is really so unlikely when we remember that composition was no doubt usual, and if we do not accept either Appleton's or Binding's view a serious difficulty remains.

was 25 *asses.*" In all probability this refers merely to blows such as do not result in serious injury. It is unlikely that the Romans of the fifth century B.C. were very susceptible to insult, and, if we imagine that *iniuria* can here refer to the innumerable different kinds of attack on a man's personality which it covered in the later law, it is impossible to explain how they could all be punished by the same fine. There is indeed evidence that the XII Tables punished the singing of defamatory verses, and that capitally, but it seems that this was the only case of defamation with which they dealt, and that they treated it as a case of disturbance of the public peace, not as a private delict.[1,2]

D. Other delicts and the general character of the law of delicts. In addition to these main rules for the chief offences against the person and against property, the fragments of the XII Tables contain a number of scattered provisions for penalties, some of which would not, in a developed system, come under the heading of delict at all, but must be so classed here precisely because the cases they concern are dealt with by the imposition of penalties, that is, are treated as delicts. Thus if a depositee fails to return the thing deposited with him he is liable, like the thief, to an action for "double", and not, as in the later law, regarded as having merely broken his contract.[3] Similarly the tutor who embezzles the property of his ward has to pay "double",[4] whereas in later law, though this action survived,[5] the relations between a tutor and his ward were regulated generally by an action which has no delictal character and is placed by Justinian under the heading of quasi-contract.[6]

The picture given by this description of almost all that has survived of the decemviral legislation with respect to delict is an interesting one, for it shows that Roman law was at the time of the XII Tables in a state of transition from voluntary to compulsory composition for private wrong.

---

[1] Tab. VIII. 1. The severity of the punishment seems sufficient proof of this. There appears, though it is not certain, to have been a provision of the XII Tables separate from that concerning defamatory verses (*carmen famosum*), which dealt with *mala carmina*. If so, then this provision probably referred to magical incantations; *v.* Bruns, I. 29.

[2] A further difference between the law of the XII Tables and that of later times is that, whereas in the later law only intentional acts could count as *iniuriae*, the XII Tables probably included unintentional injuries to the person. There is no direct proof of this, but the general rule of early Roman, as of all early, law is that the penalty follows the act regardless of intention; *v.* Mommsen, *Strafrecht*, 796 and 836, n. 4.

[3] Tab. VIII. 19; cf. *supra*, 166.   [4] Tab. VIII. 20.
[5] As *actio rationibus distrahendis*.   [6] I.e. the *actio tutelae*; *v.* J. 3. 27. 2.

In nearly all cases, so far as we can see, the law already insists that the party wronged shall accept a pecuniary penalty in lieu of exercising his primitive right of vengeance, and fixes an amount at which the penalty is to be assessed, but in the cases of *membrum ruptum* and manifest theft[1] it is still open to him to insist on vengeance of a sort, though this too is now regulated. The reason why the manifest thief is more hardly treated than one who is not caught in the act is probably that the law is not yet strong enough to interfere with the vengeance of a man whose anger has had no time to cool.

But if the simple system of vengeance or composition at the option of the party wronged has almost disappeared already at the time of the XII Tables, the law of delict not only then, but long afterwards, retained many traces of its origin in the system of compensation. Throughout the history of Roman law it remains true that a delictal action dies with the wrongdoer, and the reason is no doubt that vengeance was only permissible against the wrongdoer, not against his heir. Originally it was also probably true that the action died with the victim of the wrong because his heir would not feel the same thirst for vengeance, and this rule remains even in the developed law for some actions, especially that for *iniuria*, which was held to be of a particularly vengeful character.

Again, the whole system of "noxal" actions[2] which remains in existence throughout the history of the law bears, on its face, the traces of its origin in the idea of vengeance. It was the rule that, if a slave or a child under power committed a delict, an action known as "noxal" lay against the master or father, in which he had the choice either to surrender the wrong-doer (*noxae deditio*) or to pay what a free person would have had to pay had he committed the same delict. Originally this meant that the person wronged had the right to take vengeance on the wrongdoer, but that the father or master could buy off that vengeance; obviously the slave or child could not do so himself, for he had no property with which to pay. If before the action was brought the slave changed hands or the child was adopted into another family, then it was the new master or father who was liable, again clearly because the primary right was to vengeance, and the payment of damages merely a possibility open to the domestic

[1] Here too the party wronged might accept compensation if he liked; D. 2. 14. 7. 14: *Nam et de furto pacisci lex permittit*, where *lex* no doubt refers to the XII Tables.

[2] *V.* de Visscher, "Les actions noxales et le système de la noxalité d'après ses origines et la loi des XII Tables" (*Revue générale du Droit, de la Législation et de la Jurisprudence*, 1918–19); "La nature juridique de l'abandon noxal", *R.H.* IX (1930), 411–471.

superior for the time being to ransom his inferior. If the child was emancipated or the slave manumitted, the liability was transferred to him himself, and he had to pay just as if he had not been under power when he committed the delict; for the liability to vengeance is not affected by any change in status or family relationships.[1]

If we turn to the nature of the penalties imposed for the different delicts, we see that the XII Tables, like other primitive systems, are detailed and rigid; the code tries to lay down exactly what is to happen in every case, so that when the question of guilt is decided nothing is left to the discretion of the judge. In particular the fixed money penalties must be noticed, the 25 asses, for instance, which is always the penalty for simple *iniuria*, and for the cutting down of each tree,[2] although, no doubt, the severity of the blow and the value of the tree might vary considerably from case to case. In the later law, as we shall see, the praetor found it necessary to improve on this very rough and ready method by introducing an action for *iniuria* in which it was left to the judge to estimate the damages payable in any particular case according to his view of the seriousness of the offence,[3] and similarly in the case of the trees he substituted an action for double the amount of the loss inflicted.[4] The early penalty on the other hand is always a fixed sum or a simple multiple of a definite quantity—the value of an article—not, as sometimes in the later law, of something which is harder to calculate, the loss inflicted on the person wronged by the delict (*id quod interest*).[5]

There is no doubt either that, in the main, the Roman law at the time of the XII Tables has the primitive principle that a man is responsible for his acts irrespective of his state of mind,[6] no distinction being, as a

[1] De Visscher (*Études de droit romain*, 109–134 = *St. Bonfante*, III. 233–248) distinguishes between two types of delict, those against the person (*iniuria*) and those against property (*noxa* = damage to property and *furtum*). The former originally gave rise simply to talion, the latter to a right to get satisfaction by acquiring the person of the wrongdoer. In both the acceptance of composition became compulsory, but in different ways. For *iniuria* there was a fixed *poena*, for the other cases the requirement of *damnum decidere*, and the difference comes out clearly in the system of noxality. At civil law noxal actions existed only in the case of offences against property; for *iniuria* they were introduced by the praetor; Gai. IV. 76.

[2] *Supra*, 88.   [3] Gai. III. 24.   [4] Lenel, *E.P.* 326.

[5] *V. D.* 47. 2. 27 pr., which, if it is interpolated, is no less useful as evidence of the law in Justinian's day. In *Cambridge Legal Essays* (1926), 203–222, I have tried to show that at the time of the XII Tables the multiplication was not of the value at all, but in kind, so that the man who stole a cow, for instance, had to give two cows.

[6] Cf. Mommsen, *Strafrecht*, 85.

rule, drawn between intentional, negligent, and accidental acts, but this principle was no longer applied without exception. One of the very few things that we know about the law of murder is that a distinction was already made between intentional and unintentional killing, for a fragment tells us that "if the weapon sped from his hand rather than was thrown by him", then a ram was "substituted"[1]—probably given to the agnates—a relic of the time when the agnates of the slain man were entitled to take vengeance on the slayer.

A similar distinction between an intentional and an unintentional act was also made, as we have seen, in the case of arson,[2] but otherwise, so far as the fragments go, the act alone seems to have been taken into consideration.

---

[1] Tab. VIII. 24; cf. *infra*, 324, n. 5.
[2] *Supra*, 174.

Chapter XII

THE LAW OF PROCEDURE AT THE TIME OF THE XII TABLES

In the history of Roman law there are to be found, apart from differences of detail, three systems of procedure—that of the *legis actiones*, the formulary system, and *cognitio extraordinaria*. The periods during which these systems were in use overlapped each other, but broadly it may be said that the *legis actio* system prevailed until the passing of the *lex Aebutia*, probably in the second half of the second century B.C.,[1] that the formulary system was that chiefly used from the last century of the republic until the end of the classical period and that *cognitio extraordinaria* was the system in use in post-classical times. At any rate, for the purposes of the XII Tables we have only to consider the first of these types of procedure—the *legis actiones*.

In any discussion of procedure three main questions have to be asked: (i) How does a man who wants to set the law in motion against another begin; how, that is, does he get the other into court? (ii) How is the trial conducted when the parties are before the court? (iii) Supposing that the judgment is in favour of the plaintiff, how is it enforced against the defendant? We have therefore to consider (i) Summons, (ii) Trial, (iii) Execution.

§ I. SUMMONS (*IN IUS VOCATIO*)

This process was the simplest that can well be imagined; the man who wished to begin legal proceedings summoned his opponent orally, wherever he might find him, to follow him to court (*in ius*—before the magistrate), and it was the duty of the opponent to obey the summons. If he refused, the summoner called the bystanders to witness and then proceeded to use force, for the state as yet, and for a long time afterwards, provided him with no help. If the defendant was sick or infirm with age he had to be provided with a beast to carry him but he could not insist on a cushioned carriage.[2] The only way in which a defendant could escape from the duty of obeying the plaintiff's summons was by finding a *vindex*, i.e. one who would guarantee his appearance before the magistrate when

---

[1] *Infra,* 228.

[2] Tab. I. 1: *Si in ius vocat ito. Ni it antestamino: igitur em capito.* 2: *Si calvitur pedemve struit, manum endo iacito.* 3: *Si morbus aevitasve vitium escit, iumentum dato. Si nolet arceram ne sternito.* We know that these provisions stood at the beginning of the XII Tables, for Cicero (*de leg.* 2. 4. 9) refers to the whole code by the initial words *si in ius vocat.*

wanted, and, as the plaintiff could not be expected to let a substantial opponent go merely on the guarantee of some impecunious bystander, the XII Tables laid down that where the defendant was a member of the wealthier class (*assiduus*) the *vindex* must be one also.[1]

§ II. TRIAL

The trial of an action under the *legis actio* procedure (and also later under the formulary system) was characterised by a remarkable division of the proceedings into two stages, the first of which took place before the magistrate (*in iure*), under whose supervision all the preliminaries were arranged, while the second, in which the issue was actually decided, was held before a *iudex*,[2] who was neither a magistrate nor a professional lawyer, but was appointed by agreement between the parties.[3,4]

[1] Tab.1.4: *Assiduo vindex assiduus esto; proletario iam civi quis volet vindex esto.* The exact position of the *vindex* (who also appears in execution by *manus iniectio*, *infra*, 189) is uncertain. Some authorities regard him as a substitute who took over the whole liability of the defendant, i.e. became the actual party to the action, but the general view is that he was a mere guarantor for the defendant's appearance. Opinions are divided on the question whether he had actually to go with the plaintiff and give his guarantee to the magistrate or merely gave the guarantee on the spot to the plaintiff with the result that he could be made responsible afterwards if the defendant did not appear. Lenel (*E.P.* 68) inclines to the latter view but *v.* also Wenger, 93.

[2] Besides *iudices* there might also be *arbitri*, already apparently at the time of the XII Tables (*v.* Tab. XII. 3). The difference was perhaps that the *arbiter* had a greater discretion. Boards of *recuperatores* were also used, originally probably only for international matters (*v. supra*, 100) but no trial could be a *iudicium legitimum* unless it were before a single *iudex*; *v.* Gai. IV. 104.

[3] The phrase *in iudicio* commonly used in modern books for the proceedings before the *iudex*, as opposed to those before the magistrate, does not appear to be warranted by the sources, and it is better to say *apud iudicem*. According to Wlassak, *Prozessgesetze*, II. 26–51, followed by Wenger, 181, *iudicium* meant the proceedings from *litis contestatio* until judgment, but there are some passages, especially Cic. *Part. Or.* XXVIII. 99, which go to show that it might also have the narrower meaning, *v.* Buckland, *Classical Review*, XL (1926), 83.

[4] The origin of the bipartite arrangement, which goes back as far as we can trace Roman history, is unknown. Wenger, 23, 50–51, supposes that under the monarchy the kings were the judges (as is indeed the Roman tradition, Cic. *de Rep.* V. 2. 3, Pomponius, D. 1. 2. 2. 1), but that there existed also a custom of purely voluntary submission to arbitration. In the republic there was, in his view, a compromise which took from the magistrate (now representing the king) the power of direct adjudication, but at the same time placed the arbitrator under magisterial control. See however Koschaker, *Z.S.S.* XLVII. 508–510, who points out that this view assumes the expulsion of the kings to have been due to democratic tendencies, which in fact did not appear at Rome until several centuries later. Against Wenger also Levy, *Z.S.S.* XLVI. 370–372.

It was never possible to do without this agreement, so that a case could never be tried unless the defendant consented to the appointment of the *iudex*, but the *iudex* was more than a mere private arbitrator because, unless for some special reason the parties wished to select a man for themselves, he was always chosen from a list of qualified persons kept for the purpose by the magistrate (*album iudicum*)[1] and because the decision which he subsequently gave was no mere arbitrator's award but a judgment, recognised by the state and giving rise to execution proceedings. Above all, it must be remembered that, though the defendant had to agree to the *iudex* before a trial could take place, the magistrate had means at his disposal for putting pressure on an obstinate defendant, which might amount (at any rate in the later law) to giving the plaintiff possession of the whole of his property.[2]

A. PROCEEDINGS *in iure*. It is in this stage that the highly formal character of the system makes itself evident. Once before the magistrate[3] the plaintiff had to set the proceedings in motion by making his claim in a set form of words appropriate to his cause of action. The defendant then (if he disputed the matter) replied similarly in set words and the magistrate intervened, again in a prescribed form, so that the case might be sent for trial before the *iudex*. It was these forms of spoken words (for the procedure was entirely oral) which constituted the actual *legis actiones*, and the forms laid down had to be followed so exactly that if a plaintiff made the slightest slip he failed in his action.[4] Thus Gaius records[5] that a man who wished to sue for the destruction of his vines and used the word "vines" in his claim lost his case because the clause in the XII Tables[6] under which he was suing spoke only of "trees". Had he used the word "trees" all would have been well, for vines are trees, but

---

[1] This list originally contained the names of senators only; in the later republic the staffing of the courts was one of the great political questions and the lists were made up of senators or *equites* according as one or other order was politically predominant. At times there was a compromise.

[2] *Missio in bona* leading eventually, if the defendant remains obstinate, to sale of his property (*bonorum venditio*).

[3] After the institution of the praetorship the magistrate concerned was normally the *praetor*, but originally the only magistrates with *imperium* and hence the only ones with jurisdiction were the consuls, or, in the period between the XII Tables and the institution of the praetorship the military tribunes with consular power (*supra*, 13). It must be remembered too that the magistrate could not sit on all days but only on those which were marked *F* (*fasti*) in the calendar or on those marked *C* (*comitiales*) if no *comitia* were in fact held on them. Days on which he might not sit were marked *N* (*nefasti*).

[4] Gai. IV. 30.   [5] IV. 11.   [6] *Supra*, 174.

his failure to use the right word was fatal. From this example[1] we can see that where the claim was based on a statute it had to follow exactly the wording of the statute, but there must also have been forms of claim not directly based on any statute but the product of customary law, and in either case it was presumably the pontiffs, in their capacity of advisers to the magistrate, who finally decided whether a form was admissible or not.[2] When Gaius came to describe the *legis actiones* (which were almost completely obsolete in his day[3]) he said that there were five kinds (*modi*) of *legis actio*,[4] but it is clear that these *modi* were only general moulds in which the action might be cast, and that within these moulds each cause of action had its own appropriate form. In any case, so far as the procedure for beginning an action at the time of the XII Tables is concerned, we need only discuss one of the five *modi*—*sacramentum*—for, of the remainder, two (*manus iniectio* and *pignoris capio*) are primarily methods of execution,[5] and of the other two, one (*condictio*) is certainly and the other (*iudicis arbitrive postulatio*) very possibly later than the XII Tables.[6]

The form of proceedings by *sacramentum* differed according as the claim was *in rem* (a *vindicatio* or claim of ownership especially) or *in personam* (a claim to enforce an obligation). As to the former we are well informed, for Gaius' description is fairly full;[7] unfortunately the manuscript is defective where he deals with the latter.[8]

(i) *Legis actio per sacramentum in rem* (*vindicatio*). Where the thing

---

[1] Gaius also says (IV. 11) that the forms were called *legis actiones* "either because they were provided by statute...or because they were adapted to the words of the statutes themselves and so were adhered to as unchangingly as statutes". On this passage v. Lenel, *Z.S.S.* XXX. 340 *sqq.*

[2] It was always the custom at Rome, both in private and in public life, not to take important decisions without the advice of a *consilium* and the pontiffs probably sat originally on the *consilium* of the consul as did later the jurisconsults on that of the *praetor*. The *ius Flavianum* (*supra*, 88) was a collection of forms of action accepted by pontifical jurisprudence, and that this collection could grow is shown by what Pomponius says of the *ius Aelianum* (D. 1. 2. 2. 7, *supra*, 89) which was composed "because with the growth of the state there were some forms lacking". Note that in the story about the "vines" Gaius (IV. 11) does not say that the magistrate dismissed the case but that "there was a *responsum* that he had lost his case", and no doubt as a result of that *responsum* the magistrate dismissed it.

[3] Gai. IV. 31.   [4] Gai. IV. 12.

[5] Cf. Buckland, 609: "*actio* did not necessarily imply litigation; it was a process for the enforcement of a right".

[6] In any case we know hardly anything about it.

[7] Gai. IV. 16–17.   [8] Gai. IV. 14–15.

claimed was movable it had to be present in court and the plaintiff began by grasping the thing and saying (e.g. if it was a slave) "I assert that this man (?with all accessories) is mine by Quiritarian right; see, as I have said, I have put my wand upon him" (*Hunc ego hominem ex iure Quiritium meum esse aio secundum suam causam*;[1] *sicut dixi, ecce tibi, vindictam imposui*). He then laid a wand (*vindicta*) on the slave. There were now two courses open to the defendant; he might admit the claim either expressly or by his silence, in which case the plaintiff took the slave away with him, and the matter was at an end.[2] If however the defendant did not wish to give way he himself made a claim in the same words and with the same gestures as the plaintiff. The praetor then called on both of the parties to loose their hold (*Mittite ambo hominem*), so that we have here clearly a stereotyped sort of struggle between two people for the possession of a thing which each of them grasps, and the struggle is ended by the intervention of a third party; the form of litigation reproduces the self-help which was the predecessor of litigation.[3] After the praetor's intervention the parties take up the dialogue again. The plaintiff[4] says: "I demand this; will you say on what ground you have made your claim?" (*Postulo anne dicas qua ex causa vindicaveris*), and the defendant answers: "I have done right and thus I have laid my wand on him" (*Ius feci sicut vindictam imposui*).[5] Plaintiff: "Seeing that you have claimed unrighteously I challenge you to a *sacramentum* of five hundred *asses*" (*Quando tu iniuria vindicasti, D aeris te sacramento provoco*). Defendant: "And I you" (*Et ego te*). The *sacramentum* was a sum of money[6] which had originally to be deposited, later promised with security,[7] as a sort of stake by each of the parties and was forfeited to the public use by the one

[1] The meaning of *causa* in this connection is uncertain.

[2] Wenger, 103, and others think that there was an *addictio* by the magistrate in such case, but this view rests on the evidence of the procedure in *in iure cessio*, which is probably fallacious, for *in iure cessio* is not merely a collusive action; cf. *supra*, 150.

[3] See, however, Levy-Bruhl, *St. Bonfante*, III. 81–90.

[4] Gaius (IV. 16) says with greater accuracy "he who had made the first vindication", for strictly, as each has to claim that the thing is his, neither is more of a plaintiff than the other. Cf. *supra*, 144.

[5] The exact meaning is doubtful.

[6] Fifty *asses* if the matter at issue was worth under 1000 asses, 500 if it was worth 1000 or more, except that a question of liberty could always be raised for a stake of 50. Originally the amounts were probably assessed in oxen and sheep. The stakes appear to have been deposited at one time with the pontiffs (Varro, *L.L.* v. 180, Bruns, II. 54) and the loser's no doubt forfeited to the gods whom his perjury had outraged.

[7] *Praedes, v.* Gai. IV. 16. Cf. *infra*, 188, n. 2 and 309.

that eventually lost the case. As however *sacramentum* literally means
"oath" it is supposed that, originally at any rate, the parties each made
an oath as to the justice of their claims,[1] and that what the judge had to
decide was which oath was justified, the loser forfeiting a certain sum as
a penalty for his false oath. In any case, in historical times it was the
money that mattered, and the process was a sort of bet, except for the fact
that the winner did not profit by the loser's stake, which went to the
state.

Once the "bet" was made it was the business of the magistrate to
assign the interim possession of the thing claimed to one or other of the
parties who had to give security that if he turned out not to be entitled he
would return it together with any fruit that had accrued meanwhile.[2]
Where the thing claimed was an immovable it appears that originally the
parties went and transacted part of the ceremony at least on the disputed
land, and later there was a pretence of doing so.[3] A clod of earth, Gaius
says, was used to represent the land and the parties spoke their words and
made their gestures over it "as if it were the whole thing that was present".[4]

(ii) *Legis actio per sacramentum in personam.* Here we have fewer
details as to the form of words used, but the proceedings must clearly
have been simpler, as there was no thing of which both parties claimed the
ownership, and no need therefore for any touching or wands or interim
possession. The plaintiff asserted whatever it was that he claimed as
owing to him from the defendant, saying "I assert that you owe me"
(*Aio te mihi dare oportere*),[5] and perhaps also adding the ground for the
claim, and the defendant denied the debt (if he wished to dispute the
matter). Then no doubt there followed the challenge to the *sacramentum*,
as where the action was *in rem*, and the appointment of the *iudex*. If
the defendant did not wish to dispute the plaintiff's claim, he must
admit it; it was not here possible for him, as in *sacramentum in rem*,
merely to remain silent, for there was here no thing that the plaintiff
could take away with him; the plaintiff wanted the defendant to pay him
something or do something for him, and the defendant must therefore
either admit the claim or dispute it in such a way that it could be tried.

---

[1] Or perhaps only as to their good faith; cf. Wenger, 119.
[2] The assignment of interim possession, i.e. until the action had been tried,
was called *vindicias dicere*, and the sureties *praedes litis et vindiciarum*; Gai. IV. 16.
[3] *V.* Festus, s.v. *superstites* and *vindiciae*, Bruns, II. 42 and 46; Cic. *pro Mur.*
XII. 26; Gell. XX. 10.
[4] Gai. IV. 17; cf. Gell. *loc. cit.*   [5] Val. Probus, IV. 1.

If he admitted it, the effect of such admission before the magistrate was already at the time of the XII Tables[1] equivalent to that of a judgment, so that execution could proceed just as if there had been a trial followed by a judgment for the plaintiff.[2]

The last proceeding *in iure*, whether the *sacramentum* was *in rem* or *in personam*, was the appointment of the *iudex*,[3] always, it must be remembered,[4] with the concurrence of both parties, and the arrangement of the trial before him for the next day but one (*in diem tertium sive perendinum*). The critical moment however was that at which the parties "joined issue" by agreeing on the trial of their difference as formulated in their assertions and counter-assertions, and this was called *litis contestatio*, probably because it was originally preceded by a solemn calling upon the bystanders to witness (*testari*) what took place.[5] The chief reason why this moment was so important was that from then onwards the plaintiff's right was held to have been "consumed", i.e. even if judgment was not obtained, no fresh action could be brought on the same claim.

It sometimes happened that the proceedings *in iure* could not be terminated on a single day; in this case, in order to avoid the necessity for a fresh *in ius vocatio*, sureties of a special sort (*vades*) had to "go bail" for the re-appearance of the defendant; this sort of suretyship (*vadimonium*) was replaced at a later date by an ordinary stipulation made by the defendant himself and guaranteed by later forms of suretyship, but it is

[1] This is shown by the treatment of confession and judgment together in Tab. III. 1: *Aeris confessi rebusque iure iudicatis* xxx *dies iusti sunto;* cf. *infra*, 189.

[2] At least if the admission was that a definite sum of money was owing. We do not know what happened if the defendant admitted liability, e.g. for damage to property but did not agree to the sum claimed by the plaintiff, or if he admitted liability for the delivery of a certain slave, but there was no agreement as to the value of the slave. The question is bound up with the question whether judgment could be for anything other than a sum of money under the *legis actio* system; in the formulary system it could only be for money and many authors are of opinion that this rule also held for the *legis actio* system. If so, then presumably where the admission was of liability for something not a definite sum of money there was a special proceeding (possibly by *iudicis arbitrive postulatio*) for assessment; *v.* Wenger, 109 *sqq.*

[3] Originally the appointment was made at once but by the *lex Pinaria* (of unknown date) an adjournment of thirty days was prescribed between the end of the *sacramentum* proceedings and the meeting for the appointment (Gai. IV. 15), presumably for the purpose of giving the parties time to come to terms. As in other cases *vadimonium* would be used to secure the presence of the defendant after the adjournment.

[4] *Supra*, 181.

[5] Festus, s.v. *Contestari* (Bruns, II. 5): *Contestari litem dicuntur duo aut plures adversarii, quod ordinato iudicio utraque pars dicere solet:* "*testes estote*".

important to notice its existence at the time of the XII Tables as a separate kind of contract and one of the procedural forms out of which the stipulation itself very probably grew. For the adjournment at the end of the proceedings *in iure* for the purpose of meeting again before the *iudex* no bail was needed, because, as we shall see, the *iudex* could condemn a defendant who failed to appear even in his absence, and this was considered sufficient guarantee that he would not fail.

Such, in outline, was the nature of the proceedings *in iure* in the *legis actio* period. There are many points, not only of detail but of substance, on which our information fails us. We do not know, for instance, exactly how proceedings were begun. In the subsequent formulary system the plaintiff had to let the defendant know what the case was about, probably[1] by showing him the draft of the formula which he proposed to use (*editio actionis*), and he had to ask the magistrate to allow the action (*postulatio actionis*). Something of the sort must presumably have been necessary under the *legis actio* system as well, but we have no details. The chief point round which discussion rages is the position of the magistrate himself, but this question, being intimately bound up with the formulary procedure, must be left for discussion, together with that system.[2]

B. PROCEEDINGS *apud iudicem*. The proceedings before the *iudex* appear to have been from the earliest times free from restrictions of form. The *iudex* sat in some public place in the city;[3] he could hear cases even on days when no proceedings *in iure* could take place, and, like the magistrate, he was assisted by a *consilium* of advisers. Proceedings began with a brief statement of the case by the parties.[4] Then came the actual trial, conducted as a rule by advocates who spoke on behalf of their clients and produced the evidence on which each side relied. This evidence might be either that of witnesses or of documents, though until well into the empire the testimony of witnesses was preferred, and no doubt documentary evidence would be extremely rare in early times. There were of course, at any rate in the developed law, some rules of evidence, as for instance the general principle that the burden of proof rests on the plaintiff, but in the main the judge had complete freedom in

[1] *V.* Wlassak, *Prozessformel*, 72 and 99.

[2] *V. infra*, 224–226.

[3] Tab. I. 7: *Ni pacunt, in comitio aut in foro ante meridiem caussam coiciunto. Com peroranto ambo praesentes.*

[4] Called *causae coniectio*, *v.* Gai. IV. 15. Under the formulary system the *formula* itself would inform the *iudex* what the case was about.

weighing the evidence that the parties put before him. He had, as is already laid down in the XII Tables, to hear both sides,[1] unless one of them did not appear by midday and had no valid excuse, for the law laid down that in that case he could give judgment for the party who was present.[2] Serious disease and an appointment made for a trial of some matter with a foreigner[3] are the only excuses of which we know. The hearing had to come to an end at sunset,[4] but, at any rate in later times when advocates had learnt to make long speeches, adjournments were common in important cases.

When both parties have finished, the *iudex* withdraws to consider his judgment with the help of his *consilium*. If he is unable to come to a decision he can swear that "the case is not clear to him" (*sibi non liquere*) and the magistrate can then release him from his duty.[5] The parties will have to go back to the magistrate and get another *iudex* appointed.[6] In the ordinary way, when he could make up his mind, he delivered his judgment (*sententia*) orally at once, but he must do so in the presence of all parties, for a party is not bound by a judgment given in his absence. The judge is quite free as regards the form of his decision which may be either with or without reasons.

§ III. EXECUTION

There remains the question how a judgment is enforced if the defendant against whom it is pronounced does not voluntarily comply with it. In modern law we think of execution as directed towards the fulfilment of the actual judgment; if the defendant will not do himself whatever it is that he is ordered to do—hand over the possession of a thing, pay a sum of money, or whatever it is—then the state will, so far as possible, take steps to secure the desired result itself; it will, for instance, seize the thing in question and hand it over to the successful plaintiff or seize and sell sufficient of the defendant's property to enable it to pay the requisite sum of money to him. This is not the standpoint of early law; execution is there regarded rather as a method of putting pressure on a

---

[1] *Ambo praesentes*; cf. *supra*, 186, n. 3.

[2] Tab. I. 8: *Post meridiem praesenti litem addicito*. When it was the defendant who was absent the plaintiff had probably to produce some evidence of his case, but as there would be no one to contradict it, there would generally be no difficulty; cf. Buckland, 638.

[3] *Morbus sonticus* and *status dies cum hoste*; v. Tab. II. 2.

[4] Tab. I. 9: *Solis occasus suprema tempestas esto*.

[5] Gell. XIV. 2. 25.

[6] For the difficulties involved in any change of *iudex* v. Buckland, 715.

defendant who is obstinate in order to break his will and make *him* do whatever it is he ought to do. It is therefore directed almost exclusively against the person of the defendant, for it is thus that he can be made to suffer most effectively; only in exceptional cases is execution against the property employed. It must also be noticed that in this early period it is the business of the plaintiff to carry out the execution proceedings; for this he needs the authorisation of the magistrate but the magistrate does not act for him. For the discussion of details it is again necessary to distinguish between actions *in rem* and *in personam*.

A. ACTIONS *in rem*. Here the need for execution can arise only if the judgment goes against the person to whom interim possession has been awarded,[1] for if it is in his favour then there is no more to be done. In most cases, at any rate, where the defeated interim possessor did not give up the thing of his own accord, execution proceedings would be against the *praedes litis et vindiciarum*, who had gone surety for him at the beginning of the trial, for the purpose of their existence was precisely to facilitate execution.[2] Whether it was also possible to proceed against the party himself is disputed.[3] It may be that there could be further proceedings for an assessment of the amount payable in default of restitution and that when this amount was ascertained execution could proceed as on a judgment *in personam*.[4]

B. ACTIONS *in personam*. Under this heading we have to consider in strictness only the *legis actio per manus iniectionem*, which is the only method of execution for judgment debts and goes against the person of the debtor. It will be convenient however to discuss also the *legis actio per pignoris capionem*,[5] which is a method of execution against the property, permissible in exceptional cases for the execution of certain debts without judgment.

---

[1] *Supra*, 184.

[2] We do not know exactly what the position of the *praedes* was and what exactly they promised. The most plausible conjecture is that they bound themselves to see that if judgment went against their principal he would fulfil it, but that there was also an arrangement by which, if they failed to induce him to fulfil, they themselves should be quit of liability on paying a sum of money instead of being exposed (as was perhaps once the case) to the rigours of execution against the person; *v.* Wenger, 122.

[3] Mitteis, *Festgabe für Bekker* (1907), 122, says it is obvious that no liability attached to the party himself. But *v.* Koschaker, *Z.S.S.* xxxvii, 358.

[4] *V.* Buckland, 621.　　　　　　　　　　　[5] Cf. *supra*, 182.

(i) *Manus iniectio*. Thirty days of grace must be allowed after admission in court[1] or judgment; if not paid within this period the creditors could seize the debtor and take him before the magistrate.[2] If the debtor still could not or did not pay, and if no *vindex* came forward, then the creditor could take the debtor away with him and keep him in captivity; the XII Tables lay down that he may "bind him with cord or with fetters of fifteen pounds weight or more". While he remained thus in captivity the debtor was still a free man, owner of his property and capable of contracting, at least to the extent of coming to some arrangement with his creditor. If he still did not pay and did not manage to come to any arrangement he might be kept thus for sixty days, but he must be produced on three consecutive market-days[3] before the magistrate in the *comitium*, and the amount of the debt must be publicly announced, in case someone should take pity on him and pay on his behalf or perhaps to give other creditors an opportunity of asserting their rights.[4] If nothing was done by the end of the sixty days, the debtor could be killed or sold as a slave abroad; if there were several creditors they could cut the body up into pieces corresponding to the amount of their debts, but the XII Tables added that no responsibility attached to them if they cut too much or too little.[5]

The frightful severity of this process of execution, which is vouched for by the fragments of the Tables,[6] shows clearly that the law of debt was still regarded as part of the law of delict; the creditor who is not paid what is owed him has suffered a wrong; he desires to take vengeance on his debtor and the law permits him to have his way. The process described is, clearly, merely a regulation of vengeance, of the primitive seizure of the debtor by the creditor. The state already regulates the procedure by requiring the presence of the magistrate and by laying down that certain delays must be allowed, but the seizure still takes place. The only possibility of escape is the appearance of a *vindex*; by this is meant

---

[1] *Confessio in iure*; cf. *supra*, 185, n. 1.

[2] In later times, at any rate, there was a ceremonial "seizing" (*manus iniectio*) before the magistrate and a set form of words was used. The formula is preserved in Gai. IV. 21.

[3] Probably the last three market days (*nundinae*) of the period of sixty days; *v.* Buckland, 619, n. 10.

[4] Beseler, *Beiträge*, IV. 104.

[5] It has been held by some that this famous clause is not to be taken literally but refers to a partition of the property of the debtor. Most modern authorities however regard a literal interpretation as more in accordance with the spirit of primitive law; *v.* e.g. Wenger, 214–5; Kübler, 51; Bonfante, I. 131.

[6] Tab. III. 1–6.

a person who prevents the removal of the debtor into captivity by himself offering to dispute the matter, not only at his own risk, but, almost certainly, at the risk of having to pay double the amount owing if he fails to dispute it successfully.[1] It is almost certain, also, that even the *vindex* could not dispute the merits of a case which had once been decided by judgment, but could only dispute the validity of the judgment itself,[2] or its sufficiency as a basis for *manus iniectio* on the ground, for instance, that the debt had already been paid, or that the debtor had already made some arrangement with the creditor.[3]

The extreme severity of the process was mitigated in some way by the *lex Poetilia* (? 326 B.C.) already referred to in connection with *nexum*.[4] This law, apparently, made killing and selling into slavery abroad illegal; presumably it also authorised detention beyond the sixty days allowed by the XII Tables in order that the creditor might use the labour of the debtor, for otherwise, if he had had to let him go free, there would have been no effective process for execution at all. Gaius[5] in describing the result of failure to provide a *vindex* says simply that the debtor was "led home and bound".

How far execution against property accompanied *manus iniectio* we do not know. It is clear that the debtor remained owner of his property during his sixty days' captivity, for the XII Tables[6] say expressly that if he wishes he is "to live on his own", but whether, after the sixty days, his property went with his person to the creditor is uncertain. In any case the question would not be of great practical importance for a man would almost always part with his last shred of property before allowing *manus iniectio* to take place.

(ii) *Pignoris capio*.[7] This "taking of a pledge" was the seizure of a piece of property belonging to a debtor as a means of putting pressure on him to pay the debt. The seizure had to be accompanied by the speaking of a solemn form of words, but it did not have to be in the presence of a magistrate and so some authorities, says Gaius, doubted whether it should be classed as a *legis actio* at all. It does not appear that the pledge could be sold; probably, if the debtor proved obdurate, it was destroyed.

---

[1] Cf. *infra*, 199.

[2] E.g. on some formal ground, or on the ground that one of the parties had not been present when it was delivered.

[3] Cf. Buckland, 619.

[4] *Supra*, 167; de Visscher, *Études de droit romain*, 313–326 (= *Mél. Fournier*, 755–765), believes that it concerned *nexum* only and had no reference to execution.

[5] IV. 21. [6] Tab. III. 4. [7] Gai. IV. 26–29.

In any case *pignoris capio* was never a general method of execution, nor was it used for judgment debts. It was allowed only in a very limited number of cases, in some by custom, in others by the XII Tables themselves. All these cases appear to be such as concern the state or religion, and the probability is, therefore, that it was primarily a state privilege, allowed to individuals only by a kind of delegation when it was recognised that their claims were of peculiar public importance.[1]

[1] Cf. Buckland, 624. The two cases concerned with religion, and said to have been introduced by the XII Tables, have already been mentioned incidentally (*supra*, 165, n. 5; 166, n. 2). The customary cases mentioned by Gaius are all those where an individual has been placed under a duty to provide a soldier with money, either for his pay (*aes militare*) or, if he were a knight, for the purchase or upkeep of his horse. This last burden (*aes hordearium*) is said (Livy I. 43) to have been placed on unmarried women, presumably because, though they might be possessed of property, they could not be rated in the census (Greenidge, 74). Pay is said to have been taken over by the state in 406 B.C. The remaining case of *pignoris capio*, mentioned by Gaius as having been introduced *lege censoria* (i.e. presumably in the terms of a contract laid down by the censors), is that of the tax-farmers (*publicani*) who were allowed to use this method to enforce the payment of taxes. Here the idea of delegation by the state appears most clearly.

Chapter XIII

PRIVATE LAW FROM THE XII TABLES TO THE FALL OF THE REPUBLIC: PROCEDURE

It was in this period that the foundations were laid for the great edifice of the classical law. The four centuries which intervene between the compilation of the XII Tables and the beginning of the Principate saw the growth of Rome from a small city-state to be the mistress of a great empire, and the increasing complexity of life which this expansion brought about was necessarily accompanied by an increasing complexity of the law. In 450 B.C. the Romans were still a community of peasant-proprietors, organised largely on the basis of the *gens* or clan, whose life could be regulated by a few comparatively simple institutions; in 31 B.C. they were a diversified population, in which the gentile organisation had ceased to have any importance, and their law, as a result of foreign conquest and the spread of commercialism, was already marked by that individualism which was to become one of its most distinctive features.

There is great difficulty in dealing satisfactorily with the law of this period, for the direct sources from which we can obtain any information are very scanty, and such as exist belong mainly to the latest period.[1] In general we have to take the law as we know it to have existed in the time of the great classical jurists, and, since we cannot suppose it to have sprung into existence fully developed, deduce the earlier state of affairs

---

[1] Chief among these must be reckoned the works of Cicero (106–43 B.C.). Many of the speeches were actually delivered before the courts, though mostly in criminal cases, and thus necessarily contain much legal material, but the philosophical writings are also of great importance. The *Republic* and the *Laws*, though professedly descriptive of the ideal state, are to a considerable extent based on idealisations of actual Roman practice and they, as well as the other works, contain many legal anecdotes. Even the letters often refer to legal matters, especially, of course, to Cicero's private affairs. *V.* Costa, *Cicerone Giureconsulto*, 2nd ed. Bologna, 1927. Other authors of importance are the elder Cato (*supra*, 90) and Varro (B.C. 116–27), whose *de lingua Latina* contains many explanations of legal technical terms and was the chief source from which was drawn indirectly Festus' work *On the Significance of Words*. The comedies of Plautus (254–184 B.C.) are full of legal allusions, but have to be used with great care, for the plots are taken from Greek originals, and even where the dramatist uses Roman technical terms we can be by no means sure that he has made the necessary alterations in the facts to make them fit. Terence (185–159 B.C.) is of less value than Plautus as his works are much closer copies of the Greek originals. Cf. Kipp, 186–187.

as well as we can from the internal evidence of the institutions themselves, helped out by the little that the Roman jurists themselves tell us of the history of the law, by stray references in non-legal writers, especially the historians, and, to some extent, inscriptions. Even so it is not only details which remain doubtful; there is plenty of room for differences of opinion even on such fundamental matters, for instance, as the development of the contractual system which we find existing in the early empire.

Before proceeding to deal with the substantive law it will be best to begin by continuing the history of procedure at the point where it was left at the end of the last chapter, because the procedural changes were not only of great importance in themselves, but a condition precedent to much of the substantive development. The chief creative instrument was, in the later part of our period, as in the early empire, the praetorian edict, and it was to a great extent through the *formula* that the praetor worked. The system of procedure, under which the question for decision between the parties is put to a *iudex* in a form of words (*formula*) authorised by the praetor, is indeed the system with reference to which the main body of Roman law was worked out. It is thus impossible to understand the development of the law without some knowledge of this procedure.

§ I. CHANGES IN THE SYSTEM OF *LEGIS ACTIONES*

Even before the introduction of the formulary procedure (and the date and manner of its introduction are much disputed) considerable changes must have been made by way of suiting the old system to altered conditions. In the first place the number of actual forms of words to be cast in one or other of the "moulds" of *legis actiones* was presumably increasing continuously as new grounds of action came to be recognised, either by legislation or by custom, and we have some evidence of this process in the statement of Pomponius that Sextus Aelius composed a book of actions to supplement that of Flavius "because, with the growth of the state, some forms of action were lacking".[1] This can only mean that since Flavius' time new forms had in fact been recognised and that Aelius put them in his "book of precedents"; he cannot possibly have created them on his own authority.[2]

---

[1] D. 1. 2. 2. 7: *Augescente civitate quia deerant quaedam genera agendi, non post multum temporis spatium Sextus Aelius alias actiones composuit et librum populo dedit, qui appellatur ius Aelianum*; cf. *supra*, 89 and 182, n. 2.

[2] Cf. Lenel, "Der Prätor in der legis actio", *Z.S.S.* xxx. 343. We can compare in a general way the growth in the number of writs in the twelfth and early thirteenth centuries; *v.* Holdsworth, *H.E.L.* I. 398; *Sources and Literature of English Law*, 21.

Apart from this gradual development the only changes of which we have any definite knowledge are those introduced by legislation and mentioned by Gaius in his account of the *legis actio* procedure. Though there is great difficulty in dating the individual laws, they appear to belong to the period stretching from about the middle of the third to about the end of the second century B.C., and they tend, not only to a certain simplification of procedure, but more particularly towards ameliorating the position of the poor litigant who had no kin able and willing to help him. The system of *sacramentum* meant that each plaintiff or defendant had to find a considerable sum of money for the stake, or, in the later period, find friends who would go surety for him in the requisite amount,[1] and in the case of *manus iniectio* the defendant's position was still worse, for he could not defend himself at all, but had to find a *vindex* who would undertake the cause at the risk of having to pay double if he failed in the defence. The harsh use of the judicial machine by the rich against the poor was a question of political importance throughout the republic, and it must have become increasingly acute with the breakdown of the old gentile system.[2] The influx of new citizens made it more difficult for a poor man to find the friends whose help he needed in litigation.[3]

A. INTRODUCTION OF *legis actio per condictionem*. One of the most important changes made in the old system was the creation of a new *legis actio*—that *per condictionem*. Of this Gaius[4] says that it was introduced by a certain *lex Silia* for the recovery of definite sums of money (*certa pecunia*) and by a *lex Calpurnia* for all "definite things" (*certa res*).[5]

---

[1] Cf. *supra*, 183. That 500 *asses* was a large sum is clear from the fact that a penalty of 300 was inflicted for the serious offence of breaking another's bone; *v. supra*, 174.

[2] Including the protection of "clients" by the *gens* to which they were attached.

[3] Cf. Jobbé-Duval, *Études sur l'histoire de la procédure civile chez les Romains* (1896), 28. In early law the man without family is a man without rights. It is worth noticing that the period of these reforms (slight as they are) seems to correspond with the appearance of democratic tendencies at Rome about the end of the third and beginning of the second centuries B.C. Cf. also the laws relating to suretyship (*infra*, 310–311), which were probably the result of agitation on the part of the popular party.

[4] IV. 19.

[5] A claim for *certa res* is a claim for the conveyance either of a specific thing already identified ("the slave Stichus", "the estate at Tusculum") or of a definite quantity of fungible things of a definite quality ("a thousand sesterces", "a hundred bushels of *the best* African corn", "a hundred jars of *the best*

The dates of these laws are unknown, for, though they are generally assigned to the middle of the third century B.C., the evidence for this date is quite unreliable.[1] Of the nature of the proceedings by *condictio* we know only that they included, and probably began with, a summons by the plaintiff to the defendant to appear on the thirtieth day to appoint a *iudex*;[2] it was from that summons that the procedure took its name, for, says Gaius,[3] "*condicere* in ancient speech was equivalent to *denuntiare*". It seems that one advantage over *sacramentum* was greater simplicity; for there was no need for elaborate ritual, and the proceedings began where those in *sacramentum* left off, with the arrangement to appoint a *iudex*. Even more important however was the comparative cheapness, for the loser did not, as in *sacramentum*, forfeit a sum of money to the state. On the other hand it is probable that already, in the *legis actio* period, *condictio*, if for a definite sum of money, was characterised by a feature which ensured that the loser forfeited a sum of money to the successful party. This was the *sponsio et restipulatio tertiae partis*, i.e. the plaintiff said to the defendant, "Do you promise to pay me so and so much (one-third of the sum at issue) if judgment goes in my favour?"[4] The defendant promised and then proceeded in his turn to stipulate for a payment of a similar sum if judgment went against the plaintiff. These two stipulations formed a bet on the result of the trial, the object of which was to discourage vexatious litigation by imposing a penalty on the

Campanian wine"). Any other claim is one for an *incertum*, in particular where the claimant alleges that the other party is under an obligation to perform any act other than a conveyance of property (*v.* D. 45. 1. 68; 74; 75). The question is of special importance with respect to stipulations. Where it was desired to bring an action on a stipulation for *certum* the proper action was *condictio*; where the stipulation was for *incertum*, the action (under the formulary system) was *actio ex stipulatu* (*v.* Gai. IV. 136, 137; D. 12. 1. 24). The close connection between *condictio* and stipulation suggests that the introduction of the *legis actio per condictionem* may have had something to do with the recognition of the stipulation as a binding contract (*v. infra*, 290), but it is unlikely that the *leges Silia* and *Calpurnia* first made stipulations actionable, as Gaius (IV. 20) says that claims which were enforced by *condictio* had previously been enforceable by *sacramentum* or *iudicis arbitrive postulatio*, and that he does not know why the new form was introduced (cf. Buckland, 617).

[1] Cf. Girard, 1051, n. 4.

[2] Presumably this summons took place *in iure* and had, like every part of a *legis actio*, to be in set terms; *v.* Buckland, 617; Wenger, 123.

[3] IV. 17 A; cf. Festus, s.vv. *condicere* and *condictio*. Bruns, II. 5: *Condicere est dicendo denuntiare* and *Condictio in diem certum eius rei quae agitur denuntiatio*.

[4] The exact form of the stipulations is uncertain, but *v.* Gai. IV. 180 and Lenel, *E.P.* 238.

unsuccessful plaintiff or defendant. This penalty, unlike the loser's stake in *sacramentum*, goes to the winner.[1,2]

B. PROCEDURE *per sponsionem*. Another simplification of procedure, this time for the decision of questions of property, which also almost certainly goes back to the time of the *legis actiones*, is the device of trying questions of ownership indirectly, by means of a stipulation. The plaintiff says to the defendant, "Do you promise to pay me twenty-five sesterces if the slave (e.g.) in question is mine by Quiritarian right?" and the defendant promises. Action is then brought for the twenty-five sesterces, and the *iudex* in deciding whether these are owed or not has necessarily to decide the question of ownership, which is the object of the proceeding, for the twenty-five sesterces are a purely nominal sum and are not even in fact paid.[3] The advantage of this process is that even if the

[1] That a similar *sponsio* and *restipulatio* existed where the claim was for *certa res* is improbable (Buckland, 618, n. 7; Girard, 1051), though it is so held by Jobbé-Duval (*op. cit.* 196–206); it did not exist in the *condictio certae rei* of the formulary system and it seems impossible to explain its disappearance if it had once existed.

[2] Another point which is disputed is whether there might be a *iusiurandum in iure delatum* (*necessarium*). Under the formulary system where there was a *condictio* for *certa pecunia*, and in some other cases (*v.* Buckland, 633), the plaintiff might offer the defendant the chance of deciding the matter by his oath. If the defendant accepted the offer and swore that the claim was unfounded the plaintiff lost the action. The defendant might, however, refuse to swear and "refer" the oath to the plaintiff, and then, if the plaintiff swore that the claim was justified, the result was as if judgment had been given. If the defendant refused either to swear or to "refer" he was treated as one who would not defend himself properly and liable to have pressure put upon him by *missio in bona*, i.e. by the praetor's putting the plaintiff in possession of his property. If the plaintiff to whom an oath had been "referred" refused to take it, then the matter was also settled, for the praetor would refuse him his action if he tried to begin again (*denegatio actionis*); *v.* Wenger, 115, n. 68. Jobbé-Duval (*op. cit.*) bases his theory of *condictio* largely on this theory of the oath. Before the introduction of *condictio* he thinks that compurgation was the usual practice, i.e. that the defendant in order to clear himself had to get a number of his kinsmen to come and support his oath with theirs. He holds too (28) that the *vindex* and the *praedes* were co-jurors. The introduction of *condictio* made the position of the man who had no kin to help him in this way easier by permitting other methods of disproof, but the oath remained a possibility. As against this theory it must be pointed out that the evidence for compurgation in Roman law is very slight, Jobbé-Duval's chief support being a statement by Dionysius of Halicarnassus (II. 75) that "the magistrates and courts dealt with most disputes by means of oaths".

[3] In Gaius' time when the indirect method *per sponsionem* was used the *summa sponsionis* was usually claimed by an ordinary formulary *condictio*, but that the procedure dated from before the formulary system is made highly probable by

trial is by *sacramentum* it is *sacramentum in personam*, where the formalities are simpler than in the case of *sacramentum in rem*, and as the amount formally at issue is only very small, the stake is only 50 *asses*, whereas if the object whose ownership was disputed was valuable it would have to be 500 *asses* in *sacramentum in rem*. Once *legis actio per condictionem* had been introduced, the nominal amount of the stipulation could be claimed by this form and so no stake forfeited to the state at all. Of course the mere decision on the stipulation in his favour did not secure to the plaintiff the surrender of his thing. In order that he should be able to enforce this the defendant had to make another promise by stipulation by which he undertook, in effect, if the decision on the first stipulation went against him, either to restore the property with interim profits or pay the value.[1]

For this promise he had to find sureties, whose function was consequently similar to that of the *praedes litis et vindiciarum* in *legis actio per sacramentum in rem*, and the promise was therefore called *stipulatio pro praede litis et vindiciarum*.[2]

C. INTRODUCTION OF *manus iniectio pura*. The ancient process of *manus iniectio* has been described above as a method of proceeding to execution when judgment had been obtained,[3] and as applicable, very probably, even without judgment in the case of debts contracted by *nexum*.[4] Gaius[5] after describing its nature goes on to explain that its application was extended by a number of statutes which permitted its use also in the case of other debts; one of the statutes was the *lex Publilia*, which permitted the *sponsor* (surety) who had paid a debt on behalf of the principal debtor to use *manus iniectio* against the principal debtor if he were not reimbursed within six months; another was the *lex Furia de sponsu*, which gave similar rights to one of several *sponsores* or *fidepromissores* who had been forced, contrary to the provisions of that law, to pay the creditor more than his share of the debt.[6] In both these cases

the fact that it was claimed by *sacramentum* if the case came before the centumviral court, which used the old procedure (Gai. IV. 95). In any case the process could hardly have been invented at a time when the more effective and simpler *formula petitoria* (*infra*, 268) was already in existence.

[1] *V.* Lenel, *E.P.* 516 *sqq.*   [2] Gai. IV. 94.
[3] *Supra*, 189.   [4] *Supra*, 168.   [5] IV. 22.
[6] The date of *lex Furia de sponsu* is unknown, but it must be later than 241 B.C., the date of the creation of the first province (Sicily, *supra*, 68), for it was later than the *lex Appuleia* which presupposes the existence of provinces (Gai. III. 122); *v.* Girard, 805, n. 4. For the date of the *lex Publilia* we have even less evidence, but it appears to be one of the numerous laws in connection with suretyship

the *manus iniectio* was *pro iudicato*, i.e. the words "as if on a judgment" were added to the words spoken when the seizure was made, and the position of the defendant was similar to that of a judgment debtor, in particular with regard to the necessity for a *vindex*; if none such appeared he had either to pay or be led away to captivity, and the *vindex* could only prevent this result by taking over the defence himself at the risk of having to pay double the amount due if it were found to be really owing. We cannot, however, imagine that in this case the burden of proof was on the *vindex*, for that would mean that anyone by merely alleging e.g. that he had paid as *sponsor* for the defendant could force the defendant to find a *vindex* who would prove the negative.[1]

Other statutes, Gaius then goes on to say, introduced a different kind of *manus iniectio* for various debts, namely *manus iniectio pura*; in these cases there was no need for a *vindex*, the defendant being allowed to "ward off the hand of the plaintiff himself and himself defend the action".[2] Finally, by a certain *lex Vallia*, all *manus iniectio* except that on a judgment and that under the *lex Publilia* was made *pura*,[3] and the process therefore became merely a method of beginning an action available in particular

which were passed about the end of the third or beginning of the second century B.C.; cf. Girard, 808. According to Juncker (*Gedächtnisschrift für E. Seckel* (1927), 241) the position before the *lex Publilia* was probably that the principal debtor who failed to reimburse his surety simply became the property (slave?) of the surety and the *duplum* was regarded as a sort of ransom. The evidence for this view is slight though it is likely enough that, as pointed out by Koschaker (*Z.S.S.* xxxvii. 361), the *lex Publilia* did not introduce a new liability but made easier the conditions of one which already existed.

[1] Cf. Buckland, 621.

[2] Gai. IV. 23. The instances are (*a*) the *lex Furia testamentaria* giving *manus iniectio* for a fourfold penalty (Ulp., Reg. I. 2) against anyone not coming under one of the classes excepted from the provisions of the law, who had received more than 1000 *asses* by way of legacy or *donatio mortis causa* from the same person; and (*b*) the *lex Marcia* providing for the recovery of interest illegally exacted. The date of the *lex Furia* appears to lie between 204 and 169 (Girard, *Mél.* I. 101; *Manuel*, 1046; *contra*, Mitteis, R.P.R. I. 52, n. 30); that of the *lex Marcia* is unknown.

[3] Gai. IV. 25. Girard (*Manuel*, 1001; *Mél.* I. 101 and 124) holds that the *lex Vallia*, which appears from Gaius (*sed postea*...) to be later than the *lex Furia testamentaria*, was also earlier than the *lex Aebutia*, on the ground that the innovation in *legis actio* procedure is not likely to have taken place after the introduction of the formulary system by the *lex Aebutia*, and therefore places it in or near the first half of the second century B.C. This argument is of course not accepted by those who differ from Girard as to the date of the *lex Aebutia*, and it is also pointed out (Mitteis, R.P.R. 52, n. 30) that, as the *lex Aebutia* certainly did not abolish *legis actiones*, the old form of procedure might still have received statutory modification at a later date. Cf. *infra*, 228–229.

cases and characterised by the liability of the defendant to condemnation for double if his defence were unsuccessful. Some writers, it is true, hold that there was no such double liability, and there is in fact no direct evidence of it, but without it the process would have no advantage over the ordinary form of procedure by *sacramentum* or *condictio*, and it is difficult to see why it should ever have been invented.[1]

D. INSTITUTION OF THE CENTUMVIRAL AND DECEMVIRAL COURTS. Among the changes in the *legis actio* system we can include the setting up of two new courts before which proceedings " *in iudicio* " might take place—the *centumviri* and the *decemviri stlitibus iudicandis*.[2] The *centumviri* were a panel, numbering in fact during the republic 105 persons, from which the actual court (*consilium*) had to be selected for each particular case. We do not know the method of selection, nor the usual number forming a *consilium*, but some indication is given by the fact that under the empire, when the number on the panel was 180, the *centumviri* usually sat in four divisions.[3] The jurisdiction of the court included the whole field of civil law *vindicationes* in the widest sense of that word, and in particular *hereditatis petitiones* (claims for inheritance),[4] but this jurisdiction was not exclusive;[5] such actions could equally well be brought before a single *iudex*, and it is probable that they were in general only brought before the *centumviri* when a matter of some importance was involved. The presidents of the courts were in the latest days of the republic at any rate ex-quaestors.[6] The preliminary proceedings *in iure* were always before one of the two city praetors,[7] and were always by *legis actio per sacra-*

---

[1] Buckland, 622. Mitteis (*Z.S.S.* XXII. 116) holds that the doubling was characteristic of *m.i. pro iudicato* only, and Juncker, *op. cit.* 241, even thinks that the original *vindex* was not liable for double.

[2] I.e. literally, ten men for the trial of cases.

[3] Mommsen, *Abriss*, 249, conjectures that there were originally three divisions each consisting of thirty-five members.

[4] This is nowhere stated in so many words but is deduced from numerous accounts of cases before the *centumviri*, v. Wlassak, P.-W., s.v. *centumviri*, col. 1940. They also dealt especially with the *querela inofficiosi testamenti* (Buckland, 327), though this was probably not strictly a *hereditatis petitio*; indeed the working out of the law on this subject, if not its initiation, is due to the practice of this court; v. Wlassak, *loc. cit.*

[5] Wlassak, *op. cit.* cols. 1941–1942, and *Prozessgesetze*, I. 111 *sqq.*

[6] Pomponius, D. 1. 2. 2. 29, attributes the introduction of the x *viri* to the need of presidents for the *centumviri*, but as they are not found exercising this function at the end of the republic, either they must have lost it or Pomponius must be mistaken. For the former view Wlassak, *op. cit.* col. 1937, for the latter Mommsen, *Staatsr.* II. 608, n. 2; *Abriss*, 249.

[7] Gai. IV. 31.

mentum.[1] Presumably it was the parties who in the first place decided whether to ask for a trial before the *centumviri* or not, but whether the praetor was bound to grant such a request if made is unknown.[2]

It was formerly held that the institution was one of great antiquity, dating back even to the time of the monarchy, but it is now agreed to be of comparatively late origin.[3] That it cannot be earlier than 241 B.C., the year in which the number of tribes was raised to 35, seems clear from the statement of Festus[4] that the panel was constituted by taking three persons from each tribe, and indeed the earliest trial known to have been held before the centumviral court did not take place until about a century later.[5] In the generation preceding Cicero it was a court where *causes célèbres* were heard and the greatest orators appeared;[6] its reputation, at any rate from the orator's point of view, fell in the latest days of the republic,[7] but rose again under the empire when the absence of openings for political oratory made judicial opportunities of addressing considerable audiences more valuable.

Of the *decemviri* even less is known, partly because they ceased to have any separate existence when Augustus made them[8] into presidents of the centumviral courts. Pomponius[9] speaks of them as being instituted after the creation of the *praetor peregrinus*, and the earliest mention we have is an inscription[10] referring to a certain M. Cornelius Scipio Hispanus,

[1] Even after the otherwise complete supersession of the *legis actiones* by the formulary system, *v. infra*, 229, n. 1. It was the use of the *festuca* (wand) in *sacramentum* which caused the spear to be used as a symbol of the court (Gai. IV. 16).

[2] Wlassak, *op. cit.* col. 1945.

[3] Wlassak (*op. cit.* col. 1935, and *Prozessgesetze*, II. 291) thinks that it may very probably have been introduced by the *lex Aebutia* itself.

[4] Festus, s.v. *centumviralia*, Bruns, II. 5.

[5] That of C. Hostilius Mancinus probably shortly after 146 B.C., Cic. *de Or.* I. 40. 181; *v.* Girard, 1038, n. 5.

[6] Most famous of all cases was the *causa Curiana* in which the great jurist Q. Mucius Scaevola and the great orator L. Licinius Crassus appeared on opposite sides in a question of inheritance, the former arguing for a strict, the latter for a more equitable interpretation of the law; *v.* Cic. *de Or.* I. 57. 242 *sqq.*; Brutus, XXXIX. 144–145.

[7] Tac. *Dial.* XXXVIII.

[8] Or re-made them; *v. supra*, 199, n. 6.

[9] D. I. 2. 2. 29.

[10] *C.I.L.* I. 38; *v.* Girard, *Org. Jud.* I. 23, n. 2. Livy (III. 55) mentions certain *iudices decemviri* as being included with tribunes and aediles of the plebs in a *lex* of 449, but it is now generally agreed that these must have been purely plebeian officials and unconnected with the later court for which both patricians and plebeians were eligible; *v.* Wlassak, *Prozessgesetze*, I. 139 *sqq.*

praetor peregrinus in 139 B.C. and *decemvir* a few years earlier. It may be that they were originally appointed by the praetor, but at the end of the republic they were elected in the *comitia tributa* and counted as magistrates. Their jurisdiction appears to have been confined to matters involving liberty.

Both the *centumviri* and the *decemviri*, dating as they do from about the same period as the first criminal *quaestiones*,[1] represent a moment in Roman legal history when the state was beginning to take a hand in the actual appointment of judges, instead of leaving the matter to the agreement of the parties, but, so far as civil (as opposed to criminal) law is concerned, the experiment was without further effect, and the normal tribunal remained the single *iudex*, appointed at the *litis contestatio* by the parties themselves.

§ II. THE FORMULARY SYSTEM

A. NATURE OF THE SYSTEM. The chief difference between the *legis actiones* and the formulary system is summed up by Gaius when he says[2] that the result of the *lex Aebutia* and the *leges Iuliae* was to introduce litigation *per concepta verba*, i.e. by words adapted in each case to the particular matter in dispute between the parties, the phrase being used in contradistinction to the *certa verba*—the unalterable forms—which had been characteristic of the *legis actiones*.[3] Under the new system the question at issue is submitted to the *iudex* in a form of words making plain to him that if he finds certain assertions of the plaintiff to be true it is his duty to condemn the defendant, and that if he does not find them true he is to absolve him. Thus in a claim for a definite sum of money (to take the simplest *formula* as an example) the form is *si paret Numerium Negidium Aulo Agerio*[4] *sestertium decem milia dare oportere, iudex Numerium Negidium Aulo Agerio sestertium decem milia condemnato,*[5] *si*

---

[1] *Infra,* 325.   [2] IV. 30.   [3] *V.* Gai. IV. 29.

[4] In the pattern *formulae* (*infra,* 204) the name of the plaintiff (he who brings the action—*agit*) is always given as *Aulus Agerius*, that of the defendant as *Numerius Negidius* (he who pays—*numerat*—and denies—*negat*). The parallel sometimes drawn between these names and the Richard Roe and John Doe of English law is a little misleading, for these latter persons are actually feigned to exist and act for certain purposes, whereas the Roman names mean no more than the *A.B.*'s and *C.D.*'s of our books of precedents.

[5] It used to be generally assumed that the *formula* was a command of the praetor to the *iudex*, who was thus addressed in the second person, and this view was supported by the MS. of Gaius which in IV. 43 and IV. 46 gives the forms *condemna, condemnate* and *absolvite*, which can only be used for the second person. Now however Wlassak's view (*Der Judikationsbefehl der römischen Prozesse—*

non paret absolvito (if it appear that Numerius Negidius ought to pay ten thousand sesterces to Aulus Agerius, the judge is to condemn Numerius Negidius to pay Aulus Agerius ten thousand sesterces, if it does not appear he is to absolve). What is now done *in iure* is to lay down the *formula*; *apud iudicem*, as before, the actual trial takes place and the *iudex* gives his decision. As under the old system, it is only by co-operation between the parties that a case can be sent for trial before a *iudex*; but this co-operation now consists in agreement on the terms of the *formula*, whereas before it had consisted in the speaking of the set words necessary for joinder of issue. As before, agreement is also necessary as to the person of the judge, and, as before, an obstinate defendant may be coerced into agreement by the magistrate.

The actual stages in the process were as follows. Summons could still take place in the old form of *in ius vocatio*, but this was usually replaced by a *vadimonium*, i.e. the defendant instead of accompanying the plaintiff immediately into the presence of the magistrate promised (by stipulation) to appear on such and such a day. When summoning his opponent the plaintiff had to make it clear to him what the claim was and this notification was known as *editio actionis*;[1] when, on the appointed day, the parties came before the magistrate, a second *editio actionis* took place, in which the plaintiff placed before his opponent and the magistrate the draft *formula*, drawn no doubt usually with the help of his legal adviser,[2] on which he proposed that the case should be tried.

At the same time occurred the *postulatio actionis*—the request by the plaintiff to the magistrate that he would grant the action, i.e. order a *iudex* to undertake the trial on the *formula* indicated. The defendant, also no

---

v. esp. 242) that it is the parties who are the authors of the *formula*, and that they refer to the *iudex* in the third person (let him condemn—absolve) is very generally accepted, in particular (though with some hesitation) by Lenel, *E.P.* 114. Lenel points out (*Z.S.S.* XLIII. 574) that it is quite possible to accept Wlassak's view that the *formula* represents the instructions of the parties to the *iudex* and yet hold that they addressed him in the second person. He compares the form of will given by Gai. II. 174 in which the testator having begun in the third person, *L. Titius heres esto*, went on in the second *cernitoque in diebus ... quibus scies poterisque*, etc.

[1] Lenel, *Z.S.S.* XV. 385–392; *E.P.* 59–62. Wlassak, *Die klassische Prozessformel*, 72 *sqq.*, thinks that the plaintiff had actually to present the defendant with a draft of the formula he intended to use. Wenger, *Praetor u. Formel* (1926), 8–20, considers that this, though usual, was not essential.

[2] On the jurists' activity as advisers to the parties and the magistrate and its effect on the growth of the *formula v.* especially Wlassak, *Prozessformel*, 25 *sqq.*

doubt usually acting on professional advice, might declare himself satisfied with the draft or he might demand alterations, in particular the insertion of an *exceptio*, and the magistrate, who also had his legal advisers, would take part in the proceedings by indicating what form of words he would allow.[1] When once the form of words was arranged there remained the question of the *iudex*, and only when he had been chosen[2] and his name inserted in the draft was the case ready for *litis contestatio*.[3] This now takes the form of a formal proposal by the plaintiff to go to trial on the issue as now defined, and an equally formal acceptance by the defendant. Very probably the plaintiff actually handed the document containing the completed *formula* to the defendant. As under the old system witnesses were called upon to attest the joinder of issue and in all probability affixed their seals to the document.[4] The final agreement of the parties is the culminating point of the proceedings *in iure*, but the agreement is no mere submission to arbitration; the proceedings *apud iudicem* to which it is the preliminary are a trial authorised by the state, because they need, in addition to the co-operation of the parties, the order of the magistrate to the judge to undertake the duty of hearing and determining the case. It is by his power of giving this order (*iussum iudicandi*), or refusing it, that the magistrate retains in the last resort his complete control over litigation.[5]

B. THE EDICT AND THE *Formula*. The new system, by reason of this supreme control, gave a new importance to the position of the

[1] He could threaten a plaintiff who would not accept certain modifications with denial of action, and a defendant who refused to accept a formula in a certain form with the use of his powers of coercion.

[2] As before the parties can agree upon a judge of their own choice, or, if they do not, one is chosen from the magistrates' list (*album iudicum*). The parties however always retain the right to reject a judge who does not suit them.

[3] Lenel, *Z.S.S.* XLIII. 570, holds (in opposition to Wlassak) that it might be possible in exceptional cases to proceed to *litis contestatio* before the *iudex* was appointed. See also Wenger, *Praetor u. Formel*, 59–83.

[4] The document was very probably in the familiar double form (*infra*, 424). V. Wenger, *Z.S.S.* XLII. 633; *Institutionen des r. Prozessrechts*, 184.

[5] The conception of *litis contestatio* as a contract between the parties, and of the *formula* as an instruction to the judge emanating from the parties, is due to Wlassak, who has developed it in a whole series of works (*v.* Wenger, 3) in which he directs his attack against the older view represented especially by Keller (*Über litis contestatio und Urtheil*, 1827). This older view regarded the magistrate as the author of the *formula* which contained his orders to the *iudex*, and the *litis contestatio* as consisting in the whole proceedings *in iure*, and in particular in the "giving" of the *formula* by the magistrate. Wlassak's views are now almost universally accepted.

magistrate. As no *formulae* were laid down by law and the particular *formula* to be used in each case needed his *iussum* to make it effective, he could, if so minded, assent to the use of a *formula* even if such *formula* had no basis in the civil law; and, on the other hand, where a party sought to enforce a civil law right he could render such right nugatory by refusing his concurrence to the *formula* proposed. The general principles by which he intended to be guided in this matter were, like his other rules, set out in the *edictum perpetuum*. The praetor however did more than merely announce that in such and such cases he would "grant an action".[1] He also set out in his *album* patterns of the *formulae* which he would permit to be used,[2] and this he did, not only where the action itself was one of his own creation, but also where a *formula* was needed for causes of action already existing at civil law. Thus where the cause of action was, for instance, a loan of money, there was no need for the praetor to say that he would grant an action, because such a loan created a civil law obligation, and all that was needed was that the plaintiff should have indicated to him a *formula* for claiming a definite amount of money due at civil law.[3] Where, on the other hand, the plaintiff's cause of action was the fraud of the defendant, a fact which, by itself, gave no claim at civil law, the edict said: "If it be alleged that fraud has been committed, and there be no other remedy available on the facts, and the cause appear to me to be a just one, I will grant an action, provided that not more than a year has passed since proceedings might have been begun".[4] Then followed the pattern *formula*, which was probably much in the following form: "If it appears that, as a result of fraud on the part of Numerius Negidius, Aulus Agerius[5] mancipated[6] the estate with which this action is concerned to Numerius Negidius, and provided that not more than a year has passed since proceedings might have been begun, then, unless restoration be made in accordance with the directions of the *iudex*,[7] the *iudex* is to condemn Numerius Negidius to pay to Aulus Agerius as much

---

[1] And occasionally that he would not allow one; *supra*, 97, n. 1.

[2] Originally in an appendix; *infra*, 363.

[3] For the *formula* v. *infra*, 218, n. 3.

[4] *Quae dolo malo facta esse dicentur, si de his rebus alia actio non erit et iusta causa esse videbitur intra annum, cum primum experiundi potestas fuerit, iudicium dabo.*

[5] For these names of the plaintiff and defendant respectively v. *supra*, 201, n. 4.

[6] This is merely an example of an act involving loss which might be induced by fraud. In the particular case the particular method by which the fraud had caused the plaintiff loss would be set out.

[7] For explanation of this *clausula arbitraria* v. *infra*, 217.

money as shall be the value thereof; if it does not appear, he is to absolve".[1]

In addition there are set out, in an appendix, the forms of words to be used for the different *exceptiones*[2] which may be introduced, at the instance of the defendant, into the *formula* in particular cases.

It is obvious that the exact formulation of the issue to be tried in these forms of words was a matter of great importance, and that the praetor, who had the last word in the formulation, exercised a vast influence on the growth of the law in this way. It is also obvious that there is a great deal to be learnt as to the substance of the law from the study of the *formula*, because it expresses in precise language exactly what are the powers and duties of the *iudex* in each case. It may even be said that the invention of this instrument of procedure, at once flexible and precise, was not only a sign of the Roman genius for law, but also, to some extent, a cause of the success which the Roman jurists achieved. We must therefore say something here in more detail of the structure of the *formula*—the "parts" of which it might be made up, and of the different classes of *formulae* which were in use.

C. THE "PARTS" OF THE *Formula*. (i) *Intentio*. Beyond the appointment of the *iudex* or *recuperatores* (*Titius iudex esto*; *Titius Maevius ...recuperatores sunto*), which appears at the head of each *formula*, the most important part, appearing in almost[3] all *formulae*, is the *intentio*. It is here, as Gaius says,[4] that the plaintiff formulates what it is that he

---

[1] *Si paret dolo malo Numerii Negidii factum esse, ut Aulus Agerius Numerio Negidio fundum quo de agitur mancipio daret, neque plus quam annus est, cum experiundi potestas fuit, neque ea res arbitrio iudicis restituetur, quanti ea res erit, tantam pecuniam iudex Numerium Negidium Aulo Agerio condemnato; si non paret absolvito.* It must be noticed how the *formula* is made to fit exactly the conditions for granting the action laid down in the edict. For both edict and *formula v.* Lenel, *E.P.* 114–115. [2] *Infra,* 209.

[3] In some cases (especially *actio iniuriarum*) the *formula* consists of a *demonstratio* followed by *quantum bonum aequum videbitur condemnato* or similar words, so that there is no *intentio* which can be separated from the *condemnatio*, and in partition actions, before the *condemnatio* was added to the *adiudicatio* (*infra,* 207), there was no *intentio* separate from the *adiudicatio*. For the problems connected with these "*formulae* without *intentio*" *v.* Buckland, 652; Wenger, 133, n. 3, and literature there quoted, especially Audibert, "Formules sans intentio", in *Mél. Girard,* I. 35–65. De Visscher, *Études,* 359–434 (= *R.H.* IV (1925), 193–252), holds that *intentio* is confined to *formulae in ius* and that the *si paret* clause of *formulae in factum* has a quite different nature. But *v.* Lenel, *Z.S.S.* XLVIII. 1–20.

[4] IV. 41: *Intentio est ea pars formulae qua actor desiderium suum concludit.* This definition, which really only fits *intentiones in ius*, is probably taken over from the *legis actio* period; Lenel, *Z.S.S.* XLVIII. 13.

claims as his right, and so it is here that is crystallised the question at issue between the parties. Thus in the *actio certae creditae pecuniae*,[1] the *intentio* is the clause "if it appear that the defendant owes the plaintiff ten thousand sesterces", that being precisely what the plaintiff claims, and the question whether he is entitled or not being precisely what the *iudex* has to decide. In this case the claim is for a *certum*[2] and hence the *intentio* is *certa*, i.e. it describes the claim exactly, but there are also many cases where the *intentio* is *incerta*, and there we find not "if it appear...", but "whatever it appear..."—not *si paret*, but *quidquid paret*. Thus e.g. in an action on a stipulation for an *incertum* the *intentio* reads "whatever on that account the defendant ought to pay to or do for the plaintiff".[3]

In a few cases the *intentio* stands alone, without anything further; this happens in what we should call "actions for a declaration", i.e. where no remedy is sought, but the court is only asked to decide a certain question, whether e.g. *A* is the freedman of *B* or not. These *formulae* are called *praeiudiciales*.[4]

(ii) *Condemnatio.* Much more commonly, of course, the plaintiff wants not only a declaration but a condemnation, and *condemnatio* is the name given to the clause "in which the *iudex* is given the power of condemning or absolving".[5] Thus in the *actio certae creditae pecuniae* this clause runs "condemn the defendant to pay the plaintiff (ten thousand) sesterces; if it do not appear absolve him".[6] In this case, as there is a definite sum of money mentioned in the *intentio*, so there is the same definite amount mentioned in the *condemnatio*, which is consequently *certa* also. The *iudex* has only the choice of condemning in that sum or absolving. But this is not usually the position. Generally the *iudex* has himself to fix the amount of money for which he will condemn (if he finds for the plaintiff), and the *condemnatio* clause only indicates to him how he is to arrive at the sum. He may e.g. be told to take the value of something,[7] or a multiple

---

[1] Cf. *infra*, 219, n. 1.   [2] Cf. *supra*, 194, n. 5.

[3] *Quidquid paret Nm. Nm. Ao. Ao. dare facere oportere*, Gai. IV. 41, 131.

[4] "Pre-judicial", because the decision is generally needed as a preliminary to further litigation. It was e.g. forbidden that a freedman should summon his patron *in ius* without special authorisation from the magistrate. If *A* wanted to bring an action against *B* and *B* alleged that he was *A*'s patron this question would have to be decided before the case could proceed.

[5] Gai. IV. 43.

[6] *iudex Nm. Nm. Ao. Ao. sestertium* X *milia condemnato; si non paret absolvito.*

[7] Either *quanti ea res est* (i.e. at the time of *litis contestatio*) or *quanti ea res erit* (i.e. at the time of *condemnatio*), e.g. in a *condictio* for a *certa res* the whole formula reads as follows: *Iudex esto: s.p. Nm. Nm. Ao. Ao. tritici Africi optimi modios centum dare oportere, quanti ea res est, tantam pecuniam condemnato; s.n.p.a.* For *q.e.r. erit v.* e.g. *infra*, 217, n. 1.

of some value,[1] or simply "whatever amount of money seems right and just to him".[2] Where the *intentio* is *incerta*, the *condemnatio* simply tells the *iudex* to condemn for "that amount", i.e. the value of "whatever it appears that the defendant ought to pay to or do for the plaintiff".[3] In some cases the judge's discretion is further limited by a clause (*taxatio*) which fixes a maximum above which he cannot go.[4] But in any case it is for a sum of money only that the judge can condemn; he cannot condemn the defendant to hand over a house or a slave to the plaintiff, or to perform any service for him, or do anything else whatsoever except pay him a sum of money.[5] The explanation of this apparently inconvenient rule of *condemnatio pecuniaria* is not known for certain, but the most plausible conjecture is that the *condemnatio* really represents the fixing of an amount of money, by the payment of which a defaulting party can escape execution against his person (bondage) to which the man he has wronged would otherwise be entitled.[6] Whatever the origin of the rule it remained in force throughout the formulary system, and, although, as we shall see,[7] pressure might be put upon an obstinate defendant to fulfil his obligations, in the last resort all that could be done was to order him to pay a sum of money.

(iii) *Adiudicatio.* This name is given to the clause appearing in the *formulae* of partition actions[8] which entitles the *iudex* to assign the whole or part of the subject matter of the action to one party as his sole property: "let the *iudex* adjudge what should be adjudged (? to him to whom it should be adjudged)".[9]

(iv) *Demonstratio.* In certain cases the *formula* begins (after the nomination of the judge) with a *quod* (whereas) clause, the object of which

---

[1] E.g. in *actio furti nec manifesti* "*quanti ea res fuit cum furtum factum est, tantae pecuniae duplum iudex Nm. Nm. Ao. Ao. c.s.n.p.a.*" (Lenel, *E.P.* 328).

[2] *V. infra*, 216, on *actiones in bonum et aequum conceptae.*

[3] *V.* e.g. the *formula* of *bonae fidei* actions, *infra*, 215, n. 1.

[4] The *taxatio* may mention a specific sum (*v.* Gai. IV. 51) or the judge may be restricted in some other way, e.g. to a certain fund, as in the *actio de peculio et in rem verso.*

[5] Gai. IV. 48.

[6] *V.* Wenger, 136, and literature there quoted, especially Koschaker, *Z.S.S.* XXXVII. 355–359. That the English common law courts could also only give damages and not specific performance appears to be not a real parallel but a coincidence, for the rule is due only to the early disappearance of "real" actions.

[7] *Infra*, 217.

[8] *Supra*, 157.

[9] Gai. IV. 42 gives *quantum adiudicari oportet, iudex Titio adiudicato*, but *Titio* can hardly be right; Lenel, *E.P.* 207.

is to define the issue to which the *intentio* relates.[1] If e.g. the seller brings an action on the contract of sale (*actio venditi*) the *formula* reads as follows: "Whereas the plaintiff sold to the defendant the slave who is the object of this action, which sale is the matter involved in this case, whatever on that account the defendant ought in good faith to pay to or do for the plaintiff, that (i.e. the value thereof) the *iudex* is to condemn the defendant to pay to the plaintiff; if it does not appear he is to absolve".[2] Here the words "whereas...case" form the *demonstratio*, "whatever... plaintiff" the *intentio*, and the remainder the *condemnatio*. A *demonstratio* is only found in actions *in personam* where the *intentio* is *incerta*, thus in all *bonae fidei* actions and in the *actio ex stipulatu*, not in *condictiones* or in actions *in rem*.[3]

(v) *Praescriptio.* There were originally two sorts of *praescriptio*: (a) *pro actore* (on behalf of the plaintiff), (b) *pro reo* (on behalf of the defendant).

(a) The *praescriptio* in this case was a clause limiting the scope which the action would otherwise have. Thus if a stipulation had been made for a number of payments at different dates and one or more, but not all, were overdue, the promisee, if he wished to sue on these, inserted a clause "let only those payments which are due be the object of the action".[4] If he did not insert this clause, *litis contestatio* would "consume" his right and he could never bring an action for the remaining instalments when they, in their turn, became payable.

(b) Certain defences, subsequently raised by *exceptio*, were originally raised by *praescriptio*, e.g. in some cases an action might not be brought if its decision would prejudice that of another and more important issue. Originally if the defendant wished to make use of this rule as a defence he inserted a *praescriptio* in which the judge was told to deal with the matter only if it would not prejudice the more important case.[5]

---

[1] Gai. IV. 40.

[2] *Quod As. As. No. No. hominem quo de agitur vendidit, qua de re agitur, quidquid ob eam rem Nm. Nm. Ao. Ao. dare facere oportet ex fide bona, eius iudex Nm. Nm. Ao. Ao. c.s.n.p.a.*; Lenel, *E.P.* 299. All *b.f. iudicia* (cf. *infra*, 214) have exactly parallel *formulae*.

[3] The difficulty with *formulae* containing a *demonstratio* is that they appear to be illogically constructed. The *quod*-clause apparently states a fact and yet the truth or falsehood of this fact is one of the matters which the *iudex* has to decide; one would have expected "whereas the plaintiff alleges that he sold..." or something of the sort. Further, the clause *si non paret absolvito* seems logically to demand a previous *si paret condemnato*, which is not there. For suggested historical explanations v. literature quoted by Wenger, 134, n. 10.

[4] *Ea res agatur cuius rei dies fuit*, Gai. IV. 131.

[5] Gai. IV. 133.

Demonstratio, intentio, adiudicatio and *condemnatio* are the only "parts" of the *formula* enumerated as such by Gaius,[1] but, as we have seen, they do not by any means all of them appear in every *formula*. Nor, on the other hand, do they exhaust the possible contents of the *formula*. In any concrete case it might include additions by which the attention of the judge was directed to special defences put forward by the defendant, answers by the plaintiff to these defences, and so on. To these we must now turn.

(vi) *Exceptio.* An *exceptio* is a clause, the effect of which is to direct the judge not to condemn, even though he finds the *intentio* proved, if he also finds a further set of facts to be true. It is thus always a conditional clause with a negative, i.e. beginning "if not" or "unless", and it is used where the defence is not a denial of the right asserted by the plaintiff, but an allegation, that even though that right may exist, it is unjust that the defendant should be condemned.[2] If, for instance, in a claim for money lent the defence is that the money was never received, or that it has already been returned, the defendant can allow the simple *formula* "if it appear that the defendant ought to pay the plaintiff ten thousand sesterces" to stand, because, if the judge believes him, then he must find that the money is not owed; but if the defence is that the plaintiff agreed (informally) not to sue for the money, then, as an informal pact of this sort has no effect on the existence of the obligation at civil law, if the *formula* is left as it is the judge will be bound to condemn. The defendant can therefore insist on the insertion of an *exceptio pacti*, so that the instruction to the *iudex* reads: "If it appear that the defendant ought to pay the plaintiff ten thousand sesterces and if there has not been an agreement between the plaintiff and the defendant that that money should not be sued for, the judge is to condemn, etc."[3] The result of this form is that if the judge finds that such a pact was in fact made he must absolve the defendant.

The power of authorising such *exceptiones*, which, if proved, will result in the plaintiff's losing his case although his right is perfectly good at civil law, is, equally with the power of granting actions, a source of the praetor's influence on the growth of the law, and the rules concerning these *exceptiones* are just as much part of the *ius honorarium* as are those

---

[1] IV. 39; v. Buckland, 649. *Praescriptio* has been mentioned together with them above for the sake of convenience.

[2] Gai. IV. 116.

[3] *S.p. Nm. Nm. Ao. Ao. sestertium decem milia dare oportere et si inter Am. Am. et Nm. Nm. non convenit ne ea pecunia peteretur, iudex Nm. Nm. Ao. Ao. sestertium decem milia c.s.n.p.a.* (v. Gai. IV. 119).

concerning praetorian actions, but it must not be thought that all *exceptiones* are due to praetorian initiative. In a considerable number of cases rules introduced by a *lex* or a *senatus consultum* are made effective by means of an *exceptio*. If, for instance, it was desired to plead in answer to a claim for the repayment of a money loan, that the loan was contrary to the provisions of the *sc. Macedonianum*, which forbade such loans to sons under power, an *exceptio* had to be inserted, and similarly where the defence was that the transaction on which the plaintiff founded his claim was contrary to the *lex Cincia*.[1] The form of the *exceptio* was usually in these cases "if in this matter there has been no contravention of any statute or senatus-consult",[2] it being left apparently to the defendant to make clear *apud iudicem*, if necessary, what was the *lex* or *senatus consultum* on which he was relying.[3] The reason why the rules under these statutes were enforced by means of *exceptiones* and not by treating the forbidden transaction as void were not the same in all the cases,[4] but the use of this praetorian method is a good example of the way in which the *ius honorarium* and the civil law worked in together; nothing could be further from the truth than to conceive of them as antagonistic systems working in opposition to each other.

(vii) *Replicatio*. It may happen, as Gaius says, "that an *exceptio* which *prima facie* appears just, really acts unjustly against the plaintiff, in which case an addition is needed to assist the plaintiff".[5] This addition is called a *replicatio*, and is in the form of a clause which tells the *iudex* to condemn even though the facts alleged in the *exceptio* are true, if a further set of facts is also true. If, for instance, a pact not to sue has been made and after that another pact whereby the debtor releases the creditor from that pact and permits him to sue again, in order that he may have the advantage of this second pact it is necessary to allow him to put in the *formula*, in answer to the debtor's *exceptio pacti*, a *replicatio pacti*, so that the whole formula reads: "If it appear that the defendant ought to pay the plaintiff ten thousand sesterces, and there has not been an agreement...that the

---

[1] Forbidding gifts above a certain maximum except between near relatives; *v. supra*, 85.

[2] *Si in ea re nihil contra legem senatusve consultum factum est*; Lenel, *E.P.* 513. The case might e.g. be that of *A* who is suing on a gratuitous promise which *B* has made by stipulation to pay him a sum of money larger than that allowed by the *lex Cincia*.

[3] In some cases an *exceptio in factum* specifying the statute was used; *v.* Lenel, *loc. cit.*

[4] *V.* Buckland, 653.

[5] IV. 126.

money should not be sued for, or if afterwards there was an agreement that it might be sued for, the judge is to condemn, etc."[1]

The *replicatio* was not necessarily the last word; the *formula* might be extended by a *duplicatio*, a *triplicatio*, or even further.[2,3]

D. CLASSIFICATION OF *Formulae*. (i) *Formulae of civil and of praetorian actions.*

All *formulae* fall first of all into two classes according as they are used for civil or praetorian actions, for, as already observed, there are some cases where the praetor merely authorises a *formula* for the enforcement of a right already existing at civil law, and others where the right only exists because the praetor "gives the action". But the praetor does not always act in exactly the same way when he allows an action which falls outside the civil law, and we can distinguish three different sorts of *formulae* according to the different types of *actiones honorariae*.

(a) *Formulae* with a fiction. In some cases where one definite requirement for a civil law action is absent and it is desired that an action should nevertheless be permitted, the praetor exercises his powers by authorising a *formula* in which the *iudex* is simply told to assume that that requirement is present and decide accordingly. Thus the *actio furti* proper lies only between citizens, but if the thief is a foreigner an action may nevertheless be brought against him and the *formula* will be similar to that of the civil law action, but contain a fiction; it will say not "if

---

[1] Gai. IV. 126.   [2] Gai. IV. 128–129.

[3] The Roman *exceptiones, replicationes*, etc. have often been compared with the pleas, replications, rejoinders, etc. of the old English system of pleading, and there is indeed this central point of resemblance, that the object of both systems was the formulation, *by the allegations of the parties*, of the issues to be tried between them. In the English, as in the Roman procedure agreement is necessary before the case can proceed (*v*. Stephen, *Pleading* (15th ed.), 137–138, quoted by Holdsworth, *H.E.L.* III. 627–628). This resemblance is all the more striking now that we know, through Wlassak's investigations, that it is the parties and not the praetor who are the actual authors of the formula (cf. *supra*, 201, n. 5). But the differences are as great as the resemblance. In form the English pleadings were separate allegations of fact put into the mouths of the parties, whereas the Roman allegations are in the form of clauses conditioning a condemnation. Secondly, in the English system there had always to be a plea in answer to the declaration, even if it were only a direct traverse, whereas, if the Roman defendant's answer is a traverse he need only accept the formula as proposed by the plaintiff. Also, although an *exceptio* is often called a "plea in confession and avoidance", the defendant is not, as in the English system, necessarily taken to admit the truth of the plaintiff's first statement. In some ways the English system, though infinitely more developed, is more closely comparable with the system of the *legis actiones*, where the issue is also formulated by assertion and counter-assertion of the parties.

he ought (i.e. at civil law) to pay damages as a thief", but "if he ought, were he a Roman citizen, to pay damages as a thief".[1]

(b) *Formulae* in which a different name appears in the *condemnatio* from that which appears in the *intentio*. This occurs where a right which, at civil law, belongs to *A* is to enure, at praetorian law, for the benefit of *B*, or *vice versa*, a right which, at civil law, avails only against *A* is, at praetorian law, to be made the ground of an action against *B*. For instance if *A* has authorised his son *B* to purchase a thing from *C*, then, at civil law, *B* alone is liable on the contract, but this is one of the cases in which the praetor allows an action against the father on the son's contract, and the *formula* will run something like this: "Whereas *B*, by authorisation of *A*, when he was in *A*'s *potestas*, bought such and such a thing from *C*, which thing is the subject matter of the present action, whatever on that account *B* ought in good faith to convey to or do for *C*, thereto the judge is to condemn *A*, etc."[2]

(c) *Formulae in factum conceptae.* Where there is no analogy in the civil law sufficiently close for the use of a fiction, and the case cannot be met in the manner described under (ii), the *formula* used is one *in factum concepta*, i.e. there is no reference to a civil law conception such as "owing" (*dare oportere*) or "owning" (*alicuius esse ex iure Quiritium*), but the judge is simply told to condemn, if he finds certain facts described in greater or less detail in the *intentio* to be true, if not to absolve. Thus, in the example given by Gaius of an action for a penalty against a freedman who has begun proceedings against his patron without special permission, the *formula* is as follows: "If it appear that such and such a patron has been summoned to court by such and such a freedman contrary to the edict of such and such a praetor, the *recuperatores* are to condemn that freedman to pay that patron ten thousand sesterces; if it do not appear they are to absolve".[3]

Opposed to such *formulae in factum conceptae*, are those *in ius*

---

[1] *Quam ob rem eum, si civis Romanus esset, pro fure damnum decidere oporteret.* A fiction was similarly allowed where it was the victim of the theft who was a foreigner, Gai. IV. 37. Among the most important "fictitious" actions is the *actio Publiciana, ibid.* 36; cf. *infra,* 273.

[2] Lenel, *E.P.* 278. The *formulae* of the other *actiones adiecticiae qualitatis* were similar in the respect here considered. Equally important examples of the same device are the *formulae* used by and against representatives (Gai. IV. 86), and purchasers of bankrupt estates (*Rutiliana species actionis, v.* Gai. IV. 35).

[3] Gai. IV. 46: *Recuperatores sunto. Si paret illum patronum ab illo liberto contra edictum illius praetoris in ius vocatum esse, recuperatores illum libertum illo patrono sestertium decem milia condemnanto* (MS. *condemnate*); *si non paret absolvunto* (MS. *absolvite*). The amount of the penalty is not certain, *v.* Lenel, *E.P.* 69.

conceptae,[1] i.e. where the *intentio* refers not merely to the existence of certain facts, but to the existence of certain civil law relationships, in particular those of "owning" and "owing". For instance in a *condictio* for a definite sum of money the *intentio* is "if it appear that the defendant owes..." (*dare oportere*); in an action on sale it is "whatever the defendant ought to convey or do in good faith..." (*quidquid dare facere oportet ex fide bona*); in a *vindicatio* it is "if it appear that the thing is the property of the plaintiff at Quiritarian law" (*Ai. Ai. esse ex iure Quiritium*). Included among *formulae in ius conceptae* are thus not only those of civil law actions, but also those of praetorian actions with fictions or change of persons, because here too the *intentio* refers to the civil law conceptions of "owning" and "owing", the formula of the *actio Publiciana* being, for instance, "if the thing in question would have been the property of the plaintiff at Quiritarian law, had he possessed it for a year" (*si...anno possedisset tum si eius ex i. Q. esse oporteret...*).[2,3]

In addition to the main distinction between the *formulae* of civil and praetorian actions and those between different classes of praetorian *formulae*, there are also a large number of variations in type corresponding to differences in the nature of the right asserted by the plaintiff and the nature of the relief to which he is entitled either by civil or praetorian law. The *formula* is not, of course, a complete instruction to the *iudex* as to the law which he is to apply, but it does indicate briefly what it is that

---

[1] Gai. IV. 45.

[2] The difference between *formulae in ius* and *in factum conceptae* cannot be expressed simply by saying that in the one case it is a question of law and in the other one of fact which is submitted to the judge. In either case the judge has to decide all questions whether of law or of fact which arise; whether e.g. *A* owes *B* money depends not only on law but on fact, and similarly questions of law might, no doubt, arise in the action against a freedman for beginning proceedings against his patron without leave, whether for instance the act complained of amounted to an *in ius vocatio* or not.

[3] The exact meaning of *actio in factum* (as distinguished from action with a *formula in factum concepta*) is disputed. One view is that it is simply equivalent to *actio praetoria*, i.e. would include actions with a fiction and actions with change of persons. Wenger (152, *q.v.* for literature) believes that *actio in factum* can never mean anything but one with *formula in factum concepta*. Such *formulae* might be granted for a special case and then forgotten, but they might also form precedents and result in the inclusion of a new pattern formula in the edict; when this happened the action would nevertheless continue to be called *in factum*. The expression *actio utilis*, which is also frequently found, apparently covers all praetorian actions which are based on civil law analogies, whether they have *formulae in factum* or with a fiction or of any other sort. The terms *actio in factum* and *actio utilis* thus overlap to some extent. *V.* Lenel, *E.P.* 203; Wlassak, *Prozessformel*, 88.

the plaintiff demands, and what the duty of the *iudex* is, and its form therefore varies with the variations in the nature of the claim, and the nature of the relief which it is possible to grant. Among the more important distinctions and categories are the following:

(ii) *Formulae of actions in rem and actions in personam.* Whether an action is *in rem* or *in personam* is immediately clear from the structure of the *formula*, for when a man is claiming *in rem*, the defendant's name does not (apart from exceptional cases)[1] appear in the *intentio*[2] at all, in a claim *in personam* it necessarily does. Thus in the typical case of a *vindicatio*,[2] because the plaintiff is only asserting a relationship between himself and the thing he claims, the *intentio* runs "if it appear that the thing belongs at Quiritarian law to Aulus Agerius", whereas if he is claiming *in personam*, i.e. is alleging that some other person is under a duty towards him, then to make the extent of his assertion clear it is necessary that the name of the person from whom he claims, i.e. the defendant, should be mentioned. In an *actio certae creditae pecuniae* therefore the *intentio* reads "if it appear that *Numerius Negidius* ought to pay Aulus Agerius...".

(iii) *Formulae of actiones bonae fidei*[3] *and of actiones not bonae fidei.* In a number of actions *in personam* where the *intentio* is *incerta* (*quidquid dare facere oportet*), there are added the words *ex fide bona*, the judge being thus definitely instructed to take "good faith" into account, and to condemn for an amount representing what the defendant ought to do in accordance with good faith. Of this nature are for example all the actions on consensual contracts.[4] Thus if *A* has sold *B* a slave and wishes to

---

[1] The *intentio* of the *actio negatoria* does mention the defendant's name, but this is necessary to define the extent of the real right that the plaintiff is claiming; *v.* Buckland, 677. So also with the *actio prohibitoria*, Lenel, *E.P.* 190. The category of actions said to be *in rem scriptae*, because although *in personam* they do not mention the defendant's name in the *intentio*, appears to be of Byzantine origin. The chief example formerly given was the *actio quod metus causa*, but Schulz, *Z.S.S.* XLIII. 240 *sqq.*, has now shown that in classical law this action lay only against the author of the threats.

[2] In the *condemnatio* the name of the defendant necessarily always appears, as it is he who, failing restitution, will be condemned to pay money to the plaintiff.

[3] The classical phrase is *iudicia bonae fidei*.

[4] The list given by Gaius (IV. 62) includes the actions on *emptio venditio*, *locatio conductio*, *negotiorum gestio*, *mandatum*, *depositum*, *fiducia*, *pro socio* and *tutela*. Most editions give also *actio rei uxoriae*, but Biondi (*Iudicia bonae fidei* (1920), 178 *sqq.*) has shown that this is probably a mistaken reading of the MS. and that the *actio rei uxoriae* was not *b.f.* in classical times (*v.* Lenel, *E.P.* 302–307). On the other hand we must add to Gaius' catalogue almost certainly the *actio commodati* (*v.* Lenel, *E.P.* 253) and possibly the *actio pigneraticia* (*ibid.* 255). In the case of *depositum* and *commodatum* the existence of an alternative (and

claim the price or enforce any other claim arising out of the contract the
formula will read as follows: "Whereas *A* sold to *B* the slave in question,
which matter is the subject of this action, whatever on that account *B*
ought to convey to or do for *A* in accordance with good faith, that
sum the judge is to condemn *B* to pay *A*; if it do not appear he is to
absolve".[1] The practical importance of the insertion of the words *ex fide
bona* is considerable. In particular two points should be noticed.[2]

(*a*) Inherence of *exceptio doli.* If the defence to an *actio venditi,* for
example for the price of goods sold, were that the defendant had been
induced to enter into the contract by the fraud of the plaintiff, there is
no need (as there would be if the contract were one of stipulation) for him
to insist on the insertion of an *exceptio doli* in the formula. He can simply,
apud iudicem, raise the point that it is unfair for him to be condemned in
such circumstances, and the judge, if he finds the facts to be as the
defendant alleges, will have to absolve him.[3]

(*b*) Possibility of set-off (*compensatio*). In the ordinary way, if *A*
brought an action against *B, B* could not originally plead in answer that
A was under an obligation to him (*B*); *B* must, if he wished to enforce
that obligation, bring a separate action against *A*. In the case of *b.f.
iudicia* however it was already in Gaius' time possible for the judge to take
account of such counterclaims, provided that they arose out of the same
transaction. Thus e.g. if *A* and *B* are partners and *A* is suing *B* for a share
of profit made by *B* out of partnership business amounting to 10,000
sesterces and *B* wishes to claim from *A* 3000 sesterces, *A*'s share of expenses incurred by *B* on partnership business, it is open to the judge to
take this into account and condemn *B* only for the difference, 7000
sesterces.[4]

---

earlier) *formula in factum* is proved by Gai. IV. 47, and it may also be regarded as
certain for *pignus* (Lenel, *E.P.* 254) and *negotiorum gestio* (*ibid.* 102). In Justinian's time, when the phrase *iudicium bonae fidei* has lost the very definite
signification that it had in the formulary period, the list of *b.f.* actions is considerably enlarged; *v.* J. 4. 6. 28.

[1] *Quod As. As. No. No. hominem q.d.a. vendidit, q.d.r.a. quidquid ob eam rem
Nm. Nm. Ao. Ao. dare facere oportet ex fide bona eius iudex Nm. Nm. Ao. Ao.
condemnato, s.n.p.a.*

[2] For other points *v.* Buckland, 680; *Manual,* 363.

[3] Whether the *exceptio pacti* is similarly "inherent" in *b.f. iudicia* is open to
some doubt. D. 18. 5. 3 says *bonae fidei iudicio exceptiones pacti insunt,* but the
fragment is certainly interpolated. Siber, *Z.S.S.* XLII. 77; Stoll, *Z.S.S.* XLIV.
41 *sqq.,* and Biondi, *op. cit.* 22. Biondi holds that the *exceptiones metus* and *rei
iudicatae* were also "inherent", *op. cit.* 37 *sqq.*

[4] Gai. IV. 61–63.

In the later law it became possible to plead set-off to actions which were not *bonae fidei*, but the subject is too complicated and disputable for discussion here.[1]

In the law of Justinian's time the antithesis to *actio bonae fidei* was *actio stricti iuris* (or *strictum iudicium*), but it is improbable that the classical law had any inclusive expression of this sort;[2] the variety of actions which were not *bonae fidei* was too great for them all to be included under one heading, and it has long been recognised that in any case the classification could not be exhaustive.[3] Instead, therefore, of attempting to formulate a definition of a "strict action", it will be better to indicate some of the principal classes of action which are not *bonae fidei*.

(i) *Actiones in bonum et aequum conceptae*. Most closely allied to *iudicia bonae fidei* are these actions, where a phrase referring the *iudex* to equitable considerations is also found in the *formula*, but not in the same position. Instead of the words *ex fide bona* in the *intentio* there is here a clause (following a *demonstratio*) referring the *iudex* to his feeling of justice for the amount for which he is to condemn. Thus the *formula* of the *actio iniuriarum* (*aestimatoria*) ran something as follows: "Whereas ...Aulus Agerius was (e.g.) struck in the face by Numerius Negidius... whatever amount of money the *recuperatores* think right and fair that N. N. should be condemned to pay A. A. on that account that amount of money...they are to condemn N. N. to pay A. A. etc."[4,5]

(ii) *Actiones arbitrariae*. The rule of *condemnatio pecuniaria*[6] is a clumsy one; there are many cases in which damages are an insufficient remedy and the plaintiff should be given, not a sum of money, but that to which

---

[1] J. 4. 6. 30; Buckland, 696–700; Girard, 748–755.

[2] Pringsheim, *Z.S.S.* XLII. 649–651; Biondi, *B.I.D.R.* XXXII (1923), 61–72.

[3] Wenger, 155, n. 13; Buckland, 679; Girard, 1082. In any case the distinction only fits non-penal actions *in personam* with a formula *in ius*. Thus *condictiones* (*infra*, 217), the *actio ex stipulatu* and the *actio ex testamento* are counted as "strict" because the *intentio* runs *si paret dare oportet* or *quidquid dare facere oportet*, but the words *ex fide bona* are not inserted.

[4] *Quod...Ao. Ao. pugno mala percussa est...q.d.r.a., quantam pecuniam recuperatoribus bonum aequum videbitur ob eam rem Nm. Nm. Ao. Ao. condemnari, tantam pecuniam...recuperatores Nm. Nm. Ao. Ao. c.s.n.p.a.* The manner in which the defendant's name appeared in the *demonstratio* is uncertain; Lenel, *E.P.* 399.

[5] List of actions having similar *formulae*, Buckland, 686, n. 8; Girard, 1084, n. 3. *Formulae* of this kind appear to have been used especially where sentimental as well as pecuniary damage had to be considered; Costa, *Profilo*, 57. On the whole subject *v.* now Pringsheim, *Z.S.S.* LII. 78–155.   [6] *Supra*, 207.

he has a right. The formulary system, though it retained the rule that in the last resort the judge could only condemn for a sum of money, knew in some cases, of a roundabout way in which pressure might be put on the defendant, if unsuccessful, to induce him to fulfil his primary duty instead of waiting to be condemned in damages. This was achieved by the insertion in the *condemnatio* of a clause which had the effect of making the judge's duty to condemn the defendant in damages dependent on the defendant's not fulfilling his original duty. Thus to take the most important case as an example, if A. A. brings a *vindicatio* against N. N. to recover his property, there will appear after the *intentio* ("if it appear that the property in question belongs to A. A. at Quiritarian law") a *condemnatio* in the following form: "and N. N. do not make restitution to A. A. in accordance with the directions of the *iudex*, the *iudex* is to condemn him in the value thereof, etc."[1] If therefore the judge finds for the plaintiff he must announce the fact and give the defendant an opportunity of complying with his findings;[2] only if the defendant fails to comply will he proceed to a condemnation; otherwise he must absolve.

The defendant, it must be noticed, is under pressure to comply, because, if he does not do so, the judge will allow the plaintiff to assess the value of what he claims on oath (*ius iurandum in litem*) himself, and the plaintiff is not likely to be too modest in his assessment.[3]

The list of *actiones arbitrariae* (i.e. of actions with the clause referring to the directions—*arbitrium*—of the judge) includes, in addition to the *rei vindicatio*, also all other actions *in rem*[4] and some actions *in personam*, e.g. the *actio doli* and the *actio quod metus causa*.[5]

(iii) *Condictiones.* Under the rubric *si certum petetur* in the edict there

---

[1] *neque ea res arbitrio iudicis Ao. Ao. restituetur, quanti ea res erit tantam pecuniam iudex Nm. Nm. Ao. Ao. c.s.n.p.a.*

[2] The word commonly used for this finding of the judge is *pronuntiare*, v. H.-S. s.v.

[3] The judge is not bound to accept the plaintiff's figure but, at any rate where the defendant's refusal to restore appeared to be inexcusable, he would presumably do so. This is indeed given as the rule in D. 12. 3. 2, but the passage is very probably interpolated; v. Biondi, *Studi sulle actiones arbitrariae e l'arbitrium iudicis* (1913), 198.

[4] Except probably those whereby praedial servitudes were claimed; Lenel, *E.P.* 193.

[5] There is considerable doubt as to the list; v. Buckland, 659. It has even been urged (Biondi, *op. cit.*) that *actio arbitraria* was unknown as a technical term for this class of action in classical times. *Contra*, Lenel, *Festgabe für Sohm* (1914), 201–223. V. also Lenel, *E.P.* 113, and Biondi, *B.I.D.R.* XXXII. 70, n. 1.

were two[1] pattern *formulae*, one for use when it was a definite sum of money that was claimed, the other for the claim of any other *certa res*.[2] The former (already quoted several times as an example) ran: "If it appear that N. N. ought to pay A. A. 10,000 sesterces, the judge is to condemn N. N. to pay A. A. 10,000 sesterces; if it do not appear he is to absolve".

The latter was: "If it appear that N. N. ought to convey to A. A. 100 bushels of the best African corn the judge is to condemn N. N. to pay A. A. the value thereof; if it do not appear he is to absolve".[3]

It is characteristic of both these *formulae* that they allege a civil law debt (*dare oportere*) without mentioning in any way the cause of action. They were used, in fact, in some cases where the cause of action was a contract—if *A* had lent *B* a sum of money or a sack of corn (*mutuum*), if *B* had promised *A* a sum of money or any other *certa res* by stipulation[4] —but they were also used in a number of non-contractual cases. If, for instance, *A* had paid *B* 10,000 sesterces in the mistaken belief that he owed *B* that sum, he could get the money back by an action of this sort as money paid when it was not owed (*indebitum*). Indeed a number of causes of action came to be recognised because these *formulae* were available for cases where it was difficult to assign a definite cause of action for the plaintiff while it was felt to be unjust that the defendant should retain the money (or other thing) that he had got,[5] e.g. if *A* had given money to *B* as a dowry because *B* was going to marry his daughter, and the marriage in fact never took place. The word used for bringing an action of this sort was *condicere*,[6] and hence *condictio* may be said to be an action alleging a civil law debt, but not mentioning any cause of action.[7] In this sense it is opposed, not only to praetorian actions, but

---

[1] Lenel, *E.P.* 232. Perhaps a third, with a slave instead of the hundred bushels of corn, served as a model for claims of a "species" as opposed to those of a "genus"; Lenel, *E.P.* 240.   [2] *Supra*, 194, n. 5.

[3] *S.p. Nm. Nm. Ao. Ao. sestertium decem milia dare oportere iudex Nm. Nm. Ao. Ao. sestertium decem milia c.s.n.p.a.* and *S.p. Nm. Nm. Ao. Ao. tritici Africi optimi modios centum dare oportere quanti ea res est tantam pecuniam Nm. Nm. Ao. Ao. c.s.n.p.a.* Though the *intentio* is *certa* in both cases the *condemnatio* of the second form is *incerta* because the judge has to arrive at a money value of the corn for himself.

[4] Or where money was owing under a literal contract.

[5] Cf. *infra*, 294.

[6] Thus Gaius (III.91), in explaining the possibility of claiming return of *indebitum*, says *proinde ei condici potest* "*si paret eum dare oportere*" *ac si mutuum accepisset.* The word is used presumably because actions with such *formulae* took the place of the old *legis actio per condictionem.*

[7] Originally only claims for a *certum* could be made in this way. For the *condictio incerti v.* Buckland, 683; Lenel, *E.P.* 156–158.

also to civil law actions with a *demonstratio*, whether "strict" (e.g. *actio ex stipulatu*) or *bonae fidei*.[1,2,3]

E. TRIAL AND EXECUTION. The formulary system appears to have brought with it no important change in the proceedings *apud iudicem*. All we can say with any certainty is that the brief statement of the case with which the trial had previously opened[4] had now become unnecessary, as the *formula* itself was sufficient to inform the judge what the case was about.[5] Judgment too was delivered as before.[6] We do however find great changes when we come to execution, the most important innovation being the introduction of execution against the property of the judgment debtor. Not that execution against the person was abolished; it remained, on the contrary, normal throughout the classical period,[7] and common even in the late empire, but already in the last century of the republic it was no longer the only possibility.[8] Apart from this change the most

---

[1] We cannot say that this usage was at all strict in the classical period, for the following reasons: (i) the name for the action claiming *certa pecunia* was *actio certae creditae pecuniae*, not *condictio* (Lenel, *E.P.* 234); (ii) Gaius says (IV. 5) that actions *in personam* with an *intentio* referring to *dari fieri oportere* are called *condictiones*, and again (IV. 18) that a *condictio* is an action *in personam* with an *intentio* claiming *dari oportere*. The definition would include *actio ex stipulatu* (although that has a *demonstratio*) and even the *actio certi ex testamento* although that certainly contained a reference to the cause of action (Lenel, *E.P.* 367). This however is a minor matter of terminology—the important thing is to realise in what cases these particularly simple *formulae* were used.

[2] The difficulties in understanding *condictio* come in part from the close connection here between the substantive law and the law of procedure. If *condictio* is the name of a certain type of action it is also the name under which a very important class of "quasi-contractual" causes of action have always been known to the Roman lawyer. For the very considerable literature *v.* Girard, 648; Rabel, 470; Wenger, 123.

[3] The three categories here given do not by any means exhaust the types of action which are not *b.f.* Actions not *b.f.* include all those *in rem*, all *in factum*, all *condictiones* and a few actions which, though "strict", state the ground on which they are brought.

[4] *Supra*, 186.

[5] If, as is probable (*supra*, 203), a document with an inner and outer writing was used, the inner writing would be opened.

[6] *Supra*, 187.

[7] The *lex Rubria* allows the local magistrates to order *ductio* (XXI. 15), but reserves *missio* for the praetor (XXII. 47).

[8] *Missio in possessionem* followed by *bonorum venditio* certainly existed in 81 B.C., the date of Cicero's *pro Quinctio*, though judgment is not actually mentioned as one of the grounds on which it might be granted (v. 19. 60). Girard (*Manuel*, 1110; *Mél.* I. 91–94) supposes it to be necessarily later than the *lex Aebutia*, because it gives the *bonorum emptor* praetorian actions (cf. *infra*, 225), but not

important reform is that it is no longer permissible to proceed at once to execution after the days of grace; instead we find the curious system that the judgment creditor must first bring another action, this time an action on the judgment—*actio iudicati*. As in the case of every other action, there must be summons and *editio actionis*, but the cause of action is now the judgment itself. In the normal case, however, there will be no *litis contestatio* and no trial before a *iudex*, because it is usually hopeless for the defendant to dispute the judgment. He will generally either pay if he can, or, if he cannot, will admit his liability and then execution will begin. It may, however, happen that he does wish to dispute the matter. He cannot, of course, dispute the judgment on its merits,[1] but he may wish to plead that it is invalid, e.g. for want of jurisdiction or want of form, or that he has already satisfied it. If he does this there will be *litis contestatio* and trial in the ordinary way, but there are two rules which must have effectively discouraged frivolous defences; first that the defence will not be admitted at all unless the defendant furnishes security,[2] and secondly that if he loses the case he will be condemned in double the amount of the original judgment. The result is thus in effect much the same as it was under the system of *manus iniectio iudicati* where no trial could take place unless the defendant found a *vindex*, and condemnation was similarly for double if the defence was unsuccessful.[3]

If the defendant neither pays nor defends[4] the *actio iudicati* then the magistrate issues his authorisation to the plaintiff to take him away into custody (*duci iubet*), that is to say, his position is the same as it would have been under the system of *manus iniectio* after the abolition of the creditor's right to kill or sell his debtor.[5]

much later, as P. Rutilius (the inventor of the appropriate *formula, v.* Gai. IV. 35) appears to have been praetor at the latest in 118 B.C. The procedure is generally believed to have been modelled on that used previously by the magistrates to exact debts due to the state (Girard, *Manuel, loc. cit.*). It appears to have been used first in private matters where the debtor made personal execution impossible by remaining in hiding—*qui fraudationis causa latitabit; v.* Lenel, *E.P.* 415.

[1] Appeal is an innovation of the empire; *v. infra,* 406.

[2] Gai. IV. 102. This must no doubt sometimes have been a hardship to poor and friendless persons who really had an honest defence.

[3] *Supra,* 190.

[4] The possibilities are payment, defence, admission of liability (*confessio*) and refusal to defend, i.e. failure to concur in the steps necessary for *litis contestatio.* In either of the last two cases the praetor could order *ductio*, for he could always do this on confession or failure to defend in an action for *certa pecunia* (Lenel, *E.P.* 410), and an action on a judgment is necessarily for *certa pecunia.*

[5] *Supra,* 190.

But the magistrate may also now authorise execution against the goods of the debtor. In this case he issues a decree putting the judgment creditor in possession of all the debtor's property (*missio in bona*); the creditor then advertises the seizure in order to give other creditors the chance to come in and claim also; at the end of thirty days the creditors meet and elect a *magister* from among their number who is to proceed to the sale. This *magister*, after the lapse of a further period of days, during which he prepares a list of the property and of the debts, then sells the goods to the highest bidder (*bonorum venditio*),[1] that is to say to the person offering the creditors the highest percentage on their debts. If, for instance, the buyer offers a quarter (5s. in the £ as we should say), then he is given a right to the debtor's assets,[2] in return for which he has to pay each creditor a quarter of what the debtor owed that creditor.

The process, it will be seen, is in effect bankruptcy; at this period in Roman law a creditor must make his debtor bankrupt in order to enforce the payment of the smallest sum that the debtor will not pay voluntarily; he cannot just take one piece of property sufficiently valuable to satisfy his debt and sell that. The method is clumsy, for it often means imposing much greater hardship on the debtor than is necessary to secure the creditor his rights. But from the ancient point of view there was no objection to this; the object was not that the state should do for the creditor what the debtor would not do, but that the state should help the creditor to put pressure on the debtor and punish him if he did not pay his debts, a result normally accomplished by locking him up, but one which could also be achieved by taking away all his property; that the creditor was also paid was a secondary, not a primary, consideration.

The relationship between the two forms of execution is to some extent doubtful. We do not know whether *missio in bona* always accompanied the authorisation to imprison the debtor, or whether personal execution was possible without execution against the goods; normally at any rate the two would go together. It seems clear however that the creditor could waive his right to imprison and rely on *missio* alone.[3] In any case there existed, probably only from the time of Augustus[4] how-

---

[1] Gai. III. 77–79.

[2] He has an interdict to recover property in anyone else's possession (Gai. IV. 145) and can bring a "Rutilian" action against the judgment debtor's debtors, in which the *intentio* will contain the judgment debtor's name, the *condemnatio* his own (Gai. IV. 35). Cf. *supra*, 212, n. 2.   [3] Wenger, 223.

[4] It is referred to as *cessio e lege Iulia* (e.g. Gai. III. 78), i.e. probably Augustus' law on procedure of 17 B.C., though Mommsen (*Röm. Gesch.* III. 536) refers it to Caesar; cf. also Costa (*Cicerone Giureconsulto*, II. 48), who is doubtful.

ever, a method by which the debtor could in many cases escape execution
against his person. This was by making a voluntary surrender of his
property (*cessio bonorum*) to his creditor or creditors. This surrender took
the place of the forcible putting in possession by the magistrate and led
similarly to a sale of the property, but it had great advantages for the
debtor. He escaped the *infamia* which resulted from an enforced sale and
he remained for ever free from danger of imprisonment for his debt.[1]
Not all persons however could avail themselves of this means of escape;
it was closed probably not only to those whose insolvency was due to
their own fault, but also to those who had no property worth the mention
to hand over to their creditors.[2]

F. Origin of the Formulary System; date and effect of
the *lex Aebutia*. According to Gaius[3] the abolition of *legis actiones* and
substitution of the formulary system was the result of a certain *lex Aebutia*
and two *leges Iuliae*. This brief statement leaves us in doubt as to a
number of important questions. We do not know whence came the idea
of the new procedure, the date of the *lex Aebutia* (though that of the *leges
Iuliae* is relatively certain),[4] or what the relationship was between the

---

[1] If the creditors were not paid in full and the debtor afterwards acquired
enough property to make it worth while (J. 4. 6. 40; D. 42. 3. 4; 6; 7), the
creditors might bring another action against him and proceed to another sale,
but in such action he had the so-called *beneficium competentiae*, i.e. in the
condemnatio of the *formula* was a clause limiting the condemnation to *id quod
facere potest*, i.e. what the defendant had. He could therefore always pay the
amount of the judgment and need not suffer personal execution. The debtor
whose goods had been forcibly taken had similarly the *beneficium competentiae*,
but only for a year, whereas the man who had made *cessio* had it for ever (Lenel,
E.P. 432). In the law of Justinian's day the *beneficium* meant that the debtor
was allowed to retain the necessaries of life; Buckland, 694; cf. Wenger, 229.

[2] Woess, *Z.S.S.* XLIII. 485–529. There is very little direct evidence for either
of these exceptions but there certainly must have been exceptions, for otherwise
all insolvent debtors would have made *cessio*, and yet we know that personal
execution survived.

[3] IV. 30: *Per legem Aebutiam et duas Iulias sublatae sunt istae legis actiones,
effectumque est ut per concepta verba, id est per formulas, litigemus.* Cf. Gell. XVI.
10. 8: *sed enim...omnisque illa duodecim tabularum antiquitas, nisi in legis actionibus centumviralium causarum, lege Aebutia lata, consopita sit....*

[4] They were almost certainly part of the procedural legislation of Augustus.
There is some difficulty about the number of laws on this subject. Wlassak,
Prozessgesetze, I. 191 *sqq.*, holds that there were three in all, one dealing with
iudicia publica and two with *iudicia privata*, of which one concerned Rome itself
and the other *municipia*. Almost the only reason for believing that there were two
concerning *iudicia privata* is the statement of Gaius (n. 3, *supra*), and Girard

statutes. All that is clear is that the *lex Aebutia* cannot have abolished *legis actiones* altogether, for if it had there would have been nothing left for the *leges Iuliae* to do.

That the formulary system was a new invention introduced suddenly by statute is unlikely; such changes are seldom made at one stroke,[1] and there is indeed some evidence that a form of procedure, apparently copied from the Roman *formula*, was in use for settling disputes between Greek cities under the authority of the Roman senate at a time when the *lex Aebutia* had almost certainly not yet been passed.[2] The most probable conjecture is that the system arose in courts where the Roman magistrate exercised jurisdiction over foreigners and his *imperium* was consequently untrammelled by any *lex*, either therefore in that of the *praetor peregrinus* at Rome or in those of the governors of the provinces. In dealing with foreigners a *litis contestatio* in Roman form would have been impossible, and on the other hand it was necessary that the *recuperatores* should be informed in some way of the question they were to decide; the *formula* then very probably grew up out of their instructions.[3]

This much is very generally agreed, though proof is lacking; the great cleavage of opinion concerns the question whether the use of the new procedure between citizens and in Rome itself was made possible only by the passing of the *lex Aebutia* or had existed before, and this question

(*Manuel*, 1059; *Z.S.S.* XXXIV. 341 *sqq.*) prefers to explain this by supposing that the jurists cited the two laws dealing with *publica* and *privata iudicia* as if they were a single enactment, although here, of course, only private (i.e. civil) jurisdiction was in question. The date of the law *iudiciorum publicorum* is given by Girard (*Z.S.S.* XXXIV. 356) as 17 B.C., that of the law *iudiciorum privatorum* as 17 or 16 B.C.

[1] The great reform of English procedure by the Judicature Act of 1873 was preceded by piecemeal legislation, the most important of which was included in the Common Law Procedure Acts of 1852–1860.

[2] Partsch, *Die Schriftformel im römischen Provinzialprozesse* (1905), especially 51, where one such case is shown to have been tried not long after 190 B.C.

[3] There is some evidence that the practice may have been derived from a pre-Roman system in use in some of the provinces. We know that both in Sicily (*v.* Cic. *in Verr.* II. 2. 15, 37; 17, 42) and in Egypt (Mitteis, *Chrest.* No. 50) there was a system by which notice of action had to be registered by the plaintiff with the court. It may be that these notices, which would contain some account of the case, served as a basis for the instructions to the jurymen; *v.* Girard, 1034 and 1056, and Fliniaux, *N.R.H.* XXXIII (1909), 535–549. V. however also Mitteis, *Z.S.S.* XXIX. 470, where he withdraws his opinion that *dicam scribere* was necessarily an extra-judicial act. For the view that the formulary system was first used where peregrines were concerned *v.* Wlassak, *Prozessgesetze*, I. 165; II. 301–302; Mitteis, *R.P.R.* 50; Jobbé-Duval, *Mél. Cornil*, I (1926), 527.

is not a mere minor matter of procedural history. It must, on the contrary, considerably affect our general view of legal development during the republic, for it was the formulary system which made much of that development possible, and if we suppose that its use between citizens was unknown until the time of the *lex Aebutia* some advances have to be put at a surprisingly late date.

None the less Girard has, in a number of works, elaborately supported the view that until the passing of the *lex Aebutia* the only system available for suits between citizens was that of the *legis actiones*, and that the great powers of the magistrate, in particular that of refusing actions (*denegatio actionis*), did not exist until that time.[1] His main arguments may perhaps be summarised as follows. Gaius[2] says definitely that it was as a result of the *lex Aebutia* and the *leges Iuliae* that *formulae* came to be used by "us" (i.e. citizens), and this statement is confirmed in the only other passage, that from Gellius,[3] which throws any direct light on the matter. Gaius also says[4] that the *legis actiones* were so called either because they were introduced by *leges* or because they had to be fitted exactly to the words of *leges*, and that "at that time the edicts of the praetor, by which a number of actions were introduced, were not yet in use". In another passage[5] we are told that "in those times (i.e. of the *legis actiones*) *exceptiones* were not used at all as they are now", and the granting of *exceptiones* is of course, like the granting of the *formula* itself, a matter on which the last word rests with the magistrate. The change in the magistrate's position is thus shown to be due to the *lex Aebutia*; before then he was something of an automaton; if a citizen used the proper words for beginning a *legis actio* and another made the proper reply, the praetor had to repeat the words laid down for him, whatever he thought about the rights and wrongs of the matter, just as a returning officer must accept the candidature presented in proper form of a person whose election to Parliament he would regard as a misfortune to his country.[6] That this was in fact still the position in the middle of the second century B.C. is, in Girard's opinion, confirmed by the number of *leges imperfectae* and *minus quam perfectae* passed at about that time.[7] The *lex Furia testamentaria*[8] for instance, which fixed a maximum value for legacies,

---

[1] *Manuel*, 1057; Z.S.S. xiv. 11–54 (= N.R.H. xxi (1897), 249–294) and xxix. 113–169 (both reprinted *Mél.* i. 67–174); v. also *Org. Jud.* i. 217.

[2] iv. 30.   [3] *Supra*, 222, n. 3.   [4] iv. 11.

[5] iv. 108.   [6] *Mél.* i. 145.

[7] For discussion of these *leges*, v. Mitteis, R.P.R. 24, n. 4; 247; Lenel, Z.S.S. xxx. 335; Buckland, *Main Institutions*, 3.

[8] *Supra*, 85.

gave the heir an action for recovery against a legatee who had received a legacy of a greater value; it would have been simpler to have directed the magistrate to refuse the action which the legatee had to bring against the heir in the first instance to claim his legacy, and the only reason why this was not done was, according to Girard, that the magistrate had not yet the power of refusing actions at all. The facts furthermore, in so far as we know them, are said to bear out this train of argument. Until nearly 125 B.C. there is no example of *denegatio actionis*, of praetorian actions or in general of the new procedure. Then "we seem to pass from one geological stratum to another".[1] In 127 or 126 we have evidence of an argument in court which clearly implies the right of the praetor to refuse an action;[2] 118 was almost certainly the date of the praetorship of P. Rutilius, the inventor of the *formula* used by the *bonorum emptor*;[3] and in 118 at latest we have the first inscription testifying to the new procedure in the *lex Latina tabulae Bantinae*.[4]

The details of this elaborate argument are, as will be seen from the notes, open to some criticism, but it is the central position, the view that the magistrate was powerless to influence the course of procedure right

[1] *Mél.* I. 89.

[2] Cic. *de Orat.* I. 36. 166. Ridicule is here poured on two orators on account of their ignorance of law. The one arguing for the plaintiff insisted that an action should be granted, the effect of which would have been, as the amount claimed was greater than that allowed by the XII Tables, that the *iudex* would have had to dismiss the case for *plus petitio*; his opponent failed to see that this would be greatly to his client's advantage and strenuously argued against the admission of the action. (The story has not quite lost its moral to-day; it is not always wise to try to have an opponent's faulty pleading struck out.) But this is not really the first example of *denegatio actionis* that we have; according to Livy XLI. 9 a senatus-consult was passed in 177 B.C. which forbade the magistrates to permit manumissions unless the manumitter swore that the act was not undertaken for the purpose of circumventing the laws against the admission of *socii* and Latins to the citizenship (cf. *supra*, 60). As manumission took the form of a collusive *vindicatio in libertatem*, this means that the magistrate would have to refuse the action if the oath were not taken. Girard replies (*Mél.* I. 141) that for the magistrate to do this on the authority of the senate is quite a different thing from his doing it on his own initiative, but it is not easy to see how even the senate's authorisation could enable a magistrate to do something which lay outside the bounds of his *imperium*; cf. Buckland, 625. *V.* also Mitteis, *R.P.R.* 40; Wlassak, *Z.S.S.* XXVIII. 91.

[3] But it seems fairly clear that there must have been magisterial actions before. In D. 19. 1. 38. 1 an opinion of Sextus Aelius on an *arbitrium* concerning sale is quoted (*si per emptorem steterit quominus ei mancipium traderetur per arbitrium indemnitatem posse servari*). This can only refer to something outside the *legis actio* system—either the *b.f.* action itself or a predecessor; Mitteis, *R.P.R.* 48. *V.* however Girard, *Mél.* I. 79 and 155.　　　　[4] Lines 9–10 (Bruns, I. 50).

up to the passing of the *lex Aebutia*, which is the most vulnerable part of Girard's theory. Can we conceive that, if this had been the state of affairs, if a whole people had been accustomed to regard its magistrates as mere automata to be put in motion by the speaking of certain set words, they should then have accepted a law which would give to these same functionaries the power to allow or refuse actions as they thought fit, and, by their power over the drafting of the new *formulae*, to create at their will entirely new rules of law?[1] Girard seems to regard this increase in the magistrate's importance as to a large extent the fortuitous result of the power now given to him to direct whether the trial should be by *legis actio* or by *formula*, but, on his own showing, the development of praetorian law must have been very rapid from the moment of the change, so that it can hardly have been unforeseen or unintentional.

An even more powerful, if indirect, argument against Girard lies in the impossibility of understanding the growth of Roman law and the relationship between *ius civile* and *ius honorarium* without supposing that magisterial actions (even between citizens) existed in pre-Aebutian times. If we accept Girard's theory we have to suppose that the consensual contracts—even sale and hire—did not become actionable until 125 B.C. or thereabouts, a supposition which appears quite incompatible with the stage of civilisation to which Rome had attained well before that date. If, on the other hand, we follow Mitteis' views the development becomes intelligible.[2] Originally there was presumably a time when the inelastic system of *legis actiones* sufficed for a primitive community, but from a very early period there must have been also some form of procedure depending on the magistrate alone and free from the formalities of *litis contestatio* for dealing with persons who were not citizens, very probably for clients, certainly for foreigners. It is generally agreed that in this type of procedure the judge—or rather the *recuperatores*—had to consider the rules of the growing *ius gentium*, in particular the formless contracts. Does it not follow, seeing that *ius gentium* is valid for all peoples (including Romans) that, at any rate at the request of the parties, the *praetor urbanus* might permit similar procedure to be used between citizens? And as this course came to be more commonly taken would it not also probably happen that the magistrate would, where necessary, compel an unwilling party to submit to it? Particularly important in this connection

---

[1] Lenel, *Z.S.S.* xxx. 333. The whole article ("Der Prätor in der legis actio", 329–354) is of great importance for the questions here discussed; cf. Huschke, *Analecta Literaria* (1826), 216.

[2] *R.P.R.* 42.

is Mitteis' view of the relationship between *ius civile* and *ius honorarium*. He points out that for a number of *bonae fidei iudicia* (sale, hire, *mandatum* and *societas*) the praetor's *album* never contained an edict promising the action, but only a pattern *formula*, whereas for others (e.g. *depositum*, *commodatum*, *negotiorum gestio*) there was both an edict and a *formula*. How, without any indication from the praetor, was a judge confronted with one of these *formulae* (in the case, for instance, of a formless sale) to assume a civil law duty (*dare facere oportere*) if nothing had gone before to make such an assumption a natural one? Mitteis explains this by supposing that there had been so long a tradition of praetorian protection in these cases (probably by *actio in factum*) that a *iudex*, given the ordinary *formula* of *b.f.* actions, would have no difficulty in finding e.g. that the buyer of goods by an informal contract "ought in good faith" to pay the price thereof. On Mitteis' view the spheres of *ius civile* and *ius honorarium* were not, in earlier times, so strictly delimited as they subsequently became; there was, on the contrary, a constant process of "reception"[1] by the civil law of principles which had first been worked out in purely magisterial procedure, and it is this reception which accounts for the absence of any edict in the case, for instance, of obligations resting on consensual contracts; these had already passed into the civil law before it became usual to embody all praetorian practice in the edict.

One obvious difficulty presents itself on this view. If there existed magisterial actions with *formulae* before the *lex Aebutia*, what was the point of passing that law and what were its effects? Mitteis' answer is[2] that it first raised the status of formulary trials to that of *iudicia legitima*, whereas before they had only been *iudicia imperio continentia*, in other words, recognised them as fully Roman trials with the various technical superiorities of such trials over those of lesser status.[3]

---

[1] This reception continued in classical times, and the clearest instance of it is to be found in the double *formulae*—*in ius* and *in factum*—which exist in the case of certain contractual obligations (e.g. *commodatum* and *depositum*, v. Gai. IV. 47). Of these the *formula in factum* is known to be the earlier. The reason is that it was only after the *formula in factum* had been in use for some time that the praetor could give one *in ius* (in the ordinary *b.f.* form) and assume that a *iudex* would know the ordinary legal consequences of the contract.

[2] *R.P.R.* 52. Mitteis is here following the theory put forward by Wlassak, *Prozessgesetze, v.* especially I. 166; cf. also Sohm, 668.

[3] For the distinction and its consequences v. Gai. IV. 103–109. To be *legitimum* a trial must be in Rome, or within the first milestone, all parties must be Romans and there must be only a single judge; if any one of these conditions is lacking the trial is merely "dependent on the *imperium*", and can only continue as long as the magistrate who granted the action in the first place remains in office.

As to the actual date of the law, theories again vary considerably. Girard holds that it must be later than 149 B.C., in which year the *lex Calpurnia repetundarum* allowed provincials who had suffered from the extortion of Roman governors to bring an action for recovery by *legis actio per sacramentum*; had any other procedure been available this, Girard thinks, would not have been chosen.[1] On the other hand there is evidence of the new state of things in 127 or 126, so that Girard dates the law between 149 and 127 or 126. If however we once give up Girard's assumption that *denegatio actionis* and other magisterial powers are necessarily post-Aebutian it is impossible to fix the date in this way. Mitteis himself does not even accept the argument from the *lex Calpurnia*. All he regards as certain is that the *tripertita* of Sextus Aelius (consul 198)[2] presuppose the *legis actiones* as the only system in use for *iudicia legitima*, and that consequently the *lex Aebutia* must be later than the time of their publication, probably indeed a good deal later, since the law of the late republic and early empire is still permeated by a formalist spirit which it would hardly have retained if the change in procedure had come at the beginning of the second century B.C. Nor can we suppose that the period between the *lex Aebutia* and the final victory of the formulary system brought about by the *leges Iuliae* was a very long one. Mitteis' arguments thus come, so far as the date is concerned, to much the same result as Girard's, though by a very different route.[3]

The question of the relationship between the *lex Aebutia* and the *leges Iuliae* is, on the whole, less difficult. It is quite clear that in the time of Cicero (i.e. before the *leges Iuliae*) both *legis actiones* and *formulae* were in use, for there are references in his works to all the *legis actiones* (except probably that *per condictionem*)[4] and several examples of *formulae*, both *in rem* and *in personam*, as well as a general statement that there were *formulae* "for all matters".[5] After the *leges Iuliae* we hear nothing of *legis actiones* except in the cases in which Gaius tells us that the old

[1] Mitteis (*R.P.R.* 52, n. 30) replies that *formulae* were never used in trials before a permanent court such as that set up by the *lex Calpurnia* (*v. infra*, 325).

[2] Cf. *supra*, 89.

[3] Wlassak himself is even less definite. He thinks that all we can say for certain is that the law is later than Sextus Aelius and was already in force in Cicero's time, the most reliable proof of its existence being found in the *pro Flacco*, XXI. 50 (59 B.C.), though it was probably then already not recent; *v.* *Z.S.S.* XXVIII. 110, n. 2.

[4] The references are collected by Jobbé-Duval, "La legis actio avec formule à l'époque de Cicéron", *Mél. Cornil*, I (1926), 517–590 at 542 *sqq.*

[5] *Pro Roscio Com.* VIII. 24.

procedure survived.[1] It is therefore most widely held that what the *lex Aebutia* did was to make the *formula* an alternative to the *legis actio*, at the choice of the parties,[2] while the *leges Iuliae* did away with the old procedure altogether.[3]

G. PRAETORIAN REMEDIES OTHER THAN ACTIONS. The history of procedure during the republic must not be left without some mention of those praetorian remedies which lie outside the system of actions, but contributed hardly less than the actions and *formulae* to the growth of the *ius honorarium*. The activity of the magistrate in the ordinary procedure leading to an action is a result of that part of his function known as *iurisdictio*; it is true that this is ultimately dependent on his *imperium*, as indeed the duty of the *iudex* to try the issue is imposed upon him by a command from the magistrate,[4] but here the *imperium* is in the background; more immediately obvious are the activities of the parties, and

[1] IV. 31. The only real exception was that when a case was to go before the centumviral court (*supra*, 199) the formalities of the *legis actio per sacramentum* were first gone through before the *praetor urbanus* or *peregrinus*. Gaius further mentions the practically unimportant case of *damnum infectum*, where in practice a praetorian procedure by means of stipulation had superseded the theoretically possible *legis actio*. It also remained true that where collusive actions were used for creating or transferring rights (*manumissio vindicta*, *cessio in iure*) the form was always that of the *legis actio*. The explanation of the exceptions is that *litis contestatio* by agreement on a formula is intimately bound up with the appointment of the single *iudex*; where this is not needed, either because, as in *in iure cessio*, there is no question to try, or in the case of centumviral matters because the court is already constituted, then the only procedure possible is the old one; *v.* Sohm, 670.

[2] With the magistrate, now admittedly armed with full powers, to settle the matter in case of disagreement.

[3] This view, put forward by Wlassak, *Prozessgesetze* (*v.* especially I. 103 *sqq.*), has been very generally accepted—e.g. by Girard, *Mél.* I. 67; *Manuel*, 1056; Mitteis, *R.P.R.* 52, n. 30 (*v.* also Sohm, 669); Lenel, 337; Wenger, 20; Declareuil, *Rome the Lawgiver*, 71. Cuq, however, holds that the *lex Aebutia* abolished the *legis actio per condictionem* only and substituted the use of a *formula*. As Girard points out (1056, n. 2) this would mean that the most recently introduced and least cumbersome of the *legis actiones* was abolished first. Jobbé-Duval ("La legis actio avec formule à l'époque de Cicéron", *Mél. Cornil*, I (1926), 517–590) has again put forward the view expressed by him, *N.R.H.* XXIX (1905), 16. I, that what the *lex Aebutia* did was to add a *formula* to the *legis actiones*, i.e. after the accomplishment of the *legis actio* the praetor gave his instructions to the judge in a *formula*. The evidence for this view appears to be slight, *v.* Girard, 1056, and Wlassak, *Prozessgesetze*, I. 62 *sqq.*, where he argues against a somewhat similar view of Bekker's.

[4] *Supra*, 203.

in the process by which they reach the necessary agreement the magistrate acts rather as a helper than as one armed with powers of command. With the remedies we have now to discuss, the position is different; here we have to deal with orders issued by the praetor as a holder of *imperium*[1] and independent of any agreement between the parties such as is needed for the joinder of issue in an action. These orders are however issued for the purpose of the administration of justice; the rules which the praetor adopts with respect to their issue, or at least some indications of them, appear in the edict, and, as we shall see, the praetor generally avoids using direct means of enforcing obedience, so that any dispute concerning them will very often lead to an action which has to be tried in the ordinary way.

The remedies which we have to consider under this head are of four kinds: (i) Praetorian stipulations, (ii) *Missiones in possessionem*, (iii) *In integrum restitutiones*, (iv) Interdicts.[2]

---

[1] Hence they are not as a rule available in the courts of the municipal magistrates. In the case of *damnum infectum* the praetor delegates the power of exacting the stipulation and granting the first *missio* (*infra*, 233) but reserves the more drastic second *missio* for himself; D. 39. 2. 1; 4. 3.

[2] That all four types of remedy existed before the end of the republic is clear, but otherwise their history raises many difficult questions, the answers to which depend in part on the view taken of the magistrate's powers before the *lex Aebutia*. Some interdicts, it is agreed, must have existed before that law, for there is a clear reference to the interdict *utrubi* in Plautus' *Stichus* (acted 200 B.C.), 5. 4. 14, and about 190 B.C. we find a form of words obviously based on that of the interdict *uti possidetis* in use for the settlement of a dispute between two Greek cities (Partsch, *Schriftformel*, 28, 51; cf. *supra*, 223). From the latter example it would also seem likely that the procedure was by this time out of the stage in which the magistrate settled everything himself (*infra*, 237), for the decision is referred to the assembly of a third city just as in a private matter it is referred to a judge. That *missiones* were known to Q. Mucius Scaevola (consul 95 B.C.) is clear from D. 41. 2. 3. 23 and, since he is there quoted as making a distinction between different kinds, they can hardly have been quite new in his time. A stipulation *damni infecti* is reported (Pliny, *H.N.* xxxvi. 2 (2)) to have been exacted as early as 123 B.C. (cf. Karlowa, II. 1241), and the rather archaic form given in D. 46. 8. 18 also points to an early date (Lenel, *E.P.* 552, n. 1). With *restitutiones* the question is more difficult. Girard, of course, holds (*Manuel*, 1128; *Organisation Judiciaire*, I. 206) that they must be later than the *lex Aebutia*, before which, in his view, it would have been impossible for the magistrate to refuse an action on a cause valid at civil law, or to grant an *actio rescissoria* (cf. *infra*, 234, and Karlowa, II. 1104). He even holds that where *restitutio* co-exists with an action and an exception, as in the case of *metus*, *dolus* and minority, the *restitutio* is the last to appear (*Manuel*, 446, n. 4); for the contrary view in case of *metus*, Karlowa, II. 1064–1065. However that may be, *restitutio* for *metus* certainly existed in 59 B.C. (Cic. *pro Flacco*, xxi. 49), and other cases are pretty certainly

(i) *Praetorian stipulations*. In some cases the praetor[1] supplements what he considers to be the deficiencies of the civil law by ordering one party to make a promise to the other, such promise being in the form of a stipulation, and giving to the promisee a right, or at least a remedy, which he would not otherwise have. Thus if *A*'s house is in a dangerous condition and likely to fall and damage *B*'s land, *B* can insist on *A*'s promising to pay damages for any harm that may be done (*cautio damni infecti*—i.e. damage threatened—"not done").[2] If without such promise having been exacted the house fell and did damage, *B* would have no claim against *A* unless he could show that *A* had been guilty of some wilful or negligent act such as would make him liable under the *lex Aquilia*, and this would, of course, not always be the case. Again, suppose that *A* has been left the ownership and *B* the usufruct (life-interest) in an estate, *A* must, it is true, already at civil law, refrain from actively injuring the property, as for instance by cutting down all the timber; but he is, at civil law, under no obligation to do any positive acts to keep it in repair; also at civil law he (or his heir) is under no active obligation to hand over the estate to the owner on the cessation of the usufruct, though of course he has no right to remain on the land. The praetor, on the other hand, will insist that the usufructuary makes a promise to the owner that he will perform active duties, will look after the property as a careful man should and return it when the usufruct is at an end (*cautio usufructuaria*).[3,4]

older. The rubric of the edict promising *restitutio* on account of absence (*Ex quibus causis maiores* XXV *annis in integrum restituuntur*) points to a time when this was the only reason for which persons above the age of twenty-five could get *restitutio*, and this is indeed probably the earliest case, except that of minors, which very probably goes back to a date not long after the *lex Plaetoria* (*infra*, 247); cf. Karlowa, II. 1082.

[1] The aediles, although not invested with *imperium*, also used their powers of coercion to insist on the making of stipulations with relation to matters within their jurisdiction. These stipulations were of great importance in the history of sale; *v. infra*, 303.

[2] That there was a liability at civil law is clear from Gaius' statement (IV. 31; cf. *supra*, 229, n. 1) that procedure by *legis actio* was possible. What the *legis actio* was we do not know, but it is suggested that it may have been *pignoris capio*; *v.* Buckland, 619; Karlowa, II. 481. In any case the praetorian law here completely superseded the civil.

[3] *Usurum se boni viri arbitratu et, cum usus fructus ad eum pertinere desinet, restituturum quod inde exstabit*; D. 7. 9. 1. pr.

[4] Sometimes a mere promise was enough, sometimes there had to be security as well, e.g. in the case of *damnum infectum* if the occupier was not the owner; D. 39. 2. 7. pr.; 13. 1.

The methods by which the praetor enforces these stipulations are not always the same. In the case of usufruct the praetor would simply refuse the usufructuary failing to make the promise the action for claiming the estate from the owner.[1] In the case of *damnum infectum*, if the stipulation was refused, the praetor made an order entitling the person whose land was threatened to enter into possession of the dangerous building (*missio in possessionem*),[2] and if opposition was offered to the entry and the damage was done, there was an *actio ficticia*, i.e. one in which the judge was told to condemn for as much as would have been payable had the stipulation been made.[3] Direct methods of constraint are not evidenced in classical times, though they may have been used.[4]

Whatever the method used it is clear that the praetor's insistence on the making of the stipulation in fact altered and amplified the law, and the rules of this part of the *ius honorarium* were, like the rest of it, to be discovered from the edict. An appendix gave the forms to be used in each case, and scattered among the earlier provisions were to be found individual edicts concerning their application. Whether in any particular case a stipulation had, according to these rules, to be made, was a question which the praetor decided himself, if necessary after hearing argument; there is no place here for reference by means of *formula* to a *iudex*.[5]

(ii) *Missiones in possessionem. Missio* is an authorisation by the praetor to enter into possession, either of a particular thing (as with *damnum infectum*), or of the whole of a person's property (as in the case of execution).[6] Sometimes it merely entitled the person authorised to enter and hold the property concurrently with the person to whom it belonged, sometimes it gave full possessory rights, with authority to eject the owner and eventually become owner by usucapion. The primary object of such *missiones* was to put pressure on the person to whom the goods belonged, as we have seen in the case of the person who failed to "defend himself properly",[7] or failed to carry out a judgment, but, as we have also seen,

---

[1] D. 7. 1. 13. pr. If the usufructuary were in possession of the thing the owner could claim it (*vindicatio*) and if the usufructuary pleaded his usufruct in an *exceptio* the owner would have a *replicatio* alleging that the stipulation had not been made; D. 7. 9. 7. pr.

[2] *Infra*, 233. [3] Lenel, *E.P.* 372.

[4] Wenger, 234. *Multae* and *pignora* are mentioned J. 1. 24. 3, but this passage is probably not classical.

[5] For technical distinctions between different classes of stipulations *v.* Buckland, 437 and 728.

[6] *Supra*, 221. In some cases it might be a *hereditas*, not a single thing nor yet the whole of a person's property.

[7] *Supra*, 181.

it might have the further purpose of enabling the creditor to get paid by having the goods sold if the pressure proved ineffective. It was also used where there was no one on whom pressure could be put, as where the creditors of a deceased person who leaves no heir are put in possession of his property and allowed to proceed to *bonorum venditio*.[1] Or again it might be a purely provisional measure, as where the mother of an unborn child is put in possession of the property which the child will inherit if it is born alive, but which will go to someone else if it is not.[2] The rules differ very considerably in the different cases, but again we can take *dammum infectum* as an example. If the stipulation ordered by the praetor were refused, there was first a *missio in rem* which entitled the complainant to enter into the dangerous building, but not to eject the owner. If this proved of no avail a second decree would issue giving full possession,[3] which, if the other party remained obdurate, would ripen into ownership after the time for usucapion had elapsed.[4] Again here, as with stipulations, the praetor did not as a rule use direct force if his commands were disobeyed. In the particular case of *dammum infectum*, if opposition was offered to the entry of the person authorised to take possession there was, as we have seen,[5] a fictitious action, at which it was assumed that the desired stipulation had been made.[6] In other cases other means were used. Thus where the *missio* was the result of a judgment, and in connected cases,[7] there was an action for damages against anyone who prevented the persons authorised from taking possession of anything forming part of the estate.[8] When *bonorum venditio* had taken place, the *emptor* had an interdict to enable him to recover anything belonging to the estate which was not voluntarily surrendered to him.[9] An action of course involves reference to a *iudex*, and so, as we shall see, does an interdict, so that, where opposition was offered to the magistrate's order, there would in fact usually be a trial *apud iudicem* before the matter was decided. The importance of *missiones* can hardly be exaggerated; on them depended, in the last resort, the working of a system in which no trial could take place without the concurrence of the defendant, and no

[1] Gai. III. 79.
[2] D. 37. 9; Lenel, *E.P.* 347. It was only available where the child would be a *suus heres*.
[3] D. 39. 2. 7. pr.   [4] D. 39. 2. 5. pr.; 12.
[5] *Supra*, 232.
[6] There was also an interdict forbidding interference with the entry of one authorised to take possession; Lenel, *E.P.* 469.
[7] I.e. those called *rei servandae causa*; *v.* Buckland, 724.
[8] Lenel, *E.P.* 424.   [9] Gai. IV. 145.

judgment be executed except by the sale of the whole of the judgment debtor's estate.

(iii) *In integrum restitutiones.* In some cases the praetor's way of dealing with the possibility that general rules of law may have inequitable results is to annul the result which he considers inequitable by restoring the party injured to his original position (*in integrum*). Thus if a man has been prevented by absence abroad in the public service from taking steps to interrupt another's possession of his land, with the result that that other has been able to complete usucapion, the praetor will restore him to his original position by decreeing that the usucapion is to be held not to have taken place; or if a man has been induced by threats (*metus*) to make a mancipation of his property, the praetor may decree that the conveyance is to be held not to have taken place. Particularly important too is the rule that a minor (i.e. one under twenty-five years of age) may get *in integrum restitutio* if his inexperience has led him to enter into a transaction which turns out to be disadvantageous, even though he cannot show that the other party actually took advantage of his youth.[1] The praetor does not, of course, act arbitrarily in granting this relief, and like his other remedies it is provided for by clauses in the edict. As, however, it is the praetor himself who decides in each case whether *restitutio* is to be granted or not, he does, in some of the edicts, leave himself a considerable liberty; that concerning minors, in particular, reads simply: "If a transaction with a person under twenty-five years of age be alleged, I will take such steps as each particular case shall call for".[2]

The actual grant by the praetor is only a necessary preliminary to which effect is given by other proceedings. These consist most commonly of an *actio rescissoria*, i.e. the person benefiting by the *restitutio* is allowed to bring the action which would have been open to him but for the event whose effects have been rescinded by the praetor.[3] Thus, where land has been usucaped owing to absence, the original owner brings a *vindicatio* with the fiction that the usucapion has not taken place, and the *formula* reads something like this: "If the land in question had not been usucaped by Numerius Negidius, then if that land ought, by Quiritarian law, to be the property of Aulus Agerius, etc."[4]

---

[1] Cf. *infra,* 247–248.

[2] *Quod cum minore quam viginti quinque annis natu gestum esse dicetur, uti quaeque res erit, animadvertam*; Lenel, *E.P.* 116.

[3] For other possibilities *v.* Buckland, 723.

[4] The exact form of the fiction is uncertain, *v.* Lenel, *E.P.* 123. For another case of *actio rescissoria* cf. Gai. III. 84.

(iv) *Interdicts*. Literally *interdictum* means a prohibition, but the word came to be used for all praetorian orders of a certain class, whether positive or negative in form.[1] These orders are issued by the praetor, not on his own initiative, but on the application of some person who either considers himself aggrieved or thinks that some public interest is in danger:[2] they are in a stereotyped form which is set out for each sort of case in the edict,[3] and lead, where there is any opposition, to a trial before a *iudex* or *recuperatores*. Suppose, for instance, that *A* has let *B* occupy a farm *precario*, i.e. on condition that *B* returns it at any moment that *A* chooses to ask for it back,[4] and that when *A* does so ask for it, *B* refuses to give it up. *A* goes to the praetor, and the praetor issues an order to *B* in the following form: "What you hold *precario* from *A*, or by your own wilful wrongdoing have ceased so to hold, that you are to return to him".[5] Now this order is carefully framed so as to leave open the question whether *B* really does hold the farm *precario* from *A* or not, and is equivalent to an order "if you hold *precario*...you are to return". Of course if *B* recognises that the praetor's order does apply to him and gives up the farm, the matter is at an end, but if he does not, the question has now to be decided whether, in not returning the farm, *B* has been guilty of disobeying the praetor's order or not. Only if he does so hold *precario* from *A* has he been guilty, and this is what, in effect, the *iudex* will have to decide. Two methods of procedure are possible, one, no doubt the older, *per sponsionem*, and the other *per formulam arbitrariam*.

(a) *Per sponsionem*. The parties by means of stipulations (*sponsiones*) make a sort of bet. *B* promises to pay *A* so-and-so much[6] if he has

---

[1] Gai. IV. 139 says that *decretum* was the proper word when something was ordered to be done, *interdictum* when something was forbidden.

[2] Certain interdicts were *popularia*, i.e. could be brought by anyone whether personally affected or not, e.g. *ne quid in loco publico vel itinere fiat* for the prevention of unauthorised building on public land; *v*. D. 43. 8. 2. 2.

[3] In cases where the form set out did not exactly fit, an *interdictum utile* might be granted; cf. the discussion of *actio utilis, supra*, 213, n. 3.

[4] *Precarium* is distinguished from loan (*commodatum*) by the intentional absence of any contractual relation between the parties; neither has any action against the other arising out of the relationship; *v*. Sohm, 279, n. 13.

[5] *Quod precario ab illo habes aut dolo malo fecisti ut desineres habere, qua de re agitur, id illi restituas*; Lenel, *E.P.* 486.

[6] How great the amount was in classical times is unknown. Originally it was probably the full value of the plaintiff's interest in the matter estimated by him on oath. At a time when the *iudicium secutorium* (*infra*, 236, n. 3) did not yet exist this would have been the only way in which the plaintiff could get full satisfaction. With the invention of the *iudicium secutorium*, this reason no longer applied, and the full value appears to have been merely a maximum beyond which the praetor would not allow the parties to go. Cf. Lenel, *E.P.* 471; Girard, 1124; Buckland, 739, n. 6.

disobeyed the interdict, and *A* promises to pay *B* a similar amount if *B* has not disobeyed it. *A* and *B* then bring actions against each other in the ordinary way[1] for these sums; the question to be decided in the two actions is of course exactly the same and they are sent to the same *iudex* to try. The *iudex*, in order to decide whether there has been disobedience or not, must go into all the facts of the case, and in particular must find out whether the land claimed was held *precario* by *B* from *A* or not, for, if it was, *B* has disobeyed the interdict, if it was not, although he has disregarded it, he has not disobeyed it.[2] If the *iudex* finds that *B* has disobeyed, then he must condemn *B* in the first action, and absolve *A* in the second; if he finds that *B* has not disobeyed he must absolve *B* in the first action and condemn *A* in the second. The loser thus pays a penalty in any event, but, if *B* is the loser, the mere decision on the stipulations does not give *A* his land back. There is therefore in this case a third action, also sent to the same *iudex* (but necessitating no further trial because the point at issue has already been decided), in which the *iudex* is instructed to condemn *B* to pay the value of the land unless he restores it to *A* (*iudicium secutorium*).[3] Here again, as we have seen with actions *in rem*,[4] there is no specific restitution; in the last resort the *iudex* can only award damages, but the defendant is given the chance of escaping condemnation by making restoration.

(b) *Per formulam arbitrariam.* In certain classes of interdicts it is possible for the defendant to avoid the risk involved in the *sponsiones* by asking, before he leaves the presence of the praetor, for the appointment of an *arbiter*. A *formula arbitraria*[5] will then issue at once and the case will be tried on that; the result will then be exactly the same as it would be under the other procedure except that the defendant will not, if he loses, have to pay the penalty, and that the plaintiff will similarly be free from penalty if the case is decided in favour of the defendant.

Such, in the barest outline, is the procedure on this very important and common type of praetorian remedy. Interdicts served all manner of

---

[1] In classical times these would be *actiones certae creditae pecuniae*; under the *legis actio* system *condictio* or *sacramentum* would have been available.

[2] Cf. Buckland, 737.

[3] Gai. IV. 165, 167. The exact wording of the *formula* is not known, but at any rate it contained a *clausula arbitraria* (cf. *supra*, 216) where the interdict was exhibitory or restitutory. In the case of prohibitory interdict there is more difficulty; *v.* Lenel, *E.P.* 450–451. There can be no doubt that the *iudicium secutorium* is later than the *sponsiones*, for it could not exist under the *legis actio* system. Cf. *supra*, 235, n. 6, and Lenel, *Festgabe für Sohm* (1914), 207.

[4] *Supra*, 217.

[5] The *formula* is here quite uncertain (*v.* Lenel, *E.P.* 449), but the effect was that the defendant either had to put matters right or pay damages.

purposes. Some were no more than cogs in the procedural wheel,[1] some were devised to safeguard public rights;[2] others were the vehicles of immensely important praetorian innovations and amplifications of the civil law, as in particular the interdict *quorum bonorum*, by means of which the praetor carried through a great part of his reform in the law of succession.[3] Of even greater significance, if we consider not merely Roman law but the history of law in general, were the interdicts by which the praetor protected possession. This was a matter outside the civil law, but, as we shall see,[4] the praetor made it a rule that an existing possession, whether rightful or wrongful, must not be disturbed except by making a proper claim in a court of law. If I am in possession of land belonging to you and you take it from me, the praetor, by means of an interdict, will force you to return it to me quite regardless of your ownership, and you will not be able to get it again except by the proper action, the *vindicatio*, which is open to owners who are out of possession of their things. The interdicts are, in fact, the most far-reaching of magisterial remedies and a very considerable appendix to the edict was needed to include all of them; they are also that form of procedure which most clearly shows the magistrate not merely as an intermediary who helps the parties to come to an issue, but as a superior who can command.[5] It is true that this command leads in historical times to a trial, but it is highly probable that there was originally a personal investigation of the facts by the praetor before he issued the command,[6] and that this system only had to be given up because of an intolerable pressure of business on the single judicial magistrate. It should be noticed in this connection that interdicts have to a certain extent a "police" character; many are concerned with public ways and rivers; a number, such as those regulating possession, are provisional—the peace must be kept until the question at issue is settled in a lawful way; one protects the tenant who is prevented by his landlord from moving out with his goods,[7] and others regulate disputes between neighbours.[8] All are further characterised by comparative rapidity of procedure; the praetor can issue them on *dies nefasti* and they can be tried outside term time.[9]

---

[1] E.g. *interdicta secundaria*, Gai. IV. 170. [2] *Supra*, 235, n. 2.
[3] *Infra*, 260. [4] *Infra*, 268.
[5] Gaius begins his account of interdicts (IV. 139) by saying: "In certain cases the praetor or proconsul uses his authority directly for the settlement of controversies" (*principaliter auctoritatem suam...interponit*).
[6] Which would then naturally not be in the hypothetical form subsequently used.
[7] *De migrando*; Lenel, *E.P.* 490.
[8] E.g. *De glande legenda*; Lenel, *E.P.* 487.
[9] Cf. Wenger, 71, 237, 245; Costa, *Profilo*, 105.

Chapter XIV

PRIVATE LAW FROM THE XII TABLES TO THE FALL OF THE REPUBLIC: THE LAW OF THE FAMILY AND OF SUCCESSION

§ I. MARRIAGE

A. BETROTHAL. Marriage at Rome, as elsewhere, was preceded normally by engagement. This, in early times, took the form of reciprocal promises[1] (*sponsiones*) between the intending husband or his father and the father or guardian of the woman. The consent of the woman herself was almost certainly not needed if she was in her father's power, and perhaps not even that of a son under power.[2] The contract appears to have been enforceable originally in the sense that if either party broke off the engagement an action lay against him for damages, but it was certainly not enforceable in classical times, when all restrictions on the freedom of the parties were regarded as improper, and it had indeed probably ceased to be so long before the end of the republic.[3] Whether by this time the old form of *sponsio* had already been replaced by an informal agreement (as in classical times)[4] is unknown, but for breaking off the engagement a mere formless notice (*renuntiatio*) was sufficient. Even in classical times this could be sent by a father without his daughter's assent, if she

[1] D. 23. 1. 2.

[2] D. 23. 2. 21. Solazzi (*B.I.D.R.* XXXIV (1925) 1–6) argues that the consent of the *filia familias* was not required even in classical times.

[3] Gellius, IV. 4, quoting Veratius' account of a statement of Servius Sulpicius, says that *sponsalia* had been enforceable in the law of Latium until the *lex Iulia* (90 B.C.), when all the Latins received the citizenship and so came under Roman law. This shows pretty clearly that they were no longer enforceable in Roman law at this period, but original Roman law can hardly have differed from the allied systems of Latium in so important a particular, though it is easily comprehensible that it should have developed the more modern principle earlier; cf. Karlowa, II. 178. Varro, *L.L.* VI. 70, 71, also seems to regard the contract as enforceable. That it was not enforceable in classical times does not mean that it was without legal importance; the engagement created an affinity in some respects similar to that resulting from marriage. Thus a prospective father-in-law could not be forced to give evidence against his daughter's fiancé (D. 22. 5. 5) and gifts which would be invalid under the *lex Cincia* between unrelated persons were permissible between betrothed persons (Fr. Vat. 302). On the whole question *v.* Corbett, *The Roman Law of Marriage* (1930), 8–17.

[4] D. 23. 1. 4.

was in his power,[1] and probably at one time the same had been true in the case of sons.

B. Marriage. We have already seen that marriage without *manus* appears to go back as far as the XII Tables, if not further.[2] When it became common we do not know,[3] but it is clear that by the end of the republic it was the rule and *manus*, though it still existed, the exception. In this later form of marriage the woman not only does not pass into the power of her husband, but does not even become a member of his (agnatic) family. If her father is still alive she remains under his *potestas*; if he is dead she is *sui iuris* and has a tutor appointed in the same way as if she had remained single. To her children she is not related according to the civil law, for they are in the *patria potestas* of her husband. No ceremony of any kind was required for contracting a marriage of this sort; all that was necessary was the consent of the parties, and, if they were under power, of their *patres*,[4] together with the *de facto* beginning of conjugal life. It was usual for this to take place by a ceremonial bringing of the bride to the bridegroom's house, where she was lifted over the threshold and received from the bridegroom the symbolical gifts of fire and water.[5] But this was not legally necessary; any other actual beginning of life as husband and wife was sufficient. Thus marriage might be contracted by the bringing of the bride to the house of the bridegroom in his absence provided he signified his consent by letter or message,[6] or the

---

[1] D. 23. 1. 10.   [2] *Supra*, 116.

[3] The earliest references which can be quoted appear to be Ennius (239–169 B.C.), Cresphontes (quoted Auctor ad Herenn. II. 24; *v.* Merry, *Fragments of Roman Poetry*, 53), where a father is represented as divorcing his daughter without her consent, which shows that she must have remained in his *potestas*, and Plautus, *Stichus*, I. I. 13–32. These references cannot be explained as mere translations from the Greek originals, for it appears that in Greek law the father had no power to dissolve his daughter's marriage; *v.* Levy, *Gedächtnisschrift für Seckel* (1927), 154.

[4] In the case of a woman *sui iuris* the *auctoritas* of the tutor was not necessary, as it was for *coemptio*, but it appears from later legislation that he and the relatives had some say in the matter; *v.* Buckland, 114, n. 2. Solazzi (*B.I.D.R.* XXXIV. 1–28) tries to show that even in classical times the consent of a *filia familias* herself is not needed, but it is difficult to see how consent (of a sort) could be dispensed with in a system which regards marriage as a *de facto* matter, unless the girl is carried struggling into the husband's house. The question is quite different from that of betrothal.

[5] Symbolical apparently of her share in the most necessary elements of human life; *v.* Festus, s.v. *aqua et igni*, Bruns, II. 2.

[6] D. 23. 2. 5.

couple might take up their residence together in the bride's house.[1] On the other hand the mere fact that the bride has been brought to the bridegroom's estate is not enough to constitute marriage, if it be clear from the fact that she is staying in a separate building that the parties have not yet actually set up their common household.[2] The setting up of a common household is, of course, compatible not only with marriage but with concubinage, but, as already noticed,[3] it would usually be quite clear from the attendant circumstances when marriage was intended,[4] and there was further a presumption in favour of marriage when the parties were of equal social standing.[5]

There were, of course, certain fundamental conditions for the validity of the marriage; the parties must have *conubium*, be above the age of puberty, of sound mind and not related within the prohibited degrees. With respect to this last point the rules became progressively less strict; thus marriages between first cousins, originally forbidden, were known already towards the end of the third century B.C.[6]

Of the legal relationships set up between husband and wife by the marriage there is little to say, for under the system of free marriage such relationships can hardly be said to exist. Where the marriage is dissoluble at will by either of the parties it is idle to impose a duty for instance on the husband to support his wife, and such did not in fact exist. We only hear of vague duties such as those of protection and respect.[7] So far as property was concerned, the separation (apart from the dowry) was complete; it even became the rule that gifts between husband and wife were invalid.[8]

---

[1] *V.* Levy, *Ehescheidung* (1925), 69. If, as is said in D. 23. 2. 5, the woman cannot, in the same way as the man, be married in her absence, it is because her entry into the husband's house is the normal thing, whereas his entry into hers in her absence would not be equally unequivocal evidence of the beginning of matrimonial life.

[2] D. 24. 1. 66. 1.

[3] *Supra*, 116.

[4] Preceding betrothal, festivities, and, in particular, the drawing up of *instrumenta dotalia*, documents concerning the dowry, which could only exist where there was lawful marriage.

[5] D. 23. 2. 24; 39. 5. 31 pr.

[6] Livy xx (*Hermes*, IV. 372), quoted by Karlowa, II. 175; cf. Tac. *Ann.* XII. 6.

[7] *V.* Buckland, 106.

[8] The object of this rule is said to be that the spouses should not be led by affection to deprive themselves of their property (D. 24. 1. 1), and that no material considerations should enter into married life (D. 24. 1. 3 pr.). The text of D. 24. 1. 1 says that the rule is one introduced by custom, but it is held by

C. DIVORCE. Where marriage was without *manus* divorce was entirely free to either party. As marriage began by the *de facto* beginning of life as husband and wife, so it ended if such community of life was broken by the action of either spouse. This does not, of course, mean that mere separation constituted a divorce any more than mere living together constituted marriage; it must be the intention of one of the parties to treat the separation as putting an end to the marriage and such intention must, normally at any rate, be made clear to the other spouse.[1] The husband might send his wife from the house, using perhaps the traditional formulae,[2] or the wife might leave it declaring that she considered the marriage at an end. No particular form was laid down, but as such declarations are usually only made when personal intercourse between the spouses has become painful, it was usual for a written or oral message to be sent, and *repudium* or *nuntium mittere* became a common expression for divorcing.

In the less usual case of marriage with *manus*, the *manus* could still only be broken by a re-mancipation undertaken by the husband,[3] and this he could no doubt undertake when it pleased him;[4] in the classical law a woman married with *manus* could apparently also insist on being freed; she repudiated her husband in the same way as a woman married without *manus*, and could then insist on re-mancipation;[5] but how long this had been the rule is unknown.

By the end of the republic divorce had become extremely frequent, at any rate in the high society of the capital, of which alone we have any real knowledge, and this was a state of affairs that Augustus set himself, without much success, to remedy. The change from the primitive

some scholars that this is interpolated and that it was really due to a provision in the marriage laws of Augustus; *v.* Alibrandi, *Opere giuridiche e storiche*, I. 593 *sqq.*, followed by Windscheid-Kipp, III. 47, n. 1. At any rate it is subsequent to the *lex Cincia* (*supra*, 85), for husband and wife were "excepted persons" under that statute.

[1] Levy, *Ehescheidung*, 84. Where one spouse has been missing for so long that there is no reasonable likelihood of being able to re-establish communication with him, the marriage appears to be *ipso facto* at an end, so that the other spouse can marry again without sending any *repudium*; *v.* Levy, *Gedächtnisschrift für Seckel* (1927), 147–165.

[2] *Supra*, 117.

[3] I.e. where the *manus* resulted from *coemptio* or *usus*. For divorce in confarreate marriage *v. supra*, 117.

[4] For the difficulties which would arise if the wife refused to be present for the re-mancipation ceremony *v.* Levy, *Ehescheidung*, 41.

[5] Gai. I. 137 A. The text is defective, but *v.* Levy, *op. cit.* 40, n. 1.

austerity of Roman family life had no doubt been gradual, but the Romans themselves tended to date it from the famous case of Sp. Carvilius Ruga who, apparently in 234 B.C.,[1] divorced his wife, not on account of any fault on her part, but because she was childless. That this case became so well known [2] seems to show that at that date what was common in the later republic was still something unusual if not unprecedented.

D. DOWRY. Dowry (*dos*) is always a gift to the husband coming from the side of the wife and intended as a contribution to the expenses of married life, which fall upon the husband. So long as marriage with *manus* was the rule, the property of a woman *sui iuris* necessarily passed to her husband on her marriage, and in the case of a daughter under power it was usual for the father to provide for his daughter by giving a dowry to her husband; to the daughter herself he could, of course, not give it. It was also possible for persons other than the father who were interested in the wife to provide for her in the same way. When the marriage was without *manus* it was perfectly possible (if the woman was *sui iuris*) for her to own property and to have property given her, but it nevertheless remained usual for a dowry to be given to her husband on the marriage. If this was given by her father it was called *dos profecticia*, if by the woman herself or any other person *dos adventicia*.[3] Neither where the marriage was with *manus*, nor where it was not, does there appear to have been originally any legal duty on the husband or his heirs to return the dowry when the marriage came to an end. Where there was *manus* the wife, if she survived her husband, shared with the children on intestacy, or might be provided for by will; if the wife predeceased the husband the dowry remained with him as part of the family property which, in the normal course of events, he would transmit to his children. Where there was no *manus* the position was still satisfactory; the wife could be provided for by will if her husband predeceased her, and to give her a claim to the return

---

[1] *V.* Kübler, 33. But the dates given by ancient authors vary widely; *v.* Corbett, *op. cit.* 227.

[2] It is mentioned by Gellius (IV. 3; XVII. 21), Valerius Maximus (II. I. 4), Dionysius (II. 25), and Plutarch (*Qu. Rom.* XIV); *v.* Karlowa, II. 188.

[3] It was not necessary that property should be transferred at once; it might be promised. Anyone could bind himself to give a dowry by the ordinary contract of stipulation, but certain persons could bind themselves by a formal oral promise (*dictio dotis*) even though it was not (as was necessary in a stipulation) preceded by a question, and consequently without necessarily meeting the promisee. The persons to whom this rule applied were the woman herself, her debtor acting with her authorisation and her father or other male ascendant related solely through males (Ulp. VI. 2).

of the dowry would have meant depriving the children of the marriage of all hope of succession since, at this period, a woman could make no will, and her property would go on her death, not to her children (who were in the agnatic family of their father), but to her own agnates. In the rare cases of divorce (always at the instance of the husband) it was apparently usual for the husband to sit in judgment on the wife and either give her back part of her dowry, if the fault were a minor one, or refuse to return any of it if she had been guilty of serious misconduct, but this was a matter of custom, not of law.[1] The change must have come when divorce became more frequent, especially divorce where no fault was imputed to the wife, or at her instance. If in such cases the husband did not choose to return the dowry a woman still of marriageable age might be left without provision and thus find difficulty in contracting another marriage. We find consequently, in the developed law, quite a different state of affairs. In many cases the person giving the dowry would actually make a stipulation for its return on the dissolution of the marriage,[2] but even where this was not done, the wife had a special action (*actio rei uxoriae*) for the return of her dowry or part thereof to herself, when the marriage was dissolved by divorce or predecease of the husband; only if the marriage was dissolved by her death did the husband retain the dowry.[3] This action was almost certainly *in bonum et aequum concepta*, and the husband could make deductions in some cases, as, in particular, in case of divorce occasioned by the wife, for her misconduct (*propter mores*), and for children, one-sixth being allowed for each child up to three.

The origin of this action is obscure, but the most probable view appears to be that it originated in agreements for the return of an equitable portion of the dowry in case of divorce, which it became the custom to make at the time of the marriage when the increasing frequency of divorce made this a contingency which had to be taken into account. Later an action would be granted even if the parties had not taken this precaution. The agreement cannot have been by stipulation for it was probably not until the empire that it became possible to make a stipulation for an indefinite sum such as an "equitable portion",[4] which is

---

[1] Speech of Cato reported in Gell. x. 23: *Vir, cum divortium facit, mulieri iudex pro censore est; imperium quod videtur habet. Si quid perverse taetreque factum est a muliere, multatur; si vinum bibit, si cum alieno viro probri quid fecit, condemnatur.* For discussion v. Karlowa, II. 212.

[2] In such case the dowry was said to be *recepticia*; Ulp. VI. 5.

[3] Even then he did not retain it if it was *profecticia* and the giver himself was still alive; he had however the right to retain one-fifth for each child; Ulp. VI. 4.

[4] *Infra*, 290.

precisely what, according to our only authority,[1] these agreements did provide for.[2] It is thought, however, that the praetor may have given validity to an informal pact made with this object.[3] In any case the liability of the husband to return the dowry goes back well into the republic. It is related[4] that in 160 B.C. the heirs of L. Aemilius Paulus had to pay back the dowry to his wife and were hardly able to find the money by selling the whole of his movable property, while in 121 B.C. the claim of C. Gracchus' widow was held justified by Q. Mucius on the ground that the riot in which Gracchus was killed had been caused by his own fault.[5] Both these cases refer to claims where the marriage was dissolved by death, and the rule requiring return of the dowry on divorce was probably earlier.[6]

§ II. *PATRIA POTESTAS* AND BONDAGE

The milder manners of the later republic did not bring about any change in the legally despotic power of the father over his children; in 63 B.C. it was still possible for A. Fulvius to be executed by his father's orders for having been concerned in the Catilinarian conspiracy.[7] Mancipation of children still existed, not only as a device for achieving the objects of emancipation and adoption,[8] but as a reality in the case of noxal surrender,[9] and was probably still occasionally used as a way of setting children to work where the father could not usefully employ them himself.[10] But the status of the bondsman had probably already changed considerably for the better, for Gaius records that such a person could

---

[1] Boethius, *v. infra*, n. 6.

[2] Also where marriage was with *manus* a stipulation would be useless to the wife.

[3] *V.* Mitteis, *R.P.R.* 53.

[4] Polybius XVIII. 18; XXXII. 8; Plutarch, *Aem. Paul.* IV; Livy, *Epit.* XLVI.

[5] D. 24. 3. 66. pr.

[6] Another view as to the *actio rei uxoriae* is that of Esmein (*N.R.H.* XVII (1893), 145–171), who thinks that it originated as a penal action against the husband who divorced without good cause. The chief objection to this view would appear to be that the words *quod melius aequius erit*, which were certainly part of the *formula* of the *actio rei uxoriae* (Lenel, *E.P.* 304), are given as part of the *cautio rei uxoriae* by Boethius (ad Cic. *Top.* XVII. 65), which would be strange if the action had no connection with the *cautio*. In any case some features of the action, in particular the fixed fractions which may be retained in certain cases, appear to be due to specific legislation probably under Augustus; *v.* Lenel, *E.P.* 304, n. 5. For the literature of the subject *v.* Rabel, 514; Biondo Biondi, *Actiones arbitrariae*, 154.

[7] Sallust, *Cat.* XXXIX. 5.   [8] *Supra*, 118–119.

[9] *Supra*, 176. It still existed in classical times; Gai. I. 141.

[10] It is maintained by Cugia, *Profili del tirocinio industriale* (1921) (quoted *Z.S.S.* XLVII. 531), that mancipation was used in order to apprentice a son to a trade.

insist on obtaining his freedom *censu*, even against the will of his master,[1] and this is a rule which can hardly have arisen during the empire, when the *census* was very rarely taken. So far as proprietary relationships are concerned the old rule that all acquisitions go to the father also remained untouched, though it became common for sons, like slaves, to have *peculia*. These would be all the more necessary as civilisation became more urban and the son no longer usually worked with his father on the land. In the plays of Plautus they appear already as a well-recognised institution, so that they were certainly not new at that time. Action against the father on the son's contract could be brought in the same cases as against the master on the contract of his slave.[2]

§ III. GUARDIANSHIP

A. *Tutela.* The XII Tables had dealt only with tutors appointed by will or right of kinship. At some time previous to 186 B.C. was passed a *lex Atilia*,[3] which laid down that where an incapable person *sui iuris* was without a tutor the *praetor urbanus* should appoint one with the co-operation of the majority of the tribunes of the plebs. It may well be that the praetor had had the right of nomination before, and that the *lex Atilia* really restricted his power by bringing the tribunes into the matter,[4] but even so the increasing attention paid to the magisterial or "dative" guardianship shows how the idea of *tutela* as a public duty was superseding the early conception of it as an advantage to the guardian. More important however in this respect was the introduction of the *actio tutelae*, a *bonae fidei* action, in which the tutor could be called upon to account for any loss that the ward had suffered by his fault (intentional or negligent) in administering the estate. This action existed at any rate at the time of Q. Mucius Scaevola,[5] and shows a great advance on the

[1] Except where he had been noxally surrendered, and in the cases where there was a trust (*fiducia*) for re-mancipation to the father; Gai. I. 140. In I. 141 Gaius says that an *actio iniuriarum* will lie for dishonouring treatment of a person *in mancipio*, but it is impossible to say how far back this rule goes.

[2] *Infra*, 265–267.

[3] Gai. I. 185. The date must be earlier than 186 B.C., for the woman whose information led to the discovery of the Bacchanalian conspiracy of that year had a tutor appointed by the praetor and tribunes; Livy XXXIX. 9. Gaius, *loc. cit.*, mentions that a similar power of appointment was given in the provinces to the governors by a *lex Iulia et Titia*; if this was a single law it must have been passed in 31 B.C., but there were more probably two separate laws; *v.* Girard, 224, n. 2.

[4] Mitteis, *R.P.R.* 41, n. 4.

[5] It appears in the list of *b.f. iudicia* quoted by Cicero, *de Off.* III. 17. 70, from Scaevola.

earlier law according to which the tutor had only been liable if he actually embezzled the property of the ward.[1] This action however only lay in the case of guardianship over boys and girls; in that of adult women no such action was ever developed, because the position of the tutor was here quite different. He did not administer the woman's fortune at all; she administered it herself, and only needed the tutor's authorisation for certain classes of transactions.[2] In fact, although the lifelong guardianship of women remained, it was only as a burdensome technicality left over from an earlier stage of civilisation. Tutors, other than those holding *tutela legitima* as parents or patrons,[3] could be forced, if necessary, to give their authorisation to transactions which the woman desired to carry out, and a method was devised whereby a woman could get a different guardian in place of one whom she disliked. For this purpose a *coemptio* (called *coemptio fiduciae causa*[4] to distinguish it from one entered into on marriage) was used. The woman made a *coemptio* with some man—it did not matter with whom—and thus fell under his *manus*; this man then mancipated her to the person whom she wished to have as her tutor, and he (who now held her *in mancipio*) manumitted her, thereby becoming her tutor in the same way as a man who manumitted a female slave became her tutor.[5] The original *coemptio* needed, it is true, the authorisation of the tutor, but this could, as we have seen, generally be enforced. It was also possible for a husband when appointing by will a tutor for his wife *in manu* to leave her to choose the individual, and he might even give her the right to choose a new one as often as she liked.[6] In such a case it is clear that the burden was not a serious one at all.

B. *Cura.* (i) *Furiosi and prodigi.* Here too there was a development, in some respects obscure, of magisterial appointment, in addition to the agnatic and gentilician rights recognised by the XII Tables. Both in the case of the lunatic and in that of the spendthrift the praetor came to have the right to appoint in default of agnates, and though there was never any

---

[1] I.e. by the *actio rationibus distrahendis*; *supra*, 175.

[2] Gai. I. 190–192.   [3] Gai. I. 192.

[4] I.e. "for the purpose of a trust", the trust being one for manumission imposed by the *coemptionator* on the person to whom he mancipated; *v.* Buckland, 120.

[5] The *tutela* was however *fiduciaria* whereas that of the patron was *legitima*; Gai. I. 166 A. The use of *coemptio* for the purpose of changing tutors is not actually attested before Gaius (I. 115), but the mention of *coemptio* for the purpose of getting rid of *sacra* by Cicero (*pro Mur.* XII. 27) immediately after that of the powerless tutor suggests that it was already known in his time.

[6] Gai. I. 150–154.

strictly legal right to appoint by will, it became the rule that the magistrate should confirm an appointment so made by the father of the incapable person.[1] It seems also clear that the interdiction of the spendthrift, originally confined to inherited property and probably only to that inherited on intestacy,[2] could, in later law, extend to all property however acquired, but in this matter, as in many others, it is impossible to give even approximate dates.[3] At no time does there appear to have been any *lex* granting the power of appointment to the magistrate; it seems to have been regarded as inherent in the *imperium*.

(ii) *Minoris*. More significant of the change in the conception of guardianship was the rise of an entirely new kind of *cura*, that over young men above the age of puberty but under twenty-five (*minores*). This sort of guardianship was never anything but an institution for the benefit of the ward, and curators of this sort were never appointed except by the magistrate. The first step away from the old system whereby a youth was considered fully adult as soon as he had reached the age of puberty was taken apparently by a *lex Plaetoria*, probably passed about 200 B.C.[4] This statute permitted an action to be brought against anyone taking advantage of the inexperience of a young man under twenty-five[5] (*circumscriptio adulescentium*). What exactly was the nature of this action[6] is disputed, but the law evidently had the effect of making people chary of dealing with minors, for in a play of Plautus we find a young man complaining that the law about being twenty-five years old will be the ruin of him, since everyone is afraid to lend him money.[7] Transactions with minors became still more dangerous when the praetor began to grant them *in integrum restitutio*,[8] not only if advantage had been taken of them, but

[1] Not attested before classical times; *v.* D. 27. 10. 16. pr.

[2] *Supra*, 121.

[3] The interdiction of a prodigal who had received property under the will of his father is attested for the year 92 B.C. by Valerius Maximus, III. 5. 2; *v.* Collinet, *Mél. Cornil*, 1. 153.

[4] There is a clear reference to it in Plautus' *Pseudolus* (acted 191 B.C.), I. 3. 69, and possibly in his *Rudens* (acted about 192 B.C.), V. 3. 24.

[5] It is possible that this was for a time, during the early empire, interpreted as meaning men who had entered upon their twenty-fifth year, i.e. as we should say, men of twenty-four; *v.* Brassloff, *Z.S.S.* XXII. 169–194, commenting on the *oratio Claudii* (Bruns, I. 198).

[6] It is generally said, mainly on the strength of *Tab. Heracl.* 112, Bruns, I. 108, that there were two actions, one criminal (*iudicium publicum*), and the other private, for recovery of the amount lost or a multiple thereof. Duquesne, however (*Mél. Cornil*, I. 217–244), shows that there was probably but a single *actio popularis*.

[7] *Pseud.* I. 3. 69.   [8] *Supra*, 234.

even if, without any fraud on the side of the other party, they had been led by their inexperience into an unprofitable transaction—had, for instance, bought something for more than it was worth. The dangers which persons transacting business with minors thus ran could however be minimised if, before concluding the transaction, the minor received the consent of some experienced adult appointed by the praetor to consider whether it would be advantageous. Perhaps the consent of such a *curator* did not exclude an action under the *lex Plaetoria*, and it certainly did not exclude an application for *in integrum restitutio*,[1] but it would make the success of either much less probable, and thus anyone doing business of importance with a minor would generally insist on a curator's consent. Whether the *lex Plaetoria* itself provided for the nomination of curators is uncertain,[2] but at any rate the practice became common. A curator of this sort, however, was not, like the curator of a lunatic or a spendthrift, appointed once and for all; he had to be asked for and nominated for each transaction. In classical times there were some cases —those in which a man could not avoid doing business with a minor— in which a minor had to allow the appointment of a curator,[3] but we have no evidence that any of these go back to republican times.

§ IV. SUCCESSION

A. TESTAMENTARY SUCCESSION. The chief feature here is the development of the mancipatory will and the final disappearance of the earlier forms, but something must also be said of the so-called "praetorian will", that is to say of the recognition by praetorian law for certain purposes of documents which might not fulfil the civil law requirements for a valid will.

(i) *Disappearance of the early forms of will.* That the wills *comitiis calatis* and *in procinctu* had become obsolete by the time of Cicero is clear, but no precise date can be given. Cicero states definitely that wills *in procinctu* were no longer made,[4] and they are last recorded as occurring in 143 B.C.[5] For the comitial will we have no evidence.[6]

---

[1] C. 2. 24. 2.

[2] The only text which speaks of tutors in connection with the *lex Plaetoria* is *H.A., Vita Marci*, x; *v.* Buckland, 169.

[3] *V.* Buckland, 170.   [4] *De nat. deor.* II. 3. 9.

[5] Vell. Pat. II. 5. The mention in Cicero, *de Or.* I. 53. 228, hardly helps as to date.

[6] Labeo (quoted by Gell. xv. 27) is the earliest authority to mention it at all, and he speaks of it in the past tense, but we can be fairly sure that if it had existed in Cicero's time some mention would have survived.

(ii) *The mancipatory will (testamentum per aes et libram).*[1] We have a clear description of the manner in which wills of this sort were made in classical times from Gaius,[2] and as the previous history of the institution is almost completely a matter of conjecture it will be as well to begin with this description, and discuss the theories of its original nature afterwards. According to Gaius the testator first writes out his will, which must, at this period, contain the nomination of an heir,[3] on wax tablets, then he gets together the usual personnel of a mancipation, the five witnesses and the balance-holder, and a man to act as *familiae emptor* ("purchaser of the estate"). He then goes through a formal ceremony of mancipating his estate to the *familiae emptor*, such ceremony being exactly like any other mancipation, except that the transferee (the *familiae emptor*), instead of speaking the ordinary words,[4] makes use of a more complicated formula: "I say that your *familia* and *pecunia* are at your orders and in my custody, and be they bought to me with this piece of copper so that you may make a will in accordance with the public statute".[5] Then follows something quite different from the proceedings in an ordinary mancipation. Whereas in an ordinary mancipation the transferor is silent,[6] here the testator takes an active part in the proceedings. He takes the prepared tablets in his hand and says: "As it is written on these tablets and wax, so I give, bequeath and declare, and so do you, Quirites, bear me witness".[7] This speech, says Gaius, is called the *nuncupatio*, and by it the testator confirms generally the specific directions given in the tablets.[8]

Now in classical times the whole ceremony is merely a legally necessary form, not a real conveyance. It does not matter who the *familiae emptor* is, for he takes no rights and comes under no duties by the transaction.[9]

[1] Cf. *supra*, 126.   [2] II. 104.

[3] *Supra*, 127.   [4] *Supra*, 145.

[5] *Familiam pecuniamque tuam endo mandatela tua* (MS. *tuam*) *custodelaque mea esse aio, eaque* (the words *esse aio, eaque* are not in the MS.) *quo tu iure testamentum facere possis secundum legem publicam hoc aere esto mihi empta.* Some people add, says Gaius, after *hoc aere* the words *aeneaque libra*.

[6] Cf. *supra*, 148.

[7] *Haec ita ut in his tabulis cerisque scripta sunt, ita do, ita lego, ita testor* (MS. *testator*), *itaque vos, Quirites, testimonium mihi perhibetote.*

[8] Sealing by the witnesses, the *libripens* and the *familiae emptor* for the purpose of subsequent identification of the document was usual, and may have been legally necessary, for the edict concerning *bonorum possessio secundum tabulas* in Cicero's time spoke of seals "not less in number than the law requires" (cf. *infra*, 255, n. 2), but neither Gaius nor Justinian (Inst. 2. 10. 2) mentions this requirement.

[9] "He is brought in", says Gaius, II. 103, "for form's sake (*dicis gratia*) in imitation of the ancient law."

No effect whatever is produced until the testator dies, and then the person who succeeds to the rights and duties is the heir nominated in the will, who is also liable for the legacies, if any. Further the testator, as long as he lives, can always entirely invalidate the whole proceeding by making another will.

Clearly this had not always been the position. As the choice of the form of mancipation and the whole nature of the proceeding shows, the *familiae emptor* had originally had the property really conveyed to him, and this type of Roman will is an example of the rule that testamentary forms commonly originate in bilateral transactions *inter vivos*.[1] Gaius himself clearly distinguishes an earlier state of affairs in which the *familiae emptor* "took the place of an heir and for that reason the testator gave him instructions as to what things he wished given to each person".[2] Gaius further[3] represents the mancipatory will as originating in a device adopted by persons who were in danger of death and could not wait for the next opportunity of making a will in the normal way before the *comitia*. In such an emergency the testator (if one can call him so) conveys his property to a friend, who will presumably outlive him, and asks the friend to make such dispositions as he himself would have made had he been able to make a comitial will. This friend (the *familiae emptor*) has then, like an English executor, to dispose of the property in accordance with the testator's instructions. The instructions were no doubt originally oral, and there was no mention of any heir, the nearest thing to an heir being the *familiae emptor* himself.

This much is clear, but there are many points of difficulty and dispute, among them the following:

(*a*) Did the conveyance originally take effect at once, so that if the testator survived the immediate peril he had no property and had to live on the bounty of the *familiae emptor*,[4] or was the effect put off until his death? The probability is that its effect was put off. The form of words spoken recognises that the ownership acquired by the *familiae emptor* is not an ordinary one but a "custody" and, subject to the testator's instructions, existing further only "so that he may make a will". This would be mere verbiage if the effect were not postponed until the testator's death.[5]

---

[1] Cf. *supra*, 131, n. 1. See also Pollock's notes on Maine, *Ancient Law*, chap. VI.
[2] II. 103; cf. also 105.   [3] II. 102.
[4] Maine, *Ancient Law*, 183: "Still we must believe that, if the Testator did recover, he could only continue to govern his household by the sufferance of his Heir".
[5] The object of these words was probably to bring the mancipatory form under the provisions of the XII Tables respecting wills, though those provisions were intended originally for the comitial form.

(*b*) Was there any method of forcing the *familiae emptor* to carry out the instructions, or was there simply an unenforceable trust? Here again the careful construction of the form of words seems to put a legal limit on the ownership transferred. There is indeed no reference to a *fiducia* (trust) as in some other cases where mancipation is used to effect purposes other than those of a mere conveyance,[1] but there is a direct reference to the instructions of the testator, and this again would hardly be present if it had had no legal importance.[2]

(*c*) Was the *familiae emptor* a universal successor in the sense in which a *heres* was? It may well be that if the testator's instructions did not cover the whole of his property the *familiae emptor* could retain the beneficial ownership of what was left over, and this fact would account for Gaius' reference to him as being *heredis loco*, for the heir also retained what remained after he had distributed the legacies, but that mancipation can in early times have been deemed capable of transferring the abstract "inheritance" seems unlikely, for the simple reason that this abstract conception is not primitive at all.[3] On the crucial question whether or not the *familiae emptor* was liable for the debts of the deceased we have no evidence.[4]

Not only are these and other questions[5] unsettled, but it is clear that

---

[1] As in *fiducia cum amico* and *cum creditore*; *v.* Gai. II. 59, 60; *infra*, 295.

[2] See also Weiss, *Z.S.S.* XLII. 102–114. Weiss' theory (*v.* especially 112) is that the *custodela* of the *familiae emptor* meant simply that he had to keep the things at the disposal of the legatees. In his view the legacies were all originally *per vindicationem* (cf. *infra*, 253) and the legatees could consequently fetch the things as soon as they became theirs at the testator's death. This theory has the advantage of explaining *how* the legatees enforced their rights, which is a difficulty if we dismiss the theory of a mere unenforceable trust. For a different view *v.* Sohm, 586–590.

[3] Cf. *supra*, 129, n. 4. On the other hand it is pointed out by Jörs (224, n. 4) that *familia* ought to have the same meaning here as it has in the words of the XII Tables dealing with intestate succession. If the agnate was an heir then the *familiae emptor* must, in his view, also have been one.

[4] Of course if the *familiae emptor* was not liable for the debts it is difficult to say exactly what did happen. It may be that the rules were not as definite as could be wished, and that the need for someone who would be liable for them was precisely one of the reasons which led the later jurists to insist that an heir not only might but must be appointed. It was not the private citizen himself so much as the authorities who insisted on universal succession. Cf. Kniep, *Gai. Inst. Commentarius*, II. §§ 97–289, p. 95. If, as Korošec (*Die Erbenhaftung nach römischem Recht*, 1927) thinks, obligations were intransmissible the difficulty vanishes. Cf. *supra*, 131, n. 3.

[5] E.g. whether it was possible to make a will of this sort if one had *sui*, *v.* Kübler, 62; what connection, if any, there was between the validity of the mancipatory will and the clause *cum nexum faciet*, etc., *supra*, 146.

the answers may, and indeed in some cases must, have been different at different periods. There was never any legislation turning the old mancipatory will in which the *familiae emptor* played an active part into the new one in which he was a mere cipher, and the development must have been a gradual one, culminating at the moment when the jurists first recognised that a *heres* could be appointed by the testator's instructions. Once that had become possible the importance of the *familiae emptor* must have immediately declined, though technicalities which testify to his original position remained even in the classical law.[1] When this change took place we cannot tell; Lenel puts it as late as about the beginning of the second century B.C.,[2] but there can be no doubt that by Cicero's day, when the old forms had disappeared, the evolution was complete. By then too the testator's instructions were already written down in the normal case and remained secret until his death, but it seems certain that there existed also the possibility of an oral will, the ceremony being exactly the same except that the dispositions were spoken by the testator and hence necessarily known to the witnesses.[3]

(iii) *Restrictions on institution.* The testator, whether he has *sui* or not, is free to choose his heir or heirs as he wishes,[4] but if he has *sui* whom he wishes to exclude he cannot simply pass them over in silence. In the case of a son he must put in a clause disinheriting him expressly (*nominatim*), otherwise the will will be entirely void.[5] If he has other *sui* (grandchildren or daughters) he must at least put in a clause saying that all not instituted heirs are to be disinherited; otherwise the omitted persons will be able to come in and share with those instituted.[6] The reason for these rules is, no doubt, that the *sui* are regarded as having a sort of dormant ownership in the estate of their father even during his lifetime, and, at his death, if they are heirs they succeed without the need for any express acceptance.

---

[1] No person in his power or in whose power he was or in the same power with him could be a witness; Gai. II. 105–108. Another trace is probably to be found in D. 48. 18. 1. 6; *v.* Sohm, 589; Mitteis, *R.P.R.* 287.

[2] *Essays in Legal History* (ed. Vinogradoff), 141.

[3] Horace is said by Suetonius (*Vita Horatii, sub fin.*) to have made a will orally in favour of Augustus because he was too ill to observe the usual form; see Girard, 860, n. 1. The form of the *nuncupatio* must, of course, have been slightly different in these cases from that given by Gaius.

[4] Provided the person chosen has *testamenti factio*.

[5] Gai. II. 123.

[6] Gai. II. 124. The rules given in the text are those stated by Gaius. There was still some doubt about details when Cicero was a child (*v. de Or.* I. 38. 175), but, in spite of some controversy, it seems clear that the general rule is old; *v.* Girard, 905, n. 1.

The power of the father is great enough to exclude them, but this power must be exercised expressly and not by implication.[1] The rules of disherison are thus restrictions of form; the testator can do as he likes, provided he takes the proper steps. The only restriction of substance introduced during the republic with respect to the institution of heirs is that of the *lex Voconia* (168 B.C.), which forbade the institution of women as heirs by persons rated in the highest (i.e. wealthiest) class at the census.[2]

(iv) *Legacies.* A legacy is always regarded by the jurists as a lessening (*delibatio*) of the inheritance,[3] a disposition which decreases the amount that the heir or heirs would otherwise take. This conception is perhaps not an original one (at any rate as regards the mancipatory will), for it is obviously inapplicable if that form of will began by containing no institution of an heir at all, but it is fundamental in the developed law. The "lessening" might take either of two forms—*per vindicationem* or *per damnationem.*[4] A legacy *per vindicationem* is one in which the testator has used the form *do lego* ("I give, bequeath") or an equivalent, and the result is that, as soon as the will becomes operative by the entry of the heir, the ownership in the thing bequeathed passes to the legatee, who can then bring a *vindicatio* to obtain it from the heir or anyone else who happens to possess it. A legacy *per damnationem*, on the other hand, is given by the words *heres meus damnas esto dare*[5] ("Let my heir be *damnas* to convey") or an equivalent; it gives no right *in rem* to the legatee, but imposes an obligation on the heir. The thing bequeathed (if it was the property of the testator) passes, like the rest of the property of the deceased, to the heir, but the legatee can bring an action (*in personam*) against the heir to force him to transfer it. It is even possible by this method to bequeath things which do not belong to the testator; the heir is then under an obligation to get the thing if he can and transfer it to the legatee, or, if he cannot, to pay its value. This form was particularly useful for giving legacies of sums of money. A pecuniary legacy *per vindicationem* was only good if the testator actually owned coins to the

---

[1] Cf. *supra*, 123, n. 3.

[2] Gai. II. 274. The scope of the statute was perhaps originally wider; *v.* Buckland, 290, n. 10.

[3] D. 30. 116. pr.

[4] Two less important forms, per *praeceptionem* and *sinendi modo*, are known to the classical law, Gai. II. 192, but the former is a variation of *per vindicationem* and the latter of *per damnationem*, and the antiquity of both is disputed; *v.* Buckland, 234, n. 7.

[5] For the word *damnas v. supra*, 168.

requisite amount when he died,[1] for only so could he pass ownership in the coins, but however little actual cash a man owned he could impose a duty on his heir to pay a sum of money, which the heir could then raise in any way he thought fit. Of these two main types of legacy that *per vindicationem* is probably the older, for the words *do lego* which are used in giving it are precisely those which the testator uses in his *nuncupatio*,[2] and this likeness further goes to support the view that the mancipatory will consisted originally only of legacies. Legacies *per damnationem* on the other hand cannot have been given in this type of will before the will appointed an heir on whom they could be charged.

(v) *Restrictions on legacies.* Even after the institution of an heir had become a definite requirement of the mancipatory will, there seems to have remained a tendency to comply in form with the demands of this rule by nominating an heir, while neglecting the substance of it by giving away so much in legacies that little or nothing was left to the heir. One result of this practice was that heirs often found that it was not worth their while to accept the inheritance, and refused to enter, thus causing the whole will to fail, and a series of statutes had to be passed to remedy matters.[3] The first of these was the *lex Furia* (*testamentaria*), of unknown date,[4] which forbade legacies of more than 1000 *asses* to be given except to certain persons closely related to the testator. It did not have the desired effect because by giving a sufficient number of legacies, none of which exceeded 1000 *asses*, the largest estate might be exhausted and nothing left for the heir. No greater success attended the provision of the *lex Voconia* which forbade any legacies to be greater than the amount which remained for the heir,[5] for again, provided there were a large enough number of legacies, although no one individually exceeded the heir's share, that share might still be too small to make it worth his while to accept. The matter was not finally settled until the passing of the *lex*

---

[1] A legacy of non-fungible things could not be given *per vindicationem* unless the testator owned them *ex iure Quiritium* both when he made the will and when he died. For fungible things ownership *ex i. Q.* at death sufficed; Gai. II. 196.

[2] Cf. *supra*, 249. On the whole question v. especially Wlassak, *Z.S.S.* XXXI. 196 *sqq.*, and other literature quoted by Kübler, 63, n. 3.

[3] Gai. II. 224–227.

[4] It is probably later than the *lex Cincia* (204 B.C.) and certainly before the *lex Voconia*; Girard, 975, n. 7. For the machinery of the law cf. *supra*, 85.

[5] The combined result of this with the other provision of the *lex Voconia* (*supra*, 253) was that no person rated in the first class of the census could leave a woman more than half his property. Some scholars hold that there was an exception in the case of daughters, but the evidence is not convincing. For literature v. Girard, 870; Kübler, 196.

Falcidia (40 B.C.), which enacted that if the amount of the legacies exceeded three-quarters of the estate the heir might cut them all down proportionately and so retain a quarter for himself.

(vi) *The "praetorian will"*. The praetor could not make an heir but he could grant *bonorum possessio*, which meant that he could grant to persons of his choice the right to use certain remedies which would enable them to get possession of the goods of the deceased. Whether they would be able to keep what they had got is another question, which has to be answered differently according to the circumstances and the period, but at any rate they could get possession in the first instance.[1] The rules governing the praetor's choice of persons to whom he will grant *bonorum possessio* are set out in the edict and extend both to testamentary and intestate succession. For the moment, however, we are concerned only with testamentary succession. So far as this is concerned the praetor based his action on the view that the whole formality of mancipation and nuncupation was so much useless ceremonial. What was important was that the testator's dispositions should be committed to writing and that the document in which they were contained should be identifiable by the seals of persons who could testify that it was genuine. The praetor therefore promised *bonorum possessio secundum tabulas* (i.e. in accordance with the tablets) to any person nominated heir in tablets sealed with the requisite number of seals, i.e. seven,[2] for, so far as the praetor is concerned, the *familiae emptor* and the *libripens* are just two witnesses in addition to the five required by civil law for mancipation. This *bonorum possessio* was given whether the civil law ceremonies had been gone through or not, so that if they had been gone through the person nominated in the tablets was both heir at civil law and entitled to *bonorum possessio*; if they had not been gone through he was entitled to *bonorum possessio* only, and the document may be called a "praetorian will".[3]

At what date *bonorum possessio secundum tabulas* was first granted is unknown, but it was already in existence in the time of Cicero.[4]

(vii) *Praetorian rules of disherison*. As the civil law will is subject to certain restrictions with respect to *sui*,[5] so the praetorian will is subject

---

[1] Cf. *infra*, 260.

[2] The edict as revised by Julian (*infra*, 362) said definitely that there must be "not less than seven seals". In Cicero's time we know however (*in Verr.* II. 1. 45. 117) that the words were "not fewer than the law requires" (cf. *supra*, 249, n. 8), but whether that meant five or seven is not clear; *v.* Lenel, *E.P.* 349.

[3] This phrase was not used by the Romans, and in some respects documents of this sort did not attain the efficacy of a will; *v.* Buckland, 285–286.

[4] *Supra*, n. 2.   [5] *Supra*, 252.

to analogous restrictions with respect to the praetorian class corresponding to *sui*—the *liberi*.[1] In Gaius' time all male *liberi* must be disinherited
nominatim if they are not to succeed; only females can be excluded *inter
ceteros*. If these rules are not complied with the omitted person can
claim *b.p. contra tabulas*, i.e. contrary to the dispositions in the tablets.
These rules, or at any rate *b.p. contra tabulas*, go back as far as Labeo,[2]
but cannot be much older, as the class of *liberi* had not yet been defined
in Cicero's time.[3]

B. INTESTATE SUCCESSION. (i) *Civil law*. The civil law rules of
succession as laid down by the XII Tables remained unchanged throughout the republic, except in one[4] particular, the restriction of the agnatic
rights of females. By the law of the later republic only sisters, not more
remote female agnates, could inherit on intestacy, whereas there had been
no such limitation originally.[5] This change was apparently not due to
legislation, but to the *interpretatio* of the jurists, and is said by Paulus[6]
to have been made "on the principle of the *lex Voconia*". This probably
means that it took place after the passing of that statute, but it may
only mean that it was produced by the same tendency which produced
the *lex Voconia*, a tendency to restrict the power and luxury of women
by restricting their chances of sharing the great fortunes which were
becoming common at Rome.[7]

(ii) *Praetorian law*. More important and destined to have much more
far-reaching effects were the reforms brought about by the praetor's
edict, for it was the praetor who first recognised the claims of the cognatic, as opposed to the agnatic, system of relationship, i.e. of blood-
relationship traced through females as well as through males and
independent of *potestas*. Here again it will be well to mention briefly the
classical system, which is well known, before indicating how far the
reforms had got by the end of the republic.

---

[1] *Infra*, 257.

[2] D. 37. 4. 8. 11; *v*. Girard, 910, n. 4.

[3] *Infra*, 257, n. 5.

[4] There may also have been the change from corporate to individual succession
by the *gentiles*; *supra*, 124.

[5] *Supra*, 124.   [6] *Sent*. IV. 8. 20 (22).

[7] Some modern scholars have thought that the restriction must be older on the
ground that the complete equality of males and females is inconsistent with a
primitive system, but the evidence brought forward is insufficient to upset the
uniform Roman tradition; *v*. Kübler, *Z.S.S.* XLI. 15–43. Against, Kübler;
Brassloff, *Studien zur r. Rechtsgeschichte*, I Teil (1925), reviewed, *Z.S.S.* XLVII.
440–445.

In classical times, so far as ordinary cases of succession to freeborn persons was concerned,[1] the praetor had four classes of persons to whom he offered *bonorum possessio ab intestato* in turn:

(*a*) *Liberi* ("children"). This is an extended class of *sui*, i.e. it includes all who are *sui* together with those who would have been *sui*, but for *capitis deminutio minima*,[2] in particular emancipated children.

(*b*) *Legitimi*, i.e. all who have a civil law claim, including *sui* and *agnati*, but not *gentiles*, whose rights are obsolete by classical times.

(*c*) *Cognati*, i.e. blood-relations up to the sixth degree,[3] without distinction of male and female lines, the nearer relation excluding the more remote, as was the case with agnates under the civil law system.

(*d*) *Vir et uxor*. Failing any of the earlier classes the husband might get *bonorum possessio* to his deceased wife or the wife to her deceased husband. This refers only to marriage without *manus*, because where there was *manus* the woman could own nothing, and if her husband predeceased her would be a *sua heres* to him.

It will be seen that this system breaks with agnation in favour of cognation in two respects, first in the category of *liberi*, for here it disregards the element of *potestas*, and secondly by giving rights to *cognati* as such, but the breach must not be exaggerated. The category of *liberi*, like that of *sui*, exists only on the death of a *paterfamilias*; the praetor gave children no right of succession to their mother except as cognates, and *cognati* come in only after all *agnati*, so that the remotest agnate will exclude, for instance, an uncle or a first cousin on the mother's side.

In republican times the praetorian categories had not yet assumed their classical form. After the words promising *b.p. secundum tabulas* there followed immediately words promising *b.p.* to those persons who had a civil law claim,[4] i.e. the *legitimi*; the class of *liberi* had not yet apparently come to be recognised, and the *legitimi* still included the *gentiles*.[5] The rights of cognates also do not appear to have been as yet recognised expressly in the edict. Probably the edict merely said that if there was no

[1] Special rules applied where the deceased had been emancipated; *v.* Buckland, 384.

[2] Except that children given in adoption were not included so long as they remained in their adoptive family, and adopted children were not included if they had been emancipated.

[3] Seventh in one case, that of second cousins once removed.

[4] Cic. *in Verr.* II. 1. 44. 114.

[5] *In Verr.* II. 1. 45. 115. It is probable too that *sui* were not yet included as *legitimi*; *v.* Sohm, 568, n. 8.

claim under a will or under the civil law rules of intestacy the praetor
would grant *bonorum possessio* to the person whose claim appeared most
just.[1] But there are instances of grants to cognates who of course may well
have been the persons whom such an edict was primarily intended to
benefit.[2]

C. ACQUISITION OF *hereditas* AND OF *bonorum possessio*. *Sui
heredes* acquire the rights and duties of an heir immediately on the death
of the deceased, but an *extraneus* upon whom an inheritance devolves does
not become *heres* until he has manifested his acceptance of the position.[3]
In the classical law such manifestation might be made in either of two
ways.[4] Normally it was by *pro herede gestio* (acting as heir), i.e. by doing
some act, such, for instance, as selling the goods or providing the slaves
with food, which showed that the *extraneus* regarded himself as heir.[5]
But sometimes a much more formal method called *cretio* was used, which
consisted in the speaking of a solemn formula in which the chief words
were *hereditatem adeo cernoque* ("I enter and decide upon the inheritance").[6] Acceptance in this way was only necessary in classical times
where it had been prescribed in a special clause of a will,[7] and therefore
only took place in the case of testamentary succession, but it is held by
many scholars that originally it had a much wider scope and was in fact
the only method by which an *extraneus* could acquire an inheritance
immediately, whether it came to him under a will or on intestacy. It
would be strange indeed if the highly formal system of early Rome had
allowed so important a matter as the entry upon an inheritance to take
place informally, and there is no other ceremony of which we have any
trace.[8] It is also probable that *cretio* included originally more than the

---

[1] Cic. *Part. or.* XXVIII. 98.

[2] *V.* Cic. *pro Cluent.* LX. 165, and quotations Kübler, 190, n. 4.

[3] Cf. *supra*, 123.

[4] The text of Gaius, II. 167, mentions also *nuda voluntas* (informal declaration
of intention) as a way of acquiring an inheritance, but there is considerable doubt
whether this correctly represents the classical law; *v.* Kniep, *Gai. Inst. Commentarius*, II. §§ 97–289, pp. 307–311; Sohm, 567, n. 7. At any rate it seems clear
that Labeo did not yet know of it; D. 29. 2. 62. pr.

[5] Ulp., *Reg.* XXII. 26.

[6] Gai. II. 166. Though it was no doubt usual to have witnesses they were
probably not necessary; Buckland, 313; "Cretio and Connected Topics" (*Revue
d'histoire du droit*, III (1922), 239–276) at 241.

[7] The object of the clause, which always contained a time-limit, was to ensure
that the heir made up his mind whether to accept or not within a reasonable
time. There was no limit at civil law otherwise; *v.* Buckland, 313.

[8] Girard, 923–924; Sohm, 567; Karlowa, II. 896; Buckland, *op. cit.* 249.
Contra, Lenel, *Essays in Legal History* (ed. Vinogradoff), 124.

mere speaking of the words, that, as the word *adeo* suggests, it necessitated physical entry upon the land of the deceased.[1] How informal acceptance by *pro herede gestio* came to be equally effective remains a problem.[2]

Unlike *hereditas*, *bonorum possessio* is never acquired simply by the death of the person whose estate is in question. It has always to be asked for from the praetor, and one of the chief characteristics of the praetorian system is that it has to be asked for within a limited time. For each class there is a period (usually 100 days, but a year in the case of children and ascendants) during which it is open to them to claim, and then the next class has its chance. Thus, if the deceased died intestate leaving an agnatic first cousin and a maternal uncle as his only relatives, the cousin has first claim; if he fails to ask for *b.p.* during 100 days the maternal uncle can claim as cognate. It is true that the cousin is also a cognate (he is a blood-relation), but as such he will be postponed to the uncle, for an uncle is in the third degree of relationship whereas a first cousin is in the fourth. Only if the uncle fails to claim can the cousin now come in. This system of "succession of orders and of grades" (i.e. of one class to another and of a more remote relative within the same class on the failure of a nearer) is purely praetorian, and is among the praetor's most important innovations. At civil law if there was e.g. a *suus*, and he did not want the inheritance, no right passed to the agnates; if there was an agnate and he failed to accept no right passed to the *gentiles*. Similarly, if there was a nearer agnate who failed to accept, a remoter agnate had no right. The object of the praetor, on the other hand, was to multiply successors, to see, as Gaius says, that no one should die without a successor.[3]

D. Remedies of the heir and of the *bonorum possessor*. The civil law heir, no matter what his title to the inheritance, succeeds to the rights and duties of the deceased, so far as they are transmissible.[4] Having thus become owner of the goods which the deceased owned, he can bring a *vindicatio* to recover any of such goods if they are not in his possession; being now creditor where the deceased was creditor, he can use the same action (whatever it might be in the particular case) for recovering the debt as the deceased might have done. But, in addition, he has an action in his

---

[1] Sohm, 567, n. 7.

[2] It is not mentioned by Cicero, but was evidently known to Labeo, D. 29. 2. 62. pr.; Buckland, 313, n. 3.

[3] Gai. III. 33.   [4] Cf. *supra*, 128.

capacity as heir—the *hereditatis petitio*—which is the proper one for him to bring where the question to be raised is whether he or the defendant is entitled to the succession. Thus, if he finds a horse which he believes to have belonged to the deceased in the possession of a third party, X, and X on being asked to give it up refuses on the ground that the horse never belonged to the deceased or that he bought it from the deceased before he died, the proper action for settling the matter is an ordinary *vindicatio*; but if X's reply is, "I agree that the horse belonged to the deceased when he died, but in fact I am his successor, not you", the proper action is the *hereditatis petitio*.[1] So also if a third party, on being asked to pay a debt which he owed to the deceased, refuses to do so on the ground that he himself is heir and the debt has thus been cancelled, *hereditatis petitio* is the proper action.

The *bonorum possessor* as such has neither the particular actions nor the *hereditatis petitio*; the praetorian grant simply means that he can use certain praetorian remedies, of which the earliest and probably the only one existing in republican times was the interdict *quorum bonorum*.[2] This interdict enabled him to get possession of any of the goods of the deceased which were in the hands of any person who held *pro herede* or *pro possessore*, i.e. who believed himself (rightly or wrongly) to be heir, or knew that he had no title, and did not put forward any ground of possession independent of inheritance.[3] It was thus possible for the *bonorum possessor* to get possession even from the heir himself, if there was one. True, the heir could sometimes in classical law, always originally,[4] get back possession from the *bonorum possessor* by means of the *hereditatis petitio*, but that does not mean that the interdict *quorum bonorum* was useless. In the first place it enabled the *bonorum possessor* to be defendant in any action that was brought—he could get the goods and force the person who alleged himself to be heir to prove his case; secondly, if he retained possession long enough, he would become owner of the property by usucapion, and then any claim by the heir would be too late; thirdly,

---

[1] If the plaintiff insisted on bringing the *vindicatio* he would be defeated, originally by a *praescriptio*, later by an *exceptio praeiudicialis*; v. Gai. IV. 133.

[2] Cf. *supra*, 237. It was already known to Cicero, v. *ad fam.* VII. 21; *Top.* IV. 18. For the words of the interdict v. Gai. IV. 144.

[3] Gai. IV. 144. In the law of Justinian's day a person was said to possess *pro herede* when he alleged that he was heir even though he knew this to be untrue, but this was not the classical use of the term; Siber, II. 391. For the difficulties involved see especially Lenel, "Die Passivlegitimation bei der *hereditatis petitio*", Z.S.S. XLVI. 1–18.

[4] *Infra*, 261.

there might be no heir at all, in which case his possession would be unchallengeable and necessarily ripen into ownership by usucapion. Further, it must be remembered that the person entitled to *bonorum possessio* would very often be the heir himself; if, in such case, he availed himself of the praetor's offer, he had the advantage of being able to use the praetorian remedy (*quorum bonorum*), which was more expeditious than the *hereditatis petitio*.[1]

E. ORIGIN OF *bonorum possessio*. The chief historical importance of *bonorum possessio* lies in its use as an agency for the reform of the old law of succession—*supplendi* or *corrigendi iuris civilis gratia*—but it is unlikely that in its origin it was at all revolutionary. Even in Cicero's time, as we have seen, the praetor's scheme differed but very slightly from that of the civil law, the only class of intestate successors who were recognised being in fact the *legitimi*—those entitled at civil law. It was not until later that the class of *liberi*, in which the praetor definitely broke with the civil law, was recognised, and, though cognates might be admitted to *bonorum possessio*, they do not appear to have been specifically mentioned in the edict. In any case, if *bonorum possessio* did come to be granted to someone who was not civil law heir, it is clear that the civil law heir, if there was one, would always be able, at this period, to succeed in a *hereditatis petitio* against him, provided, of course, that he brought his action before the *bonorum possessor* had had time to usucape. In fact, whereas in the classical law the praetor would sometimes uphold his own nominee against the civil law heir,[2] in Cicero's time *bonorum possessio*, if given to someone other than the heir, was always *sine re*, i.e. ineffective against the heir. In its origin then *bonorum possessio* was almost certainly

---

[1] In the classical law (and probably since Labeo's time, *v.* Girard, 965, n. 2) the *bonorum possessor* could also sue the debtors of the deceased and be sued by his creditors by actions in which there was a fiction that he was heir (Gai. IV. 34). Until these were invented he could apparently do nothing more than get the *res corporales* by the interdict *quorum bonorum*. Where he succeeded in usucaping them, according to the older theory (Gai. II. 54), he was regarded as usucaping the inheritance, and was, consequently, it is to be presumed, liable for the debts in proportion to the share he had usucaped (Leist in Glück's *Erläuterung der Pandekten, Serie der Bücher* 37, 38, I. 172). That the edict of the pontiffs (Cic. *de leg.* II. 19, 47–20, 50) concerning liability for *sacra* had any application to liability for debts is denied by Mitteis, *R.P.R.* 98, n. 12.

[2] This was done by giving the *bonorum possessor* an *exceptio doli* against the *hereditatis petitio* of the heir. *V.* e.g. Gai. II. 120, which describes how *bonorum possessio secundum tabulas* became *cum re* as against agnates by reason of a rescript of Antoninus Pius.

given *adiuvandi iuris civilis gratia*, i.e. to provide persons who were already civil law heirs with additional praetorian remedies, but what the motive was which determined the praetor to act in this way remains a matter of much dispute.

According to one theory, that of Leist,[1] the central idea of *bonorum possessio* is to be found in the praetorian system of "succession of orders and degrees". The civil law gave no right to a more remote agnate if the nearest did not accept the inheritance open to him, or to the *gentiles* if there were agnates who failed to accept; further, at civil law, if there was an heir nominated under a will, intestate succession did not open until it was certain that he would not accept, either by reason of his death or his repudiation,[2] and there was nothing to force him to make up his mind within a reasonable time. It might thus happen very easily that an inheritance was vacant, without anyone to protect it, a state of affairs necessarily dangerous and particularly so at Rome, where the rule was that anyone might seize on any portion of a vacant inheritance and usucape it in one year even though he was not in good faith.[3] The praetor therefore, so Leist supposes, gave to all those who would be entitled at civil law, in turn, the chance of getting possession of the inheritance, by which he means, not merely the corporeal assets, but a possessory right to the position of heir, so that they would be able to bring all necessary actions and be liable to be sued by the creditors. This procedure was in the interest of all parties—the heir himself, other possible claimants, the creditors and the pontiffs, who would thus have someone on whom they could fix the responsibility for the *sacra*. If it so happened that possession was granted to a non-heir there was always the possibility that the real heir would make it *sine re* by claiming in time, but meanwhile the inheritance was protected. The idea of this provisional regulation of the inheritance was, according to Leist's view,[4] actually taken by the praetor from Athenian law, for at Athens any claimant to an inheritance, not being a son of the deceased, could only get possession of the inheritance after an application to the magistrate, followed by proceedings in which the claims of any other claimants were investigated, and even after he had obtained possession he was liable to be ousted by any other person who

---

[1] In Glück's *Erläuterung der Pandekten, Serie der Bücher* 37, 38, 1. Also published as *Der römische Erbrechtsbesitz in seiner ursprünglichen Gestalt*, 1870.

[2] Repudiation, for which no formalities were prescribed, sufficed in classical law, but it is doubtful whether originally there was any way in which a testamentary heir could repudiate so as to open the succession to the intestate heir; *v.* Sohm, 569. [3] *Supra*, 154, n. 2.

[4] *Gräco-italische Rechtsgeschichte* (1884), 89–90.

could successfully bring the Athenian equivalent of *hereditatis petitio* against him.[1]

Sohm[2] goes even further than Leist in an attempt to explain the Roman system by reference to Athenian institutions. At Athens, if a man had a son, he could not make a will, and no one else could be his heir; in such a case, therefore, there could be no dispute as to the inheritance, and the son could take possession of the property of the deceased on his own initiative; if there was no son, the claimant, whether under a will or on intestacy, needed magisterial authority before he could enter. Similarly, in Sohm's view, originally there could be no will at Rome if there was a *suus heres*. The succession of the *suus heres* is presumed in the XII Tables, whereas of the agnates and *gentiles* it is said, *familiam habento;*[3] this means that the *suus* alone, being the physical representative of the deceased, is deemed to succeed also to his possession, and can use force if his entry is opposed, whereas other successors only become heirs by the act of taking possession (*cretio*), and, if this is opposed, need the authorisation of the magistrate. *Bonorum possessio* thus, according to Sohm's view, began as a magisterial decree authorising *extranei* (whether claiming on intestacy or under a will) to take possession, and this view is supported by reference to the first words of the edict in its old form—*si de hereditate ambigitur*[4]—if there be dispute as to the inheritance, i.e. according to Sohm, because of the non-existence of *sui heredes*.

There is much to be learnt both from Leist's original theory and from Sohm's development of it, but they both involve the assumption that the grant of *bonorum possessio* was a grant of the "inheritance" as such, and not merely of the corporeal assets. This means that the *bonorum possessor* (even if not heir) must have been able to sue and be sued in the same way as an heir, and Leist indeed says that the actions with a fiction date from the time when *bonorum possessio* was first given to a non-heir.[5] This is a very difficult assumption to make, for the interdict *quorum bonorum* is probably considerably older than the fictitious actions. Interdicts date in the main from the *legis actio* period, fictitious actions from the time of the formulary system,[6] and, while the interdict *quorum bonorum* was clearly known to Cicero,[7] the first trace of the fictitious actions dates from the

---

[1] For this procedure *v.* also Lipsius, 577–584.
[2] 566 *sqq.*   [3] *Supra*, 123–124.
[4] Cic. *in Verr.* II. I. 45. 117; Lenel, *E.P.* 349.
[5] *Op. cit.* (*supra*, 262, n. 1), 102.
[6] A. Schmidt, "Die Anfänge der *bonorum possessio*", *Z.S.S.* XVII at 327.
[7] *Top.* IV. 18; *ad fam.* VII. 21.

time of Labeo.[1] It is thus probably better to follow the opinion of those scholars who regard *bonorum possessio* in its origin as simply a scheme for the regulation of the possession of the goods of a deceased person pending the settlement of the question of inheritance by *hereditatis petitio*.[2] If two people were about to dispute the title to a thing by *hereditatis petitio* under the old system of *legis actio sacramento*, the interim possession of it would have to be assigned to one or other of them, just as was the case with an ordinary *vindicatio*, and the praetor might very well settle this question by assigning it to the one who appeared *prima facie* to be entitled according to the civil law; originally this would have been done after investigation by the praetor himself: later, the machinery of an interdict would be used in this as in other cases. Often, no doubt, the parties would content themselves with this procedure, and the *hereditatis petitio* would never need to be tried. According to this theory, then, the interdict *quorum bonorum* would have had an origin very similar to that of the other possessory interdicts,[3] in the desire of the praetor to grant the advantage of possession to the person who appeared to be *prima facie* entitled; it is also pointed out that the words *si de hereditate ambigitur* may well have referred to the proceedings by *hereditatis petitio* for which the interim assignment of possession was first needed.

[1] *V.* Girard, 965, n. 2.
[2] Girard, 844 *sqq.*, and quotations there; Buckland, *Manual*, 235.
[3] *Infra*, 272.

Chapter XV

PRIVATE LAW FROM THE XII TABLES TO THE FALL OF THE REPUBLIC: THE LAW OF SLAVERY AND MANUMISSION

The old civil law had recognised the humanity of the slave only by admitting that he could acquire rights for his master and by allowing him to become a citizen on manumission.[1] By the end of the republic praetorian rules had modified this position only in two directions: (*a*) by admitting that in certain circumstances the slave might not only acquire rights for the master but also lay him under an obligation, (*b*) by allowing that certain acts, not falling under any of the forms of civil law manumission and not resulting in citizenship, might give a slave the right to protection against the exercise by the master of his rights of ownership.

(*a*) Here the praetor carried out his innovation by granting actions against the master on transactions entered into by the slave.[2] These actions fall into two classes, according as they are based on the idea that a master who has authorised his slave to contract must be responsible for the contract, or on the idea that the master who has allowed the slave to administer a *peculium* for himself must be prepared to lose the *peculium* if the slave administers it badly. To the former class belong the *actiones quod iussu*, *exercitoria* and *institoria*, to the latter the *actio de peculio et in rem verso* and the *actio tributoria*.

The *actio quod iussu* enabled a person with whom a slave had made a contract which was authorised by his master to sue the master on the contract for the full amount owing. The *actio institoria* concerns the general authorisation implied in the appointment of a slave as manager of a business; if any person contracted with the slave in connection with the business which he was appointed to manage he could sue the master for the full amount by this action. Almost exactly the same rules applied where the slave was appointed master of a trading ship, but here the action was called *exercitoria*.[3] These actions, it must be noticed, greatly increased

---

[1] *Supra*, 135.

[2] The name *actiones adiecticiae qualitatis* usually given to these actions, though not Roman, is useful.

[3] From *exercitor*, i.e. the person who takes the profit of a ship, her owner or charterer. *Institoria* is derived from *institor*, a business manager. These actions were also available if the agent was free. Gai. IV. 71.

the usefulness of slaves, for they made it possible for masters to use their slaves as agents, a thing which had been impossible under the old law when slaves could only acquire rights for their masters and not put them under obligations. The *actio de peculio et in rem verso* also enables the master to be sued on his slave's contract, but there are two important features which distinguish this case from those that precede. There is no need for any authorisation—indeed the action lies even if the master forbade the transaction; all that is necessary is that the slave should have a *peculium*.[1] But, on the other hand, the master's liability is limited; he is only liable up to the amount of the *peculium* and for any proceeds of the transaction by which he has profited, if, for instance, the slave has borrowed money and used it to pay a creditor of his master's. In estimating the amount of the *peculium* the master could deduct any debts due from the slave to himself,[2] but, on the other hand, must include any debts due from himself to the slave—"debts" meaning here not actionable debts (for there could be no action between a master and his slave), but unenforceable debts arising out of transactions between the slave and the master, because so far as practice went the *peculium* was treated as the slave's property. He could, for instance, "sell" a thing to his master and the result would be that the price of the thing had to be reckoned as part of the *peculium* even before the master gave it to the slave, because he already "owed" it.[3] The *actio tributoria* shows a difference in this respect. If the slave traded with his *peculium* or with part of it to the master's knowledge and the fund so created was at any time insufficient to pay all the creditors, it was the master's business (if required to do so) to divide what remained up fairly in proportion to the debts; in such a case he might not deduct first what was "owing" to himself, but had to treat himself just as he would any other creditor. If any creditor thought he was not being treated fairly in this respect he could sue the master by this action.

The whole field of these *actiones adiecticiae qualitatis* is a good example of purely praetorian law-making right outside the province of the civil law. Several edicts laid down the circumstances in which the different actions would be allowed, and in the *formulae* the praetorian devices of fiction and change of person between the *intentio* and the *condemnatio*

---

[1] *V. supra*, 80.

[2] Or, what comes to the same thing, to any other member of the *familia*.

[3] In the law of Justinian's day such obligations are called "natural", but it is questionable whether this is a classical use of the word; *v.* Siber, "*Naturalis obligatio*", *Gedenkschrift für Mitteis* (Leipzig, 1926), 1–85.

were employed.[1] E.g. the *formula*, in the case of a purchase made by a slave on the authorisation of his master, ran something as follows: "Whereas A. A. with the authorisation of N. N. sold a toga to Stichus at a time when Stichus was in the power of N. N., whatever on that account Stichus, if he were free, would have in good faith to pay A. A., thereto the judge is to condemn N. N. etc."[2] A great deal of the elaboration of the law in connection with these actions is of course due to the work of the classical jurists, but that the actions themselves were known by the end of the republic seems clear. The *actio quod iussu*[3] and the *actio tributoria*[4] were both known to Labeo,[5] the *actiones institoria*[6] and *de peculio*[7] to Ser. Sulpicius,[8] and the *exercitoria*[9] to Ofilius.[10]

(*b*) The "informal" methods of manumission. It happened sometimes that a master who failed for one reason or another[11] to use recognised methods of manumission, nevertheless declared that he wished a slave of his to be free. This had no effect at civil law, but, provided certain conditions had been complied with, the praetor would not allow the master to go back on his word to the extent of forcing the slave to work for him again; he would, in fact, refuse the master his *vindicatio in servitutem*. For all other purposes however the slave remained a slave, and the children of a woman were slaves of her owner. It was not every informal declaration that had this effect; the praetor only acted if the master had provided the slave with some evidence which he could subsequently adduce if the declaration were called in question, either by writing him a letter or by making the declaration before witnesses. Hence there are said to be two kinds of informal manumission, that *per epistolam* and that *inter amicos*, for the "friends" are here present as witnesses.[12]

---

[1] *Supra*, 212.
[2] Lenel, *E.P.* 278.
[3] D. 15. 4. 1. 9.
[4] D. 14. 4. 7. 4; 9. 2.
[5] For dates *v. infra*, 387.
[6] D. 14. 3. 5. 1.
[7] D. 15. 1. 17.
[8] Dates *supra*, 91.
[9] D. 14. 1. 1. 9.
[10] Dates *supra*, 91.

[11] E.g. because being only "bonitary" owner he was not competent to use one of the civil law methods, or because being deaf or dumb he was similarly incompetent; *v.* Paul. *Sent.* IV. 12. 2.

[12] Wlassak, *Z.S.S.* XXVI. 367–431, objects to the term "informal manumission", as these conditions were in fact insisted upon, but these conditions can hardly be called rules of form in the same sense as those of manumission *vindicta* are; they are practical requirements for evidentiary purposes—thus there was no rule as to the number of witnesses needed for *inter amicos*.

Chapter XVI

PRIVATE LAW FROM THE XII TABLES TO THE FALL OF THE REPUBLIC: THE LAW OF PROPERTY

§ I. OWNERSHIP AND POSSESSION

The chief development in this part of the law is the working out of the absolute conception of ownership and the differentiation of possession as something quite distinct from ownership through the growth of the possessory interdicts. As we have seen,[1] the oldest type of *vindicatio*, the *legis actio sacramento in rem*, was really a claim to the better right to possess; neither party could, strictly, be said to be either plaintiff or defendant, for both had to assert a claim to the thing in dispute, and interim possession was not necessarily given to the party who had had possession when proceedings began. But we have also seen[2] that there was developed, in the later republic, the procedure *per sponsionem*; in this procedure we can already say that one party is plaintiff and the other defendant, and that the plaintiff must claim an absolute right, because the bet formed by the two *sponsiones* is on the question whether he is owner *ex iure Quiritium* or not. The same question is also put directly to the *iudex* in the still later type of procedure *per formulam petitoriam*.[3] These actions lie only at the suit of one who is out of possession against one who is in possession,[4] and if the plaintiff does not prove his case the defendant retains the thing. If it is not clear which of the parties is actually in possession the question can be settled by special interdict proceedings. Possession thus becomes a conception quite separate from that of ownership and protected by quite separate remedies.

§ II. THE POSSESSORY INTERDICTS

To understand the importance of possession it is necessary to understand the interdicts by which it was protected. The characteristic of these interdicts is that they protected possession as an existing state of fact without reference to its rightfulness or wrongfulness,[5] and the result of their existence is that if anyone wishes to disturb an existing possession

---

[1] *Supra*, 144. [2] *Supra*, 196.

[3] I.e. where the *intentio* is *si paret rem...ex iure Quiritium Ai. Ai. esse*; cf. *supra*, 214.

[4] Cf. Buckland, 258, n. 12; Girard, 366.

[5] Except that it must not have been obtained *vi*, *clam* or *precario* from the other party; *infra*, 270.

he can only do so by means of a regular judicial proceeding in which he himself proves a title.

The Romans themselves divided possessory interdicts into three classes, according as they served the purpose of acquiring, retaining or recovering possession (*vel adipiscendae vel retinendae vel reciperandae possessionis causa comparata*).[1] An example of the first class is the interdict *quorum bonorum*, which enables the *bonorum possessor* to get possession of the goods of the deceased.[2] This is possessory in the sense that it deals with possession only; no question of superior title may be raised by the defendant; if, for instance, he thinks that he is heir and has a better right to the goods than the *bonorum possessor*, he must nevertheless give them up and will have to make good his title, if he can, in a separate *hereditatis petitio*. But these interdicts of the first class are not relevant to the present discussion, because, as their name shows, they do not protect an existing possession, but are a means of obtaining a new one. The remaining two classes we must consider.

(i) *Interdicta retinendae possessionis causa comparata.* Of these there were two, one, *uti possidetis*, for use where the property concerned was immovable, the other, *utrubi*, for use where it was movable.

(a) *Uti possidetis.* The simplest way of understanding this interdict is to take the case where it is used as a preliminary to a *vindicatio*. If two people are in dispute as to the ownership of a piece of land, it is usually quite clear that one possesses and the other does not, but it may happen that each claims to be actually in possession; one may say that he has mown the grass, the other that he has pastured his beasts on the stubble, and each may claim that his act amounts to the exercise of possession. Which is right is decided by the interdict proceedings. The praetor issues an order, addressed to both parties, forbidding any interference with the existing state of possession;[3] each party then does some act (for form's sake) which, if the other possesses, amounts to such interference, and the question which of them has thus disobeyed the praetor's order is tried on *sponsiones* and *restipulationes*.[4] Interim possession is granted to the party who makes the higher bid for it, i.e. offers to pay the higher sum should he get it and be found subsequently not to have been entitled.[5]

---

[1] Gai. IV. 143.   [2] Cf. *supra*, 260.

[3] *Uti eas aedes quibus de agitur nec vi nec clam nec precario alter ab altero possidetis, quo minus ita possideatis vim fieri veto*; Lenel, *E.P.* 470.

[4] Cf. *supra*, 235. The interdict being "double" there is need for two bets, (i) that *A* has disobeyed, (ii) that *B* has disobeyed, and consequently for four stipulations.   [5] Gai. IV. 167.

If it turns out that the interim possessor is the person entitled, i.e. really did possess at the beginning of the proceedings, he of course remains in possession and will be defendant in the *vindicatio*; if the other party turns out to be entitled, possession will have to be handed over to him, and he will have the desirable position of defendant. The interesting thing to notice is that the whole proceeding is "double", as the *legis actio sacramento in rem* was; there is no plaintiff and no defendant, and interim possession pending the settlement of the question at issue has thus to be given to one or other, but the question at issue is now simply that of the actual possession, and in no way prejudices further proceedings to settle the right of ownership. This use of *uti possidetis* as a preliminary to *vindicatio* is typical, but it might, of course, happen that the party defeated in the interdict rested content with that decision and never brought a *vindicatio*, and it appears that in the developed law the interdict could even be brought to safeguard existing possession against interference where the person interfering did not claim to possess himself.[1] It is also generally agreed that *uti possidetis* might be used in certain circumstances to recover a possession which had been lost.[2] The interdict, from a very early date, contained words which limited the praetor's protection to such possession as had not been obtained *vi, clam* or *precario* (violently, clandestinely or as tenant-at-will) from the other party to the proceedings. If, therefore, *A* was found to be in possession but it was also found that he had obtained that possession by violently ejecting *B*, then it is clear that *B* in exercising the formal force did not disobey the praetor's order. It is not quite so clear that *A* disobeyed it, but it appears that he was held to have done so and consequently had to give up possession to *B*.

(b) *Utrubi*.[3] Where a movable object was concerned, the praetor's order was framed so as to give possession not to the person who was found to have it at the moment when proceedings commenced, but to the one who had had it for the greater part of the last year. It is obvious therefore that this interdict might be used to regain possession—if e.g. *A* had had possession for the last five months, but *B* for the seven months preceding, then *B* could recover from *A*. Otherwise the effect was similar to that of *uti possidetis*.

[1] Girard, 302, n. 1, quoting D. 43. 17. 3. 2–4; Buckland, 734, n. 4.
[2] Girard, 301; Buckland, 734.
[3] *Utrubi vestrum hic homo quo de agitur nec vi nec clam nec precario ab altero fuit, apud quem maiore parte huiusce anni fuit, quo minus is eum ducat vim fieri veto*; Lenel, *E.P.* 489; Gai. IV. 150–152, 160.

(ii) *Interdicta reciperandae possessionis causa comparata*. Of these there were two, or perhaps at one time three.

(*a*) *Unde vi*.[1] This enabled a man to regain possession of land from which he had been ousted violently. It had two forms according as the violence complained of had been "armed" or "ordinary". The chief difference was this: if *A* complained that *B* had ousted him by ordinary violence, it was sufficient answer for *B* to show that *A* himself had previously got possession *vi, clam* or *precario* from *B*; if *A* complained of armed violence such defence was not open to *B*.

(*b*) *De precario*.[2] This enabled the man who had let another have a thing *precario* to get it back.

(*c*) Perhaps there existed at one time an interdict *de clandestina possessione* enabling a person who had lost possession by the clandestine entry of another to get it back. As the two other recuperatory interdicts correspond to two of the limbs of the clause *nec vi nec clam nec precario* found as a defence in other interdicts, so it is thought that there must have been one corresponding to the third limb.[3]

§ III. ORIGIN OF THE POSSESSORY INTERDICTS

Of the origin of the possessory interdicts nothing is known for certain. One old theory, which still has adherents, is that they were originally developed for the protection of the interest in public land which settlers had acquired by occupation;[4] such interest was, of course, not ownership, and consequently an occupier deprived of his enjoyment could not avail himself of the *vindicatio*; the praetor consequently, according to this view, provided protection by interdict.

It is true that persons who occupy public lands are frequently referred to as *possessores*, but nevertheless there are serious objections to the theory. As is pointed out by Jhering,[5] a dispute about *ager publicus* would not be a matter for the jurisdiction of the praetor, but for administrative action on the part of the magistrates, in particular the censors, whose duty it was to manage state property, and, above all, it is difficult to see how a remedy, originally intended for the protection of legitimate interests in public land, could have subsequently been used for the

---

[1] Gai. IV. 154; Lenel, *E.P.* 461 *sqq.*
[2] Cf. *supra*, 235.
[3] Girard, 304, n. 1; Buckland, 735, n. 11.
[4] Niebuhr, *Röm. Geschichte*, II. 161 *sqq.* Followed by Savigny, Dernburg and others; *v.* Kübler, 156; Girard, 300.
[5] *Besitzwille*, 124, n. 1.

totally different purpose of protecting mere *de facto* possession of private property. Jhering's own view[1] is that the original purpose of the possessory interdicts was to form a substitute for the procedure of *vindicias dicere* in actions *in rem*, so that instead of granting interim possession according to his own discretion, the praetor now caused the question who was actually possessor to be investigated by means of the interdict procedure, and saw that the party who was successful in the interdict remained in possession until the action was decided. There are difficulties about this theory too,[2] but it is still probably the best that has been advanced; it corresponds closely with the utterances of the Romans themselves concerning the purpose for which the interdicts existed, and it provides an explanation of these interdicts parallel to that suggested for the interdict *quorum bonorum*.[3,4] For the dates of introduction of the different possessory interdicts we have but little evidence. That *uti possidetis* was already known in the middle of the second century B.C. seems clear from the very close copy of its wording used to decide a dispute between two Greek cities about 140.[5] *Utrubi* is said to be referred to by Plautus in 200 B.C., but the reference is very doubtful.[6] On the other hand Terence, in 161 B.C.,[7] seems pretty clearly to refer to the clause concerning violent, clandestine and "precarious" possession. *Unde vi* is spoken of by Cicero[8] as a remedy known "to our ancestors", but details are lacking. It is likely enough that the earlier form of the interdict was that concerning "ordinary" violence, and that the form concerning armed violence only arose in the troubled days of the civil wars, when the edict concerning robbery also became necessary.[9]

[1] *Grund des Besitzschutzes*, 76 *sqq.*

[2] Karlowa (II. 318) points out that the assignment of *vindiciae* came right at the end of the old procedure *in iure* as described by Gaius (IV. 16) and that it would not be possible to insert at this point a possibly lengthy investigation of the facts of possession. Somewhat similar arguments, Ubbelohde, in Glück's *Erläuterung der Pandekten, Serie der Bücher* 43, 44, v. 630 *sqq.* Cf. Cuq, *N.R.H.* XVIII (1894), 12–14.

[3] Cf. *supra*, 264.

[4] Another view is that it was simply a question of the need for a more summary remedy than *vindicatio* where a person's possession was interfered with, and that this need became noticeable when the extension of Roman territory made disputes concerning land at once commoner and more difficult to settle quickly; Karlowa, *loc. cit.* If the need for more summary process was the driving force, the case is closely parallel to that of the English possessory assizes; *v.* Holdsworth, *H.E.L.* III. 8.

[5] Partsch, *Schriftformel*, 19; cf. *supra*, 223.

[6] *Stichus*, v. 4. 14 and v. 5. 9.   [7] *Eunuchus*, II. 3. 27.

[8] *Pro Tull.* XIX. 44.   [9] *V.* Karlowa, II. 1207; cf. *infra*, 287.

§ IV. THE *ACTIO PUBLICIANA* AND THE DEVELOPMENT OF "BONITARY" OWNERSHIP

The *actio Publiciana* is the action which is allowed under the praetorian edict to a man who, after possessing a thing in such circumstances that he would in time usucape it, loses possession of it before the time for usucapion has elapsed. Such a man can clearly not bring a *vindicatio* because he has not yet become owner, but the praetor desires that he should be able to get the thing back from subsequent possessors who have no better right than himself and therefore permits him to bring this action, the *formula* of which contains a fiction[1] that the time for usucapion has already run, i.e. the judge is told to condemn if the thing in question would have become the property of the plaintiff *ex iure Quiritium* had his possession lasted long enough. It must be noticed that the fiction only extends to the lapse of time; whether the plaintiff's possession was such as to lead to usucapion the judge must of course investigate.

Now an action of this sort would benefit two classes of possessors who had not got good title to the thing they possessed,[2] (*a*) the possessor who was not owner because the person from whom he had acquired the thing was not owner, and (*b*) the possessor who was not owner because of some defect in the method by which the thing had been acquired, in particular, where a *res mancipi* had been received by mere *traditio*. The position, however, of these two classes is not the same, because possessors of the first class (whom we will call "*bona fide* possessors") will be protected only against persons who have no better title than themselves, whereas those of the second class (whom we will call "bonitary owners") will be protected even against the Quiritarian owner. The way in which the praetor brings this result about is best seen by examples.

(i) *Bona fide possessor.* If *A* sells and delivers to *B* a thing which in fact belongs to *X*, and *B* receives it in good faith, *B* (provided there has been no theft) will become owner in one or two years (according as the thing is a movable or immovable). If now before the time has elapsed the thing gets into the hands of *C*, *B* can get it back by the *actio Publiciana*;[3] but if it gets back into the hands of *X*, its real owner, the *actio Publiciana* will not be successful, because, although it is true that *B* would have been

---

[1] Gai. IV. 36. For *formulae* with a fiction cf. *supra*, 211.

[2] Cf. *supra*, 155–156, on the functions of *usucapio*. Whether the *formula* was exactly the same in the two cases is disputed; Lenel now holds that it was, *E.P.* 170.

[3] In some cases of course a possessory interdict would be available, but by no means in all.

owner had his possession continued long enough, X is allowed to plead his ownership as a defence. X puts into the *formula* an *exceptio iusti dominii*, i.e. a clause telling the judge not to condemn even if B would have been owner had his possession lasted long enough, if in fact X is owner.[1] It is, of course, also open to X at any time so long as B possesses and the time for usucapion has not elapsed to bring a *vindicatio* against B.

(ii) *Bonitary owner.* If A sells and delivers (*tradit*) to B a slave (*res mancipi*) which is his (A's) property, B does not become owner at once *ex iure Quiritium*, but will do so in time by usucapion. If he loses possession to C he can therefore use the *actio Publiciana* in the same way as the mere *b.f.* possessor. But unlike the mere *b.f.* possessor he can use the *actio Publiciana* successfully even against A (who has remained owner *ex iure Quiritium*) if the slave happens to get back into A's possession. It is true that A can put in the *exceptio iusti dominii*, but B will meet this by a *replicatio rei venditae et traditae*,[2] i.e. the judge will be told to condemn even if the thing is the defendant's (A's) property if it be further shown that the defendant sold and delivered it to the plaintiff (B). If A tries to take advantage of his Quiritary ownership and bring a *vindicatio* against B then B will use the *exceptio rei venditae et traditae*,[3] i.e. the judge will be told not to condemn if the property belongs to the plaintiff (A) if the plaintiff sold and delivered the thing to the defendant. In fact the praetor treats failure to mancipate a *res mancipi* as a mere technicality and regards anyone who seeks to rely on it as unworthy of consideration; the recipient he supplies with such remedies that he in practice has all the security and very nearly all the advantages of ownership. In such a case, where the advantage of ownership was with B and the mere nominal right *ex iure Quiritium* with A, B was said to have the thing among his goods—*in bonis*—from which phrase the Greek writers subsequently coined the word "bonitary" to express this type of ownership.[4]

---

[1] D. 6. 2. 16; 17.

[2] The existence of this *replicatio* is not directly attested, but can be inferred with certainty from the *exceptio r. v. et t.* It is also said that the *exceptio iusti dominii* is only given *causa cognita*, D. 17. 1. 57; Buckland, 193.

[3] D. 21. 3. As its name shows, the *exceptio* was originally only intended for the commonest case, i.e. where the delivery was on account of a sale, but protection was also given, apparently by allowing *exceptio doli*, where there was some different ground, e.g. an exchange, D. 44. 4. 4. 31. The *exceptio* was available to successors in title of the transferee and against successors in title of the transferor, D. 21. 3. 3.

[4] *Bona* is the praetorian expression for property, no distinction being drawn by the praetor between *res mancipi* and *nec mancipi*; cf. *bonorum possessor*, etc. In

Like the "praetorian will", this "bonitary" or "praetorian" ownership exemplifies the dislike of the praetorian system for the old formal requirements of the civil law, requirements whose importance it greatly diminished by providing remedies for those whose rights were defective because some piece of ceremonial had been omitted. Obviously once the position described above had been reached there was little danger if a buyer did not insist, when buying a *res mancipi*, on having it conveyed to him by mancipation or *in iure cessio*.

By the end of the republic this development was certainly not yet complete, but it is generally held that it had at least begun. Who the Publicius was who introduced the Publician action we do not know,[1] but the action would appear to have been known already to Sabinus[2] in the early years of the empire, and it is likely enough that the *exceptio rei venditae et traditae* is earlier than the *actio Publiciana*. To give a transferee a defence against the transferor who tries to rely on his purely technical title seems a more obvious piece of equity than to provide the transferee with means

explaining the difference between ownership *ex iure Quiritium* and *in bonis* Gaius (II. 40, 41) mentions only the case of the *res mancipi* transferred by *traditio*, but it is clear that other cases too are included in the phrase *in bonis habere* for Modestinus (D. 41. 1. 52) says generally, "We are deemed to hold a thing *in bonis nostris* whenever we have an *exceptio* if we possess it and an action to recover it if we lose possession". There are also a number of different cases in which the *actio Publiciana* is said to lie, e.g. where a man has been put in possession on the ground of *damnum infectum* (D. 39. 2. 18. 15; cf. *supra*, 231), Buckland, 195. No doubt the *formula* of the *actio Publiciana* would in such cases differ from that given by Gai. IV. 36, which refers to the common case of delivery by reason of sale. Similarly the *exceptio rei venditae et traditae* would have to be altered or replaced by the *exceptio doli*. It appears from Gai. I. 167 (*in bonis mea*) and II. 40 that the lawyers of the classical age already regarded the person who held a thing *in bonis* as a kind of owner, but they had apparently not yet distinguished what modern books call "bonitary ownership", i.e. the case where the holder is completely secure against all other persons from the case of *b.f.* possession where the title is not good against the real owner but is good against others, for Modestinus' definition fits both cases; cf. Karlowa, II. 1220. The word "bonitary" is first used by Theophilus, *Paraphr.* 1. 5. 4. On the whole subject *v.* especially Appleton, *Histoire de la propriété prétorienne et de l'action Publicienne* (1889).

[1] J. 4. 6. 4 says that the action was called "Publician" because it was first put in the edict by a praetor named Publicius, but none of the Publicii known to have held the praetorship appears to fit, Girard, 375. Wlassak, *Prozessformel*, 33, suggests the Publicius mentioned by Pomponius, D. 1. 2. 2. 44, among the pupils of Servius. It is also possible that Justinian is mistaken and that the name comes from a jurist who held no office, but was the first to suggest the *formula* as adviser to a party.

[2] D. 6. 2. 15; Girard, *loc. cit.*

of attacking third parties, but such *a priori* reasoning cannot carry us very far.[1]

§ V. OWNERSHIP OF PROVINCIAL LAND

In classical law it was settled doctrine that land in the provinces belonged to the state and could not be owned *ex iure Quiritium* by any private individual, Roman or peregrine.[2] Exception was only made in the case of a few favoured localities, where the soil was assimilated for legal purposes to that of Italy, by special imperial grant of the *ius Italicum*.[3] In spite of this rule, however, rights heritable and alienable were in fact enjoyed by individuals in provincial land, and differed in practice from full Roman ownership mainly by reason of the liability to one form or another of land-tax which attached to the soil. For the protection of this quasi-ownership the ordinary *vindicatio* was of course not available, but an action analogous to the *vindicatio* was certainly given under the provincial edicts.[4]

The doctrine of state ownership in provincial land is commonly held to date from the time of C. Gracchus (tribune 123–122 B.C.)[5] and to be connected with his project for bettering the position of the Roman proletariate by securing for them the wealth of the provinces, and the idea seems certainly to have existed already in the republic.[6] It is, however, more likely that the formulation of the legal dogma dates only from the empire, and is indeed subsequent to the reign of Claudius.[7]

§ VI. OWNERSHIP BY *PEREGRINI*

Peregrini (unless they had *commercium*) could not own property *ex iure Quiritium*, and the ordinary forms of *vindicatio* could therefore not be used by them; nor could the Publician action, for it involved the

---

[1] Cf. Karlowa, II. 1223. The *actio Publiciana* cannot in any case be earlier than the *formula petitoria* of the *vindicatio* of which it is an adaptation, and the earliest trace of the *formula petitoria* is in Cic. *in Verr.* II. 2. 12. 31 (70 B.C.).

[2] Gai. II. 7: *In provinciali solo...dominium populi Romani est vel Caesaris, nos autem possessionem tantum vel usumfructum habere videmur*; cf. II. 21.

[3] *Infra,* 352, n. 4.

[4] The *formula* is uncertain. Lenel, *E.P.* 189, conjectures *Si paret Ao. Ao. fundum quo de agitur habere possidere frui licere*, mainly on the ground of Gai. II. 7 (*supra,* n. 2), and the occurrence of similar words in the *lex agraria* of III B.C. (Bruns, I. 73–89), lines 32, 40, 50, 52 and 82.

[5] Mommsen, *Staatsr.* III. 730–737.

[6] Cic. *in Verr.* II. 2. 3. 7: *Quasi quaedam praedia populi Romani sunt vectigalia nostra atque provinciae.*

[7] Tenney Frank, *Journal of Roman Studies,* XVII (1927), 141–161.

proposition that the plaintiff would have acquired ownership *ex iure Quiritium* had he possessed long enough. There can be no doubt however that their property was in fact protected, perhaps by actions with a fiction, and their relation to such property must therefore be classed as one of the inferior modes of ownership known to Roman law.[1]

§ VII. *IURA IN RE ALIENA*

A. PRAEDIAL SERVITUDES. By the end of the republic the number of servitudes recognised by law had grown considerably, but it was not, and never became, the rule at Rome that parties could attach the character-istics of a servitude to any restriction on the ownership of land that they chose.[2] Of the rustic servitudes which appear on Justinian's list[3] (beyond the original rights of way and *aquae ductus*), *aquae haustus* was already known to Cicero as well established,[4] *pecoris ad aquam adpulsus* to Trebatius,[5] and others may be equally old. At no time was there, it appears, a special pattern *formula* in the edict for any rustic servitude except the rights of way and *aquae ductus*;[6] the *formula* would have to be drafted specially in each case.

Urban servitudes, too, had long been in existence. The need for these came, as has been said,[7] with the growth of urban life and the raising of buildings above the ground floor, a practice which goes back at least to the end of the third century B.C.[8] A number of the servitudes known to the later law are actually attested by republican writers; thus *stillicidium* (the right to let rain-water drop onto a neighbour's land) and *flumen* (where the water flows in a continuous stream) are mentioned by Varro,[9] and Cicero treats of *iura parietum, luminum, stillicidiorum* as three definite groups.[10]

The whole law on the subject was, it is clear, already considerably developed, and *servitus* was already a term for a definite class of rights,[11] but the absolute nature of these rights had not yet been worked out, i.e. they were not yet fully recognised as being *in rem*, capable of assertion against any person whatsoever; strictly the action by which a servitude is claimed (later called *actio confessoria*) availed only against the *dominus*.[12]

---

[1] Buckland, 190; Girard, 380.

[2] Note especially the rule that the servitude must in some way add to the advantages of the dominant tenement, not be a merely personal advantage to the owner; D. 8. 1. 8 pr.; 15 pr.; 19.

[3] J. 2. 3. pr. and 2.   [4] *Pro Caec.* XXVI. 74.

[5] D. 43. 20. 1. 18.   [6] Lenel, *E.P.* 192.   [7] *Supra,* 159.

[8] Livy v. 55.   [9] *L.L.* v. 27.   [10] *De Or.* I. 38. 173.

[11] Karlowa, II. 496, though as Buckland points out (259) it was not very ancient.

[12] This was still true in classical times; *v.* Rabel, 448 and literature there quoted.

B. *Ususfructus* AND *usus*. Usufruct is the right of using and taking the fruits of property belonging to another, *salva rerum substantia*,[1] i.e. without the right of destroying or changing the character of the thing, and lasting only so long as the character remains unchanged.[2] It is usually for the life of the person entitled and cannot be for a longer period, and it thus corresponds most closely to what we call a "life interest". *Usus* is a similar right, but to the use of the thing only, not including the taking of fruits. Rights of this nature are classed in the law of Justinian's day as "personal servitudes",[3] because they exist for the benefit of individuals as such, without reference to the ownership of any particular piece of property, whereas praedial servitudes enure to the advantage of the owner for the time being of a particular piece of land, but this classification we know now to date from the end of the classical period at the earliest.[4] They can exist over either movable or immovable property.

We do not know precisely when either of these rights came to be recognised, but usufruct was well known to Cicero,[5] and we hear of a question concerning it that was debated by the jurists of the second century B.C.[6] It may well be that it arose about the first half of the third century B.C.,[7] very probably as a method of providing for the widow where marriage was without *manus*.[8] There can be little doubt that it occurred first as the result of legacies, and legacy remained always the main source of the "personal servitudes". *Usus* is probably of later origin, for the jurists treat it as a variation of the more normal usufruct and apply the rules worked out for usufruct to it by analogy.[9,10]

---

[1] J. 2. 4. pr.

[2] V. Buckland, *Manual*, 162, but see also *Main Institutions*, 145 *sqq*.

[3] D. 8. 1. 1. The Institutes, following Gaius, distinguish "servitudes" from usufruct; J. 2. 2. 2 and 3; Gai. II. 14.

[4] Buckland, 268; *L.Q.R.* XLIII (1927), 326.

[5] E.g. *pro Caec.* VII. 19.   [6] Cic. *de fin.* I. 4. 12; D. 7. 1. 68.

[7] Karlowa, II. 534.

[8] Buckland, 268.

[9] D. 7. 8. 1. 1; Karlowa, II. 540.

[10] The rule that a servitude cannot impose a duty to act on the owner of the servient tenement was already formulated by Aquilius Gallus (D. 8. 5. 6. 2), and is clearly based on a sharp distinction between servitude and obligation. Perhaps the exception whereby in *oneris ferendi* the servient owner is under a duty to repair the wall is a survival from a time when this distinction was not so clearly recognised. Early Germanic law, in which the idea of obligation was undeveloped, felt no difficulty in imposing a duty to act (e.g. a rent charge) as the correlative of a right *in rem*, and consequently treats as property many of the rights which in Roman and modern law fall under the heading of obligations; cf. Holdsworth, *Historical Introduction to the Land Law*, 90 and 98.

C. *Conductio agri vectigalis* AND *superficies*. The classical law knew of two further rights in relation to land, both arising from a sort of lease, which had already through praetorian legislation almost completely attained to the status of rights *in rem*, a process which was completed in Justinian's time. *Conductio agri vectigalis* (which became *emphyteusis* under Justinian) arose from the grant of a heritable and alienable lease of land, by the state or municipalities in return for a comparatively small rent, payable by the tenant for the time being (and thus constituting a burden on the land). *Superficies* was a somewhat similar grant for building purposes. The practice of granting leases of this sort had apparently begun in republican times, but it is unlikely that the praetor as yet gave remedies which assimilated the position of the tenant to that of a holder of a right *in rem*.[1]

---

[1] The chief work on the subject is Mitteis, *Zur Geschichte der Erbpacht* (1901). See also the other literature quoted by Rabel, 451–452.

Chapter XVII

PRIVATE LAW FROM THE XII TABLES TO THE FALL OF THE REPUBLIC: THE LAW OF OBLIGATIONS

In tracing the history of obligations it is necessary, more even than in other parts of the law, to distinguish the growth of theoretical conceptions, of general rules and of classifications, from the development of the actual procedural possibilities which underlay the generalisations of theory. So far as the former are concerned the end of the republic still finds the Romans comparatively backward. The word *obligatio* itself is not yet a technical term,[1] and indeed even in the classical period, when it had become technical, it did not correspond to the Byzantine and modern conception, for there still remained about it traces of its original literal meaning. *Nexum*, it is true, had long fallen into disuse, but a man who was "under an obligation" might find himself quite literally bound, if he did not discharge it, so long as execution against the person remained a normal thing. Further, at least until towards the end of the classical period, *obligatio* was a purely civil law word, and did not include those cases where a man was liable because a praetorian action lay against him.[2] With other familiar words the position is similar. "Contract" seems to us a fundamental conception, denoting the formation of an obligation by agreement, and this was the Byzantine meaning also; but the Latin for an agreement is *conventio* or *pactum*,[3] and it was by no means every agreement which gave rise to an obligation. *Contractus* is simply the verbal noun formed from *contrahere* (literally, "to tie"), and it is used elliptically for *contractus negotii* or *obligationis*, whether what we call a "contract" was involved or not. Logically there was no reason why it should not be used of obligations contracted by delict, but usage seems to have confined the word to *negotia* (transactions), in opposition to delict.[4]

---

[1] The verb *obligare* is old in juristic use, e.g. Varro (*L.L.* VII. 105), quoting Mucius: *quae per aes et libram fiant ut obligentur* (*supra*, 167, n. 2), but it is not confined to "obligations". Plautus uses it of pledge (*Truc.* II. I. 4: *aedes obligatae sunt ob amoris praedium*), as indeed the classical lawyers still do (e.g. D. 20. 4. 21). The noun *obligatio* is rare before Gaius; Cicero uses it, e.g. *ad Brut.* I. 18. 3, but without any definite legal implication; *v.* Buckland, 406; Mitteis, *R.P.R.* 86.

[2] Buckland, 409; cf. Perozzi, *Le obbligazione romane* (1903), 135 *sqq.*

[3] Bonfante, "Sui *contractus* e sui *pacta*" (*Scritti Giuridici*, III. 136).

[4] Bonfante, "Sulla genesi e l' evoluzione del *contractus*", *Scritti Giuridici*, III.

At the end of the republic indeed terminology had not got even as far as this, for, though Cicero uses the word *contrahere*, he does not use the noun.[1] Still less was there any classification of obligations into those arising from contract and delict, or of contracts according to their different methods of formation.

If, however, we turn from abstract conceptions and classifications to the actual remedies available in the courts, we can see that the main skeleton of the classical structure was already in existence before the republic came to an end. Most of the long process by which this great change from the rigidity of the XII Tables took place is obscure; we have no clear knowledge, for instance, of the origin of the stipulation, the most important formal contract of the developed law, and even the time at which such a vital contract as that of sale became actionable is still a matter of dispute. On the other hand, so far, at least, as the last century of the republic is concerned, it is clear that the main agent in the change has been the praetor. His activity consists partly in giving actions under the *ius honorarium*, where, though there is already the possibility of action under the *ius civile*, the civil action displays some objectionably archaic feature, such as the *addictio* under the *actio furti manifesti*.[2] Largely, however, the praetor acts by granting actions where the civil law would have given none at all. Primarily, it seems, all such actions are conceived of as penal; the praetor wishes to punish a wrongful act of the defendant, and this is still his object where the action merely gives the plaintiff reparation for the loss occasioned by the wrong. But in some cases the wrong could only be committed provided there existed already a certain relationship between the parties, and this relationship might, in fact, be one that had been brought about by agreement.[3] Thus if *A* has lent *B* a

107–124; Mitteis, *R.P.R.* 147. The payment of an *indebitum* would be as much a *negotium* as the payment of money by way of loan, and it is clear from Gai. III. 91 that the two cases were traditionally treated together as "contracts" made *re*, though Gaius himself criticises the arrangement. In his Institutes (III. 88) Gaius only mentions two categories of obligations, *ex contractu* and *ex delicto*, and it is easy to see that, so long as *contractus* retained its original significance, this classification was an exhaustive one. In the *Aurea* according to the Digest (44. 7. 1 pr.) Gaius added a further miscellaneous category of obligations arising *ex variis causarum figuris*, but this passage is suspected of interpolation. Even stronger suspicion rests on D. 44. 7. 5, where quasi-contractual and quasi-delictal obligations are mentioned.

[1] Costa, *Cicerone giureconsulto*, I. 202. How different even Labeo's terminology was from that to which we are accustomed can be seen from D. 50. 16. 19.

[2] *Supra*, 170.

[3] Levy, *Privatstrafe und Schadensersatz*, 13.

horse and *B* fails to return the horse, the praetor gives an action for damages; primarily this is to punish *B*, but, clearly, only a borrower can commit the particular offence which *B* has committed, and, on analysis, borrowing is seen to mean receiving a thing for use on agreeing, expressly or impliedly, to return it. Thus, to later theory, the action will appear one to enforce fulfilment of an agreement, and borrowing (*commodatum*) will be regarded as what we call a contract. Actions of this sort, resting, as they did, solely on the *ius honorarium*, had a *formula in factum concepta*,[1] but in some cases we know that there existed, in addition to the *formula in factum*, a *bona fide* action with a *formula in ius*,[2] and in others, where only the *bona fide* action is known, it is conjectured that an *actio in factum* preceded it.[3] What has happened apparently in these cases is that what was originally purely praetorian law has been "received" into the civil law, for the *actio in ius* of course implies a civil law duty. Exactly how far this process had gone by the end of the republic it is impossible to say, and in the case of some relationships, contractual or otherwise, which we find recognised by *b.f.* actions, a previous stage of recognition by praetorian *actio in factum* is unlikely,[4] but this, at any rate, is one way in which progress was made towards the complexities of the later law.

In the more detailed discussion which follows, the usual classification under contract and delict will be preserved for the sake of convenience, but it must be remembered that the terminology is in advance of the time of which we are speaking, and that contract often grows up out of delict. It will also be necessary to discuss some obligations usually classed under quasi-contract in close connection with contract.

§ I. DELICT

A. THE CIVIL LAW DELICTS AND THEIR EXTENSIONS. (i) *Iniuria*. (*a*) Praetorian reforms. These are here of a twofold nature: (1) the praetor substitutes for the old actions, involving talion or fixed penalties, actions of his own in which the penalty is always pecuniary and is always variable at the discretion of the court according to the gravity of the offence (*actio aestimatoria*); (2) he makes actionable a number of offences which

---

[1] *Supra*, 212.

[2] *Commodatum* and *depositum*, Gai. IV. 47; cf. *infra*, 297.

[3] *Negotiorum gestio* and possibly *mandatum*; cf. *infra*, 307–308.

[4] *Infra*, 297. Wlassak, however, *Prozessformel*, 22, goes so far as to say that the recognition of an enforceable duty at civil law (*oportere*) must always have been preceded by an *actio in factum* resting on the *imperium* of the magistrate.

were unpunished by the XII Tables, thus carrying the conception of *iniuria* far beyond that of physical assault.

(1) First under the heading *de iniuriis* in the praetor's *album* stood a "general edict" promising a court of *recuperatores* to assess damages where *iniuria* was alleged.[1] It is probable that the original intention of this edict, traces of which are found as early as Plautus,[2] was not to extend redress beyond those cases already covered by the XII Tables, but merely to modernise the procedure and the penalty. No doubt the fall in the value of money had helped to make the old fixed penalties ridiculous, as is illustrated in the anecdote of L. Veratius, who is said to have amused himself by slapping people in the face and then ordering a slave who followed him with a bag full of money to pay each of them the 25 *asses* fixed by the XII Tables.[3] But we know now that the praetorian action is closely modelled on Greek parallels and it is probable that Greek influence was decisive in its introduction.[4]

(2) After the general edict came a number of special edicts dealing with particular cases of non-physical *iniuria*—*convicium* (insult), *adtemptata*

---

[1] The plaintiff assessed the damages himself and the court could condemn for the sum claimed or less; where the *iniuria* was *atrox* the praetor in effect fixed the sum (Gai. III. 224). There is considerable difficulty about the composition of the court. Gellius (XX. 1. 13) says clearly that the edict promised *recuperatores*, but Gaius speaks of a single *iudex* and so do others, e.g. Auctor ad Herenn. II. 13. 19; *v*. Lenel, *E.P.* 397; Hitzig, *Iniuria*, 62; Girard, *Mél. Gérardin*, 255–282; Wlassak, *Prozessgesetze*, I. 179, II. 309.

[2] *Asinar.* II. 2. 104, where *pugno malam si tibi percussero* seems to be a humorous allusion to the pattern *formula*, Lenel, *E.P.* 398.

[3] Quoted from Labeo by Gellius, XX. 1. 13.

[4] Hitzig, *Iniuria*, 60 *sqq.*, 71 *sqq.*, takes the model to have been the δίκη αἰκίας, i.e. for assault, but Partsch (*Archiv für Papyrusforschung*, VI. 62) holds that the *iniuria* of the "general edict" is the equivalent of the Greek ὕβρις and, apparently, that it had from the beginning the wide meaning which it certainly possessed later. If this is so it is difficult to see why the special edicts (which appear to be later) were needed, a difficulty already felt by Labeo (D. 47. 10. 15. 26). It seems more likely that the original meaning was a restricted one, subsequently extended by analogy with the special edicts and, no doubt, through the influence of Greek terminology. A curious stage intermediate between that of fixed penalties and complete freedom of assessment is evidence for Alexandria in the third century B.C. by *P. Hal.* 1. 205–207, according to which there is a fixed penalty for one blow whereas for several assessment is permitted. Apparently the absurdity was first felt when it came to multiplying the fixed penalty by the number of blows. The Romans need not have gone through this stage themselves, but may have taken the final result straight from some Greek system; Partsch, *loc. cit.* 59. On the noxal *actio iniuriarum* and its relation to Greek law *v*. de Visscher, *Études*, 327–349 (= *Revue d'histoire du Droit*, XI (1931), 39–55).

pudicitia (e.g. following a respectable woman) and defamation—and with *iniuriae* to slaves and persons under power. The penalty was, of course, always assessable. That these special edicts were later than the general one is probable, but well before the end of the republic the meaning of *iniuria* itself (i.e. under the general edict) had been extended far beyond that of physical assault,[1] and in the classical law it is a very wide conception indeed, covering not only our law of assault and defamation but including any act which could be construed as an attack on a man's honour or dignity, even e.g. a refusal to allow him to use the public baths.[2]

(*b*) *Lex Cornelia*. This statute of Sulla's (about 81 B.C.) provided specially for three cases of forcible *iniuria*—*pulsare* (blows), *verberare* (explained as blows which hurt)[3] and *vi domum introire* (forcible entry into a house). The action under the statute was of a criminal nature in so far as it was tried by a *quaestio*,[4] but counted as private[5] and could be brought only by the person wronged, whereas anyone could prosecute in a criminal action. The penalty is not known for certain, but was probably pecuniary.[6] It has been held that, until late in the classical period, no ordinary praetorian *actio aestimatoria* could be brought in the cases covered by the statute,[7] but the better view appears to be that the statute merely provided an alternative procedure for those cases.

(ii) *Furtum*. How long the system of the XII Tables remained untouched we do not know, but it may have been until towards the end of our period, for there is no trace of the praetorian edicts on the subject before Labeo.[8] The praetor, according to Gaius,[9] retained the civil action for double value in case of *furtum nec manifestum* and the actions *concepti* and *oblati* for triple value; for *furtum manifestum* he gave an action for fourfold. The old search *lance et licio* evidently

---

[1] Auct. ad Herenn. II. 26. 41 already rejects the view that it did not extend beyond blows and *convicium*, and Labeo, D. 47. 10. 15. 26, held the special edict against defamation to be superfluous.

[2] D. 47. 10. 13. 7. [3] D. 47. 10. 5. 1.

[4] This appears from the remains of the rules concerning the composition of the court preserved in D. 47. 10. 5. pr.

[5] D. 3. 3. 42. 1.

[6] Mommsen, *Strafrecht*, 804, relying on D. 47. 10. 37. 1, holds that the plaintiff fixed the sum, the court being bound either to condemn for this sum or acquit.

[7] Girard, *Mél. Gérardin*, 278–282. But this view seems inconsistent with Gaius' treatment (III. 220) of *verberatio* as an ordinary case of *iniuria* without any mention of the *lex Cornelia*; v. Lenel, *E.P.* 397.

[8] Costa, *Storia*, 321; Huvelin, *Études sur le furtum*, 567.

[9] III. 190–191.

became obsolete,[1] and that "in the presence of witnesses" alone survived. Where permission to make such search was refused, self-help was no longer allowed[2] and the praetor gave an *actio furti prohibiti* for fourfold. Justinian mentions also a praetorian *actio furti non exhibiti*[3] which lay against a person who refused to give up a stolen thing found after search on his premises. This action, which is not mentioned in any other text, was presumably for fourfold also. If this is right then the rule of the XII Tables that in such a case the theft was deemed to be manifest was not held to apply *ipso facto* to the praetorian remedy, and the praetor had to make it clear that he too treated the two cases in the same way. The right to kill the thief who came by night or who defended himself with a weapon by day no doubt continued to exist; indeed it was probably not until post-classical times that it sank to a mere right of self-defence.[4]

(iii) *Damage to property*. The date of the *lex Aquilia*, which became the foundation of the law on this subject, is not known. It was certainly later than the XII Tables, for Ulpian says[5] that it partially repealed their provisions, and it would appear to have been subsequent to 287 B.C., for it was strictly not a *lex* but a *plebiscitum*,[6] and a plebiscite would probably not have had the force of law before the passing of the *lex Hortensia* in that year. On the other hand it had apparently been in existence some time about the middle of the second century B.C., for it was commented on by M. Junius Brutus.[7]

We know of three chapters of the law, but only the first and third concerned damage to property.[8] The first dealt with the unlawful killing

---

[1] Gellius, XVI. 10. 8, ascribes its disappearance to the *lex Aebutia*, but little reliance can be placed on his heterogeneous list of antiquities abolished by that statute.

[2] *Supra*, 172.   [3] J. 4. 1. 4.

[4] That D. 9. 2. 5 has been interpolated is shown by comparison with Coll. VII. 3. 2–3; *v*. Karlowa, II. 776, n. 2.

[5] D. 9. 2. 1. pr.   [6] D. 9. 2. 1. 1.

[7] D. 9. 2. 27. 22. For Brutus *v. supra*, 90. The date 287 B.C. found in some modern books rests on two remarks of Byzantine authors which connect the law with a time of political dissension. Theophilus (*Paraphr.* IV. 3. 15) says "at the time of the secession" and the Scholiast on B. 60. 3. 1 (Heimb. 5. 263: κἂν κυρίως) says "when the plebs was in revolt against the senate and seceded from it". As the latest secession was in 287 it is concluded that this was the date. But (*a*) the law is of a non-political character, (*b*) Theophilus and the Scholiast probably had no independent evidence, but, not knowing much early history, jumped to the conclusion that the *lex Aquilia* was connected with political strife because it was a plebiscite.

[8] For the second *v*. Gai. III. 215.

of slaves or four-footed *pecudes*[1] belonging to others, the third with
"burning, breaking or smashing" any other property. The third chapter,
at any rate as interpreted later,[2] included also minor injuries to slaves and
pecudes. The measure of damages under the first chapter was the highest
value the slave or animal had borne during the preceding year, that under
the third the highest[3] value which had attached to the thing in question
during the preceding thirty days. No satisfactory explanation of this
curious reckoning seems ever to have been given.[4]

The *lex Aquilia* is peculiarly interesting historically as it affords
examples of development both by *interpretatio* and by praetorian action.

(*a*) Interpretation. According to the text of the statute only the actual
value of the thing could be recovered by way of damages, but interpretation, going back at least as far as Labeo,[5] allowed the plaintiff to include
consequential damages as well, if e.g. the thing destroyed was one of a
pair, so that the loss suffered was greater than the value of the individual
thing.[6] Further, the text of the third chapter ran "*si quis...usserit,
fregerit, ruperit...*", and strictly *rumpere* only means "to break", but the
republican jurists already interpreted it as equivalent to *corrumpere*, "to
spoil", thereby bringing all other sorts of injury within the statute.[7]

(*b*) Praetorian actions. Apart from this extensive interpretation of
rumpere, the words of the third chapter and the word "kill" of the first
were strictly construed at civil law. Hence "causing death", as opposed
to "killing", did not give grounds for an action at civil law, nor did
damage done to a thing without physical contact. Already, however, in
Labeo's time a person who caused a slave's death by giving him poison to
drink was liable to a praetorian *actio in factum*,[8] and similar actions were
given where the damage was not considered direct enough for a civil
action under the third chapter.[9] Equally important was the granting of
praetorian actions to persons who, although not owners, had an interest
in the property (e.g. to the usufructuary), whereas the words ·of the
statute mentioned the owner only.[10] But there seems to be no evidence
that this step was taken before the empire.

---

[1] Explained, J. 4. 3. 1, as including all beasts which graze.

[2] For a suggestion as to its original meaning *v*. my article, *L.Q.R.* xxxviii.
220–230.

[3] This word was not in the text but was held to be implied, Gai. III. 218.

[4] Rabel (456, n. 2) says that it is an attempt to get at the real amount of the
·damage, but this does not explain the strange method adopted.

[5] D. 9. 2. 23. 4.   [6] Gai. III. 212.

[7] Ulpian, D. 9. 2. 27. 13, refers the extension to the *veteres*.

[8] D. 9. 2. 9. pr.   [9] D. 9. 2. 27. 35.   [10] D. 9. 2. 12.

(iv) *Violent damage to property and rapina.* Among the four main delicts treated by Gaius in his Institutes is robbery (*rapina*), which is simply theft accompanied by violence.[1] For this an action lay under the edict for fourfold damages provided it was brought within the year, for simple damages if brought later. The history of this action is curious and, in some respects, obscure.[2] We know that in 76 B.C. M. Terentius Lucullus, when praetor, found it desirable, no doubt on account of the disturbed state of the country, to promise in his edict an action for damage (*damnum*) inflicted violently by armed bands (*vi hominibus armatis coactisve*). It is probable that this edict was intended to deal with violent damage to property and not with violent theft, which seems to have been sufficiently covered by a previous edict, that of Octavius, dating from about 80 B.C.[3] But before Labeo's time a second clause was inserted which expressly dealt with violent theft, whether committed by a band or not, the reason probably being that the edict of Octavius had in the meanwhile been restricted, so as not to cover this case any more. In classical times both the clause about damage by armed bands and that dealing with violent theft were in the edict, but under more settled conditions the latter was the more important in practice and alone thought worthy of a place in Gaius' elementary work.

B. DELICTS RESTING PURELY ON THE *ius honorarium.* So far we have spoken only of such praetorian innovations as were in extension or alteration of provisions already known to the civil law; something must now be said of those which gave actions where the civil law saw no wrong at all. Some of these really belong to the law of procedure and were required for perfecting the machinery of justice. Such e.g. were the provisions giving actions for damages against anyone who refused to obey the decree of a municipal magistrate,[4] and against anyone who forcibly removed a person who had been *in ius vocatus*.[5] Other actions, unconnected with procedure, but of minor importance, were that for corrupting a slave,[6] and that which lay against a surveyor who fraudulently made a false report on the acreage of a field.[7] But the most important praetorian delicts were *metus* and *dolus*, for here the praetor introduced new general principles which were to influence the law through all its branches.

---

[1] Gai. III. 209.
[2] For the following description see Schulz, *Z.S.S.* XLIII. 216 *sqq.*
[3] Cf. *infra*, 288.   [4] Lenel, *E.P.* 51.   [5] *E.P.* 73.
[6] *E.P.* 175; Gai. III. 198.   [7] *E.P.* 219.

(i) *Metus*. In the classical law there were three possible remedies available to a person who had been induced by threats to do some act which was detrimental to him—*in integrum restitutio*,[1] *exceptio* and action. Of these the action appears to be the oldest, and to date back to the praetorship of an Octavius about 80 B.C.[2] In its original form it lay, apparently, only for actual deprivation of property by violence or through menaces,[3] and was for four times the value of the property. Subsequently the reference to violence was dropped, but the action was made available in all cases where a man was induced by threats to perform any act by which he suffered loss, whether this was a legal transaction such as the conveyance of property or a physical act such as pulling down a house.[4]

(ii) *Dolus*. Originally, in accordance with formalist principles, there was no redress for mere deceit any more than for threats. If a man had been cheated e.g. into making a conveyance of his property he had made it none the less, and perhaps in very early times the deceit was not even regarded as morally reprehensible.[5] No remedy was found until Aquilius Gallus, in Cicero's words, "produced the *formulae de dolo*".[6] We cannot say for certain whether this refers to the *actio* or the *exceptio doli*, but the probability is that here, as in the case of *metus*, the action came first. It was, like the *actio metus*, *arbitraria*, but it gave only simple damages for the loss which had been inflicted by the fraud, and was only available provided the plaintiff had no other remedy open to him.[7]

§ II. CONTRACT

A. FORMAL CONTRACTS.   (i) *The disuse of nexum*. The *lex Poetilia*[8] does not appear actually to have abolished *nexum*, but to have led to its

---

[1] *Supra*, 234.

[2] Cicero, *in Verr*. II. 3. 65, 152, refers to it as *formula Octaviana*, but which Octavius was its author is uncertain; *v*. Schulz, *op. cit.* 217.

[3] *Quae per vim et metum abstulerant*, Cic. *loc. cit.*; cf. *ad Quintum fr.* I. 1, 7, 21.

[4] Schulz, *op. cit.* 220.   [5] Cf. Maine, *Ancient Law*, 277.

[6] *De Off*. III. 14. 60; in *de nat. deor.* III. 30. 74 Cicero speaks of *iudicium de dolo*, which points to the action rather than the exception. Aquilius was praetor with Cicero in 66 B.C., and hence the action is usually assigned to that date. The difficulty however is that he is known (Cic. *pro Cluent.* LIII. 147) to have acted when praetor as president of the *quaestio ambitus*. Girard, 450, thinks he probably held the peregrine praetorship at the same time (cf. Costa, *Storia*, 332), but perhaps it was in his capacity as legal adviser to a magistrate and not as a magistrate himself that he was the author of the *formula*, in which case the date may be any time during his activity as a lawyer; *v*. Wlassak, *Prozessformel*, 25 *sqq*.

[7] For the *formula v. supra*, 205, n. 1.

[8] Cf. *supra*, 167.

disuse;[1] indeed it seems to have remained a theoretical possibility even in classical times, for Gaius speaks of *solutio per aes et libram* as being appropriate for dissolving an obligation contracted by the scales and copper.[2] According to Girard[3] the effect of the law was to abolish the possibility of proceeding immediately to execution without first getting judgment, and as this left *nexum* with no advantage over the simpler forms of contracting an obligation which were coming into existence, it gradually fell out of use.

(ii) *Stipulatio.*[4] In the developed law stipulation is a form of contract by which any agreement can be made actionable by the simple expedient of reducing it to the form of an oral question and answer. The person to become promisee says e.g. "Do you promise to pay me 10,000 sesterces?" or "Do you promise that you will build a house according to such and such specifications?" and the other answers "I promise". No witnesses and no writing are required. Already in the republic there was considerable freedom of choice as regards the words which could be used,[5] but originally it seems clear that they had to be "*Spondesne?*" "*Spondeo*", for the use of this particular word was always confined to citizens, whereas the stipulation, if other words were used, was *iuris gentium.*[6]

We speak of stipulation as a formal contract because it requires for its validity that the parties should meet and formulate their agreement in an oral question and answer, but the form is about the simplest which can be imagined, and so flexible an institution is certainly not primitive. Nor indeed is there any trace of its existence in the fragments of the XII Tables. It is, on the other hand, known to Plautus,[7] and certainly prior

---

[1] Cic. *de Rep.* II. 34: *Omnia nexa civium liberata nectierque postea desitum.*

[2] III. 173. It may be however that the obligations to which Gaius refers are those which may arise as a result of mancipation and are enforced by the *actiones auctoritatis* and *de modo agri* (*supra*, 149); *v.* Kniep, *Gai. Inst. Commentarius*, III. §§ 88–225, p. 374.

[3] Girard, 514.

[4] There were two very much less important forms of verbal contract—*dictio dotis*, the promise of a dowry, and *iusiurandum liberti*, the oath by which a slave on manumission promised certain services to his former master. Both of these differ from stipulation in that only the promisor need speak—there is no preceding question by the promisee; *v.* Gai. III. 95–96. *Dictio dotis* was perhaps originally enforceable as an accessory to the enforceable promise to give in marriage, *v.* Costa, *Storia*, 341; *iusiurandum liberti* was perhaps first recognised by the praetor, *ibid.* 342.

[5] For varieties *v.* Gai. III. 92. "*Dabis?*" "*Dabo*" is as old as Plautus, *v. Pseud.* IV. 6. 16.

[6] Gai. III. 93.   [7] *Pseud.* IV. 6. 7; *Curc.* IV. 1. 12; *Rud.* V. 3. 25.

to the *lex Aquilia*.[1] It was first used for promises of money, then for promises of other *res certae*, and not until the empire perhaps for promises to perform acts.[2]

The origin of the stipulation is thought by many to lie in the practice of making promises under oath,[3] and one of the chief arguments in favour of this view is that the word *spondeo* appears to have religious associations.[4] It is also pointed out that there existed outside the sphere of the ordinary civil law, a form of *sponsio* which was used for making treaties with foreign states,[5] and this international form is said to have been originally a double oath, the representative of each party swearing that the conditions of the treaty would be observed.[6] The evidence for this theory is, however, distinctly meagre, and the different view put forward by Mitteis[7] has now many adherents. According to this view stipulation originated as a contract of suretyship, and probably as a form of suretyship given in the course of judicial proceedings, such e.g. as the parties to a *legis actio sacramento* give to the magistrate to guarantee the payment of the *sacramentum*.[8] We have already seen that in some systems of law there is a development of this sort—first when *A* goes surety for *B*, *A* alone and not *B* is liable, then *B* is allowed to go surety for himself, so that "duty" and "liability" fall upon the same person.[9] Now this development certainly took place at Rome in the case of an old kind of surety—the *praes*[10]—and, in Mitteis' view, *sponsio* grew up out of an

---

[1] Otherwise the second chapter (Gai. III. 215) could not have dealt with the *adstipulator*. For the suggestion that the introduction of the stipulation was connected with the *lex Silia v. supra*, 194, n. 5.

[2] Girard, 521, n. 3, thinks the use of stipulation for *facere* goes back as far as Cato, and relies on *de re rust.* 144. 2. 5 and 146. 2. 5 (Bruns, II. 47 and 49), but D. 45. 1. 81 shows that the question was still open in Celsus' time (cf. 45. 1. 68 and 137. 7), and Cato may well be referring to stipulations with a money penalty for non-performance of the act promised.

[3] See e.g. Girard, 516; Kniep, *Gai. Inst. Commentarius*, III. §§ 88–225, pp. 90–157.

[4] See especially Festus, s.v. *spondere* (Bruns, II. 40), where the word is said to be taken from the Greek σπονδαί, literally "drink-offerings", but also meaning "treaty", because it was customary to make such offerings when concluding a treaty. [5] Gai. III. 94.

[6] Mommsen, *Abriss*, 292; *Staatsr.* I. 249.

[7] *Aus röm. u. bürgerlichem Recht, Festschrift für Bekker* (1907), 107–142; also *R.P.R.* 27 and 266 *sqq.* For literature see there and Sohm, 62–63 and 405.

[8] *Supra*, 183. [9] *Supra*, 161–163.

[10] In an inscription found at Puteoli referring to a building contract (Bruns, I. 374) the debtor is described at the end as being also surety—*idem praes*; cf. Festus, s.v. *manceps* (Bruns, II. 13).

arrangement of this kind, but here there followed a further development, also to be found in other systems,[1] by which the arrangement of going surety for oneself turned into a method of making binding promises in a more general way. It is impossible even to summarise the arguments here, but one important piece of evidence may be mentioned. Although *spondere* means "to promise" the noun *sponsor* does not mean "one who promises", but "one who goes surety" (in a particular way), and it is difficult to explain this fact except, in accordance with Mitteis' view, as the survival from the original usage.[2]

(iii) *The literal contract.* Of this contract little is known for certain, as Gaius,[3] almost our only authority, describes rather the use to which it was put than the way in which it was formed. It appears, however, that *A* might become the debtor of *B* for a sum of money by a fictitious entry made in a cash-book of *B* (the creditor)[4] (*codex accepti et depensi*) alleging that *B* had paid out that sum of money by way of loan to *A*. It is clear that the consent of *A* must have been needed to make such an entry binding, for otherwise a man could have made anyone his debtor in this way, but Gaius says nothing of such consent, and we do not know whether it had to be given in any particular form.[5] Gaius tells us of two uses to which the contract might be put:

(a) *Transscriptio a persona in personam.* If *A* owed *B* 10,000 sesterces and it was desired to substitute *C* for *A* as *B*'s debtor (e.g. because *C* owed *A* a similar sum and the position could be simplified by cutting him out altogether), then this might be achieved by entering in *B*'s book a fictitious loan of 10,000 sesterces to *C*.

Presumably, in order to make the cash-book correspond accurately with the cash-box there was also made at the same time a fictitious entry of the receipt of the money from *A*.

---

[1] V. Brunner, in Holtzendorff, *Enzyklopädie der Rechtswissenschaft*, I. 139; Pollock and Maitland, *History of English Law*, II. 184; Holdsworth, *H.E.L.* II. 83 *sqq*.

[2] V. Gai. III. 155 *sqq*. and *infra*, 310.

[3] Gai. III. 128–133. In addition we have an account, probably of little authority, in Theophilus, *Paraphr.* III. 21, a fragmentary inscription dating from the middle of the first century A.D. (Bruns, I. 353), and a number of references in legal and lay literature, for which see Costa, *Storia*, 342 *sqq*., where there is also a full account of modern literature.

[4] The nature of the book is disputed; the view given in the text may be described as the orthodox one, v. Buckland, 460.

[5] Cic. *pro Rosc. com.* I. 1–2 refers to the *iussus* of the debtor, and from Gai. III. 138 it would appear at least that the presence of the debtor was not required, but the paragraph looks like a gloss and so has little authority.

(b) *Transscriptio a re in personam.* If *A* owed *B* 10,000 sesterces because e.g. *B* had sold him goods, this debt could be turned into a debt owed under a literal contract by entering fictitiously in *B*'s book that *B* had lent *A* 10,000 sesterces, the book being here again made to correspond with the cash-box, by a fictitious entry of the receipt of the 10,000 sesterces owed by reason of the sale. The object of such a transaction might be to give the creditor an easily provable debt enforceable by the simple and profitable [1] remedy of *condictio* instead of the *bonae fidei* action under the original contract, and the debtor might have to agree to such a course, because e.g. the creditor made it a condition of granting him further credit.

Gaius carefully distinguishes from these fictitious entries (*nomina transscripticia*) what he calls *nomina arcaria*, i.e. entries which recorded payments actually made by way of loan, where the binding element lay, not in the written entry (which was merely evidence), but in the actual payment of the money (*mutuum*). But the literal contract itself is probably a survival from the time when a mere informal *mutuum* did not give rise to an action. [2] It may well be that with the disuse of *nexum* [3] the need was felt for a new form by which a lender could secure to himself an action for the repayment of his loan and that this form was found in the entry of the debt in his account book. Then, according to the usual formalist principle, if this form of entry had been observed, the debt was held to exist whether there had been actual payment or not. The entry thus came to be useful for creating an actionable debt whatever the reason might be for which the parties wished to create it. [4] Gaius indeed only mentions the two uses described above, but this does not prove that there were not others at an earlier date; perhaps it was possible, e.g. when there really was a loan, to provide for interest by entering a larger sum than that actually paid. [5] How old the institution is we cannot say; book-keeping with entries of loans and repayments certainly existed at the beginning of the second century B.C., [6] but this does not necessarily

---

[1] *Supra,* 195.

[2] *V.* Kniep, *Gai. Inst. Commentarius,* III. §§ 88–225, p. 205.

[3] Cf. Girard, 528.

[4] I.e. became what continental writers call an "abstract" transaction, as opposed to a "causal" one, and created liability as a modern cheque does without reference to the reason for which it is given.

[5] Livy (xxxv. 7) describes how Romans got round the laws fixing a maximum rate of interest by transcriptive entries which made it appear that Italian *socii* (who were not originally subject to these laws) were parties to the transaction. It may be that the entries were of the sort described in the text.

[6] *V.* Livy *loc. cit.,* which refers to the year 193 B.C., and Plautus, e.g. *Truc.* I. 1. 52; IV. 2. 36.

mean that fictitious entries were already known. In Cicero's day, on the other hand, they were clearly in common use,[1] and by the classical era the institution had already become practically obsolete.

B. INFORMAL CONTRACTS. (i) *Mutuum and the quasi-contractual obligations giving rise to condictio*. In the classical law if *A* handed *B* money with the intention that it should be a loan and *B* received it with the same intention, the transaction was called *mutuum* and *A* could bring a *condictio* to recover the amount.[2] The obligation arising in this way was said to be one contracted *re*, i.e. the transfer of the money was necessary in order to create the obligation to return an equal sum; if no money had been in fact transferred, then there could be no *mutuum*. When formless loans of this sort first became actionable we do not know, but it was certainly well back in republican times.[3] The question is perhaps not of such great practical importance as would appear at first sight, because the formless loan could never give the right to recover a greater sum than was actually lent, and gratuitous loans were comparatively rare. If interest was to be charged, it was necessary, even in classical times, to make a special stipulation to this effect, and perhaps, at one time, the literal contract had been used for a similar purpose.[4] In all probability *mutuum* first became actionable not because it was recognised specifically as a contract worthy of enforcement, but by reason of the recognition of a general principle that if *A* had been enriched at the expense of *B* without any justification, then *B* should have an action to recover the amount of the enrichment.[5]

In the classical law a number of such cases are recognised, and the remedy is always *condictio*. Thus, if *B* has paid *A* a sum of money under the mistaken belief that he owes it, he has a *condictio* for recovery (*condictio indebiti*). Similarly, if *B* has given *A* money to manumit a slave

---

[1] *Pro Rosc. com.* IV. 13; V. 14; *de Off.* III. 14. 59: *Nomina facit.*

[2] The contract is also possible with other "fungible" things, e.g. corn. Its essential points are that the things lent should pass into the ownership of the borrower and that the parties should intend a duty to arise in the borrower to return an equal amount of similar things; *v.* Gai. III. 90.

[3] Phrases such as *Si quis mutuom quid dederit* (*Trin.* IV. 3. 43) in Plautus do not actually prove more than the existence of loan as an economic fact, but in Cicero's day we have proof that formless loan was actionable, e.g. *pro Rosc. com.* v. 14, where Cicero, enumerating the possible grounds of action for a claim of *pecunia certa*, says: *haec pecunia necesse est aut data aut expensa lata aut stipulata sit. Data* must here include loan, though it may include other things as well.

[4] *Supra*, 292; Kniep, *op. cit.* 202.

[5] Cf. Girard, 539.

within a certain time and A fails to manumit, B can get the money back by *condictio* (*condictio causa data causa non secuta*). *Mutuum* is really a similar case; if B has lent A money and A does not return it, A has been enriched unjustifiably at the expense of B. The principle that unjustifiable enrichment should be recoverable by the person at whose expense it has occurred was actually expressed early, for it is attributed by Sabinus[1] to the *veteres*, i.e. the republican jurists, but there is no need to suppose that it did not exist until it was expressed. Some authors indeed connect the recognition of debts of this sort with the introduction of the *legis actio per condictionem*,[2] but this assumption is unnecessary. Debts recoverable by *condictio* seem, at least in some cases, to have been recoverable previously by *legis actio sacramento*,[3] and there is no reason to suppose that the range of facts which would support the assertion *aio te mihi dare oportere* had not been extended so as to include the debts we are discussing before the introduction of *condictio*. The history of our own law teaches us that such processes are inevitably gradual. There can be little doubt, however, that the abstract nature of *condictio* (at least under the formulary system)[4] helped to extend the number of cases where a debt was assumed, for it was obviously easier for a *iudex* (or his professional adviser) to recognise that what was claimed "ought to be paid" than it would have been for a pleader to define exactly the cause of action if the *formula* had not absolved him from this duty in such cases. As Rabel puts it,[5] "*condictio*, seeing that it was a *formula* which did not mention the cause of action, was excellently adapted to cover those cases in which it was desired to allow a claim for recovery, not because the plaintiff had a special justification for his claim, but because the defendant had no sufficient justification for retaining what he had got".

When "contract" came to connote the idea of agreement,[6] *mutuum* of course could be classed as a contract, whereas the obligation arising from the payment of *indebitum* had, since there was no agreement, to be called quasi-contractual,[7] but the origin of the two lies in the same idea, as does also that of the other non-contractual *condictiones* which modern authors place with *indebitum solutum* under the heading of quasi-contract.

(ii) *Fiducia and the "real" contracts other than mutuum*. *Fiducia*, or *pactum fiduciae*, is not an independent contract but an agreement subsidiary to a conveyance by mancipation or *in iure cessio* imposing a trust upon the transferee with reference to the thing conveyed, most frequently

---

[1] D. 12. 5. 6.   [2] E.g. Costa, *Storia*, 356.   [3] Cf. *supra*, 194, n. 5.
[4] *Supra*, 218.   [5] Rabel, 470.   [6] Cf. *supra*, 280.
[7] *V. J*. 3. 27. 7.

a trust for reconveyance of the thing in certain circumstances.[1] Thus, if a man thought for some reason that his property would be safer in the hands of a friend than in his own, he could convey it (by mancipation or *in iure cessio*) to the friend with a *fiducia* for reconveyance on demand or when the particular danger which he had in mind had passed (*fiducia cum amico*).[2] The friend would in the meanwhile be technically owner and able to exercise all the rights of an owner, for instance to vindicate the thing if it got out of his possession. More important however was *fiducia cum creditore*—a form of pledge. Here a debtor, in order to secure his debt, conveyed some piece of his property to his creditor with a *fiducia* for reconveyance if and when the debt was paid. Something more will have to be said later about this arrangement under the heading of "real security",[3] but for the moment the important point is the *fiducia*. This was at all times a purely informal agreement,[4] and its informality as well as the word *fiducia* (*fides*) points to a time when it was unenforceable, and the transferor had to rely on the faith of his friend or creditor.[5] Already some way back in the republic, however, this was no longer the case, and an *actio fiduciae* lay against a transferee who was guilty of a breach of trust. The first mention of this action occurs in a list of *bonae fidei iudicia* quoted by Cicero from Q. Mucius,[6] but the probability is that the action is older than Mucius, for some words quoted by Cicero from the *formula* are of a peculiar and archaic character.[7] Very probably it was the first departure from the old principle of giving effect only to formal transactions and was the prototype of the actions of good faith.[8]

Depositum, commodatum and pignus. These three contracts (deposit,

[1] The trust might also be for the manumission of a person either free (see e.g. *supra*, 246, n. 4) or slave who was mancipated, or for the further transfer of property to a third party; *v*. e.g. D. 39. 6. 42.

[2] Gai. II. 60. [3] *Infra*, 314.

[4] This seems to be proved by the words *pactum conventum* in the *formula Baetica* (Bruns, I. No. 135, p. 334), but is disputed by Karlowa, II. 567.

[5] Some writers, e.g. Sohm, 60, regard the *fiducia* as actionable under the words of the XII Tables (VI. 1): *cum nexum faciet mancipiumque uti lingua nuncupassit, ita ius esto*, but see *supra*, 146.

[6] *De Off*. III. 17. 70. Plautus uses the word (e.g. *Bacch*. III. 3. 9), but nothing can be deduced as to the possibility of an action from his use.

[7] *Ut inter bonos bene agier oportet*, *Top*. XVII. 66; *de Off*. III. 15. 61; 17. 70; *ad fam*. VII. 12.

[8] Lenel (*E.P.* 293) now thinks that, even in classical times there was but one *formula* which was *in factum* and was preceded by a *legis actio in factum* (*Z.S.S.* XXX. 339 *sqq*.); he explains the position of *fiducia* in Q. Mucius' list by saying that the jurists regarded the reference to the "conduct of good people" as equivalent to a reference to good faith.

loan for use, and pledge) are classed by Justinian with *mutuum* under
"obligations contracted *re*".[1] They are all "real" in the sense that there
is needed for their formation (in addition to the agreement of the parties)
only the handing over by one party to the other of a thing which is the
object of the contract, and that the main duty which arises under the
contract is that of the recipient to return the thing.[2] Late[3] analysis thus
places them with *mutuum*, but Justinian is careful to point out the
differences; whereas the borrower in *mutuum* becomes owner of what he
borrows and has only to restore an equal quantity of similar things, the
borrower in *commodatum*, the depositee and the pledgee do not become
owners and have to return the identical thing received. Now it is obvious
that, from the economic point of view, *pignus* and *depositum* cover the
same ground as *fiducia cum creditore* and *fiducia cum amico*, and it may be
that *fiducia cum amico* was also used to effect the purposes of a *commodatum*.[4] The technical legal difference is great, for the recipient under
fiducia becomes owner, whereas in the other cases he does not, but from
the point of view of the layman both *pignus* and *fiducia cum creditore* are
ways of raising money on security, and both *depositum* and *fiducia cum
amico* are ways of getting someone to look after property. It is also clear
that the "real" contracts are the simpler and, when recognised, would
tend to supersede *fiducia*. It is consequently sometimes said that they
are simplifications of *fiducia*, but it is very doubtful whether this
accurately expresses the historical process. *Fiducia* could only be attached
to *mancipatio* and *in iure cessio*, and would hence be inappropriate to *res
nec mancipi*, and yet people must, in fact, have delivered *res nec mancipi*
by way of loan, deposit or pledge, without transferring the ownership
therein, before they were protected by the development of special actions.
Even then they would not be entirely without protection, for the owner
who had lent or deposited his thing could vindicate it, and was perhaps
also protected by the law of theft.[5] The position of the pledgor would be

[1] J. 3. 14.
[2] The pledgee only if and when the debt is paid.
[3] How late is uncertain. In his Institutes Gaius does not mention any of the
three under the heading "obligations contracted *re*" (III. 90–91). On the other
hand the quotation from his *Aurea* in D. 44. 7. 1 is closely parallel to Justinian's
Institutes and mentions them all. How far this latter passage is genuine and, if
not genuine, how old it is, is disputed; *v.* Arangio-Ruiz, *Mél. Cornil*, 1. 83 *sqq.*
[4] Girard, 554, n. 5; Costa, *Storia*, 362. *Contra*, Karlowa, II. 570.
[5] Girard, 558–560. For this kind of protection cf. Pollock and Maitland,
H.E.L. II. 186: "If the gage was not restored the claim for it would take the
form 'you unjustly detain what is mine'". For *depositum* there was also the old
action under the XII Tables, *supra*, 166.

similar if the debt had been paid, but what happened if he attempted to vindicate before then we cannot say.

As has been indicated already, the first specific recognition of these "real contracts" was by praetorian *actiones in factum* having a delictal character, and it was only later that *actiones in ius* also became available.[1] This latter process had only just begun when the republic came to an end, for, though the *actio depositi in ius* appears to have been known to Cicero, the corresponding action for *commodatum* was probably, that for *pignus* certainly, not yet in existence.[2]

(iii) *The consensual contracts and the quasi-contractual relationships of negotiorum gestio and tutela.* In the classical law there are four contracts said to be concluded *consensu*, i.e. nothing more is necessary for their formation than the agreement, no matter how expressed, of the parties.[3] These are *emptio venditio* (sale), *locatio conductio* (hire), *societas* (partnership) and *mandatum* (agency). All were in existence well before the end of the republic, and all appear in the list of *bonae fidei iudicia* quoted by Cicero from Q. Mucius,[4] though this does not necessarily prove that they were already recognised as consensual. In no case except that of *mandatum* is there any trace of an *actio in factum*, and it is improbable that one ever existed.[5] So long, however, as the history of procedure before the *lex Aebutia* remains as obscure as it is at present, we can have no detailed knowledge of the stages by which the consensual contracts came to be recognised, and their history before the time of Q. Mucius must remain almost wholly conjectural.

The grouping of the four contracts together is, no doubt, like the other institutional classifications, an achievement of theoretical jurisprudence dating from the early empire, and we can see that historically the four fall into two distinct groups, the one consisting of *emptio venditio* and *locatio conductio*, which are commercial relationships, the other of *societas* and *mandatum*, which appear to have had their origin in the family.[6] In sale and hire the parties are men whose interests are opposed, and each

---

[1] *Supra*, 282. The date of these *actiones* is quite uncertain. According to Girard's argument (*Manuel*, 556, n. 4 and 560) they cannot have existed before the *lex Aebutia*, because, until then, in his view, the praetor had no power to create actions (cf. *supra*, 224). Lenel, on the other hand, *Z.S.S.* xxx. 345 *sqq.*, argues in favour of the existence of a *legis actio in factum* for *commodatum*.

[2] Costa, *Storia*, 364–369. The existence of an *actio pigneraticia in ius* is doubtful even for the classical period; Lenel, *E.P.* 255.

[3] Gai. III. 135–137.   [4] *De Off.* III. 17. 70.

[5] Lenel, *Z.S.S.* xxx. 353.   [6] Cf. Costa, *Storia*, 372.

seeks to make a bargain which will be profitable to himself,[1] whereas partnership and mandate are both of a fiduciary nature and require that the parties should have special trust in each other,[2] a point which is clearly illustrated by the rule that condemnation in an *actio pro socio* or *mandati* leads to *infamia*.[3] It is more dishonourable for one partner to try to overreach another, than for a seller to try to overreach a buyer.

(*a*) *Emptio venditio* and *locatio conductio*.[4] (1) *Emptio venditio*. (*α*) Theories of origin. There can be no doubt that at Rome, as elsewhere, sale began by being an exchange in which the parties carried out their respective parts of the bargain simultaneously and left no obligations outstanding, but beyond this point there is no agreement as to the origin of the contract or the date at which it first became consensual. Many solutions have been offered, and it may be that there is an element of truth in all of them, but the difficulty has not been solved because the story was probably a long and complex one which can never be reconstructed without some evidence of the actual decisions of the courts, any more than it would have been possible to reconstruct the history of contract in early English law without the evidence of the Year Books. Among the chief hypotheses are the following:

Hypothesis of development from state contracts.[5] According to this view both sale and hire originated in the imitation, by private persons, of arrangements which had existed from time immemorial in the practice of the state. The typical public sale was that of booty by the quaestor on behalf of the state. The magistrate in these cases published the conditions of the sale orally or in public notices and the bargain was concluded when a bid made by the private purchaser was accepted by the magistrate without any further formality. If difficulties arose, the magistrate himself decided them on equitable grounds, and this procedure became a pattern for the subsequent *b.f. iudicia* on private contracts.

It may, of course, well be that these public contracts did have an influence on the development of informality in private contracts, but the

---

[1] In the English phrase the contract is "at arm's length".

[2] Cf. Cic. *pro Rosc. Amer.* XXXIX. 112: *Neque mandat quisquam fere nisi amico.*

[3] Gai. IV. 182; D. 3. 2. 1. But only condemnation in the "direct", not in the "contrary", action.

[4] The careful separation of the two is itself not primitive but the work of legal theory; *v.* Rabel, 465; Mommsen, *Z.S.S.* VI. 264. In Cato, *de agr. cult.* CXLIX (Bruns, II. 50), an agreement for the use of land as pasture during the winter is still treated as a sale.

[5] Mommsen, "Die römischen Anfänge von Kauf u. Miethe", *Z.S.S.* VI. 260–275; Cuq, 354–355.

real difficulty of knowing what actions the private parties used is not touched, and, without any evidence, it is difficult to accept the view that the administrative process used by the magistrate in dealing with public contracts could have formed the model for the totally different private procedure before a *iudex*.

Hypothesis of double stipulation.[1] According to Bekker and a number of other writers, the earliest method of concluding a contract of sale which was not to be executed at once was by recourse to the universal method by which any undertaking could be rendered actionable—the stipulation. The buyer, it is supposed, stipulated for the delivery of the thing, the seller for the payment of the price.

That stipulation played some part in the development of sale is certain,[2] but there are great difficulties in supposing that these double stipulations were the origin of the contract; if they had been we should have expected the actions, like other actions on stipulations, to have been strict and not *bonae fidei*, and, above all, it is strange, on this hypothesis, that in the forms of sale given by Cato there is no suggestion that the whole contract was confirmed by stipulation though he recommends that there should be stipulations for certain special points.[3]

Hypothesis of a "real" stage in the evolution of sale. Another view, advocated especially by Pernice,[4] supposes that before sale became consensual there was a stage during which it was "real", in the sense that the seller could bring an action for the price if he had delivered, but only then, and that there was no action by which the buyer could enforce delivery. Comparison with other systems would appear to support this view,[5] but the positive arguments in its favour are not as strong as was thought at one time,[6] and the comparatively late development of the

[1] Bekker, *Aktionen*, I. 157; Girard, *Manuel*, 570; Jhering, *Geist*, III. (4th ed.) 202.   [2] *Infra*, 301–304.

[3] *V.* especially *de agr. cult.* CXLVI (Bruns, II. 49); cf. Cuq, 454.

[4] *Labeo*, I. 456 *sqq.*

[5] For English law *v.* Glanvil, X. 14, quoted by Holdsworth, *H.E.L.* III. 414, n. 2.

[6] (*a*) The rules that risk passed on the conclusion of the contract and that for usucapion *pro empto bona fides* is needed both at the time of the contract and at the time of delivery, quoted by Pernice in support of his view, may equally well be relics of the time when delivery and payment were simultaneous.

(*b*) The *exceptio mercis non traditae* (Gai. IV. 126 A) does not prove that the seller had to deliver before he could sue for the price, for Gaius is referring to actions brought by bankers, not *ex vendito*, but on stipulations for the price of goods sold by auction; Girard, 567, n. 3; Lenel, *E.P.* 503.

(*c*) Varro, *R.R.* II. 2. 6 (Bruns, II. 63), after giving the form of stipulation which

contracts known to be "real" makes an early application of the principle improbable.[1]

Hypothesis of original formation by payment of arra.[2] In the classical law the function of *arra*, or earnest, was purely evidentiary,[3] i.e. it served to mark the moment when the parties had ceased chaffering and had definitely concluded a bargain. But in other systems, and particularly in Greek law, it served a different purpose, that of a kind of pledge that the bargain would be carried out; the rule in some Greek systems, at any rate, being that if the party who had given the earnest failed to complete the contract he lost his earnest, and if the other party failed he had to give the earnest back with as much again.[4] The position was then that although there was no possibility of action to enforce fulfilment, the party who failed to fulfil lost the amount of the earnest. It may be that some similar rule existed in early Rome and that the practical binding secured in such cases resulted finally in the rule that the mere consent, even without *arra*, would be sufficient to constitute obligations on either side.

This suggestion, though not unlikely in itself, is without sufficient evidence to warrant its acceptance, and in any case does not, any more than the other suggestions, bridge the gap in our knowledge of the actions by which the parties enforced their rights. The most plausible answer to the question of the origin of the *b.f.* actions is that they were

the buyer of sheep should exact as to their soundness, says: *Cum id factum est, tamen grex dominum non mutavit, nisi si est adnumeratum; nec non emptor pote ex empto vendito illum damnare, si non tradet, quamvis non solverit nummos; ut ille emptorem simili iudicio, si non reddit pretium.* From this Pernice argues that the seller had to deliver first and that this is a relic of the time when there was no obligation until he had delivered. But the words can equally well mean that the buyer can insist on delivery even before he has paid, provided he is ready and willing to pay, and that the seller can similarly insist on payment provided he is ready and willing to deliver. It is true that Varro does not actually say of the seller that he can secure payment *quamvis non tradiderit*, but this seems to be implied in the comparison he makes between the positions of seller and buyer; had he meant to contrast their positions he would have said *at ille non potest emptorem damnare simili iudicio nisi ipse tradidit.*

The argument from the rule that the ownership in the thing only passes if payment has been made falls to the ground if Pringsheim is right in his view that this rule is post-classical (*v. infra*, 521). In the passage quoted from Varro Pringsheim (*Der Kauf mit fremdem Geld*, 73) takes *adnumeratum* to refer, not to payment of the price, but to the counting of the sheep on delivery.

[1] Girard, 569; v. Mayr, *Röm. Rechtsgeschichte*, I. 2. 81.

[2] v. Mayr, *op. cit.* II. 2. II. 59 *sqq.*

[3] Gai. III. 139.

[4] V. Mitteis, *Grundzüge*, 185.

first introduced in the courts where foreigners were concerned and then borrowed from the *ius gentium* by the *ius civile*. There is no trace of any *legis actio* for sale, and we have seen that the formulary system itself very probably originated in the peregrine court.[1] We have seen also that *formulae* were probably possible even between citizens before the *lex Aebutia*, so that formless sale may have become actionable in this way at a fairly early date.[2] How early we cannot say; the evidence from Plautus is ambiguous[3] and the fact that Sextus Aelius (consul 198 B.C.) is said to have given an opinion as to an *arbitrium* in connection with sale[4] is not conclusive, for we cannot be sure that it is the *b.f. formula* with which he was concerned.

(β) Liability of seller for defective title. The primary duty of the seller in the classical and later law is to deliver possession of the thing sold (*vacuam possessionem tradere*); he is not bound, as he is usually in modern systems, to convey ownership therein,[5] i.e. the buyer cannot complain merely because he discovers that he has not become owner on delivery, if he has not actually suffered some loss by reason of the defective title. If, however, there has been eviction,[6] or if, without actual eviction, the buyer has lost the benefit of his bargain, then he can make a claim against the seller. Such loss without eviction may happen if, for instance, the buyer keeps the thing, but only because he buys off the claim of the real owner, and thus has to pay twice for the same thing.

The history of these rules is to be found in the stipulations which ordinarily accompanied sales.[7] We have seen that where a buyer had received a thing by mancipation he could, if subsequently evicted, bring an *actio auctoritatis* for double the purchase price, provided he had warned the seller of the threatened action. This was only possible in the case of mancipation, but where, for one reason or another, the thing was not mancipated,[8] it was customary to provide for the seller's liability

[1] *Supra*, 223.
[2] Lenel, *Z.S.S.* xxx. 353.
[3] Girard, 570, n. 3.
[4] D. 19. 1. 38. 1; *supra*, 225, n. 3.
[5] Sale of Goods Act, 1893, §§ 1 and 62 (1); German Civil Code, § 433; Swiss Law of Obligations, § 184.
[6] For the meaning of "eviction" *v. supra*, 149.
[7] Girard, 589, and literature there quoted.
[8] E.g. because it was not *res mancipi* or because one of the parties was a peregrine. Even where there was mancipation it would be necessary for there to be a stipulation if the obligation were to be guaranteed by sponsors or fide-promissors, and it is to this guarantee that the phrase *satisdatio secundum mancipium* (Cic. *ad Att.* v. 1. 2; *tab. Baetica*, Bruns, I. 334) probably refers; Lenel, *E.P.* 546.

by exacting from him a promise by stipulation that in the event of eviction he would pay double the purchase price (*stipulatio duplae*), i.e. to copy the liability arising *ipso facto* from mancipation; or, if the parties preferred, the stipulation might be simply for the purchase price (*simplae*), this being apparently common where the article sold was of no great value.[1] There was also used sometimes a stipulation wherein the seller promised that the buyer "should be allowed to hold" the thing (*habere licere*). The original meaning of this stipulation and its relation to the *stipulatio simplae* is disputed,[2] but it may well be that in its original form it meant that the seller and his successors in title would not do any act to prejudice the position of the buyer, and, in particular, that they would not attempt to get back the thing sold by relying on the greater right which the older possession would *prima facie* give them. At a time when absolute ownership was not yet recognised this was a real danger, and one which was certainly guarded against by other peoples who, like the early Romans, had only a relative conception of ownership.[3]

Be that as it may, it is clear that, with the growth of the conception of *bona fides*, it came to be regarded as inconsistent with good faith not to make the promises which were usual, and, if in any particular instance they had not been made, an *actio empti* could be brought by the buyer to insist on the seller's making them. This stage had been reached at any rate by the time of Neratius[4] (late first century and early second century A.D.). Finally it was admitted that even if the stipulations had not been made at all the *actio empti* could be used by the buyer to get what he would have got if they had been made, and that was the classical position.[5]

The rule that the seller is not bound to convey title is often said to arise from the fact that sale is a contract *iuris gentium*, the argument being that it would have been impossible, when dealing with foreigners, to insist on the transfer of ownership of which they were incapable.[6] It seems however at least equally likely that the reason is a different one. Handing over possession is a necessary ingredient of a sale from the beginning of things; beyond that the seller's duties were those contained in the usual

---

[1] Varro, *R.R.* II. 10. 5 (Bruns, II. 64): *solet...aut si mancipio non datur, dupla promitti, aut, si ita pacti, simpla.* For restriction of *stipulatio duplae* to valuable things *v.* D. 21. 2. 37. 1.

[2] Girard holds (*Manuel,* 598; *N.R.H.* VIII (1884), 434 = *Mél.* II. 147) that they were the same, what the plaintiff got in an action being his *interesse*. *Contra,* Rabel, *Haftung des Verkäufers wegen Mangels im Rechte* (1902), 31, 132 *sqq.,* 140 *sqq.*

[3] Rabel, *op. cit.* 30–72.

[4] D. 19. 1. 11. 8.

[5] Girard, 592.

[6] E.g. Girard, 584.

stipulations, against eviction and *habere licere*, i.e. the seller promised to refrain from attacking the possession himself and to prevent others from attacking it. He did not promise ownership because that conception was lacking, and he remained free from any duty to convey ownership because at the time when his obligations crystallised the conception of absolute ownership was still undeveloped.[1]

(γ) Liability of seller for latent defects. Roman law, like other systems, began with the principle that no liability attached to the seller for defects in the thing sold, whether or not they were noticeable at the time of the sale; the buyer bought the thing "as it was".[2] In classical law it was indeed recognised that the seller was liable (in the *actio empti*) if he knew of the defect and fraudulently concealed it, but probably even this stage had not yet been reached by the end of the republic.[3] It was, of course, possible to provide by stipulation that the seller should be liable in case the thing turned out to have some particular defect or defects, and it is clear from the forms given by Varro that this was frequently done. Thus he says, for instance, that when oxen are sold the buyer stipulates that they are "healthy and free from noxal liability".[4] Further development was achieved through the action of the curule aediles, who, having charge of the market-place, were able to make regulations concerning the sales which took place there.[5] We know of two edicts dealing with the matter, one of which concerned the sale of slaves, the other the sale of beasts.[6] The slave edict certainly dates from republican times, and indeed appears to have existed already in the first half of the second century B.C.;[7] the edict concerning beasts is later, but also appears to have existed by the end of the republic.[8] The object of the aediles was, no doubt, to punish fraudulent sellers,[9] and the two classes

---

[1] Cf. v. Mayr, *op. cit.* II. 2. II. 65: "This (rule) too was presumably a result of sale by mancipation which, at least originally, did not give absolute ownership, but only a relative claim for warranty against the *auctor*".

[2] Rabel, 464.

[3] Haymann, *Haftung des Verkäufers für die Beschaffenheit der Kaufsache* (1912), 44 *sqq.*

[4] *R.R.* II. 5. 10, 11 (Bruns, II. 63).   [5] Cf. *supra*, 49.

[6] *Iumenta*, literally beasts of burden, but a special clause made it clear that all *pecora*, especially e.g. cattle, were included; D. 21. 1. 38. 5.

[7] Cato (d. 152 B.C.) is quoted on the meaning of *morbus* in D. 21. 1. 10. 1; *v.* Haymann, *op. cit.* 23. Cicero mentions the edict *de Off.* III. 17. 71.

[8] Labeo is quoted on sows by Gellius, IV. 2. 8, and Ofilius on mules in D. 21. 1. 38. 7.

[9] D. 21. 1. 1. 2; in D. 21. 1. 23. 4 the aedilician actions are actually called "penal".

of dealers with which their edict was concerned were clearly particularly suspect, but the result of their action was to import into sales which fell within their jurisdiction entirely new rules of law; as Girard says, "they made private law instead of mere police regulations".[1] The great change which they made consisted in placing upon the seller the responsibility of knowing the defects of the slave or beast that he sold. In the case of slaves they required that an actual stipulation should be made, in which the seller promised to pay damages if any one of a number of particular defects appeared,[2] and it may be that this was originally all that they did. Later, however, both in the case of slaves and in that of beasts, even where no stipulation had been made, if a defect appeared of which the buyer had not been warned,[3] he could claim either rescission of the contract (by an *actio redhibitoria*) or a rebate in the purchase price corresponding to the difference which the defect made to the thing's value (*actio quanto minoris*).[4]

In the classical law it seems clear that the principles of the aedilician edict were applied to sales of slaves and beasts even outside the market-place, but that the extension had gone any further is very unlikely. There is indeed a text in the Digest which attributes to Labeo the statement that the rules applied indiscriminately to sales of all things, movable or immovable, but this is almost certainly interpolated and so evidence for the law of Justinian's day only.[5]

(2) *Locatio conductio.* Under this heading were included three different types of agreement, *l.c. rei*, the hire of a thing, movable or immovable, *l.c. operarum*, the hire of services, and *l.c. operis*, the giving out of a job to be done, e.g. the building of a house, the repair of a garment, the transport of merchandise.[6] It is important to realise that

---

[1] Girard, 600.   [2] D. 21. 1. 28.

[3] The seller either of a slave or a *iumentum* was liable for *morbus* and *vitium*, the latter including such faults as a propensity to take fright easily; D. 21. 1. 43. pr. Slaves had further to be guaranteed against noxal liability, a tendency to wander and being fugitives; D. 21. 1. 1. pr.

[4] *Actio redhibitoria* was available for six months, *actio quanto minoris* for twelve; D. 21. 1. 48. 2.

[5] D. 21. 1. 1. pr., *v.* Haymann, *op. cit.* 37 *sqq.*

[6] In *l.c. rei* and *l.c. operarum* the person who pays the money is the *conductor*, he who provides the thing or the services the *locator*; in *l.c. operis* the one who pays the money is the *locator*, the one who does the job the *conductor*. The origin of this rather confusing terminology is probably to be found in the literal meaning of the words. *Locare* is to "place" a thing with another, whether that other is to enjoy the use of it or to do work on it; the workman similarly "places" himself and his services with the employer who "takes him with him".

the renting of land and dwellings was not treated on different principles from the hire of a chattel, so that what corresponds to the English law of landlord and tenant is to be found under the heading of *l.c. rei*.

There is no more agreement about the origin of *locatio conductio* than there is about that of *emptio venditio*. Mommsen, as we have seen,[1] attributes both to the imitation by private persons of contracts concluded informally by magistrates on behalf of the state, the typical *l.c. operarum* of public law being the contract by which the magistrate hires the services of lictors and other free attendants, while the contracts of the censors formed the model both of *l.c. rei* and *l.c. operis*, for they were the magistrates chiefly concerned both with the leases of public land, where the state received money, and with the placing of contracts for public works, where the state paid the money.[2] Girard, here too, thinks that reciprocal stipulations were first used,[3] while others assume a stage during which the contract was "real", in the sense that it did not become binding until executed on one side, in particular in the case of *l.c. rei*.[4] So far as *l.c. rei* is concerned it is suggested[5] that the lease of land was the earliest example of this type of contract, and that such leases first became common when, as a result of the *lex agraria* of 111 B.C., a great deal of land, formerly held on lease from the state, became the private property of the *possessores*. These people were then able to let off portions of their land on definite leases, whereas before, since their own title was not secure, they had only been able to give it *precario*, i.e. in such a way that they could put an end to the tenancy at their own will. Only subsequently, on this view, were the same principles extended to the leases of houses and the hire of movables.[6]

(b) *Societas* and *Mandatum*. (1) *Societas*. The Roman *societas* has a wider meaning than the English "partnership", for it includes any agreement for the common exploitation of capital or labour for a common purpose, whether that purpose be profit or not. Its scope too may vary from *societas omnium bonorum*, in which the parties agree to own all their present property in common and share future acquisitions, to *societas unius rei*, i.e. for a single transaction. Between these two extremes lie *s. unius negotiationis* (partnership in a single branch of business) and *s. universorum quae ex quaestu veniunt* (in which the parties share all acquisitions made by any type of business transaction).

---

[1] *Supra*, 298.
[2] *Z.S.S.* VI. 268.
[3] *Manuel*, 604.
[4] Costa, *Storia*, 396; Pernice, *Labeo*, I. 466 *sqq.*
[5] Costa, *Locazione di cose nel dir. rom.* (1915)—summarised *Z.S.S.* XLVII. 529.
[6] For the priority of leases of land cf. Jhering, *Besitzwille*, 123.

The oldest form is probably *s. omnium bonorum*, itself apparently the development of a more primitive arrangement known as *consortium*, whereby coheirs, instead of dividing their inheritance, continue to enjoy it in common, this being often the most practical course to pursue, in the case, for instance, of a small farm.[1] Whether the other forms of *societas* have the same origin is more doubtful; they are, in classical law, treated as species belonging to the same genus as *s. omnium bonorum*; they are equally characterised by *fraternitas*;[2] condemnation results in *ignominia*,[3] while, on the other hand, the *socius* cannot be condemned for an amount greater than his resources permit (*beneficium competentiae*).[4] On the other hand, it is urged that the objects of a commercial partnership are so different from those of *s. omnium bonorum* that its origin must have been different, though the *s. omnium bonorum* may subsequently have influenced its rules.[5] The truth is, presumably, that there existed in early law many sorts of arrangement, each having its own rules, and that it was juristic abstraction which brought them under one head, just as it brought all the different arrangements for providing goods and services in return for money under the two carefully distinguished categories of *emptio venditio* and *locatio conductio*.

One form of *societas unius negotiationis* needs special mention, that entered into by *publicani*, i.e. tax-farmers and other persons who paid the state money in return for permission to exploit public resources, such e.g. as the state salt-works.[6] These *publicani* formed a powerful capitalist class in the later republic and it is clear that their contracts differed from ordinary *societates* not only by reason of their complicated organisation, the magnitude of their undertakings, and their relationship to the state, but also in the legal relationship of the partners *inter se*.[7] It also appears that in addition to the *socii* proper there were persons who contributed capital and shared in the profits without taking any part in the manage-

---

[1] A few examples are mentioned by historians, e.g. Livy XLI. 27; *v.* Girard, 611; cf. also D. 17. 2. 52. 8. The old phrase used in this connection was *ercto non cito*, i.e. "no summons to division having been made"; *v.* Gell. 1. 9. 12; Festus, s.v. *sors* and s.v. *erctum citumque*, Bruns, II. 40 and 8. All the cases of *s. omnium bonorum* mentioned in the sources where it is possible to see who the parties are refer to relations except D. 34. 1. 16. 3, where they are husband and wife; *v.* Pernice, *Z.S.S.* III. 85, n. 1. Karlowa, II. 653, denies the connection with *consortium*.

[2] D. 17. 2. 63. pr. (interpolated in form but not in substance, Lenel, *E.P.* 298).

[3] Gai. IV. 182.

[4] D. 42. 1. 22. 1; Lenel, *E.P.* 298. [5] Pernice, *Labeo*, I. 443 *sqq.*

[6] D. 39. 4. 12. 3; 13. pr. [7] See e.g. Buckland, 513.

ment and without risking more than the amount of their contributions. There is no clear evidence that these "shares" (*partes*) were alienable,[1] but they obviously provided opportunities for investment. It is sometimes asserted on the strength of one text[2] that *societates publicanorum* could, unlike ordinary partnerships, have a corporate personality, but there is some difficulty in seeing why an association formed to undertake a temporary contract (usually for five years) should have needed incorporation. One suggestion is that the corporate bodies were not the *societates* formed to undertake the particular contracts, but more permanent associations of persons commonly engaged in such business for the protection of their common interests.[3]

(2) *Mandatum*. *Mandatum* is a contract by which one party undertakes gratuitously to perform some service for the other. The principal (*mandator*) can, by an *actio mandati directa*, obtain damages if the undertaking is not carried out properly and can insist on the agent's handing over to him any advantage accruing through its performance; the agent, on the other hand, has an *actio contraria* to secure reimbursement of his expenses.[4]

The date at which it first became possible to bring an action on mandate is not known; it must have been after the passing of the *lex Aquilia*[5] and before 123 B.C., for in that year it is said that Sextus Iulius as praetor refused to grant an action against the heirs of the agent, whereas a few years later another praetor, Livius Drusus, allowed one in such cases.[6] Girard holds that this doubt about transmissibility points to an *actio in factum*,[7] but there is no direct evidence for one and the *actio mandati* appears with the actions on the other consensual contracts in Q. Mucius' list of *b.f. iudicia*.[8]

---

[1] Mitteis, *R.P.R.* 413.

[2] D. 3. 4. 1. pr.: *vectigalium publicorum sociis permissum est corpus habere.*

[3] Cohn, *Zum röm. Vereinsrecht*, 158 *sqq.*, quoted by Mitteis, *op. cit.* 405.

[4] Biondi, *Iudicia bonae fidei*, 61 *sqq.*, holds that there was in classical law only a single action, which might be brought by either party, the claims on both sides being considered together, and that the distinction between "direct" and "contrary" actions here as well as in *negotiorum gestio* is Byzantine. *Contra*, Lenel, *E.P.* 296.

[5] Because the second chapter gave the principal creditor an action against the *adstipulator* who fraudulently released the debtor; such action would have been unnecessary had the *actio mandati* already existed, for the *adstipulator* is necessarily the agent of the principal creditor and can be sued on the mandate if he causes loss to his principal; *v.* Gai. III. 215–216.

[6] Auct. ad Herenn. II. 13, 19.

[7] 619, n. 2. There was probably a *formula in factum* of the *actio contraria* for a special case; Lenel, *E.P.* 296. [8] *Supra*, 295, n. 6.

(c) *Negotiorum gestio* and *tutela* (quasi-contract). Closely allied to *mandatum* are the quasi-contractual relationships of *negotiorum gestio* and *tutela*. In both these cases there is an agent who acts in the interests of a principal, but there is no contract (according to later ideas)[1] because there is no agreement, for the *negotiorum gestor* is precisely a person who "carries on affairs" which concern another without any instructions, and the tutor, though he acts on behalf of his ward, is appointed, not by agreement with the ward, but by the law. These agents are however responsible for the proper management of their principals' affairs, and can, within limits, secure reimbursement of their expenses. As in the case of mandate, the action brought by the principal is the *actio directa*, that brought by the agent the *actio contraria*. According to one view[2] the *actiones n.g.*, *tutelae* and *mandati* are all descended from a single earlier *actio n.g.*, with a wider scope than that of the developed law, which had in it a "real" element in so far as it lay only if the agent had actually performed some act of administration, but lay in such case whether there had been previous authorisation or not. This view is however abandoned by most authorities. Cicero, though he knew the *actio mandati* both in its "direct" and in its "contrary" function, apparently knew the *actio n.g.* only as a direct action.[3] It is also now generally agreed that the *actio n.g.* was of praetorian origin and was originally *in factum* only,[4] whereas there is no reliable evidence of an *actio in factum* either in the case of mandate[5] or in that of *tutela*,[6] both of which appear in Q. Mucius' list of *b.f. iudicia*, whereas *n.g.* does not. It is however now very generally held that the respective spheres of the *actio mandati* and the *actio n.g.* were not originally, or even in classical law, the same as those assigned to them by the Byzantine system. To the Byzantines an agent who has any authority at all is a mandatary, while a *negotiorum gestor* is a person who intrudes unasked into another person's affairs. In the earlier law, on the other hand, it seems that *actio mandati* lay only where there was special authorisation for the act done, and that anyone acting under a general authority (in particular a *procurator* in the original sense of "general agent") was a *negotiorum gestor*.[7] It is now

---

[1] *Supra*, 280.

[2] Wlassak, *Zur Geschichte der n.g.* (1879), followed by Costa, *Storia*, 373 *sqq.*

[3] Cic. *Top.* XVII. 66; *v.* Girard, 663. See also against Wlassak; Karlowa, II. 672; Pernice, *Z.S.S.* XIX. 162; Partsch, *Studien zur n.g.* I.

[4] There was an edict promising the action, which would be unparalleled in the case of a civil action; Lenel, *E.P.* 101; Girard, 663.

[5] *Supra*, 307.   [6] Lenel, *E.P.* 319.

[7] Frese, "Prokuratur und *n.g.*", *Mél. Cornil*, I. 352 *sqq.*

generally held that the edict promising *actio in factum n.g.* mentioned definitely the case of one who carried on the affairs of another in that other's absence,[1] and the most common case was probably precisely that of a *procurator* who had been appointed with general authority to act in the absence of his principal.[2] At any rate a *procurator* is commonly regarded, even by the classical lawyers, as one who *negotia gerit*,[3] and the *actio n.g.* is the only one available to or against a *curator*,[4] who is certainly not a person who pushes himself into other people's affairs.

C. SECURITY. The law of obligations is completed by the law of security, i.e. of the methods by which a creditor seeks to guard himself against the possible insolvency of his debtor. Such security may be either personal or real according as the creditor obtains a right against a third person who will be liable for the debt in addition to the debtor himself, or a right over a piece of property which he can use in some way to satisfy himself if the debtor does not pay the debt. The two institutions take widely different paths, but in their origin they are not so different. The primitive (personal) surety is, as we have seen,[5] a hostage, i.e. a person who is "liable", not in addition to, but instead of the person whom we call the "principal debtor"; if the principal pays, the surety is released. So too, in the earliest times, with real security; the debtor has the right to release the thing pledged by paying his debt, but if he does not the thing is "liable", i.e. the creditor keeps it.[6] Personal security appears to have developed at an earlier stage in Roman history than did real security; it was a social duty to become surety for one's relations and friends, and we have already noticed the importance of this practice in connection with procedure.[7] Even in the law of classical times and later, when security is needed for procedural purposes, it is almost exclusively in the form of suretyship that it is required.

(i) *Personal security.* The original nature of suretyship is visible, in historical times, only in the *praedes*, who, as we have seen, probably engaged themselves instead of, not in addition to, the "principal debtor".[8] In historical times, however, *praedes* only occur where security has to

---

[1] Partsch, *op. cit.* 10 *sqq.*; Lenel, *E.P.* 101.
[2] Frese, *op. cit.* 346.
[3] Mitteis, *R.P.R.* 233, n. 97.
[4] Some texts describe it as *utilis*, but these are probably interpolated; *v.* Buckland, 538, n. 20; Lenel, *Z.S.S.* xxxv. 203 *sqq.*
[5] *Supra*, 162.   [6] Cf. *infra*, 313.
[7] *Supra*, 194.   [8] *Supra*, 188.

be given to the state or in connection with *legis actio sacramento*,[1] and for private as well as most procedural matters the form of suretyship used is quite a different one, in which the surety makes a promise by stipulation, by which he becomes indebted to the creditor in addition to the person who may now be described quite properly as the "principal debtor". Three forms of such *adpromissio* are described by Gaius,[2] *sponsio*, *fidepromissio* and *fideiussio*, which last is of considerably later origin than the other two, and may not have come into use until after the end of the republic. *Sponsio* is probably the oldest form; here the surety is asked *idem dari spondes?* and replies *spondeo*, the use of this word being confined, as in the case of ordinary stipulations, to Roman citizens.[3] The *fidepromissor* is asked *idem fidepromittis?* and in this form the contract is open to peregrines as well. Otherwise there is no difference between the effects of the two forms;[4] both enable the creditor to take his choice of suing either the principal debtor or the surety;[5] both can be used only to guarantee obligations which have themselves been created by stipulation; in neither case is the heir of the original surety liable, and both forms were subjected to restrictive legislation which began some two centuries before the end of the republic. The first statute was a *lex Apuleia* which enacted that where there were several *sponsores* or *fidepromissores* any one of them who had paid more than a proportionate share of the debt might recover the excess from his co-sureties. A little later the *lex Furia*[6] went

[1] It is held by some authorities, e.g. Girard, 797, that *praedes* as well as *vades* were never used except for contracts with the state and for procedural purposes. This view is *prima facie* supported by Festus, s.v. *praes* (Bruns, II, 26): *Praes est is qui populo se obligat interrogatusque a magistratu si praes sit, ille respondet: praes.* But see Mitteis, *Festschrift für Bekker*, 121.   [2] III. 115–127.

[3] Probably the promise had at one time to be made immediately after that of the principal debtor, but this can no longer have been so at the time of the *lex Cicereia* (*infra*, 311) for it is clear from what Gaius says that there might be several sureties who did not know of each other's existence; *v.* Girard, 798, n. 3.

[4] Except that only the *sponsor* has the *actio depensi*, *supra*, 197.

[5] But *litis contestatio* with one will make it impossible for an action to be brought against the other, and the creditor will thus always sue the surety if there is any doubt about the solvency of the principal debtor. To this extent the surety is in the same position as a correal debtor, and it has been contended (E. Levy, *Sponsio, fidepromissio, fideiussio*, 79 *sqq.* Berlin, 1907) that there was originally no legal distinction between correality and suretyship, the correal debtor being merely in some cases one who entered into his obligation for the purpose of guaranteeing a debt which did not concern him personally, and that the first legal recognition of the accessory nature of his debt was by the *lex Cicereia*; *contra*, Mitteis, *Festschrift für Bekker*, 119.

[6] This statute was confined to suretyships in Italy, whereas the *l. Apuleia* applied in the provinces as well.

further by providing, so far as sureties in Italy were concerned, that the debt should be divided by the number of *sponsores* or *fidepromissores* living at the due date and that any one who had been made to pay more than his share should have an action, exercisable by *manus iniectio*, against the creditor for recovery.[1] It also enacted that *sponsores* and *fidepromissores* should be released from their liability two years after the due date of the debt. The restriction of liability to a proportionate share where there were several sureties made it important for each surety to know how many others there were, and a *lex Cicereia* completed the system by requiring that the creditor should state openly the amount of the debt and the number of sureties, and that if he did not the surety could secure his release. A further restriction was introduced by a *lex Cornelia*, which, with some exceptions, forbade any one man to be surety for any one other for a greater amount than 20,000 sesterces in the same year.[2]

The object of all this restrictive legislation was presumably to lighten the burden cast upon sureties and so make it easier for people in need of credit to obtain the necessary security, but apparently it overshot its mark by reducing too greatly the value of the surety to the creditor, and this led to the introduction of the new type of surety, the *fideiussor*, to whom none of the restrictions (except that of the *lex Cornelia*) applied. The *fideiussor*, like the older sureties, entered into his obligation by stipulation, being asked *id*[3] *fide tua esse iubes?* but this method could be used to

---

[1] Girard thinks that the surety must have been forced to pay by a judgment in an action (cf. *supra*, 85, on *leges imperfectae*). *Contra*, Lenel, *Z.S.S.* xxx. 336.

[2] There is no direct evidence for the dates of any of these statutes, but it is clear from Gaius that the order was *l. Apuleia, l. Furia, l. Cicereia, l. Cornelia*. The author of the *l. Cicereia* may have been C. Cicereius who was praetor in 173 B.C. (Livy XLII. 1) and the use of a *praeiudicium* (Gai. III. 123) where one would have expected an *exceptio* points to a time when the formulary procedure was at any rate still undeveloped. The *l. Apuleia*, on the other hand, since its provisions extended to the provinces, cannot well have been passed earlier than 241 B.C., the date of the first province (*supra*, 68). The *l. Cornelia* may well be due to Sulla (*circa* 81 B.C.), but there is no evidence to prove this. Girard thinks that as it applied to *fideiussores* it must necessarily be later than the introduction of *fideiussio*, but the words of Gaius seem equally compatible with a subsequent extension of its provisions to a new type of surety; *v.* Girard, 800; Levy, *op. cit.* 118; Kniep, *Gai. Inst. Comm.* III. §§ 88–225, 187 *sqq.*

[3] The MS. of Gaius reads, somewhat doubtfully, *idem*, but other authorities give *id*, e.g. D. 45. 1. 75. 6; *C.I.L.* III. 934 (Bruns, I, 352): *id fide sua esse iussit Titius Primitius*. Whether the distinction between the *fideiussor's id* and the *idem* of the older sureties points to a fundamental difference in the newer institution, as Pernice holds (*Z.S.S.* XIX. 182), is doubtful. Gaius' complete silence is against Pernice's view; Levy, *op. cit.* 79 *sqq.*

guarantee any sort of obligation whether it had been created by stipulation or in any other way. There is, however, no trace of *fideiussio* in Cicero and it is probable that it did not exist until the time of Labeo.[1]

In addition to the three adpromissory types of suretyship there were in the classical law two others which were free from rules of form, *mandatum pecuniae credendae* and *constitutum debiti alieni*. The origins of both go back to the republic, but neither was developed until imperial times. *Mandatum pecuniae credendae* is the use of mandate to achieve the purposes of suretyship. If *A* gives *B* a mandate to lend money to *C*, *A* has in effect become surety for *C*, because if *C* fails to repay, *B* will be able to bring an *actio mandati contraria* for reimbursement against *A* on the ground that he has suffered loss by carrying out *A*'s instructions. This method had evidently been tried before the end of the republic, because Servius Sulpicius denied its validity on the ground that the *mandator* himself had no interest in the fulfilment of the mandate; Sabinus however thought differently, and in classical times it was extremely common.[2]

Constitutum was an informal promise to pay an already existing debt, enforceable by a praetorian action. In classical times the debt might be one owed by the promisor or by a third party, and in the latter case there was clearly a kind of suretyship. Only *constitutum* of a debt owed by the promisor, however, seems to be evidenced for republican times.[3]

(ii) *Real security*. The origins of real security at Rome are uncertain. Probably the earliest form to develop was *pignus*, in the sense already discussed of the delivery of possession by way of pledge.[4] This, it is often said,[5] would in early times have given the creditor mere *de facto* security because, before the development of the formulary procedure and of *exceptiones*,[6] the debtor, if he had not transferred ownership, could have successfully vindicated the thing as his own even before

---

[1] Levy, *op. cit.* 123.   [2] Gai. III. 156.

[3] Cic. *pro Quinct.* v. 18. The action was probably originally intended to punish the breach of faith committed by a person who received an extension of time on condition of promising to pay at a definite future date. The *receptum argentarii*, which was fused by Justinian with *constitutum*, used commonly to be thought an ancient institution of the *ius civile* (e.g. Karlowa, II. 758–761). *Contra*, Lenel, *E.P.* 132 *sqq.* There appears to be no reliable trace of its existence in republican times.

[4] *Supra*, 295.

[5] E.g. Girard, 815; Pappulias: ἡ ἐμπράγματος ἀσφάλεια κατὰ τὸ ἑλληνικὸν καὶ τὸ ῥωμαικὸν δίκαιον (Leipzig, 1909), 219.

[6] Before the introduction of possessory interdicts the creditor would, on this view, have had no protection even against third parties.

paying the debt, though he would usually be restrained from doing so by fear of the severe measures which the creditor could take against him if he did not pay in the end. It is, however, difficult to conceive that the early Roman creditor would have been satisfied with such very poor security and, though we cannot tell exactly what the legal position was, we can be fairly sure that if the debt were not paid at the due date the creditor simply kept the thing.[1] This, at any rate, is what analogy with other early systems of law would lead us to suppose, for it is clear that both in Greek and in Germanic law the original position is that the pledge, like the personal surety, is primarily given in satisfaction of the debt, and that all that the debtor retains is a right of redemption up to a certain date for the amount of the debt.[2] Roman law, it is true, goes a very different way in its developed state, when the pledge is merely accessory to the personal debt, and the normal thing is for the creditor (if not paid) to have to sell the thing pledged in order to pay himself out of the proceeds, and to hand over any excess to the debtor, just as he remains entitled to claim from the debtor any amount by which the sale price falls short of the amount of the debt.[3] But this proves, not that Roman law was unlike cognate systems in its infancy, but that here, as in other cases, the legal genius of the Romans enabled them to develop in a peculiar way institutions which they originally shared with other peoples. Be that as it may, there certainly developed at a fairly early period a different institution, also closely parallel to institutions of other systems, which served the purposes of real security in a different way.

---

[1] Manigk, P.-W., s.v. *hyperocha*, 17th half-volume, col. 295. Cf. Art. *hypotheca, ibid.* col. 355; Rabel, 494. A somewhat different form of agreement is seen in Cato, *de agr.* 146. 5 (Bruns, II. 49), where the articles pledged are to become the property of the landlord-pledgee if removed from the land. The earliest reference to *pignus* seems to be in the "Latin treaty" quoted by Festus, s.v. *Nancitor* (Bruns, II. 16): *Si quid pignoris nanciscitur, sibi habeto.* So far as it goes this supports the view given in the text, but as it refers to international law it is of little help.

[2] For early Greek law at any rate there can be no doubt, *v.* e.g. Lipsius, 702 and Manigk, P.-W., s.v. *hypotheca,* col. 355. For English law *v.* Pollock and Maitland, *H.E.L.* II. 184: "In the case of the gage there probably was at first no outstanding duty on the side of the debtor when once the gage had been given...he handed over something of sufficient value to cover and more than cover the debt; the debt was satisfied; the only outstanding duty was that of the recipient of the gage, who was bound to hand it back if within due time its giver came to redeem it".

[3] That the old conception survived even in classical times is shown by the practice of inserting a special clause which reserved the creditor's right to exact any deficiency from the debtor; as Pomponius says, D. 20. 5. 9. 1, the creditor had exactly the same right in any case.

This was *fiducia*, the contractual aspect of which has already been discussed.[1] Here the ownership in a thing was conveyed to the creditor by mancipation or *in iure cessio*, and the debtor consequently lost all rights *in rem* with respect to the thing, retaining only his personal action against the creditor if the creditor alienated the thing before the debt fell due or in any other way broke the agreement. In classical times it was evidently usual for there to be a special term in the agreement allowing sale,[2] and if the thing fetched more than the amount of the debt the excess had to be paid to the debtor;[3] also, the creditor could probably not simply keep the thing as his own if the debt were not paid unless there were a special clause (*lex commissoria*) allowing him to do so, just as there had to be such a clause if he were to retain a *pignus*. But these rules are no doubt comparatively late developments; originally and probably still in Cicero's time the rule was simple: if the debt remained unpaid after it had become due the creditor was freed from his duty to re-convey.[4]

The last form of pledge to develop was that known, at least to the law of Justinian's time, as *hypotheca*,[5] i.e. the pledging of a thing by mere agreement, without the transfer of either ownership or possession. Clearly there were grave inconveniences about both *fiducia* and *pignus*. In the first place these both meant that the debtor was deprived of the use of his thing, unless, as sometimes happened, it were given back to him either *precario* or on hire, and secondly the credit-raising value of the thing was necessarily exhausted by a single pledging, for a thing cannot be conveyed or delivered successively to two creditors even though the amount of the first debt be very much smaller than the value of the thing. The first case in which it became possible (among private persons) for a thing to be pledged by mere agreement was apparently that of the agricultural tenant who desired that the effects which he brought on to the land (*invecta et illata*) should be available as security to the landlord for the payment of the rent. Obviously he could not be deprived of the possession of them for they were probably all that he had, and the land could

---

[1] *Supra*, 294. The word *fiducia* occurs in Plautus, e.g. *Trin.* I. 2. 80, but the institution is probably older; v. Manigk, P.-W., s.v. *Fiducia*, col. 2290. For comparison with the English law of mortgage v. Hazeltine, Preface to Turner *The Equity of Redemption* (Cambridge, 1930).

[2] *Formula Baetica* (Bruns, I. 334), 12–15.   [3] Paul. *Sent.* II. 13. 1.

[4] Manigk, *op. cit.* col. 2299; Cic. *pro Flacco*, XXI. 51.

[5] The classical use of the word is disputed; v. Fehr, *Beiträge zur Lehre vom r. Pfandrecht* (Upsala 1910). But see also Manigk, s.v. *hypotheca* in P.-W., coll. 364 *sqq*.

not be worked without his slaves, beasts and agricultural implements. If then he had agreed that they were to be pledged it was allowed that the landlord should have an interdict (*interdictum Salvianum*) which enabled him to obtain possession of them if the rent were not paid when it fell due.[1] This was available only against the tenant himself, but a praetorian action (*actio Serviana*) was later allowed whereby the landlord could get possession of the things even from third parties into whose hands they had come, e.g. by purchase from the tenant. This action was subsequently generalised, so that it lay when any debtor had agreed that a thing belonging to him should be pledged for his debt, and the creditor could thus claim the thing wherever it was if the debt were not paid when it fell due.[2] Once he had got the thing he was in exactly the same position as if it had been pledged to him from the first by delivery of possession. It was at one time commonly held, owing to the Greek name, *hypotheca*, under which the institution commonly appears in the Corpus Juris, that its introduction was due to Greek influence, but it is now generally agreed to be of native growth. *Pignus* and *hypotheca* are treated throughout as one and the same thing;[3] in some cases possession is transferred at once, in others it is not, but that is all. The word *pignus* is freely used for both cases and indeed occurs in the *formula* of the very action which made pledge without possession possible.[4] It is clear too that the particular case from which *hypotheca* arose was one which was but a slight extension of the original principle. The land onto which the tenant's goods are brought is in the possession of the landlord, though they themselves are not, and it was doubtless the feeling that they were to some extent within the landlord's control which prompted this departure from the original necessity of possession.[5]

As to date—the existence of pledge without possession is attested for Cato's time (234–149 B.C.) by a clause in his form of contract for the sale

---

[1] Gai. IV. 147.

[2] Justinian (Inst. IV. 6. 7) distinguishes *actio Serviana* available to the landlord from the *actio quasi Serviana* or *hypothecaria* used by ordinary hypothecary creditors, but this distinction is probably interpolated; Lenel, *E.P.* 493.

[3] D. 13. 7. 1. pr.: *Pignus contrahitur non sola traditione, sed etiam nuda conventione, etsi non traditum est*; Manigk, *op. cit.* coll. 347 *sqq.*

[4] *Actio Serviana*; Lenel, *E.P.* 494.

[5] An institution of public law may also have formed a precedent—the *praedia subsignata*, i.e. lands which pledged to the state or a municipality apparently without any actual handing over to officials. The officials could seize them if the debt were unpaid, and here too it is no doubt the overwhelming power that the state has of enforcing its rights which makes the original delivery unnecessary. Cf. Manigk, *op. cit.* col. 347.

of olives on the tree, which provides that everything which the purchaser brings into the olive-yard is to serve as security for payment,[1] and a similar clause with respect to slaves and cattle in the form for a sale of pasture, there being in the latter case a further clause which provides that any litigation concerning the matter is to take place at Rome.[2] The litigation contemplated may at that time have been interdictal, but the *actio Serviana* itself also dates probably from some way back in the republic. It was certainly of praetorian origin and yet there is no trace of any edict promising it, a fact which goes to show that it came into existence before the practice of issuing edicts had become common[3] and therefore probably before the *lex Aebutia*.

[1] 146. 5 (Bruns, II. 49).

[2] 149. 7–8 (Bruns, II. 50).

[3] Manigk, *op. cit.* col. 353; Pappulias, *op. cit.* 330. *Contra*, Girard, 818, who supposes the reform still unknown to Labeo.

Chapter XVIII

CRIMINAL LAW IN THE REPUBLIC

§ I. ORIGINS

In early Roman law, as in other early systems, a great part of the field covered by modern criminal law falls within the province of the ordinary civil law of delict. We have seen already, for instance, that theft and assault, typical crimes according to modern law, led only to private actions at the instance of the party injured, though the result of such action might be the infliction of a physical penalty upon the wrongdoer.[1] It is, however, remarkable that at Rome, from the earliest times of which we have any knowledge, murder appears to have been punished at the instance of the state[2] and almost all traces of the blood-feud have disappeared.[3] So far as criminal law existed at all there appear to be in the early records two distinct strata. On the one hand, there are the secular crimes of treason (*perduellio*) and murder, to which may perhaps be added the evasion of military service; on the other, there are a number of offences, largely concerned with family relationships, which were evidently held to be of a religious nature and were visited by sanctions of a religious character. Thus, according to a law attributed to Romulus, the man who sold his wife was to be sacrificed to the infernal gods,[4] and Servius Tullius is said to have enacted that the child who struck his parent was to be "sacred" to the gods of his parents.[5] In the XII Tables we find the rule that he who cuts another's corn by night is to be crucified[6] as a sacrifice to Ceres, as well as the more famous *patronus si clienti fraudem fecerit sacer esto.*[7] It may well be that some of these recorded rules date from a period before the justice of the state superseded that of smaller groups—perhaps the *gentes*—and that only a few of them were

---

[1] *Supra*, 170 and 174.
[2] *Quaestores parricidii* (officers who, as their name shows, were connected with public trials for murder) were mentioned in the XII Tables (Tab. IX. 4).
[3] *Infra*, 324.
[4] Plut. *Qu. Rom.* XXII (Bruns, I. 6); cf. *supra*, 118, n. 1.
[5] Festus, s.v. *plorare* (Bruns, II. 23).
[6] Tab. VIII. 9. *Suspensum* refers to crucifixion, *v.* Mommsen, *Strafrecht*, 918.
[7] Tab. VIII. 21. According to Dionysius (2. 10. 1, Bruns. I. 4) Romulus already enacted that those guilty of offences against the law of patron and client should be deemed traitors and that anyone could kill them as a sacrifice to Dis.

taken over by the state together with the primitive religious sanction.[1]
Some certainly disappeared, for there is no indication that any public
tribunal ever tried the offence of wife-selling or that of striking a parent,
which latter would, in historical times, have been purely a matter for the
domestic jurisdiction of the *paterfamilias*. It is even difficult to believe
that a public tribunal can ever have been called upon to decide whether
the religious and moral duties of a patron towards his client had been
carried out. It must also be noted that the implications of the phrase
sacer esto are a matter of dispute, but it seems clear that the criminal
would normally suffer death.[2]

§ II. FROM THE XII TABLES UNTIL THE INTRODUCTION OF THE
QUAESTIONES PERPETUAE

It was not until the last century of the republic had been nearly reached,
that any permanent provision was made for the establishment of special
tribunals to try criminal cases. Before that time all criminal jurisdiction
was a matter for the magistrates and for the assemblies of the people.
Every sentence must be pronounced by a magistrate in the first instance,
but the rules of *provocatio*[3] mean that if the sentence is one of death or
imposes a fine above a certain limit it cannot be executed (in the case of
a citizen) unless it has been confirmed by the people. One most unfortunate result of this system was that the criminal law never attained to the
same degree of certainty as did the civil. When a magistrate ordered the
infliction of some penalty he might be doing either of two things; he
might be acting as a judge who ordained a punishment for an infraction of
the law, or he might be exercising his general powers of *coercitio*, i.e.
of enforcing his commands upon recalcitrant persons, but no clear
distinction was ever drawn between the two functions[4] and (unless the
matter was one which would come before the people) no procedural forms

---

[1] Cf. Costa, *Crimini e Pene da Romolo a Giustiniano*, 27.
[2] The difficulty arises largely from the definition given by Festus, s.v. *sacer*
(Bruns, II. 33): "A *sacer homo* is one whom the people has condemned on account
of crime; it is not lawful (*fas*) for him to be sacrificed, but one who kills him is
not condemned for murder (*parricidium*)". This seems to point to "sacredness"
as a kind of outlawry, an idea which does not fit at all well with the sacrificing to
particular gods of which instances are given above, nor with the view commonly
held (Mommsen, *Strafrecht*, 900 *sqq.*) that all capital punishment at Rome
was in the nature of a sacrifice. For a possible explanation *v.* Strachan-Davidson,
I. 8 *sqq.*   [3] *Infra*, 320.
[4] Mommsen attempts to find a distinction, *Strafrecht*, 475; for the difficulties
involved *v.* Strachan-Davidson, I. 96 *sqq.*

were laid down in either case. It was for the magistrate to inform himself, as he thought fit, by witnesses or otherwise, of the matter, and then to issue his decision. If he had himself witnessed the offence there would be no need for evidence. He might, of course, act on the information of a private individual, but the informer did not become a party to an action as did the plaintiff in a civil suit. Further, if the matter came before the people, they did not regard themselves as a court bound to administer the law; they were sovereign and, even if they agreed with the magistrate as to the guilt of the accused, might find reasons for pardoning him,[1] just as they might acquiesce in a sentence which involved a stretching of the law if political feeling led them to do so. Their function, in fact, was more closely akin to that exercised in the English system by the Crown than to that exercised by the Court of Criminal Appeal.

The magistrates who could use coercive powers included in the first place the holders of *imperium* (dictator, consuls, praetors), but, by ancient custom, these officers always acted through delegates when the case was one which would give the accused, if convicted, the right of appeal to the people.[2] If the charge were one of *perduellio* these delegates were the *duoviri perduellionis*, appointed or elected for each occasion;[3] in other cases the duty fell upon the quaestors, the *quaestores parricidii*, mentioned in the XII Tables and a few other authorities, being probably not separate officers but identical with the urban quaestors of historical times.[4] Capital jurisdiction could also be exercised by the tribunes, although they, of course, had no *imperium*. The tribunes were especially concerned with political offences, this function of theirs having arisen originally from their position as heads of the plebeian community who used what were, in effect, revolutionary powers to punish any person, in particular patrician magistrates, who had infringed the rights of the *plebs*. After the end of the struggle between the orders, the tribunes, now in fact, though not in law, the magistrates of the whole state, continued to exercise similar functions, especially against magistrates and others guilty of abusing public authority with which they had been entrusted.[5] In the later

---

[1] This is precisely what they did in the legendary case of Horatius (Livy I. 26); there was no doubt that he had murdered his sister and the II viri had to pronounce sentence on him, but the people pardoned him because of the victory which he had won. Cf. Quintilian, VII. 4. 18: *apud populum...et ubicumque iuris clementia est, habet locum deprecatio.*

[2] Cf. *supra*, 49.

[3] Elected according to Mommsen, *Strafrecht*, pp. 154 and 587. *Contra*, Strachan-Davidson, I. 153.

[4] Strachan-Davidson, I. 152.   [5] Mommsen, *Strafrecht*, 156.

republic tribunician procedure entirely superseded the ancient form of trial by the II *viri perduellionis*.[1] A considerable amount of criminal jurisdiction also fell to the aediles (both curule and plebeian), who had *coercitio*, though no *imperium*, and could pronounce minor penalties. They were especially concerned with police offences in the markets and the streets, and were also apparently the magistrates who usually ordered the infliction of fines for various offences; e.g. usury[2] or gambling, created under special *leges*.[3]

According to tradition, *provocatio* against a capital sentence had been possible during the monarchy, but only with permission of the king, and became a right of the citizen in the first year of the republic by the passing of a *lex Valeria*. The magistrate's power of fining was said to have been originally unlimited, but to have been restricted, already before the XII Tables, by the rule that no fine greater than thirty oxen and two sheep might be imposed on any one person on one day, and this amount was a little later expressed in money as 3020 *asses*.[4] The supposed *lex Valeria* of 509 B.C. is probably only a reflection of a real *lex Valeria* on the same subject of 300 B.C.,[5] but it is generally held that *provocatio* must have existed by the time of the XII Tables, because they enacted that only the *comitia centuriata* might decide *de capite civis*.[6] There were several other laws which confirmed and extended the right and finally, in 123 B.C., C. Gracchus attempted to prevent others from suffering his brother's fate by securing a plebiscite which forbade any magistrate on any excuse to put a citizen to death without trial before the people, and probably made any such execution equivalent to murder.[7] There were, of course, limits to *provocatio*; in the first place only citizens had a right to

---

[1] The attempt to revive it against Rabirius (who was defended by Cicero) in 63 B.C. was defeated by a technicality, *v.* Strachan-Davidson, I. 189.

[2] Mommsen, *Strafrecht*, 849.

[3] For censors *v. supra*, 52. The *pontifex maximus* had the power of punishing priests subject to him. In the case of unchastity of a Vestal virgin this power extended to her accomplice, and no *provocatio* was possible.

[4] There are contradictory accounts of this legislation, *v.* Mommsen, *Strafrecht*, 50.

[5] Cf. *supra*, 10.

[6] Tab. IX. 2. Lenel, however (323), thinks that this provision was merely intended to prevent capital sentences from being inflicted by the plebs under tribunician presidency.

[7] Mommsen, *Strafrecht*, 258; Strachan-Davidson, I. 144. For the *senatus consultum ultimum*, which was held at any rate by the senatorial party, to free the magistrates from *provocatio*, *v. supra*, 34 and Strachan-Davidson, I. 240 *sqq.*

it,[1] and for a long time it did not prevail against the sentence of a dictator. The exceptional magistracies, e.g. that of Sulla, during the revolutionary period, were expressly exempt from *provocatio*, and it was probably only during the second century B.C. that the citizen obtained any right of appeal against a sentence pronounced against him *militiae*, i.e. in any part of the world except in Rome or within the first milestone from the city (*domi*). There appear indeed to have been some cases in which a magistrate inflicted, not indeed the death penalty, but deprivation of liberty within the city; thus in 138 B.C. a certain Matienus was scourged and sold as a slave for deserting the army,[2] and persons who failed to inscribe themselves on the census list for the purpose of evading military service seem to have been regularly treated in this way.[3] Perhaps the explanation is that even within the walls military crimes were subject to a sharper *imperium* than civil offences, or the theory may have been, as Cicero explains, that such persons by neglecting their duties as citizens had forfeited a citizen's rights.[4]

If there was to be *provocatio*, but not otherwise, the proceedings had to take a prescribed form.[5] First the magistrate must summon the accused to appear before him on a certain date (*diei dictio*). On the day mentioned he begins his investigation (*anquisitio*), which must take place in a public *contio* so that the people, who may have to consider the matter on appeal, can acquire the necessary information. This investigation must be adjourned at least twice, with at least one day's interval between hearings. Little is known of the procedure, in which the magistrate, no doubt, had a very free hand. As at other *contiones*, he could allow selected persons to speak, and this meant that the accused generally had the assistance of counsel. At the end of the proceedings, the magistrate gives his decision. If this is an acquittal the matter is at an end; if, however, he sentences the accused either to death or to a fine greater than the maximum allowed to his discretion, the accused can appeal to the people, whose vote is taken when the usual twenty-four days' notice required

---

[1] Including those *sine suffragio*; Strachan-Davidson, I. 142. Mommsen holds (*Strafrecht*, 143) that women had no right of *provocatio* though he admits that they were sometimes tried by the people on charges brought by the aediles. For arguments against this inherently improbable view *v.* Strachan-Davidson, I. 141 *sqq.*

[2] Strachan-Davidson, I. 111.   [3] Gai. I. 160.

[4] *Pro Caec.* XXXIV. 99.

[5] Most of our information comes from Cicero, *de domo*, XVII. 45, and from the *commentarium vetus anquisitionis* of M. Sergius preserved by Varro, *L.L.* VI. 90 (Bruns, II. 59).

for resolutions has expired. There is no further discussion or evidence; as in other cases, the people simply accept or reject the magistrate's proposal. If the sentence is one of death, then, by the XII Tables, the only assembly which can authorise its execution is the *comitia centuriata*, but the only magistrates who can summon the *centuriata* (those with *imperium*) are precisely those who must not pronounce a sentence which will be subject to appeal.[1] The magistrate who has pronounced the sentence will consequently always have to obtain the loan of his power of summons from a consul or praetor. Perhaps there was a standing delegation of this power to the quaestors for the purposes of their criminal work,[2] but it is clear that a tribune wishing to bring a citizen before the people on a capital charge had to "ask for a day for the *comitia*" from a magistrate with *imperium*.[3] If there was no question of the death penalty the other assemblies were competent.[4]

It was, no doubt, originally within the power of the magistrate who initiated criminal proceedings to use his *coercitio* for the purpose of arresting the accused and keeping him in custody,[5] so that if the people did not pardon him the sentence might be executed. But even if such arrest did take place any tribune might use his *auxilium* to set the prisoner free, and, though this was perhaps not usually done during the earlier republic in the case of ordinary malefactors, it is clear that persons of consideration and especially political offenders could always count on being freed in this way. From the second century B.C. it seems to have become the practice that all accused persons should remain at liberty until the people had actually decided against them, a custom or rule which had the remarkable result that the death penalty was hardly ever inflicted (on citizens) because the accused always left Rome before it could be pronounced.

After the criminal had left, it was usual for the *comitia* to pass a decree of "interdiction of fire and water" against him.

The exact legal effect of this is disputed, but it certainly had the result that he could not return without making himself liable to be put to death.[6]

The justice administered by magistrates and *comitia* seems to have sufficed in normal times for the requirements of the early and middle

---

[1] *Supra*, 319.
[2] *Contra*, Strachan-Davidson, I. 157–158.
[3] See e.g. Livy XXVI. 3. 9.   [4] Mommsen, *Strafrecht*, 169.
[5] Imprisonment was never regarded by the Romans as a normal form of punishment in itself; cf. D. 48. 19. 8. 9: *Carcer enim ad continendos homines, non ad puniendos haberi debet.*
[6] Strachan-Davidson, II. 23 *sqq.*; Mommsen, *Strafrecht*, 971 *sqq.*

republic, but occasionally in special circumstances other measures were taken. Special instructions to investigate a particular crime might be given to a magistrate with *imperium* by a *lex* or plebiscite, and in such cases there was no *provocatio*, the people having given up its rights in advance. At other times the senate appears to have taken upon itself the responsibility of authorising the magistrates to use their coercive powers to the full, and in these cases too the magistrates, perhaps without strict constitutional propriety, sometimes carried out their sentences without allowing *provocatio*.[1] The most famous instance of this procedure occurred in 186 B.C. at the time of the "Bacchanalian conspiracy".[2] The senate, shocked by the excesses of crime and vice which the new cult of Bacchus had introduced, empowered the consuls to hold an enquiry and decreed that participation in the cult should be deemed a capital offence. Large numbers of persons of both sexes, citizens as well as others, were put to death, and there was apparently no appeal. These special *quaestiones* may to some extent have served as precedents for the introduction of the later *quaestiones perpetuae*.[3]

Of the substantive law little can be said here; it was, as has been explained, lacking in definition, and, from the nature of the tribunals which administered it, contained a much greater element of arbitrariness than the civil law.

Treason had, of course, been punished by the state from the earliest times, the first word used in this connection being *perduellio*.[4] Literally *perduellis* means "an enemy", and the crime of *perduellio* is committed by a Roman when in any way he acts in a manner hostile to his country, especially of course if he actually adheres to an external enemy. Another crime against the state, of later origin and never very clearly marked off from *perduellio*, is *maiestas* (*crimen imminutae maiestatis*), i.e. any act calculated to diminish in some way the greatness or authority of the Roman people.[5] Definitions of treason are seldom precise, but the Romans

[1] See however Mommsen, *Strafrecht*, 257, n. 2.

[2] See especially Strachan-Davidson, I. 232 *sqq*. The chief authorities are Livy XXXIX. 8–19 and the inscription known as *Sc. de Bacchanalibus* (Bruns, I. 164).

[3] But Maine's theory (*Ancient Law*, 339 *sqq*.) that the *quaestiones* were regarded as committees of the legislature cannot be accepted; *v.* Strachan-Davidson, II. 16–19.

[4] Festus, s.v. *hostis* (Bruns, II. 11).

[5] Mommsen, *Strafrecht*, 538, thinks that the *maiestas* in question was originally that of the tribunes of the *plebs* and that crimes against the state only came to be included because, in the developed republican system, it was the tribunes who prosecuted; *v. supra*, 319. For contrary arguments *v.* Schisas, *Offences against the State in Roman Law* (1926), 7 *sqq*.

do not seem to have attained even a moderate degree of precision in the matter, and trials for *maiestas* were decided mainly on political considerations.

Murder, as we have seen, was also treated as a crime very early, but details are difficult, partly owing to uncertainties of terminology. There is no word exactly corresponding to the English term, and the oldest word —*parricidium*—is not only of uncertain origin but is used in different senses. In the Latin of historical times it means sometimes, in accordance with its supposed derivation from *pater*, the killing of a father[1] or other ascendant,[2] and sometimes, as in Pompey's *lex de parricidio* (? 70 B.C.), the killing of any near relation.[3] But Festus says that at one time it included the killing of any person uncondemned, and he quotes in support of his view a law of Numa's which enacted that, if anyone intentionally killed a free man, he was to be a "parricide".[4] Possibly the original meaning of the word was "blood-feud", and *paricidas esto* in Numa's law meant "let there be an avenger of blood". The blood-feud presumably existed at some time among the Romans, as among other peoples, but the state was evidently very early strong enough to suppress it, and take the punishment of murder into its own hands.[5] It may then have happened that the word for blood-feud came to mean such killing as would previously have justified the feud. Subsequently, when ordinary murder no longer actually led to the death penalty, and the terrible punishment of the sack[6] was reserved for those who murdered their relations, the original meaning of *parricidium* was forgotten, and its supposed connection with *pater* gave it the narrower significance.[7]

---

[1] E.g. Cic. *pro Rosc. Amer.* XXII. 62 *sqq.*

[2] D. 48. 9. 9. 2.   [3] Cf. *infra*, 325, n. 5.

[4] Bruns, II. 21: *Si qui hominem liberum dolo sciens morti duit, paricidas esto.*

[5] The only trace of the feud which remains is in the law of Numa quoted by Servius (in Verg. *Ecl.* IV. 43; Bruns, I. 10; II. 79), which enacted that in the case of involuntary homicide a ram was to be given to the agnates of the deceased. Cf. Tab. VIII. 24, *supra*, 178.

[6] According to Modestinus, D. 48. 9. 9. pr., the criminal was scourged, sewed in a leather sack with a dog, a cock, a viper and an ape, and thrown into the sea, but there are many variations of this ancient penalty; Mommsen, *Strafrecht*, 922.

[7] The above explanation is suggested by Lenel, *St. Bonfante*, II. 1–13. For review of Lenel, de Visscher ("La formule *Paricidas esto* et les origines de la juridiction criminelle à Rome", *Études*, 435–482 (= *Bulletins de l'Academie Royale de Belgique. Classe des Lettres*, 5ᵉ serie, XII. No. 6, pp. 298–332, Brussels, 1927)) and Meylan (*L'Etymologie du mot parricide*, Lausanne, 1928) *v.* Juncker, *Z.S.S.* XLIX. 593–613. Other explanations, e.g. Mommsen, *Strafrecht*, 612; Costa, *Crimini e Pene*, 20.

A few other crimes which endangered life, arson in particular, seem to have been assimilated to murder and punished in the same way—almost certainly by death.[1]

Beyond treason and murder we know of a few other offences which were the subject of special *leges*, such, for instance, as those passed in 181 and 159 B.C. concerning *ambitus*[2] (bribery at elections), but such statutes were rare, and it is not until the last century of the republic that the development of the criminal law is much furthered by statutes.

§ III. THE *QUAESTIONES PERPETUAE*

Criminal justice in the late republic was administered mainly by permanent courts, known as *quaestiones perpetuae*, which were established by a number of different statutes. The first of these statutes of which we have any knowledge was a *lex Calpurnia* of 149 B.C. which provided for the trial of provincial governors accused of extortion (*res repetundae*).[3] Other laws followed, and Sulla, by a whole series of *leges Corneliae*, reduced the practice to a system, afterwards completed by further statutes.[4]

These laws did not merely provide new machinery for the trial of offences, nor, on the other hand, did they merely enact new rules of substantive law. They each made provision for the establishment of a court consisting of a magistrate and a number of jurors to try some particular offence or class of offences, and at the same time laid down with greater or less particularity[5] the law to be applied by the court which they set up, as well as the punishment to be inflicted. This was still in some cases death,[6] but the execution (of citizens) in fact hardly ever took place. Not only, as we have seen, might the accused withdraw before judgment was pronounced, but it appears that about the beginning of the first century B.C. magistrates were definitely forbidden by statute to

---

[1] Mommsen, *op. cit.* 646.   [2] Mommsen, *op. cit.* 866.

[3] The action under this law was more of the nature of a civil action for the return of what had been wrongfully taken and the procedure was by *sacramentum*, *Lex Acilia*, line 23 (Bruns, I. 63); cf. Girard, *Org. Jud.* 104.

[4] Courts for the following crimes existed under Sulla's scheme: *repetundae*, sacrilege and peculation, murder (*de sicariis et veneficis*), *ambitus*, *maiestas*, forgery of wills and coinage offences, and special cases of *iniuria*. Later laws dealt with kidnapping (*plagium*) and violence (*vis*). V. Mommsen, *Strafrecht*, 203.

[5] The *lex Pompeia de parricidio* e.g. defines carefully the degrees of relationship which will bring murder under its provisions; D. 48. 9.

[6] Levy, *Die römische Kapitalstrafe* (1931), 14 *sqq.*, against the hitherto dominant view.

arrest the accused, even after judgment, without giving him time to depart.[1] It was thus possible for an accused person to await the result of the trial, and, if it went against him, still escape with nothing worse than the banishment imposed by *aqua et igni interdictio*.

The jurisdiction of the *comitia* was not abolished, but it necessarily fell into disuse as the sphere of the *quaestiones* extended, for there was never any question of *provocatio* from the decision of one of these tribunals.[2] The normal president of the *quaestio* was a praetor, and the raising of the number of praetors to eight by Sulla was intended to provide six such presidents in addition to the urban and peregrine praetors who were mainly concerned with civil jurisdiction. There were, however, usually not enough of these magistrates to cope with the amount of business, and it was possible for the presidency to be assigned to persons not actually holding office, or to an individual chosen from the jury. The rules for the composition of the jury varied according to the particular statute under which the trial was being held, the usual procedure being that a list of some hundreds was chosen (sometimes by lot) from the general panel of those qualified to serve, and then reduced by a complicated process of challenging by accuser and accused to the number required by the statute, usually between thirty and seventy.[3] The staffing of the jury courts was a matter of great political importance throughout the revolutionary period, and, according to the fortunes of political warfare, sometimes the senate and sometimes the *equites* were in power,[4] but in any case it must be noticed that the jurors were always men of substance, the lowest class ever admitted being the *tribuni aerarii*, who ranked apparently immediately below the *equites*.

Technically the introduction of the *quaestiones* produces no infraction of the principle that it is for a magistrate (or a person acting as magistrate) to investigate crimes and to pronounce the fitting penalties; the jury is called a *consilium*, and is, in form, a body similar to the *consilium* which he chooses himself to assist him in making any other important decision. But in practice the position is entirely altered, for the *consilium* in a criminal trial is chosen in accordance with the provisions of a *lex*, the way in which they are to vote is laid down, and their vote decides the matter. The president does not even sum up to the jury, and altogether does

---

[1] Levy, *op. cit.* 19.

[2] Nor was tribunician *intercessio* possible, Mommsen, *Strafrecht*, 219.

[3] No attempt can be made here to deal with the very difficult questions involved. For some of the difficulties *v.* Strachan-Davidson, II. chap. XVII.

[4] Cf. *supra*, 181.

not play nearly such an important part in the trial as does an English judge.

The new procedure also means that the magistrate no longer acts on his own initiative in beginning a prosecution. Anyone may lodge the name of a person, whom he wishes to accuse, with the president of the appropriate *quaestio* (*nominis delatio*), and the president, if he thinks there is any case, will " receive the name ", i.e. put it down on the list of persons for trial. Then the trial takes the form of "contradictory" proceedings between the accuser and the accused, evidence being produced by the parties and not by the president, though the accuser may have the assistance of public officials in collecting it. The reform thus substituted an "accusatory" for an "inquisitorial" form of criminal justice,[1] and this remained, in spite of many practical exceptions, the theoretically normal procedure even during the empire—a fact of considerable importance in the later history of European law in general.[2]

[1] But the close analogy which Mommsen (*Strafrecht*, 192) saw between proceedings before a *quaestio* and an ordinary civil suit has now been disproved by Wlassak, *Anklage u. Streitbefestigung im Kriminalrecht der Römer* (1917); *Anklage u. Streitbefestigung, Abwehr gegen Ph. Lotmar* (1920).

[2] Pollock and Maitland, *H.E.L.* II. 656.

Chapter XIX

THE CONSTITUTION UNDER THE PRINCIPATE

§ I. THE BEGINNINGS OF THE PRINCIPATE[1]

For a hundred years before Augustus finally became supreme, republican institutions had failed to function with any degree of smoothness, and Rome had become familiarised with arbitrary powers placed in the hands of individuals. The sovereignty of the *comitia* made it possible, as a rule, to give a legal basis to such powers by securing a vote of the people, but in fact such a vote was little more than a formality which presented no difficulty to the man or men who commanded a sufficient army. Most far-reaching had been the powers conferred on Sulla and on Julius Caesar, both of whom bore the title of "dictator", though their office had little more than the name in common with the temporary and constitutional dictatorships of the republic. After the assassination of Caesar (44 B.C.) Mark Antony conciliated republican sentiment by securing an enactment which abolished the dictatorship for ever, and the title was never again borne by any Roman. Nevertheless, as Cicero put it, Caesar's death had done away with the "king" only, not the "kingship".[2] The rival leaders could not be restrained within the bounds of the republican constitution, and when, in 43 B.C., the three most powerful, Mark Antony, Octavian (then but twenty years old) and Lepidus, had come to an agreement between themselves, it was easy for them to secure a resolution of the people appointing them "triumvirs for settling the republic" for five years. Their power in fact continued for longer than the five years originally laid down, the continuation being probably again legalised by a popular vote, though it appears that this was passed some little time after the first period had elapsed.[3] In 36 B.C. Lepidus, after an unsuccessful revolt against his colleagues, dropped out of the triumvirate, and a new honour—subsequently of great importance—was conferred upon Octavian by an enactment granting him the "power of a tribune" for life.[4]

---

[1] The literature on the Augustan constitution is immense. For the more recent work *v.* de Francisci, *St. Bonfante*, I. 13.

[2] *Ad fam.* XII. I. I.

[3] The matter is controversial; *v.* Holmes, *The Architect of the Roman Empire*, 231–245.

[4] Perhaps only *sacrosanctitas* was given in 36 B.C., the full tribunician power being conferred later in 30; *v.* Holmes, *op. cit.* 222.

After the end of 33 B.C., when, so it appears, the second term of office allotted to the triumvirs expired, the legal position is obscure. But the law mattered very little; Octavian was master in the West and his victory over Antony and Cleopatra at Actium in 31 B.C. made him master in the East as well. In that year he was indeed consul, but this office alone would not account legally for the position he held; actually, though not in name, he was an unconstitutional dictator.

Once his authority was unchallenged and peace restored throughout the empire, Octavian desired to put an end to the unconstitutional position and to begin afresh. In 28 B.C. all the previous illegal acts of the triumvirate were cancelled, and at the beginning of 27 B.C., in his own words, Octavian "transferred the state from his power to the management of the Senate and People of Rome".[1] In a speech to the senate he renounced his extraordinary powers and the ordinary republican constitution *ipso facto* revived. This purported restoration of the republic has however always been regarded as the beginning of the empire.[2] In fact it would have been impossible for Octavian to retire even if he had wished. The tranquillity of the Roman world rested upon his enormous prestige, and the old republican system had really broken down before he was born. Some system had to be put in its place, and that system could only survive if it left room for him as supreme power in the state. The solution adopted involved as little break as possible with republican tradition. The authority of the *comitia*, of the senate and of the magistrate was not touched, but there were concentrated in the hands of Octavian sufficient powers to make it possible for him to control the whole administration of the state. These powers individually were such as had been known to the republican system or at any rate involved, each in itself, no very great departure from republican practice. What was new was their concentration in the hands of a single individual and the absence *de facto* of any time limit. For there is no doubt that the arrangement was meant to be permanent. One cannot tell what Octavian thought at that time about the succession to the position he had created for himself, but his subsequent dynastic plans show that he did not contemplate the possibility of a real return to the republic.

---

[1] *Monumentum Ancyranum*, VI. 13–16: *In consulatu sexto et septimo, postquam bella civilia extinxeram per consensum universorum potitus rerum omnium rem publicam ex mea potestate in senatus populique Romani arbitrium transtuli.* This inscription is one of the most important sources of our knowledge of Augustus; it contains an account of his career written by himself in the last year of his life.

[2] Dio Cassius, LII. I, says that from this moment the Romans "began again to be ruled by a monarch".

Outwardly perhaps the most striking sign of the change was the assumption by Octavian, at the request of the senate, of the name "Augustus", by which he has ever since been known. The use of honorific cognomina by distinguished persons and even their conferment by the senate was not unknown in republican times, but the title itself was unprecedented. It was a rare word and had a strong religious flavour about it, its meaning being almost equivalent to our "holy"; in Greek it is rendered by σεβαστός, "worshipful", a word which perhaps conveyed more meaning to the bulk of the population than did the Latin term.[1] His real power Augustus apparently intended at first to base mainly upon the consulship, which he continued to hold until 23 B.C. But the consulship as it had existed in the later republic did not give him all that he needed, for since the time of Sulla it had been an office confined to Rome and Italy and giving no military power, the armies being all under the command of provincial governors. He consequently received also the proconsular *imperium*[2] for a period, in the first instance of ten years, but with the possibility of renewal, which gave him the necessary standing outside Italy. He did not however retain the administration of all the provinces. Those which were peaceful he returned to the senate, and they were henceforth governed by proconsuls of the republican type, but the frontier provinces in which troops were stationed (with the single exception of Africa) remained under his command and were actually administered by legates whom he appointed.

In 23 B.C. Augustus made a change in his position so far as the basis of his power in Italy was concerned, by laying down the consulate, to which he thereafter only permitted himself to be elected occasionally. One objection to the earlier system may have been the scarcity of consulars (i.e. men who had held the consulship), which necessarily resulted if the princeps filled one of the two available places every year,[3]

[1] Mommsen, *Staatsr.* II. 771.

[2] Augustus' *imperium* during the years 27–23 is never actually called *proconsulare*, but is generally so described, on Mommsen's arguments and authority (*op. cit.* II. 845), in modern books. Another view is that it was not yet proconsular, but consular, and that its completeness was a return to the early republican idea of the consulship; *v.* Pelham, Smith's *Dictionary of Antiquities*, s.v. *princeps*. From 23 onwards Augustus certainly had proconsular *imperium*, and this was superior even in the senatorial provinces to that of the individual proconsuls, Dio Cassius LIII. 32. O. Th. Schulz considers that even after 23 the princeps had an *imperium* which was consular as well as proconsular and was a complete return to the *imperium* of the ancient republic, *Vom Prinzipat zum Dominat*, 11.

[3] Even after 23 there would not have been sufficient to fill posts reserved for consulars if the practice of holding the consulate for less than the full period of

but probably Augustus' main reason for the change was that he found the annual election and the necessary association with a colleague incompatible with his supreme authority. Instead of the consulate he henceforward used the tribunician power as the chief basis of his authority in Rome. This power he had already had before, but in some way he now brought it into greater prominence, as is evident from the fact that the years of the tribunician power are dated from this year.[1]

The tribunician power evidently suited Augustus' purposes admirably. It was free from the inconvenience of colleagueship, for the ordinary tribunes were not regarded as in any way the colleagues of the princeps, who indeed, as a patrician, would have been ineligible for the tribunate proper; it provided the necessary powers of summoning the senate and people, and power of veto enabled the princeps to invalidate the act of any other magistrate. No less important, though less tangible, were the advantages conferred by the ancient *sacrosanctitas* or inviolability attached to the person of the tribune, which meant that any indignity in act or word offered to him might be treated as a crime.[2]

The two main bases of Augustus' power, the *proconsulare imperium* and the *tribunicia potestas*, were supplemented by a number of minor powers which in the aggregate were almost equally important. Thus he had the right, formerly reserved for the people, of declaring war and making peace,[3] as well as that of concluding such treaties as he saw fit.[4] He had special rights with respect to the senate beyond those implied in his tribunician power, including the right to put a proposal before it by letter, and he also exercised considerable influence over the composition of that body, partly through his powers of "recommending" candidates for the magistracies which carried with them the right to a seat, and partly in other ways.[5]

a year had not been adopted. The increasing need for consulars in the imperial service led to increasing interference by Augustus in the elections and thus to interference with the senatorial government generally; Marsh, *The Founding of the Roman Empire* (2nd ed. Oxford, 1927), chap. IX. *V.* especially the lists (246) of consular holders of imperial posts in the periods 22–13 B.C. and 12 B.C.–A.D. 3 respectively.

[1] Thus in the last year of his life (A.D. 14) Augustus describes himself as being in the thirty-seventh year of his tribunician power, *Mon. Anc.* I. 28–30; *v.* Mommsen, *op. cit.* II. 795 and 873.

[2] The power of an ordinary tribune was confined to the city, but this limitation did not apply to the emperor. Exactly why not is hardly clear; *v.* Mommsen, *op. cit.* II. 880.

[3] *V.* Mommsen, *op. cit.* II. 954.

[4] *Lex de imp. Vesp.* (Bruns, I. 202), I: *foedusve cum quibus volet facere liceat ita, uti licuit divo Aug.*   [5] *Infra*, 334.

It appears that Augustus also already had a general power "to do all things which he should deem to be for the benefit of the state".[1] These words were probably intended to give the fullest possible executive power, but to the question of their exact meaning we shall have to recur.[2] In 12 B.C., on the death of Lepidus, who had succeeded Julius Caesar in the chief pontificate, Augustus also became *pontifex maximus*, and this position was always subsequently held by the princeps.[3]

§ II. THE DEVELOPMENT OF THE PRINCIPATE

A. THE POWERS OF THE PRINCEPS. The legal basis of the princeps' powers as it had once been established by Augustus remained almost unaltered throughout the duration of the principate. In spite of the preservation of republican forms Augustus was himself supreme, and the most autocratic of his successors needed for the enforcement of their will but little that he had not already had. On strict republican theory the most significant change was perhaps the assumption by Domitian in A.D. 84 or 85 of a permanent censorship,[4] the chief advantage of which was that it gave him complete control over the senate. Augustus had refused the offer of a *cura legum et morum*,[5] which would have included censorial powers, no doubt because he considered that such an office would make the independence of the senate too obviously unreal, but these considerations did not weigh with Domitian, who detested the senate. After his assassination the title of censor was never assumed, even temporarily, by any emperor, but the necessary functions of the office continued to be carried out by the emperor as such.[6]

Far more important than any technical change was the gradual penetration of imperial authority, without the assumption of fresh legal powers, into all departments of government and the recognition of the new system as normal and necessary, so that even on the death of an emperor only a few visionaries could ever regard the restoration of the republic as a real possibility. This process, in its turn, was not without

[1] *Lex de imp. Vesp.* 16–20. [2] *Infra*, 371.

[3] For an admirable discussion of some questions connected with the imperial title *v.* McFayden, *The History of the Title Imperator under the Roman Empire* (Chicago, 1920), especially p. 47, where the point is stressed that the aim of Augustus' titulary was not to indicate his legal position, but to appeal to men's imaginations.

[4] Dio Cassius LXVII. 4.

[5] *Mon. Anc.* I. 37–39. It would have made him in fact dictator under another name.

[6] Mommsen, *op. cit.* II. 945.

influence on the view which the lawyers took of the imperial attributes. Originally there is no doubt that the princeps was regarded as a citizen, subject like all other citizens to the laws, though the senate might, and occasionally did, exempt him from the operation of particular rules, such, for instance, as those imposing disabilities on unmarried and childless persons. Domitian and his successors frequently usurped this senatorial privilege of dispensation and it came finally to be recognised as an imperial right. Henceforward if the emperor acted in contravention of any rule from which dispensation was possible, he was held to have given himself the necessary dispensation. It was in this sense, and in this sense alone, that the lawyers of the later classical period spoke of the emperor as *legibus solutus*,[1] though the phrase meant much more under the dominate, and played an important part in the development of autocracy on the basis of Roman law in European history.[2] Still more significant than the dispensing power was the legislative power of the emperor. This, as we shall see, was also a growth of customary law, and was recognised already in the time of Hadrian.[3]

B. THE ANCIENT ELEMENTS OF THE CONSTITUTION. Of the three elements which went to make up the republican constitution, the people, the senate and the magistrates, it was the first which suffered the most obvious curtailment of its power on the establishment of the principate. In form indeed no change was made even here by Augustus, and the dogma of popular sovereignty continued to play a part in legal theory even in the late empire,[4] but from the first, legislation by the people was merely the ratification of the emperor's wishes, and, though not uncommon under Augustus, became progressively rarer, until it ceased altogether at the end of the first century.[5] The elections were transferred already by Tiberius from the people to the senate,[6] and the only popular function which survived the first century was that of conferring the tribunician power upon a new emperor.[7] Augustus, as we have seen, deprived the

---

[1] D. 1. 3. 31; cf. *Lex de imp. Vesp.* 20 *sqq.* (Bruns, I. 203). For discussion v. Mommsen, *op. cit.* II. 750 *sqq.*

[2] Esmein, *Essays in Legal History* (ed. Vinogradoff, 1913), 201 *sqq.*

[3] *Infra*, 370.   [4] *Infra*, 434.

[5] The last known instance is an unimportant *lex agraria* under Nerva; D. 47. 21. 3. 1.

[6] Tac. *Ann.* I. 15. For some doubts as to the consular elections in the first century v. Greenidge, 372.

[7] The vote of the *comitia* was really only a formality confirming a previous decree of the senate; Mommsen, *op. cit.* II. 875; Schulz, *op. cit.* 221. Very probably, except in the earlier years of the principate, the assembly did not

people of one of its most ancient prerogatives by accepting the power to make peace and war, and the judicial functions of the assemblies, which had fallen into disuse before the end of the republic, were not revived.

Unlike the people, the senate received a considerable accession of dignity with the inception of the principate. In 29–28 B.C. and again in 18 B.C. Augustus purged it of some undesirable elements which had entered under Caesar and the triumvirate, and fixed its number permanently at 600. Membership, as before, was normally obtained after holding the quaestorship, and this meant, when the elections had been transferred to the senate, that the numbers were kept up by co-optation, except in so far as the princeps influenced the elections. But there were considerable changes in the qualifications for a senatorial career. In the republic already the senate had become *de facto* largely hereditary, because members of the old families were generally elected to the magistracies,[1] but Augustus turned this principle into one of law. Under the principate the senatorial order became a new type of nobility consisting partly of persons qualified by birth and partly of those admitted by the princeps. This result was secured by a rule that no one except the son of a senator might stand for the vigintivirate, a necessary preliminary to the quaestorship, unless he had the special authorisation of the princeps. Such authorisation was signified by permission to wear the *latus clavus*, or broad stripe on the tunic, which thus became the badge of the senatorial order. Imperial control also made itself felt in other ways, partly by influence on the elections[2] and partly by censorial or quasi-censorial functions. When acting as censor the princeps could not only remove members, but could grant membership directly, by *adlectio*, and grant such rank (e.g. *inter tribunicios*, *inter praetorios*) as he pleased, though *adlectio* to consular rank did not take place until the third century.[3] Augustus also instituted a property qualification of 1,000,000 sesterces

actually vote, but only signified its approval by acclamation. Public meetings may have been occasionally summoned for other purposes, for it is related of Alexander Severus (*H.A. Al. Sev.* 25. 11) that he "held many *contiones* after the manner of the ancient tribunes and consuls"; *v.* Schulz, *op. cit.* 187. But this part of the *H.A.* is particularly suspect; Baynes, *The Historia Augusta* (Oxford, 1926), 118–144.   [1] *Supra*, 16.

[2] It is necessary to distinguish between *commendatio*, which is a legal right and secured definitely the election of the candidate (*Lex de imp. Vesp.* 10–14, Bruns, I. 202), and *nominatio*, which probably gave merely *de facto* influence; Greenidge, 349.

[3] Mommsen, *op. cit.* II. 942.

and a yearly revision of the list of members, at which the names of the deceased were removed, as well as of those who no longer had the necessary property (unless the emperor chose to make it up by gifts), and of those who failed, as was now essential, to take an oath to observe the *acta* of the emperor.[1]

With these changes in composition there came an entire change in the position which the senate held in the state, and this change cannot be described merely by pointing to the overwhelming power of the princeps. What happened was that the senate became, at the expense of the *comitia*, the representative of the republican element in the constitution. In fact the *comitia* had become an absurdity before the end of the republic, and the principate drew the necessary inference by transferring those powers not exercised by the emperor to the senate,[2] including that of electing magistrates and that of actual legislation. In addition, so far as imperial administration permitted, the senate continued to exercise those general powers of supervision which it had had during the republic, but its rôle was now definitely secondary. Its control of foreign policy it lost entirely, though the emperor might ask or allow it to receive embassies from foreign nations; the provinces which remained under its jurisdiction were those where no great questions of policy were likely to arise, and it lost such control of the army as it had ever had. The old treasury of the republic, the *aerarium*, remained under senatorial control, though the emperor had a share in the nomination of the officials in charge.[3] But the importance of the *aerarium* was greatly diminished by the establishment of a new imperial treasury, the *fiscus*,[4] which provided the bulk of the money needed for public purposes throughout the empire, and received not only the taxes from the imperial provinces but a considerable amount of revenue from the senatorial provinces as well.[5] The emperor also, as the expenses of his government increased, appears to have had large sums voted to him out of the *aerarium* itself.[6]

The republican hierarchy of magistrates was retained almost intact by the principate, but, like the rest of the republican machinery, it now

[1] Mommsen, *op. cit.* II. 946.
[2] This is clearly stated by Pomponius, D. I. 2. 2. 9: *Deinde quia difficile plebs convenire coepit, populus certe multo difficilius in tanta turba hominum, necessitas ipsa curam rei publicae ad senatum deduxit*; cf. J. I. 2. 5.
[3] These varied from time to time; Mommsen, *op. cit.* II. 1010; Greenidge, 394.
[4] V. *infra*, 345, n. 4.
[5] Mommsen, *op. cit.* II. 267, 1005.
[6] Mommsen, *op. cit.* II. 1006. M. Aurelius still made a point of requesting the senate to vote the money; Dio Cassius LXXI. 33.

functioned mainly on the non-political side of government and was, in the most important spheres of administration, superseded by the new imperial civil service.

Nevertheless the consulship was still the highest titular office in the state open to a subject and a great object of ambition; and still, if there were a vacancy in the principate, the responsibility of government rested for the moment with the consuls. Even in normal times, too, they must have had a sufficiency of real business to transact, for beyond the presidency of the senate in its ordinary and its judicial capacities they had also some important judicial functions of their own. Thus they appear, sometimes at least, to have sat alone to hear what were technically appeals to the senate in civil matters,[1] and Augustus already entrusted them with the enforcement of *fideicommissa*, a duty which they later shared with a special *praetor fideicommissarius*.[2]

Claudius added the appointment of tutors to their functions, but under M. Aurelius this also was transferred to a special praetor, perhaps because the consulship changed hands so frequently.[3] For it must be remembered that each pair now only held office for a few months, those who were elected at the beginning of the year being considered most highly honoured and giving their names to the whole year.

Praetors were appointed in numbers varying from ten to eighteen, and were now, as under the late republic, confined almost entirely to judicial or quasi-judicial work. The urban praetor continued to be the chief magistrate for civil suits between citizens so long as the formulary system lasted, and the peregrine praetorship apparently lasted until Caracalla's edict of A.D. 212 conferred the citizenship on nearly all the inhabitants of the empire.[4] Praetors continued to preside over the criminal *quaestiones perpetuae*, until these too were superseded; one praetor presided over the work of the centumviral court,[5] and, as we have seen, praetors were used for jurisdiction in connection with *fideicommissa* and for the appointment of guardians. One was appointed by Nerva for the decision of cases arising between the *fiscus* and private individuals.[6]

The number of quaestors which had been raised by Caesar to forty was reduced to twenty by Augustus,[7] and a further change was the lowering of the minimum age from thirty to twenty-five.[8] As before, two quaestors

---

[1] Mommsen, *op. cit.* II. 106–107.
[3] J. I. 20. 3; *H.A. Marc. Aur.* 10, 11.
[4] *Infra*, 353. Mommsen, *op. cit.* II. 226.
[5] Mommsen, *op. cit.* II. 225.
[7] Mommsen, *op. cit.* II. 527–528.

[2] *Infra*, 401 and 410.
[6] Pomponius, D. I. 2. 2. 32.
[8] Greenidge, 184 and 364.

bore the title *urbani*, but, except for a short period, they had no longer the control of the *aerarium* and their exact functions are uncertain. Two of the remainder were in the direct service of the emperor (*quaestores Augusti*), who probably was entitled to them as proconsul, and used them mainly for communications to the senate. The remainder were, as under the republic, assistants to the consuls or to the proconsuls of the senatorial provinces, those in the provinces now bearing the title *pro praetore*.[1] Among their duties in the provinces was that of exercising a jurisdiction similar to that of the curule aediles at Rome and issuing the corresponding edict. There were no quaestors in the imperial provinces, no doubt because there the governor himself was only a delegate, and Gaius tells us that the aedilician edict was not issued.[2] What steps, if any, were taken to supply its place is not stated. Even in the early principate the importance of the aediles diminished considerably. Caesar had raised their number to six by adding two plebeian *aediles Ceriales* for the purpose of supervising the corn supply. But this duty had to be taken over already in Augustus' reign by a special imperial prefect,[3] and most of the real work in connection with the police of Rome was done by the prefect of the city. Trials before the people under the presidency of the aediles had become very rare before the end of the republic[4] and disappeared entirely under the empire, but a minor criminal jurisdiction remained, and in Nero's time it was still worth while to issue a new regulation limiting the amount of the fines they could inflict.[5] The civil jurisdiction of the curule aediles continued to exist and it would seem from Gaius' language[6] that they still issued their edict in the middle of the second century A.D., but this, like the praetorian edict, had then been standardised and no longer gave to the promulgating magistrate any opportunity of developing the law.[7]

For tribunes the empire had even less use than it had for the aediles, since all their real power was merged in the superior *tribunicia potestas* of the emperor himself. Nevertheless they continued to be elected and it was a necessary step for a plebeian in his *cursus honorum* to become either aedile or tribune between holding the quaestorship and the praetorship.[8] *Intercessio* was still legally possible but only very occasionally used in quite minor matters of administration,[9] and possibly also on appeal from

[1] Mommsen, *op. cit.* II. 247.
[2] Gai. I. 6. [3] *Infra*, 343.
[4] Mommsen, *op. cit.* II. 496.
[5] Tac. *Ann.* XIII. 28; Mommsen, *op. cit.* II. 514.
[6] I. 6. [7] *Infra*, 363.
[8] Dio Cassius LII. 20. [9] Tac. *Hist.* IV. 9.

a decree of a judicial magistrate.[1] A minor criminal jurisdiction also survived.[2] Augustus abolished the II *viri viis extra urbem purgandis* and also probably the four *praefecti Capuam Cumas*, whose jurisdiction had become superfluous with the reorganisation of municipal government.[3] The XXVI virate of the republic thus became a XX virate. The X *viri stlitibus iudicandis* lost their jurisdiction in matters concerning freedom and became presidents of the centumviral courts,[4] but the remaining minor magistrates continued to exercise some at any rate of their earlier functions. The tenure of an office included in the vigintivirate was, as we have seen, apart from special imperial favour, a necessary preliminary to the quaestorship and a senatorial career. At the end of the principate the only republican offices which still survive with any real functions at all are those of consul, praetor and quaestor, and the functions even of these have been constantly diminished by encroachments of the emperors themselves or of their officers. The practical consequence of election which bulked most largely in the minds of the holders was probably the expense which they would be bound to incur in the provision of public games and other festivities. Tribunes and aediles appear *de facto* to have ceased to exist, though the titles may still have been conferred and a corresponding rank in the senate granted. The vigintivirate can be traced at the beginning of the third century, but whether it fell into disuse before Diocletian or was only abolished by his or Constantine's reforms is unknown.[5]

C. THE IMPERIAL CIVIL SERVICE. One reason for the failure of the republic to govern satisfactorily the vast territories over which it held sway was the absence of any organised body of civil servants to support and assist the constantly changing magistrates. This defect was remedied by the principate, which introduced for the first time in Roman history a trained, paid and permanent service, responsible to the princeps himself, which was able to reduce chaos to order, but finally developed all the

---

[1] This seems to be the best explanation of Juvenal VII. 228—*rara tamen merces quae cognitione tribuni non egeat*. If the schoolmaster could not get his fee he would apply first to the *extraordinaria cognitio* of the praetor, for there could be no ordinary civil liability in such a case (D. 50. 13. 1. pr.), and if he got no satisfaction there he might perhaps appeal, as under the republic, to a tribune; Greenidge, 371 and Appendix II. It has also been suggested that the tribunes were given some special jurisdiction, *v.* Girard, 621, n. 3.

[2] And was limited, like that of the aediles under Nero, Tac. *Ann.* XIII. 28. 3.

[3] Mommsen, *op. cit.* II. 610.

[4] *Ibid.* 608.   [5] *Ibid.* 594.

worst vices of a bureaucracy and was among the contributing causes of the downfall of the empire. It is important to have some idea of this service, not only in order to understand how the empire was governed, but also from the legal point of view, because many of the officials came to have powers of jurisdiction, and because with the growth of the emperor's own powers of jurisdiction it became necessary for him to have a staff of officials and advisers to assist him in this as in his other tasks.

The civil service as it appears at Rome is the outcome of the princeps' position as a magistrate. He is no monarch with ministers who are necessarily also ministers of the state; he is a magistrate, and expected, like other magistrates, to carry out his duties himself. But for his enormous sphere of activity he needs more help than other magistrates. In part this help is provided by delegates who are themselves in a quasi-magisterial position, analogous to that held by some magisterial delegates under the republic; such are his prefects, who may be compared with the *praefecti Capuam Cumas*, who exercised a jurisdiction delegated by the praetor,[1] and the legates through whom he governs the provinces under his control.[2] But the bulk of his assistants come into existence simply as members of his household such as any other wealthy Roman might have, and only gradually is it realised that, since the business of the princeps is in fact for the most part state business, these assistants are in fact government officials. The free choice of these officials by the princeps is never restricted by law, and the service remains quite separate from the hierarchy of republican offices which, as we have seen, continues to exist; but rules concerning the classes of persons who may be appointed to the different posts are laid down by the emperor or grow up by custom, and are rigidly observed. In this connection we may note three points particularly.

(i) *The use of freedmen.* In the household of a wealthy Roman freedmen and even slaves were commonly used in responsible positions as business agents, estate managers, accountants and secretaries, and at first the emperors continued this practice in their own households. The result was that men of this sort sometimes occupied positions of the very greatest importance, and were given the opportunity of amassing enormous fortunes. The climax was reached under Claudius, in whose reign, or at least in the latter part of it, the imperial freedmen became the

---

[1] *Supra*, 55. But the emperor's prefects are always chosen by him himself, whereas the *praefecti Capuam Cumas* were elected.

[2] The position of the *curatores, infra*, 341, n. 3, is similar.

real governors of the empire. With the gradual recognition that the emperor's service was the state service this system could not continue, and the more influential posts were reserved for members of the equestrian order by the reforms of several emperors and in particular of Hadrian.[1]

(ii) *The distinction between senatorial and equestrian posts.* For some purposes, even in the imperial service, senators were always employed, so that the holding of these posts might be part of a senatorial career fitting in with the tenure of the ordinary republican magistracies. But it was felt that the loyalty of a senator might be divided, for he was a member of the corporation which was to some extent a rival of the emperor in the government of the state and hence from the beginning there were some very important posts from which senators were excluded, and which together with the great bulk of responsible posts throughout the service were in the hands of *equites*. These are the *equites equo publico* of the republic,[2] but the corps was reorganised and enlarged by Augustus, and knighthood became a type of nobility with its own insignia[3] and privileges, second only to senatorial rank and *de facto*, if not *de iure*, hereditary.[4] The emperor, however, might admit whom he wished and admission was in effect permission to enter upon a public career. Free birth and good character were essential as was also a property qualification of 400,000 sesterces,[5] control being exercised by a special bureau *a censibus equitum Romanorum*.

(iii) *The relation between the civil and military services.* In the public life of the republic there had never been any clear separation between civil and military office. The *imperium* of the highest magistrates included the power of command in the field as elsewhere; the tribunate of a legion counted as one of the minor magistracies, and during a public

---

[1] *H.A. Hadr.* 22. 8.

[2] The word *eques* however seems still to have been used, as under the republic, in a secondary sense of those who had the property qualification, without being given the public horse; Greenidge, 402.

[3] Especially the narrow stripe (*angustus clavus*) on the tunic, and the golden ring (which senators also wore). In the later principate permission to wear the golden ring was freely granted and it came to mean no more than free birth, either real or fictitiously acquired by imperial grant; Kübler, P.-W., s.v. *Equites Romani*, col. 286.

[4] Against *de iure* inheritance Mommsen, *op. cit.* III. 500, and A. Stein, *Der römische Ritterstand* (Munich, 1927), but *v.* Kübler, *loc. cit.* and *Z.S.S.* XLVIII. 651 *sqq.*

[5] This, it should be noticed, is not a great sum, when we consider that the better paid procurators received 200,000 sesterces yearly; cf. Rostovtzeff, *Social and Economic History of the Roman Empire*, 175.

career a man would in most cases see some military service on the staff of a general, even if he did not ever hold an independent command of his own. This system was continued by the early principate; the young man of senatorial rank regularly served as a military officer before being elected to a magistracy, and the *equites* who held posts under the emperor were also men who had served in the army, and might again have military duties to perform. Hadrian however introduced innovations in this as in other respects, by separating the civil from the military career. In his time and later it was possible to enter the emperor's service without being a soldier, the post first held being often that of an *advocatus fisci*.[1] Septimius Severus did, in a sense, bring about a renewed militarisation of the service by increasing the number of offices open to *equites* as opposed to senators, and by the possibilities of promotion which he opened to the rank and file of the army. Under him indeed a procurator-ship was often the reward of long military service. Nevertheless his officials were by no means all soldiers, as the tenure of the praetorian prefecture by Papinian in his reign shows.[2]

D. CLASSES OF IMPERIAL OFFICIALS. One important class of imperial officers has already been mentioned, the *legati Caesaris pro praetore*, who were governors of the imperial provinces. These legates were in the earlier principate uniformly of senatorial rank, but a movement in favour of employing *equites* began at the end of the second century and culminated under Gallienus in the complete exclusion of senators from all positions involving military command.

Apart from provincial governors the chief imperial officials were the prefects, the procurators, the secretaries and the members of the imperial council.[3]

(i) *The Prefects.* (a) *Praefectus urbi.* The prefect of the city was originally a mere delegate appointed in case of the temporary absence of the emperor, but the office became a permanency owing to Tiberius' continued residence away from Rome in the latter part of his reign, and under subsequent emperors the prefect remained in office even when the emperor was present. His duties included generally the maintenance of order in the city, and he had under his command the urban cohorts, in effect a police force numbering between 4000 and 6000 men. He early

[1] Hirschfeld, *Die Kaiserlichen Verwaltungsbeamten*, 51.
[2] Cf. *infra*, 396.
[3] Of rather less importance were senatorial *curatores* appointed, generally, by co-operation between the emperor and the senate, e.g. for public works in Italy and the conservancy of the Tiber; *v.* Greenidge, 413; Karlowa, I. 539.

assumed criminal jurisdiction, and in the end became the chief criminal court not only for Rome but for the district within 100 miles. Civil cases he could take if they affected public order, but this was rare. The office was one which made most obvious to the Roman populace that they had now a master and appears to have been unpopular at first.[1] Its offensiveness was however to some extent mitigated by its ancient name,[2] and by the fact that senators, almost without exception of consular rank, were always appointed.

(b) *Praefectus praetorio.* The famous praetorian guard, which exercised such great influence on the choice of the emperors and was responsible for the fall of several of them, came into existence as the development of a republican institution. It had long been the practice for every general to have a body-guard, *cohors praetoria,* consisting of soldiers with higher pay and other privileges, and Augustus, as permanent *imperator,* turned this body into a standing force consisting of nine cohorts of 1000 men each. Recruits were drawn from Italy only and, until the time of Severus, this was the only military force stationed within the Italian borders. At first the only commander was the emperor himself, but, later in his reign, Augustus appointed a prefect, and the office thus created came to be the highest in the empire next to the principate itself.

From the first the *praefectus praetorio* was no mere soldier; he was chief of staff to the emperor, and since the emperor's powers as proconsul were both civil and military, he was the chief adviser and executive officer for both spheres.[3] The actual influence of the prefect depended very largely, as is always the case with a chief of staff, upon his own and his commander's personality, but it might be, and frequently was, very great, simply because he was the natural person to do anything that the emperor did not do himself. Most of his powers were thus legally the powers of the emperor, but he had also powers of his own. In particular he had a mass of judicial work, and, by the end of the principate, it seems that he was also responsible for the provisioning of the army as a whole.[4]

The great position held by the praetorian prefect made him a possible rival to the emperor himself, and the emperors were, not without reason, jealous of their powerful subordinates. It is this fact which accounts for the rule, observed with but few exceptions until the time of Alexander Severus, that the prefect should not be a senator but an *eques,* and it also

---

[1] Mommsen, *op. cit.* II. 1063.

[2] It had existed under the monarchy and maintained a shadowy existence during the republic; Pomponius, D. 1. 2. 2. 33.

[3] Stein, *Geschichte,* I. 54. [4] Mommsen, *op. cit.* II. 1120.

accounts in part for the common practice of appointing two or three persons to occupy the office jointly. In part however this must be ascribed to the increase in the amount of business to be done.

(c) *Praefectus annonae*. The provisioning of the city had always been one of the cares of the Roman government and difficulties had led at times to the creation of extraordinary magistracies, notably that held by Pompey in 67 B.C., when he was entrusted with the command against the pirates, who intercepted the sea-borne supplies on which Rome depended. Such was really also the *cura annonae* undertaken by Augustus at a time of shortage in 22 B.C. At first he appointed *curatores* of senatorial rank as his deputies in the matter, but towards the end of his reign a prefect was appointed and the office became a permanency.[1] The chief duty attached to it was that of seeing to the provision of sufficient corn at reasonable prices for the Roman market and for this purpose the prefect had a number of subordinates in Italy and in the provinces; with the provision of the corn doles to the city populace, he apparently had no direct connection.[2] The prefecture was an equestrian office, and like the other imperial posts acquired both a criminal and a civil jurisdiction in matters which arose out of the functions with which it was concerned.

(d) *Praefectus vigilum*. According to the republican system the officials chiefly concerned with the duty of dealing with fires at Rome were the III *viri capitales*, but they were not alone, and Mommsen[3] reckons that at any fire there were twenty-four people entitled to give orders, a circumstance which did not make for efficiency. Augustus took the matter in hand in A.D. 6 and created a fire-brigade, consisting of seven cohorts, each numbering 1000 to 1200 men, organised under the command of a prefect of equestrian rank. The post became one of great importance and its holder a high police officer second only to the prefect of the city. He tried criminal cases of minor importance and appears in the third century to have obtained a civil jurisdiction in some cases.

(e) *Praefectus Aegypti*. Egypt had come under the dominion of Augustus after Actium and was henceforward part of the Roman empire, but, by reason of its great strategic and economic importance, it was not treated as an ordinary province. The emperor himself succeeded to the position previously held by the kings and, instead of appointing a senatorial governor, kept a closer hold on the country by means of a prefect of equestrian rank. Senators were not even allowed to set foot on

---

[1] Mommsen, *op. cit.* II. 1041.
[2] Mattingly, *The Imperial Civil Service of Rome*, 91.
[3] *Op. cit.* II. 1055.

Egyptian soil without special permission.[1] The prefecture became one of the greatest prizes in an equestrian career, yielding in rank only to that of the praetorian guard, but the position was anomalous, and special arrangements were necessary to enable the prefect to exercise civil jurisdiction, such as an ordinary governor exercised in virtue of his *imperium*.[2]

Other officials with the title of prefect were the *praefecti vehiculorum* (postmasters), generally of equestrian rank, and at one time *praefecti alimentarii* were in charge of charitable funds for the relief of poor children.[3]

(ii) *Procuratores. Procurator* is a word taken from private law, and means an agent entrusted by his principal with the management of property.[4] A wealthy Roman might have several such agents, one e.g. for each of a number of estates, and they would nearly always be freedmen, i.e. persons who though dependents were free, and thus had the capacities, such as that for representation in a lawsuit, which were necessary for their duties. The imperial procurator was originally just such an agent appointed to manage some part of the emperor's property, to collect moneys due to him and for similar purposes, but the vast extension of the wealth belonging to the emperor and its use in reality as state property made these procuratorships into offices of such importance that already in the early principate the higher ranks were filled by men of the equestrian class.[5] In time there came to be a whole hierarchy of such officials graded according to the pay they received,[6] and promoted from one post to another on a fairly uniform principle. Some were employed at Rome where the central office was presided over by a *procurator a rationibus*,[7] who became in effect the Finance Minister of the emperor. More, naturally, were to be found in the provinces, where they collected taxes and looked after the emperor's property. The wasteful system of tax-farming which had been in use under the republic was not given up at once, but gradually replaced either by direct collection or by collection which, if not strictly direct, was closely supervised by the procurators.[8]

---

[1] Tac. *Hist.* I. 11; *Ann.* II. 59. [2] Tac. *Ann.* XII. 60.

[3] No reference is here made to the purely military prefectures.

[4] It has also the special meaning of "representative in litigation"; Gai. IV. 82 *sqq.*

[5] These alone bore the honourable title of *procurator Augusti*; Karlowa, I. 538.

[6] There were four classes, *trecenarii* (HS 300,000), of whom there were very few, *ducenarii* (HS 200,000), *centenarii* (HS 100,000) and *sexagenarii* (HS 60,000).

[7] Later *rationalis*. [8] Rostovtzeff, *op. cit.* 467.

Even in those cases where taxes, such e.g. as the *portoria* (customs duties), were still farmed to *publicani*, the machinery for checking fraud and extortion was much improved. Procurators were sent not only to imperial provinces, but also to those under senatorial government. In the former the chief procurator held a position analogous to that of a quaestor in a senatorial province and was in charge of the local branch of the fiscus. Though inferior in rank to the governor he held an independent mandate from the emperor and friction between the two was not uncommon.[1] In the senatorial provinces, where the proconsul had his own quaestor and legates, the imperial procurator stood apart from the main work of government and only represented the interests of the fiscus. In addition to the chief *procuratores provinciarum* there were, in both types of province, procurators with special functions, in particular for the administration of the great estates which were acquired in increasing numbers by the emperors. Originally these were simply part of the undifferentiated property of the emperor, but their administration was separated and placed under special *procuratores patrimonii* in the time of Claudius. Later, under Septimius Severus, there was created a further department, the *res privata Caesaris*, made up chiefly of confiscated lands, which gradually overshadowed the old *patrimonium* and finally swallowed it up altogether,[2] the *procurator rei privatae* becoming the equal in importance of the *procurator a rationibus*.[3,4]

Procurators were not however confined exclusively to financial business; in a number of cases officers bearing this title were placed in charge of whole imperial provinces as governors—such, for instance, were

[1] Mattingly, *op. cit.* 118.

[2] The *patrimonium* still apparently existed in the fourth century; Stein, *Geschichte*, I. 62. The relationship between it and the *res privata* is not yet fully cleared up.

[3] Mattingly, *op. cit.* 22.

[4] The *fiscus* was, no less than the *patrimonium*, at the absolute disposal of the emperor, and Mommsen held that it too was, in strict law, his property (*Staatsrecht*, II. 998 *sqq.*). Ulpian says *res fiscales quasi propriae et privatae Caesaris sunt* (D. 43. 8. 2. 4), and Mommsen points out that, as the vast possessions of the fisc could not, in fact, be allowed to pass to anyone but the successor to the throne, some emperors got out of the difficulty by transferring the fortune which they had at their accession to their children, whom they emancipated for the purpose, thus saving it from falling into the mass of imperial property. General modern opinion is however against Mommsen, and regards the *fiscus* as a fund devoted to state purposes, having a separate existence and only said to belong to the emperor in much the same way as in modern monarchies state property is said to belong to the Crown. See Rostovtzeff, P.-W., s.v. *fiscus*, coll. 2400–2402; Mitteis, *R.P.R.* 350, n. 7.

Pontius Pilate and Felix in Judaea—but the provinces were usually small, or the arrangement of a temporary nature.[1]

Jurisdiction in matters connected with the imperial finances was first given to the procurators by a *senatus consultum* passed in the reign of Claudius.[2] This jurisdiction, however, does not seem to have been exclusive,[3] and Nerva entrusted such matters to a special praetor.[4] But this reform appears to have had reference to Rome and Italy only and not to have been a lasting one. Each procurator decided those cases which affected his own department, but appeal lay from him to the emperor, in earlier times directly, in the late principate apparently first to the *rationalis* or *magister rei privatae* as the case might be, and thence to the emperor.[5] The procedure used was of course that known as *cognitio extra ordinem*,[6] for the procurators were not magistrates, and thus had no power to authorise a trial by a *iudex* according to the formulary system.

(iii) *The Secretaries*. As the emperor's chief accountant, *a rationibus*, had developed into a Finance Minister with a great body of officials under him, so the imperial secretaries also developed into Secretaries of State at the head of departments, and, from the time of Hadrian onwards, were, almost without exception, members of the equestrian order. But it must be remembered that the Roman emperors, for the most part, ruled as well as reigned, and transacted a surprising amount of business of all sorts themselves, so that the secretaries were, except for the size of their staffs, more like those of a Tudor monarch than like the Secretaries of State of to-day.

The two chief departments were those *ab epistulis* and *a libellis*. Of these the former dealt with the great mass of imperial correspondence, whatever it might concern and whether it was directed to governors, to civil or military officers or to foreign states, and it was also the department chiefly concerned with the appointment of imperial officials. In the second century the work was so heavy that there was one secretary *ab epistulis Latinis* and another *ab epistulis Graecis*, the former being the more important.

The office *a libellis* was concerned with petitions, of which great numbers were naturally addressed to the emperor. These petitions included those requests for advice on points of law out of which there grew in the second century the regular practice of settling cases by

[1] Mattingly, *op. cit.* 127–149. [2] Tac. *Ann.* XII. 60; Suet. *Claud.* 12.
[3] Mommsen, *op. cit.* II. 1022. [4] *Supra*, 336.
[5] This was so at any rate in the fourth century; Stein, *op. cit.* 63.
[6] *Infra*, 402.

imperial rescript.[1] It was consequently necessary that the head of the department (and, no doubt, some of his subordinates), should have legal knowledge, and the post was in fact held by several distinguished lawyers, including Papinian and Ulpian, both of whom subsequently became praetorian prefects.

Another officer of some importance for legal purposes was the *a cognitionibus*, who, as the name implies, was concerned with the judicial work of the emperor, but perhaps only in those cases where the imperial council was not consulted.[2] The post ceased to exist comparatively early, and its duties were merged in those of the *a libellis*.

A memoria was the title of an official, at first of subordinate rank, whose original duty appears to have been to reduce to writing speeches and oral decisions made by the emperor, and to prepare the necessary material for them. The post however grew in importance and its holder's duties came to include the preparation of patents for the appointment of imperial officers as well as the issue of permits for the use of the imperial post, a privilege which was rigidly restricted. In the dominate it became equal if not superior to the offices *ab epistulis* and *a libellis*.

(iv) *The Imperial Council*.[3] The ancient Roman custom of calling a *concilium* before making any important decision was followed by the emperors, who might, of course, summon any persons they chose for this purpose, and one might have expected that something in the nature of a regular Privy Council would grow up. Indeed in the latter part of his reign Augustus was assisted by a standing council consisting of the magistrates for the time being and fifteen senators, and Tiberius instituted a permanent council of twenty persons, including both senators and men of equestrian rank. Later emperors however, with the exception of Alexander Severus, seem to have preferred to retain the power of choosing their counsellors as they felt inclined for each particular occasion, and a permanent body was created only for legal work, for which a technical training was particularly desirable. Here again the innovation is due to Hadrian, who, we are told, always had among his council when he sat as judge not only his "friends", but also certain jurisconsults whose appointment had in all cases been approved by the senate.[4] These councillors, at any rate when they were men of equestrian

---

[1] *Infra*, 375.
[2] Karlowa, I. 545. According to Premerstein, P.-W. IV. 221, he was concerned with organisation of the court—prepared the cause list, etc.
[3] Mommsen, *op. cit.* II. 988–992.
[4] *H.A. Hadr.* 18. 1.

and not senatorial rank, were paid, and in the third century we find them divided into classes according to the amount of their salaries in the same way as the procurators. As the emperor's judicial functions shaded off into his powers as a lawgiver, there can be no doubt that these men were also the real authors of a great deal of imperial legislation.

E. SUCCESSION TO THE PRINCIPATE. NATURE OF THE CONSTITUTION. The principate began by being in part, at any rate, an extraordinary magistracy, and it never entirely lost its magisterial character. There was consequently at no time any acknowledged legal system of succession even when it had become obvious that the institution was a permanency. What we have to ask therefore is this: "How did people come to occupy such a position that the usual powers of the princeps were conferred upon them?" and this is, in the main, not a legal question at all.

We may say that there were four chief factors at work, heredity, choice by a predecessor, choice by the army, and choice by the senate. All of these four were closely connected and their relative importance varied greatly from one case of succession to another.

Especially closely connected were the first two, for the choice of an emperor generally fell upon one of his sons if he had any, and the expression of his choice, if he had no sons, was normally by adoption. But this is not the whole story. Choice was frequently made clear by granting to the person chosen a share in the imperial power, and here we can distinguish two separate periods. In the earlier the position of the co-regent is, even in form, definitely subordinate to that of the princeps himself, in the later there are two emperors, and, though the senior may take by far the greater share in the government, they are legally on a footing of equality. The change came when Marcus Aurelius, immediately on his accession, insisted that the senate should confer on his adoptive brother, L. Verus, exactly the same honours and titles as he himself received, and thereafter there were a number of cases in which two Augusti ruled over the empire. When this happened legislative enactments, for instance, bore the names of both emperors,[1] whereas previously the single emperor's "minor colleague", as he may be called, has taken no part in legislation. The existence of two Augusti of course simplified greatly the question of succession; on the death of one, the other continued to hold office and might or might not himself cause a co-regent to be appointed.

---

[1] Thus a number of enactments bear the names of Severus and Antoninus (i.e. Caracalla).

But choice and heredity by no means suffice to explain the whole troubled history of the succession. It is common knowledge that the troops, especially the praetorian guard, played a considerable part in the matter, and on more than one occasion, even before the long horrors of the third century, armies from different parts of the empire, each wishing to raise its leader to the throne, had fought the question out by force of arms. Where armed forces are willing to fight for such a cause they can naturally impose their will upon an unarmed and unorganised population, but this element of force is itself sometimes connected with the element of heredity, for the loyalty which made the Roman soldier willing to fight for his general often extended to that general's family, at any rate after the general had become emperor, and some of the worst of Rome's emperors were really imposed on her in this way.[1] But even though the army could, and often did, force its nominee upon an unwilling senate, there were occasions, as in the case of Nerva, and later of Tacitus, when the senate was able to exercise a real choice.

Given these facts as to the succession and bearing in mind the imperial powers already discussed, how are we to construe, from a legal point of view, the nature of the constitution?

Mommsen's[2] view was that, from the point of view of law, the principate was not conferred at all, but assumed by the individual emperor, either at the invitation of the senate, or, more frequently, at that of the army. The invitation by the army was, in his opinion, identical in law with the acclamation of a general as *imperator* after a victory, a well-known republican custom, which gave to the general concerned the right to use that title officially thereafter. Mommsen even goes so far as to say "any armed man had the right to make anyone else, if not himself, emperor".[3] Of course the number and strength of the "armed men" might make all the difference to the possibility of their carrying their nominee to real power, but it made no difference to the legal quality of their act, and, if there were several nominees, each was legitimate until overthrown by another. On this view it is not difficult to see why Mommsen went on to describe the principate as "autocracy tempered by legally permanent revolution",[4] and to say that there "never was a system of government which had lost so completely the conception of legitimacy as the Augustan principate".[5]

---

[1] Domitian had received neither proconsular *imperium* nor tribunician power during the reign of Titus, and the senate would hardly have accepted him but for the action of the praetorian guard.

[2] *Op. cit.* II. 842.

[3] *Ibid.* 844.   [4] *Ibid.* 1133.   [5] *Ibid.* 844.

This startling conclusion drawn by the greatest master of Roman constitutional history has not remained unchallenged, but there is still no agreement. Some scholars hold that, from the legal point of view, the principate was but the continuation of the republic, and that, throughout, the sovereignty rested with the senate as representing the people of Rome.[1] Others can only give the name of absolute monarchy to a constitution in which the constant conferment of powers on a single man made it clear that there was no law but his will;[2] while others again, basing themselves on another famous description of Mommsen's, classify the principate as a "dyarchy",[3] in which the sovereignty was shared between the princeps and the senate.

No one of these explanations can really tell the whole truth of the matter,[4] for none of them can satisfactorily draw the distinction between law and fact. Like the British constitution, that of Rome was unwritten, and changed imperceptibly as the *de facto* methods of exercising governmental power hardened into conventions which, whether called law or not, became inseparable from the legal elements. It was thus that the senate had become the governing body in the republic, and it was thus that the public law of the empire was formed. The powers attributed to the emperor were defined by reference to offices well known to the republic; a lawyer might have said that their concentration in the hands of a single man was accidental, but in fact it was vital, and became a convention of the constitution from which further deductions were constantly being made. The property of this multiple magistrate becomes, as we have seen, state property and his servants obtain judicial powers, both developments being a logical inference not from his magisterial position, but from his personal supremacy. Even a right to legislate comes to be recognised, but so gradually that no one can point to a definite date. In the formation of this conventional constitution, the most varied factors play a part, traditional reverence for republican institutions, the brute force of the army, dynastic sentiment, oriental ruler-worship, and many others. The final result was the undisguised autocracy of Diocletian, but the process by which it was reached was a continuous one, and the principate was

[1] O. Th. Schulz, *Das Wesen des römischen Kaisertums der ersten zwei Jahrhunderte* (1916); *Vom Prinzipat zum Dominat* (1919); *Die Rechtstitel und Regierungsprogramme auf römischen Kaisermünzen* (1925).

[2] Dessau, *Geschichte der römischen Kaiserzeit*, I. 132.

[3] Mommsen, *op. cit.* II. 748.

[4] See especially Schönbauer, "Wesen und Ursprung des römischen Prinzipats", *Z.S.S.* XLVII. 264–318, to which article I owe part of what appears in this section.

never capable of being fitted into the ready-made categories, of "monarchy", "aristocracy" or even "dyarchy". Nor indeed is it sufficient to think of the princeps merely as a magistrate, even in the earliest period. That his supremacy was personal as well as official is expressed most clearly by the title "Augustus", which connotes no magisterial powers at all, but is yet the highest that the princeps bears. The same point too comes out clearly in the *Res Gestae* of Augustus, when he says that he had greater "weight" (*auctoritas*) but no greater power than his colleagues in the magistracy.[1] It may be that he was thinking of the idea of a princeps, as it had already been conceived by some during the republic,[2] i.e. a man who, without holding any office not open to others, is able by his personality to guide the policy of the state. Pericles had guided the policy of Athens in this way, for he held no office at variance with the constitution. But Augustus added the force of arms to the force of personality, and he did not, like Pericles, lose his power before his death.

---

[1] *Mon. Anc.* VI. 21–23. That the Greek ἀξίωμα represents the Latin *auctoritas* (not, as Mommsen thought, *dignitas*) is now made certain by the discovery of fragments of another inscription; *v.* Ramsay and Premerstein, *Monumentum Antiochenum* (Leipzig, 1927), 6 and 96.

[2] In particular, Cicero, e.g. *de har. resp.* XXVIII. 60; but as Schönbauer points out, *op. cit.* 313, Cicero was not thinking of a single princeps at all.

Chapter XX

CLASSES OF THE POPULATION AND THE GOVERNMENT OF THE CITIES UNDER THE PRINCIPATE

§I. THE EXTENSION OF THE CITIZENSHIP

The extension of citizenship to the whole of Italy was complete before the end of the republic,[1] and with the principate began the policy of extending it also gradually to the provinces, both by the foundation of colonies and, more frequently, by direct grant to already existing communities. Citizenship might also be given to individuals, especially in connection with military service, either to enable a provincial to serve in the legions or to reward members of the auxiliary forces who had served their time and received an honourable discharge.[2] The grant, whether to a community or an individual, was now always made by the emperor alone, possibly by virtue of a special clause in the *lex* conferring *tribunicia potestas*,[3] possibly by tacit assumption of a right which had been given to extraordinary magistrates in republican times.[4] The emperor also frequently

[1] The inhabitants of Cisalpine Gaul, who had become Latins by the *lex Pompeia* of 89 B.C. (*supra*, 66), were given the full citizenship in Caesar's time, probably by the *lex Roscia* mentioned in the *Fragmentum Atestinum* (Bruns, I. 101). For difficulties as to date, *v.* e.g. Abbott and Johnson, *Municipal Administration in the Roman Empire*, 322 *sqq.*

[2] Many Latins must also have become citizens by holding office or becoming *decuriones* in their own towns. Gaius, I. 96, tells us that there were two sorts of Latin right in this respect, the *maius Latium*, whereby all *decuriones* became Roman citizens, and the *minus Latium*, whereby only magistrates had this privilege.

[3] Mommsen, *Staatsr.* II. 888. No. III of the edicts of Augustus recently found in Cyrene (*Z.S.S.* XLVIII. 426) seems to refer to special *leges* or *scc.* conferring on the emperor the right to grant *immunitas* together with citizenship; *v.* Schönbauer, *Z.S.S.* XLIX. 399.

[4] The extension of the citizenship to Italy had always been taken to imply that the new citizens owned their land according to Roman law, and, of course, that any other Roman could do so similarly. This consequence was not deemed to follow when citizenship was granted to communities outside Italy. Here (*supra*, 276) the principle prevailed that the soil was the property of the Roman people or of the emperor and as such liable to taxation. Freedom from taxes was granted by conferring the *ius Italicum*, which assimilated the soil to that of Italy and thus also made it a *res mancipi*. For a list of communities, almost all colonies, whose soil had *ius Italicum v.* Mommsen, *Staatsr.* III. 807–808.

conferred Latin rights on Western communities which were not yet considered fit for full citizenship. In the East, where city life was already developed, this was not done. Nor was Latinity ever given to individuals, except in the anomalous case of "Junian" Latins, i.e. certain classes of freed slaves who received this status in accordance with legislation of the early empire, if there was a flaw in their manumission.[1] In A.D. 212 a great extension of citizenship was made by the Emperor Caracalla. The exact scope of this famous *constitutio Antoniniana* is a matter of doubt.[2] Ulpian, Dio Cassius and others[3] speak as if it had turned all the inhabitants of the empire into citizens, but it is clear that even after 212 there were considerable numbers who did not possess the citizenship,[4] and the difficulty is to discover what was the nature and scope of the limitation. A papyrus which is believed to have contained a copy of the decree[5] is so fragmentary that its discovery has increased, rather than diminished, the uncertainty. As first restored and interpreted by P. M. Meyer, it appeared to exclude from the grant of citizenship those known as *dediticii*, which Meyer himself conjectured to be equivalent to the payers of full poll-tax.[6] In his view, therefore, the great bulk of the agricultural population, including especially the native Egyptian peasants, remained *peregrini*, and the constitution did little more than enfranchise the citizens of the municipalities. But if this were right, our ancient authorities could hardly have spoken of the extension of the citizenship without mentioning so serious a limitation, and in fact it seems that the native Egyptians did become citizens.[7] Probably then the limitation was of narrower scope

---

[1] Gai. I. 16, 22, 23; III. 56. See Buckland, 78 and 93–94; cf. also *supra*, 60.

[2] For literature *v*. P. M. Meyer, *Z.S.S.* XLIV. 587; XLVI. 264–267, 314; XLVIII. 595–597; L. 512–513; de Zulueta, *Journal of Egyptian Archaeology*, XIV. 151–152; XV. 131.

[3] Ulpian in D. I. 5. 17; Dio Cassius LXXVII. 9; *H.A. Sept. Sev.* I; Augustinus, *De civitate dei*, 5. 17; *Nov.* 78. 5.

[4] Diplomas granting citizenship to ex-soldiers were still given; Mommsen, *Ges. Schr.* V. 402 *sqq.*, 419 *sqq.*; Meyer, *Z.S.S.* XLVI. 265. Even in Justinian's time it was considered worth while to abolish definitely Junian Latinity and *dediticia libertas*; J. I. 5. 3; C. VII. 5 and 6.

[5] *P. Giess.* 40. I; Mitteis, *Chrest.* No. 377; Abbott and Johnson, *op. cit.* No. 192. Bickermann, *Das Edikt des Kaisers Caracalla in P. Giess.* 40 (1926), holds however that what the papyrus contains is not the *const. Ant.* itself, but a supplementary enactment of A.D. 213, giving citizenship to "barbarian" immigrants.

[6] *P. Giess.* I. 29–33; *Jurist. Papyr.* 2; already, before the discovery of *P. Giess.* 40, Meyer had conjectured (*Heerwesen der Ptolemäer u. Römer in Aegypten* (1900), 136 *sqq.*) that payers of poll-tax were excluded from the benefit of the *const. Ant.*; cf. Wilcken, *Grundzüge*, 55 *sqq.*; Rostovtzeff, *Social and Economic History*, 300, 369.

[7] Bickermann, *op. cit.* 27–37, followed by Schönbauer, *Z.S.S.* LI. 291, 295.

than Meyer believes, but none of the rival restorations and explanations of the papyrus is satisfactory, and the problem remains at present unsolved. From the political point of view the matter is not as important as might appear. Citizenship no longer implied either real political power or immunity from taxation, so that the case was really one of levelling down rather than levelling up, and Dio[1] actually says that Caracalla's true motive was to make more persons liable to those taxes which were only paid by citizens.

§ II. LOCAL GOVERNMENT

When all the inhabitants of Italy had become Roman citizens it became a logical necessity that the local constitutions, previously those of independent city-states living under their own law and merely in alliance with Rome, should be reorganised as instruments for the local government of communities which now merely formed part of a larger whole. This reorganisation was indeed gradually completed, but the process by which it was achieved is obscure. Something was done by individual *leges datae*,[2] and it is probable that Julius Caesar either passed or intended to pass a statute laying down a model constitution for the municipalities.[3] At any rate in the early empire a considerable degree of uniformity had been attained and the form of constitution adopted was also used for those provincial communities which received the citizenship. There were indeed always a number of local variations, due either to local conditions or to the ancient traditions of the community concerned—sometimes as old as those of Rome herself—but the general scheme was the same. The difference between colonies and *municipia*, formerly of importance, had come to be one of name only, and even the "Latin" cities were organised on lines sufficiently similar to those of the citizen communities for all to be treated together in this very summary treatment of an obscure subject.

---

[1] *Loc. cit. supra*, 353, n. 3.

[2] An example is the *lex municipi Tarentini*; Bruns, I. 120; Abbott and Johnson, *op. cit.* No. 20.

[3] The doubt is due to the disputed character of the *Tabula Heracleensis*, commonly called *lex Iulia municipalis* (Bruns, I. 102; Abbott and Johnson, *op. cit.* No. 24; Hardy, *Six Roman Laws*, 136–163). Savigny (*Verm. Schr.* III. 279 *sqq.*) held this to be a law of Caesar's passed in 45 B.C. providing a model constitution for Italian towns, and some authorities still agree (e.g. Kipp, 43). Premerstein (*Z.S.S.* XLIII. 45–152) thinks it consists of uncorrected drafts prepared by Caesar and put into force by Antony with the rest of Caesar's *acta* after his assassination without receiving the necessary revision. For literature *v.* Premerstein, *loc. cit.*; Peguero, *Mél. Cornil*, II. 383–423.

The constitutions were, as might be expected, models on a small scale of the constitution of Rome, with a popular assembly, consisting of citizens divided into tribes or *curiae*, a council of *decuriones*, corresponding to the senate at Rome, and annual magistracies. The magistrates were usually four in number, II *viri iure dicundo*, who corresponded to the Roman consuls, and II *viri aediles*, generally ranking below the former, who carried out duties similar to those of the Roman aediles. Occasionally, however, six or eight magistrates are found. They were elected, in the earlier period, by popular vote, but this practice seems to have fallen into disuse in nearly all cities before the end of the principate. By then municipal office was usually regarded as a burden which those eligible tried to avoid if possible, and Ulpian[1] speaks as if election by the *ordo decurionum* were the usual thing. Thus the development in the municipalities followed, after an interval, what had taken place at Rome. Every five years the II *viri iure dicundo* had to undertake a census of the city and they were then called *quinquennales*. Like the censors at Rome, they had to make up a list of the senate, which usually numbered 100. They had to choose ex-magistrates in the first instance and fill up the remaining places from other qualified persons. Private law legislation could not take place in a Roman municipality, for its citizens were subject to Roman law, but minor variations seem to have been permitted in a few cases by the original charter of the city.[2] Administrative decrees however were of course possible and there was considerable independence in matters of finance. The power to impose local taxation appears indeed not to have existed generally, but the cities derived income from the lands and other property which they possessed, from monopolies, from fines and other sources.[3] Administration was the work of the *decuriones*, not of the assembly. The II *viri iure dicundo* presided over the *decuriones*, but, as the name implies, their chief duties were judicial. They, or courts under their presidency, had exercised criminal jurisdiction of some importance in republican times,[4] but this was taken from them under the principate and transferred to imperial authorities, the municipal magistrates being left with no more than minor powers of police.[5] Their civil jurisdiction was more important, though limited to cases involving small sums,[6] and

---

[1] D. 49. 4. 1. 3. In the fourth century some towns in Africa apparently still elected their magistrates in the assembly; C. Th. 12. 5. 1.
[2] Mommsen, *Staatsr.* III. 811–812.
[3] For a summary of municipal finance *v.* Abbott and Johnson, *op. cit.* 138–151.
[4] *Lex municipi Tarentini*, I. 4 *sqq.*
[5] Mommsen, *Strafrecht*, 225–228.   [6] *Infra*, 411.

further by the principle that the municipal magistrates could not exercise rights, such as that of *missio in bona* or *in integrum restitutio*, which depended on *imperium*.[1] Acts of voluntary jurisdiction—manumissions *vindicta*, adoptions and *in iure cessiones*—since they all required the use of the *legis actio*, were not normally within their power, but the right of using the *legis actio* might be given in exceptional cases,[2] and the magistrates of the Latin cities could certainly allow manumissions, presumably by a process of local law parallel to the Roman *legis actio*, which resulted in the slave's becoming a Latin.[3]

Apart from the municipalities with Roman or Latin rights there were of course, before Caracalla, great numbers of cities which remained purely peregrine. Not only was this so in the East, where urban life was old, but also in the West and in Africa, where Rome herself encouraged the foundation of municipalities. Technical differences still existed between "federated" or "free" states and those which were definitely subject,[4] but the difference was little more than technical, for the imperial government did not hesitate, when occasion arose, to interfere with the former,[5] and the latter were *de facto* left for the most part in the enjoyment of their own institutions.

The Greek cities had, of course, constitutions of widely varying types, and Roman influence was at first limited to minor changes, or changes in the direction of oligarchical as opposed to democratic institutions. In the West, where the constitutions themselves were of Roman origin, they were from the first oligarchical. In some cases, especially in Gaul, where city life was undeveloped, the existing tribes were treated as *civitates*, or municipal units, and appear to have remained in part under the government of their own native aristocracy.[6] Imperial interference was to a great extent provoked by the incompetence of the local authorities. Before the end of the first century A.D. the practice of sending *curatores* to deal with the disorganised finances of the municipalities had begun and the appointment of these officers subsequently became general. At first they were of senatorial or equestrian rank, but in the third century the local senates appointed members of their own order. The office of *curator reipublicae* thus became a municipal one, and its history was partly

---

[1] D. 50. 1. 26.　　　　　　　　　[2] Paul. *Sent.* II. 25. 4.
[3] *Lex Salpensana*, 28 (Bruns, I. 146).　　[4] Cf. *supra*, 68.
[5] An official was sent by Trajan to reorganise the free cities of Greece. Pliny (*Ep.* VIII. 24) advises him to deal tenderly with them in view of their glorious past.
[6] Reid, *Municipalities of the Roman Empire*, 178.

repeated in the fourth century, when local corruption again led to the appointment of imperial officials, now known as *defensores civitatum* because they were intended to protect the interests of the poorer classes.[1]

The constitution of Caracalla naturally gave a great impetus towards uniformity and, though the stages are unknown to us, it appears that by the time of the dominate the ordinary Roman municipal constitution with *decuriones* had become general throughout the empire.[2] With the extension of the citizenship the *raison d'être* of local sovereignty had ceased to exist, and well before the end of the principate it had become clear that everywhere the city institutions were for local government only and the local authorities entirely dependent on the central government.

§ III. CLASSES OF THE POPULATION

We have seen that the old distinction between citizens, Latins and peregrines, though it continued to exist, became of diminishing importance. On the other hand distinctions, originally purely social, acquired legal significance, so that even when all men, or nearly all, were citizens there was still no equality. The senatorial and equestrian classes formed a higher and a lower imperial nobility, the former certainly, the latter very probably, hereditary.[3] Both were recruited in increasing proportions from provincials, for in this respect, as in others, the principate saw the levelling of the provinces with Italy. Next to these imperial orders came the local governing classes in the municipalities, for, as we have seen, the tendency in local government was towards aristocracy. Not only was a property qualification required for membership of the local senates,[4] but before the end of the principate office had become very largely a matter of hereditary right and duty. The *curiales*, i.e. the members of official families, in fact took a place in the municipality similar to that held by the senatorial class in the empire at large, and both, together with the *equites*, were privileged persons, *honestiores*, in the eye of the criminal law.[5] The rest of the population were *humiliores* or *plebeii*, which latter word had thus assumed quite a different meaning from that which it bore

---

[1] Abbott and Johnson, *op. cit.* 90–93; cf. *infra*, 443.

[2] An important step towards uniformity was the introduction of a council (βουλή) for the government of the capitals of the nomes (counties) in Egypt by Septimius Severus. Hitherto these towns had been, in law, merely part of the nome; Wilcken, *Grundzüge*, 38–43.

[3] *Supra*, 340.

[4] At Comum 100,000 sesterces; Pliny, *Ep.* I. 19.

[5] *Infra*, 408.

under the republic. "*Plebeii*", says Paulus, "cannot hold magistracies reserved for *decuriones.*"[1]

Among the upper classes in the provinces—before Caracalla's constitution—the Roman citizens formed a peculiarly privileged class, but in the East it is clear that the members of the Greek cities were also regarded as privileged.[2] If they attained the citizenship they did not forfeit their membership of their own city,[3] and indeed in Egypt a man had to become a citizen of Alexandria before he could become one of Rome.[4] Gradations also existed among the lower classes, but the great cleavage was in reality between the well-to-do city-dwellers and the rest of the population. Fostering city life seems to have exhausted the efforts of the government for the well-being of its subjects and the condition of the agricultural population was often miserable enough. In Egypt at any rate, where, owing to the papyri, our knowledge is most extensive, forced labour and heavy taxation were the lot of the *fellaheen* in Roman times as during the rest of their history. But it was not only in Egypt that this was true, and with the decline of wealth and prosperity the note of compulsion becomes dominant. Before the principate comes to an end we can see the beginning of the colonate, the institution which in the later empire was to bind great numbers of peasants to the soil in the manner of the mediaeval villein.[5]

If the lower classes were bound to labour at their hereditary tasks, the lot of the *curiales* was sometimes scarcely more desirable. Wealthy citizens had to contribute large sums to the public expenditure of their cities, and office involved such great financial liabilities that in the later principate those eligible had to be forced to serve as magistrates. Should they attempt to escape they could be forced to serve,[6] though conditions had not yet become as bad as they did later, when office itself was used as a punishment.[7]

Like municipal office a military career was also gradually becoming hereditary, as was the membership of certain guilds, those, for instance, of transport workers, which were bound to labour in the service of the state. The iron system of the later empire, in which all vital occupations became compulsory and hereditary, was in fact prepared already in the century preceding Diocletian.

---

[1] D. 50. 2. 7. 2. Freedmen were excluded by a definite enactment, the *lex Visellia* of A.D. 24, but they, as well as actors, criers and others whose professions excluded them, could (if sufficiently wealthy) become priests of the imperial cult and enter the ranks of the *Augustales*, a sort of minor municipal order.

[2] See e.g. Schönbauer, *Z.S.S.* XLIX. 396 *sqq.*

[3] Mommsen, *Staatsr.* III. 699. This is the opposite of the old rule of incompatibility, *supra*, 62.   [4] Pliny, *Ep.* X. 6 (22).

[5] *Infra*, 448–452.   [6] D. 50. 4. 9.   [7] C. Th. 12. 1. 16; *infra*, 447.

Chapter XXI

SOURCES OF LAW IN THE PRINCIPATE

§ I. THE OLD SOURCES

A. CUSTOM. In a famous text Justinian, following Ulpian, divides the law into *ius scriptum* and *ius non scriptum*.[1] By *ius non scriptum* only custom is meant; all other law, that derived from *responsa prudentium* and magisterial edicts, as well as that enacted by *leges*, *plebiscita*, *senatus consulta* and imperial constitutions, is classed as written.[2] It is thus clear that the term "written law" is being used in a perfectly literal sense, not in the modern sense in which it is equivalent to enacted or statute law.[3] *Responsa prudentium* are not statutes but they exist in writing and the law which they lay down is thus classed as written. Customary law on the other hand is unwritten because it can be discovered, not by reading any document, but only by observing what people actually do.

The general principle that custom can create law is recognised in numerous texts, and some rules and institutions (not a great number) are ascribed to a customary origin,[4] but no Roman writer appears to have thought deeply about the matter, and, as soon as we ask detailed questions, either of theory or of practice, we come upon difficulties. The only theoretical justification for the validity of custom given by the jurists is that it is based upon the consent of the people. Julian puts this most forcibly when he says "since statutes themselves bind us only because they have been accepted by the judgment of the people, it is right that what the people has approved without any writing should be binding on all. For what does it matter whether the people declares its wishes by

---

[1] J. 1. 2. 3; D. 1. 1. 6. 1. Interpolated, according to Perozzi, *Istituzioni di diritto romano* (2nd ed. 1928), I. 42.

[2] Pomponius, D. 1. 2. 2. 5, classes the law arising from *disputatio fori* as unwritten, perhaps because he was writing before Hadrian's enactment concerning *responsa* (*infra*, 366). However Perozzi, *loc. cit.*, holds the words *sine scripto* to be interpolated here and in § 12 *eod.* Cf. Baviera, *Scr. Giur.* I. 62.

[3] Blackstone, *Commentaries*, I. 63.

[4] E.g. the interdiction of prodigals (Paul. *Sent.* III. 4. 7; D. 27. 10. 1. pr.); pupillary substitution (D. 28. 6. 2. pr.); the prohibition of gifts between husband and wife (D. 24. 1. 1), though this rule is now held by some to be statutory (*supra*, 240, n. 8); *patria potestas* (D. 1. 6. 8. pr.); prohibited degrees (D. 23. 2. 8; 39. 1).

vote or by its actual conduct?"[1] These words may appear disingenuous in the mouth of a jurist who wrote at a time when supreme power had passed from the people to the emperor, but it must be remembered that the theory of popular sovereignty remained, not only in the principate, but much later. Even so, however, the explanation is unsatisfactory, for the number of persons who actually have occasion to follow any particular custom can scarcely ever amount to a majority of the citizens entitled to vote.

The practical rules which modern systems have evolved for testing the validity of an alleged custom are in fact partly taken from Roman texts, but the Roman rules themselves never received any exact formulation. At no time was it laid down how old a custom must be, and, though it is said that custom cannot prevail against reason,[2] this text is post-classical and is not further explained. The greatest difficulty has always been felt about the relation between custom and statute. If, as Julian's theory has it, custom is itself a sort of statute, then it follows of necessity that a statute can be repealed as easily by the growth of a contrary custom as by another statute, and this is expressly stated by Julian. On the other hand the same constitution which denies the validity of a custom against reason says that it cannot prevail against statute. From the frequent repetition of the theory given by Julian[3] and from the actual examples of statutory rules said to have fallen into disuse,[4] we can probably say that the general classical opinion would have been that custom could prevail against statute. The contrary text is not only post-classical, but, it has been suggested, was intended to deal with a case in which some provincials, in spite of the extension of Roman law to them by the *constitutio Antoniniana*, desired to assert the validity of their native law, on the ground that its rules had survived as local custom and, so far as the locality was concerned, abrogated the Roman law.[5] The fact is that too many different things are included by the different expressions which we translate "custom" (*mos* (*maiorum*), *mores*, *usus; consuetudo*), and too little distinction is drawn between them for us to formulate rules with any certainty. Sometimes what is meant is that an institution forms part of the primeval Roman law,

[1] D. 1. 3. 32. 1. But *v*. Steinwenter, "Zur Lehre vom Gewohnheitsrechte" (*St. Bonfante*, 11. 419–440), who regards the whole theory as a post-classical importation from Greek philosophy.

[2] C. 8. 52. 2: *Consuetudinis ususque longaevi non vilis auctoritas est, verum non usque adeo sui valitura momento, ut aut rationem vincat aut legem* (A.D. 319).

[3] J. 1. 2. 9; Ulp. 1. 4; D. 1. 3. 35; cf. Cic. *de Inv.* 11. 22. 67.

[4] Cap. 11 of the *lex Aquilia* (D. 9. 2. 27. 4, interp.); the penalties laid down by the XII Tables for *iniuria* (J. 4. 4. 7); *lex Genucia* on usury; Appian, *Bell. Civ.* 1. 54; Val. Max. IX. 7. 4.　　　　　[5] Mitteis, *Reichsrecht*, 163.

and here *mos* or *mores* is generally used;[1] sometimes the practice of the courts is meant, or a series of precedents which the Romans do not distinguish from what a modern lawyer calls custom.[2] Custom is not clearly distinguished from usage,[3] nor general from particular custom, though it is to the latter that many of the texts refer,[4] and there can be no doubt that local custom was, even after the *constitutio Antoniniana,* admitted as a subsidiary authority.

On the whole however it remains true to say that in the classical period custom, at any rate as we understand it, was not a very fruitful source of law, except indeed in the constitutional sphere, where the Romans did not recognise it, for, as we have seen, much of the emperor's power, and indeed partly that of the senate, cannot be attributed strictly either to any enactment or to the application of existing republican rules. But in the sphere of private law the main development takes place—apart from legislation—by juristic and judicial interpretation.

B. LEGISLATION BY THE POPULAR ASSEMBLIES. A number of *leges* of fundamental importance for the subsequent history of the law were passed through the *comitia* in the reign of Augustus. These included laws concerning marriage and divorce,[5] manumission,[6] and legal procedure.[7] Although in some cases they bear the names of the consuls who actually put them before the assembly, they were all part of the emperor's policy and passed at his wish. The *lex Papia Poppaea* indeed of A.D. 9, which imposed disabilities on unmarried and childless persons, can hardly have been welcome to the proposing magistrates, who were both unmarried. A few *leges* were passed in the succeeding reigns, especially under Claudius,[8] who in this as in other respects showed his love for ancient republican forms, but, although Gaius still speaks of *leges* and *plebiscita* as existing sources of law, the practice of popular legislation had in fact disappeared by the end of the first century A.D.[9]

---

[1] E.g. *patria potestas,* cf. *supra,* 259, n. 4; Allen, *Law in the Making,* 40.

[2] D. 1. 3. 38: *Nam imperator noster Severus rescripsit in ambiguitatibus quae ex legibus proficiscuntur consuetudinem aut rerum perpetuo similiter iudicatarum auctoritatem vim legis obtinere debere.* In D. 47. 11. 9 there is clear reference to the custom of the proconsul's court in punishing offences peculiar to the province.

[3] I.e. usages which have no binding authority in themselves but are deemed to be implied in a contract unless the parties expressly exclude them; *v.* Allen, *op. cit.* 91. Salmond, *Jurisprudence,* 211 *sqq.,* uses "conventional custom" in this sense. For usage used to explain provisions of a will *v.* D. 32. 65. 7.

[4] E.g. C. 8. 53. 1.

[5] *L. Iulia de maritandis ordinibus; l. Iulia de adulteriis coercendis; l. Papia Poppaea.* [6] *L. Aelia Sentia; l. Fufia Caninia.*

[7] *Leges Iuliae, supra,* 222. [8] E.g. Gai. I. 157. [9] *Supra,* 333.

C. THE EDICTS OF THE MAGISTRATES. The empire brought with it no immediate change in the legal position of those magistrates whose edicts created the *ius honorarium*, but their independence suffered, like that of all the other organs of the state, from the new all-embracing authority of the princeps. Changes were still occasionally made in the edicts, but additional clauses were seldom inserted except in order to carry out the provisions of other law-making agencies, especially *senatus consulta*,[1] but sometimes even *leges*.[2] Even the theoretical power to alter the *ius honorarium* was, however, evidently deemed in the long run to be incompatible with the emperor's supremacy, and came to an end in the reign of Hadrian.

Our accounts of this important reform are extremely meagre and late,[3] but it is clear that the great jurist Salvius Iulianus was entrusted with the task of revising the praetorian edict, and that this, in its new form, was in some way confirmed by a *senatus consultum* passed at the emperor's wish.[4] Exactly how much Julian did is uncertain. One change in arrangement

[1] *Infra*, 368. Independent action of Cassius as praetor is mentioned, but it does not appear to have resulted in permanent changes in the text. In D. 44. 4. 4. 33 he is said to have omitted the *exceptio metus*, but it was evidently restored. In D. 4. 6. 26. 7 he is said to have issued an edict promising *in integrum restitutio* if the court were prevented from sitting by the proclamation of a public holiday, but this does not seem to have been incorporated in the permanent *edictum*, for the passage goes on to say that Celsus approved of the principle, which he would not have been likely to do if there had been a clause embodying it specifically. D. 29. 2. 99 refers to a special case. On D. 42. 8. 11 *v.* Lenel, *E.P.* 500, n. 2. Pliny (*Ep.* V. 9. 3) refers to a *breve edictum* issued by a praetor who presided over some special court in which he announced his intention of enforcing a *sc.* concerning gifts to advocates. It was perhaps an old *sc.* which had not been observed, for the excitement of which Pliny speaks clearly shows that the praetor need not have issued it had he not wished, and the centumviral praetor adjourned his court to consider whether he should follow the example or not.

[2] The *l. Papia Poppaea* gave in some cases *bonorum possessio* (not *hereditas*), e.g. Gai. III. 50, and the praetor put a clause in his edict granting *b.p.* wherever a statute required it (Lenel, *E.P.* 360); *v.* Buckland, 9. There is no definite instance of a clause put in at the emperor's wish, except perhaps D. 43. 4. 3. 3 (Lenel, 351), but the edict in several places (e.g. D. 3. 1. 1. 8; 4. 6. 1. 1) puts *decreta principum* on a level with *leges*, etc.

[3] *C. Tanta*, § 18; C. 4. 5. 10. 1; Eutrop. VIII. 17; Aurelius Victor, *de Caes.* XIX. 2; *Epitome Legum* (Zachariae, *Jus Graeco-Rom.* II. 280). The date of the revision is probably between 130 and 138. Appleton, *N.R.H.* XXXIV (1910), 791; Girard, 11 (= *Mél.* I. 219), would put it before 129 on the ground that Julian's *Digesta*, which presupposed the revision, must have been begun before 129 as he appears not to know of the *sc. Iuventianum* of that year. But this is very doubtful. Appleton, *loc. cit.*; Krüger, 94, n. 9; Kipp, 55, n. 24.

[4] *C. Tanta*, § 18.

he is known to have made. Hitherto the pattern *formulae* had, it seems, all appeared together at the end of the edict, as one of the appendices, whereas he placed each one after the clause promising the action for which the *formula* was intended, or, if there was no such clause, he fitted them in where they appeared to be most appropriate.[1] He is also known to have introduced one new substantive rule (the *nova clausula Iuliani* concerning a particular case of *bonorum possessio*),[2] and may well have introduced a great many more.[3] But in any case the actual changes which were made did not constitute the chief innovation. The great change was that henceforth the individual praetor could not make any alteration in the edict. He did indeed continue to publish it as his edict when he entered upon his office, so that the distinction between *ius civile* and *ius honorarium* persisted, but as a source of new law the edict ceases to come into consideration. Provision was apparently made in the confirmatory *senatus consultum* for necessary alterations to be introduced by imperial legislation,[4] but there is no evidence that such alterations were incorporated in the text. Gaius for instance, when he speaks of a rescript altering the rules of *bonorum possessio*[5] (a matter of the *ius honorarium*), says nothing of any change in the text, nor is there anything to show that the numerous *actiones utiles* allowed on the authority of the jurists found any mention.

Our accounts speak only of one edict, but it is clear that the revision must have embraced not only the urban edict but those of the *praetor peregrinus* and the curule aediles also, for these magistrates cannot have been allowed to retain powers which were taken from the *praetor urbanus*. It has been suggested that the urban and peregrine edicts were fused,[6] but Gaius speaks of them as separate,[7] and the silence of our few authorities is easily explained by the fact that they all lived long after the extension of the citizenship by Caracalla. Gaius also speaks of the aedilician edict as a separate document, and commentaries were written on it. In later times those commentaries were evidently treated simply as appendices to their authors' commentaries on the praetorian edict,[8] but the evidence

---

[1] Wlassak, *Edict und Klageform*, 22 *sqq.*; Girard, *Mél.* I. 300 *sqq.*

[2] D. 37. 8. 3.

[3] A correction in the edict *de eo quod certo loco dari oportet* is almost certain; Lenel, *E.P.* 243.   [4] *C. Tanta*, § 18, *sub fin.*   [5] II. 120.

[6] Rudorff, *Zeitschr. f. Rechtsgesch.* III. 21, quoted by Krüger, 95. But they were probably largely identical; Lenel, *E.P.* 3.   [7] I. 6.

[8] This explains why the Florentine *Index auctorum* ascribes eighty books instead of seventy-eight to Paulus' commentary on the edict, and eighty-three instead of eighty-one to Ulpian's, the last two in each case being those on the aedilician edict.

seems hardly to justify our saying that Julian himself treated one edict as an appendix to the other.[1]

The provincial edicts give rise to a difficulty. Gaius speaks as if each governor still promulgated his own, and one would imagine that local circumstances would require the preservation of differences. On the other hand Gaius also wrote a commentary *ad edictum provinciale*, which looks as if there had been only one, and the fragments of this work in the Digest show that the text on which he commented was largely identical with that of the urban edict.[2] The explanation is probably that there was one part, largely borrowed from the urban edict, which was common to all provinces, and that this was revised by Julian, whereas the special parts for each province were dealt with in some other way by imperial instructions.[3]

In addition to the edicts issued at the beginning of their term of office and consisting almost wholly of matter taken over from their predecessors, the provincial governors could publish edicts dealing with special matters. A number of such edicts issued by the prefects of Egypt have been preserved,[4] some, especially that of Ti. Iulius Alexander of A.D. 68[5] (which forbade imprisonment for debt), of great interest. The Egyptian edicts at any rate appear to have remained in force even after their authors had ceased to be governors.[6]

Apart from the governors of imperial provinces, the new imperial officials did not follow the republican practice of issuing general edicts when they entered upon their offices,[7] but they could naturally give general instructions within their sphere when they thought it necessary, and a constitution of A.D. 235[8] recognises a kind of subordinate legislative

---

[1] As Lenel does, *E.P.* 48; *contra*, Krüger, 95, n. 15.

[2] As Lenel points out (*E.P.* 5) the subsequent unification of law throughout the empire would necessarily mean that the compilers would have no use for those parts of the commentary which dealt with rules peculiar to the provincial edict. The existence of a provincial edict is attested for Egypt in A.D. 244; Wilcken, *Z.S.S.* XLII. 135.

[3] Wlassak, *Provinzialprozess*, 28, thinks that the edict on which Gaius commented was "an urban original containing only what was applicable to all or nearly all provinces, imposed upon governors perhaps by a *senatus consultum*".

[4] See Wilcken, *Z.S.S.* XLII. 137–139.

[5] Bruns, I. 243.

[6] Wilcken, *Z.S.S.* XLII. 139 *sqq.*

[7] It is also noticeable that the consuls and praetors concerned with jurisdiction *extra ordinem* (e.g. *fideicommissa, supra,* 336) did nothing of the sort.

[8] C. I. 26. 2.

power in the prefects of the praetorian guard, by commanding that general instructions given by them were to be observed provided they were not contrary to *leges* or imperial constitutions. The practice is probably older than the constitution.[1]

D. *Responsa prudentium* AND THE *ius respondendi*. *Responsa prudentium* continued in the principate to be an increasingly important source of law, but in this case, as in that of *edicta*, it was evidently felt that complete independence would be incompatible with the new regime, and Augustus already took steps to bring the jurists under his influence. The method he adopted was characteristic. He did not openly interfere with the right of any jurist to say or write what he pleased, but he distinguished certain of the more eminent among them by giving them the right to give *responsa* "with the emperor's authority".[2] This right is the famous *ius* (*publice*) *respondendi*, and most of the great jurists of the principate probably possessed it. It is unlikely that Augustus' act made the *responsa* of the favoured jurists legally binding on the courts,[3] or indeed that it could have done so. Such a rule would have required legislation and he never assumed the power of a legislator. But it is obvious that his innovation must, in the circumstances of the period, have made an immediate distinction between the *responsa* of those jurists who had the emperor's authority and those who had not. The *iudex* who disregarded one of the former would have to be a bold man. Pomponius, who tells us of Augustus' action, also mentions a change of form in the giving of *responsa*. Formerly the jurist had written to the *iudex* or evidence of his opinion had been given by the party who had consulted him; now the *responsa* were always in writing and though given to the party were

---

[1] Kipp, 95.

[2] Pomponius, D. 1.2.2.49: *Et, ut obiter sciamus, ante tempora Augusti publice respondendi ius non a principibus dabatur, sed qui fiduciam studiorum suorum habebant, consulentibus respondebant: neque responsa utique signata dabant, sed plerumque iudicibus ipsi scribebant, aut testabantur qui illos consulebant. primus divus Augustus, ut maior iuris auctoritas haberetur, constituit, ut ex auctoritate eius responderent: et ex illo tempore peti hoc pro beneficio coepit.* It is curious that we have direct evidence only of two persons who possessed the *ius respondendi*, Massurius Sabinus, to whom it was given by Tiberius (D. 1.2.2.48), and an otherwise unknown Innocentius, who probably lived in Diocletian's reign (Krüger, 296); but it is probable that all those jurists who published works called *responsa* had it, and indeed that most of the jurists quoted in the Digest did.

[3] Before the discovery of Gaius' Institutes (*infra*, 394), when the only texts known were that of Pomponius and J. 1.2.8, this was the general view (Buckland, 22). It has also been held by many modern scholars, e.g. Krüger, 121; Jörs, 20.

sealed,[1] obviously in order that they should not be tampered with on their way from the jurist to the *iudex*. This precaution again shows that, even if the *iudex* was not technically bound by the *responsum*, it would, if coming from a "patented" jurist, in fact always settle the case. Apart from Pomponius the chief text concerning the matter is Gaius' definition of *responsa prudentium*.[2] These, he says, "are the decisions and opinions (*sententiae et opiniones*) of those who have been given permission to lay down the law (*iura condere*)". This in itself points to an authoritative "laying down", but Gaius goes on to say that by a rescript of Hadrian "if the opinions of all of them agree the view thus expressed has the force of statute; if however they disagree, the *iudex* can follow whichever opinion he wishes". The interpretation of these words is a matter of difficulty. Some scholars hold that Hadrian, using the legislative power which he had and Augustus had not, made *responsa* legally binding on the *iudex*,[3] whereas before they had only been "persuasive". But even if this is right it is not clear whether a single *responsum*, if uncontradicted by one of equal authority, was sufficient, or whether all the "patented" jurists of the time had to be consulted. If the latter, then the burden on the parties and the amount of unnecessary work entailed would be very great, and if the former then it seems strange that the rescript should have been needed at all, for it appears that authorised *responsa* had in effect become binding before Hadrian's time. Seneca already says of them that they "are valid", whether reasons for them are given or not.[4] Nor is it likely that the rescript was merely intended to settle the obvious difficulty about conflicting *responsa*, for that must have arisen long before.

It is therefore more probable that Gaius is not referring to *responsa* given for the particular case which was being tried, but to the citation as precedents of *responsa* given in previous cases. Indeed he does not confine himself to *responsa* in the strict sense at all, but (if the word

---

[1] *Supra*, 365, n. 2. It is probable that the oral testimony of the party was already in republican times supported by a document attested by the seals of witnesses. The innovation may then have consisted either (i) in requiring that the jurist should himself seal as a method of authenticating the document, or (ii) in requiring that the document must now always issue from the jurist himself. If, as is probable, the document was always in the double form (*infra*, 424) the latter is more likely, but it is quite possible that there had to be both the seals of the witnesses to secure the inner writing against alteration and the seal of the jurist to authenticate the opinion as his. See Wenger, P.-W., s.v. *signum*, col. 2427.

[2] I. 7.   [3] Buckland, 24.

[4] *Epist.* XCIV. 27.

opiniones is genuine)[1] includes opinions expressed by patented jurists in their writings generally. It may be that an undesirable practice had grown up of citing the text of works published by a patented jurist as if it were the text of a statute and so binding in itself, and that Hadrian's rescript was intended to make it quite clear that only a definite common opinion to be discovered from the works of the jurists was to be taken as law.[2] This would have been a restatement of what was already true during the republic, when the *interpretatio* of the jurists made civil law, with the important restriction that now only the opinions of those who had the *ius respondendi* were to count.[3]

Another question raised is this. *Responsa* were addressed not only to private persons and *iudices*, but also to magistrates.[4] It might be said, for instance, that in such and such a case the praetor should "give an action". Was the magistrate in any sense bound? Almost certainly not. No emperor could have placed the magistrates of the senate and people under the authority of men who had received the imperial patent without making it clear that the "dyarchy" of princeps and senate was at an end.[5] Nor can we imagine that there would have been much point in such an enactment. The praetor, even if he had not much knowledge of law himself, would have eminent jurists on his *consilium* and, if he were presented with a *responsum* which did not commend itself, he could easily negative its effect by getting a contrary opinion.

This consideration supports the view that there was never any legislation defining in exact terms the binding authority of *responsa*, even on *iudices*. Their force would be a matter of degree, varying according to the person concerned. For the magistrate they would be "persuasive" only, for the *iudex*, and probably for the imperial official trying a case by *cognitio*,[6] normally "authoritative", but further than that one cannot go.

---

[1] It is suspected e.g. by Kniep, *Gai. Inst. Commentarius*, I. 105, and Buckland, 25. Krüger, 124, says that one must suppose that Gaius was mixing up the binding force of individual *responsa* with that of *communis opinio*. But if one takes Gaius to refer to the *communis opinio* only the text is comprehensible and there is no need to suppose it corrupt; cf. Wlassak, *Prozessformel*, 41.

[2] Kipp, 111. Somewhat similarly Lenel, 360. Jörs, 21, is also of opinion that Hadrian's rescript refers to the citation of *responsa* as precedents. As he points out C. 6. 37. 12 and C. 5. 71. 4 provide actual examples of such citation by a party in his petition to the emperor, and in *P. Oxy.* 237. VIII. 2 an opinion given to a governor of Egypt is quoted.

[3] Wlassak, *op. cit.* 41, n. 3.

[4] Wlassak, *op. cit.* 42, gives a list of examples, among them D. 9. 3. 5. 12; 3. 5. 20.

[5] Wlassak, *op. cit.* 45.

[6] Wenger, *Praetor u. Formel* (1926), 113.

English law presents a sufficiently close parallel in its treatment of precedent. The practitioner knows well enough for ordinary purposes when he can quote a case in the confident anticipation that the court will follow it, if it considers it in point, but Parliament has never passed any enactment on the subject and the writers of text-books do not agree in their accounts of the matter.[1]

Whatever the exact technical value of *responsa* may have been it is clear that the jurists were the chief instrument of legal development throughout the principate. Of the chief personalities and their writings something will be said in the next chapter, but writing was not their only or even their chief activity. Wlassak's investigations have given us a clearer idea of the importance of their work as advisers to the parties, the *iudices* and the magistrates. They were also active on the council of the emperor himself. When the principate came to an end, the formulary system of procedure also ceased to be in use, and with it the peculiar influence which the jurists had been able to exercise ceased. The latest author of a work known as *responsa* was Modestinus, who was also the last of the "classical" jurists. It is indeed said that the *ius respondendi* was given to a certain Innocentius, who probably lived in the time of Diocletian, but nothing else is known about him.[2] Henceforward the completely autocratic nature of the constitution does not permit of any law-making which does not come directly from the emperor, and, though of course imperial legislation was in fact the work of professional lawyers, their names do not appear on the enactments which they drafted.

§ II. THE NEW SOURCES

A. *Senatus consulta.* We have seen that in republican times, though the senate had great influence on legislation, it could not pass general enactments in the same way as the sovereign assembly. In the later principate it undoubtedly could do so, and Gaius mentions *senatus consulta* next after *leges* and *plebiscita* as sources of law.[3] He adds, however, that there had been doubts about the matter, and there was certainly no specific enactment, imperial or popular, conferring legislative power.[4] The change may be said to have come about as the combined result of two tendencies, that by which the senate assumed more and more the task of guiding the magistrate in his use of the *ius*

---

[1] Allen, *Law in the Making*, 149 *sqq.*   [2] *Supra*, 365, n. 2.
[3] I. 4; cf. D. I. 2. 2. 9 (Pomponius) and D. I. 3. 9 (Ulpian).
[4] The transference of elections to the senate by Tiberius (*supra*, 333) had no connection with legislation.

edicendi, and its general tendency to take the place of the *comitia* as representing the republican element in the constitution. Advice to magistrates had, of course, always been the function of the senate, and when given to a magistrate with jurisdiction might result in a change in the *ius honorarium*. From the beginning of the empire *senatus consulta* which thus indirectly alter the law become common, the first known being the *sc. Silanianum* of A.D. 10, which was put into effect by a clause in the edict.[1] Similarly the *sc. Vellaeanum* (A.D. 46), which forbade women to become answerable for the debts of others, was enforced by granting them an *exceptio* if they were sued on such an engagement.[2] The same means were used, in accordance with the *sc. Macedonianum*,[3] to make irrecoverable loans of money to *filii familias*. The first *sc.* of which one can be quite certain that it produced direct effect on the law without the intervention of the praetor is the *sc. Tertullianum* of Hadrian's reign,[4] which conferred civil law rights of succession in certain cases on a mother whose child had died intestate, but some scholars hold that even earlier *scc.*, e.g. *sc. Neronianum*[5] and *Hosidianum*,[6] had civil law effect.[7] The explanation seems to be that the distinction between *ius civile* and *ius honorarium*, never perhaps as rigid as some modern authors believe, was becoming relaxed already early in the empire. We have seen that even *leges*, which certainly could make civil law, were sometimes enforced by praetorian machinery,[8] and the use of *scc.* for direct legislation does not necessarily mean that the older method was at once abandoned.

Many of the *scc.* of the empire are in so far like *leges* that they bear the names of the persons who proposed them, but this resemblance is a little misleading, for the designation is never official. A number have no names at all; one, the *sc. Macedonianum*, is called after the person whose crimes occasioned its enactment, and in any case the form in which the proposer's name appears is different from that in use for *leges*.[9] That the senate ever

---

[1] D. 29. 5; Lenel, *E.P.* 364.

[2] And by restoring to the creditor the action against the original debtor where he had lost it through the invalid *intercessio* of the woman; Lenel, *E.P.* 287. The form of this *sc.* shows the relation between the senate and the praetor most clearly. *Arbitrari senatum recte atque ordine facturos ad quos de ea re in iure aditum erit, si dederint operam, ut in ea re senatus voluntas servetur*; D. 16. 1. 2. 1.

[3] Passed in the reign of Vespasian.

[4] *V.* Girard, 61.   [5] Krüger, 90, referring to Gai. II. 198.

[6] Bruns, I. 200.

[7] Lenel, *Ursprung u. Wirkung der Exceptionen* (1876), 49 *sqq.* He refers also to the *scc.* quoted D. 38. 4. 1. pr. and D. 40. 5. 51. 4.   [8] *Supra*, 362.

[9] A lengthened adjectival form ending in *-anum* of the *nomen* or even *cognomen* is used; Krüger, 91.

exercised much initiative in legislation is unlikely. Sometimes indeed the formulation of the measure was left to it,[1] but it was generally recognised that the emperor was the real author,[2] and the text of the measure itself may mention that it was he who desired the consuls to take the opinion of the senate.[3] He could of course propose *scc.* himself, but he could also do what no other senator could, namely have a proposal read (by a *quaestor*) without being present himself, and it appears to have been customary for the reading to take place even when he was there. Latterly all that the senate did was to confirm the emperor's "speech" (*oratio*), and the later jurists refer to the speech itself as if it were the authority, and not the confirmatory *sc.*[4] One example of such an *oratio* which has been preserved leaves no doubt that this represents the true state of affairs, for the emperor uses the words "I will forbid".[5] In fact, in the next period, the *oratio* merges into the *edictum* as a direct expression of the emperor's will, which may be promulgated to the senate as to other persons. The last mention of any confirmation by that body comes from the reign of Probus (276–282), who is said to have allowed it to confirm by its own *scc.* the laws which he promulgated.[6]

B. *Constitutiones principum.* We have seen that Augustus himself did not assume legislative power and that he even directly repudiated the *cura legum et morum* when it was offered to him.[7] Nevertheless the influence of the emperor on the development of law was from the first very great, and by the middle of the second century A.D. it was recognised by the jurists that he could actually make law.[8]

There can be little doubt now that this rule is of customary origin, though both Gaius and Ulpian give a different explanation. Gaius says

[1] This appears to have been so in the case of the *sc. Iuventianum*; cf. A.D. 129, D. 5. 3. 20. 6.

[2] Mommsen, *Staatsr.* II. 899, points out that no one but the emperor is ever called *auctor senatusconsulti.*

[3] See the *sc.* quoted in Augustus' edict, recently found in Cyrene; Premerstein, *Z.S.S.* XLVIII. 428. For the already considerable literature on these edicts (especially *Die Augustus-Inschrift auf dem Marktplatz von Kyrene* by Stroux and Wenger, *Abh. d. Bay. Akad.* XXXIV (1928), 2) *v.* Premerstein, *Z.S.S.* LI. 431–459.

[4] *Or. Severi*, D. 24. 1. 23; *Or. d. Marci*, D. 2. 15. 8. pr.; D. 40. 15. 1. 3.

[5] D. 27. 9. 1. 1.   [6] *H.A. Prob.* 13. 1.

[7] *Supra*, 332.

[8] For a view that the texts are untrustworthy and that during the principate the power of the emperor was limited to authentic interpretation and instructions within the sphere of his *imperium*, *v.* Kreller, *Z.S.S.* XLI. 262–272. It is generally admitted that *regia* in D. 1. 4. 1. pr. is an interpolation, but there seems to be insufficient reason for suspecting the text of Gaius.

that there has never been any doubt but that what the emperor lays down is as good as statute because he himself receives his *imperium* by a statute (*lex*).[1] Ulpian is a little more explicit. "Everything", he says, "which the emperor decides has the force of statute, since by the royal law passed concerning his *imperium* the people gave to him and put into his hands all its own *imperium* and power."[2] The *lex* referred to is presumably that conferring the *t ribunicia potestas*, but we know of no clause therein which contained such a delegation of sovereign power. The words "he is to have the right and power to do all things...which he considers in the interest of the state"[3] cannot have had this meaning, at any rate originally, for the text says that Augustus had the same power, and Augustus' refusal of the *cura legum* would have been an absurdity if he had accepted the same thing in a slightly different form. Indeed, had complete legal sovereignty been meant, the rest of the enactment would have been meaningless. It is however quite possible that it was this clause which Gaius and Ulpian had in mind. They were trying to explain the legislative power of the emperor, which in their day had become an accomplished fact, and they had difficulty in doing so satisfactorily. What Gaius says is, strictly, no explanation at all. Because a man has received his powers by statute he does not necessarily have the power himself to make statutes. It is also surprising to be told that there had never been any doubt about the matter,[4] though we can well believe that such doubts had not been openly expressed. In fact the growth was gradual. From the first the emperor had numerous ways of expressing his wishes and was in a position to interpret the law. With the consolidation of his position his interferences with existing law had become more open, and, since there was no one who could dispute their authority, they came to be regarded as binding. When the jurists reckoned imperial enactment as one of the sources of law they were merely recognising a constitutional convention as part of the law of the constitution.

[1] I. 5: *Constitutio principis est quod imperator decreto vel edicto vel epistula constituit. nec unquam dubitatum est quin id legis vicem obtineat, cum ipse imperator per legem imperium accipiat.*

[2] D. 1. 4. 1. pr. and 1: *Quod principi placuit legis habet vigorem: utpote cum lege regia, quae de imperio eius lata est, populus ei et in eum omne suum imperium et potestatem conferat: quodcumque igitur imperator per epistulam et subscriptionem statuit vel cognoscens decrevit vel de plano interlocutus est vel edicto praecepit, legem esse constat. haec sunt quas vulgo constitutiones appellamus.* Cf. Pomponius, D. 1. 2. 2. 11: *Constituto principe datum est ei ius ut quod constituisset ratum esset.*

[3] *Lex de imperio Vespasiani, supra*, 332.

[4] As Gaius says there had been about *scc., supra*, 368.

Throughout the principate, however, traces of the original position of the princeps remain. Not only does he continue at times to act through the senate, but he continues to legislate, even independently of the senate, in the forms which had existed before he was recognised as a legislator. For imperial enactments are not all in the same form, and even the most general word used to describe the various forms— *constitutio*—was not strictly a technical term.[1]

Gaius mentions three types of *constitutiones*: *edicta*, *decreta* and *epistulae*. We can adopt this classification for the purpose of discussion, but under the heading of *epistulae* we must speak of *rescripta* and *subscriptiones*, which Gaius no doubt intended to include in the more general term. We must also say something of *mandata*, which, though never actually called *constitutiones* by a Roman writer, were also instructions through which new rules of law might be introduced.[2]

(i) *Edicta*. Since the emperor is a magistrate he can, like other magistrates, make known his orders and intentions, but whereas the spheres of other magistrates are limited, his embraces the whole business of the state, and his edicts may deal with the most varied matters. One, for instance, of Claudius, which is preserved in an inscription, settles the status of the Anauni by granting them the citizenship, which they have been enjoying *de facto* for some time previously.[3] Several others of a more general nature are known to us, such as those of Augustus and Claudius forbidding women to become answerable for the debts of their husbands,[4] and another of Claudius which enacted that a slave who was abandoned by his master on account of sickness should become a Junian Latin.[5] The famous *constitutio Antoniniana* of A.D. 212 was an edict.[6]

Originally an edict was an oral proclamation, and it was still possible

---

[1] Ulpian says—*supra*, 371, n. 2—"which we commonly call *constitutiones*". The sentence however might be a gloss.

[2] Among the types of imperial legislation it is also possible to include *leges datae*, i.e. charters to municipalities, which the emperor alone could now grant. Such are the leges *Salpensana* and *Malacitana* (Bruns, I. 142 *sqq.* and 147 *sqq.*), both dealing with municipalities in Spain and dating from Domitian's reign. As opposed to a *lex data*, a *lex dicta* is a regulation issued by a person for the governance of property belonging to him. Such regulations issued by the emperor for mines or lands forming part of his domains were of public importance, and so also in a sense imperial legislation. The chief example preserved in an inscription is the *l. metalli Vipascensis*, Bruns, I. 289.

[3] Bruns, I. 253.

[4] D. 16. 1. 2. pr. The rule was subsequently extended to all *intercessio* whether for husbands or others by the *sc. Vellaeanum*.

[5] D. 40. 8. 2.   [6] *Supra*, 353.

for an emperor to promulgate one orally.¹ But this must have been a very exceptional proceeding, and the usual practice was for the edict to be published in writing. The words of the emperor were then prefaced by the date, his name and titles and the word *dicit* (The emperor says...), in the present tense,² a form which is presumably referable to the original oral proclamation.

The edicts of ordinary magistrates took effect only during their term of office, and thus, logically, those of the emperor, whose office was lifelong, should have lost their validity at his death. It seems however, though the matter is much disputed for the earlier principate, that this consequence was not drawn. It is true that there are instances in which edicts of successive emperors concerning the same matter are mentioned,³ but this does not necessarily mean that they were not valid unless repeated, for we cannot be sure that the later enactment did not contain some fresh provision. Certainly edicts of emperors are quoted long after their deaths without any suggestion that they have been renewed,⁴ and this appears to be so even when the emperor's memory has been officially held up to execration by the senate.⁵ It is agreed, at any rate, that, in the late principate, when the emperor had in fact become the sole legislator, there was no need for renewal.

(ii) *Decreta*. The emperor had great judicial powers, both on appeal, and, if he thought fit, as judge of first instance.⁶ In trying a case he always uses *cognitio*, i.e. investigates the matter himself and does not send it to a *iudex*, and his decisions, like those of other magistrates after *cognitio*, are known as *decreta*.⁷ He may also have occasion to give an interlocutory decision.⁸ Primarily, like other judges, he is concerned to apply the

---

¹ Technically the *oratio* of M. Aurelius to the troops, quoted *Fr. Vat.* 195, was an oral edict.

² As opposed to *dixit* in accounts of *decreta*, *infra*, 374.

³ D. 16. 1. 2. pr.; cf. *supra*, 372, n. 4; D. 40. 15. 4.

⁴ The most striking instance of this is quoted by Wilcken, *Z.S.S.* XLII. 134, from Pliny's correspondence with Trajan (*Ep.* x. 79 (83) *sqq.*). Wilcken also relies on the analogy of the prefect's edicts, cf. *supra*, 364.

⁵ Krüger, 115, quoting D. 48. 3. 2. 1 and Gai. 1. 33.

⁶ *Infra*, 400.

⁷ There is also a wider meaning in which *decreta* include imperial enactments generally, e.g. D. 1. 1. 7. pr. and frequently in the praetorian edict, e.g. D. 4. 6. 1. 1; 43. 8. 2. pr.; Kipp, 70.

⁸ D. 1. 4. 1. 1: *vel de plano interlocutus est. De plano*, literally "from the level", is used in opposition to *pro tribunali*, "on his judgment seat", and means that the decision may be given outside the ordinary course of judicial procedure, and even on an *ex parte* application, e.g. D. 38. 15. 2. 1.

existing law, but, as the highest authority in the state, he naturally allows himself considerable freedom of interpretation, and sometimes goes so far as to introduce definitely new principles.[1] Though the Romans had no general theory of the binding force of precedent, it was different with these imperial decisions. They were, as we should say, authentic interpretations of the law,[2] and as such could not be questioned even if they went beyond what was strictly interpretation. They were thus recognised with other methods by which the imperial will was expressed as binding statements of law for all future cases,[3] and are freely quoted by the jurists.[4] Generally only a summary of the facts and the decision is given, but sometimes the exact words of the emperor are reported, introduced by the word *dixit* (The emperor said...). Occasionally even the arguments of counsel or incidental remarks of the emperor[5] may be quoted, so that the whole reads like a much abbreviated English report.

(iii) *Epistulae, rescripta and subscriptiones. Epistula* in its most general sense means simply a letter, and *rescriptum* means the written answer of the emperor to a question or petition addressed to him in writing. It is consequently also an *epistula* in the general sense. Of rescripts there were two main classes, *epistulae* (in the narrow sense) and *subscriptiones*.[6]

(a) *Epistulae* (in the narrow sense). These were answers to officials or public bodies, such for instance as municipalities, who had asked the emperor for instructions, for the settlement of some dispute, or perhaps for some indulgence. They were couched in the usual form of a letter, beginning with the names of the sender (the emperor) and the addressee, and a greeting (*salutem* or *salutem dicit*), and ending with the usual form "farewell" (*vale* or *valete*). They were prepared in the department *ab epistulis*, and, just as to-day a man signs a letter which may be written for him by his secretary, so this "farewell" was written by the emperor himself, for the ancient signature does not, like ours, consist of the name merely, but of a phrase to which the name may or may not be added.[7]

---

[1] E.g. the famous *decretum d. Marci*, D. 4. 2. 13 and 48. 7. 7.

[2] I.e. interpretation which comes from a source equivalent to that of the law to be interpreted.

[3] Fronto, *ad Marcum imp.* 1. 6: *Tuis decretis, imperator, exempla publice valitura in perpetuum sanciuntur*, etc.

[4] Paulus compiled two collections of them; cf. *infra*, 397.

[5] E.g. D. 28. 4. 3; 32. 97.

[6] The clear-cut distinction here made is taken from Wilcken's brilliant article in *Hermes*, LV (1920), 1–42.

[7] Steinacker, *Die Antiken Grundlagen der frühmittelalterlichen Privaturkunde* (1927), 112.

The original letter was then sent to the addressee, in the case of officials normally by the imperial post. Communities might have sent a special delegation with their original request and the answer would then be handed to the delegates.[1]

(b) *Subscriptiones.* Private persons were not in general allowed to send letters to the emperor. Their petitions (*libelli*) had to be handed to him in person, or by a representative.[2] The answers were then prepared by the department *a libellis* and were set underneath the petitions themselves. The form, since the addressee is present, is different from that of the *epistula*, which is a letter to one who is absent. Though the names of the emperor and addressee are given, the greeting is absent, and the emperor writes simply *scripsi* (I have written) or *subscripsi*.[3] The original is not given to the petitioner—it remains in the imperial archives—but he can obtain a certified copy of it.

Both *epistulae* and *subscriptiones* may deal with matters of the most various kinds according to the nature of the request or petition which they answer, and many, either because they were of a purely administrative nature or for some other reason, would have no influence on the development of the law. The *subscriptio* for instance of Antoninus Pius, permitting a certain Acutianus to take a copy of a judgment given by Hadrian which interested him,[4] can hardly have been of interest to the legal profession at large. But many rescripts concerned matters of the greatest interest, such, for instance, as the famous *epistula* in which Trajan replied to Pliny's requests for instructions about the treatment of the Christians.[5] Above all, from the time of Hadrian onwards it became the practice for a litigant to address a petition to the emperor asking for his decision upon a point of law involved in the case. He would, of course, have to set out the facts, and the emperor's answer would apply only if the judge who subsequently tried the matter found the facts to be as stated. But so far as the law was concerned the emperor's decision settled the matter, in much the same way as the *responsum* of a jurist, though with even greater

---

[1] *Epistula* of Vespasian to the Saborenses, Bruns, I. 255.

[2] In Egypt *libelli* could be handed to the prefect for transmission to the emperor; Wilcken, *op. cit.* 21 *sqq.* Similar arrangements may have existed in other provinces.

[3] Before he does so an official certifies that the text laid before the emperor corresponds with his instructions. This is (according to the view here adopted) the explanation of the word *recognovi* ("I have verified") found e.g. in the rescript of Gordian to the Skaptopareni; Bruns, I. 263–264. See Wilcken, *op. cit.* 6.

[4] Bruns, I. 257.

[5] *Ep.* x. 97 (98).

authority. The process was, however, only applicable where the case was to be tried by *cognitio*.

It was also possible for a judge (again only an official using *cognitio*)[1] to ask for direction from the emperor on a point of law which came before him (*relatio*). He then stated the facts as he saw them (though the parties had to see the statement and might add their own versions),[2] and the emperor decided on the law. Most rescripts were however directed to private persons, and of these a great number are preserved in Justinian's *Codex*. In these rescripts, as in *decreta*, the emperor normally applies existing law, and it is indeed surprising to see what elementary legal propositions they sometimes contain. But often the point which he had to decide was an uncertain one, and he might lay down quite a new rule by rescript just as well as by decree. We know of a number which were thus of great importance in the development of the law.[3]

(iv) *Mandata*. These were instructions given by the emperor to subordinate officials,[4] in particular provincial governors,[5] including not only his own legates in the imperial provinces, but also the proconsuls of those governed by the senate.[6] As in the case of the ordinary mandate of private law, the instructions lost their force with the disappearance of either the principal or the delegate, and thus needed renewal when the emperor died or the governor was replaced. Gradually, by successive renewals, a body of standing instructions was built up, in much the same way as the praetorian edict was evolved through the repetition of the same regulations by successive praetors, and the mandates concerned with different provinces would also frequently contain similar provisions. In this manner a number of important general principles were first introduced, mainly in connection with soldiers and administrators, and it must be noticed that they were not merely regarded as a matter between the emperor and his subordinate, but as rules which could be relied on by private persons. Most famous of all such rules is perhaps that which permitted soldiers to make a will without observing any of the formalities required of civilians.[7] It is clear from this, and from the way in which

[1] And probably only one from whom appeal lay direct to the emperor; Kipp, 73, n. 36.

[2] C. 7. 61. 1. 2.   [3] E.g. J. 1. 8. 2; Gai. II. 120; C. 8. 41. 3. pr.

[4] Example of form, D. 47. 11. 6.

[5] *Mandata* to a *curator aquarum* are also mentioned; *v.* Krüger, 110, n. 73.

[6] Who, though not his delegates, were subordinated to him by reason of his *imperium proconsulare maius*.

[7] D. 29. 1. 1. For other examples *v. e.g.* D. 1. 16. 6 (forbidding gifts to proconsuls), D. 23. 2. 65 (forbidding marriage between officials or soldiers with women of the province in which they are serving. The marriage is void *iure civili*).

the jurists quote *mandata*, that they were in effect binding declarations of his will by the emperor, and thus "had the force of statute". That they are not actually classed as *constitutiones* is an accident of terminology, due perhaps to their almost exclusively provincial character.

(v) *Publication of constitutiones*. The edicts of the emperor, like those of other magistrates, were published in the first instance by being put up (*proposita*) on a white board (*in albo*) at his place of residence, i.e. normally at Rome, where however they only remained for a short time. If it was held desirable they might be similarly published elsewhere. Thus an edict of Claudius concerning the Jews was ordered to be put up by the local authorities throughout Italy and the provinces for thirty days.[1] *Decreta*, which would normally be made known to the parties at once, were recorded in the records of the imperial court (*commentarii*), and private individuals might obtain copies of them.[2] The treatment of rescripts differed according as they were *epistulae* or *subscriptiones*. The originals of the former were sent to the addressees, a copy being retained, no doubt, in the files of the department *ab epistulis*, but if the matter was of importance the emperor might order his instructions to be published.[3] In the case of *subscriptiones* the practice was that the original petition, with the answer written beneath it, should be put up in public and that the petitioner or his agent should obtain a certified copy of it.[4] It is probable that several of these rescripts, already stuck together on a roll, were put up together at intervals of a few days and that these small rolls were then put together in chronological order and retained in the archives. When the original petition had been forwarded by a provincial governor this process would take place in the province, a roll of copies only being kept at Rome.[5] *Mandata*, being instructions to officials, would not normally be published at all, but we know that Antoninus Pius, when proconsul of

[1] Joseph. *Antiq.* XIX. 5. 3.

[2] Cf. *supra*, 375, n. 4. The sending of a copy as in *C.I.L.* IX. 5420 (Bruns, I. 255) must have been exceptional.

[3] *B.G.U.* 140 (Mitteis, *Chrest.* No. 373) is the Greek translation of an *epistula* of Hadrian giving children of soldiers (who were illegitimate since soldiers were not allowed to marry) the right to claim *b.p. unde cognati*. At the end the emperor says that he wishes his concession to be published to the men.

[4] The system is most clearly shown by the inscription from Skaptoparene (Bruns, I. 263). It was formerly held (e.g. Karlowa, I. 651) that only those rescripts which were of some general interest were *proposita*. Wilcken (*op. cit.*; cf. *Archiv für Papyrusforschung*, IX (1930), 15–23) has now made it clear that all *subscriptiones* were put up, but not *epistulae*, unless for some special reason. The *subscriptio* of Skaptoparene, which certainly was *proposita*, is of no general interest whatever.

[5] Wilcken, *op. cit.* 26, 35–37.

Asia, thought fit to publish a chapter of the *mandata* issued to him,[1] and no doubt other governors on occasion did the same.

There was thus some provision for notification to the public of certain types of imperial legislation, but it was of a temporary nature at best, and no steps were taken officially to keep the legal profession informed. It had to obtain the necessary knowledge through the writings of jurists who had, in many cases, taken part in drafting the legislation as officials or members of the emperor's council. Persons of rank may also have been allowed access to the archives.[2] The earliest definite collection of which we know is that of Papirius Iustus which included constitutions of the *divi fratres* and M. Aurelius alone, and, as we have seen, Paulus made two collections of *decreta*. As a rule neither author gives the text of the enactment in full. It was not until the time of Diocletian that collections of the texts were made available in the *codices Gregorianus* and *Hermogenianus*.[3]

(vi) *The use of constitutiones as precedents.* None of the methods by which the emperors legislated were exclusively methods of legislation. Indeed their power to make new law arose from the fact that what they laid down in various ways which were not legislative came to be accepted as the expression of the highest authority in the state. *Decreta* and procedural rescripts were primarily judicial decisions, *mandata* were administrative instructions, and even *edicta* sometimes dealt with matters of very limited interest. There was thus nothing in the form of a constitution which made it clear whether the emperor had intended to lay down a general rule or not. It is said of Trajan that he refused to answer petitions (*libelli*) for fear that a concession intended as a personal favour should be used as a precedent in different cases.[4] In post-classical times there was legislation restricting the use of imperial constitutions beyond the case for which they were intended,[5] but in the classical period the only rule appears to have been that some constitutions were personal and that such concessions to a particular person on account of his merits were not to be extended beyond that person.[6] In other words, it must be gathered from

---

[1] D. 48. 3. 6. 1.

[2] There are a number of references in the Corpus Juris to rescripts contained in the *semestria* of M. Aurelius (e.g. J. 1. 25. 1; D. 2. 14. 46); *v.* Karlowa, 1. 654. Wilcken, *op. cit.* 37, n. 4, suggests that these may have been rolls of (copies of) epistolary rescripts, the more common *subscriptiones* being, according to him, bound up in three-monthly rolls.

[3] *Infra*, 478.   [4] *H.A. Macrin.* 13, quoted Kipp, 74.   [5] *Infra*, 475.

[6] Ulpian, D. 1. 4. 1. 2: *Plane ex his quaedam sunt personales nec ad exemplum trahuntur: nam quae princeps alicui ob merita indulsit vel si quam poenam irrogavit vel si cui sine exemplo subvenit, personam non egreditur.*

the tenor of the constitution itself whether it is meant to be general. In some cases this would be immediately obvious from the wording,[1] and as a rule a statement of law, new or old, contained in a rescript would be authoritative. In other cases the reverse would be clear, e.g. the grant of citizenship to a person or a community would not mean that others, even if they could prove that their case was similar, would be entitled to demand it likewise. One can readily believe that in the classical period a trained lawyer can have had little difficulty as a rule in knowing how to treat any given constitution.

[1] E.g. D. 4. 2. 13; 27. 1. 6. 2; 42. 1. 31.

Chapter XXII

LEGAL SCIENCE DURING THE PRINCIPATE

§ I. THE WORK OF THE JURISTS

It is to the jurists of the principate that Roman law owes its fame and its influence on subsequent generations. The way had indeed been prepared during the republic, and there is no break between the work of Caesar's contemporaries and their successors under Augustus, but there was a development of interest in legal matters and an increase in the amount of legal literature produced. In some degree this was perhaps due to the introduction of the *ius respondendi*, which gave to some jurists an official position such as they had not enjoyed before, but to a much greater extent it was the result of the more settled conditions which the empire brought with it, and to the shifting of interest from politics to administration. Oratory could now no longer suffice as a means of winning distinction in public affairs, and the only alternative to military service was jurisprudence. As under the republic, the jurists were as a rule public men. Most of them were of senatorial rank and many held high office in the imperial service as well as magistracies of the old type. Some however appear to have acted only as teachers and writers, or, like Sabinus, to have combined these activities with the work of a "respondent". In any case it was their close connection with the actual administration of the law which gave to the Roman jurists their peculiar qualities. It has often been remarked that they had little interest in legal theory, and, except in elementary works, cared little for the arrangement of their material. Their definitions, though often giving the gist of the matter, will generally not bear close investigation,[1] nor are they concerned to elaborate general conceptions.[2] Being educated men they were naturally acquainted with current philosophical ideas, and in isolated instances a distinction or a decision may be assigned to some definite doctrine of one school or another.[3] It is also true that no constructive lawyer can keep his ideas of social and moral values out of his legal work, even if he wishes to do so,

---

[1] See Buckland, 61, on the definition of slavery given in J. 1. 3. 1.

[2] We have seen that the conception of contract was not yet fully developed in classical times (*supra*, 280, n. 4) and though the jurists constantly treat of the invalidity of various forms of disposition they never distinguish between what is void and what is voidable; *v.* Lenel, 357.

[3] *V.* D. 18. 1. 9. 2; 41. 3. 30 and *infra*, 385, n. 5.

and one can find a connection between the individualism of contemporary philosophy and the legal system, which, as it has been said, knows nothing between the state and Titius. But there is no attempt to elaborate a philosophy of law and the Roman jurists owe their fame to their success in solving practical problems. Though they might not be able to define the concepts with which jurisprudence must work, these concepts were present to their minds in sufficient numbers and with sufficient clarity for their practical purposes, and a whole host of them have passed into modern law, where they have been subjected to the analysis which the Romans were able to do without. A comparison with the practical lawyers by whom English law has been and is still being developed immediately suggests itself. In both systems the concrete question which requires a direct answer is the basis, and the men who are concerned to give that answer have in their minds continuously the procedure of the courts with which they are in daily contact. At Rome, as in England before the abolition of the forms of action, the procedural often dominated the substantive aspect of the matter.[1] But the way in which the practitioner exercises his influence is very different in the two systems. In England, apart from "the practice of conveyancers", all that is really effective is the judgment of a judge who decides a case, whereas at Rome the jurist had many ways of asserting himself. He was, it is true, sometimes actually a judge, especially in the later principate when the great prefectures had acquired wide judicial powers and were held by eminent lawyers; he was also in a position not unlike that of a judge when he gave a *responsum* which, when conveyed to a *iudex*, would settle the legal question raised by an actual case. But the influence of the jurists in other ways was at least equally important. They continued, as under the republic, to advise the magistrates on the composition of their edicts (though the importance of this function diminished), and we have seen that a large number of their *responsa* were addressed to magistrates.[2] There can be little doubt that it was the jurists on the *consilium* of a magistrate who really decided, as a rule, whether a new *formula* was to be accepted, or an old one allowed in a new application, just as it was a jurist who, in the first instance, had drafted the *formula* for the litigant to produce. We have seen, too, that much of the imperial legislation, whether judicial or direct, was in reality the work of the jurists on his

[1] Though this is less true under the formulary procedure than under the *legis actiones*, the *formulae* themselves came to be looked on as technical traps; *v.* C. 2. 57. 1: *Iuris formulae aucupatione syllabarum insidiantes cunctorum actibus radicitus amputentur.*   [2] *Supra,* 367.

council. Maine, speaking of *responsa prudentium*, says: "the authority by which this part of the Roman jurisprudence was expounded was not the *bench* but the *bar*",[1] but this statement contains only a small part of the truth, for not only were the jurists not "the bar", they were frequently very near "the bench", if not actually on it.

The practical nature of the jurists' interests comes out very clearly in their writings. Apart from works definitely intended for beginners, these are all constructed on the casuistic principle, i.e. the discussion of cases, actual or hypothetical, is much more frequent than the abstract statement of legal principle. And in arrangement, again with the exception of elementary books, the jurists prefer to follow the traditional order of Sabinus or of the edict to inventing a more logical scheme for themselves. Uniform tradition no doubt made the works easy of reference for the practitioner and this was the object in view. The English alphabetical "abridgments" served a similar purpose.

It is impossible to classify the different types of legal literature with any precision, for naturally the author's treatment differs in each case, and books which bear similar titles are often very different in contents, but, very roughly, the following main categories may be distinguished.

(a) Text-books for beginners, *institutiones* or *enchiridia*. These treat of the civil law and the *ius honorarium* together under each heading. We know of no such work before the second century, but the manuals of that period were probably based on older works.

(b) Scarcely distinguishable from *institutiones* are the works called *regulae*, *definitiones* or *sententiae*, which also contain short statements of the law, intended however, partly at least, for practitioners as well as students. The arrangement is in some cases looser than that of *institutiones*.

(c) General works on the *ius civile*. Some of these were called *libri ad Sabinum* or *ex Sabino* because they were based on the *libri* III *iuris civilis* of Massurius Sabinus. Others go back further and base themselves on the eighteen books on the civil law by Q. Mucius, whose arrangement was different in some respects from that subsequently adopted by Sabinus. Among the civil law books can also be counted the commentaries on the XII Tables.

(d) Commentaries on the edict. These are treatises not only on the *ius honorarium*, but also on much of the *ius civile*, which is treated in connection with the paragraphs of the edict to which it is relevant. The edict was now the chief text for the lawyer, and the separate civil law works tended to become subsidiary to the commentaries.

[1] *Ancient Law*, 32.

(e) *Digesta*, i.e. treatises on the law as a whole. The matter dealt with in the commentaries on the edict comes first, and then follows the purely civil law. Criminal law (*de iudiciis publicis*) is also included.

(f) *Responsa, quaestiones*, etc. *Responsa* are collections of actual answers given in the course of the writer's practice, sometimes with the addition of those of other jurists. The method of presentation varies, some authors reproducing the answers very nearly as given, whereas others change the form so much that only the title of the work betrays its origin. As contrasted with *responsa*, *quaestiones* and *disputationes* contain cases which come in the main, not from actual practice, but from the author's discussions with his pupils. *Epistulae* include cases, some actually from practice, in which the jurist was asked his opinion by letter, often by a former pupil.

(g) Commentaries on individual *leges* or *senatus consulta* and other monographs of various sorts.

Our knowledge of these writings and of the jurists generally is mainly derived from the excerpts from their writings preserved in Justinian's Digest, where each excerpt is preceded by the name of the author and the work from which it is taken, together with the number of the volume in the case of works consisting of several volumes. These references (now called "inscriptions"), together with the references by one jurist to another, have enabled scholars to put together all the excerpts from each work and arrange them according to the number of the volume from which they are quoted.[1] It has thus been possible to obtain in many cases a good idea of the nature and arrangement of the original works. The bulk of the classical literature must have been very considerable. Justinian says that in the Digest the works excerpted have been reduced to one-twentieth of their original length.[2] The Digest in the most commonly used modern edition fills a volume of nearly 1000 large double-column pages, so that on this basis the original works would fill twenty such volumes. In fact, however, there must have been a great deal more. Justinian is referring only to the works used by his compilers and by his time much had perished or was known only in abridgment.[3]

---

[1] By far the most important work of this sort is Lenel's *Palingenesia Iuris Civilis* (Leipzig, 1889).

[2] *C. Tanta*, § 1.

[3] Lenel, 365. Justinian (*loc. cit.*) speaks of 2000 books (*libri*) containing 3,000,000 lines (*versus*), but Labeo is said to have left 400 books; Pomponius must have written some 300 and Paulus and Ulpian nearly as many each, so that all the authors together must have left many more than 2000. The *liber*, or roll of papyrus, in the case of prose works contained on an average between 1500 and

The dating of the individual works and of their authors has to be deduced very largely from internal evidence supplied by the fragments themselves, such e.g. as references to emperors,[1] to other jurists, or to enactments whose date we happen to know. Occasionally we find an autobiographical detail such as Ulpian's mention of his birthplace.[2] It is in the Digest too that there is preserved the fragment of Pomponius' *enchiridion* already frequently quoted. Some scraps of information are occasionally to be got from the rest of Justinian's compilations. Independently of Justinian but little has survived, for the obvious reason that the works became obsolete on the publication of the Digest and were not recopied.[3] Of the few survivals something will be said later. Apart from them and from Justinian there are occasional references in the historians and other writers, and a few inscriptions of importance.

§ II. THE TWO SCHOOLS

Before speaking of the individual jurists and their writings it is necessary to say something of the two "schools" into which they were divided in the earlier principate—the Proculians and the Sabinians. Famous as these schools are they present a problem which has never been satisfactorily solved. All we know of them for certain can be very briefly summarised. Pomponius says that Labeo and Capito (in the time of Augustus) "first created what may be called two sects", and that whereas Labeo was a very able man, learned in many branches of knowledge and an innovator in law, Capito held fast by traditional doctrines.[4] He then says that their respective successors, Nerva (the elder) and Massurius Sabinus, "increased the disagreements", and proceeds to enumerate the subsequent leaders on each side, so that we get the following lists:

Proculians	*Sabinians*
Labeo	Capito
Nerva (the elder)	Massurius Sabinus

2500 lines of some thirty-five letters each. Where a work extended over several books, an attempt was usually made to make the divisions of the subject-matter correspond with the physical division into *libri*, but this was not always found possible; *v.* Krüger, 150.

[1] Where an emperor is called *divus* he is certainly already dead. *Imperator noster* or *princeps noster* means the reigning emperor, who is also sometimes called *imperator* simply.

[2] *Infra*, 398.   [3] This is not strictly true in the West.

[4] D. 1. 2. 2. 47: *hi duo primum veluti diversas sectas fecerunt: nam Ateius Capito in his quae ei tradita fuerant perseverabat, Labeo, ingenii qualitate et fiducia doctrinae, qui et ceteris operis sapientiae operam dederat, plurima innovare instituit.*

Proculians	Sabinians
Proculus, Nerva (the younger), Longinus	Cassius
Pegasus	Caelius Sabinus
Celsus (the elder)	Iavolenus
Celsus (the younger), Neratius	Valens, Tuscianus, Iulianus

Pomponius also says that the schools initiated by Labeo and Capito were called *Proculiani* and *Cassiani* respectively.[1] In addition to the information from Pomponius we know (mainly through Gaius, who proclaims himself a Sabinian) of a number of individual questions on which the members of the two schools held opposing opinions. After Gaius we know of no jurist who belonged to either of the schools, so that it is assumed that they came to an end not much later. Outside legal literature the chief references of interest are a passage from Pliny[2] in which he refers to Cassius as *Cassianae scholae princeps ac parens*, and a rhetorical contrast in Tacitus between Labeo and Capito, in which Labeo appears as the incorruptible republican while Capito is subservient to the new imperial regime.[3]

That this political difference between the two founders was not perpetuated by their followers seems clear. There is no trace of it in the recorded controversies, and one of Capito's successors actually suffered exile under Nero for his supposed adherence to republican principles.[4] Nor is there any real evidence that the followers of Labeo were, like him, any freer from the bonds of tradition than were their rivals. It has been suggested that the difference was mainly a philosophical one, the Proculians being adherents of the Peripatetic (Aristotelian) system whereas the Sabinians were Stoics.[5] There is probably some truth in this, but it explains only a small part of the controversies, and if it had been the gist of the matter it would hardly have been left for modern ingenuity to find it out. It thus seems necessary to conclude that the difference between the two schools was personal rather than doctrinal, and that the recorded controversies were handed on by two different sets of teachers to their

---

[1] D. 1. 2. 2. 52.   [2] *Ep.* VII. 24.

[3] *Ann.* III. 75. For an equally studied but longer contrast *v.* Gibbon, *The Decline and Fall of the Roman Empire*, ed. Bury, IV. 459.

[4] Cassius; cf. *infra*, 389.

[5] The clearest case is that of *specificatio* (Gai. II. 79), where the Proculians give the ownership, in accordance with the Aristotelian doctrine of εἶδος (form), to the person who makes a thing up, whereas the Sabinians give it to the owner of the material, the Stoic οὐσία. Sokolowski, *Die Philosophie im Privatrecht*, I (1902), 69–111. But see Kunkel, *Z.S.S.* XLIX. 488.

pupils. Some sort of organisation is indicated by the way in which Pomponius speaks of one jurist as "succeeding"[1] another in each school, but what the nature of this organisation can have been remains obscure. That the schools cannot have been mere places of instruction in law seems clear. Such did indeed come into existence in the early empire with the growing demand for an education which would enable young men to enter upon a procuratorial career, and in the second century there were, according to Gellius, numerous *stationes ius publice docentium aut respondentium*[2] in Rome. But these were private establishments, no doubt organised, like the schools of rhetoric, by the teachers for profit, and it is quite impossible to suppose that most of the men who are mentioned as heads of the Sabinian and Proculian "schools", many of them of consular rank and constantly engaged in public affairs, could have had either the time or the inclination to teach in such establishments. That Sabinus, who never rose higher than equestrian rank, was supported by the fees of his students is mentioned by Pomponius as something exceptional. The least unsatisfactory conjecture[3] is perhaps that the famous "schools" were rather more in the nature of aristocratic clubs formed for the discussion of legal matters and centring round a distinguished jurist. The members would be the pupils of this jurist in the sense that they attended his consultations in the traditional way which had come down from republican times. It may be that subscriptions were paid, but hardly salaries.

Whatever form the organisation took, it is doubtful whether it went back as far as one would imagine from what Pomponius says. The schools are not called after Labeo and Capito, but after Proculus and Sabinus, and Proculus was not even Labeo's immediate successor. Sabinus did indeed succeed Capito, but the earlier name for the school appears to be *Cassiani*, and Cassius came after Sabinus. It seems as if later writers, knowing of some connection between Labeo, Nerva and Proculus on the one hand, and between Capito, Sabinus and Cassius on the other, pushed the origin of the schools back beyond the times of their real founders, Proculus and Cassius. In our own day an attempt has been made[4] to carry the two lines back further still and make the Sabinians appear as the

---

[1] Whereas in dealing with earlier jurists he says merely *post hos fuit* or *ab his profecti sunt.*   [2] XIII. 13.

[3] Ebrard, *Z.S.S.* XLV. 134 *sqq.*, but I cannot agree with the other views expressed there.

[4] By Carlo Arno in *Scuola muciana e scuola serviana* (1922) and other works; *v.* account by H. Krüger, *Z.S.S.* XLVI. 392–401 and (not mentioned there) *Nuovi studi su Cassio* (Modena, 1925).

successors of Servius Sulpicius and the Proculians as followers of Q. Mucius. The thesis cannot be said to have been proved, and in their origin as in their nature the schools still remain a mystery.

§ III. THE CHIEF INDIVIDUAL JURISTS

M. ANTISTIUS LABEO was the most prominent jurist of the early empire. His father, also a lawyer, committed suicide on hearing of the defeat of the republican party at Philippi (41 B.C.), and, as we have seen, the son remained staunch to the political opinions of his father. Occasionally this showed itself in a somewhat pedantic insistence, despite the changed circumstances, on the rules of the ancient republican constitution.[1] Labeo held the praetorship, but refused the consulate although it was offered him by Augustus.[2] He survived long enough to discuss the *l. Papia Poppaea* (A.D. 9) in his writings, but must have died before A.D. 22. In his youth he was a pupil of Trebatius, but "heard" many other jurists and was learned in other branches of knowledge as well as in jurisprudence. The originality of his mind, which Pomponius mentions, is shown not only by the quality of such fragments of his as survive but also by the innumerable quotations from him to be found in later writers. He is said to have divided his time so as to spend six months in the year at Rome with his students and six months in retirement writing his books. At his death he left 400 volumes.[3] In the Digest there are a number of direct excerpts from his work as well as a mass of indirect quotations. His writings included a work on pontifical law, a commentary on the XII Tables, commentaries on the urban and the peregrine edicts, *responsa* (at least fifteen books), *epistulae* and *pithana* (opinions on special points), which last were epitomised and commented on by Paulus. After his death appeared the *posteriores*, which were subsequently epitomised by Iavolenus.

C. ATEIUS CAPITO, though evidently considered by his contemporaries the rival of Labeo, did not have anything approaching equal influence on

---

[1] According to Gellius (XIII. 12) Capito said of him *agitabat hominem libertas nimia atque vecors*, and told a story that he had refused to appear before a tribune when summoned, on the ground that though tribunes had a right to take people into custody when present themselves (*prensio*) they had no right to send for them (*vocatio*).

[2] Pomponius, D. I. 2. 2. 47. Tacitus, *Ann.* III. 75, says that Augustus secured Capito the consulate before the usual time in order to raise him in rank above Labeo, but this does not necessarily conflict with Pomponius' statement.

[3] D. I. 2. 2. 47.

posterity. He was consul in A.D. 5 and died in 22. In politics, as we have seen, he was an adherent of the empire, and he is said to have been something of a time-server.[1] His works consisted, so far as is known, of *coniectanea* (miscellany), in at least eight books, at least seven books *de iure pontificio*, and one book *de officio senatorio*.

MASSURIUS SABINUS, from whom the Sabinian "school" derived its name, occupies a unique position in the history of the law. He did not belong to the aristocracy, but only rose to the rank of *eques* late in life. He held no public office and lived mainly on the fees of his students. Nevertheless he was given the *ius respondendi* by Tiberius.[2] He was still alive in the reign of Nero, for his opinion on the *sc. Neronianum* is quoted.[3] His chief work consisted of three books *iuris civilis*. Its comparatively small size seems to show that it was of a more general character than Q. Mucius' eighteen books on the same subject. The Digest contains no direct quotation but the scheme of arrangement has been made out from the books subsequently based on it.[4] Other works were *libri ad Vitellium*,[5] a commentary on the urban edict, *responsa*, *de furtis*, *adsessorium* (perhaps a book of cases which had come under his notice when he was acting as assessor to a magistrate), and perhaps a commentary on the *lex Iulia de iudiciis privatis*.[6]

M. COCCEIUS NERVA (the father), head of the Proculian school, was consul before A.D. 24 and subsequently *curator aquarum*. He was an intimate of Tiberius, but committed suicide, so Tacitus says, because the close insight which his position gave him into the evils of the time made him desire to quit life before he himself was corrupted.[7] We do not know the titles of any of his books, but he is frequently quoted by later writers. The Emperor Nerva was his grandson.

NERVA (the son) is little known. He wrote a work *de usucapionibus*. Ulpian refers to a story that he gave *responsa* at the age of seventeen.[8]

PROCULUS. Nothing is recorded of his life, except that he "succeeded" Nerva the elder as head of his school, and that he was very influential,[9] as we can well believe, seeing that the school bore his name. His *epistulae* are used in the Digest, and some writers quote his notes on Labeo.

C. CASSIUS LONGINUS, on the other hand, is well known. He came of a great family and was, on his mother's side, the great-grandson of

---

[1] *Supra*, 385.
[2] D. 1. 2. 2. 48, 50.
[3] Gai. II. 218.
[4] *V.* Krüger, 164–165.
[5] A jurist who probably lived during the Augustan age; Krüger, 159.
[6] Gell. XIV. 2. 1.
[7] *Ann.* VI. 26.
[8] D. 3. 1. 1. 3.
[9] D. 1. 2. 2. 52.

Servius Sulpicius. In addition to being head of the Sabinian school he held the urban praetorship[1] and the consulate (A.D. 30), and was governor of Asia (40–41) and of Syria (47–49). He was banished under Nero in 65 to Sardinia because he retained among the portraits of his ancestors one of the Cassius who had been concerned in the assassination of Julius Caesar.[2] He was recalled by Vespasian in whose reign he died. Mercifulness was not one of his virtues,[3] but his reputation for legal knowledge must have been unequalled. His chief work was one on the *ius civile*, which is known partly from quotations by other authors and partly from excerpts in the Digest from Iavolenus' *libri ex Cassio*. The arrangement differed in important particulars from that of Sabinus.[4] He also wrote *libri ad Vitellium*.

CN. ARULENUS CAELIUS SABINUS succeeded Cassius as head of the Sabinians. He was consul in 69 and Pomponius says that he was very influential under Vespasian.[5] He wrote a treatise on the aedilician edict[6] and probably other works.

PEGASUS succeeded Proculus and was *praefectus urbi* under Vespasian.[7] He is frequently quoted but no title of any of his works is known. He was so learned that he was said to be " a book, not a man ".[8] Whether he was connected with the two *scc.* passed *Pegaso et Pusione consulibus*[9] is unknown.

PLAUTIUS, who must have been about contemporary with Pegasus, wrote a work which was the basis of several later books. It dealt mainly with *ius honorarium*.

IAVOLENUS PRISCUS,[10] successor to Caelius Sabinus as head of the Sabinian school, was consul, commandant of several legions, and governor in turn of Britain, *Germania superior* (A.D. 90), Syria and Africa. Pliny, writing in 106 or 107, says that there were doubts about his mental health, but the incident which he relates seems to argue nothing worse than absence of mind, and may even have been intended as a joke. Pliny admits that he attended to business, was summoned to the imperial council and gave *responsa*.[11] In any case he was one of the most influential

---

[1] On his activity in this office *v. supra*, 362, n. 1.
[2] D. 1. 2. 2. 52; Tac. *Ann.* XVI. 9; Suet. *Nero*, 37.
[3] Tac. *Ann.* XIV. 43–44. [4] Krüger, 169. [5] D. 1. 2. 2. 53.
[6] Gell. IV. 2. 3; D. 21. 1. 14. 3. [7] D. 1. 2. 2. 53.
[8] Scholiast to Juvenal, IV. 77. [9] Gai. I. 31 and II. 254.
[10] His full name was C. (or L.) Octavius Tidius Tossianus Iavolenus Priscus (*C.I.L.* III. 2864).
[11] *Ep.* VI. 15. He attended a reading of poetry by Passienus Paullus and, when Paullus began with the words *Prisce iubes...*, he interjected *Ego vero non iubeo*. Perhaps he had been asleep and woke up with a start

of the jurists. There are excerpts in the Digest from his fourteen books of *epistulae*, fifteen books *ex Cassio*, five books *ex Plautio* and from two epitomes of Labeo's *posteriores*. He had the distinction of being Julian's teacher.[1]

TITIUS ARISTO, extolled both for learning and character by his friend Pliny in a letter written about A.D. 100,[2] was a member of Trajan's council, and acted both as consultant and advocate. Notes of his on Labeo's *posteriores*, Sabinus' *ad Vitellium* and perhaps Sabinus' *ius civile* are quoted, and Pomponius quotes his *decreta Frontiana*, a work of doubtful nature, in the Digest.[3]

P. IUVENTIUS CELSUS[4] succeeded his father (of whom little is known) as head of the Proculians. He was praetor in 106 or 107, twice consul (the second time in 129) and a member of Hadrian's council. His style is downright, but his reputation for rudeness seems to be based on rather meagre evidence.[5] His chief work was his *Digesta* in thirty-nine books, from which there are many excerpts in the Digest. He also wrote *epistulae*, *commentarii* and *quaestiones*.

SALVIUS IULIANUS, the last known head of the Sabinian school, has already been mentioned in connection with the revision of the edict. His home was in Hadrumetum (Africa) and his career as given in an inscription found at Tunis was one of great distinction.[6] Hadrian, whose quaestor he was, gave him double the usual salary on account of his learning, and he became subsequently tribune, praetor, prefect of the *aerarium Saturni* and the *aerarium militare*, consul (148), *pontifex*, governor of *Germania inferior* (under Pius), of *Hispania citerior* (under the *divi fratres*) and finally of Africa. He died probably in the reign of the *divi fratres*. As a lawyer he was a pupil of Iavolenus. His chief work, *Digesta* in ninety books, was written after the revision of the edict and probably entirely during the reign of Antoninus Pius.[7] It is much quoted

---

[1] D. 40. 2. 5.

[2] *Ep.* I. 22. He was also the recipient of a letter from Pliny in 108 or 109; *Ep.* VIII. 14.

[3] D. 29. 2. 99.

[4] His full name, P. Iuventius Celsus Titus Aufidius Oenus Severianus, is given in D. 5. 3. 20. 6.

[5] Pliny, *Ep.* VI. 5, recounts a dispute between him and a certain Nepos in the senate during which both used rather unparliamentary language, and an answer of his (D. 28. 1. 27) begins "Either I do not understand what you are asking me or your question is extremely stupid".

[6] *C.I.L.* VIII. 24094; Mommsen, *Z.S.S.* XXIII. 54 *sqq.*

[7] See however Kipp, 123, and literature there quoted.

by later writers and extensively used in the Digest. Other works were, *de ambiguitatibus liber sing.*, *ad Urseium Ferocem* (four books), and *ad Minicium*. A number of his decisions and opinions are also known through the *quaestiones* of Africanus.[1]

Julian and Celsus are the chief names in what may be called the earlier classical period which began with the reign of Hadrian. They were heads of rival schools and a certain personal rivalry may perhaps be deduced from the fact that they never quote each other in any of the fragments which have been preserved. Julian was probably the greater of the two, and some modern authorities would regard him as the greatest of all the Roman jurists, not excluding even Papinian.

NERATIUS PRISCUS is mentioned by Pomponius together with Celsus as head of the Proculian school.[2] He was consul and member of the council under Trajan and Hadrian, and is probably identical with the L. Neratius Priscus mentioned in an inscription as prefect of the *aerarium Saturni* and governor of *Pannonia*.[3] His *regulae* (fifteen books), *responsa* (three books) and *membranae*[4] (seven books) are used in the Digest and other works are known from quotations.

SEXTUS POMPONIUS is known only from his writings and from quotations by other jurists. So far as is known he held no office and, as no *responsa* of his are quoted,[5] it is supposed that he did not have the *ius respondendi*. He may have been a teacher and was certainly a most voluminous author. His *liber singularis enchiridii*, already frequently quoted, must have been written after 129,[6] but still during Hadrian's reign, and probably before Julian's revision of the edict, for otherwise it would be strange that he should say nothing about this reform. He wrote two great civil law works, thirty-five or thirty-six books *ex Sabino* (under Hadrian) and thirty-nine *ad Q. Mucium* (under Pius), a commentary on the praetorian and aedilician edicts, which probably ran into something like 150 books, and several other works. His object seems to have been to compile a complete survey of the work done up to his time in the sphere of private law, and he does not figure as a man of much creative power.[7]

---

[1] *Infra*, 392.
[2] D. 1. 2. 2. 53.
[3] *C.I.L.* IX. 2454/5.
[4] I.e. written on parchment.
[5] In his *epistulae* (e.g. D. 4. 4. 50) he sometimes answers questions by jurists, but these were probably his pupils; Krüger, 193.
[6] For he mentions Celsus' second consulate (D. 1. 2. 2. 53).
[7] He is sometimes said to have been a Sabinian, but the only evidence for this is that in D. 45. 3. 39 he is quoted as saying *Gaius noster*, which was supposed to refer to C. Cassius. The passage is however now generally held to be interpolated, and the compilers mean their own favourite Gaius.

SEXTUS CAECILIUS AFRICANUS was in all probability a pupil of Julian's.[1] His *quaestiones* (nine books) contain almost exclusively decisions of Julian (though Julian's name is only occasionally mentioned) with some critical observations. The excerpts in the Digest have the reputation of being particularly difficult to understand. Some of our evidence about the XII Tables comes from an account in Gellius of a discussion in which Africanus upheld their excellence.[2]

GAIUS. Of Gaius we know at the same time more and less than of any other classical jurist. His Institutes are the only classical work which has come down to us in anything like its original state, but we know nothing at all of his life, except the very little which can be deduced from his writings, and even his name is a mystery, for the one we know is merely a *praenomen*. He must have been born at latest in Hadrian's reign,[3] and appears to have been writing the Institutes in 161.[4] He lived at any rate until 178, for he wrote a commentary on the *sc. Orfitianum* of that year.[5] On his own showing he was an adherent of the Sabinian school. So far as we know, he held no public office, and he is not quoted by any contemporary or subsequent classical jurist. The absence of any *responsa* of his and the manner in which he is mentioned in the "Law of Citations" of 426[6] make it almost certain that he did not have the *ius respondendi*. He was presumably a teacher and his works evidently became very popular in the post-classical period, when by the "Law of Citations" they were placed on a level with those of the great writers of the Severan age. With Justinian's compilers he was a favourite author, presumably because of his clear style and excellent methods of presentation, and because his Institutes had been used as a text-book for first-year students for centuries.

It has been sought to explain the mystery of Gaius' name and personality by assuming that he was a provincial, living and teaching in one of the Greek-speaking provinces of the East, where local custom might account for the use of a single name.[7] In favour of this view it is urged that he

---

[1] D. 25. 3. 3. 4.　　　　　　　　　[2] Gell. xx. 1.

[3] D. 34. 5. 7 pr.: *nostra quidem aetate...mulier ad divum Hadrianum perducta est....*

[4] In the first book (§§ 53, 74, 102) and earlier part of the second book (§§ 120, 126, 151 A) Antoninus Pius (who died A.D. 161) is referred to as *imperator*, whereas in II. 195 he is *divus*. In II. 177–178 it is also noticeable that Gaius does not mention a constitution of M. Aurelius (Ulp. Reg. XXII. 34) which altered the law as there set out.　　　[5] D. 38. 17. 9.　　　[6] *Infra*, 468.

[7] Mommsen, *Ges. Schr.* II. 26 *sqq.* Followed by many, e.g. Bremer, *Rechtslehrer*, 77 *sqq.*; Kalb, *Roms Juristen*, 83; Kniep, *Der Rechtsgelehrte Gaius*, 9 *sqq.* Mommsen conjectures that the province was Asia, Kniep that it was Bithynia.

wrote on the provincial edict, that he occasionally mentions foreign legal systems[1] and that he was acquainted with the laws of Solon.[2] All the arguments however fall far short of proof, and against them must be set the facts that Gaius, in spite of some Graecisms of which any educated Roman might be guilty, wrote admittedly in excellent Latin, that he was quite certainly a Roman citizen[3] and that he could hardly have spoken as he did of the contrast between Roman and foreign law unless he had felt himself to be a Roman by origin also. It seems further unlikely that a provincial jurist should have been so definitely an adherent of one of the schools as Gaius obviously was, for there is no evidence whatever that their organisation extended beyond the capital. Another theory is that the works which we know under the name of Gaius were originally written by C. Cassius and re-edited by another jurist about the year 161.[4] Cassius is indeed occasionally referred to as "Gaius",[5] but the alternative name of his school was *Cassiani*, not *Gaiani*.[6] He is also referred to in the works of Gaius as "Cassius", which would be strange if he were their original author.[7] We must thus content ourselves with leaving the riddle still unsolved. Its solution, did we but know all the facts, would perhaps be found in some accident of manuscript tradition.

Besides the Institutes Gaius wrote *libri ex Q. Mucio*,[8] the commentary on the provincial edict already mentioned, in thirty books, together with two books on the aedilician edict,[9] a commentary on the urban edict, of which Justinian's compilers could only find ten books,[10] *de fideicommissis* (two books), *de tacitis fideicommissis l. sing.*, *de manumissionibus* (three books), *de verborum obligationibus* (three books), *libri singulares* on the law of dowries, the *sc. Tertullianum*, *sc. Orfitianum*, *ad legem Glitiam*, *de formula hypothecaria*, *de casibus*, fifteen books *ad legem Iuliam et Papiam*, a commentary on the XII Tables in six books (the last such commentary

[1] Inst. I. 55, 193; III. 134.
[2] D. 10. 1. 13; 47. 22. 4.
[3] He constantly speaks of the Romans as "we", e.g. I. 55, IV. 37.
[4] Kalb, *Jahresber. f. Altertumswiss.* LXXXIX. 231; CIX. 40.
[5] D. 24. 3. 59; 35. 1. 54. pr.; 46. 3. 78. Cf. Roby, *Introduction to the Study of Justinian's Digest*, CLXXV.
[6] *Supra*, 385.
[7] Kipp, 128, n. 23.
[8] Only known from Gaius' own reference, I. 188.
[9] In the Florentine Index (XX. 1) thirty-two books are mentioned, the last two being no doubt, as in other cases (*supra*, 363, n. 8), those on the aedilician edict, but if the provinces were in question one would have expected it to be called quaestorian.
[10] Florentine Index, XX. 3.

known), *regulae* in three books and in a *liber singularis*, and seven books of *res cottidianae*. Parts of this last work, also called *aurea*,[1] are used in Justinian's Institutes.

Gaius' Institutes (four books) occupy a place apart. An abridgment of them in two books is contained in the *lex Romana Visigothorum*;[2] there are a number of excerpts from them in the Digest, and they were known to have formed the basis of Justinian's Institutes, but it was not until 1816 that Niebuhr discovered a manuscript in the cathedral library at Verona which Savigny immediately recognised as containing the original work. The MS., which dates probably from the fifth century, is a palimpsest, some works of St Jerome having been written over the original text, and is particularly difficult to read on account of the numerous mistakes made by the copyists and the free use of abbreviations. The importance of its discovery for the history of Roman law can hardly be overestimated, for it is the only one giving the work of a classical jurist in its original form which we possess. Only about a fifth of it is missing,[3] and what is preserved contains a great deal, especially in relation to procedure, which later compilations, whether made in the East or in the West, omitted as no longer of practical value. It also enables us to follow in detail the famous threefold arrangement of the subject-matter of the law according as it concerns "persons", "things" or "actions". That Gaius invented this classification is unlikely. He himself makes no such claim but speaks as if it were already well known, and there are slight indications that the *regulae* of Neratius, who was older than Gaius, followed the same arrangement.[4] In fact it is probable that Gaius based his book very largely on some previous work. In one or two places it looks as if he did not understand the reasons for the order which is adopted,[5] and there are some peculiarities best explained in this way.[6]

---

[1] *Res cottidianae* is presumably the original title; it means "everyday" or "elementary" matters; an author could hardly call his own book "golden". Gaius when he mentions *commentarii* on *bonorum possessio* (III. 33) and succession to freedmen (III. 54) probably refers to the relevant books on the edict and the *lex Iulia et Papia* respectively (Krüger, 203).

[2] *Infra*, 481.

[3] Three pages are lost and some passages cannot be deciphered. Recently discovered papyrus fragments (*P. Oxy.* XVII. 2103) are discussed by de Zulueta, *L.Q.R.* XLIV. 198–208; E. Levy, *Z.S.S.* XLVIII. 532–555 and *St. Bonfante*, II. 277–287; Collinet, *R.H.* VII (1928), 92–97. Some help is provided by the "Autun Gaius"—fragments of a poor commentary dating probably from the fifth century.

[4] Buckland, 56–57.　　　　　[5] Krüger, 208, n. 51 and 209, n. 52.

[6] E.g. III. 91, where the receipt of an *indebitum* is still classified as a "real contract", but a criticism is added.

Kniep, in his great edition of Gaius,[1] has attempted to distinguish this original from the additions made by Gaius as well as from the post-Gaian additions (which undoubtedly exist) in the manuscript, but it can hardly be said that the attempt has succeeded in detail.[2]

A suggestion (which is perfectly compatible with the view that Gaius was basing himself on an earlier work) is that the book as we have it really consists of notes prepared for the purpose of a lecture.[3] That books have sometimes originated in this way is well known,[4] but the excellence of the style rather militates against this theory.[5]

Great originality cannot in any case be claimed for Gaius. He seems rather to have taken Pomponius as a model and attempted to sum up the results of other workers in the field of private law, but we can well believe that he was an excellent teacher, and the popularity of his works in later ages is not difficult to understand.

VENULEIUS SATURNINUS wrote de stipulationibus (nineteen books), de interdictis (six books) and several other works. Most of his writing at any rate was done after Hadrian's death. He is perhaps to be regarded as a Sabinian.[6]

L. VOLUSIUS MAECIANUS, probably a pupil of Julian, was a member of the council under Pius and the divi fratres, and perhaps prefect of Egypt under Pius.[7] He wrote quaestiones de fideicommissis (sixteen books), de iudiciis publicis (fourteen books), a book on the lex Rhodia in Greek,[8] and also a little book on the "parts of the as", i.e. as used in designating fractions of an inheritance,[9] and for other purposes. This last, which is hardly a law book, was written for M. Aurelius, who as a youth studied law under Maecianus. It has survived complete.

PAPIRIUS IUSTUS has already been mentioned as author of the first collection of imperial constitutions known to us.[10]

FLORENTINUS, who must have been alive after the death of Pius,[11] wrote Institutiones (twelve books), parts of which were used for Justinian's

[1] Jena, 1911–1917 (Gai. books I–III only).
[2] According to Arno (cf. supra, 386, n. 4) the work originated in the school of Servius, v. Z.S.S. XLVI. 395.
[3] Dernburg, Die Institutionen des Gaius, ein Kollegienheft aus dem Jahre 161 n. Chr. Geb. (1869).
[4] The most famous examples are some of Aristotle's works.
[5] Kipp, 129.
[6] D. 45. 1. 138. pr., where his emphatic sed ego cum Proculo sentio seems to show that agreement with Proculus was something unusual.
[7] References, Kipp, 132; Krüger, 200.
[8] V. the famous D. 14. 2. 9.
[9] Cf. J. 2. 14. 5.
[10] Supra, 378.
[11] D. 41. 1. 16, divus Pius.

Institutes. He anticipates the arrangement of modern books by putting the law of inheritance at the end.

ULPIUS MARCELLUS was a member of the council under Pius[1] and M. Aurelius.[2] His chief work was his *Digesta* in thirty-one books, which is freely quoted by subsequent writers, especially Ulpian, and much used in Justinian's Digest.

Q. CERVIDIUS SCAEVOLA was chief legal adviser to M. Aurelius.[3] His works included *Digesta* in forty books, twenty books of *quaestiones* and six of *responsa*. The cases with which he deals often came from the provinces and the facts are sometimes given in the original Greek. This does not however mean that he was himself a Greek; it only proves his widespread popularity as a consultant.[4] His answers are characterised by extreme brevity and by absence of reasons for the decision. Modestinus speaks of him together with Ulpian and Paulus as a leader among the jurists.[5]

AEMILIUS PAPINIANUS. This is the most famous name in the whole history of Roman jurisprudence. There are numerous references to Papinian's pre-eminent qualities,[6] and, under the "Law of Citations", his opinion tipped the balance if the authorities on either side were equal in number.[7] He is believed to have been a Syrian by birth,[8] was assessor to the *praefecti praetorio*, probably under M. Aurelius,[9] chief of the department *a libellis* under Septimius Severus, and then, probably from 203, himself *praefectus praetorio*,[10] in which capacity he accompanied the emperor to Britain (208). In 212 he was executed by the orders of Caracalla, because, so it is said, he refused to compose a justification of the murder by Caracalla of his brother and co-regent, Geta.[11]

His most important works were thirty-seven books of *quaestiones* (which might rather have been called *digesta*, for they contain little which

---

[1] *H.A. Pius* 12. 1.   [2] D. 28. 4. 3. pr.

[3] *H.A. Marc. Aur.* 11. 10.   [4] Krüger, 217.

[5] κορυφαῖοι τῶν νομικῶν, D. 27. 1. 13. 2.

[6] *C. Th.* 4. 4. 3. 3: *auctor prudentissimus iurisconsultorum*; *C. Omnem*, § 1: *sublimissimus*; *C. Deo auctore*, § 6: *summi ingenii*.

[7] *Infra*, 468.

[8] Because *H.A. Carac.* 8 says that he was a brother-in-law of Severus whose second wife, Julia Domna, came from Hemesa (Homs).

[9] D. 22. 1. 3. 3.

[10] In 205 at any rate he shared the position with Maecius Laetus; *C.I.L.* VI. 228.

[11] *H.A. Carac.* 8. The famous, though perhaps mythical, answer was "it is not so easy to justify murder as to commit it". Bury (*Note to Gibbon*, I. 135) says that the real cause of Papinian's death was probably his unpopularity with the soldiers, whose wishes Caracalla was always ready to humour.

is the outcome of "disputations") and nineteen books of *responsa*, which differ from the *responsa* of most jurists in that the form of question and answer is usually obliterated. They include *responsa* of earlier jurists as well as his own.

CLAUDIUS TRYPHONINUS wrote notes on Scaevola's *digesta* and twenty-one books of *disputationes*. He was one of Severus' councillors.[1]

CALLISTRATUS, a Greek, as is shown by his name and his awkward Latin, wrote, under Severus and Caracalla, six books *de cognitionibus*, the first work dealing specially with *cognitio extraordinaria*. He also wrote several other treatises.

TERTULLIANUS wrote *de castrensi peculio l. sing.* and *quaestiones* (eight books). The former is mentioned by Ulpian in the eighth book *ad Sabinum* which was written in the time of Caracalla.[2] Whether he is identical with the famous theologian of the same name is much disputed.[3]

IULIUS PAULUS was a pupil of Scaevola,[4] assessor to Papinian when *praefectus praetorio*,[5] head of the department *a memoria*,[6] member of the imperial council at the same time as Papinian,[7] and himself *praefectus praetorio* under Alexander Severus, probably at the same time as Ulpian.[8] His works, which were extremely voluminous, included a commentary on the edict in eighty books (the last two on the aedilician edict), *ad Sabinum* (sixteen books), *responsa* (twenty-three books), *quaestiones* (twenty-six books), commentaries on a number of *leges* and *senatus consulta*, works on the duties of various officials (e.g. *de officio praefecti urbi*), works based on earlier writings,[9] notes on Julian, Scaevola and Papinian, two collections of *decreta*,[10] and some elementary works—two books of *institutiones*, seven books of *regulae* and *regularum liber singularis*. The five books of *sententiae* which were current under Paulus' name are now generally held to have been a collection of passages from different works by him compiled in post-classical times.[11] Opinions as to the value of his writings are very various. Jhering regarded him as a doctrinaire, capable of

---

[1] D. 49. 14. 50.
[2] D. 29. 2. 30. 6.
[3] The chief argument in favour is the statement by Eusebius (*Hist. Eccl.* II. 2. 4) that the theologian was "a man intimately acquainted with the laws of the Romans". For literature *v.* Kübler, 279. For identification also Beck, *Römisches Recht bei Tertullian u. Cyprian* (1930), 39–43.
[4] So it seems from D. 40. 12. 23. pr. and 28. 2. 19.
[5] D. 12. 1. 40.
[6] *H.A. Pescenn.* 7. 4.
[7] D. 29. 2. 97.
[8] *H.A. Pescenn.* 7. 4. See Krüger, 228, n. 8.
[9] Cf. *supra*, 387.
[10] *Supra*, 378.
[11] *Infra*, 472.

denying the facts of life if they conflicted with his theories,[1] while other writers speak of him in the highest terms.[2] In any case his reputation in later times and his influence were immense. About one-sixth of the Digest is taken from his works; the *sententiae* enjoyed particular popularity, and their inclusion in the *l. Romana Visigothorum* meant that they became one of the chief sources from which the nations of the West drew their knowledge of Roman law.

DOMITIUS ULPIANUS was born at Tyre.[3] At some time he served on the *consilium* of a praetor,[4] and he was, together with Paulus, assessor to Papinian when *praefectus praetorio*.[5] He is said to have held the office *a libellis*,[6] but when is not clear. One report says that Heliogabalus banished him in 222,[7] but if this is right he must have been recalled immediately after the accession of Alexander Severus, for in a constitution dated March 31st, 222, he is mentioned as *praefectus annonae*[8] and in one dated Dec. 1st of the same year as *praefectus praetorio*.[9] He was the young emperor's chief legal adviser and continued to hold the prefecture until 228, when he was murdered by the mutinous guards. His literary work belongs almost entirely to the reign of Caracalla, probably because in his later years he was too much occupied in public business to be able to write. Its volume was nevertheless very great, almost equal to that of Paulus. The chief works were eighty-three books on the edict (the last two on that of the aediles) and *ad Sabinum* (fifty-one books), which was probably unfinished. Among the others were *de appellationibus* (four books), *disputationes* (ten books), *de fideicommissis* (six books), *de omnibus tribunalibus* (ten books), *responsa* (two books), works on special offices (e.g. *de officio praetoris tutelaris l. sing.*), and, for beginners, *institutiones* (two books) and *regulae* (seven books).[10] In his works generally it seems that Ulpian intended to cover the whole field of law and to make direct references to previous authorities unnecessary.[11] His own citations are innumerable, and he is commonly regarded as lacking in originality, but, given his purpose, the charge seems to do less than justice to one whom

---

[1] *Besitzwille*, 281 sqq.

[2] E.g. Seckel, quoted Berger, *Teilungsklagen*, 45, n. 2.

[3] D. 50. 15. 1. pr., though this perhaps means only that his family came from there; Karlowa, I. 740.

[4] D. 4. 2. 9. 3.   [5] *H.A. Pescenn.* 7. 4.

[6] *Ibid.*   [7] *H.A. Heliogab.* 16. 4.

[8] C. 8. 37. 4.   [9] C. 4. 65. 4.

[10] The *l. sing. regularum* is probably not authentic, *infra*, 472. Nor are the six books of *opiniones*, *infra*, 473.

[11] Krüger, 250.

Modestinus classes with Scaevola and Papinian among the *coryphaei*,[1] and who appears among the primary authorities in the "Law of Citations". In any case the completeness and clarity of Ulpian's work caused the compilers of Justinian's Digest to use him more than any other writer, for about one-third of the whole work consists of excerpts from his writings.

AELIUS MARCIANUS was a younger contemporary of Paulus and Ulpian. His chief works were sixteen books of *institutiones* and five of *regulae*.[2]

HERENNIUS MODESTINUS was a pupil of Ulpian,[3] and held a *praefectura vigilum* between the years 226 and 244.[4] In a constitution of 239 he is mentioned as having given a *responsum*.[5] He wrote, among other works, *differentiae* in nine books, *regulae* (ten books), *pandectae* (twelve books), *responsa* (nineteen books) and *de excusationibus* (six books). This last was in Greek, from which fact it is sometimes assumed that Greek was his native language. More probably it was intended to introduce this part of family law[6] to those who had recently become citizens through Caracalla's enactment. Modestinus is one of the primary authorities in the "Law of Citations", but owes this great distinction to the fact that he is the latest of the truly classical jurists rather than to his intrinsic merits.[7]

---

[1] D. 27. 1. 13. 2; cf. *supra*, 396, n. 5.

[2] On Marcian *v.* Buckland, *Studi Riccobono*, I. 275–283 (1932).

[3] D. 47. 2. 52. 20.

[4] *Lis fullonum*, Bruns, I. 406, where he appears as one of the prefects who gave judgment in the course of some protracted litigation.

[5] C. 3. 42. 5.

[6] I.e. valid grounds for refusing guardianships.

[7] The latest jurists whose works are used in the Digest are Hermogenianus and Arcadius Charisius. Both are usually assigned to the fourth century on the ground that they know the rule that no appeal lies from the decision of the praetorian prefect which was enacted by Constantine in 331 (C. 7. 62. 19); *v.* Kübler, 375–376. Krüger, however, 254–255, would assign both to the third century.

Chapter XXIII

JURISDICTION AND PROCEDURE
IN THE PRINCIPATE

§ I. GENERAL

The history of the Courts and of judicial procedure during the principate is closely parallel to that of the government as a whole. Republican institutions were not abolished, but new imperial institutions grew up by their side, with the result that they became atrophied and finally perished. This process however was not complete until the principate had given way to the dominate, and here, as in other departments of public life, it was the provinces that took the lead, while Rome herself retained the relics of republicanism longer than any other part of the empire.

The chief new factor is the all-pervading power of the emperor. This must be taken as a fact in the judicial sphere as elsewhere, though it is difficult to find any definite constitutional foundation for his jurisdiction as it was actually exercised. He had *imperium* and therefore *iurisdictio*, but from the first he occupied a position which was quite different from that of any other magistrate. He might assume jurisdiction in the first instance in any matter, civil or criminal, arising anywhere within the empire, either of his own motion or, more usually, in accordance with the prayer of a party. He might hear appeals, and, as we have seen, he might, without hearing the whole case, decide questions of law by rescript. Though some of the emperors managed to transact a surprising amount of judicial business in person, it was of course necessary to restrict appeals within narrow limits and to lighten the burden further by delegation. A delegate might be appointed specially for a particular case, and this indeed seems to have been not uncommon, but there were also standing rules concerning the delegation of certain classes of cases. Augustus, for instance, already directed that appeals from Rome should go before the urban praetor, those from the provinces to a man of consular rank appointed for each. The jurisdiction exercised by the great prefects, mainly criminal at first, but civil as well in the later principate, is also, from the constitutional point of view, based solely upon delegation by the emperor of his own powers, and this kind of jurisdiction was destined, under the dominate, to become the most important of all. A rather different type of delegation consisted in entrusting to republican magistrates, consuls and praetors, special functions in connection with matters which had never given rise to trials of the ordinary sort. Thus Augustus ordered the consuls to see that certain *fideicommissa* were carried out, and this subsequently became a standing instruction applicable to all *fideicommissa*.[1] Trusts of this nature, hitherto unrecognised by the law, consequently became binding though it was never possible to bring an action under the "ordinary" procedure for their enforcement.[2] Claudius added two special praetors to relieve the consuls in this work, but one was subsequently removed by Titus.[3] Somewhat similar was the treatment of guardianship matters. The appointment of tutors at Rome lay, under earlier legislation, with the urban praetor and the tribunes,[4] but Claudius added appointment and supervision of guardians to the functions of the consuls[5] and M. Aurelius appointed a special praetor.[6] Normally these functions would not involve litigation *inter partes*, but the matter might assume the complexion of a lawsuit where a person who was appointed sought to shift the burden on to someone else whom he alleged to be better qualified (*potioris nominatio*).[7] In addition the consuls dealt with claims for *alimenta*, which were an innovation of the empire and only recoverable by *cognitio extraordinaria*,[8] and questions of status, though here the ordinary procedure was also available.[9] A praetor *de liberalibus causis* also existed, though references to him in the sources are rare.[10] Claims for payment by people who had rendered "liberal" services were also dealt with by a praetor.[11]

[1] J. 2. 23. 1.   [2] Gai. II. 278.
[3] D. 1. 2. 2. 32.   [4] *Supra*, 245.
[5] Suet. *Claud.* 23.
[6] *H.A. Marc. Aur.* 10, 11; cf. *infra*, 410.
[7] Fr. Vat. 161 *sqq.* So also there may be a dispute between a proposed tutor and the person who proposed him; *ibid.* 156.
[8] D. 34. 1. 3 *sub fin.*; cf. Jörs, *Untersuchungen zur Gerichtsverfassung der r. Kaiserzeit* (*Festgabe für Jhering*, Leipzig, 1892), 25 *sqq.* This right of children and parents to claim support from each other in case of indigence is not known to have existed before Pius, who issued constitutions concerning it; D. 25. 3. 5. 5, 7; Girard, 676.
[9] Jörs, *op. cit.* 11 *sqq.*   [10] Jörs, *op. cit.* 43 *sqq.*
[11] The services of e.g. advocates, doctors and teachers could not be the object of *locatio*, and hence no action could be brought in the ordinary way for the recovery of remuneration. Most of the relevant texts speak of *cognitio* by a provincial governor. Only one (D. 50. 13. 1. 14) mentions a praetor. This may mean that, at Rome, there was a special praetor appointed for these matters, or that either the urban or the peregrine praetor dealt with them. It is also suggested that the reference was originally to the tribunes, who may have had some connection with teachers' claims for salaries; cf. *supra*, 338, n. 1.

In all these cases, though the magistrates in question bore names belonging to the republican hierarchy, the functions which they exercised were such as they had not had during the republic, and the real basis of their authority was the imperial command.

In these "extraordinary" matters consequently there is a concurrence of the emperor's judicial and legislative powers, which illustrates at once the extent and the indefinite nature of his authority.

§ II. INNOVATIONS IN CIVIL PROCEDURE

A. *Cognitio extraordinaria*.   The chief innovation consists in the introduction, side by side with the old procedure, of a new system, commonly known as *cognitio extraordinaria*.

Jurisdiction in the Roman scheme of government was never completely separated from administration; *iurisdictio* in the technical sense was itself a derivative from *imperium*, and sometimes even the urban praetor used directly his powers of command for the settlement of what were in fact legal disputes. *Cognitio extraordinaria* is, in its origin, an extension of this method. Though the praetors at Rome continue to use and even to develop the older system, the emperor and his delegates are, from the first, free from its trammels, need wait for no agreement between the parties and need not suffer the old division of the trial into two stages. It is common to speak of *cognitio* as a type of administrative procedure, and this description expresses a considerable part of the truth, for the official uses his powers of investigation and compulsion to decide a suit between private parties as he does in the case of one which arises in the course of his administrative duties. But the process is a judicial one to which many of the rules of the older procedure apply. Judgment must still be delivered in accordance with the law,[1] and the new system of appeal serves to secure uniformity in the judgments of the various courts. The emperor himself, it is true, can travel outside the existing law if he so pleases, but he too is primarily concerned to administer the law as it is.[2] The new procedure does however imply a different attitude on the part of the state towards the process of litigation. Justice, instead of proceeding from a voluntary contract, is imposed from above, and the official no longer merely supervises a submission to arbitration, but sees that the rules laid down by public authority are enforced. This attitude is, of course, that to which we are accustomed in modern European states, and we shall see that it produced two institutions with which we are familiar,

---

[1] Cf. Buckland, 662.   [2] Cf. *supra*, 373.

but which were unknown to the earlier system—appeal and judgment by default.

The Latin word for investigating a case is *cognoscere*,[1] and it is usual to refer to the newer procedure as *cognitio extraordinaria*. This phrase, which has some support in the sources, may be retained for the sake of convenience, but it must be understood that it is purely negative,[2] and is used in contradistinction to the *ordo iudiciorum privatorum*,[3] or system requiring agreement of the parties. It itself assumed different forms at different periods and in different parts of the empire, and, of course, when the old system disappeared, became itself "ordinary". This, however, was not until the principate was over; the normal civil procedure at Rome throughout the classical period was that which used the *formula*, and it is with reference to this procedure that most of the classical literature was written.

B. DIFFERENT FORMS OF *cognitio*. The use of *cognitio* does not necessarily imply that the official whose authority is invoked tries the whole matter himself. Not only the emperor but some of his delegates (other than those appointed for a particular case) can delegate their powers, and in such cases it may still be convenient to use a *formula* in order to define the issue which the delegate is to try. When this happens the procedure does not, externally, look very different from that of the *ordo*. But there remains the fundamental difference that the judge is appointed by the official and not by agreement between the parties, even though the official may take their wishes, if they have any, into account in making the appointment. There are thus three possibilities: (i) hearing of the whole case by the official to whom it comes in the first instance, (ii) the delegation of the whole case by the official to another person (*iudex pedaneus*) who hears it in the same way, (iii) what may be called the "divided *cognitio* procedure", in which there are two stages, *editio* of a *formula* and even *litis contestatio*, as in the "ordinary" procedure, but the *iudex* derives his powers from the official and not from the parties. Until recently the existence of this third possibility was not recognised, but it is now very generally held that it must have formed a stage in the development, for it is only thus that we can explain why, though the *ordo*

---

[1] The verb *cognoscere* is used sometimes of the *iudex*, e.g. D. 28. 5. 35, but where *iudex* is used with the noun *cognitio* it is always, or nearly always, interpolated for *consul*; v. Heumann-Seckel, s.v. *cognitio*.

[2] Wenger, 26, n. 20.

[3] This expression is not found in the sources, but is also convenient; Wenger, 27, n. 21.

had certainly disappeared by Diocletian's time, the sons of Constantine in 342 still found it necessary to issue a constitution abolishing *formulae*.[1] In all probability the development began in the provinces where, from the first, the position was different from that which existed at Rome. In the governor's hands were concentrated powers which at Rome were divided among several magistrates, and whereas at Rome the praetor was bound by law to the forms of the *ordo*, there was nothing but tradition to bind the governor. He might, and in imperial as well as in senatorial provinces did, use the *ordo*,[2] but any difficulties would be got over by his supreme powers. In particular the difficulty of finding suitable *iudices* agreed on by the parties might be overcome by his appointing one of his own subordinates. But this does not mean that the whole of the old procedure had to go by the board. As much of it as was useful could be retained, if only because it was impossible to invent something new to take its place immediately. When and how this "divided *cognitio* procedure" came to Rome is unknown, but it may well be, as Wlassak conjectures, that it first appeared in the courts of the *iuridici* in Italy and was then brought to the capital.[3] This however can, in any case, only have happened right at the end of the classical period.

C. CHANGES IN THE METHOD OF SUMMONS. PROCEDURE BY DEFAULT. In the *ordo* it was, as we have seen, the business of the plaintiff to get the defendant before the magistrate;[4] in *cognitio*, on the other hand, the state official began to take a part, not only in the trial, but in the summons. It appears that there were three principal forms— *litterae, edictum* and *denuntiatio*.[5] *Litterae* were used if the defendant lived at a distance from the place where the tribunal sat.[6] The plaintiff had to obtain a letter of authorisation from the tribunal, which he then took to the local magistrates, who summoned the defendant and returned the letter to him with a note thereon that this had been done.[7] *Edictum*,

---

[1] C. 2. 57. 1 (*infra*, 454, n. 1). On the whole question see especially Wlassak, *Zum r. Provinzialprozess* (1919); Wenger, 252 *sqq.* For a summary of the former see de Zulueta, *Literature on Roman Law*, 1918–1920 (The Year's Work in Classical Studies, 1920).

[2] Wlassak, *op. cit.* 8 *sqq.* But there is no trace of the Roman formulary procedure in the Egyptian papyri (*ibid.* 4), and it was probably not used in districts governed by procurators (*ibid.* 6).

[3] Wlassak, *op. cit.* 59–82; *Iuridici, infra*, 412.   [4] *Supra*, 179 and 202.

[5] The three are mentioned together; Paul. *Sent.* v. 5 A. 6 (7); D. 40. 5. 26. 9.

[6] Kipp, *Litisdenuntiation* (1887), 126.

[7] Fr. Vat. 162–163. For an instance of the process *v. P. Giess.* 1. 34 (Mitteis, *Chrest.* No. 75).

i.e. a written notice put up in public, was no doubt only used when the defendant could not be found.[1] *Denuntiatio*, which would seem to have been the normal method when the defendant resided within the jurisdiction of the court in which proceedings were begun, presents more difficulty. That it consisted in a notice to the defendant is clear, but what part the plaintiff himself played is uncertain. Some authorities have seen in it a private summons issuing from the plaintiff,[2] but the better opinion to-day seems to be that it always issued from an official, though, of course, at the request of the plaintiff. It might be served on the defendant by official subordinates,[3] but it might also happen that the plaintiff served the notice himself, after getting official authorisation, and this would appear to have been the practice at Rome.[4]

If this view is correct, then all three types of summons were simply different forms assumed by the magisterial *evocatio*, or right which the higher magistrates had always had of ordering a private individual to appear before them.[5] The development consists in the use of this right at the instance of another private individual as a method of beginning a private action.

This view also makes it clear why *denuntiatio* as well as the other forms of summons, if not obeyed, might lead to judgment by default. This was an impossibility under the procedure of the *ordo* because no trial could take place without the agreement of the defendant. But disobedience to *evocatio* is an offence, and one effective way of dealing with this particular offence (*contumacia*) is to proceed to try the case without the defendant. Three summonses, with stated intervals, were normally necessary before this could be done, but in special circumstances one " peremptory " edict might be sufficient.[6] The defendant's absence did not necessarily have the result that judgment went against him. The judge had still to go into the

---

[1] Kipp, *op. cit.* 124. But judgment by default seems to have been possible only if it could be shown that the defendant had knowledge of the edict; Steinwenter, *Studien zum r. Versäumnisverfahren* (1914), 40.

[2] E.g. Costa, *Profilo storico*, 151; Steinwenter, *op. cit.* 20 sqq., thinks there was both a private and an official form. For the view that it was always official see especially Wlassak, *op. cit.* 38, n. 7. Boyé, *La denuntiatio introductive d'instance* (Bordeaux, 1922), distinguishes official and semi-official types, but agrees that all are derived from magisterial *evocatio*. He rejects Wlassak's " divided *cognitio* procedure " (280 sqq.), but thinks that *denuntiatio* came also to be used to initiate proceedings under the *ordo* (316 sqq.).

[3] This is clearly the case with the παραγγελίαι in Mitteis, *Chrest.* Nos. 50–56.

[4] *Infra*, 455.

[5] Gell. XIII. 12; cf. *supra*, 387, n. 1.

[6] Paul. *Sent.* V. 5 A. 6 (7).

case, and might find against the plaintiff,[1] but naturally this would not often happen.

D. APPEAL. In the republic appeal, as we understand it, had not existed. A judgment might be called in question by defending the *actio iudicati*,[2] and the veto of a colleague or a tribune might be invoked to quash the decree of the magistrate made in the initial stages of an action or as a preliminary to execution.[3] But the judgment of a *iudex* was not a magisterial act and so not subject to *intercessio*. This rule probably continued to exist during the empire,[4] but for *cognitio extraordinaria* appeal soon became a regular institution, and the higher court not only quashed the decision of the lower, but substituted its own. It was a general rule that appeal lay from a delegate to the magistrate who had appointed him,[5] but there might be further appeals, ending finally with one to the emperor. He, as we have seen, frequently delegated the hearing of appeals by a standing order to other officers, but this did not, during the principate, necessarily prevent further appeal to the emperor himself. Thus Paulus recounts a case in which *in integrum restitutio* was refused by the praetor and by the *praefectus urbi*, but finally granted by the emperor.[6] In the dominate however judgments of the praetorian prefect were declared unappealable.[7] Notice of appeal had to be given to the court whose judgment was to be called in question, and might be given at once, orally, or within a very few days in writing.[8] In the case of appeals to the emperor the amount at issue had to be above a certain minimum,[9] and an unsuccessful appellant suffered pecuniarily.[10] No appeal from a judgment given by default was allowed.[11]

Relatio and rescript procedure[12] differ from appeal, but they both serve to show the emperor as supreme judicial authority throughout his dominions and to keep the administration of justice consistent.

[1] C. 7. 43. 1.

[2] Not, of course, on its merits; cf. *supra*, 220. There was also a rather obscure proceeding known as *revocatio in duplum*; Buckland, 642.

[3] Cicero (*in Verr.* II. 1. 46. 119) says that during Verres' tenure of the urban praetorship a crowd gathered round the seat of his colleague L. Piso to ask him to intercede against Verres' acts.

[4] This is much disputed. Perrot, *L'appel dans la procédure de l'ordo iudiciorum* (1907), thinks that appeal was possible during the empire and that it was based on an extension of the *tribunicia potestas* in 30 B.C. But see Wenger, Z.S.S. xxx. 479–482.

[5] D. 49. 3. 3; 49. 1. 21. 1.   [6] D. 4. 4. 38. Possibly an exceptional case.

[7] D. 4. 4. 17; 1. 11. 1. 1.   [8] D. 49. 1. 5. 4.

[9] D. 49. 1. 10. 1.   [10] Tac. *Ann.* XIV. 28.

[11] D. 49. 1. 23. 3.   [12] *Supra*, 375–376.

E. EXECUTION. Execution, like summons, becomes a matter in which the magistrate can use his powers of command and coercion. Judgment is not, as under the *ordo*, necessarily for money, and in some matters dealt with by *cognitio extraordinaria* the magistrate may actually carry out his decision by direct constraint.[1] When the judgment is for money, however, execution is still begun by *actio iudicati*, but this action too may be brought under the new procedure.[2]

Imprisonment for debt continued possible, but a more sensible method of execution against the goods came into existence during the second century.[3] The judgment creditor need not be put into possession of the whole of the debtor's property. Instead, court officials might be authorised to seize a sufficient part of the property and, after a delay of two months, sell it for the benefit of his creditor.[4] Here again the state does what under the older system was the business of the plaintiff.

§ III. CRIMINAL JURISDICTION

The last century of the republic had provided the *quaestiones perpetuae* for the trial of serious offences committed by Roman citizens, and these tribunals continued to exist during the first two centuries of the Christian era. Augustus himself regulated their procedure by one of his *leges iudiciariae*, and added to their number by creating a *quaestio de adulteriis* for the sexual offences which he first made punishable. He also introduced, in some provinces at least, an analogous method of trial by jury courts,[5] but these did not have any jurisdiction over Roman citizens.[6] In spite of these innovations, however, the system remained incapable of providing adequately for the needs of the empire. It was clumsy in that the constitution of the tribunal differed according to the offence, and incomplete in that a number of offences which a civilised state must take

---

[1] E.g. when he forces an heir to enter upon an inheritance which is over-burdened with *fideicommissa*, under the provisions of the *sc. Pegasianum*; Gai. II. 258; Paul. *Sent.* IV. 4. 2, 4; D. 36. 1. 4. In the case of a *fideicommissum* of liberty the person under the duty might be forced to manumit (D. 40. 5. 26. 6); if he failed to appear and judgment went against him the slaves became free without any manumission by him (*ibid.* 7).

[2] D. 5. 1. 75.

[3] The earliest known mention occurs in a rescript of Pius, quoted D. 42. 1. 31.

[4] Movables were to be taken first, then land and then, if necessary, incorporeal assets; D. 42. 1. 15. 2.

[5] See No. 1 of the edicts of Augustus recently discovered at Cyrene; Premerstein, *Z.S.S.* XLVIII. 419–531, especially 442 *sqq.*

[6] *Ibid.* 444.

upon itself to punish were not covered at all. Theft, damage to property and fraud would, for instance, normally give rise only to a civil action. Only in particular cases, as, for instance, if combined with violence, would they come within the ambit of a *quaestio* at all. The severest punishment which could be inflicted was in many cases too light, and the extension of Roman citizenship gradually made it impracticable to send all citizens accused of serious crime to Rome for trial. It was thus necessary to supplement the work of the *quaestiones* by that of other tribunals which dealt *extra ordinem* both with offences which were covered by them and with those which were not. One of these tribunals was the senate, which in its judicial as in its legislative capacity became the heir of the *comitia*.[1] It dealt however mainly with cases of political interest and those in which senators were concerned,[2] so that its influence on the development of the criminal law was not of any very great consequence. Of much greater importance were the courts of the emperor and his delegates, in particular the prefects and the provincial governors, for, so far as criminal jurisdiction over citizens was concerned, the powers not only of the former, but also of the latter, even in senatorial provinces, rested on imperial delegation. The governors' *imperium* did not include the right to try citizens on a capital charge, but such right, under the name of *ius gladii*, was given more and more frequently to individual governors, and in the third century was possessed by all who held senatorial rank.[3] Sometimes it was limited in such a way that, though the governor might try the case, sentence must not be executed without imperial sanction, and towards the end of the principate it appears to have been the rule that *honestiores* should have right of appeal to Rome, while *humiliores* were subject to the unrestricted power of the governor.[4] Appeal to Rome now meant appeal to the emperor.[5]

From the first punishments were made more severe. Even now, indeed, the death penalty was very seldom actually inflicted as the result of the verdict of a *quaestio*,[6] but *aqua et igni interdictio* was from the time of Tiberius accompanied by loss of citizenship,[7] and generally its place was taken by *deportatio*,[8] which meant not only that the convicted person

---

[1] Mommsen, *Strafrecht*, 251; Costa, *Crimini e Pene*, 82.
[2] It was a principle, several times confirmed but not always respected, that criminal jurisdiction of senators in serious matters should be exercised only by their peers; Mommsen, *op. cit.* 286.
[3] Mommsen, *op. cit.* 244.   [4] Mommsen, *op. cit.* 245.
[5] Paul. *Sent.* v. 26. 1; cf. *Acts* xxv. 11.
[6] Though this was not impossible; Mommsen, *op. cit.* 220.
[7] Dio, 57. 22; Mommsen, *op. cit.* 957.   [8] D. 48. 13. 3.

became a *peregrinus*, but that he was confined to an island or an oasis, and lost the whole of his property except such amount as might be left to him as an act of grace.[1] This however was a punishment fitted only for the higher classes; the lower in the case of similar offences were usually condemned for life to work in the mines or to less severe forced labour, whereby they lost not only citizenship, but freedom.[2] The death penalty was reintroduced in the new courts, and history furnishes sufficient examples of its infliction by the senate in political cases. In ordinary cases it was inflicted on the lower classes, but during the first two centuries it was exceptional in the case of Roman citizens of the higher social ranks. Not until about the time of Severus does it appear to have become regular even for murder and *maiestas*.[3]

In the new courts, though the magistrate could, and frequently did, deal with crime inquisitorially, i.e. by investigating on his own initiative and by any means at his disposal, the accusatory form of procedure which had been introduced for the *quaestiones* did not cease to exist. On the contrary, it remained normal throughout, and accusers were encouraged by rewards, as they were also subject to penalties for vexatious prosecution or collusion with the accused.

It will be seen that the criminal system as a whole was one in which the highest authorities in the state, the emperor and the senate, took it upon themselves to supplement the deficiencies of law and procedure, not by the enactment of new law, but by direct intervention in the interests of order. The judicial and legislative powers were insufficiently separated, and the "rule of law", towards which the *quaestiones* had been a step forward, was never established. The substantive rules created by the statutes which set up the *quaestiones* were indeed applied also when the same crimes had to be tried *extra ordinem*,[4] and some quasi-legislative help was provided by imperial *decreta* and occasional *senatus consulta*, but it was never enough to exclude arbitrariness.[5] The criminal system thus never passed through a stage of strict law, the stage in which exact differentiation and definition is necessary, and, though the jurists succeeded in elaborating some principles of value, its example was of much less consequence in subsequent history than that of the civil law.

[1] Mommsen, *op. cit.* 1010. The milder form of banishment, *relegatio*, did not affect citizenship or property.

[2] Shorter sentences, which did not imply loss of liberty, were not *opus publicum* in the technical sense; Mommsen, *op. cit.* 949.

[3] Mommsen, *op. cit.* 943. Contrast Gai. I. 128 with Paul. *Sent.* v. 23. 1.

[4] D. 48. 1. 8.

[5] D. 48. 19. 13.

§ IV. THE JUDICIAL STRUCTURE AS A WHOLE

It will be seen from what has been said that the judicial structure in the principate was complex, and that it was constantly developing. Details are by no means all known to us, but it is possible to obtain a general picture if we consider separately Rome, Italy and the Provinces. It must however be remembered that, in theory, the jurisdiction of the Roman praetor extends over citizens wherever they may be,[1] and that the emperor can intervene himself, or through a delegate, in any matter throughout his dominions. In this work he has the assistance of a *consilium*, which, as we have seen, assumed a more definite shape under Hadrian,[2] and his chief assistant is the *praefectus praetorio*. Towards the end of the principate this officer came to be regarded as having an independent jurisdiction, although of course by delegation from the emperor, and his became the highest court, if the emperor did not intervene personally, for matters arising more than 100 miles from Rome.[3]

A. ROME. For the purposes of civil jurisdiction, "ordinary" and "extraordinary" matters must first be distinguished. The former are normally dealt with throughout the principate by the "ordinary" procedure, divided into its two stages, the latter, without any such division, before special courts, in accordance with imperial instructions. "Extraordinary" matters include the appointment and supervision of guardians, claims for *fideicommissa*, for *alimenta*, for *honoraria* in return for liberal services, all of which, except the first, were innovations of the empire. Litigation involving status was also commonly dealt with *extra ordinem*. How the consuls and praetors who were charged with these matters divided the work is not fully known. In the case of *fideicommissa* it seems that the consuls took cases which involved more than a certain amount, the *praetor fideicommissarius* those which involved less.[4] The *praetor tutelarius*, whose appointment was no doubt made with the object of relieving the consuls, appears in the end to have ousted them completely.[5]

---

[1] Owing to the system of double citizenship (*supra*, 62) all citizens except those actually resident at Rome have their personal *forum* in two places, but it seems clear that no one not resident at Rome was bound to obey an *in ius vocatio* before the praetor there unless he happened to be in Rome at the time; Wenger, 35; Bethmann-Hollweg, II. 123, n. 34.

[2] *Supra*, 347.

[3] Mommsen, *op. cit.* 269.   [4] Jörs, *op. cit.* (*supra*, 401, n. 8), 9.

[5] Jörs, *op. cit.* 6, shows that they continued to act for some time after the appointment of the *praetor tutelarius*.

Concurrently with these courts, both ordinary and extraordinary, the *praefectus urbi* exercised an increasing civil jurisdiction, in addition to acting as chief criminal judge for Rome and the district within 100 miles. As a judge of first instance he appears to have dealt chiefly with matters closely connected with his police duties, for it is mentioned that he heard complaints by slaves of ill-treatment,[1] and might be approached in connection with the interdicts *quod vi aut clam* and *unde vi*,[2] presumably because these interdicts concerned violence which might disturb the public order.[3] As a judge of appeal he assumed, in the later principate, the functions originally given to the urban praetor.[4]

The *praefecti annonae* and *vigilum* were almost exclusively concerned with criminal jurisdiction, but the former acquired civil jurisdiction in matters arising out of the corn supply,[5] though the ordinary procedure was also available, and the latter also occasionally decided controversies connected with his special functions.[6] During the earlier principate, the *quaestiones* remained the principal criminal courts for offences within their jurisdiction, but they lost ground, and there is no trace of them after the time of Alexander Severus.[7]

B. ITALY. The development of municipal government under Augustus appears to have made the *praefecti iure dicundo* superfluous,[8] and civil jurisdiction was divided between the municipal authorities and the praetor at Rome, the former being limited to cases involving amounts not exceeding a certain maximum.[9] In "extraordinary" matters the jurisdiction of the consuls concerning *fideicommissa* and guardianship extended beyond the boundaries of Rome.[10] Hadrian took an important step towards the provincialisation of Italy by appointing four men of consular rank to

---

[1] D. 1. 12. 1. 8. [2] *Ibid*. 6.

[3] He also acquired jurisdiction with regard to *alimenta, ibid.* 2, but how the work was divided between him and the consuls is not known; Jörs, *op. cit.* 26.

[4] *Supra*, 400; Mommsen, *Staatsrecht*, II. 985.

[5] D. 14. 1. 1. 18; 14. 5. 8; Mommsen, *Staatsrecht*, II. 1044.

[6] D. 19. 2. 56; 20. 2. 9. Neither passage is very convincing but *v.* Mommsen, *Staatsr.* II. 1058.

[7] Mommsen, *Strafrecht*, 221.

[8] The *praefecti Capuam Cumas* were probably abolished before 13 B.C.; Mommsen, *Staatsrecht*, II. 609–610.

[9] It is possible that the matter was regulated by a second *l. Iulia iudiciorum privatorum*; Wlassak, *Prozessgesetze*, I. 190 *sqq.*; II. 221 *sqq.* The *l. Rubria* (Bruns, I. 97) fixed the limit at 15,000 sesterces; the *fr. Atestinum* (Bruns, I. 101) gives 10,000. In matters requiring urgent action (e.g. *damnum infectum*, D. 39. 2. 1) the municipal magistrates had special powers.

[10] Jörs, *op. cit.* 5.

take charge of separate districts,[1] but what their judicial functions were is unknown. In any case the institution in its original form was short-lived, but it was revived in a different form by M. Aurelius, who appointed men of praetorian rank with the title *iuridici*.[2] How many of them there were is unknown, and it appears that the boundaries of their districts varied considerably from time to time, though they never covered the district round Rome which was known as the *urbica dioecesis*.[3] It is probable that the institution was closely connected with that of the *praetor tutelarius*, whose functions they appear to have exercised within their districts. They also dealt with *fideicommissa*.[4] That they had general powers of civil jurisdiction is probable but not certain. If they had, then it may be as Wlassak suggests, that they used the "divided *cognitio* procedure" for "ordinary" matters.[5] Criminal jurisdiction they almost certainly did not have.[6] This was, in minor matters, in the hands of the municipal magistrates, while serious crimes came before the *praefectus urbi* or *praefectus praetorio*, probably already from an early date.

C. THE PROVINCES.   Some powers of jurisdiction, both before and after the *constitutio Antoniniana* of 212, were left in the hands of the city authorities,[7] but, these apart, the only magistrate with *imperium* and hence with *iurisdictio* was the governor.[8] We have already seen how he also gradually obtained even capital jurisdiction over citizens. Most of his work was done at the assizes (*conventus*), which were held regularly at important centres in the province. But the governor could not, of course, attend to every case himself, and, as under the republic, he frequently delegated his functions. In some imperial provinces there were special *legati iuridici* for the purpose,[9] but he might also use other persons. These would normally be officials when the delegation was complete and the trial proceeded throughout before the same person. Where the "divided *cognitio* procedure" was used, the *iudex* was sometimes a private indivi-

---

[1] *H.A. Hadr.* 22. 13; Jörs, *op. cit.* 51–52.

[2] Jörs, *op. cit.* 63–64, makes the date of the first appointment A.D. 163.

[3] Fr. Vat. 205, 232. There is nothing to show that the *urbica dioecesis* was identical with the district within 100 miles of Rome, which formed the limit of the urban prefect's criminal jurisdiction; Bethmann-Hollweg, II. 67; Jörs, *op. cit.* 59.

[4] Jörs, *op. cit.* 66.   [5] *Provinzialprozess*, 78.

[6] Jörs, *op. cit.* 68.   [7] *Supra*, 355.

[8] In Egypt there was a special judicial officer (*iuridicus Alexandreae*) deriving his authority direct from the emperor, but his sphere must have been limited, whereas the prefect (governor) had general powers; Mitteis, *Grundzüge*, 26.

[9] Iavolenus Priscus held this post in Britain; *C.I.L.* III. 2864.

dual, as under the formulary procedure proper, but the practice of appointing subordinate officials seems to have grown. Perhaps the reason was, as Wlassak suggests, that, in addition to the assizes, there were standing courts at the governor's usual place of residence, where he would not, as at the assizes, have available a number of jurymen summoned for the purpose. This would naturally lead to his using his own staff.[1]

Appeals from the governor's delegates went in the first instance to him,[2] but they might go further to the emperor himself.

[1] *Provinzialprozess*, 35.
[2] D. 49. 3. 2.

Chapter XXIV

GENERAL CHARACTER OF THE CLASSICAL LAW

§ I. INTRODUCTORY

The object of this chapter is not to describe, even in outline, the rules of the classical law, but only to say something of the spirit by which it was informed, and to indicate the characteristics which mark it off from the law of the preceding and subsequent ages. But first it must be realised that there are peculiar difficulties in ascertaining the true nature of the classical law. Our sources are such that it appears for the most part in Byzantine dress; in the texts, that is, of Justinian's Digest and Codex, which have been selected and, in many cases, altered, in order to fit them for their place in a compilation meant for use by a much later generation and in a greatly altered civilisation.

No doubt the alteration was not always as thorough as, from a purely legislative point of view, it should have been, but a great number of classical rules, institutions and distinctions had become obsolete by Justinian's day and references to them were omitted or altered. In particular the formulary procedure, with which the greater part of the classical law had been bound up, had long disappeared, so that those parts of the classical works which dealt with it were, for the most part, useless to Justinian's compilers. Thus it was not until the discovery of Gaius' Institutes that modern scholars had any clear idea of the nature of that system, and even now much of it remains obscure.

There is also a further difficulty. The literature of the classical period was mostly written from the standpoint of Rome, and presupposes litigation between two Roman citizens. Even when the great jurists of the capital have provincial cases in mind, they are representatives of the official point of view, which is conservative and Roman. But the system which they expounded was not, even after the *constitutio Antoniniana,* always effective in more remote parts of the empire, where the Roman law was a foreign institution, and neither officials nor litigants could command the same standard of professional advice as was available at Rome. Materials for the study of this problem are scanty even now that considerable numbers of legal papyri have been discovered in Egypt, but Mitteis has shown that, in the Eastern half of the empire, the law actually in force differed very considerably from the official system, and that, in fact, much that was of Greek origin survived.[1] Nor were the differences all due to misunderstanding of, or dislike for, the foreign law. The system of land-registration which existed in Egypt must have had the sanction of the Roman government, and yet there is no reference to it in any surviving text of the official Roman law.[2] It is, however, the law of the jurists which is of the greatest interest, for it is their work which gave to Roman law its peculiar merits, and most of what follows in this chapter is concerned with the official system.

§ II. INFLUENCES AND METHODS

The influences which were at work in the development of the law during the principate were largely the same as those which had been active during the later republic. Already then Rome had come into touch with the world outside Italy, and in particular with the older and more developed civilisation of the Hellenistic East; already her lawyers had taken some doctrines from Greek philosophy and her law had received many additions from Greek sources. Thus, as we have seen, the conception of the *ius gentium* was coloured by Greek philosophical ideas,[3] and, to mention but one practical case, the aedilician edict, with its remarkable innovations in the law of sale, was at least in part borrowed from similar provisions in the law of Greek cities.[4]

The Greek systems, being more mature, were already considerably freer from formalism than was the Roman, when contact first began, and their influence assisted the natural development in this direction. The cosmopolitan nature of the empire, the development of trade, helped in the same way to break down national idiosyncrasies, to introduce new conceptions, and to produce that individualism which is a marked

---

[1] The interaction of official Roman law and provincial custom is the chief theme of Mitteis' *Reichsrecht*. Against some of Mitteis' views *v.* now Schönbauer, *Z.S.S.* LI. 277–335.

[2] Rabel, 431. Another example of the conservatism of the jurists is to be seen in their failure to work out any consistent theory of the place of writing in legal affairs in spite of the fact that, under Greek influence, it had become universal; cf. *infra*, 424–431, and Steinacker, *Die Antiken Grundlagen der fruehmittelalterlichen Privaturkunde* (Leipzig, 1927), 74.

[3] *Supra*, 103.

[4] Partsch, "Der griechische Gedanke in der Rechtswissenschaft", in *Altertum u. Gegenwart* (Leipzig), 109. For the connection of the aediles with Greek institutions cf. Girard, *Org. Jud.* 219.

feature of the Roman law. The methods, however, of the Romans,
remained characteristic. Some innovations were of course the product of
legislation, now always openly or covertly imperial, but the chief instrument by which the law was altered was the combination of juristic
interpretation with the praetorian system. The main lines of the edict
had, no doubt, been laid down by the end of the republic, but the vast
extension of its importance was the work of the principate, and it is an
indication of this importance that, as already mentioned, in general
treatises of the later classical period, the civil law portion comes to be
treated almost as an appendix to that which deals with the edict.[1] But
the civil law does not cease thereby to exist; it exists even though its
principles may in effect cease to be applied.[2] As we have seen, the
praetorian remedies in fact modified very greatly the actual law of
inheritance, but it would be quite impossible to explain the resulting
system without reference to the civil law. As, in Maitland's phrase,
Equity was a gloss on the common law,[3] so the praetorian system was a
gloss on the civil, but the sphere of the Roman "Equity" was considerably
wider than that of its English counterpart. The actual edict, however,
represents only part of the praetorian law; it is the jurists who complete
it, as they do the text of any civil law source. Thus, though the edict has
a form for an *exceptio doli*, it is the jurists who develop the rules as to
what amounts to fraud; the edict promises to "deal with cases where it is
alleged that a transaction has been entered into with a minor", but it is
the jurists who work out more definite rules for the granting of *in integrum
restitutio*.[4] Similarly it is on the authority of the jurists that *actiones in
factum* are granted in cases where neither the civil law nor the edict has
already provided a remedy, and these, especially from the time of Julian
onwards, appear to have been one of the most fruitful methods of
development.

It is of course not only on the praetorian law that the jurists work.
Their "interpretation" applies equally to the civil law, so that the two
become parts of a coherent whole. Throughout the classical period,
however, the system continues to bear the mark of close contact with
practice, and, as a result, is lacking in the broad discussion of general
theories. Thus there was no general theory of the invalidity of acts in
the law, or even a clear distinction between contracts which are void and

---

[1] *Supra*, 382.
[2] Civil law retains even so a theoretical superiority and a civil action is
preferred to a praetorian one; Mitteis, *R.P.R.* 59.
[3] *Lectures on Equity*, 18.   [4] *Supra*, 234.

those which are voidable.[1] Nor is the question of damages ever worked out on general lines, though the jurists discuss with respect to each action "what comes into it" (*quid veniat in iudicium*). Advance is, in fact, as with us, mainly from case to case, and it is precisely the wealth of case-law (of course of a type different from our own) and the practical wisdom enshrined therein which gives to the classical law its unique value.

The following sections are intended to illustrate in rather greater detail the nature of the changes brought about. Decrease in formalism and increasingly abstract methods of thought are the most striking features which mark off the classical law from that of earlier times. The more frequent use of writing illustrates Greek influence, but in the classical period Roman law had hardly yet assimilated this element and its attitude was still very different from that which it took up in the later empire.

§ III. DECREASING FORMALISM AND RIGIDITY

We speak of a system as formal, especially with reference to its treatment of acts in the law, i.e. of acts, such as contracts, conveyances or wills, which are undertaken for the purpose of bringing about a legal consequence in accordance with the intention of the party or parties concerned. Formality in this connection has a double aspect, "external" and "internal".[2] "Externally" it means that the act in the law must be carried out exactly in the prescribed manner, with set words, gestures or accessories, and that, in their absence, an expression of the will, however clear, is ineffective. "Internally" it means that the completion of the prescribed form has the typical result, as laid down by law, even though it may be clear that the will to effect that result is absent. It also means that only a certain very limited number of results can be brought about by the exercise of the will, that it may not be possible, for instance, so to alter the effect of a conveyance, that property shall pass only at a future date, or on the fulfilment of a condition. Even modern systems of law are, it must be understood, still partly formalist, especially in the "external" sense, and a man can still, for instance, only exercise his powers of testation in the prescribed way. Thus, in England, no matter how clear it may be that a document represents the last wishes of the deceased, it will not be valid as his will unless it is attested by two witnesses.

The Roman classical law retained, however, much more of the early

---

[1] Mitteis, *R.P.R.* 236. [2] Mitteis, *R.P.R.* 255.

formalism than do modern systems. Mancipation, with its complicated ritual, was still necessary for passing the full ownership in *res mancipi*; mancipation and nuncupation were still required for the civil law validity of a will; servitudes could only be created *inter vivos* by *in iure cessio*[1]; adoption and emancipation needed the three mancipations and the intervening manumissions, and adrogation was still carried out with the old ritual before the simulacrum of the *comitia curiata*. But in a number of cases, the effect of the rule had already been mitigated by the praetorian law. Possession of a *res mancipi* received without mancipation was, in fact, so well protected under the provisions of the edict, even before it ripened into full ownership by usucapion, that it could be spoken of as a kind of ownership;[2] and, as we have seen, the praetorian law of testamentary succession required forms which were at once simpler and better adapted to the purpose of preventing interference with the testator's instructions.[3] But the "praetorian will" was not as completely effective as that made in civil law form, and in other cases, adoption for instance, there was no such mitigation at all. The development of legacies may be taken as typical of the slow and cautious advance. There were, as has been mentioned above,[4] four different types of legacy, though for the purpose of this discussion we can confine ourselves to the two more important—*per vindicationem* and *per damnationem*. Originally, it is clear, each had its peculiar form, which was, no doubt, the only valid one, the proper words for the former being *do lego*, for the latter *heres meus dannas esto dare*. By Gaius' time[5] already certain variations were allowed, but only very few. Either *do* or *lego* alone was sufficient, and indeed the effect was the same if it was said that the legatee was to "take" the thing (*sumito, sibi habeto,* or *capito*), though this was evidently considered a further relaxation. A legacy *per damnationem* could be given by saying *heres meus dato*, and, after Gaius' time, at any rate, some other forms of command were permissible.[6] But we are still very far from the principle that any form, so long as it is clear, is good enough; each particular phrase is worth discussion, and its admission is recognised as an achievement.

If we leave the matter there, however, the whole story is not complete, for at the same time, when lawyers were discussing these minutiae with

---

[1] At any rate with civil law validity. For literature *v.* Buckland, 265.

[2] The word "bonitary" used to designate it dates only from Theophilus, *Paraphr.* 1. 5. 4, but Gaius (II. 40) already says in this connection *divisionem accepit dominium ut alius possit esse ex iure Quiritium dominus, alius in bonis habere.*

[3] *Supra,* 255.

[4] *Supra,* 253.

[5] Gai. II. 193; 201.

[6] Ulp. Reg. XXIV. 4.

regard to legacies, *fideicommissa* were already recognised.[1] These were completely free from all rules of form, not even the Latin language or writing being a necessity. They could not, it is true, do what a legacy *per vindicationem* could do, i.e. transfer a right *in rem* directly to the beneficiary, but for practical purposes they were as good as legacies, and could indeed achieve results which were quite unknown to the older law. The two institutions continued to exist side by side, each with its own rules representing different stages in the evolution of law, and adding, considerably, by their coexistence, to legal complexities. Only a system such as that of Justinian's day, which had quite forgotten the procedural differences which were at the bottom of the distinction, was able to fuse them entirely.

If law was becoming less formal, it was also becoming less rigid. The two things are closely allied, but not quite the same. To say of a system that it is rigid, means that once a rule is formulated, no exceptions to it are tolerated, so that, in particular cases, the rule, good though it may be, has results which outrage the common feeling of justice. A flexible system, on the other hand, is able, by means of general overriding principles, to prevent some of these results. Thus, although it is a rule, and a good one, that a man must abide by his contract, neither the developed Roman nor the developed English law will apply the rule to a contract which has been induced by threats or fraud. But all the cases of hardship are never successfully met, and there is in all systems of law a perpetual struggle between the principle of rigidity, which makes for certainty, and that of flexibility, which makes for justice in the individual case. This struggle manifests itself most clearly as the contest between the letter and the spirit in the interpretation of statute law, but it exists also in the application of unenacted rules, and in the interpretation of other texts than those of laws, for instance wills and contracts.

The existence of this distinction, formulated as that between *scriptum* and *voluntas*, or sometimes simply as that between *ius* and *aequitas*, was perfectly well known to the Romans before the end of the republic.[2] It had been discussed at some length by Aristotle, and developed in the writings of the Greek rhetoricians whose influence in Rome was considerable. The ancient rigidity had also suffered some notable defeats in practice before the republic came to an end.[3] But all the lofty verbiage

[1] Gai. II. 246 *sqq.*
[2] Stroux, *Summum ius summa iniuria* (Leipzig, 1926).
[3] Especially the famous *causa Curiana*, mentioned e.g. Cic. *de Or.* I. 180; Stroux, *op. cit.* 5.

of Cicero and even the devotion to *aequitas* of a great lawyer like Servius Sulpicius naturally did not suffice to change the character of the ancient system at a single blow. Such a change needs, if it is to be successful, the elaboration of a technique which can only be achieved by several generations, and it was precisely this elaboration which was the work of the classical jurists. It is their mastery of technique which makes the classical lawyers superior to the Byzantines, whose desire to bring about an equitable result in every case, without a similar professional understanding, ends frequently in high-sounding phrases through which no principle capable of general application can be perceived.

An example of the increasing, but by no means perfect, flexibility of the classical law may be seen in its treatment of some of the effects of the *capitis deminutio minima*, resulting from adrogation. The old civil law rule was that the rights of the *adrogatus* passed (with the exception of some which were lost) to the *adrogator*, but that the *adrogator* was not liable for the debts. On the latter part of the rule, however, the civil law had already grafted an exception. Debts which the *adrogatus* owed as heir to some deceased person did pass to the *adrogator*, on the ground, it was said, that he became heir in place of the *adrogatus*. There can be little doubt that this exception was only allowed because the rule itself was practically inconvenient and unjust, but further than this the civil law did not go. Praetorian law, however, prevented injustice by allowing an action against the *adrogatus*, with the fiction that he had not suffered *capitis deminutio*, and (unless the action were defended by the adoptive father) allowing the goods which the *adrogatus* brought with him to be taken in execution.[1] It must not, however, be thought that all the undesirable results of *capitis deminutio* were dealt with thus satisfactorily. Usufruct, which was a highly personal right, was still lost by this "civil death", although it is clear that the rule was inconvenient, and that testators were at pains to provide against the contingency by certain drafting devices.[2]

Instances of this sort might be multiplied to any extent to show the varying degrees in which the classical law succeeded in emancipating itself from the undesired results of ancient rules, but it is at least equally important to realise how much flexibility it attained by the use of what may be called rather standards than rules. New rules could then be deduced from these standards without impairing their usefulness for the settlement of future difficulties. Of these standards, *bona fides* supplies the most striking example. No one can exhaust the meaning of "good

---

[1] Gai. III. 83–84. [2] Buckland, 272.

faith", and the acceptance of a rule, that e.g. such and such conduct on the part of a seller does not conform to the standard of faith, does not mean that other kinds of dishonest conduct may be indulged in with impunity. There had, of course, been *bonae fidei* actions before the end of the republic, but the great opportunities which this conception gave were only realised later. For instance, it was always usual in sales that the seller should, by express stipulation, make himself liable in case of eviction, but it was not until the classical period was well advanced that he was made liable even without any express promise, no doubt on the ground that it would be contrary to good faith if he attempted to escape such ordinary liability.[1]

Dolus received a similarly wide extension of application, and could include any act which did not conform with the requirements of *bona fides*. Hence the delictal *actio doli* came to be available not only, as originally, in cases of actual trickery, but much more generally where the defendant's conduct in refusing what was asked of him was contrary to *bona fides* and caused loss to the plaintiff. Thus Ulpian[2] allowed it where the defendant had given the plaintiff permission to quarry a stone on his land, and after the plaintiff had expended money on doing so, refused permission to remove the stone.[3]

A more primitive system would have been at a loss to deal with such a case. The land and the stone belonged to the defendant, and there was no contract to create a duty in him towards the plaintiff.

§ IV. INCREASING TENDENCY TOWARDS ABSTRACT METHODS OF THOUGHT

With the formalism and rigidity of a primitive system there is naturally associated a concrete method of thought, and in this respect, as in others, the classical law had by no means completely freed itself from the trammels of an earlier age. Thus its classifications were based on external features, and, whereas a modern system makes its most important distinctions according to differences in the abstract rights which a man may have, the classical law distinguished according to the more concrete remedies. It knew well, for instance, the distinction between *actio in rem* and *actio in personam*, but it was left for later ages to deduce from this

---

[1] Girard, 592.   [2] D. 4. 3. 34.

[3] See Mitteis, *R.P.R.* 317 *sqq.* Some of the developments of this action which Mitteis quotes are probably due to Justinian's compilers, Biondi, *Actiones arbitrariae*, 99 *sqq.*, but even Biondi (104) is unable to find grounds for suspecting D. 4. 3. 34.

the difference between *ius in rem* and *ius in personam*. This apparent backwardness was due to the complex system of procedure which still prevailed, and was always in the minds of the jurists, so that in any given circumstances they asked themselves, not what right a man had, but what proceeding was available. There were still several different sorts of proceeding—interdicts, *in integrum restitutiones*, *actiones* civil and praetorian, as well as the beginnings of *cognitio extraordinaria*, and each had its own peculiarities. Only in post-classical times, when the same procedure was available in every case, did it become possible to work out a man's rights first in the abstract before considering the proceeding by which they were to be enforced.

A step towards the classification of rights is, however, found already in the classification of "things" with which Gaius begins the second book of his Institutes. The chief distinction, he says, is that between things *in patrimonio nostro* and those *extra patrimonium nostrum*, the latter being those which, because they were "sacred", for instance, or "public", were incapable of private ownership. There is thus already a classification of things according to the rights which can exist over them. But Gaius goes on to distinguish between *res corporales* and *res incorporales*.[1] Corporeal things, he explains, are those which are tangible, incorporeal, those *quae in iure consistunt*, such as an inheritance, a usufruct, or an obligation, and it appears a little later that servitudes, too, are "incorporeal things". Now this distinction is, strictly, illogical, for it omits ownership altogether from the list of rights and identifies it with the thing owned. A more complete analysis would say that all rights are themselves incorporeal, though they all have corporeal objects. A cow over which I have a usufruct is no less corporeal than one I own; the difference is that in the latter case my right is greater than in the former. But if the Roman analysis is not satisfactory to the modern mind, it is none the less important to realise that there is implicit in it already a clear distinction between ownership and all other rights, and that the conception of ownership as an absolute right was, as has been mentioned, a very great achievement of the classical law. Classical law also made great strides towards the conception of servitudes as absolute rights, and here, too, a tendency to greater abstractness of thought is noticeable. Modern analysis treats servitudes as a class of *iura in re aliena*,[2] i.e. certain rights which may in a particular instance be taken out of the "bundle of rights" of which ownership consists and given to some person other than the owner, and these *iura in re aliena* are rights *in rem*, i.e. they

[1] II. 12.   [2] This expression is not Roman.

avail not only against the owner, but against all other persons whatsoever. Originally, the oldest rustic servitudes were conceived of in a very concrete manner, and the primitive mind saw, not an abstract "right of way", but a concrete path, with the result that the oldest rustic servitudes were classed as *res mancipi*.[1] Classical law, on the other hand, looked upon all servitudes as *res incorporales*, and had developed the maxim *nulli res sua servit* (no man can have a servitude over his own thing),[2] which fits admirably with modern conceptions, for it follows of necessity if servitude be defined as a right in *someone else's property*.

Nevertheless, traces of older conceptions remain. Not only was the rule that rustic servitudes were *res mancipi* retained, but it seems that a servitude might survive the abandonment of ownership in the servient tenement. This is incompatible with the definition of servitude as a right in property belonging to someone else, and is probably to be explained as a survival of the concrete view: if A has a right of way over B's estate and B abandons his estate, the path is still there, and so A's servitude continues.[3] On the other hand if, as is possible, the category of personal servitudes was already recognised before the end of the classical period,[4] this recognition shows that the conception of a *ius in re aliena* was already coming into existence, for there is little in common between personal and praedial servitudes, except that they are both (from the modern point of view) *iura in re aliena*.

In the sphere of obligations there is a similar tendency towards greater abstraction. *Obligatio* was originally conceived as the very concrete binding of one person to another,[5] such as could result, of course, only from the civil law. And such a binding was necessarily highly personal; if A is bound to B, B cannot, by his own act, bind A to C instead of to himself. In classical law much of this conception remains. Until almost the end, it appears that the word *obligatio* was still confined to civil law relationships, and, strictly, obligations remained intransferable. But *obligatio* was already classed as a *res*. This means that it was already recognised as being, from the creditor's point of view, an asset, and with this recognition came naturally the desire to make it, like corporeal assets, capable of transfer. The methods applicable to corporeal things were of course inapplicable, but an indirect process of transferring the asset by transferring the right to sue was devised, and thus "cession of

[1] Cf. *supra*, 139.   [2] D. 8. 2. 26.
[3] Buckland, "The Conception of Servitudes in Roman Law", *L.Q.R.* XLIV. 426–435. For other traces of older ideas cf. *supra*, 278, n. 10.
[4] *Supra*, 278, n. 4.   [5] *Supra*, 163.

actions" became a well-known proceeding.[1] The idea that the essence of an obligation lies in the duty which the person liable has to discharge is clearly expressed by Paulus, when he describes an obligation as that which "binds us to convey something or do something or provide something",[2] and it is probable that before the end of the classical period it was recognised that a binding of this less materialist kind existed at praetorian as well as at civil law, and consequently that the word *obligatio* might be extended to relationships recognised by the *ius honorarium*.[3]

The conception is indeed still closely bound up with the procedural conception of *actio*,[4] but there were already in the formulary system methods by which a single duty arising under an obligation might be separated from the others, and the action appropriate to the obligation brought for the enforcement of that duty alone.[5] The separation between the substantive and procedural conceptions was thus prepared, and the way open for a more abstract conception of obligation.

§ V. INCREASED USE OF WRITING

Early Roman law used writing very little, but it is clear that, under Greek influence, legal documents had become common before the end of the republic. Wills were almost always in writing; stipulations were already classed by Cicero among *res quae scripto aguntur*,[6] and though there is little evidence about consensual contracts, it can hardly be doubted that in important cases they were also generally reduced to writing, or at least that they were confirmed by a stipulation which was written down.[7]

The type of writing used was most commonly the "double document", i.e. there were two texts, of which one was sealed up, so as to prevent any alteration, while the other was open, so that the contents might be known. This type was widespread in ancient times. It was known in ancient Babylonia and other Eastern civilisations,[8] and it was also frequent in Egypt in Hellenistic times. That there is any historical

---

[1] It consisted in appointing the assignee agent to sue on behalf of the assignor and dispensing him from accounting for the proceeds of the action; Gai. II. 39.

[2] D. 44. 7. 3. pr.

[3] The matter is doubtful. Perozzi, *Le obbligazioni*, 135 sqq., holds that texts in the Digest speaking of *obligatio honoraria* are interpolated.

[4] Even the Digest (44. 7) and the Code (4. 10) have the rubric *de obligationibus et actionibus*. Buckland (*Main Institutions*, 234) suggests that the right translation of this is "Of civil and praetorian obligations".

[5] *Supra*, 208.

[6] *Top.* XXVI.

[7] E.g. D. 17. 2. 71.

[8] *V.* Jeremiah XXXII. 11 and 14.

connection between the Eastern type and the Egyptian is not certain,[1] but it is to be presumed that the Romans derived their use of such documents from people of Hellenistic civilisation. In Egypt, both before and after the Roman occupation, the almost universal writing material was papyrus, but in other parts of the Roman empire, that most commonly used for legal purposes was the diptych or triptych made of waxed tablets. From remains which have been preserved, especially those found in Pompeii[2] and in Verespatak,[3] and from a senatus-consult of Nero's time,[4] we know well enough what a document of this sort looked like. Rectangular tablets were prepared by splitting from the same wooden block, so that they fitted one another exactly, and could be joined together, by a thread passed through holes in the edges, into a little book. If, as most commonly, there were three tablets (triptych), and consequently six "pages", pages 1 and 6 remained as they were, but the interior pages (i.e. one side of the first tablet, both sides of the second and one side of the third) were hollowed out, leaving a raised edge, and coated with black wax, on which the writing was then scratched with a pointed instrument. On pages 2 and 3 was written the "interior" text, parallel to the longer side of the tablets; on page 4 and on page 5 the "exterior" text. The first two tablets were then bound together by a thread going through holes in their edges; this thread was then tied round them, its end being secured by the seals of the witnesses in a groove specially made for the purpose on page 4. The interior text was thus hidden from view until the seals were broken, while the exterior text could be read at any time.

The two texts do not necessarily always correspond exactly; in particular, it may happen that the interior writing is in an "objective" form, i.e. recounts what has been done in the third person (e.g. *dixit se accepisse*), whereas the outer is "subjective", i.e. in the first person (e.g. *scripsi me accepisse*). Of these two forms which a document may take, the "objective" is certainly the older, and Roman usage, like Greek usage before it,

[1] Mitteis, *R.P.R.* 300; Wenger, P.-W. Art. *Signum*, col. 2429.
[2] Bruns, I. 354 *sqq.*
[3] In Transylvania; Bruns, I. 328 *sqq.*
[4] Paul. *Sent.* v. 25. 6: *Amplissimus ordo decrevit eas tabulas quae publici vel privati contractus scripturam continent, adhibitis testibus ita signari ut in summa marginis ad mediam partem perforatae triplici lino constringantur, atque impositae supra linum cerae signa imprimantur, ut exteriori scripturae fidem interior servet. Aliter tabulae prolatae nihil momenti habent.* Cf. Suet. *Nero*, 17. The exact effect of the senatus-consult is doubtful. It probably means only that if the parties choose to have a document it must be in the prescribed form, not that they are bound to have a document. Its terms are inappropriate to wills, where there is, of course, no exterior text. See Wenger, *op. cit.* col. 2421.

shows a growing tendency to prefer the subjective form. The usual word for a subjective document is *chirographum*, and this word itself betrays the Greek influence. In some of the Pompeian receipts, both inner and outer texts are already chirographs in this sense, and perhaps there was a general tendency throughout the empire, as there certainly had been in Egypt, for the inner text to shrink to a mere précis of the contents of the outer, and finally to disappear.[1] At any rate there appear to be no known examples of double documents later than the third century of the empire.[2]

There was no general rule laying down what constituted the execution of a document. In particular it must be understood that the signature, as we understand it, was unknown. That is to say, there was no principle that the appending of a person's name in his own handwriting constituted the adoption by him of the document to which it was appended. If, however, a document were written in whole or in part by the person to be charged under it, its authenticity would be better evidenced than if it were wholly in someone else's handwriting. Hence arose the practice of adding a short phrase indicating adherence to a document written by someone else, of which we have seen examples in discussing imperial rescripts.[3] These phrases, which constitute the ancient signature, are in subjective form, and thus chirographs, so that there is really no hard and fast distinction between a short chirograph and a long signature.[4]

Sealing by the party was also one way in which a document might be executed; it occurs, for instance, in a number of the Pompeian receipts,[5] but it was not, so far as we know, ever necessary for the validity of a document, and it gradually lost its importance to the signature.[6]

With this sealing as a method of execution by the party must, of course, not be confused the sealing by witnesses which serves the purpose of enabling them when called upon to recognise their seals and to testify that the document in question is the one which they saw executed. Failure to acknowledge one's seal was an offence.[7] For the purpose of identification the name of each witness was written (in the genitive) opposite his seal. This, according to Ulpian, had to be done by the witness himself in

---

[1] The bronze tablets giving privileges to soldiers on their discharge certainly show a progressive shrinking of the inner text; Wenger, *op. cit.* col. 2419.

[2] Wenger, *op. cit.* col. 2429.

[3] *Supra*, 374–375.

[4] Even chirographs are not by any means always actually written by the party who makes the declaration; Mitteis, *R.P.R.* 293.

[5] Mitteis, *R.P.R.* 302.

[6] Steinacker, *op. cit.* (*supra*, 374, n. 7), 111.

[7] Mitteis, *R.P.R.* 305; Wenger, *op. cit.* col. 2391.

the case of wills,[1] but was not necessary, so far as we know, in the case of other documents.[2]

The purposes which writing may serve in connection with legal transactions are various. It may be used merely to provide evidence of an act which, whether formal or informal, is itself complete without any writing, or it may, on the other hand, be "dispositive"; i.e. it may embody, in permanent form, the expression of the will which becomes effective only through this embodiment. Such dispositive effect may again exist either because the law requires the expression of the will to be in writing or because, the law being indifferent in the matter, the parties have chosen this method of expression. Thus, in English law, an ordinary receipt is merely evidence of payment, but a promissory note is a dispositive document, for the promissor becomes bound by writing his promise, and in this particular instance writing is required by the law for the validity of the transaction.

It is a commonplace of legal history that the earlier use of writing is purely evidentiary,[3] and Roman law forms no exception to the rule. The typical acts of the *ius civile* required formalities other than writing for their validity; where writing was used, it served the purpose of recording the accomplishment of these formalities, and, as we have seen, the objective form of document was chosen. Only in two cases did the civil law develop a form of writing which was in any way dispositive. One case is the very peculiar "literal contract", and the other the mancipatory will, for the tablets do not merely record the expressed wishes of the testator; they incorporate them and are indeed the only expression thereof. In both cases, however, the act needs for its validity something more than the writing; in the literal contract there must have been the assent of the debtor, though we do not know how this was expressed;[4] and for the will, mancipation and nuncupation were needed.

The field offered by the *ius gentium* to the dispositive document was clearly wider, for it was of course open to the parties to a consensual contract to express their consent in writing if they so desired. Thus the use of documents in Greek form was by no means an impossibility, for

[1] D. 28. 1. 22. 4; cf. Paulus, D. 28. 1. 30.
[2] Mitteis, *R.P.R.* 304.
[3] This may still be so even when the form of the document is borrowed from a more advanced system which already uses writing dispositively. See Hazeltine, Preface to Whitelock, *Anglo-Saxon Wills* (Cambridge, 1930), IX. Strict Muhammadan law does not recognise a dispositive document at all; Vesey-Fitz-Gerald, *Muhammadan Law* (Oxford, 1931), 27.
[4] *Supra*, 291.

generally these could be construed as constituting a transaction known to that part of the Roman law which formed the *ius gentium*.[1] For the transactions of the *ius civile*, the Romans had to evolve their own forms, but this was not necessary for those of the *ius gentium*, and we know that the Romans living in Egypt used dispositive documents of the Greek type even for transactions between themselves.[2]

It remains to be considered whether the Greek influence did not go further. In Greek law, writing was often not merely dispositive, but abstract, i.e. in itself a binding form, like the Roman stipulation, so that, if a man had acknowledged in a document that he owed, he would have to pay, whether the other party could prove a substantive ground for the debt, or not. Thus, in particular, it appears that acknowledgments of loans were frequently given where money had not actually been received, but it was desired that a debt, as if on a loan, should exist between the parties; or, a greater amount was acknowledged than had been received, the excess representing interest.[3] Also, there was certainly a tendency in Greek law to regard agreements as unenforceable unless there was writing, whereas (with the exception of the literal contract) Roman law did not know of writing as a necessity at all.[4]

In considering how far Roman law yielded to Greek influence in these two points it is necessary to treat separately two subjects, (*a*) the written stipulation and (*b*) the document acknowledging a debt.

(*a*) *Written stipulation.* From Cicero's time it was usual to have a document where the stipulation was of any importance. This, according to Roman theory, was merely evidentiary, but a Greek would think of it differently. When the constitution of Caracalla extended the Roman law to a great number of people who had hitherto lived according to the Greek system, these people, naturally enough, did not understand the Roman principle, and, though they frequently added the clause alleging a stipulation to their written contracts,[5] they continued to see the binding

---

[1] The *ius gentium* was, no doubt, in part formed of institutions received into Roman law from foreign systems.

[2] Mitteis, *R.P.R.* 295, n. 15; cf. Steinacker, *op. cit.* 72 and 121.

[3] Mitteis, *Reichsrecht*, 468 *sqq.*

[4] Mitteis, *Reichsrecht*, 515–517, gives a list of rescripts (e.g. C. 2. 3. 17) in which the Roman emperors are at pains to correct the erroneous views of petitioners on this point.

[5] They evidently regarded the phrase *interrogatus spopondi* (ἐπερωτηθεὶς ὡμολόγηκα) as a kind of talisman giving validity to any sort of transaction; it is found attached even to a will, where of course it has no sense at all; Mitteis, *Reichsrecht*, 487.

force of the obligation where they had seen it before, i.e. in the writing, and not in the alleged stipulation, which in all probability had never taken place. This, of course, official Roman law could not accept, but it had, apparently even before 212, gone some way towards the Greek view, by admitting that if there were a document alleging a stipulation, that document should be taken as *conclusive* proof that a stipulation had been entered into.[1] It was not even, apparently, necessary that there should be a complete allegation of a stipulation, for a constitution of A.D. 200 says that if the allegation is merely that someone has promised, then it will be assumed that there was a preceding question and hence a valid stipulation.[2] In practice stipulation has thus become a written contract, except, so it seems, for one point. The parties, apparently, must still meet, as of course they would have to do for a real oral stipulation, so that the effect of a document would be nullified if the defendant could show that he did not meet the plaintiff.[3]

(b) *Written acknowledgment of debt.* For strict Roman law such an acknowledgment was of course mere evidence, but the Romans were well acquainted with the Greek point of view. Thus Gaius says "a literal obligation appears also to be created by *chirographa* and *syngraphae*, that is if a man writes that he owes or that he will pay, without there being any stipulation concerning the matter", though he adds that contracts of this sort were peculiar to *peregrini*, i.e. people of Greek civilisation.[4] The distinction between the two points of view is clear enough in theory, but in practice it is not always so obvious, and it may be that in the outlying courts of the empire it was not always observed. At any rate it is certain that mere *chirographa* acknowledging indebtedness, and documents alleging stipulation, were treated in a similar way for the purposes of the curious institution, known as *exceptio non numeratae*

---

[1] The chief text is Paul. *Sent.* v. 7. 2 (= J. 3. 19. 17). This text is not considered genuine by Riccobono (*Z.S.S.* xxxv. 291), who in his "Stipulatio ed Instrumentum" (*Z.S.S.* xxxv and xliii) has developed the view that there was no relaxation of the formal requirements for stipulation in classical times at all. He admits, however, that the writing is not merely the proof but also the instrument of the oral form, because it is referred to in the spoken words. The spoken word is the "legal baptism" of the written; *v.* "Punti", 530–531, quoting D. 44. 7. 38. [2] C. 8. 37. 1; cf. D. 45. 1. 134. 2.

[3] D. 45. 1. 134. 2. That in Paulus' time the written stipulation was thought of as dispositive is shown by the use of the present tense *spondeo* in D. 24. 1. 57.

[4] III. 134: *Praeterea litterarum obligatio fieri videtur chirographis et syngraphis, id est, si quis debere se aut daturum se scribat, ita scilicet, si eo nomine stipulatio non fiat, quod genus obligationis proprium peregrinorum est.* The distinction between *chirographum* and *syngrapha* is that the former is subjective, the latter objective.

pecuniae, which developed at the end of the classical period.[1] The use of this institution can be explained most easily by taking the simple case of fraud which consists in a moneylender's exacting a document from an intending borrower on the pretence that he will lend a sum of money and then failing to lend it. If, as was frequently the case, a stipulation had been entered into for repayment and the document recorded the stipulation, then the position, in the time of Gaius, was that the debt was owed by the supposed borrower at civil law because he had made the formal promise by stipulation; but if he were sued, he would be able to put in an *exceptio doli*. In this *exceptio* the burden of proof would of course lie upon him. It might, however, equally well happen that there was no stipulation, or allegation of one, but simply a document acknowledging indebtedness. Technically the position would then be quite different, for the moneylender's ground of action would not be a stipulation, but a *mutuum*, and the defendant would need no *exceptio*; his defence would be a simple denial of the debt, for if there had been no payment, there could be no *mutuum*, *mutuum* being a contract *re*. In effect, however, this case would be very similar to the other, for the document would be *prima facie* evidence that the money had been paid, and it would be for the defendant to rebut the evidence if he could. The reform consisted, in both cases, in permitting the defendant, within a limited period (at first one year), to invalidate the force of the document altogether by merely denying (without proving) that he had received the money. He could thereby throw upon the plaintiff the burden of proving, if he could, by some other means, that the money had actually been paid, and would only be condemned if the plaintiff succeeded in discharging this burden. On the other hand, when the limited period had elapsed, the document, it appears, became irrebuttable evidence of the debt, and the defendant would in any case have to pay.[2] The date of the reform is not known for certain, but it appears first in a constitution of 215,[3] and it has been suggested that it is connected with the *constitutio Antoniniana* of 212.[4] Now that there was but one system of law for almost all the inhabitants of the empire, there was a danger that the Greek view of documents as

---

[1] No attempt is made here to deal fully with the law on this subject. For general explanation see e.g. Buckland, 442–443; Girard, 534–537.

[2] C. 4. 30. 8. 2. Some authors however think that it would still have been possible for the defendant to plead *exceptio doli*, though of course the burden of proof would now be on him; e.g. Buckland, 443.

[3] C. 4. 30. 3. C. 4. 30. 1 of 197 is shown by another version of the same constitution, C. 8. 32. 1, to have been altered.

[4] Steinacker, *op. cit.* 87.

in themselves binding (abstract) might prevail, and the *exceptio non numeratae pecuniae* was intended to counteract this danger. On the other hand there was perhaps a partial recognition of the Greek point of view in the rule that after the requisite period had elapsed the document became conclusive evidence.

In the post-classical period the influence of Greek ideas concerning the effect of writing was to go much further, especially in connection with the registration of documents and written forms of conveyance. The beginning of the practice of registration appears indeed to fall within the classical period,[1] but whether it was due in the first instance to Greek influence or is an independent development of the voluntary jurisdiction (*in iure cessio*) of the Roman magistrates is a matter of dispute.[2]

---

[1] Fr. Vat. 266 a.
[2] Mitteis, *R.P.R.* 306; *Reichsrecht*, 551; Steinacker, *op. cit.* 77.

Chapter XXV

THE CONSTITUTION UNDER THE DOMINATE

§ I. THE IMPERIAL POWER

The half century which elapsed between the assassination of Alexander Severus (235) and the accession of Diocletian (284) was one of confusion and disaster for the empire. Plague and war, both external and civil, inflicted terrible suffering on the population; emperor followed emperor in quick succession as the caprice of the different armies and their varying successes dictated, and almost all of the ephemeral rulers came to a violent end. One actually suffered the disgrace of falling alive into the hands of an external enemy.[1] The prestige of the empire had indeed been restored under Diocletian's immediate predecessors, but it was left to him to re-establish internal order and to mitigate at least the evil of constant usurpation. He cannot be said to have achieved his object completely, for no principle of succession was able to establish itself firmly, and there were still no definite means of distinguishing between a legitimate emperor and a successful usurper. But he himself remained in power until his abdication in 305, and thereafter the empire was ruled for the most part by a number of comparatively stable dynasties.

The methods adopted to achieve stability were, in the main, three—the transformation of the imperial power into a monarchy on an Oriental model, the territorial division among co-regents and the reorganisation of the administrative machine. None of these ideas was quite new, and in many points Diocletian's system was completed by Constantine the Great, the next ruler who secured sole power over the whole of the empire. Nevertheless it was to Diocletian very largely that the empire owed its continued existence in spite of the increasing pressure of the barbarian hordes.

The rulers of the preceding epoch had been in fact supreme, but it was now intended to prevent usurpations by surrounding the imperial dignity with such a hedge of divinity that it should appear beyond the reach of any ordinary mortal. Under the new system the emperor on state occasions wears robes adorned with gold and gems as well as the diadem, or head-band of pearls, which was among the insignia of the

[1] Valerian, captured by the Persians 260.

Persian monarch;[1] he appears but little in public, and when he does it is only with full ceremony; everything connected with him, from his enactments to his bedchamber, is "sacred", and the subject who is admitted to an audience must prostrate himself in the Eastern manner.

The object of territorial division between co-regents was primarily to meet special dangers on the different frontiers, but it served also the purpose of making usurpation more difficult by placing a representative of the imperial power within reach of all parts of the empire. In 286 Diocletian raised Maximian to the position of Augustus, and in 293 each Augustus appointed a Caesar as his subordinate. It was evidently intended that this arrangement should be permanent, and that on the death or abdication of an Augustus a Caesar should take his place and a new Caesar be appointed.[2] If all went well there would thus be no gap in the succession. Each Augustus received half the empire as his territorial sphere, of which he administered part directly, while a part was placed under the immediate control of his Caesar. Thus, in the first division, Diocletian himself retained the Eastern half, with Nicomedia as his most usual place of residence, while his Caesar, Galerius, administered Illyricum.[3] Maximian continued, as from the beginning of his co-regency, to be responsible for the West, with his most usual place of residence at Milan, while his Caesar, Constantius, ruled over Gaul and subsequently, when he had overcome the usurper there, Britain.

Though Diocletian's system did not survive in the exact form which he had given it, colleagueship and partition remained usual, and from the death of Theodosius the Great in 395 the Eastern and Western halves of the empire continued separate until the fall of the Western empire in 476. But, though this was so, and though the relations between the two halves were sometimes hostile, the empire remained in theory, and indeed in something more than theory, a single whole, of which the emperors were the joint rulers as the consuls had been in republican times. The joint Augustusship was in fact the latest expression of the old Roman idea of *imperium individuum*.[4] This ideal unity found its expression in the

[1] The diadem was definitely introduced by Constantine, though it is stated to have been worn already by Aurelian and by Diocletian; Bury, *History of the Later Roman Empire*, I (1923), 10.
[2] The use of "Caesar" as a title whereby to designate a successor was of course not new, but the Caesar had not, as such, previously taken any share in the government.
[3] I.e. the territory south of the Danube from the Black Sea to the Inn and the Carnic and Julian Alps.
[4] Bethmann-Hollweg, III. 11.

exercise of the right of legislation by each Augustus for the whole empire, for, though the laws bear the names, as a rule, of all Augusti, they were not in fact the result of consultation between the colleagues, but were issued by one emperor and subsequently sent for publication to the other parts of the empire.[1] A formal expression of unity was also to be seen in the arrangements for the nomination of the consuls, for there were still normally only two, one of whom was appointed at the beginning of the year by each emperor.[2]

Diocletian's system was intended, as we have seen, to provide for the succession to the throne without intermission or revolution. In the normal case, on the death of an emperor, a son, natural or adoptive, who had already been designated by receiving an imperial title,[3] would be ready to step into his place. But the theory of popular sovereignty was, even now, not completely given up, and the empire remained, in theory, elective. As before, the co-operation of the army (or part of it) and the senate[4] was required to constitute a new emperor, and his inauguration was not complete until he had been acclaimed by the people.[5] Orientalism however added a further element to the inaugural ceremonies. From about the middle of the fifth century the emperors were almost always crowned by the Patriarch of Constantinople, but it appears that this was rather a device for avoiding the difficulties which coronation by a lay subject would have caused than a recognition that the emperor in any way owed his position to the Church, and it does not appear to have been considered legally necessary.[6]

§ II. THE ADMINISTRATIVE MACHINE

Already in the later principate, the distinctions in standing between Italy and the remainder of the empire were becoming obliterated; in the dominate the levelling process is completed and the whole empire, with the exception only of Rome and the new capital at Constantinople, is administered upon a uniform plan, which differs in several important respects from that of the earlier period. The distinction between senatorial and imperial provinces disappears entirely, and a strict hierarchy of officials, dependent now solely on the emperor, rules with a heavy

---

[1] Bethmann-Hollweg, III. 216; cf. *infra*, 477.
[2] Bury, *op. cit.* I. 17.
[3] Sometimes already "Augustus" even though he was too young to exercise real power, but sometimes "Caesar", or *nobilissimus*; v. Bury, *op. cit.* I. 7–8.
[4] For formal recognition of the senate's power to elect v. *Nov. Maiorian*, I.
[5] Bury, *op. cit.* I. 5.   [6] Bury, *op. cit.* I. 11.

hand in every part.[1] Local differences exist, and in some minor respects the Eastern empire and the Western are differently organised, but in the main, uniform grading of officials and uniform ruthlessness in exploiting the subject prevail.

One important change is seen in the altered position of the praetorian prefects. These are no longer chiefs of staff, whose business it is to assist the emperor; they are to act in principle, not with the emperor, but in his stead (*vice sacra*),[2] and there is created under them an organisation separate from the central administration and even at times competing with it. For this purpose the whole empire is divided into four great prefectures, two in the East, and two in the West, the latter, of course, ceasing to exist on the fall of the Western empire. The prefectures are then divided into dioceses, each under a *vicarius*, the dioceses in turn consisting of a number of provinces. These last, however, are much smaller and more numerous than formerly, for in most cases the older provinces have been subdivided, and Italy has been incorporated in the provincial system.[3] The two Eastern prefectures were those of the East (*Oriens*) and Illyricum. *Oriens* included the dioceses of Oriens (Syria and Palestine), Asiana, Pontus, Thrace and Egypt;[4] Illyricum included the dioceses of Macedonia and Dacia. The prefectures of the West were those of the Gauls and the Italies. The Gauls comprised the dioceses of Britain, Gaul, *Viennensis* (S. Gaul) and Spain; the Italies included Italy, W. Illyria and Africa. Italy, however, although it appears in the *Notitia Dignitatum* as a single diocese, had two *vicarii*, one for the northern provinces (*Italia annonaria*), who had his capital at Milan, the other for the southern. The southern *vicarius* resided at Rome, and was hence called *vicarius in urbe*, but Rome and the district within a radius of 100 miles was under the *praefectus urbi*, who was independent of the praetorian

---

[1] Our chief source of information on this subject and on much else connected with the organisation of the empire is the *Notitia Dignitatum*, a copy of the lists of officials in order of precedence together with illustrations of their insignia which was in the hands of the *primicerius notariorum* ("First Secretary") of the West. The Eastern list did not strictly concern him; but was sent for reference; Bury, *op. cit.* I. 26.

[2] *Infra*, 460.

[3] Finally there were over 120 provinces, Stein, *Geschichte*, I. 103. On the prefectures *v.* Stein, *Zur spätrömischen Präfecturenverfassung*, Rheinisches Museum f. Phil. N.F. LXXIV (1925), 364–380, and Seeck, *Regesten der Kaiser u. Päpste* (Stuttgart, 1919), 141–149.

[4] The ruler of the diocese of *Oriens* is however called *comes*, not *vicarius*, and the title of the Egyptian governor continues to be *praefectus*. Until about 380 Egypt formed part of the diocese of *Oriens*; Bury, *op. cit.* I. 27.

prefect.[1] The *praefectus urbi* was the only one of the older officials who gained rather than lost in importance under the new system. The removal of the emperor's court to Milan, and later to Ravenna, gave him greater independence; the *praefecti annonae* and *vigilum* and other city officers were subordinated to him, and he became the chief representative of the ancient senatorial nobility. He consequently, alone among all the dignitaries of the empire, continued to wear the toga as his official dress.

For Constantinople, which was organised on the model of Rome, and its immediate neighbourhood, there was also a *praefectus urbi* with similar functions.

Even outside the two capitals, the system of prefecture, diocese and province was not carried through the empire without exception. Two provinces, those of Africa and Asia, are exempt from the power both of the prefect and the *vicarius*, and their governors retain their ancient titles of *proconsul*, the *proconsul* of Asia being further the superior of two minor provinces.[2] The governor of Achaea is also a *proconsul*; he is subject to the *praefectus per Illyricum*, but not to the *vicarius* of the diocese of Macedonia. The other governors are in some cases *consulares* (which title, however, no longer implies that the bearer has actually held the consulship), but normally merely *praesides*.[3] In some cases, though a diocese continues to exist, it has no *vicarius* of its own, but is administered directly by the prefect.[4]

Even apart from special cases, the subordination of the diocesan and provincial governors to the prefect is not complete. The *vicarii* were appointed, not by him, but by the emperor, and, though the provincial governors were appointed on his recommendation and could be suspended by him,[5] the emperor might communicate directly both with the *vicarius*

---

[1] Under Diocletian the *praefectus urbi* had a *vicarius* of his own, but Constantine transferred the duties of this officer to the *v. in urbe*, who is therefore generally called *v. urbis Romae*; Stein, *Geschichte*, I. 183.

[2] Hellespontus and Insulae; Bury, *op. cit.* I. 27.

[3] The expression *corrector*, applied to some governors, appears to refer to their office as governor, not to their rank. A *corrector* may be a *consularis*; Karlowa, I. 857–858.

[4] The reason for this appears to be that, though the *vicarii* were originally designed as a check on the prefect, they became in course of time more and more his subordinates, so that he might in some cases find it possible to dispense with them; Stein, *op. cit.* 181–182. Justinian did away with most of the diocesan governors and the dioceses finally disappeared in the seventh century; Bury, *op. cit.* II. 339.

[5] C. I. 26. 3; I. 50. 2.

and with the provincial governor, and the prefect might communicate directly with the governor of the province. Agents of the two great financial officers of the central government continued to be sent both to the dioceses and to the provinces, and the emperor also exercised control by means of a corps of special agents (*agentes in rebus*), among whom were the *curiosi*, a type of government spy, whose duty it was to notify any infraction of the law. It was one of the chief innovations under the new monarchy that military and civil powers should be separated. The prefect consequently loses all command over the troops,[1] though he is not entirely without military functions,[2] and becomes the chief of the ordinary civil administration. It is his duty to provide for law and order in general, for which purpose he retains a subordinate power of legislation.[3] Imperial enactments of importance are commonly addressed to him for application and publication. Since, according to the Roman principle, jurisdiction goes with administration, he has also great judicial powers, especially on appeal. He is also a very important financial officer, by reason especially of his control over the *annona*. This, since the time of Diocletian, had become the most important tax of all. The misrule and disasters of the third century had led to a progressive debasement of the coinage, with the result that the old taxes, in so far as they were fixed in money, brought in only a fraction of their original value, while the falling off in trade and wealth also greatly diminished the income derived from such imposts as the customs duties and the inheritance tax. The government was thus reduced to the expedient of unsystematic requisitions in kind, in order to meet its pressing requirements, chief among which was, of course, the provisioning of the army. These requisitions, like the deliveries in kind which had to be made at times for the supply of the capital, received the name of *annona*, which was also applied to the allowances received by each soldier or official. There was indeed in this, as in other respects, a partial degeneration to the system of natural economy. Diocletian, though he took some steps to reform the currency and issued his famous edict regulating the price of commodities and of labour, did not attempt to return completely to a money economy. Instead, he systematised the *annona*. For the purpose of its assessment, a unit, known as the *iugum*, was taken, which varied in area according to the productivity of the soil, five acres of vineyard being equivalent, for

---

[1] The praetorian guard was finally disbanded by Constantine and replaced by the *scholares*.

[2] In particular the provisioning of the armies.

[3] *Infra*, 478.

instance, in Syria, to 20 acres of the best, and 40 acres of less good arable land.[1]

Such a system requires constant revision of the assessment lists. This was to be undertaken every five years, but three five-yearly periods were taken together, giving a cycle of 15 years, called *indictio*, which came to be used for dating purposes.[2] The amount to be paid on each taxable unit was fixed annually by the emperor according to the needs of the government. Had the original survey and the periodic revisions been properly carried out, there would have been little to object to in the system,[3] but in fact the resources of the time in money and administrative machinery were not equal to the immense work involved, and methods of collection did not make for a fair distribution of the burden.

As in the later principate it was the praetorian prefects who were responsible for provisioning the army, so it was they who imposed the extraordinary requisitions with which the *annona* began. Under the reorganised system they continued to supervise its collection, and each had a chest of his own into which receipts flowed.[4] In fact the resources under their control were greater than those subject to the control of the central financial officers, and indeed were increased in course of time by usurpation of revenue which should have flowed into the central treasuries.[5] With the amelioration of currency conditions after Constantine's reforms, it became common to commute both the taxes in kind and the allowances to officials and soldiers for money (*adaeratio*), a practice which subsequently became almost universal.[6]

Like the prefect, the *vicarii* and the provincial governors were now purely civil officers concerned with administration and jurisdiction, the chief military officers of the empire being the *magistri militum*, while the troops in each province were under the command of a *dux*.[7]

---

[1] Related to this land-unit was the *caput*, or unit of labour. See especially Piganiol, *L'impôt de capitation sous le bas-empire romain* (Chambéry, 1916); Lot, *L'impôt foncier et la capitation personnelle sous le bas-empire et à l'époque franque* (Paris, 1928); Bott, *Die Grundzüge der Diokletianischen Steuerverfassung* (Darmstadt, 1928).

[2] The first cycle began probably in 297; Kübler, 369; Bury, *op. cit.* I. 47.

[3] Rostovtzeff however (*Economic History*, 465) says, "Every soldier could understand it, although any fool could see that in this case what was simple was not fair and just". [4] Stein, *Geschichte*, I. 62.

[5] Stein, *Geschichte*, I. 341; *Studien zur Gesch. des Byz. Reiches* (Stuttgart, 1919), 144–145.

[6] C. I. 52. 1; Bury, *op. cit.* I. 49; Willems, *Droit public romain*, 565, 622; Baynes, *Historia Augusta* (Oxford, 1926), 114–116.

[7] Under Justinian the combination of civil and military functions again became common; Bury, *op. cit.* II. 341.

In the central administration of each half of the empire there were four civil officials who, like the *praefecti praetorio* and the *praefectus urbi*, held the highest rank—that of *illustris*. These were the *quaestor sacri palatii*, the *magister officiorum* and the heads of the two treasuries (*comes sacrarum largitionum* and the *comes rerum privatarum*).

The *quaestor s.p.* was above all a Minister of Justice.[1] It was his duty to prepare drafts of laws and answers to petitions, for which purpose he had not only to be a learned lawyer, but also, in accordance with the views of the period, a master of the stylistic elegance which should distinguish the expression of all imperial wishes.[2] He had no staff of officials himself, but used those of the great bureaux (*scrinia*), whose chiefs thus no longer conferred directly with the emperor, and ceased to be what we should call Secretaries of State.

The *magister officiorum*,[3] as his title implies, was the actual administrative chief above the heads of the *scrinia*; he commanded the new imperial guard[4] and the *agentes in rebus*, and was thus the chief instrument of imperial control over the prefectoral administration. Since it was his business to introduce foreign ambassadors, he also became to some extent a Minister of Foreign Affairs.

The two chief financial officers ranking after the *quaestor* and the *magister* were the *comes sacrarum largitionum* and the *comes rerum privatarum*, heads, respectively, of the *fiscus* and of the *res privata*.[5] Even the *res privata* served public purposes, but certain crown lands, especially those of Cappadocia, in the East, and Africa, in the West, were set aside to provide for the expenses of the imperial courts and the emperors' privy purses. The Cappadocian estates were for this purpose at an uncertain date placed under the control of the *praepositus sacri cubiculi*.[6] The word *largitiones*, now used for the treasury, is probably derived from the fact that the greatest expense was the provision of donations to the army,[7] but it is also generally held to mark the absolute position of the monarch, as it implies that all expenditure on the public service is a free gift from him.

[1] The office was probably derived from that of the *quaestor Augusti* (*supra*, 337), but it had grown enormously in importance, chiefly by the attribution of duties formerly devolving on the *praefectus praetorio*; Stein, *Geschichte*, I. 170.

[2] Cf. Symmachus, *Ep.* I. 17.

[3] V. Boak, *The Master of the Offices in the later Roman and Byzantine Empires* (New York, 1919).

[4] *Supra*, 437, n. 1.

[5] In which the *patrimonium* was now merged; *supra*, 345.

[6] After 379; Bury, *op. cit.* I. 52.   [7] Stein, *Geschichte*, I. 175.

Absolutism is also typified by the position assigned to the Grand Chamberlain (*praepositus sacri cubiculi*)[1] and the other officers of the imperial household who became in effect great state officials. The *praepositus* himself, though not a regular member of the imperial council, held the rank of *illustris*, and according to the *Notitia Dignitatum* took precedence even over the *magister* and the *quaestor*.[2] In fact, though he was generally a eunuch, his influence was very great.

The change in the constitution is also reflected in the imperial council, now called *sacrum consistorium*, probably because the members stand, while the emperor alone sits. The special judicial council[3] ceases to exist as such, but the body as a whole receives a more definite organisation. Its members fall into two classes, the *comites illustres* and the *comites spectabiles*. The former are the *quaestor*, the *magister*, and the *comites sacrarum largitionum* and *rerum privatarum*; the latter, *comites consistoriani* in the narrow sense, are also chiefly high officials, either actually serving or retired.[4] The number, no doubt, varied, but is given under Valentinian III as twenty.[5] The *praefecti praetorio*, although *viri illustres*, do not appear to have been regular members, the principle being that their administration is separate from that of the emperor himself, but there can be little doubt that if one was present at court, he would be summoned to important sittings.[6] The position of the *magistri militum* was probably the same.

The duties of the *consistorium* were not strictly defined; it had indeed to advise the emperor on all matters for which he summoned it, though we know also of some regular business.[7] It played some part in legislation and formed the council of the emperor when he sat as judge. There is no evidence, however, whether or not it had anything to do with *rescripta*.[8]

The civil service, as a whole, is now definitely separated from the army, but, by a curious paradox, it is itself organised in a military manner,[9] and *militia* is the usual word for an official position, from which real

---

[1] V. Dunlap, *The Office of Grand Chamberlain in the later Roman and Byzantine Empires* (New York, 1924).

[2] Karlowa, I. 847. [3] *Supra*, 347.

[4] According to C. 12.19.8 the *proximi scriniorum*, i.e. the under-secretaries of the great bureaux, are to be made members on retirement.

[5] *Nov. Val.* 6. 3. 1.

[6] One in each half of the empire was normally at court. On the question v. Stein, *Geschichte*, I. 170.

[7] Karlowa, I. 849. [8] Krüger, 313.

[9] This is due ultimately to the use of soldiers in large numbers for all offices by Septimius Severus.

military service is distinguished as *militia armata*. Many of the names of the different ranks are taken from the usage of the army; officials wear military uniform with indication of their rank and the military belt, *cingulum*, which word comes indeed to be used as a synonym for office. Like soldiers, civil servants who are under *patria potestas* retain complete control over their pay (*peculium quasi-castrense*).

The posts fall into two classes marked by a difference in the form of the imperial commission which, however, had in both cases to be signed by the emperor himself.[1] The holders of the higher posts (*dignitates*) changed frequently, normally every year, but the lower officials commonly passed through the various ranks in their office during a long period of service and thus acquired experience which their superiors often lacked. This, no doubt, is the reason why in imperial constitutions the members of a dignitary's staff are often threatened with more severe penalties in case of any infraction of the law than is their chief himself. The real responsibility lies with them, and this fact explains how it was possible to promote inexperienced youths to high administrative positions.

Though the office of each dignitary was naturally organised specially for the duties which it was to carry out, there was a certain parallelism of organisation and nomenclature. Thus the head of the staff was *princeps*, the next in rank *cornicularius*, the third, *adiutor*. As nearly all the administrative officers had also judicial functions, they needed assistants for this work, in which the *cornicularius* was specially concerned, other officials being the *commentariensis*, who was chiefly engaged on the criminal side, and the *ab actis*, who dealt with civil matters.

The normal way of entering the service was through the class of *exceptores*. These had originally been merely professional secretaries, whose services were used by the officials as they required them; but they came to be organised in *scholae* or corporations, and were finally classed as a type of official, though they did not as a rule have the quasi-military privileges of the higher ranks until they were promoted. Promotion throughout the service was almost exclusively by seniority, but there were exceptions, and purchase was also possible in some cases.[2] Like all other

---

[1] *Codicilli* in the case of the higher, *probatoria* in that of the lower posts. The distinction between senatorial and equestrian offices (*supra*, 340) was, since the time of Constantine, no longer observed, and senatorial rank was attached to an increasing number of posts in the imperial service, with the result that many men who entered as knights became senators before or on their retirement (*v.* Stein, *Geschichte*, I. 185). In the end the rank of *eques* disappeared (*infra*, 446).

[2] C. 3. 28. 30. 2; Karlowa, I. 879. For the later history Andréadès, *N.R.H.* XLV (1921), 232–241.

professions, that of civil servant became hereditary; owing to the privileges enjoyed, compulsion cannot have been often necessary except in the case of the *officiales cohortalini*, i.e. those employed in the *officium* of the ordinary provincial governor, who were the lowest in the scale. Slaves and freedmen were now excluded from the service, a rule which is probably connected with its military nature.

It was characteristic of the bureaucratic system that a great deal of importance was attached to exact precedence, to insignia of office and to titles. The higher posts were divided into three classes according as they carried with them the rank of *illustris*, *spectabilis* or *clarissimus*. Already in the early principate, *vir clarissimus* had been the usual designation of a senator, and the members of the higher classes were strictly *viri clarissimi et illustres* or *clarissimi et spectabiles*. The title *perfectissimus*, which came next, was given to an increasing number of subordinate officials either during their service or on their discharge, and disappeared with the gradual cheapening of these ranks in the fifth century. Titles of office might also be given merely as an honorific distinction to persons who were not in the service at all; these were called *honorarii*, as opposed both to those actually holding an office (*in actu positi*), and those who were on a kind of reserve list (*vacantes*). The title *comes*[1] especially was given frequently as a distinction. This word had been used in the principate to describe advisers chosen by the emperor to accompany him on his journeys, but it subsequently became more definitely a title, and was used, in conjunction with some descriptive phrase, to designate the holders of various offices (*comes Orientis*, *sacrarum largitionum*, etc.). Constantine introduced the division of *comites* into three classes (*primi*, *secundi* and *tertii ordinis*). Counts of the first and second class were always officials, but doctors, advocates and others who had distinguished themselves might receive the *comitiva tertii ordinis*.

To Constantine is also due the revival of the word *patricius* in a totally different sense from that which it had previously had. It was strictly a title,[2] though conferred only on those who had held the highest offices, such as that of consul, *praefectus praetorio* or *urbi*, or *magister militum*. It was not hereditary, and seems to have been chosen not so much on account of its ancient associations, as because *pater* was a polite form of address which the emperor sometimes used towards the highest dignitaries.[3]

[1] *V.* Seeck, P.-W. s.v. *comites*.
[2] It appears however to have become also an office; *v.* Picotti, *Archivio storico Italiano* (1928), IX. 1–35.   [3] J. I. 12. 4.

A class of officials separate from those employed in the imperial offices consisted of those in the employment of the municipalities. These too were bound by hereditary duty. Real self-government in the cities had almost ceased to exist owing to the close surveillance of the provincial governors, but the local senates remained an indispensable part of the organisation of the empire. In particular they were responsible for the collection of the taxes, both prefectoral and imperial, and the magistrates retained some judicial powers. The constitutions had in appearance changed little, but all life was gone from them now that compulsion was necessary to fill the offices, and the decurionate had become a hated burden from which those who were liable did their best to escape. Apart from this general decay, the chief change was the rise of the *defensor civitatis*.[1] He was originally what we should call "standing counsel" to the municipality, but exercised also minor jurisdictional powers on behalf of the II *viri iure dicundo*.[2] In 365 Valentinian I made it his special business to protect the poorer classes (*plebs*) against illegal exactions both of the tax-collecting authorities and the great landowners (*potentiores*).[3] For this purpose, men of rank, who had held either a governorship or some other high office, were to be appointed, at first by the emperor himself, subsequently by the praetorian prefect. Their judicial powers were enlarged and they were to collect the taxes from poor people themselves.[4] The innovation met with but little success. The task was thankless, and in fact men of insufficient standing and character were appointed, who became the tools of those whom they were intended to combat. In 387 it was enacted that they were to be elected by the *curiae* subject to confirmation by the prefect, and in 409, that the suffrage in this matter should be extended as well to the local notables and the local bishop and clergy.[5] The result was that the office tended to become merely another municipal magistracy, and this development was completed when Justinian laid down that all the well-to-do inhabitants of the city (*honestiores*) should be bound to undertake the office in turn for a space of two years.[6] The history of the *cura reipublicae* had been repeated.[7]

After Christianity had become the religion of the empire, better protection might in fact be obtained by the poorer classes from the bishops, who were able to use the weapon of excommunication, and received constant additions to their temporal powers, until under

---

[1] Chenon, *Le defensor civitatis* (Paris, 1889).
[2] Stein, *Geschichte*, I. 278, 344.
[3] *C. Th.* I. 29. I.
[4] *C. Th.* II. 7. 12.
[5] *C. I.* 55. 8.
[6] Nov. 15.
[7] *Supra*, 356.

Justinian they had in fact become the heads of the municipal organisation.[1]

§ III. THE SENATES AND THE REMAINING REPUBLICAN MAGISTRACIES

In spite of the acknowledged absolutism of the later empire, the senate continued to exist, and indeed in some ways acquired greater authority than it had had towards the end of the principate. There were, however, now two senates, one at Rome and one at Constantinople. Constantine the Great when he founded New Rome had already given it a senate, similar to those of the other great Eastern cities, but his son, Constantius, raised this body to imperial rank. It did not, however, acquire an influence equal to that which the Roman senate—in fact always an aristocratic assembly representative of the landowning nobility—was still able to exercise.

As in the previous period, senatorial rank is hereditary and the numbers of the hereditary members are kept up by the introduction of imperial nominees, but the conditions are very different. In the first place compulsion has to be used even here. The sons of senators enter the body as before by holding a magistracy; but the magistracy is the praetorship, now a heavy burden on account of the expensive games which have to be provided.[2] Election was again by the senate itself, but the person elected could not refuse, and in fact nominations were made ten years in advance, apparently in order that sufficient preparation, if necessary by economies, should be made.[3]

The other element was supplied by imperial officials. An increasing number of posts, both actual and honorary, carried with them the clarissimate, or the higher rank of *spectabilis* or *illustris*, and in other cases the official received senatorial rank on his discharge from the service. The emperor might also grant it to *decuriones* or city officials who had distinguished themselves. As, however, these former civil servants of one sort or another were not as a rule wealthy, they received partial, or complete, immunity from the normal burdens of the senatorial class.

With the increase in numbers of senators, the percentage actually attending the sittings became smaller. Probably only the highest class,

---

[1] Stein, *Geschichte*, 1. 345. On episcopal jurisdiction *v. infra*, 464.

[2] Of the lower magistracies, the quaestorship, which also involved games, though at smaller expense, disappeared after the fourth century; Bury, *op. cit.* 1. 18. The tribunate is still mentioned as a title conferred by the emperor (*C. Th.* 12. 1. 74. 3) but we know of no functions. The aedileship had disappeared.

[3] *C. Th.* 6. 4. 13. 2.

the *illustres*, were normally active participants,[1] and already before the middle of the fifth century the two lower ranks were dispensed from the duty of residing in the capital.[2] The distinction which thus grew up hardened into law, and thus in Justinian's day it is clear that only the *illustres* had the right to vote.[3] The functions exercised by the senate were not very many or very definite, but it is misleading to say, with some writers, that it became merely the town council of the capital. On the one hand, the actual administration of Rome and Constantinople was in the hands of the city prefects and their subordinates, and, on the other, the senate had imperial functions, mainly, it is true, ornamental, but sometimes of political importance. Thus, as we have seen, it played a part in the inauguration of a new emperor[4] and, in an exceptional case, its choice might, at any rate in the West, be of real importance.[5] It was consulted sometimes with regard to legislation,[6] and might act as a court for the trial of treason if the emperor so wished.[7] In the West it was the stronghold of the Pagan aristocracy, and not altogether subservient, as its famous controversy with the emperors concerning the removal of the altar of Victory from the Senate House evidences.[8] In the fourth century, indeed, the Roman senate was able, not only to defend, but to increase the privileges of its order, and even that of the East, at first the mere creature of the power which had called it into being, was able to make some show of independence.[9]

Above the praetorship there still remained the consulate, now a purely honorary office, without any duties except that of providing the games. The emperor nominated the holder, and, as we have seen, there was commonly one for the East and one for the West.[10] As before, the consulate was the only office which the emperors themselves deigned to hold, and it was still the highest dignity in the empire. The expense of the games, however, was a serious drawback, and in 541 Justinian decided to put an end to it, after a continuous existence of over a thousand years.[11]

[1] In 356 it was enacted that fifty members should form a quorum (*C. Th.* 6. 4. 9) although the number of senators was probably over 2000; Kübler, 333.

[2] *C.* 12. 1. 15. In 450 those living in the provinces were exempted from the praetorship; *C.* 12. 2. 1.

[3] *D.* 1. 9. 12. 1 (interp.); *Nov.* 62. 2; Kübler, 333; Bury, *op. cit.* I. 21.

[4] *Supra*, 434.   [5] As in the case of Anthemius in 467.

[6] *Infra*, 477.   [7] *Infra*, 463.

[8] Gibbon, cap. 28 (Bury's edition, III. 190); Dill, *Roman Society in the Last Century of the Western Empire*, 29 sqq.

[9] Stein, *Geschichte*, I. 343, 446.   [10] *Supra*, 434.

[11] Succeeding emperors continued to assume the title in the first year of their reigns; Bury, *op. cit.* II. 348.

§ IV. CLASSES OF THE POPULATION

The social structure of the late Roman empire is characterised by a rigid class system in which each class has definite duties to perform for the benefit of the state. The material resources of the civilised world were no longer equal to the task of defending the vast territories of the empire against the increasing pressure of external enemies. Population and wealth had decreased, partly owing to internal strife and misgovernment, partly because those parts of the empire which were economically and culturally most advanced had been exhausted in the attempt to assimilate to themselves the great mass of semi-civilised peoples whom conquest had rapidly brought within the same political organisation.[1] Had the modern development of science and machinery taken place, it might have been possible to increase wealth and population sufficiently quickly to withstand the strain, but, as matters were, compulsion was the only expedient to which the government could have recourse, and it was consequently bound to place such burdens on its subjects, either by way of taxation or labour, that the individual appeared to be merely an instrument for the preservation of the state, and compulsory social organisation reached a degree of intensity which has probably never been equalled.

The highest rank was that of the senatorial nobility. This, as we have seen, was intimately connected with the higher posts in the imperial administration. But it was no mere official nobility; the senators were also the greatest landowners, and as such had their part to play in exaction of the necessary contributions from the cultivators of the soil. They were free from municipal burdens,[2] but subject to special taxes of their own, the *follis senatorius*, a kind of land tax,[3] and the *aurum oblaticium*, originally a free gift of gold made to the emperor on festive occasions, but subsequently a definite impost. In addition they had to assume the expensive office of praetorship. Of their privileged position with respect to the administration of justice, something will be said in the next chapter.

The second order of nobility which existed under the principate, the *equites*, did not long survive. Under Constantine already, senators were in principle admitted to the offices formerly reserved for knights, and the title, *vir perfectissimus*, once distinctive of the higher ranks of the equestrian service, was given to an increasing number of subordinate officials.

[1] Rostovtzeff, *Studien zur Geschichte des r. Kolonates* (1910), 388 *sqq.*
[2] D. 50. 1. 22. 5.
[3] Abolished about 450; C. 12. 2. 2.

Equites are still mentioned in a constitution of 364,[1] but the title had already then lost all significance, except in the city of Rome, and the preservation of the constitution in Justinian's Code seems to be a piece of archaism.[2]

The third class of the principate, the *curiales*, were still, in theory, a privileged class, belonging for the purpose of the criminal law to the *honestiores* and spoken of, as a rule, with respect in imperial constitutions. In fact, however, their position was usually pitiable. Already before the end of the principate it had become necessary to apply compulsion to qualified persons in order to fill the magisterial positions.[3] Now it might even happen that enrolment was used as a punishment, and although the emperors forbade this practice,[4] they did not always observe the prohibition themselves.[5] The property qualification was fixed at no more than 25 *iugera* or 300 *solidi*,[6] liability to undertake burdens began at the age of eighteen,[7] though whether the youth became then technically a member of the council is doubtful.[8] The status was hereditary in the male line, and a father had to leave a portion of his property at his death to his sons or grandsons to enable them to meet the expenses of their position. If he were succeeded by any person not liable to the curial burdens, one-quarter went to the *curia*.[9] If a daughter succeeded, her husband had to take the burdens.[10] Illegitimate children born of concubines might be legitimated by making them sole heirs and, in the case of sons, offering them as members to the *curia*, in the case of daughters, marrying them to a *decurio*.[11] To ensure their property against dissipation, *curiales* were forbidden to alienate land without the special permission of the provincial governor,[12] and even their personal liberty was strictly curtailed; if they attempted to escape their duties by entering some other profession they could be forced to return.[13] The heaviest burden they had to bear was that of collecting the taxes; for the amount to be collected, the collector was himself liable, and in case of default by him, the magistrates by whom he had been nominated.[14]

---

[1] *C. Th.* 6. 37. 1 (*C.* 12. 31. 1).
[2] The reason may be that the privileges of the *ordo equester* for the purposes of criminal law were still regarded as valid; Kübler, P.-W. s.v. *Equites Romani sub fin.*
[3] *Supra*, 358.
[4] *C.* 10. 32. 38.
[5] *C. Th.* 16. 2. 39.
[6] *C. Th.* 12. 1. 33; *Nov. Val.* 3. 4.
[7] *C. Th.* 12. 1. 7, 19, 58.
[8] Karlowa, I. 899.
[9] *C.* 10. 35. In *Nov.* 38 Justinian enlarged the rights of the *curia*.
[10] *C. Th.* 12. 1. 124.
[11] *C.* 5. 27. 3; J. 1. 10. 13.
[12] *C.* 10. 34. 1.
[13] E.g. *C. Th.* 12. 1. 181.
[14] *C.* 10. 72. 2.

The services, civil and military, the senators and, subject to what has just been said, the *curiales* form the privileged classes. The remainder of the population takes no part in the government, and its liberty is often limited by the requirements of taxation and the system of compulsory social organisation. In the towns, especially the capitals, numbers of persons are bound by hereditary duty to become members of trade guilds and cannot escape from the task imposed upon them by the state. Among these guilds were the *navicularii*, shipowners, charged especially with the duty of transporting supplies for Rome and Constantinople, the bakers, the butchers and the porters (*saccarii*). Others, for instance the workmen in the state munition factories (*fabricenses*), were in an even worse position and were branded like slaves. The guilds, or at least some of them, originated as voluntary corporations working for the state under contract, and their members might enjoy certain privileges by reason of the services they rendered. Those, for instance, who used the greater part of their capital in the shipping trade were, in the principate, free from public burdens for five years.[1] Such immunities favoured the growth of a class, and no doubt the son usually succeeded to his father's calling and his father's capital. The existence of these classes then gave a handle to officials who were hard pressed to find the means of getting necessary services carried out. Diocletian used compulsion freely, and under Constantine the change was complete. Not only were the sons bound to their fathers' trade, but the burden might, as in the case of the *navicularii*, rest upon the guildsman's property. Anyone becoming heir to a *navicularius* or acquiring a *res navicularia* was liable to the extent of the property for the burdens placed upon the guild.[2] It was the special duty of the *defensores* and municipal magistrates to prevent members of the guilds from leaving their work, and to reclaim them if they escaped.[3] The tradespeople in the towns (*negotiatores*) were also organised in corporations, of which the main purpose was the collection of a tax (*auri lustralis collatio*), from which even the least respectable occupations did not escape. Anastasius however abolished this particular impost,[4] and the relief was evidently much appreciated.

If compulsion was applied to the inhabitants of the towns, it fell even more heavily on the rural population. The bulk of agricultural labour was carried on by *coloni*, i.e. persons who closely resembled the villeins of the middle ages in that they were bound to the soil which they cultivated, and could be reclaimed by the landowner if they escaped, while on the

---

[1] D. 50. 4. 5.
[2] Karlowa, I. 915.
[3] C. Th. 12. 19. 3.
[4] C. 11. 1.

other hand the landowner might not alienate them without the land, or the land without them. They were not all in exactly the same legal position. Some were apparently in every other way free; others, generally called *adscripticii*, were much more nearly in the position of slaves. Though capable of marriage,[1] they could not alienate their property without the permission of the lord,[2] were subject to corporal punishment, and could bring no action against the lord except in case of grave crime or an attempt to exact a larger rent than was due by custom.[3] The exact legal ground of the distinction is unknown. According to some writers *adscripticii* were those who had no land of their own,[4] but this cannot be the sole ground for distinguishing as it appears that persons who became *coloni* by prescription were in the better position.[5] The main purpose of the institution was to secure cultivation of the soil and consequently payment of taxation. The land tax proper was payable by the landlord, but the *coloni* were, it seems, themselves liable for the *annona*, which they in some cases paid themselves, in others delivered with their rent (usually in kind) to the lord, who was liable for it to the state authorities.[6]

The status was normally acquired by birth, a person being a *colonus* if his mother was a *colona* in accordance with the principle which applies to slavery.[7] If the mother was free and the father a *colonus*, the earlier rule was that, contrary to principle, the child should follow the father, but Justinian enacted that in such cases the children were to be free. The lord could, however, protect himself from the loss of prospective *coloni* by forbidding or breaking up such marriages.[8] If the parents were both *coloni*, but subject to different lords, then, according to Justinian's enactment, the children were to be divided, the mother's lord having the advantage in case of an odd number.[9] Persons might also become *coloni* by prescription if they worked on the land of another in such a position for thirty years,[10] and sturdy beggars might be assigned as *coloni* to landowners in the district.[11] Unlike slavery, the status might also be acquired by contract, which, however, needed to be enrolled in the archives.[12]

---

[1] And probably of military service, for it was presumably from among them that the landlords took the recruits whom they were bound to furnish; Karlowa, I. 921.   [2] C. 11. 50. 2. 3. Their property is called *peculium*.
[3] C. 11. 50. 2. 4.   [4] Kübler, 348.   [5] C. 11. 48. 19; 23. 1.
[6] C. 11. 48. 20. 3; Karlowa, I. 921. Piganiol, *L'impôt de capitation sous le bas-empire romain*, 46.
[7] C. 11. 48. 16; 11. 68. 4.   [8] C. 11. 48. 24.
[9] Nov. 162. 3.   [10] C. 11. 48. 18; 23. 1.
[11] C. Th. 14. 18. 1.   [12] C. 11. 48. 22.

There was no method of enfranchisement; originally thirty years *de facto* liberty in the case of a man and twenty in the case of a woman had been sufficient to break the tie,[1] but this was no longer the rule under Justinian.[2] Nor did entry into holy orders free a man, unless (under Justinian) he became a bishop.[3]

How the colonate originated is still an unsettled question,[4] but it is obvious that if a satisfactory answer is ever found it will not be a simple one. Even in its developed state the institution was, as we have seen, not uniform, and to know its history, we should have to know the history of land tenure throughout all the provinces of the empire, not only since the Roman conquest, but even before, for the Romans never began with a clean sheet, but adapted themselves in one way or another to the conditions that they found existing, and the circumstances were different in every province. One root of the colonate is to be found in the tenure of land in the Hellenistic monarchies by peasants who were outside the Greek cities and dependent directly upon the king whose serfs they were. Much of the land was acquired by the emperors, and the position of the population hardly changed at all. In Egypt under the native dynasties the king had been the only landowner,[5] and compulsory social organisation had been carried to extremes hardly reached even by the later Roman empire. With the Macedonian conquest, some measure of private property in land was created in favour of the Greek settlers, but in the main the Ptolemies stepped into the shoes of the Pharaohs.

Under the Romans there was a further development of private property, but the general system of the country was not upset. Close governmental control continued, and the system of compulsory labour could not be abandoned in a country which depended for its prosperity on the constant maintenance of irrigation works.

Africa again has a different history, of which the chief point of interest for the present purpose is the system of farming by means of *procuratores*, who managed great tracts of country on behalf of imperial or private landowners, collected the rents from the small tenants and also leased some lands themselves, which they cultivated by means of obligatory services imposed upon the tenants as a condition of their tenure.

---

[1] *C. Th.* 5. 18. 1.

[2] *C.* 11. 48. 22.

[3] Nov. 123. 4. *Curiales* on the other hand if elected bishops were to be removed and returned to the *curia*.

[4] See especially Rostovtzeff, *Studien zur Geschichte des r. Kolonates* (1910).

[5] Except the temples.

In the late republic and early principate there is no doubt that much of the agricultural labour on the great estates was done by slaves,[1] but there was an increasing tendency to substitute free tenants as the empire ceased to expand and the supply of slaves fell off. The word for tenant is *colonus*, and the tenant appears in works on private law simply as a free person who enters into the consensual contract of *locatio conductio* with the owner of the land. But this is not the whole truth; in fact he was, as we have seen, especially in the provinces, a person in a dependent position, subject very often to compulsory labour for his landlord or for the state, and often no doubt in arrears with his rent, so that he could not leave the land without forfeiting the property over which the landlord had a lien.[2]

The late empire made his dependence a matter of strict law, not everywhere at the same time or in the same way, but as part of the policy of compulsion which the needs of the government imposed upon it. One important contributory cause was the fact that with a decreased population and oppressive taxation a great deal of land fell out of cultivation and hence did not contribute its quota to the treasury. The government, unable to find tenants itself, resorted to the expedient of forcing neighbouring landowners to take over the land and become responsible for the taxes.[3] This was an ancient practice in Egypt, but it was extended to other parts of the empire and had become common already in the fourth century.[4] Imperial lands too, for which the government was no longer able to find tenants, it handed over, under one method of tenure or another, to great landowners, and with the land it assigned also its own powers over the cultivators.[5] As the pressure of fiscal needs became heavier, there was less supervision of the landowners or large leaseholders in the interests of the small tenants; provided the great men paid the taxes, for which they were responsible, the government shut its eyes to oppression.[6]

The result of these changes was that the social structure of the late empire showed some resemblances to feudalism. Not only were the cultivators bound to the soil, but their landlords acquired powers of jurisdiction over them, and became a force with which even the imperial power had to reckon. Some even kept bands of armed retainers, known

---

[1] In Egypt however slaves were never numerous.
[2] Kübler, 350.
[3] ἐπιβολή; *iunctio*. [4] Rostovtzeff, *op. cit.* 393.
[5] Wilcken, *Grundzüge*, 314 *sqq.* (Mitteis-Wilcken, *Grundzüge u. Chrestomathie der Papyruskunde*, I. I).
[6] Rostovtzeff, *op. cit.* 397.

as *bucellarii*. The practice was forbidden in 468, but such troops in the private employment of high military officers became an acknowledged feature of Byzantine armies.[1] A system of "patronage" grew up under which the inhabitants of country districts placed themselves under the protection of some powerful person,[2] such protection being especially useful against the exactions of the imperial government itself, and though the government attempted to combat the institution, the very constitutions which forbid the formation of the tie are bound to recognise it as an existing fact.

From what has been said it is clear that the new division into social classes had taken the place of the old distinction between *cives*, *Latini* and *peregrini*. The distinction between *ius civile* and *ius gentium* became obliterated and the law applied to all persons, in so far as it was not affected by their social status, was the same. The limitations of the *constitutio Antoniniana*, whatever they may have been, were neglected, and, for what it was worth, every free man counted as a citizen. Justinian tells us that the condition of *dediticia libertas* had fallen into oblivion, and that Latins (by which he means Junian Latins) were rare. He abolished both classes entirely, and, as he somewhat grandiloquently says, restored the ancient Roman rule that there should be but one sort of liberty.[3] Manumission consequently, if valid at all, gave citizenship. The only *peregrini* within the empire were the barbarians settled on the frontiers.[4]

---

[1] Bury, *op. cit.* II. 77.

[2] De Zulueta, "De Patrociniis Vicorum" (*Oxford Studies in Social and Legal History*, ed. Vinogradoff, 1); Martroye, "Les patronages d'agriculteurs et de vici au IV et au V siècles", *R.H.* VII (1928), 201–248.

[3] J. 1. 5. 3; C. 7. 5; 7. 6.

[4] Buckland, 99. Justinian avoids the word *peregrinus*.

Chapter XXVI

PROCEDURE AND JURISDICTION IN THE DOMINA|TE

As befits the system of absolute monarchy, the courts of the period were wholly dependent upon the imperial power itself, and procedure both civil and criminal lost connection with the typically republican institutions that had been preserved to a greater or lesser extent during the transitional period of the principate. Since the imperial bureaucracy was supreme throughout, there was even less distinction between the criminal and civil courts than there had been in the principate, and of criminal procedure there is little that need be said here except that the *quaestiones perpetuae* disappeared entirely, and that the dual position of the magistrate, who acted both as judge in an accusatory procedure and as investigator in the interests of order, without the need of any private accuser, continued to exist as before.[1] Imperial legislation in matters of crime was much commoner than under the principate, but was often self-contradictory as well as savage, and the vice of arbitrariness could not be eradicated in a period when legal science was in a decline. Of civil procedure there is however much that must be said before the general development of the law can be understood, and a section on this subject is prefixed to the general discussion of the judicial structure.

§ I. CIVIL PROCEDURE

A. DISAPPEARANCE OF THE FORMULARY SYSTEM. Already at the beginning of this period, the formulary system proper, resting upon a contractual *litis contestatio*, was obsolete both in the provinces and at Rome itself. A constitution of 294, which forbids provincial governors to delegate the hearing of cases to *iudices pedanei* except under pressure of business,[2] is sometimes held to have actually abolished it for the provinces, but in truth, the absence of any reference to the *iudex* of the formulary system presupposes rather that the change had already taken place.[3] At Rome, under the reformed constitution, the *praefectus urbi* is

---

[1] Cf. *supra*, 409.   [2] C. 3. 3. 2.

[3] Girard, 1140; *contra* Costa, *Profilo storico*, 142. How long before it had ceased to exist is doubtful. For Rome its existence in the time of the Severi is attested by inscriptions; Wlassak, *Provinzialprozess*, 29. Girard, 1139, n. 2, holds that its existence at that time in the provinces too is shown by C. 3. 8. 2 and 7. 53. 2, and even in Gordian's reign by C. 3. 36. 7. Wlassak, *op. cit.* 25, 29, treats these as examples of delegated jurisdiction. See however Boyé, *Denuntiatio*, 295.

the chief jurisdictional magistrate, and the *praetor urbanus*, whose court was presumably the last refuge of the ancient procedure, has ceased to have any judicial functions. But the disappearance of the formulary procedure proper does not by any means imply that *formulae* ceased altogether to be used for judicial purposes. We have already seen that in the opinion of some modern scholars there existed a hybrid type of procedure in which there was a division of proceedings into those *in iure* and *apud iudicem*, although the *iudex* was appointed by the magistrate and not by agreement between the parties. This, it is thought, continued to exist for the trial of "ordinary" matters until in 342 the sons of Constantine abolished finally "legal *formulae* with the pitfalls that they set by their minute care of syllables".[1]

But even those who do not believe in the existence of such a procedure admit that the influence of the *formulae* remained strong. Like our own forms of action, they continued to "rule from the grave" long after they had been abolished.[2] Nor was their influence confined to the survival of the substantive law which had been worked out under the classical system. For a long time the plaintiff had still to "ask the magistrate for an action",[3] and, as we shall see, the naming of actions according to the old terminology plays a part in the procedure of Justinian's day.[4] Some rules even survive which would appear to be inconvenient and to have lost the justification which they formerly had in the logic of the formulary system.[5]

With the final disappearance of the divided system, there disappeared also the distinction between "ordinary" and "extraordinary" matters. Any person who thought he had a legal claim against another now began his action in the same way, and the trial proceeded before the magistrate himself, or possibly his deputy, according to the same principles, no matter what was the historical origin of the substantive law under which he claimed. Differences which had existed within the *ordo* itself, in particular that between actions and interdicts, similarly ceased to exist, though of course the law which had come into existence through the interdicts was not affected.[6] This much however remains to be said.

---

[1] C. 2. 57. 1: *Iuris formulae aucupatione syllabarum insidiantes cunctorum actibus radicitus amputentur.* Cf. *supra*, 404. For a different view *v.* Boyé, *op. cit.* 308 *sqq.*

[2] Maitland, *Forms of Action*, 296.

[3] This was made unnecessary in 428; C. 2. 57. 2.   [4] *Infra*, 456.

[5] Diocletian (*Consultatio*, 5. 7) reaffirmed the rule that *plus petitio* resulted in complete and final loss of an action and so the rule remained until the reforms of Zeno and Justinian; J. 4. 6. 33; C. 3. 10. 1 and 2.   [6] J. 4. 15. pr. and 8.

Interdicts had in classical times had something of the nature of a summary procedure, and this characteristic was retained by the actions which took their place. There was, it is true, never any very definite type of summary procedure, but certain classes of case were exempt from the usual requirements of written pleadings and other formalities, and among these were the interdictal actions.[1]

B. SUMMONS. With the formulary system there disappeared also *in ius vocatio* (in its original sense) and *vadimonium*. It was no longer the business of the plaintiff unaided to bring the defendant before the court. But we must here distinguish two periods. In the earlier, which is that represented by the Theodosian code, the action is begun by a *litis denuntiatio*; in the time of Justinian this method has been replaced by what is called the libellary procedure.[2]

The *litis denuntiatio* appears to be a development of that which had existed already in the *cognitio extra ordinem* of the principate.[3] As before, it consists of a notice served upon the defendant at the instance of the plaintiff, but with the authorisation of a magistrate. The usual practice, at least at Rome, seems at one time to have been for the plaintiff himself to serve the notice and draw up a document attested by witnesses to prove the service (*privata testatio*).[4] But this led to abuses and was abolished by a constitution of 322 which required that, in addition to the preliminary magisterial authorisation, the plaintiff should also secure for the actual service the co-operation of an official with the right of keeping public records (*ius actorum conficiendorum*).[5] Exactly what had to be stated in the *denuntiatio* is not clear, but it would seem that it called upon the defendant to present himself before the court and remain there until the matters alleged against him should be settled,[6] and it is certain that a period of four months began to run from that moment, at the end of which both parties had to appear before the court, and the trial began.[7] If the defendant failed to appear, proceedings *in contumaciam* might be begun; if the plaintiff was absent, he lost his case, subject to the possibility

---

[1] C. 8. 1. 4. The scope of the constitution (*C. Th.* 2. 4. 6) had originally been much wider; cf. Wenger, 316.

[2] Examples of this procedure occur as early as 434, *v. P. Oxy.* 1876–1879; Collinet, *R.H.* III (1924), 722.

[3] Boyé, *Denuntiatio*, 320 *sqq.*; Fliniaux, *R.H.* IX (1930), 193–233; *contra*, Kipp, *Litisdenuntiation*, 142, 182.

[4] Cf. *supra*, 405.   [5] *C. Th.* 2. 4. 2.

[6] This is the common form of the Egyptian παραγγελίαι; *v.* Mitteis, *Chrest.* Nos. 50 *sqq.*

[7] *C. Th.* 2. 6. 1; 2. 18. 2.

of reinstatement on petition to the court (*reparatio temporum*), which must not be granted more than twice.

Of the procedure in Justinian's day rather more is known. It developed out of the older type, the chief difference being the abolition of the period of four months, which had been found inconvenient.[1] The plaintiff begins by handing in, to the tribunal within whose competence the case lies,[2] a *libellus conventionis*, which we may compare with our "statement of claim", but which also serves the purposes of a writ. In this he must make clear, as in the old *editio actionis*, the nature of his claim, for which purpose the nomenclature of the formulary system was still used, though not always understood.[3] *Plus petitio* and other mistakes, such as mentioning a wrong ground of action, were still possible, but the consequences were no longer as serious as they had been,[4] and the freedom with which amendments were permitted during the course of the trial must frequently have embarrassed the defence.[5] The plaintiff must sign the *libellus*, and must undertake with security to bring the matter to a *litis contestatio* within two months (failing which he must pay the defendant twice the amount of the costs occasioned by the omission),[6] to prosecute the cause to the end, and to pay one-tenth of the sum at issue in case judgment went against him.[7] The magistrate examines the *libellus*, and if he finds it correct on the face of it, orders it to be served on the defendant by an officer of the court, the *exsecutor*. On receipt of the *libellus*, the defendant has to pay certain fees to the *exsecutor* and to undertake (normally with security) that he will appear in court and remain there until the end of the trial.[8] Failing security he may be imprisoned.[9] He has also to acknowledge receipt of the claim and to answer it in a *libellus responsionis*,[10] though it appears that this answer need not contain more than an admission or denial of the claim,[11] and the date of

---

[1] Wenger, 265, n. 18; Boyé, *op. cit.* 328 *sqq.*

[2] Boyé, *op. cit.* 333–334.

[3] *Consult.* 5. 2; Mitteis, *Chrest.* No. 55; Wenger, 261, 265, n. 19; Collinet, *Études*, I. 193.   [4] *Supra*, 454, n. 5.

[5] J. 4. 6. 35. The defendant however had a corresponding right to put forward *exceptiones*, unless merely dilatory, at any stage in the proceedings; C. 7. 50. 2; 8. 35. 8.

[6] Nov. 96. 1.   [7] Nov. 112. 2. pr.   [8] J. 4. 11. 2.

[9] C. 9. 4. 6. 3. But the case is then tried within thirty days.

[10] ἀντιβιβλίον, Nov. 53. 3. 2.

[11] Wenger, 267, n. 26. The matter is much disputed and answers setting out the defence in more detail were certainly possible. *C.I.L.* VIII. 17,896, is quoted by Cuq, 891, n. 2, as showing that they might be four times as long as the claim, but the text is obscure.

its receipt, the object of this being to ensure that at least twenty days should be allowed to elapse before the hearing began.[1] With this limitation, it was for the plaintiff to fix the day. If the defendant failed to appear, proceedings *in contumaciam* might be begun, and if he continued absent judgment finally obtained against him.[2]

In addition to this normal method of beginning an action it was still possible to use rescript procedure.[3] The plaintiff, having obtained his rescript from the imperial office, must employ an *exsecutor* to convey it to the magistrate, who then sees that a copy is served on the defendant.[4] Justinian limited, but did not abolish this type of procedure.[5]

C. TRIAL. On the appointed day, if the defendant appeared and acknowledged the justice of the claim, judgment was given against him at once; if he did not acknowledge it, the trial began by a statement of the claim and of the defence (*narratio* and *responsio*), after which the parties had each to take an oath that they were not acting vexatiously, and counsel that they believed their clients' cases to be reasonable, not based on false statements, and that should anything of the sort come to their knowledge they would throw up their briefs.[6] This proceeding bore some outward resemblance to the old *litis contestatio*, though there was of course nothing contractual about it, and it was therefore chosen as marking the critical moment for the purpose of applying the old rules concerning *litis contestatio* in so far as these survived.[7] But the old rules were logical deductions from the contractual nature of the *litis contestatio*, and even Justinian's antiquarian zeal was not equal to the task of fitting them satisfactorily into the new procedure, based as it was on totally different conceptions.

With the formulary system there disappeared necessarily the *exceptio* in the original procedural sense of the term, but the word remained to designate the same type of defence, though it was now raised in a different way.[8] Thus if the plaintiff in his claim (to which the word *intentio* is now applied) alleges a debt, it is still possible for the defendant

---

[1] Nov. 53. 3. 1 and 2.

[2] The process might be very long; v. Steinwenter, *Versäumnisverfahren,* 193 *sqq.*

[3] Andt, *La procédure par rescrit* (Paris, 1920).

[4] Wenger, 309.

[5] Nov. 113. 1; v. Costa, *Profilo,* 199; Cuq, 891.

[6] C. 2. 58. 2. pr.; 3. 1. 14. 4.

[7] C. 3. 9. 1 (interp.); 3. 1. 14. 4. For discussion v. now especially Steinwenter, "Litiskontestation im Libellprozesse", *Z.S.S.* L. 184–211.

[8] C. 8. 35. 9.

to plead fraud, and such defence would still be called *exceptio doli*. Peremptory exceptions, i.e. those which, if proved, will defeat the claim finally, can be raised at any stage of the proceedings, but dilatory exceptions (for instance a plea that there has been a pact not to sue for a time and that the time has not yet elapsed) must be pleaded before *litis contestatio*. Now that there is no need to send all questions in a single *formula* before a *iudex* these and other matters, such as pleas to the jurisdiction,[1] can be disposed of as preliminary points, and interlocutory judgments can be given on incidental matters as appears necessary.

There is thus obviously a great increase in the flexibility of the procedure, but on the other hand the judge has no longer the freedom in estimating the value of evidence which had characterised the older system. He is an official of a bureaucratic government which is constantly binding him by new rules and threatening him with penalties if he disobeys them. Some of these rules show clearly the changes which society has undergone. Oral testimony is distrusted as against the evidence of documents,[2] and for the valuation of different types of document, careful rules are laid down.[3] The evidence of a single witness is allowed no weight at all.[4] The credibility of witnesses is to be judged by their social status;[5] those of low rank, if in any way suspect, may be put to the torture.[6] Heretics and Jews may not be witnesses where either party is an orthodox believer.[7] Rules concerning legal presumptions are introduced, i.e. the judge is bound on the proof of certain facts to infer certain other facts, either in the absence of evidence to the contrary (rebuttable presumption) or even in spite of evidence to the contrary (conclusive presumption), regardless of his own view as to the probability of the case.[8]

If the judge is now the servant of the state, he is, as such, the master of the parties, and this changed position manifests itself in several ways. It is no longer simply the business of the parties to produce such witnesses as they can persuade to come; the court issues a summons, and all except *illustres* are bound, if called upon, to give evidence on oath.[9] The examination is no longer conducted by the parties or their counsel but by the judge, though probably counsel could suggest questions to be put to a witness.[10] Much use, for the purposes of evidence, is made of

[1] C. 8. 35. 13.
[2] C. 4. 20. 1; 18.
[3] Nov. 73.
[4] C. 4. 20. 9; cf. Deuteronomy XIX. 15.
[5] C. 4. 20. 9.
[6] Nov. 90. 1.
[7] C. 1. 5. 21. pr.
[8] D. 34. 3. 28. 3 (interp.). Other examples H.-S. s.v. *praesumptio*.
[9] C. 4. 20. 16. pr.; 19. pr.
[10] Bethmann-Hollweg, III. 278.

oaths by the parties, which can be required of them either by the opposing party or by the judge according to a complex system,[1] and the judge is definitely instructed to ask questions of the parties.[2] The inquisitorial principle has thus found its way even into civil cases. It does not appear that there were any concluding speeches of counsel after the completion of the evidence; their duty seems rather to have lain in dealing with individual matters as they arose in course of the trial.[3]

D. JUDGMENT. Judgment must now always be in writing, but it has to be read out in court by the judge himself, and copies of it must be handed to the parties.[4] The rule of *condemnatio pecuniaria* is no longer in force, and the judge can therefore order a specific thing to be handed over to the plaintiff. Specific performance of obligations to do something (*facere* as opposed to *dare* or *tradere*) is however not ordered.[5] All judgments are now normally appealable,[6] although frivolous appeals are discouraged by pecuniary penalties,[7] and Justinian forbade a litigant to appeal more than twice in the same matter.[8] The appeal is always by way of rehearing and new evidence may be produced.[9] The entering of an appeal acts as a stay of execution.[10]

E. EXECUTION. If there is no appeal, or the appeal is dismissed and the judgment is not satisfied voluntarily, execution proceedings are still begun by an *actio iudicati*.[11] This is of course itself an action under the new procedure, and differs from the ancient *actio iudicati* in that the defendant, if he denies liability unsuccessfully, is no longer liable to pay twice the original amount of the judgment. If the judgment is for the delivery of a specific thing, the officers of the court seize it and hand it over to the plaintiff.[12] In the case of judgments for sums of money, execution against the person appears still to have been legal, though according to law debtors might no longer be privately imprisoned by their creditors.[13] What is clear is that, in fact, private imprisonment by

---

[1] C. 4. 1. 12.

[2] C. 3. 1. 9.

[3] Bethmann-Hollweg, III. 291.

[4] C. 7. 44 *passim*.

[5] D. 42. 1. 13. 1. Contrast C. 7. 4. 17.

[6] Nov. 82. 12.

[7] C. 7. 62. 6. 4; Nov. 49. 1. pr. Constantine, *C. Th.* 1. 5. 3, had punished the unsuccessful appellant, if rich by two years' *relegatio* and confiscation of half his fortune, if poor by two years' labour in the mines.

[8] C. 7. 70.

[9] C. 7. 62. 6. 1 and 2.

[10] Wenger, 296; Bethmann-Hollweg, III. 328; C. 7. 62. 3.

[11] *V.* Liebman, *St. Bonfante*, III. 397–405. For doubts whether this is really an action at all *v.* Buckland, *Main Institutions*, 395.

[12] D. 6. 1. 68 (interp.).

[13] Woess, *Z.S.S.* XLIII. 490.

powerful creditors was an evil which the state, in spite of repeated enactments, was not strong enough to uproot.[1]

Bonorum venditio, closely connected as it was with the old procedure, ceased to exist altogether,[2] and execution against the goods was normally by seizure and sale of sufficient of the debtor's property (*pignus in causa iudicati captum*).[3] Only in case of actual bankruptcy was a debtor's whole property sold, and then no longer in mass, for a dividend, but in detail (*distractio bonorum*).[4]

§ II. THE COURTS AND JURISDICTION

In treating of jurisdiction under the principate it was necessary to distinguish between Rome, Italy and the Provinces. Under the dominate, Italy lost her peculiar position and the judicial powers of the republican magistrates vanished almost completely even at Rome. Apart therefore from the minor municipal jurisdiction, judicial authority, both civil and criminal, was now vested in the imperial officials, divided for these as for other purposes into the three ranks of *illustres*, *spectabiles* and *clarissimi*. The chief importance of this distinction was that the two higher classes acted *vice sacra*, i.e. they were the standing repositories of the imperial jurisdiction, mainly appellate, which had grown up during the principate, and had already then been commonly delegated to some official, especially the *praefectus urbi* and the *praefectus praetorio*. This apparent simplification is however offset by a number of other factors, in particular the growth of privileged jurisdictions for special classes, the complication of the appellate system and the institution of the ecclesiastical courts. Jurisdiction still, according to the old Roman principle, goes with administration, so that the normal courts for ordinary matters are those of the provincial governors on whom the general burden of administration also rests, and appeal lies to their administrative superiors, the *vicarii* and the praetorian prefects. But in the two capitals the position was different. Here the head of the judiciary as well as of the administration was the *praefectus urbi*. Below him there were, at Rome, the *praefectus annonae*, the *praefectus vigilum* and other officials, from whom appeal lay to him.[5] The *praefectus annonae* had both civil and criminal

---

[1] Mitteis, *Reichsrecht*, 452–453.   [2] J. 3. 12. pr.

[3] Cf. *supra*, 407.

[4] This was a generalisation of a process previously applicable to persons of senatorial rank; D. 27. 10. 5.

[5] *Not. Dign. Occid.* 4. 1.

jurisdiction in connection with the corn supply, the *praefectus vigilum* was still almost exclusively a criminal magistrate for minor matters.[1] The *vicarius urbis* (like other *vicarii*, a *spectabilis*) exercised a jurisdiction which was partly concurrent with that of the *praefectus urbi*, but in case of dispute, the latter, as *illustris*, took precedence.[2] The jurisdiction of the prefect himself was not only appellate, but also of first instance. Senators had the privilege of being tried by him,[3] and it was the duty of the *praefectus vigilum* to reserve serious criminal cases for him.[4] He heard appeals not only from his own subordinates, but also by special delegation, at some periods, from provincial governors in Italy and even beyond the seas,[5] from the representatives of the imperial treasury at Rome,[6] and in some cases from the *vicarius urbis*, though from this officer, as from other *vicarii*, appeal also lay to the emperor direct.[7] From the prefect himself appeal also lay to the emperor.[8] The judicial powers of the praetors, of whom there were several, were of quite minor importance. One, we know, retained some functions in connection with guardianship[9] and *causae liberales*; *in integrum restitutio* and voluntary jurisdictions are mentioned in a constitution of Constantius preserved in Justinian's Code.[10]

At Constantinople there was no *praefectus annonae*. The *praefectura vigilum* existed but fell into disrepute, until Justinian reconstituted the office under the name of *praetor plebis*, with criminal jurisdiction only.[11] In addition there were two other praetors, for guardianship and *liberales causae*.[12] Appeal from them lay to the *praefectus urbi*, who, like the prefect at Rome, also heard appeals from certain provinces.[13]

Outside the capital the provincial governor was, as before, the centre of the judicial structure, but his position had become very different owing to his loss of military functions and the comparative smallness of the provinces. He is frequently called *iudex ordinarius*[14] and his judicial work must in fact have taken up a great part of his time, although he had the right of appointing *iudices pedanei* under pressure of business. His jurisdiction

---

[1] *Supra*, 411. [2] Bethmann-Hollweg, III. 64.
[3] In criminal cases he had to summon a council of five senators; C. *Th.* 2. 1. 4.
[4] C. 1. 43.
[5] Bethmann-Hollweg, III. 63; Karlowa, I. 867.
[6] C. *Th.* 11. 30. 49. [7] Bethmann-Hollweg, III. 64.
[8] Bethmann-Hollweg, III. 63. [9] C. 5. 35. 2. 4.
[10] C. 1. 39. 1. [11] Nov. 13.
[12] C. 1. 39. 2; Nov. 13. 1. 1.
[13] C. 7. 62. 23; Bethmann-Hollweg, III. 44.
[14] E.g. C. 1. 3. 32. pr.

is concentrated in the provincial capital and he no longer goes on circuit (*conventus*) for judicial purposes,[1] though it is still his duty to make tours of inspection.[2] Apart from privileged persons he has unlimited competence in both civil and criminal matters, and appeal lies to him from the municipal magistrates and the *defensores civitatum*.[3] Neither the *defensores* nor the magistrates exercised criminal jurisdiction of any importance,[4] but both had minor police powers and were bound to deliver offenders to the governor for trial.[5] The civil competence of the *defensores* was raised by Justinian to include suits to the value of 300 *solidi*;[6] what the maximum was in the case of the ordinary municipal magistrates is unknown, but it was probably not high, though by agreement with the parties jurisdiction might be conferred upon them up to any amount.[7]

From the governor, appeal lies normally either to the praetorian prefect or to the *vicarius*, according as the one or the other is the nearer.[8] In case of doubt the prefect, if he is willing to deal with the matter, takes precedence. From the *vicarius* appeal lies, not to the prefect, for the *vicarius* himself acts *vice sacra*, but to the emperor; from the praetorian prefect there is no further appeal, on the principle that his function is to act definitely in place of the emperor.[9] From the provinces of Asia and Africa, where the governor bears the title proconsul and the rank of *spectabilis*, there is no appeal either to *vicarius* or prefect; the proconsuls themselves act *vice sacra* on appeal, not only from their own subordinates, but from the governors of some other provinces.[10] From them appeal lies to the emperor.[11] The praetorian prefects and the *vicarii* do not, as a rule, act as judges of first instance, but they may do so on special grounds such as corruption or intimidation of the ordinary judge by some powerful litigant.[12]

The emperor himself remained competent in all cases, but in fact the amount of judicial work transacted in person was much less than during the preceding period. Regular participation in the administration of

---

[1] Theoph. *Paraphr.* 1. 6. 4; 3. 12. pr.
[2] *C. Th.* 1. 16. 12; C. 1. 40. 15.   [3] Nov. 15. 5.
[4] C. 1. 55. 5.   [5] C. 1. 55. 7; D. 48. 3. 10.
[6] Nov. 15. 3. 2.   [7] D. 50. 1. 28.
[8] *Nov. Marcian*, 1. 2.
[9] *C. Th.* 11. 30. 16: *Soli vice sacra cognoscere vere dicendi sunt*. This sentence is absent from the corresponding C. 7. 62. 19. For prohibition of appeal from *praef. praet. v.* also D. 1. 11. 1. 1.
[10] Bethmann-Hollweg, III. 43; Karlowa, I. 857.
[11] *C. Th.* 11. 30. 16. 29, 61.   [12] *C. Th.* 1. 16. 7; 1. 15. 1.

justice was hardly compatible with the monarch's sacred remoteness, and he acted normally through delegates. These were sometimes appointed for a particular case, but most of the work was done by standing commissions. Thus Theodosius II enacted that all appeals from *iudices spectabiles* should be decided by the *praefectus praetorio in comitatu* (i.e. Orientis) and the *quaestor sacri palatii*.[1] Seeing that the *vicarii* and the proconsuls were *spectabiles*, and that the judgments of the chief *iudices illustres*, the *praefecti praetorio*, were unappealable, this arrangement, which still existed in Justinian's day,[2] must have provided for a large proportion of the appeals. Even when a matter was tried by the imperial court, the *consistorium*, it appears that the emperor himself was not always present; if he was absent a report had to be made to him before any decision was given.[3] The *quaestor* probably presided. Sometimes, when important cases were to be tried, senators who were not members of the council were summoned, and Justinian made this a general rule.[4] In fact the senate thus came to be an enlarged form of the council, though the two bodies remained formally distinct, and the emperor might refer political matters to one or the other, as he thought fit.[5] Those who exercised jurisdiction on the emperor's behalf, unlike ordinary delegates, might themselves appoint delegates, and for this purpose Justinian constituted a panel of eminent persons from whom those officials whose judgment seat was in Constantinople, as well as he himself, were to choose their delegates.[6] He also laid down that these persons were to sit continuously, so that they must have had a great deal of business.[7]

Of the numerous special jurisdictions, whether for matters of a particular sort, or for privileged persons, it is possible to mention only a few. Fiscal matters went as a rule, but not exclusively, before *rationales* representing the treasury in dioceses or other aggregates of provinces,[8] and on appeal to the *comes sacrarum largitionum*; matters concerning the *res privata* to the *comes rerum privatarum* and his subordinates.[9] *Illustres* could be tried criminally only by the emperor, or a judge specially appointed by him.[10] For ordinary members of the senatorial order the rules varied; those domiciled in Rome were triable criminally only by the *praefectus urbi*;[11] those domiciled elsewhere generally by

---

[1] C. 7. 62. 32.   [2] Nov. 126. pr.
[3] Nov. 62. 1.   [4] Nov. 62.
[5] Bury, *History of the Later Roman Empire*, I. 24.
[6] Nov. 82.   [7] Nov. 82, cap. 3.   [8] Bethmann-Hollweg, III. 77–78.
[9] *V.* Kübler, 318.   [10] C. 3. 24. 3.   [11] *Supra*, 461.

the provincial governors.[1] *Officiales* were in general subject only to the jurisdiction of the dignitary under whom they served, both for civil and for criminal purposes;[2] the members of the imperial household to that of the *magister officiorum*; soldiers to that of their commanders, either the *duces* (normally *spectabiles*) or the *magistri militum* (*illustres*).[3] Ordinarily a privilege of this sort means that the privileged persons cannot be made defendants in any court except their own, but in a few cases the privilege was so strong that they were able, as plaintiffs, to force others to appear before it. Thus the tenants on the estate of the *domus divina*, whether as plaintiffs or as defendants, were under the exclusive civil jurisdiction of the *praepositus sacri cubiculi* and the *comes domorum*,[4] and the members of some trade guilds at Rome could similarly bring others before the courts of the city.[5] Attempts were evidently also made to bring civilians before the military tribunals if the plaintiff was a soldier, but this was forbidden.[6]

A new type of jurisdiction which acquired recognition during this period was that of the ecclesiastical courts. Even before Christianity became the religion of the empire, it had been common for Christians, in accordance with the dictates of the Scriptures,[7] to bring disputes between themselves before arbitrators of their own faith, especially the bishops, whose decisions would then be governed by the ordinary rules applying to arbitral awards. Church courts also dealt with matters which were of purely internal interest, such, for example, as the removal of priests for misbehaviour, excommunication of laymen, and matters of ecclesiastical administration. With the first Christian emperor, however, came a change, for Constantine not only recognised the decisions of the bishops as binding, but, if our records are to be trusted, allowed one party to a suit to bring it before the bishop for decision, even after proceedings had begun before a lay court, and even against the wish of the other litigant.[8] Be that as it may, after 398, consent was certainly necessary to give jurisdiction,[9] but with this limitation the bishop was competent for all civil matters; his judgments could be executed like those of the secular courts, and there was no appeal.[10] In fact, though strictly his position

---

[1] C. 3. 24. 1. For changes *v.* Willems, 634.   [2] C. 1. 29. 2; 12. 23. 12.
[3] C. 3. 13. 6; Bethmann-Hollweg, III. 84-85.
[4] C. 3. 26. 11.   [5] C. 11. 17. 2.
[6] C. 1. 46. 2.   [7] I Cor. VI. 1-6.
[8] *Const. Sirm.* 1. The whole question, including that of the authenticity of the Sirmondian Constitutions (cf. *infra*, 480), is disputed; *v.* Wenger, 333.
[9] C. 1. 4. 7.
[10] C. 1. 4. 8. This was however also true of arbitral awards in general.

differed little from that of an ordinary arbitrator, his court, in which justice was cheaper and quicker than elsewhere, became busy and popular, and in the later period the bishops obtained a general power of supervising the administration of justice within their dioceses.[1] With regard to privileged jurisdiction for the clergy, the imperial legislation varied. Justinian enacted that civil actions might only be brought against them in the ecclesiastical courts, but for crimes he laid down definitely that they were to be subject to the lay tribunals.[2]

The disappearance of the *iudex* in the older sense of that word, and the concentration of justice (apart from the ecclesiastical courts) in the hands of state officials, did not necessarily mean, as it does in modern communities, that the judge was always a professional lawyer. Technical assistance, such as had once been provided by the *prudentes*, was still needed and was supplied by the *adsessores* or *consiliarii*. The functions of the assessor, originally simply one of the magistrate's *consilium*, had already become sufficiently definite under the principate to be made the subject of a monograph by Paulus. Under the dominate it appears to have been usual for each official to have one, and it is a complaint made against Diocletian that he sent ignorant soldiers to act as judges without such assistants.[3] The class from which they were taken was the same as that of the *advocati*.[4] No one might be an assessor and an advocate at the same time, but Justinian definitely says that a man may return to advocacy after having been an assessor.[5] Though appointed by the magistrate whom they served,[6] they received a salary from the state and were themselves responsible for the advice they gave.[7] Their duties extended to assistance of all kinds, including the drafting of decisions; and it was sometimes only with difficulty that the magistrate, though legally competent, could be persuaded to act against their advice.[8] In Justinian's day they seem in fact to have differed little from *iudices pedanei*, for he had to lay down that officials were not to delegate the whole case to them. He only insisted however that *litis contestatio* should take place before the official himself, who must also handle the case once again and give judgment himself. For the rest the assessor was competent.[9]

Advocates were now no longer merely orators, but persons who had studied in one of the law universities. A certain number were attached to

[1] Nov. 86. 1, 2, 3.　　　　[2] Nov. 83.
[3] Lactantius, *De mortibus persecutorum*, 22. 5.
[4] Checchini, *Studi sull' ordinamento processuale*, I (1925), 110 *sqq.*
[5] C. I. 51. 14.　　　　[6] Bethmann-Hollweg, III. 131.
[7] D. 2. 2. 2.　　　　[8] Bethmann-Hollweg, III. 132.
[9] Nov. 60. 2.

each court and formed a kind of corporation with considerable privileges. Not only were their fees recognised, but a scale was laid down by law and they were subject to professional discipline.[1] In this, as in other respects, the courts in the late empire resembled those of modern times more closely than they had done in the republic or principate. This resemblance is to be seen chiefly in the exercise of jurisdiction solely by men who derived their authority from the state; but there were many minor resemblances—the transference of judicial proceedings from the open air to buildings, the swearing of witnesses on the Bible, the written record of all proceedings and the payment of court fees, though these went not to the state, but to the officials.

The likeness was, however, rather with Continental than with English procedure. Though the principle of an oral hearing was not discarded, much use was made of writing, and it is clear that there was not necessarily a "day in court" as we understand it, and as there had been, at least for proceedings *apud iudicem*, under the old system. The trial might be broken up into a number of separate investigations, and these, as we have seen, were not necessarily conducted by the same person throughout.

[1] Bethmann-Hollweg, III. 162–163.

Chapter XXVII

SOURCES IN THE DOMINATE

§ I. LEGAL SCIENCE

With the end of the classical period, *responsa prudentium* ceased to be a living source of law. The *ius respondendi* was no longer given,[1] and a period of decadence began, for which one ground was, no doubt, the disturbed condition of the empire, and the indifference—even at times the hostility—of purely military rulers. More permanent causes lay in the shifting of the intellectual centre to the East, where the Roman tradition was absent, and the rival attractions which Christian theology now offered to men of ability. This falling off among contemporary lawyers reacted on the authority of the earlier works, which came to be regarded as a body of finally settled doctrine and were known collectively as *ius*, in opposition to the imperial constitutions to which the term *leges* was now commonly applied. When the worst of the political troubles had passed, there was indeed something of a revival of jurisprudence, but it was an academic movement, and though its results were not unimportant,[2] it never produced constructive work comparable to that of classical times.

Juristic literature, both educational and practical, was dependent on the classical texts which it sought to make intelligible by epitomes and collections, and even the imperial government attempted by legislation to lighten the burden of judges who were no longer capable of approaching the classical authorities with an independent mind. It is necessary therefore, in what follows, to say something, first of this legislation, secondly of the law schools which in this period assume much greater importance than they had previously enjoyed, and lastly of the post-classical literature so far as it has survived.

A. LEGISLATION CONCERNING THE USE OF CLASSICAL LITERATURE. In dealing with the classical literature, two difficulties confronted the practitioner of post-classical times. First, since there was now an authoritative canon, it was necessary to know exactly what works formed part of it, and secondly, since independent criticism appeared no longer possible, he needed some guide to help him if all the authorities

[1] Cf. *supra*, 368.   [2] Cf. *infra*, 533.

did not speak with one voice. Both these difficulties were met by imperial legislation. Constantine in 321 introduced some simplification by "abolishing" the notes of Ulpian and Paulus on Papinian,[1] and in 327 he "confirmed" the works of Paulus, with special mention of the *Sententiae*.[2] But it was not until 426 that the matter was made the subject of a comprehensive enactment, the famous "Law of Citations" of Theodosius II.[3] By this the works of Papinian, Paulus, Ulpian, Modestinus and Gaius were constituted primary authorities, it being specially mentioned that those of Gaius were to have the same weight as the others. In addition there might be quoted the works of those who were cited by the five primary authorities, but such quotations had to be "confirmed by a comparison of manuscripts". The reason for the distinction was presumably that there were plenty of good manuscripts of Papinian, Paulus, Ulpian and Modestinus, who were the latest of the great jurists, and also of Gaius, who, though earlier, had become very popular. The text of their works was thus reliable, whereas copies of the older jurists were difficult to obtain and their text more doubtful. If there was any discrepancy between the views of different authorities, that of the majority was to be followed; if numbers were equal, the side on which Papinian stood was to prevail, and only in case there was equal division and he was silent, was the decision left to the discretion of the judge.[4] Such mechanical treatment of legal authorities shows clearly the

---

[1] *C. Th.* 1. 4. 1. The prohibition was evidently extended in practice to Marcian's notes; Const. *Deo auctore*, 6.

[2] *C. Th.* 1. 4. 2. The mention of the Sentences was probably due to justified doubts as to their authenticity; cf. *infra*, 472.

[3] *C. Th.* 1.4.3: *Papiniani, Pauli, Gaii, Ulpiani atque Modestini scripta universa firmamus ita ut Gaium quae Paulum, Ulpianum et ceteros comitetur auctoritas, lectionesque ex omni eius corpore recitentur. Eorum quoque scientiam, quorum tractatus atque sententias praedicti omnes suis operibus miscuerunt, ratam esse censemus, ut Scaevolae, Sabini, Iuliani atque Marcelli, omniumque quos illi celebrarunt, si tamen eorum libri propter antiquitatis incertum codicum collatione firmentur. Ubi autem diversae sententiae proferuntur, potior numerus vincat auctorum, vel, si numerus aequalis sit, eius partis praecedat auctoritas in qua excellentis ingenii vir Papinianus emineat, qui, ut singulos vincit, ita cedit duobus. Notas etiam Pauli atque Ulpiani in Papiniani corpus factas, sicut dudum statutum est, praecipimus infirmari. Ubi autem eorum pares sententiae recitantur quorum par censetur auctoritas, quos sequi debeat, eligat moderatio iudicantis. Pauli quoque sententias semper valere praecipimus.*

[4] Gradenwitz, *Z.S.S.* xxxiv. 274–284, holds that the law originally only laid down these rules for the five primary jurists, for whom they would have been comparatively sensible and workable, and that the comparison of MSS. originally only referred to Gaius, who was the earliest of the five. The addition of the

low level to which jurisprudence had sunk, and, if it was necessary, justifies the strictures which Theodosius, in the introduction to his Code, passes upon the lawyers of his own age.[1] In law, as Buckland puts it, opinions should be estimated by weight, not number.[2] None the less, the rules laid down remained at least theoretically in force until the time of Justinian, though one may doubt whether the secondary authorities were ever really quoted except in so far as their opinions survived in the works of the others.

B. THE LAW SCHOOLS. Private establishments in which law might be learned had existed from early imperial times, but it was not until the dominate that the schools really assumed university rank. In the West such schools existed at Rome, at Carthage and probably in Gaul;[3] in the East at Beyrout, Constantinople, Alexandria, Caesarea in Palestine,[4] Athens[5] and Antioch.[6] Most famous of all was that at Beyrout,[7] which is already mentioned as a seat of legal learning in 239.[8] Thereafter the school grew in importance, its most flourishing days being in the fifth century, the time of those teachers whom the jurists of Justinian's day revered as the "oecumenical masters".[9]

Justinian suppressed all the schools with the exception of those at Beyrout and Constantinople,[10] and Beyrout shared with the capital the honour of providing professorial members on the commissions which compiled the Corpus Juris.[11] An earthquake, however, destroyed the city in 551 and the school was transferred to Sidon.[12]

secondary authorities made nonsense of the rules, because it would be a matter of mere accident how many relevant quotations could be discovered. The difficulty, on this view, is to know how and why the change was made. Gradenwitz can only suggest that it was intended originally as a guide in their choice of authorities to the people who were to make Theodosius' projected collection of *ius* (*infra*, 479), and adopted as a direction to judges when this project had to be given up.

[1] *Nov. Th.* 1 (Krüger's edition of *C. Th.* pp. 11–12).
[2] *Text-book*, 34.
[3] Kübler, 427; Levy, *Z.S.S.* XLIX. 235.
[4] Const. *Omnem*, 7.   [5] *Infra*, n. 10.
[6] Kübler, 426. On the Eastern schools *v.* Laborde, *Les écoles de droit dans l'empire d'orient* (Bordeaux, 1912).
[7] See especially Collinet, *Histoire de l'école de droit de Beyrouth* (*Études historiques sur le droit de Justinien*, II. Paris, 1925).
[8] St Gregory Thaumaturgus, *Panegyr. ad Origenem*, cap. v.
[9] οἱ τῆς οἰκουμένης διδάσκαλοι; Collinet, *op. cit.* 125 sqq.
[10] Const. *Omnem*, 7. Athens had already been suppressed in 529; Malalas, *Chronogr.* 451.
[11] *Infra*, 486.   [12] Collinet, *op. cit.* 54 sqq.

The language used for teaching, even in the East, was originally Latin, but Greek appears to have been substituted at Beyrout towards the end of the fourth century, or early in the fifth, and a similar change probably took place at Constantinople about the same time.[1] Of the method of instruction the *Scholia Sinaitica*[2] and the *Scholia* to the *Basilica*[3] give some idea. A classical text was taken as the basis, and the lecturer added notes of his own, which consisted of references to parallel passages or imperial constitutions, the formulation of general principles, the statement and solution of difficulties, and illustrations from practice.[4] It was in fact a development of the ancient methods used in schools of rhetoric,[5] and differed widely from the system of classical times when, after the student had mastered the elements, his further education consisted chiefly in the discussion of cases. The course lasted normally four years, though some students remained for a fifth,[6] and, at any rate in the fifth century, it followed a rigid schedule. This however will be more conveniently discussed in connection with the reforms which Justinian introduced in order to fit it in with his compilations.[7]

Already in 370 the students at Rome had been placed for disciplinary purposes under the *magister census*, who was a subordinate of the urban prefect,[8] but the first mention of officially appointed professors, receiving a salary from the state, does not occur until 425, when Theodosius II laid down that there were to be at Constantinople, among other teachers, two professors of law.[9] In Justinian's day there were eight in Constantinople and Beyrout together,[10] presumably four in each. How many there were in Rome is unknown, but the school there continued to exist even after the fall of the Western empire, and after the reconquest of Italy Justinian ordered that the payment of the professors was to continue.[11]

In the second half of the fifth century at latest a certificate of attendance at a law school and sufficient knowledge became necessary for admission to practice in the courts of the *praefecti praetorio*.[12] It had to be furnished

---

[1] Collinet, *op. cit.* 211 *sqq.*

[2] *Infra*, 473.   [3] *Infra*, 511.

[4] Pringsheim, "Beryt und Bologna" (*Festschrift für Lenel*, 204–285, Leipzig, 1923), compares the scholastic methods of the teachers at Beyrout with those of the Glossators.

[5] Collinet, *op. cit.* 245.   [6] Collinet, *op. cit.* 234.

[7] *Infra*, 505.   [8] *C. Th.* 14. 9. 1.

[9] *C. Th.* 14. 9. 3 (= C. 11. 19. 1). One official professorship had probably existed for a few years already; Krüger, 392.

[10] Const. *Omnem* is addressed to eight.   [11] *Pro petitione Vigilii*, § 22.

[12] C. 2. 7. 11; 2. 7. 24. 4–5.

under oath by the professor or professors, but there is no evidence of any examination by which they tested their pupils' attainments.

C. THE SURVIVING LITERATURE.[1] An outstanding feature of the surviving post-classical literature is that it is all anonymous. Nearly all of it too has not only actually been found in the West, but is certainly, or probably, of Western origin, some indeed being known only through its use in barbarian codes. The Eastern works on the other hand have, apart from fragments, disappeared, chiefly no doubt because the compilations of Justinian rendered them obsolete in the East, and, though some were still used by the Byzantine writers, they were not recopied.

The chief Western survivals are the following:

Fragmenta Vaticana. This name has been given to the remains of a large collection containing both *ius* and *leges*, discovered by Angelo Mai in the Vatican library in 1821. It was not divided into books, but into titles only, of which seven are preserved in varying degrees of completeness. *Ius* is represented by excerpts from Papinian, Paulus, Ulpian, and a work *de interdictis* whose author is not named.[2] The constitutions which commonly, but not invariably, follow the *ius* in each title date from the years 205–372, so that the collection cannot have assumed its present form before 372. Probably however it was originally compiled in the time of Constantine, and afterwards enlarged.[3] In any case it was certainly made before 438, for some constitutions which were shortened in the *C. Theodosianus* appear in their original form.[4] The inclusion of several constitutions of Maximian points to a Western origin.

Collatio legum Mosaicarum et Romanarum. This is the modern name of a work which is headed in the MSS. *Lex dei quam praecepit dominus ad Moysen.* It consists of sixteen titles dealing with crime, delict and succession, in each of which there are a few lines from the Pentateuch in a Latin translation, and extracts from the Roman *ius* or *leges* on the same subject. The object of the author was evidently to show that the Mosaic law already contained all that was essential in the Roman system,[5] and

---

[1] The texts are easily accessible in Huschke's *Iurisprudentiae Anteiustiniani Reliquiae*, 6th ed. by Seckel and Kübler (Teubner, Leipzig), as well as in Riccobono, *Fontes* (Florence, 1909) and in Girard, *Textes*.

[2] Perhaps the part concerning interdicts of one of the great commentaries on the edict, most probably Ulpian's; Kübler, 387.

[3] Kipp, 148.

[4] Fr. Vat. 35, 37, 249.

[5] In VII. 1 he says *Scitote, iurisconsulti, quia Moyses prius hoc statuit.* Whether he was a Jew or a Christian is disputed.

perhaps to contrast its brevity favourably with the lawyers' verbosity. The jurists used are the five primary authorities of the Law of Citations,[1] and the constitutions are taken from the *codices Gregorianus* and *Hermogenianus*, together with one of 390.[2] The *C. Theodosianus* is not used, so that the work is usually dated between 390 and 438. It is probable, however, that in its original form it was earlier.[3]

Consultatio. This work was first edited by Cujas in 1577 under the title *Veteris cuiusdam iurisconsulti consultatio* from a MS. which is now lost. It is a more original production than the two previously mentioned, for it consists partly of the answers given by a jurist to an advocate who consults him, and partly of short theoretical disquisitions, in both cases however with the authorities on which the writer's opinions are based.[4] The authorities quoted are Paul's Sentences and constitutions taken from the three codices. The work dates from the later fifth or early sixth century and was probably composed in Gaul.[5]

The Sententiae of Paulus. A selection from the *Sententiae*, probably about one-sixth of the whole, forms part of the *lex Romana Visigothorum*, and additional fragments can be inserted from the Digest, the *Fragmenta Vaticana*, the *Collatio* and elsewhere. The work itself was formerly held to be authentic, but may now with some certainty be characterised as a post-classical anthology compiled from various writings of Paulus, probably already in the third century.[6]

The Epitome of Ulpian. This work, which the MS. calls *tituli ex corpore Ulpiani*, is generally regarded as an abridgment made after 320 of a *liber singularis regularum* of Ulpian. It is however doubtful whether Ulpian ever wrote such a book and the original which the compiler of the epitome used was itself probably a post-classical compilation based on Gaius' Institutes and some other classical works.[7]

---

[1] This goes to show that the Law of Citations merely confirmed what was already the practice.   [2] v. 3.

[3] Levy, *Z.S.S.* L. 278; *ibid.* 703 *sqq.* (review of Volterra, "Collatio legum M. et R.", *Memorie della R. Accad. nazionale dei Lincei, Classe di scienze morali, storiche e filologiche*, serie VI. vol. III. fasc. I. 1930).

[4] To the former series belong caps. I, II, III, VII, VII a and VIII, to the latter IV, V and VI. The two series did not originally belong together; Conrat and Kantorowicz, *Z.S.S.* XXXIV. 46–56.   [5] Krüger, 347.

[6] V. Beseler, *Beiträge*, I. 99; IV. 336–337; Rotondi, *Scr. Giur.* I. 482; Levy, *Z.S.S.* L. 272–294.

[7] F. Schulz, *Die Epitome Ulpiani des Codex Vaticanus Reginae* 1128 (Bonn, 1926), and Lenel's review *Z.S.S.* XLVII. 414. Against authenticity also Arangio-Ruiz, *B.I.D.R.* XXX. 178–219, and Albertario, *B.I.D.R.* XXXII. 73–130. Doubtful, Buckland, *L.Q.R.* XL. 199.

The Opiniones of Ulpian. These are only known from excerpts in the Digest, but their style differs so greatly from that of Ulpian that they too are probably to be regarded as post-classical.[1]

The Autun Gaius. Considerable fragments of a commentary on Gaius' Institutes were found at Autun in 1898. The work consists of a wordy paraphrase, with obvious illustrations. It was clearly intended for educational purposes only.[2]

From the East there are but two survivals:

The *Scholia Sinaitica*, fragments of a Greek work containing *scholia* (notes) on Ulpian's *libri ad Sabinum*, found on a papyrus in the monastery of Mount Sinai in 1880. They must have been written after 438, the date of the *C. Theodosianus*, and before Justinian. They are no doubt the product of a law school, perhaps of Beyrout.

The "Syro-Roman Law Book".[3] This is of a totally different character from any other legal work of antiquity. Though originally written in Greek, it is known only in a number of versions in various Oriental languages, which are of different dates and vary greatly from one another. It deals chiefly with the family, with slaves and with succession, and the law is certainly in the main Roman. Until recently, though there were divergent views concerning its date and origin, it was generally agreed that it was intended to serve a practical purpose, and the non-Roman elements which it appears to contain were commonly regarded, on the authority of Mitteis, as evidence for the survival of Oriental law in the practice of the Eastern provinces, in spite of the *constitutio Antoniniana*.[4] Sachau, who was followed by several scholars, thought that it originated in the fourth century in the patriarchate of Antioch, and was intended to assist the ecclesiastics in dealing with lay authorities and in settling disputes between Christians in the bishops' courts. Recently, however, Nallino has advanced strong arguments for a totally different view.[5] The

[1] Lenel, *Paling.* II. 1001; Rotondi, *Scr. Giur.* I. 453 *sqq.*; Beseler, *Beiträge*, II. 21.

[2] For the epitome of Gaius in the *Lex Romana Visigothorum* and the *interpretationes v. infra*, 481.

[3] *Syrisch-römisches Rechtsbuch aus dem fünften Jahrhundert*, edited with a German translation and notes by Bruns and Sachau (Leipzig, 1880). Three MSS. subsequently found were edited by Sachau (Berlin, 1907) under the title *Leges Constantini Theodosii Leonis.* A Latin translation by Ferrini is given in Riccobono, *Fontes*, II. 637–677. Literature, Kübler, 398; Kipp, 151.

[4] This law Mitteis held to be of mainly Greek origin, though with some Syrian elements; *v. Reichsrecht*, especially chap. X, on the law of intestate succession.

[5] "Sul libro siro-romano e sul presunto diritto siriaco", *St. Bonfante*, I. 201–261.

Greek original, he believes, was written about 476–480, possibly at Constantinople, and was intended for scholastic purposes. So far, indeed, was it from being practical, that the author expounds the old civil law of Rome, which had long ceased to apply, and the law of the imperial constitutions, but omits the *ius honorarium*, though he may have intended to treat of it in a separate manual. The book remained for some three centuries in well-merited oblivion, and was not translated until about the middle of the eighth century, when it happened to be found useful by ecclesiastics in Syria, Asia Minor or Mesopotamia, who required some Christian law-book because, under Muhammadan rule, they were forced to decide the disputes arising in their own community. The tradition of Roman law had quite died out among them and they consequently did not recognise the true character of the work.

§ II. IMPERIAL LEGISLATION

A. FORMS OF LEGISLATION. Already in the principate it had been recognised that what the emperor laid down had the force of law, but the forms which he used for the purpose of expressing his will were none of them directly or solely legislative.[1] In the dominate, on the other hand, it was quite definitely recognised that the emperor was a legislator, and he very frequently laid down new rules directly in legislative fashion, such rules coming to be known, in opposition to administrative or judicial acts, as *leges generales*. There was still, however, no single form invariably adopted for the purpose of promulgating such general enactments. Most commonly they were contained in a document addressed, like a letter, to some official, very frequently a praetorian prefect, who then had the duty of providing for further publication; but the document might also be addressed to the people or to some part of it, such as the inhabitants of a city,[2] or to the senate. Documents addressed to the people most closely resembled the edicts of the principate, but the word *edictum* or *lex edictalis* was also applied to those addressed to officials, and if an enactment was called an edict, this was sufficient to show that it was intended to be "general".[3] Since, however, the will of an absolute monarch must prevail, no matter how it is expressed, the emperor was not bound to these or to any other forms; multiplicity of forms continued and the distinctions between them never became very precise.[4] The emperor

---

[1] *Supra*, 372.   [2] E.g. C. 1. 1. 1: *ad populum urbis Constantinopolitanae.*
[3] C. 1. 14. 3.
[4] Thus it was possible for Justinian in his Institutes (1. 2. 6) still to use the language of classical times and refer, like Gaius, to *edicta, epistulae* and *decreta* as the types of imperial constitutions, though this explained but little of what

remained an administrator and, to some extent, a judge, and could, if he so desired, lay down a general principle in these capacities too. There was, however, less reason for him to do this now that he could legislate directly, and it was also felt that there was danger in the indiscriminate use of particular decisions as precedents in subsequent cases. A rescript, for instance, contrary to the existing law, might be obtained through unlearned or corrupt officials although no change was really intended, and cause difficulty thereafter. The legislation, however, dealing with the matter was confused and contradictory. Constantine, in 315, laid down that rescripts "contrary to law" were to have no validity,[1] but clearly such a rule was incapable of application so long as rescripts were recognised as a source of law at all, and its enactment merely shows that the legislators, though they recognised an evil, lacked the technical skill necessary to provide a remedy. Arcadius, in 398, definitely forbade the use of rescripts as authorities except in the case for which they were issued,[2] but this was evidently found inconvenient or incompatible with the supremacy of the emperor, for in 426, Theodosius II and Valentinian III, though they reaffirmed the principle, weakened it by allowing particular decisions to be used as precedents if it was definitely stated that the emperor wished them to be of general application.[3] The wording of this constitution is such as to include *decreta* as well as *rescripta*. Justinian enacted definitely that imperial judgments given in the presence of the parties were to be valid as precedents for similar cases, and also confused the matter further by insisting on a general imperial power of interpretation.[4] If this means anything, it would seem that rescripts too could be quoted as precedents, so that there is a return to the rule that they are valid as such provided they are not contrary to law, and the judge is left with the impossible task of deciding whether the emperor has merely interpreted the existing law, or travelled beyond it.

A type of constitution mentioned sometimes in connection with rescripts was the *adnotatio*. It was used for the same purposes as the rescripts and sometimes the two words seem to be synonymous.[5] In other cases, however, they are contrasted,[6] though what the difference was is

went on in his own day. *Decreta* were rare now that appeals to the emperor might be by *consultatio post sententiam*, i.e. the judge, after giving judgment, might at the wish of a party send the case, with documents, to the emperor, who then decided it by rescript; *v.* Kipp, 79.

[1] *C. Th.* I. 2. 2; cf. I. 2. 3.   [2] *C. Th.* I. 2. II.
[3] C. I. 14. 3. For an example, *v. Nov. Val.* 8. 1.
[4] C. I. 14. 12.   [5] *C. Th.* 4. 14. I. I; *Coll.* I. 10.
[6] *C. Th.* 5. 13 (14). 30; 9. 21. 10.

not clear. Possibly it is simply one of external form, and *adnotatio* means a decision placed in the margin of a petition.[1]

Another type was the *sanctio pragmatica*, but here again there is great difficulty in discovering precisely what the term means. Apparently constitutions of this sort were commonly replies to petitions either of individuals or of corporations, which contained matters of some general interest. Such, for instance, was the pragmatic sanction whereby Justinian, on the petition of Pope Vigilius, settled a number of questions which arose after the reconquest of Italy from the Ostrogoths.[2] They were not, however, always of such general interest, and Justinian, when he gave his Code the force of law, laid down that special privileges given by pragmatic sanction were not to be affected, though general rules only remained in force if not contrary to the constitutions received into the Code.[3]

Mandata are rare in this period,[4] but the illustrations to the *Notitia Dignitatum* still show the *liber mandatorum* among official insignia. The practice of issuing it, however, fell into disuse until Justinian, consciously reviving an ancient institution, prepared a general *liber mandatorum* for all *iudices medii* and *minores*.[5]

As under the principate, all written constitutions were signed by the emperor himself,[6] the phrase used for the purpose differing according to the circumstances. In the case of edicts intended to be published directly, it would order the publication.[7] If the constitution were addressed to the senate or an official there would be some form of valediction.[8] The emperor signed with a special purple ink which no one else might use on pain of death,[9] and Justinian further ordered that all enactments as a guarantee of their authenticity were to bear the counter-signature of the *quaestor sacri palatii*.[10] As before, all constitutions were recorded in the imperial archives, and those addressed to officials in their archives as well, the date of enactment (*data*) and of publication (*proposita*), and, in the latter case, also that of receipt (*accepta*) being noted. The publication

---

[1] Kübler, 378.

[2] Printed as Appendix VII in Schoell and Kroll's edition of the Novels.

[3] Const. *Summa*, § 4. [4] An example is C. 1. 50. 2.

[5] I.e. *spectabiles* and provincial governors; Nov. 17.

[6] On the form of signature and on the external features of the constitutions *v.* Seeck, *Regesten der Kaiser u. Päpste für die Jahre* 311 *bis* 476 (Stuttgart, 1919), 1–18.

[7] E.g. in *Nov. Val.* 9. 1 there are preserved at the end the words *Et manu divina: proponatur amantissimo nostro populo Romano.*

[8] E.g. *Nov. Val.* 1. 3: *Et manu divina: optamus vos felicissimos nostrique amantissimos per multos annos bene valere, sanctissimi ordinis p(atres) c(onscripti).*

[9] C. 1. 23. 6. [10] Nov. 114.

continued to be by notice, which might remain posted up as long as a year.[1] If a constitution was addressed to the senate, it was evidently deemed to be sufficiently published by being read (*recitata*) at a formal meeting and inserted in the archives.[2] Constitutions addressed to individuals were probably not published at all in this period.[3]

In style the enactments of the late empire contrast unfavourably with those of the principate. The classical lawyers had in general been free from the elaborate rhetoric which was already fashionable in their day, and the tradition of straightforward speech is still maintained in the rescripts of Diocletian's reign. Thereafter the constitutions became turgid, full of elaborate glorification of the emperor's own wisdom, and often argumentative. This rhetorical style is deliberately chosen as a form of artistic prose suitable to the expression of the emperor's commands,[4] but it frequently makes the legislator's intention very difficult to discover. Latin continued to be the language normally used, even in the East, until 534, though even before then a few constitutions were issued in Greek, or in both languages. Justinian's Novels were almost all in Greek. In 446 Theodosius II laid down an elaborate procedure for approving drafts of general enactments.[5] First they were to be debated by both the senate and the *consistorium*; then, as settled, agreed to by both bodies again, and finally read in the *consistorium* before final confirmation by the emperor. How far this procedure was actually used is doubtful. At any rate it was not intended to limit the emperor's powers, but only to secure careful consideration of proposals made by officials.[6]

When there were several emperors, the constitutions, though emanating from one, were, as we have seen,[7] issued in the name of all, and at least in theory, valid throughout the empire. This theory led, as one would have expected, to difficulties, and in 429 Theodosius II enacted that the constitutions of one emperor should not be valid in the territory of the other unless they were communicated to him and received his approval.[8] Nevertheless the practice of using the names of all the emperors continued almost down to the fall of the Western empire.

---

[1] *C. Th.* 2. 27. 1. 6.   [2] E.g. *Nov. Val.* 1. 3.

[3] Diocletian (*C.* 1. 23. 3) ordered that original rescripts, not copies, were to be sent to the parties interested; *v.* Kipp, 80; Krüger, 318. Collinet, however, believes that Beyrout was an intermediate station for the publication of rescripts of all kinds (*Syria* (1924), 359–372; *Ét. Hist.* II. 20).

[4] Cf. *supra*, 439.   [5] *C.* 1. 14. 8.

[6] Krüger, 313.   [7] *Supra*, 434.

[8] *C. de Th. cod. auct.* (*Nov. Th.* 1), § 5. Such communication did occur, but, so far as we know, only from East to West; Krüger, 331.

Subordinate powers of legislation were still exercised by the praetorian prefects,[1] and here too it seems to have been the practice for a single prefect to issue edicts in the name of all.[2]

B. The collections of constitutions. During the principate it had been the function of the jurists to keep the legal public in touch with imperial legislation, and thus when they ceased to write it became necessary to find some other guide to the increasing volume of constitutions. At first the need was met by two collections, which differed from the only classical collection known to us[3] in that they reproduced the text of the constitutions in full, but which, like it, were unofficial works. These were the *codices Gregorianus* and *Hermogenianus*, the word *codex* in this connection referring to the external form of the work, which was no longer written on a roll of papyrus, but on leaves of parchment, put together like our books, and hence much more convenient for purposes of reference. Neither *codex* has survived, but constitutions are quoted from them in later collections[4] and we also know that it was from them that the compilers of Justinian's code took the constitutions dating from before the earliest contained in the *C. Theodosianus*.[5] With respect to the date of publication and the relation of the two *codices* to each other there is much controversy,[6] but it seems clear that the *C. Greg.* is the earlier, as it is always mentioned first,[7] and contained the earlier constitutions,[8] whereas there were none in the *C. Herm.* dating from before Diocletian. Most probably both were published in Diocletian's reign, the *C. Greg.* in 291,[9] the *C. Herm.* in 295 or shortly after,[10] the latter being intended to supplement the former by giving a fairly full collection of the latest enactments.

It is true that a constitution of 295 is quoted from *C. Greg.*;[11] and that seven dating from as late as 364–365 are attributed to the *C. Herm.*,[12] but these are probably to be explained as later additions. Nothing is

---

[1] C. 1. 26. 2; cf. *supra*, 437.   [2] Krüger, 315.

[3] That of Papirius Iustus, *supra*, 378.

[4] Fr. Vat.; *Coll.*; *Consult.*; *l. R. Burg.*; *l. R. Visig.* and its appendices.

[5] C. *Haec.* pr.; *Summa*, § 1.

[6] V. especially Jörs, P.-W. IV. 1, s.vv. C. *Greg.* and C. *Herm.*

[7] C. *Th.* 1. 1. 5; C. *Haec.* pr.; *Summa*, § 1.

[8] The oldest actually quoted from the C. *Greg.* dates from 196; *Consult.* 1. 6.

[9] Rotondi, *Scr. Giur.* 1. 131–146.

[10] Jörs, *op. cit.* col. 166; Rotondi, *op. cit.* 118–131.

[11] *Coll.* 6. 4. One indeed (*Coll.* 15. 3), undated, must be of 297 or 302; Jörs, *op. cit.* 162.

[12] *Consult.* 9. 1–7.

known of the author of either collection, but both were almost certainly made in the East, possibly at Beyrout.[1,2]

The *C. Greg.* was the larger work, and was divided into books and titles, the arrangement of subjects being in the main that which had become traditional in the *digesta* of the classical jurists. The *C. Herm.* was divided into titles only, but it too must have been of considerable size, for we hear of the 120th constitution of the 69th title.[3]

In contradistinction to these *codices*, the *C. Theodosianus* was an official work. In 429 Theodosius II appointed a commission of nine persons with orders to compile a collection of all *leges generales* enacted since the time of Constantine. Obsolete constitutions as well as those still in force were to be included, for the purpose of the work was partly historical. When it had been completed it was then intended to extract from it, as well as from the earlier *codices* and from the writings of the jurists, all that was still of value, and to give to this new collection alone the force of law.[4] This plan however was apparently too ambitious. At any rate it failed, and in 435 a new commission of sixteen was appointed with different instructions. The project of including juristic writings was abandoned and the commission was given wider powers of altering constitutions for the purposes of the new arrangement, but they were still not empowered to omit any enactment merely on the ground that it was obsolete.[5]

The work was finished in just over two years, and published on Feb. 15th, 438, with effect as from Jan. 1st, 439.[6] Already before its completion it had received the approval of Valentinian III, and on Dec. 25th, 438 a copy, which had been handed by Theodosius to the prefect of

[1] The author's names were probably Gregorius (not Gregorianus) and Hermogenianus (not Hermogenes), Mommsen, *Z.S.S.* x. 347–348, but whether the latter is identical with the jurist quoted in the Digest (cf. *supra*, 399, n. 6) is uncertain.

[2] Of all the constitutions of Diocletian's reign only about three appear to have been issued by his Western co-regent, Maximian (Krüger, 321). This points to the use of Eastern archives by the compilers, though for the earlier constitutions of the *C. Greg.* some reference must have been made to those at Rome; Jörs, *op. cit.* 163. For the view that *C. Greg.* was composed at Beyrout *v.* Mommsen, *Z.S.S.* xxii. 139–144 (= *Ges. Schr.* ii. 366). Collinet, *Syria* (1924), 365, thinks the same of *C. Herm.*

[3] *Sch. Sin.* 5.

[4] *C. Th.* 1. 1. 5.

[5] *C. Th.* 1. 1. 6.

[6] *C. de Th. cod. auct.* (*Nov. Th.* 1). No reference might thereafter be made to any constitution (apart from military orders and a few others) enacted since the time of Constantine, except as it stood in the new *codex*.

Italy,[1] was laid before the Roman senate, which received it with acclamations, and gave instructions that copies were to be made for the archives and for issue to the public.[2]

The *C. Theodosianus* has not been preserved in its entirety. In the East it was superseded by Justinian's legislation, but it continued to be used in the West, and there are a number of Western MSS. containing parts of it, as well as many constitutions preserved in other works, especially the *l. Romana Visigothorum*.[3] It was divided into sixteen books, these again being subdivided into titles, in which the individual constitutions were arranged chronologically. The arrangement of the titles, as in the older *codices*, followed in the main that of the *digesta*.

A collection of later constitutions was made under Majorian. It contained some which had been sent by Theodosius II to Valentinian III and published by the latter for the Western empire in 448, some of Valentinian's, and some of Majorian's own. A selection from it is contained in the *l. Romana Visigothorum*, which has also some later constitutions, including five of Marcian's which come from an Eastern collection.

Of other enactments which have survived, the most important are the *constitutiones Sirmondi*, so called from the fact that they were first published by J. Sirmondus in 1631. They consist of sixteen constitutions, almost all concerning ecclesiastical matters, of which the latest is dated 425. The collection must have been made between that date and 438, when the *C. Theodosianus* became the only authoritative source for constitutions of this period.

[1] When he accompanied Valentinian to Constantinople on the occasion of Valentinian's marriage to Theodosius' daughter, Eudoxia.

[2] An account of this sitting was prefixed by the *constitutionarii* to the copies they made, and is printed in modern editions.

[3] For a history of the editions *v.* Kübler, 384. The only complete modern edition is in *Theodosiani Libri* XVI *cum Constitutionibus Sirmondianis et Leges Novellae ad Theodosianum Pertinentes*, edited by Mommsen and P. M. Meyer (Berlin, 1905); vol. I. part I, contains Mommsen's preface, vol. I. part 2, the Theodosian Code and the Sirmondian constitutions, vol. II. the Post-Theodosian Novels. Of Krüger's newer edition of *C. Th.* only two *fasciculi*, books 1–6 (Berlin, 1923) and books 7–8 (1926), have appeared. In this many constitutions are included which, though only known to us from Justinian's Code, must have been taken from the *C. Th.* The edition of Gothofredus (1587–1652), re-edited by Ritter (Leipzig, 1736–1745), remains valuable on account of its great commentary. Most useful in view of the many mistakes in the dating of constitutions is Seeck's *Regesten der Kaiser u. Päpste f. d. Jahre 311 bis 476* (Stuttgart, 1919).

§ III. THE BARBARIAN CODES

In strictness these codes do not form part of the sources of law of the Roman empire, for they were promulgated on the authority of Germanic kings who had established themselves on the soil of the Western empire and were, at the time of the promulgation, independent of imperial control. None the less they require mention here because they are our best authority for the development of Roman law in the West and embody Roman works not otherwise preserved. The settlement of Germanic tribes within the empire had brought with it a reintroduction of the principle of personal law, for they retained to some extent both their own organisation and their own law, while the provincials among whom they were settled continued under the Roman system.[1] When the kings became independent they did not alter this state of affairs, and in some cases actually issued separate law books, based on Roman materials, for their Roman subjects. Two of the three surviving codes are of this nature.

Lex Romana Visigothorum. This is the name now most commonly given to the code which Alaric II, king of the Visigoths, promulgated in 506 for the use of his Roman subjects.[2] It consists of *ius* and *leges*, the former being represented by extracts from the C. *Theodosianus* and the post-Theodosian Novels, the latter by an epitome of Gaius' Institutes in two books,[3] one *responsum* of Papinian, a selection from Paul's Sentences and extracts from the C. *Greg.* and C. *Herm.*[4] All parts, except the epitome of Gaius, are accompanied by an *interpretatio*, which gives an explanatory paraphrase generally, but not always, shorter than the text.

---

[1] Vinogradoff, *Roman Law in Mediaeval Europe*, 15.
[2] In the *praescriptio* found in some MSS. (Mommsen, Preface to C. *Th.* xxxii) it is called *Leges sive species iuris de Theodosiano vel (= et) de diversis libris electae*. Titles appearing in different MSS. are: *lex Romana, lex Romana Visigothorum, Corpus Theodosii, liber* or *corpus legum*. Some MSS. containing only an extract call this *breviarium Alaricianum*; Kübler, 394; Krüger, 351. The latest complete edition is Hänel's (Leipzig, 1849), but the individual parts are to be found in the editions of C. *Th.* and the collections mentioned *supra*, 471, n. 1. Conrat's *Breviarium Alaricianum* (Leipzig, 1903) gives a German translation arranged systematically, with the original text in footnotes.
[3] The matter contained in Gai. IV is omitted entirely. As it concerned procedure mainly it was quite obsolete.
[4] The reason for this treatment of the C. *Greg.* and C. *Herm.* is probably that the constitutions taken from them were rescripts and thus more like the extracts from the jurists than like the *leges generales* of C. *Th.*

Both epitome and *interpretatio* were probably taken by Alaric's compilers from existing material,[1] though they may have made alterations.

The collection was to supersede all older sources of law,[2] and to this extent had the same object as Justinian's compilations a quarter of a century later, but it was a much more modest undertaking, and the poverty of its *ius* especially, when compared with Justinian's Digest, shows how low were the intellectual standards of the West at this period.

In 654 it was repealed by Recceswind, who enacted a new code which was to apply to Goths and Romans indifferently, and thereafter it was forgotten in Spain. In other countries, however, especially France, though it had no formal validity, it continued to be used,[3] and was the chief document through which knowledge of Roman law was preserved in the West until, in the eleventh century, real study of Justinian's compilations began again.

Lex Romana Burgundionum.[4] Towards the end of the fifth century King Gundobad (474–516), in enacting a code for his Burgundian subjects, promised to do the same for the Romans also, and this promise was kept, probably by himself, certainly before the fall of the Burgundian kingdom in 534. The code differs from that of Alaric in that it consists, not of extracts from various works, but of independent statements of legal rules arranged systematically in forty-seven titles. The sources, which are only occasionally mentioned, are the three *codices*, the post-Theodosian Novels, Paul's Sentences and a work of Gaius,[5] probably the Institutes or rather an abridgment thereof. Resemblances to the *interpretatio* of the *l. Romana Visigothorum* are probably due rather to the use of similar sources than to the use of that compilation itself.[6] It is not free from Burgundian elements.

Edictum Theoderici.[7] This was promulgated by Theoderic the Great,

---

[1] Much disputed; *v.* Krüger, 353 *sqq.* for the view in the text. *Contra,* Mommsen, Preface to *C. Th.* xxxv, lxi; *Z.S.S.* xxi. 162; Conrat, *Die Entstehung des westgothischen Gaius* (1905), § 12; *Der westgothische Paulus* (1907), § 14. Other literature, Kübler, 394.

[2] Edict of Alaric, Mommsen, Preface to *C. Th.* xxxiii.

[3] See especially Wretschko's article printed in Mommsen's *Theodosianus*, I. cccvii *sqq.*

[4] Formerly called "Papian", because the MSS. generally give it after the *L.R.V.* which ends with the single *responsum* of Papinian. The corrupt heading of this was mistaken for the beginning of a new work. For a history of editions *v.* Kübler, 396. It is printed in Riccobono, *Fontes*, II. 599–630.

[5] Called *regula* (5. 1; 10. 1) and *species* (12. 2).

[6] Karlowa, I. 984; Krüger, 360; *v.* also Mommsen, Preface to *C. Th.* lxi.

[7] Editions, Kübler, 397; printed in Riccobono, *Fontes*, II. 573–596.

king of the Ostrogoths, after 493 and probably before 507.[1] It consists of 154 sections containing independent statements of legal rules, and its sources (which it does not mention) are the three *codices*, the Novels, Paul's Sentences and perhaps some other works.[2] It differs from both the other codes in that it was intended to apply to the barbarians as well as the Romans. Nor was it meant to supersede other sources, but to make the enforcement of the existing law more certain.[3] It is not called a *lex*, because Theoderic considered himself the vicegerent of the emperor. As however he was in fact quite independent of Constantinople this made no real difference.

[1] Brunner, *Deutsche Rechtsgeschichte* (2nd ed.), I. 527.
[2] In many cases the *interpretatio* is used; Krüger, 359; Mommsen, Preface to *C. Th.* lxi.
[3] This is definitely stated in the introduction.

Chapter XXVIII

THE LEGISLATION OF JUSTINIAN

Justinian was born at Tauresium, the modern Taor, in Serbia, of a peasant family, and owed his advancement to the interest taken in him by his uncle and adoptive father, Justinus. In 518 Justinus, who had risen from the ranks in the army, was proclaimed emperor, but he was then already an old man, and appears from the first to have been under his nephew's influence. In 527 Justinian became co-regent, and, on the death of his uncle later in the year, sole emperor. He was at that time about forty-five years old, and his reign, which lasted until his death in 565, was one of the most remarkable in the history of the empire. Though cold and unattractive in character, he possessed talents far above the ordinary, and excelled especially in his choice of instruments for the purposes both of peace and of war. From the first he seems to have conceived the ambition of restoring the ancient grandeur of the Roman empire, and in this he achieved a remarkable measure of success, for his generals were able to oust the Vandals from Africa, to wrest Italy, after a long struggle, from the Goths, and even to establish once more a Roman province in Spain. But these successes proved ephemeral; the resources of his subjects were exhausted by the demands which Justinian made upon them, and the cleavage between East and West was too deep to be healed by the efforts of a Latin-speaking emperor on the throne of Byzantium. In the succeeding reigns, most of the West was lost and the character of the empire became finally Eastern. Apart from conquest Justinian's chief interests lay in religion and in law, and the two features of his reign which have most impressed posterity are the building of St. Sophia, and the great codification. In the latter work his chief assistant, and possibly inspirer, was Tribonian, a man of great ability and versatility, though, it is said, of a grasping character, whose open indifference to the established religion the emperor was apparently able to overlook. He held the office of *quaestor sacri palatii* in 530, but was removed in 532 on account of the hostility shown towards him by the populace in the Nika riot, and at the time of the publication of the Digest and Code was *magister officiorum*. Subsequently however he became *quaestor* again. He died in 546.

The project of re-stating and reforming the law must have been in Justinian's mind even before he ascended the throne, for work upon it was begun almost immediately, and the codification was completed already in 534. This comprised the Institutes, the Digest and the Code, which, together with the Novels, or constitutions enacted after 534, make up the Corpus Juris, as the whole of Justinian's legislation has been called since the sixteenth century.

§ I. THE COURSE OF LEGISLATION

A. THE FIRST CODE. In a constitution[1] dated Feb. 13th, 528, a commission of ten, including Tribonian, at that time *magister officiorum*, and Theophilus, professor at Constantinople, was appointed to compile a new collection of imperial constitutions from the three old *codices* and subsequent enactments. Their powers were very wide. Everything obsolete or unnecessary was to be omitted, all contradictions and repetitions were to be removed, additions and even changes might be made, and, where convenient, several enactments might be put together. The constitutions were to be arranged in titles according to their subject-matter, and chronologically within each title.

The work was finished in a little more than a year, and the Code published on April 7th, 529, with the force of law as from April 16th.[2] Thereafter, previous enactments might be cited only as they appeared in the new collection, exception being made only for pragmatic sanctions which gave individual privileges, or contained nothing contrary to the provisions of the Code, and for imperial instructions concerning fiscal matters, which had been incorporated in the archives of officials.[3]

This Code, as will appear shortly, only remained in force until 534, and has not come down to us. A papyrus, however, containing fragments of a list of title rubrics and constitutions, has been recently discovered, and has formed the basis for some important arguments.[4]

B. THE FIFTY DECISIONS. Justinian's next task was the more difficult one of dealing with the juristic law. Theodosius, as we have seen,[5] had failed to make his projected collection, and the only guidance provided was that of the Law of Citations. This was but a makeshift which Justinian could not allow to stand, and we know that he solved the problem by making, in the Digest, a collection of excerpts from the jurists' writings, and forbidding reference to the original works. Before

---

[1] Known from its opening words as *Haec quae necessario*. It is the first of the three introductory constitutions to the (second) Code.
[2] *C. Summa rei publicae*, the second introductory constitution.
[3] *C. Summa*, § 4.   [4] *Infra*, 501, n. 2.   [5] *Supra*, 479.

he did that, however, it was necessary, or at least desirable, that the way should be made plainer by the settlement of outstanding controversies, and the abolition of certain institutions which had, in fact, become obsolete, though naturally references to them occurred in the old literature. For this purpose, a number of constitutions were promulgated, fifty of which were apparently at some time put together and published as a collection.[1] The collection has not survived, and there are great difficulties in reconstructing it, for the number of constitutions in the (second) Code, which, so far as their contents are concerned, might have formed part of it, is considerably greater than fifty, and while some have, no doubt, been broken up to fit into different titles, others have probably been suppressed altogether. Rotondi has shown that the collection was probably published at the end of 530 or beginning of 531, and contained only those "decisions" which had been published between Aug. 1st and Nov. 17th, 530, i.e. before the date when the compilation of the Digest was ordered.[2] Legislation of a similar kind continued to be passed as work on the Digest proceeded, but these later constitutions were not collected, presumably because it was already seen that a new edition of the Code, in which they could be incorporated, would become necessary.[3,4]

C. The Digest. The order for the compilation of the Digest or Pandects was given in a constitution, now known from its opening words as *Deo auctore*, dated Dec. 15th, 530.[5] It was addressed to Tribonian, then quaestor of the sacred palace, who was to choose a commission to help him. Actually he chose sixteen persons, one great official (Constantinus), four professors (Theophilus and Cratinus of Constantinople, Dorotheus and Anatolius of Beyrout) and eleven advocates.[6] The instructions were to read and make excerpts from the writings of the ancient jurists who had had "authority to compile and interpret the laws" (i.e. the *ius respondendi*), and to collect them into a single work divided into fifty books and further into titles according to the subject-

[1] *C. Cordi*, §§ 1, 5; J. 1. 5. 3; 4. 1. 16; C. 6. 51. 1. 10 B.

[2] *Scr. Giur.* 1. 232.

[3] *C. Cordi*, § 1, distinguishes between the *quinquaginta decisiones* and *alias ad commodum propositi operis pertinentes constitutiones*.

[4] For the view that the fifty decisions were intended, like the Theodosian Law of Citations, as a guide to the use of juristic literature and that at the time of their publication Justinian's plan did not include the compilation of the Digest, v. Bonfante, *Histoire*, II. 57; *B.I.D.R.* XXXII (1922), 277–282.

[5] The first of the three introductory constitutions to the Digest. It is also found in C. 1. 17. 1.   [6] *C. Tanta* (v. infra, 488), § 9.

matter. No preference was to be given to the view of the majority or to that of Papinian, but the commissioners were to choose what they thought best wherever they found it. The collection was to contain nothing superfluous or obsolete, no contradictions, no repetitions, and nothing that was already contained in the Code except where the arrangement of the material made this advisable in the interests of clarity. Full power was given to cut down and alter the texts, and this extended even to the words of ancient *leges* or constitutions which were quoted by the jurists.[1] The use of all ciphers and abbreviations was forbidden, and where, for instance, the number of a book was given this must be written out in words—a provision which was extended also to all copies which should be made.[2] One result of this has been that the "inscriptions", i.e. the words at the beginning of each fragment giving the author, the title of the work and the number of the book, are well preserved and have been of the greatest use in reconstituting the original writings and in providing material for research on the methods of the compilers.

All commentaries were forbidden, for these, Justinian thought, would only lead to doubt and confusion such as had in times past resulted from the voluminous writings by which the jurists had obscured the plain text of the praetorian edict. Only literal translations into Greek (κατὰ πόδα), *indices* and *paratitla*, were allowed.[3] By *index* is meant a short summary of the contents of a passage, while *paratitla* were collections of parallel passages. These rules are only mentioned in connection with the Digest, but it is probable that they were intended to apply to the Code and Institutes as well, for it is clear that the three works together were intended to form a complete statement of the whole law, and it would seem that exactly the same considerations would apply to all the constituent parts.[4] The penalty for breach of these rules was severe, for the delinquent was to be held guilty of *falsum* (forgery), but it is doubtful how far they were observed even in Justinian's lifetime;[5] after his death they

---

[1] *C. Deo auctore,* § 7. The diffuse language makes it difficult to pin the emperor down to a precise meaning. He says "if you find anything incorrectly expressed (*non recte scriptum*) you are to re-shape it", and was probably thinking of form rather than matter, but the person who can "re-shape" a legal text has in fact the power of legislating.

[2] *C. Tanta,* § 22.

[3] *C. Deo auctore,* § 12; *C. Tanta,* § 21.

[4] Kübler, 434. *Contra,* Krüger, 407; Peters, "Die oströmischen Digestenkommentare und die Entstehung der Digesten" (*Berichte d. sächsischen Gesellschaft der Wissenschaft, Phil.-hist. Klasse,* LXV. 1913), 105.

[5] Krüger, *loc. cit.*; Peters, *op. cit.* 42 *sqq.*

were certainly broken, and in later ages the Digest has given rise to a greater literature than any other book, except the Bible.

How the compilers carried out their instructions we know, partly from two constitutions which, in addition to *Deo auctore*, were prefixed to the Digest and are both dated Dec. 16th, 533. One of these, *C. Omnem*, is addressed to eight professors of law and deals with legal education; the other, *C. Tanta circa*,[1] gives to the Digest the force of law as from Dec. 30th of the same year, and both contain, though in the rhetorical style appropriate to imperial constitutions, a considerable amount of information. For the rest, we are almost entirely dependent on the internal evidence of the work itself, for the subsequent Byzantine legal literature, in so far as it is preserved, tells us but little, and the references to the codification in non-legal books are astonishingly rare and meagre.[2]

The number of authors shown by the inscriptions to have been actually excerpted is thirty-nine, but the amount taken from different individuals varies very greatly—from almost a third of the whole, in the case of Ulpian, to a single fragment, in that of Aelius Gallus. The instruction to use only authors with the *ius respondendi* was evidently taken to permit the citation of all those whose works had come to be reckoned as part of the canon under the Theodosian Law of Citations, for not only is Gaius well represented, but also Pomponius, and a few fragments are included from republican jurists who had lived before the time of the *ius respondendi*.[3] The bulk of the work is however taken from the late classical authors, the encyclopaedic writers, Ulpian and Paulus, together contributing about one-half. Justinian says that in all nearly 2000 *libri* containing 3,000,000 *versus* (lines) were read, and that these were reduced to 150,000 *versus*.[4] Many of the books, he adds, were unknown even by name to the most learned scholars and had only been provided by Tribonian,[5] who evidently collected a private library of rare old works. An index of authors and books used was compiled and prefixed to the Digest, but comparison with the inscriptions of the fragments shows that it is inaccurate. It omits some works actually used, and mentions some

---

[1] A Greek text (Δέδωκεν) is also given. In the Code (1. 17. 2) only the Latin is preserved.

[2] Rotondi, "La codificazione giustinianea attraverso le fonti extragiuridiche," *Scr. Giur.* 1. 340–369.

[3] There was some warrant for this in the wording of *C. Deo auctore*, § 4; *v.* Buckland, 40.

[4] *C. Tanta*, § 1. The number of *libri* is exaggerated. From the inscriptions in the Digest and from the Index it appears that about 1625 were used.

[5] *C. Tanta*, § 17.

from which no quotation appears, besides confusing separate works and making other mistakes. It does, however, add some details to our knowledge.[1]

The only instruction concerning arrangement (beyond the division into fifty books and into titles), which the commissioners received, was that they were to follow the scheme of the Code and of the Edict.[2] By the Edict was meant, not the original document, but the commentaries on it, and since the Code already followed, in the main, a traditional order based on these commentaries, the two parts of the instruction were largely identical. Actually the compilers used Ulpian's commentary as their chief guide, civil law topics being fitted in with the praetorian matter as had been done in the classical *digesta*, but with greater elaboration and important differences of method. The headings of the titles were in most cases taken from existing works, often indirectly from the rubrics of the Edict, though some were no doubt invented by the compilers themselves. The books themselves have no headings. Only in one case, that of legacies and *fideicommissa*, was the amount of material so great that a single title extends over three books.[3]

The order of the fragments within the titles appears at first sight haphazard, and indeed, except in the first few titles, there is no attempt at a scientific order. An explanation, however, of the method which the compilers used was given by Bluhme rather over a century ago,[4] and has since been generally accepted. By examination of the inscriptions, Bluhme showed that there were three main groups or "masses" of works, the excerpts from which regularly came together within each title, and further, that the order in which the excerpts from the works within each mass appeared was regularly the same. One of these masses is called "Sabinian", because it begins with the books of Ulpian, Pomponius and Paulus, *ad Sabinum*, another "Edictal", because it begins with some of the books from Ulpian's and Paulus' commentaries on the Edict, and the third, "Papinian", because it begins with Papinian's *quaestiones* and *responsa*. There is also a fourth, much smaller mass, containing only about a dozen works, commonly called "Appendix".[5] The distribution

---

[1] As it is found only in the Florentine MS. it is usually called *Index Florentinus*. The mistakes are probably best explained on Rotondi's theory (*Scr. Giur.* I. 298–339) that the index was compiled, not by a fresh examination of the inscriptions, but by collating the lists of books in the different "masses" which had been prepared for the use of the compilers.

[2] *C. Deo auctore,* § 5.   [3] Books 30–32.

[4] *Zeitschrift für geschichtliche Rechtswissenschaft,* IV (1818), 256–474.

[5] Bluhme called it "post-Papinian".

of works among the different masses appears to have been, in part, according to a system, for the main works in the Sabinian mass deal with civil law, and the main works in the Edictal mass with *ius honorarium*, while the Papinian mass includes especially those of a practical and specialist nature,[1] but in many respects it was accidental or arbitrary. The order in which the masses appear in the titles is not always the same. Most commonly the Sabinian mass comes first, then the Edictal, then the Papinian, with the Appendix, where found, last, but almost every possible order is found. In some titles only one or two masses are found, in others each appears twice over,[2] the reason being that it was originally intended to make two titles which were subsequently fused without rearrangement of the fragments. Frequently, for one reason or another, a fragment is taken out of its mass and put elsewhere, for instance because of its obvious connection with a fragment in a different mass, or because it forms a good introduction to the subject and was wanted at the beginning of the title.[3]

Bluhme's discovery of the masses is definite, and subsequent work has only been able to correct it in details, but a further conjecture, which he founded on his discovery, is also very generally accepted. This is that the compilers divided themselves into three sub-committees, to each of which was assigned the task of going through the books contained in one mass. The Appendix mass, which probably represents books which only came to hand during the course of the work, was perhaps assigned to the Papinian sub-committee, as the excerpts from it most commonly stand after those from the Papinian mass.

The scheme of titles had presumably been agreed upon beforehand, and it is supposed that after each sub-committee had dealt with its own mass, the full commission met and harmonised the contributions, striking out repetitions and discussing debatable points. Recent research has given rise to further conjectures as to the order in which the works were excerpted.[4] The commission evidently asked for imperial direction on

---

[1] Bonfante, II. 107, where he also points out the connection between this distribution and the arrangement of studies.

[2] E.g. I. 3; 23. 2.

[3] See e.g. 7. I. I. Mommsen's large edition of the Digest (Berlin, 1870) shows with each fragment the mass to which it belongs, those displaced being marked by an asterisk. In the "stereotype" edition by Mommsen and Krüger, similar information is given in a footnote at the beginning of each title. Appendix I (p. 927) contains a list of the works comprised in each mass.

[4] Longo, *B.I.D.R.* XIX. 132 *sqq.*; de Francisci, *B.I.D.R.* XXII. 155 *sqq.*; XXIII. 39 *sqq.* and 186 *sqq.*; H. Krüger, *Die Herstellung der Digesten und der Gang der Exzerption* (1922), 71 *sqq.*

certain points, and the dates of the constitutions settling the questions give some indication of the dates on which the works out of which the question arose were before the commission.

The division into books and titles was not the only one recognised. For educational purposes especially, the Digest was also divided into seven "parts", according to a scheme which is explained by Justinian in C. Tanta[1] as follows:

Part 1. Books 1–4. πρῶτα (first part).

Part 2. Books 5–11. De iudiciis.

Part 3. Books 12–19. De rebus.

Part 4. Books 20–27. Umbilicus. This "central" part includes hypotheca (bk. 20), the aedilician edict, and the stipulatio duplae (bk. 21), interest, nauticum faenus and evidence (bk. 22), sponsalia, marriage and dowry (bks. 23–25), tutela and cura (bks. 26–27).

Part 5. Books 28–36. De testamentis, including wills and codicils (bks. 28–29), legacies, fideicommissa and connected matters (bks. 30–36).

Part 6. Books 37–44. Bonorum possessio and intestacy (bks. 37–38), operis novi nuntiatio, dammum infectum, aqua pluvia arcenda, publicani, gifts inter vivos and mortis causa (bk. 39), manumission and liberalis causa (bk. 40), acquisition of ownership and possession (bk. 41), res iudicata and execution (bk. 42), interdicts (bk. 43), exceptiones, "obligations and actions" (bk. 44).

Part 7. Books 45–50. Verbal contracts, suretyship, novation, performance, acceptilatio, praetorian stipulations (bks. 45–46), private delicts and criminal law, "libri terribiles" (bks. 47–48), appeal (bk. 49), local government, public works, pollicitatio, special cognitiones, census, the meaning of words, and maxims of the law (bk. 50).

The shortcomings of this catalogue, which become even more obvious when it is compared with the list of books and titles prefixed to the Digest,[2] show how difficult even a contemporary jurist found it to explain shortly the complex and mainly traditional arrangement. It will be noticed that the first three parts are simply named, whereas the contents of the remaining four are described in some detail. The reason for this can only be that these parts corresponded to the similarly named divisions in the pre-Justinianean scheme of education, so that their contents could be taken as well known.[3]

In reviewing the work done by the compilers, Justinian admits that repetitions have not been wholly avoided.[4] Of these, some were no doubt,

---

[1] §§ 2–8.
[3] Kübler, 406; cf. infra, 505.
[2] Stereotype edition, pp. 1–7.
[4] C. Tanta, § 13 (14).

as he explains, intentional, and due to a desire to repeat the same principle in different connections. Others are the result of inadvertence, often excusable in a work of this size, but hardly so when repetition occurs within a single title. Contradictions, he says, are not to be found, and if anyone thinks he can find any, more careful consideration will show that there is some reason for the apparent discrepancy.[1] This task has however proved too difficult in some cases even for the vast mass of ingenuity lavished by later ages on the Digest, and there is no doubt that the compilers sometimes allowed differences of opinion among classical jurists to stand, and sometimes introduced fresh contradictions of their own by changing one passage and omitting to change another.[2]

Alterations in the texts, the emperor himself says, were *multa et maxima*,[3] and it was indeed obviously necessary that the compilers should make full use of their express powers in this direction if texts several centuries old were to serve as an exposition of the existing law. Their alterations, or "interpolations",[4] as they are now generally called, are however not marked in any way, so that the authors mentioned in the inscriptions of the fragments are often represented as saying what in fact they did not say. That in these circumstances the inscriptions should have been retained at all is at first sight surprising; they certainly had no practical value, for all reference to the original text was expressly forbidden.[5] Justinian gives "respect for antiquity" as the reason,[6] and there is no ground for disbelieving him. But there is also another reason. The jurists from whom the excerpts were taken had themselves cited innumerable other authorities by name; these names could not be expunged without causing confusion, and if they were left in, it would have been absurd to omit the name of the person who cited them. The titles and numbers of the books might indeed have been omitted but for "respect for antiquity", or, if we prefer to call it so, "Byzantine love of parade".[7]

---

[1] *C. Tanta*, § 15.

[2] For examples of insufficient and "slapdash" interpolation *v.* Buckland, "D. XLVII. 2 and the Methods of the Compilers" (*Rev. d'histoire du droit*, X (1930), 117–142).

[3] *C. Tanta*, § 10.

[4] An older word is "Tribonianism". Although interpolation literally means "patching", it is used to include all alterations whether by addition, omission or substitution.

[5] *C. Deo auctore*, § 7; *C. Tanta*, § 10.   [6] *C. Tanta*, § 10.

[7] Gradenwitz, *Interpolationen in den Digesten* (1887), 18; Pringsheim, *Die archaistische Tendenz Justinians, St. Bonfante*, I. 552.

The search for interpolations was already carried on by the humanists of the sixteenth and seventeenth centuries, but it was then given up, and not seriously resumed until a little over half a century ago. Since then, however, the application of much learning and ingenuity to the discovery of interpolations has changed the whole orientation of Roman law studies.[1]

The primary object of this search is to separate the classical law from the Byzantine dress in which it has come down to us, and it is therefore necessary to subject each fragment in the Digest to a "double interpretation", i.e. to ask what it tells us of the classical law as well as what it means as part of Justinian's legislation.

But modern scholars also seek to go further. It is now generally believed that many alterations were made in the classical writings before they came into the hands of Justinian's compilers, and these alterations have now to be distinguished both from the original text and from the compilers' work. When discovered, they help greatly to illuminate the development of the law in the comparatively dark period which lies between the classical age and Justinian, but most of this work still lies in the future.[2]

For the discovery of interpolations, the most various methods are available. Sometimes it is possible actually to compare the text of the Digest with that of the original work which has survived elsewhere, or to compare two quotations from the same passage in the Digest (*leges geminae*), one of which has been altered while the other has not. This is quite exceptional, but equally certain results are obtained when the text is at variance with the known facts of classical law, as where the property in a *res mancipi* is assumed to pass by mere *traditio*,[3] or when the text contains a reference to a rule which we know to have been enacted by Justinian himself.[4] More commonly, the criteria are more complex, and depend upon investigation of the style and language of a passage as well as on a careful examination of its logical coherence. The language of the

---

[1] A bibliography is given by Bonfante at the beginning of his appendix on Interpolations, II. 141–183, but almost all modern works on Roman law touch the subject. Of the *Index Interpolationum* begun by Mitteis there have been published so far Vol. I, covering books 1–20, Supplement I, covering books 1–12 (Weimar, 1929), and Vol. II, covering books 21–35 (1931).

[2] Closely connected with this study of pre-Justinianean interpolations in the Digest is the study of alterations made in post-classical times in those writings which have come down to us outside the Corpus Juris; *v.* Bonfante, II. 184–189.

[3] E.g. D. 17. 1. 27. 1. Several examples H.-S. s.v. *mancipare*.

[4] Compare e.g. D. 30. 1 with C. 6. 43. 1 and J. 2. 20. 2; or D. 19. 1. 44 with C. 7. 47. 1. 1.

compilers, who were Greek-speaking Orientals, differed widely from that of the classical jurists who either spoke Latin as their native tongue, or at least used it habitually, and the rhetorical style of the sixth century forms an even greater contrast with the straightforward diction of the classical period. Study of the language used in Justinian's constitutions, and in passages in the Digest known on other grounds to be interpolated, has shown that a considerable number of words and phrases are themselves an indication of interpolation, or at any rate enough to arouse suspicion,[1] and that the same is true of certain constructions, such as an ablative absolute[2] or a *nisi* clause[3] tacked on at the end of a sentence.[4] But style and manner of thinking go together, and one reason at least for the popularity of the *nisi* clause with the compilers is that they frequently wish to retain the classical statement, but to qualify it by referring to some principle which, in their eyes, is paramount to the rule enunciated. Thus rules for the construction of wills are frequently followed by some such clause as "unless it be clearly shown that the testator wished otherwise". The classical jurist had deduced the intention of the testator purely by construing the words he had used, but to the compilers, the paramount rule is that the testator's wish is to be decisive, and evidence can be given that in the particular case the testator had an intention different from the meaning which, according to the rules of construction, attaches to the words he has used.[5]

Very frequently again the hand of the compilers is betrayed by a lack of logic or coherence in the text, which shows that it cannot have been written as it stands by a single author, or where this might be possible, at any rate that it cannot have been written by a person of the intellectual standing of the classical jurists. In their desire to shorten the texts, the compilers have often cut out a part of the discussion, and especially, where several views have been quoted, they have very naturally left only that one of which they approved. They have, however, seldom taken care to smooth over the cuts, and sometimes they have thus made it possible for us to see that they have attributed to a jurist the precise opposite of the opinion which he actually held.[6] In some cases again, the language

---

[1] See especially Gradenwitz, *Interpolationen*, 45 *sqq.* and Beseler in all parts of his *Beiträge*.

[2] E.g. D. 18. 1. 57. 3.

[3] On these clauses *v.* Eisele, *Z.S.S.* x. 296–322.

[4] Change of language does not however necessarily imply change in the law; Buckland, "Interpolations in the Digest", *Yale Law Journal*, XXXIII. 343–364.

[5] Gradenwitz, *op. cit.* 170 *sqq.*

[6] E.g. D. 18. 6. 19. 1, which can be compared with Fr. Vat. 12.

they have used is such that it betrays the legislator who can enact a rule as opposed to the jurist who can only draw conclusions.[1] This is especially clear when some definite period or sum is mentioned, for which there is no authority in classical law, as, for instance, when it is said that a usufruct held by a corporation expires after a hundred years,[2] or that twenty *aurei*[3] have to be paid by a slave manumitted in a will, if the will is upset by the *querela inofficiosi testamenti*.[4] Another indication is the appearance of scholastic distinctions which recall the lecture-room rather than the court, and are alien from the practical spirit of the classical law.[5]

Mistakes have no doubt been made in this search for interpolations;[6] some writers have trusted too much to their own sense of style and to preconceived notions as to the nature of Byzantine institutions. It will also probably be shown in an increasing number of cases that earlier alterations have been mistakenly attributed to the compilers of the Digest. But many results are assured beyond reasonable doubt, and of these something will be said in the next chapter, when the contrast between classical and Byzantine law is discussed.

The three years which lie between the constitution ordering the compilation and its actual publication have always been regarded as but a short time for so great a work, and they seem still shorter now that we know what an amount of interpolation was involved. It has consequently been suggested more than once that there must have existed already an unofficial collection of a similar character to the Digest which the compilers could use as a foundation for their work. Peters,[7] the chief upholder of this view, believed such a "pre-digest" to have been compiled by the teachers in the law schools belonging to the generation preceding Justinian, and to have contained already a great many of the interpolations. But this view cannot be accepted.[8] If it were correct, much of what Justinian says in the introductory constitutions is not merely exaggerated self-adulation, but a tissue of lies which would have been quite transparent to

---

[1] E.g. D. 25. 1. 3. 1: *Nos generaliter definiemus*.

[2] D. 7. 1. 56.

[3] This word is always interpolated, the rule being that one *aureus* is substituted for 1000 sesterces; *v.* J. 3. 7. 3.

[4] D. 5. 2. 8. 17; 5. 2. 9.   [5] E.g. D. 19. 5. 5. pr.; 18. 1. 57.

[6] *V.* Buckland, *loc. cit.*; Lenel, *Z.S.S.* XLV. 17–38.

[7] *Op. cit. supra*, 487, n. 4. The same thesis was propounded by Hofmann, *Die Kompilation der Digesten* (1900), but the work met with no approval.

[8] Against it, though all agree in appreciation, *v.* Lenel, *Z.S.S.* XXXIV. 373–390; Mitteis, *ibid.* 402–416; Rotondi, *Scr. Giur.* I. 87–109.

his contemporaries. He could not, without making himself ridiculous, have described the collection and use of nearly two thousand books and have said that it had hardly been hoped to finish in ten years, if everyone knew that all his compilers had done was to make additions to an already existing collection. In fact, when one considers that there were sixteen members of the commission and that the standard of the work done does not in any way approach what would be demanded of a similar undertaking in our own day, the achievement of the compilers is not so surprising. Bluhme already suggested that they worked in sub-committees, and it seems probable that most of the work must, in the first instance, have been done by individual members, who, very likely, only brought what they considered important to the notice of their colleagues. Further, it is not necessary to postulate a "pre-digest" in order to see that pre-Justinianean interpolations may have facilitated the process. No doubt these could not be of the same nature as some of those made by Justinian's compilers, for they could not give definite decisions of old problems, or introduce completely new rules; but in course of time the texts had suffered alteration through the inclusion of explanatory glosses, and such glosses might actually include new dogmatic conceptions.[1] The literature of the schools included, we know, collections of parallel passages and explanatory notes,[2] which must also have been of great assistance. It is of course true, as Peters points out, that the fortnight which lies between the publication of the Digest and the date on which it came into force was too short a time for any practitioner to assimilate a new work of this size, but even on his own showing there were very considerable differences between the pre-Justinianean collection and the Digest, and the time would have been too short for anyone to go through the whole and make the necessary comparison. The fact must be accepted that Justinian was too eager to set the seal of achievement on his work to allow such considerations to weigh with him. In a fortnight it cannot have been possible for copies, even if they were already prepared, to have obtained more than a very limited circulation.

Of the many manuscripts in which the text of the Digest is preserved,[3] one, the Florentine, is of unique importance. A note in a Lombard hand of the ninth or tenth century shows that it was at that time in Italy, and in the twelfth century we know that it was in Pisa. After the conquest of

---

[1] Mitteis, op. cit. 414.   [2] Infra, 506.

[3] See especially Mommsen's Preface to his large edition, and Jur. Schr. II. 107 sqq.; Kantorowicz, "Über die Entstehung der Digestenvulgata", Z.S.S. XXX. 183–271 and XXXI. 14–83.

Pisa by the Florentines in 1406 it was brought as a valuable piece of booty to Florence, where it has been ever since. It was probably written in Italy, possibly at Ravenna.[1] Its date cannot be later than the seventh century and is more probably the second half of the sixth, so that in any case it is remarkably close in time to Justinian's own reign. It is not free from errors and omissions, but some of these were corrected by a hand different from that of any of the scribes, and probably by reference to a manuscript other than the one from which the text was copied. There are only a few fragments of manuscripts of like age. In Italy and in the West generally, the Digest fell into oblivion from early in the seventh century, and was not studied again until the eleventh. Thereafter manuscripts multiplied, especially to supply the needs of the great school of the Glossators at Bologna, for which reason the common text of these MSS. is known as *litera Bononiensis* or Vulgate. It is the great merit of Mommsen to have established that they all go back to a single archetype (not preserved), which was itself copied from the Florentine. It was however corrected by reference to a MS. which was independent of the Florentine, and it is thus in some cases of value in restoring original readings where the Florentine is corrupt. The MSS. of the eleventh and twelfth centuries omit the Greek parts of the Digest, those of the thirteenth sometimes represent them by a translation derived from the Florentine. Since the Glossators were interested in law only, those parts which were of purely historical interest, such as the introductory constitutions, were also generally omitted, and the inscriptions were much abbreviated. The MSS. are seldom complete, but generally contain only one of the three parts into which the Digest was divided in the Middle Ages. These were: *Digestum vetus* (up to end of D. 24. 2), *Infortiatum* (thence, to the end of book 38), and *Novum* (remainder), part of the *Infortiatum* (from the words *tres partes* in D. 35. 2. 82 to the end) being further distinguished as *Tres Partes*. This curious nomenclature is said by one of the Glossators[2] to arise from the fact that Irnerius, the founder of the school, at first knew only of the first part, and that he then, on coming into possession of the third, distinguished the two as "old" and "new". Subsequently he got to know the second, but without the *Tres Partes*; when these too came to light, he called the second part *Infortiatum*, i.e. "reinforced".

---

[1] Kantorowicz, *Z.S.S.* xxx. 193.

[2] Odofredus (thirteenth century). Placentinus (twelfth century) says that the *Tres Partes* originally formed the beginning of the *D. Novum*, and that they were subsequently transferred to the *Infortiatum*, which got its name from this reinforcement; Savigny, *Geschichte des r. Rechts im Mittelalter*, iii. 426 *sqq.*

The actual division has recently been explained as due to the conceit of some copyist who, having to make some divisions, hit upon the idea of making one where the subject-matter concerned separation (i.e. between D. 24. 2: *De divortiis et repudiis*, and 24. 3: *Soluto matrimonio*, etc.), and another where it concerned "new work" (i.e. before 39. 1: *De operis novi nuntiatione*). Having thus got his three parts, he wrote the words *tres partes* in large letters when he got to them in D. 35. 2. 82, and so gave later copyists the idea of making a division here too, though the words actually occur in the middle of a sentence.[1]

D. THE INSTITUTES. The Digest was to be taken into use immediately in the law schools, but it was, as Justinian knew,[2] too difficult a work for the student to begin with, and consequently a new introductory text-book was needed to take the place of Gaius' Institutes which had for centuries served the purpose. Since commentaries were forbidden it could clearly not be left to private enterprise to provide this, and already in 530 an official manual was in contemplation.[3] Orders for its compilation were given, probably before the Digest was complete,[4] to Tribonian, Theophilus and Dorotheus, and the result of their labours was published on November 21st, 533, under the title *Imperatoris Iustiniani Institutiones*. The Institutes are however not only a text-book; they have themselves the validity of an imperial statute,[5] and came into force on the same day as the Digest—December 30th, 533.[6]

The orders of the compilers were that they should produce a new book, based on the classical institutional works, and especially on the Institutes and *res cottidianae* of Gaius,[7] leaving out unnecessary obsolete matter, but including some mention of the earlier law. These instructions were carried out, and the Institutes of Justinian follow closely the arrangement of those of Gaius. Like them, they treat of "persons", "things" and "actions" in four books, but these books, unlike those of Gaius, are divided into titles, and the fourth, which in Gaius' Institutes is devoted solely to "actions", begins already with obligations *ex delicto*, the last part of "things". The reason for this change is, no doubt, that most of

---

[1] Kantorowicz, *Z.S.S.* XXXI. 59 *sqq.*   [2] J. 1. 1. 2.

[3] *C. Deo auctore*, § 11.

[4] *C. Imperatoriam maiestatem* (Introductory constitution to the Institutes), § 3, does indeed speak of the Digest as completed, but it was at any rate not yet published; cf. Kübler, 411. *Contra*, Krüger, 367; Kipp, 155.

[5] *C. Imp. mai.* § 6.   [6] *C. Tanta*, § 23.

[7] In *C. Imp. mai.* § 6 and *C. Omnem*, § 1 the emperor shows his partiality by speaking of *Gaius noster*; cf. D. 45. 3. 39 (interp.).

what Gaius had said concerning actions had to be cut out as obsolete, and it was desired to keep the books of approximately equal length. There are also added two titles on *officium iudicis* and on criminal law, which correspond to nothing in Gaius. A great part of the text is taken almost verbatim from the Institutes and *res cottidianae* of Gaius, but the compilers used also the Institutes of Marcian, Florentinus and Ulpian, and perhaps those of Paulus.[1] These they almost certainly had before them in the original, but passages from more advanced works were probably taken from the excerpts in the Digest.[2] There are several references to Justinian's own legislation which must be new, but, taken as a whole, the Institutes are no less of a compilation than the Digest, the only difference being that there are no inscriptions to show from whom each passage comes,[3] and that the whole is put into the form of a lecture by the emperor to his students, the *cupida legum iuventus*, who are addressed in the introductory constitution. There cannot thus be interpolations in the sense of passages attributed to an author who did not write them, but in fact the position is exactly the same as with the Digest. The texts used by the compilers of the Institutes had not reached them unadulterated, and they necessarily themselves made further alterations in order to bring the law up to date. The actual work was presumably done by the two professors, Tribonian reserving to himself only the general supervision, and it has been shown on stylistic grounds that books 1 and 2 are probably by a different hand from books 3 and 4. It is therefore generally agreed that Theophilus must have been responsible for the one pair of books and Dorotheus for the other, but there is not enough evidence for us to identify the work of either.[4]

Manuscripts of the Institutes are numerous, for the work was always that most in demand in the West. None however, except a small fragment, is earlier than the ninth century.

E. THE SECOND CODE. Since 529 there had been enacted not only the "Fifty Decisions", but a large number of other constitutions, so that the first Code was no longer a reliable guide to the statute law. Soon after the completion of the Digest orders were consequently given to Tribonian, Dorotheus and three advocates (all of whom had been on the

---

[1] Krüger, 385.
[2] Bonfante, II. 134; Krüger, 386.
[3] For analysis of sources *v.* Zocco Rosa, "Iustiniani Institutionum Palingenesia", *Annuario dell' istituto di storia del diritto romano*, IX (1905), 181 *sqq.* and X (1908), 1 *sqq.*; also published separately. Review by Kübler, *Z.S.S.* xxx. 433–437.
[4] For literature *v.* Kübler, 413; Krüger, 387.

Digest commission) to prepare a second edition containing the new matter.[1] Constitutions which dealt with several different subjects were to be cut up and each part put in its appropriate title, and the commissioners were again given wide general powers of omission and alteration.[2] The work was published under the title *Codex repetitae praelectionis* on Nov. 16th, 534, with the force of law as from Dec. 29th of the same year. Thereafter no reference might be made either to the first edition or to the subsequent constitutions except in the form in which they appeared in the new Code.[3]

The Code is divided into twelve books, each again subdivided into titles, which are generally shorter and more numerous than those of the Digest. Within each title the constitutions are arranged in chronological order, and provided with inscriptions showing the emperor from whom they emanate and the addressee, as well as "subscriptions" giving the date of emission or publication,[4] and sometimes the place. Some bear the subscription *sine die et consule*, in accordance with Justinian's specific orders that when the compilers found constitutions undated in the old *codices* or among the later collections, they were to make this clear.[5] The arrangement is based on that of the older *codices*, more especially on that of the *C. Gregorianus*,[6] and so indirectly on that of the Edict.

Book 1 treats of ecclesiastical law,[7] of the sources of law and the duties of the higher officials; books 2–8 of private law; book 9 of criminal law, and books 10–12 of administrative law. For constitutions previous to 312 (the date of the earliest in the *C. Theodosianus*), the only sources were the *CC. Gregorianus* and *Hermogenianus*. To this fact is no doubt due the great number of rescripts included, especially of the time of Diocletian. Full use was made of the powers of alteration and omission, and in many cases the exact nature of the alteration can be seen by comparison with

---

[1] We do not know how soon, but the names of the commissioners and their instructions are repeated in the third introductory constitution (*Cordi*), under which the Code was promulgated.

[2] *C. Cordi*, § 3.

[3] The exceptions allowed under the first Code (*supra*, 485) were evidently intended to stand; *C. Cordi*, § 5.

[4] D. = *data*: P.P. = *proposita*; cf. *supra*, 476.

[5] *C. Haec*, § 2. Absence of date was to have no effect on the validity of constitutions included in the Code. Constantine's enactment forbidding the use of undated constitutions (*C. Th.* 1. 1. 1) is received in Justinian's Code with the significant change of *edicta sive constitutiones* into *beneficia personalia* (C. 1. 23. 4).

[6] Rotondi, *Scr. Giur.* 1. 153.

[7] This is an innovation due to Justinian's piety; in *C. Th.* ecclesiastical law comes in the last book.

the remains of the older *codices*. Preambles were regularly omitted and only the operative part of a constitution included; constitutions were divided and different parts placed in different titles according to their subject-matter, and occasionally separate constitutions were fused together.

Other changes were made, as in the Digest, in order to bring the matter up to date, and to secure harmony; in some cases merely to substitute more pedestrian language for the turgid style of the fourth century, which was even more elaborate than that of the sixth. The methods available for the discovery of these interpolations, where no direct comparison can be made, are similar to those used in the case of the Digest, but not the same. There is not so much difference in the style of the imperial chancery at different periods as there is between that of the classical jurists and Justinian's compilers, and the same logical tests cannot be applied to the ornate style of the constitutions as to that of the juristic writings. Considerable progress has however been made, though less, so far, than in the case of the Digest.

Since the second Code alone has been preserved, there is considerable difficulty in discovering its relation to the first, and in knowing how much alteration had already been made by the first commission. Recent investigations go to show that more was done by the second commission than was formerly assumed.[1] The papyrus which contains fragments of an index of the first Code gives definite proof that some new titles were inserted and that individual constitutions were deleted as well as inserted.[2] It is also clear that, in accordance with Justinian's orders, the new constitutions issued since 529 were treated in the same way as the older ones, their preambles omitted, and their contents dismembered where it was desirable to introduce different parts into different titles. It has also been possible in some cases to show some definite changes which must have been made by the second commission in constitutions which were already contained in the first Code,[3] and it is indeed *a priori* likely that the greater number of changes necessary in order to bring the texts up to date were made by the second commission, as most of Justinian's reforming legislation was enacted after 529, and there were also the reforms brought about by independent interpolations in the Digest to

---

[1] Rotondi, *Scr. Giur.* I. 237; Schulz, *St. Bonfante*, I. 335–360.

[2] *P. Oxy.* xv. No. 1814. It contains, in a very fragmentary state, a list of title headings and inscriptions of constitutions of Book I, Titles 11–16; *v.* Krüger, *Z.S.S.* XLIII. 561–563, and Bonfante, *B.I.D.R.* XXXII. 277–282 (both with text).

[3] Schulz, *loc. cit.*

be considered. It is however denied by the most competent authorities, that the arrangement of the second Code was influenced by that of the Digest.[1]

The manuscript tradition of the Code[2] is not nearly so good as that of the Digest. From very early times abbreviations were used in spite of Justinian's orders, inscriptions and subscriptions were cut down and notes derived from the jurists of the sixth century included in the text. Fragments of a text produced in this way are preserved in a palimpsest at Verona dating from the sixth or seventh century, the only MS. we have which ever contained the whole Code, including the Greek constitutions. In later times, no complete MSS. were used; the last three books were separated from the first nine, which were reduced by the omission of the Greek constitutions and others (especially those repealed by the Novels or represented in the Institutes) to about a quarter of their original content. From the ninth century onward, the abridgment was enlarged again by reference to complete MSS. which then still existed, until towards the end of the eleventh century fairly complete texts replaced the abridgment. The three last books were not restored to their original place, but copied separately from the complete texts. In most MSS. they are combined with the Institutes and the *Authenticum*[3] into a single volume called *Volumen* or *Volumen Parvum*. Even after this development much was still omitted, the Greek constitutions especially, which only began to be restored, chiefly from the Basilica, by the humanists of the sixteenth century. The modern text, as given especially in Krüger's editions,[4] is the result of minute work on many sources, including the C. *Theodosianus* and others previous to Justinian.

F. THE NOVELS. With the publication of the second Code, the work of codification was complete, but Justinian foresaw that new developments might require further legislation and in fact continued to legislate freely during the remainder of his reign, though less in the later than in the earlier years.[5] Most of the Novels concern public or ecclesiastical matters, and of those which concern private law several were occasioned by doubts which had arisen as to the effect of previous legislation.[6] Such

---

[1] Krüger, 388; Rotondi, *Scr. Giur.* I. 153.

[2] Krüger, 425 *sqq.* [3] *Infra*, 504.

[4] "Critical" edition, 1877, and vol. II. of the Berlin "stereotype" edition of the Corpus Juris.

[5] This fact is commonly attributed to the death of Tribonian in 546. *Contra*, Krüger, 399. As the great legislative period comes to an end already in 540 there seems little reason to follow the general view. [6] E.g. Novv. 19, 44, 150.

doubts Justinian, when he forbade commentaries, had already ordered to be referred to himself for decision.[1] He did not, however, confine himself to interpretations, and there is a considerable amount of new private (especially family) law in the Novels, such, for instance, as the complete remodelling of intestate succession.[2] The general tendency of the legislation was towards a recognition of the actual facts of Byzantine practice; it did not, like so much of the compilation itself, look backwards towards the pure Roman law.

It is in the Novels only that we have complete specimens of Justinian's constitutions in their original state, not cut down, divided up or altered, as in the Code. They begin regularly with a preamble (called in the editions *praefatio*) setting out the occasion and purpose of the enactment, and end regularly with a form of words (called *epilogus* in the editions) ordering its enforcement. The body of the enactment is, where necessary, divided into chapters, sometimes dealing with unrelated subjects. Some of the Novels are of great length, such for instance as Nov. 22, which has forty-eight chapters, and is in fact a code of Christian marriage law; others are quite short. Almost all, except those addressed to Latin-speaking provinces, were published in Greek; a few were in both languages.[3]

In the prefatory constitution to the Code, Justinian had announced his intention of issuing an official collection of subsequent enactments under the title *Novellae Constitutiones*.[4] This intention was however never carried out,[5] and only unofficial, or perhaps semi-official, collections were made. Of three such we have, in different ways, fairly full knowledge.

(i) The most complete is that known as the Greek Collection, or the Collection of 168 constitutions, which was the one used by the compilers of the Basilica.[6] It cannot have been completed before the reign of Tiberius II (578–582), for it includes three constitutions of his as well as

---

[1] *C. Tanta,* § 21. 　　　　　　　　[2] Novv. 118 and 127.

[3] Krüger, 400.

[4] *C. Cordi,* § 4. Publication is not actually mentioned, but, since preservation in the archives went without saying, the words must be taken to have this meaning.

[5] Joh. Scholasticus (Heimbach, *Anecdota,* II. 208), who made a collection of ecclesiastical constitutions about 550, says that he had to gather them from various places. Passages in Byzantine authors which mention a collection of "new laws" appear all to be based on a misunderstanding of Malalas, who is really referring to the Code (Rotondi, *Scr. Giur.* I. 355 *sqq.*). The statement of Paulus Diaconus (*Hist. Lang.* I. 25) is based on a misapprehension as to the nature of the *Epitome Iuliani;* Krüger, 399.

[6] Kroll, Preface to Novels (vol. III of "stereotype" edition of Corpus Juris), iv.

four of Justin II (565–578). Two constitutions appear twice over,[1] and in one case the Greek and Latin texts of a single one are counted separately.[2] The three (or perhaps four) last are not imperial constitutions, but enactments by praetorian prefects. Up to Nov. 120 the order is, except occasionally, chronological, and based probably on a collection made in Justinian's reign, not earlier than 544. The remainder is not arranged on any principle, and includes some constitutions which, although dating from before the second Code, were not included in it.[3] Our knowledge is based almost entirely on two MSS., a Venetian one of the thirteenth and a Florentine one of the fourteenth century. In both, the Latin constitutions, which no doubt appeared in full in the original collection, are either omitted or represented by a Greek summary. In the Venetian MS. there follow, after the collection proper, thirteen constitutions of Justinian, there called "edicts". Two are doublets of enactments which were in the collection but are missing in this MS.[4] One gives a Greek version of a Latin constitution which had been in the original.[5] The collection, like the other Greek sources, was not used by the Glossators. It was only brought to light by the humanist schools of the fifteenth and sixteenth centuries.

(ii) The oldest collection is that represented by the *Epitome Iuliani*, which contains 124[6] constitutions in an abridged Latin version. Its author, Julianus, is described as a professor in Constantinople, and it must date from Justinian's reign, for he is referred to as *imperator noster*. The order, though partly chronological, is confused. The latest constitution included dates from 555, and this fact, together with the use of Latin, makes it probable that the work was intended for use in Italy, where promulgation of the Novels had been ordered in 554.[7]

(iii) There is more doubt about the date and nature of the *Authenticum*. This is also a Latin collection, in which the Latin constitutions appear in the original, the Greek in a literal translation. It contains 134 constitutions dating from between 535 and 556, arranged, with some variations, in chronological order up to No. 127.[8] What follows is a later addition. The name *Authenticum* is said to have been given to the collection because

---

[1] Nov. 75 = 104; Nov. 143 = 150.   [2] Nov. 32 = 34.

[3] Krüger, 405, n. 39.

[4] Ed. 1 = Nov. 8 (Corpus Juris, III. pp. 78 *sqq.*); Ed. 6 = Nov. 122.

[5] Ed. 5 = Nov. 111.

[6] Or rather 122, since two are repeated.

[7] *Pro petitione Vigilii* (Corpus Juris, vol. III. Appendix VII), 11. The Digest and Code had already been published in Italy (*ibid.*).

[8] = Nov. 134.

Irnerius, in whose time (11th–12th centuries) it is first mentioned, originally doubted its authenticity, but subsequently changed his mind and preferred it to the *Epitome Iuliani*.[1] He held that it was the official collection made by Justinian's orders for promulgation in Italy,[2] and this theory fits well enough with the date of the latest constitution and the literal nature of the translation, which is in accordance with Justinian's rule.[3] But most modern authorities disagree.[4] The translation, which was apparently made by a man whose knowledge of Greek was poor, who used a corrupt text and was without legal training, is generally considered too bad for an official version, and an official collection would not have omitted the pragmatic sanction, *pro petitione Vigilii*, which ordered the promulgation of the Novels in Italy. The probability however appears to be that it dates from the sixth century, and it may be that it is semi-official in the sense that it consists of Latin versions made at different times by scribes in the office of the prefect of Italy at Ravenna.[5,6]

§ II. LEGAL EDUCATION

The instructions which Justinian gives in *C. Omnem* for the use of the compilation in the law schools are preceded by a short account of the previous arrangements.[7] To his contemporaries this was no doubt clear enough, but it is not now perfectly intelligible. In their first year, says Justinian, students learnt the Institutes of Gaius and four *libri singulares*: 1, dowry; 2, *tutela*; 3 and 4, wills and legacies; in their second, the *prima pars legum*, with the omission of some titles (although, as he explains, it was absurd that anything except the Institutes should come before a "first part") and selected titles from the *partes de rebus* and *de iudiciis*; in their third, the remainder of these parts and eight out of the nineteen books of Papinian's *responsa*, and even of these much was omitted, so that

---

[1] Savigny, *Geschichte des r. Rechts im Mittelalter*, III. 491 *sqq.*

[2] This view is accepted by Zachariae, *Sitzungsber. d. Berliner Akademie der Wissensch.* (1882), 993 *sqq.*; Karlowa, I. 1021; and in part by Noailles, *Les collections des Novelles de L'empereur Justinien* (1912), 170 *sqq.*

[3] For translations from Latin into Greek, *supra*, 487.

[4] Krüger, 403; Kübler, 419.

[5] Bonfante, II, 69, quoting Tamassia, "Per la storia del' Autentico", *Atti del R. Istituto Veneto di scienze*, IX. ser. VII. Mommsen however, *Z.S.S.* XXI. 155 = *Ges. Schr.* II. 376, with whom Krüger, 403, apparently agrees, thinks that the eleventh century is more likely.

[6] The best modern edition, that of Schoell and Kroll (vol. III of stereotype Corpus Juris), is primarily a reconstruction of the Greek collection, with the text of the *Authenticum*, where it exists, in parallel columns.

[7] § 1.

"their thirst remained unslaked"; in their fourth year they read the *responsa* of Paulus by themselves and attended no lectures. A period of only four years of study is here mentioned, but from what is said in *C. Imperatoriam maiestatem* it would appear that, sometimes at least, a fifth year was devoted to the study of imperial constitutions.[1] What is meant by *partes legum* is not explained. Peters[2] regarded the use of the expression as an indication that there must have existed already, before Justinian's time, a "pre-digest", whose divisions could be referred to in this way, but we have seen that this theory cannot be accepted. The general view is that the parts of the commentaries on the Edict, especially that of Ulpian, are meant. These were the chief basis of legal education and no doubt there were many omissions and additional references or notes which had become traditional in the schools. In the *Scholia Sinaitica* (which are notes on Ulpian's work *ad Sabinum*) the reader is several times recommended to omit certain passages, and Justinian himself says that a good deal was left out as unsuitable for educational purposes. What the four *libri singulares* were is also disputed. Some take Justinian's words to mean that they, like the Institutes, were by Gaius, in which case they might be either special works or the parts of his commentary on the Edict.[3] More probably, however, since the subjects[4] correspond to the chief divisions in the books on the civil law, these books are meant, and in particular Ulpian's *libri ad Sabinum*, which we know to have been used in the schools.[5,6]

Justinian's own arrangement was as follows[7]: In their first year, the men had lectures on the Institutes and the first part ($\pi\rho\hat{\omega}\tau\alpha$) of the Digest; in their second either the *pars de iudiciis* or the *pars de rebus* and on the first books in each of those divisions which corresponded to matters treated in the old *libri singulares*: dowry, *tutela*, wills and legacies (i.e. books 23, 26, 28 and 30); in their third year, they took whichever of the two *partes* (*de iudiciis* and *de rebus*) they had not taken in their second year, as well as

[1] Cf. *supra*, 470.   [2] *Op. cit.* (*supra*, 487, n. 4), 57 *sqq.*
[3] Kniep, *Der Rechtsgelehrte Gaius* (1910), 23 *sqq.*
[4] *Res uxoria, tutela, testamenta, legata.*
[5] Krüger, 396; Collinet, *Ét. Hist.* II. 225.
[6] Great difficulty is caused by Justinian's statement that six *libri* were all that the students learnt from their professors. Some, believing the words to refer to the first year only, think that Gaius' Institutes were (as in the West, *supra*, 481) reduced to two books, which, with the four *libri singulares*, would make up the required six. More probably the six are meant to include all that was taught in the three years of lecturing, and are to be understood as (i) Institutes, (ii) *ll. singulares*, (iii) *prima pars*, (iv) *pars de iudiciis*, (v) *pars de rebus*, (vi) *responsa Papiniani*; v. Kübler, 429 *sqq.*   *C. Omnem*, §§ 2–6, cf. *supra*, 491.

books 20–22. In their fourth year they attended no lectures, but had to study by themselves what remained of the fourth and fifth *partes* of the Digest (i.e. books 24, 25, 27, 29, 31–36), and the fifth year was similarly devoted to the private study of the Code. The seventh and eighth *partes* of the Digest (books 37–50) formed no part of the course, but were to be read in each man's own time, including, evidently, the period after he had begun to practise. From the alternations of the parts *de iudiciis* and *de rebus* it would seem that the same professor lectured to the same batch of students in their second and third years, for otherwise there would have had to be two separate courses in each year on the same subject, or second and third year students would have had to attend the same lectures.[1]

It is indeed probable that the lectures were so arranged that each student attended those of the same professor throughout his university career.[2]

Students of the various years all had their special names already before Justinian's time. Freshmen were *dupondii*, "two-pounders", though what the name meant is undiscoverable.[3] Second and third year men were called, from the nature of their studies, *edictales* and *Papinianistae* respectively; fourth year men were λύται, perhaps because they were already capable of solving problems for themselves.[4] Justinian forbade the use of the term *dupondius*, which he says is frivolous and ridiculous— it had no doubt been originally students' slang—and substituted for it the title *Iustiniani novi*—"Justinian's freshmen".[5] The names for the second, third and fourth years he retained, and in order to find a justification for still calling third year men *Papinianistae*, he hit upon the device of putting a quotation from Papinian at the beginning of each title in the 20th book, the first of the three *libri singulares* (20–22) which they had to

---

[1] Neither of these solutions seems possible for the rigid system established by Justinian, though it is true that Zacharius, in his life of the Patriarch Severus, writing of Beyrout in 487 or 488, describes himself when a freshman as attending the same lecture as Severus, then in his second year, and as leaving with the other freshmen when the second year work began; Collinet, *op. cit.* II. 194; Peters, *op. cit.* 62. *V.* also the retranslation of the Syriac text into Greek, *ibid.* 109.

[2] Collinet, *op. cit.* 195. If the argument from the alternation of the parts *de iudiciis* and *de rebus* has any weight this must have been the rule before Justinian also.

[3] Kübler, 431, gives some conjectures.

[4] Krüger, 398, says that the word cannot have the passive meaning "freed" (i.e. from lectures). But ἀφέτης can mean a freedman.

[5] *C. Omnem*, § 2.

read. He also allowed them to celebrate as heretofore the day on which
they entered on the course of study which was illuminated by this famous
name.[1] Fifth year men were called *prolytae* (perhaps = "advanced
lytae"). Ragging—*ludi*—especially of freshmen, such as Zacharius also
mentions, but describes as harmless,[2] was forbidden in the strongest
terms.[3]

§ III. THE HISTORY OF JUSTINIAN'S LEGISLATION IN THE EAST

The influence of Justinian's legislation in the West is part of the
general history of European law, and lies outside the scope of this book,
but in the East, the history of the law, though mainly one of decadence,
is continuous,[4] and did not indeed come to an end even with the Turkish
conquest, for the ecclesiastical courts maintained considerable independence and continued to administer the Romano-Byzantine system.

Justinian's compilation gave rise immediately to a series of works of
which the chief object was to render it more easily accessible to a Greek-
speaking population. The emperor had allowed not only translations but
also *indices* and *paratitla*, and it seems that even in his lifetime the limits
of this permission were not closely observed,[5] partly perhaps because of
a certain ambiguity in the terms themselves and partly because it was
impossible to prevent the circulation of lecture notes. At any rate there
were among the writers two of the compilers themselves. Theophilus
wrote an extended Greek version of the Institutes, now known as the
"Paraphrase",[6] and an *index* to the first three parts of the Digest, which
was however much more than a mere summary, for it included a paraphrase of the text together with historical and other notes.[7] Dorotheus
also wrote an *index* to the Digest, which followed the text more closely.[8]

---

[1] *C. Omnem*, § 4.   [2] Collinet, *op. cit.* 107.   [3] *C. Omnem*, § 9.

[4] For a general account *v.* Collinet, *Cambridge Medieval History*, IV. 706–725.

[5] *Supra*, 487.

[6] Latest edition by Ferrini, 1884–1897. Ferrini himself denied the authorship
of Theophilus, but see Zachariae v. Lingenthal, *Z.S.S.* x. 257–258; Kübler, 434–
436.

[7] It was probably based on lecture notes, as is indicated by the fact that only
those books on which lectures were given were included. See however Peters,
Die oströmischen Digestenkommentare, 46 *sqq.*, where the view is expressed that
Theophilus commented on a "pre-digest"; cf. *supra*, 495.

[8] Not published before 542 as he quotes Nov. 115 of that date; Heimbach, VI.
36, n. 3. He probably also wrote παραγραφαί (notes), though this is denied by
Peters, *op. cit.* 44 and 85, on the ground that these would have fallen under
Justinian's prohibition of commentaries. For papyrus fragments believed to
belong to Dorotheus' version *v.* La Pira, *B.I.D.R.* XXXVIII. 151–174.

Works on the Code were written by Thalelaeus and Isidorus,[1] both professors addressed in *C. Omnem*, and of about the same period is the version of the Digest by Cyrillus, which consists of short summaries giving the effect of each text without reference to the original form and has been called "perhaps the most remarkable intellectual achievement of the time".[2] Rather later, though still perhaps dating from Justinian's reign, is the *index* to the Digest by Stephanus, who is described as a professor, and whose work is almost certainly based on lectures which he delivered. It was very full, containing a broad version of the text together with extensive notes and quotations from other authors, especially Theophilus.[3] Later again, between about 570 and 612,[4] lies the work of a man known to us only (from the scholia to the Basilica) as "Anonymus". It appears that he was the author of two monographs, one on legacies and *donationes mortis causa*, the other on discrepancies in the Digest,[5] of a version of the Digest with notes, and of the collection known as the "Nomocanon in fourteen titles".[6] According to Peters'[7] theory the vast majority of the notes on the Digest consisted of extracts from the works of previous authors, and these, together with a few notes by the author himself, were written in the margins round the text. Each extract was prefixed by the name of the writer from whom it was taken, but those of the author himself naturally had no prefix. When the MS. was copied these nameless notes received the prefix "Anonymus" ($\tau o\hat{v}$ '$A\nu\omega\nu\dot{v}\mu o\nu$),

[1] Thalelaeus' work was much more extensive than that of Isidorus and is particularly important for its frequent references to the earlier law. A version of the Codex was also composed by a certain Anatolius but he was probably not identical with the one mentioned in *C. Omnem*; *v.* Kübler, 438. Whether these writers also wrote on the Digest is doubtful; *v.* Peters, *op. cit.* 97; Heimbach, VI. 47–49, 61–63.

[2] Krüger, 409. He is generally said to have written under Justin II (565–578), but Lawson has shown, *Z.S.S.* XLIX. 228–229, that there is really no evidence for this statement. He may however be identical with the Quirillus mentioned in Nov. 35 of A.D. 535.

[3] He refers to Theophilus, Thalelaeus and Dorotheus as "late"; Heimbach, VI. 51; Peters, *op. cit.* 39–41.

[4] Peters, *op. cit.* 11–24.

[5] Of the former nothing remains; extracts from the latter, $\pi\epsilon\rho\grave{\iota}$ $\dot{\epsilon}\nu\alpha\nu\tau\iota o\phi\alpha\nu\epsilon\iota\hat{\omega}\nu$, are quoted in the scholia to the Basilica as if '$E\nu\alpha\nu\tau\iota o\phi\alpha\nu\acute{\eta}s$ were the name of a man.

[6] "Nomocanon" means a collection in which secular sources, $\nu\acute{o}\mu o\iota$, and ecclesiastical sources, $\kappa\alpha\nu\acute{o}\nu\epsilon s$, of Church law are combined.

[7] This is one of the chief theses of his *Oströmische Digestenkommentare*. See also review by Mitteis, *Z.S.S.* XXXIV. 402–416, and Lawson, *L.Q.R.* XLVI. 486–501, XLVII. 536–556. For the view that there were two Anonymi *v.* Kübler, 437.

which they retained subsequently when transferred to the MSS. of the Basilica. Such *catenae* (chains) of excerpts are common in theological works of the period, and in them also are found excerpts headed "Anonymus" or similarly.

After the early seventh century the use of the whole Corpus Juris seems to have become too great a burden. At any rate the production of literature apparently ceased, and the next legislative effort was much more modest in size. This was the Ecloga ('Εκλογὴ τῶν νόμων),[1] published about 740 by Leo the Isaurian, the first Iconoclast emperor, and his son Constantine Copronymus. It describes itself as a selection from the Institutes, Digest, Code and Novels of Justinian, but also as altering these enactments in the direction of greater humanity. In fact it contains much that is new and is intended to make the law more consonant with Christian principles. From some time between about 600 and 800 date also probably three small collections of rules on special subjects, the Sea-law, the Farmers' Law and the Soldiers' Law, but it is not now thought that they had any connection with the Iconoclast emperors.[2]

The rise of the Macedonian dynasty under Basil I (867–886) produced a reaction in law as in other matters against the innovations of the Iconoclasts, and Basil set himself the task of restoring and "purifying" the legislation of Justinian. He projected a complete compilation, but all that was actually achieved in his own reign was the Procheiron and the Epanagoge. The Procheiron ('Ο πρόχειρος νόμος),[3] published about 879, is a manual intended to take the place of the heretic Ecloga, but in fact retains a good many of its innovations. The Epanagoge ('Επαναγωγὴ τῶν νόμων)[4] was apparently merely a draft and never received legislative sanction.[5] Under Basil's son, Leo the Wise (886–911), the great compilation, now known as the Basilica ('Ο βασιλικὸς νόμος or Τὰ βασιλικὰ νόμιμα),[6] was completed. It is by far the most important legal

[1] Zachariae, *Collectio Librorum Iuris Graeco-Romani* (Leipzig, 1852); Spulber, *L'Églogue des Isauriens, Texte, Traduction. Histoire*, Cernautzi (Rumania), 1929, English translation by Freshfield, Cambridge, 1926. For a brief account of some of the changes introduced v. Bury's edition of Gibbon, vol v. Appendix II.

[2] Zachariae, *Geschichte des Griechisch-Römischen Rechts* (1892), 17, 249–250, 315–316, held them to be official legislation of the Iconoclast emperors, but see now Ashburner, *The Rhodian Sea-Law* (1909) and *Journal of Hellenic Studies*, xxx. 85–108.

[3] Zachariae, Heidelberg, 1837. English translation by Freshfield, Cambridge, 1928.

[4] Zachariae, *Collectio Librorum Iuris Graeco-Romani* (Leipzig, 1852).

[5] Zachariae, *Geschichte des Griechisch-Römischen Rechts*, 85.

[6] Edited by Heimbach in six volumes, Leipzig, 1833–1870. Vol. VI contains

monument of post-Justinianean times. In it are fused into a single whole, consisting of sixty books, subdivided into titles, all parts of Justinian's compilation. Within each title the relevant parts of the Digest, Code and Novels, and in some cases of the Institutes, are collected, the fragments of each work being usually retained in their original order.[1] Of the inscriptions only the names of the jurists, usually in abbreviated form, are retained. In some titles parts of the Procheiron are incorporated. The language is, of course, Greek throughout, the Latin originals being represented by the Greek versions of the sixth and seventh centuries. Theophilus is used for the Institutes, Anonymus and sometimes Cyrillus for the Digest, Thalelaeus especially for the Code. Some changes were however made, and, in particular, Greek equivalents were regularly substituted for the technical terms which had been preserved in the original Latin by the earlier writers.[2]

No complete MS. of the Basilica has survived, but there are a considerable number containing parts of the text from which very nearly the whole work can be reconstructed. Some of the MSS. have in the margins a very full apparatus of so-called "scholia". Some of these, the "old scholia", consist chiefly of extracts from sixth and seventh century writers, and were probably added to the texts of the Basilica in the tenth century;[3] the "new scholia", which are the result of work subsequent to the publication of the Basilica, were then introduced in a later revision probably of the thirteenth century.[4] If the theory of the *catena* of the Anonymus[5] is correct, then the insertion of the "old scholia" was in the main, so far as the text corresponding to the Digest was concerned, a restoration of that *catena* to its original place round the Greek version which had been extracted under Leo to form the text of the Basilica.[6]

A revival of legal studies took place in the reign of Constantine Monomachus (1042–1054), who re-established a chair of legal studies at Constantinople.[7] No great new work was compiled, but there was a continual

his "Prolegomena" and "Manuale", the latter being an attempt to assign each part of the text and scholia to its origin. Supplements were published by Zachariae in 1846, and by Ferrini and Mercati in 1897.

[1] On the order of the titles v. Lawson, *L.Q.R.* XLVI. 494–501.

[2] Heimbach, VI. 55, 123.

[3] Peters, *op. cit.* 8, quoting Zachariae, *Jahrbücher für Deutsche Rechtswissenschaft*, 1844, 1083 *sqq.*, and 1847, 594 *sqq.*; Heimbach, VI. 121–124.

[4] Heimbach, VI. 212–215.

[5] *Supra*, 509–510.

[6] Cf. Lawson, *L.Q.R.* XLVI. 489–490.

[7] Zachariae, *Geschichte des Griechisch-Römischen Rechts*, 29.

working over and epitomising of earlier sources. Among what remains may be mentioned the so-called "Tipucitus", a work of reference dating from the late eleventh or twelfth century,[1] the Peira (Πεῖρα ἤγουν διδασκαλία ἐκ τῶν πράξεων τοῦ μεγάλου κύρου Εὐσταθίου τοῦ Ῥωμαίου), a collection of decisions given by a judge of the eleventh century,[2] and the Hexabiblos, a compendium published by Harmenopulos, a judge at Thessalonica, about 1345.[3] Though this last has been called "a miserable epitome of the epitomes of epitomes", it is interesting as having survived in use up to the present day.[4]

---

[1] The name Τιπουκεῖτος is made up from the title τί ποῦ κεῖται, "What is to be found where". The book has been much used for restoring lost parts of the Basilica. Parts of it are given by Heimbach, vol. II. 742–753; the first twelve books were published at Rome by Mercati and Ferrini in 1914, books 13–23 in 1929, also at Rome, by F. Doelger (v. review, Z.S.S. L. 713–721).

[2] Zachariae, Ius Graeco-Romanum, I. 1856.

[3] Edited by Heimbach, Leipzig, 1851. English translation of part VI, on Torts and Crimes, by Freshfield, Cambridge, 1930.

[4] This use is however now theoretical rather than practical. By a decree dated Feb. 23rd, 1835 it was laid down for the Kingdom of Greece that the Hexabiblos should be in force, subject to contrary custom or practice of the courts, pending the promulgation of a Civil Code. As the Civil Code has not yet been published the decree retains its validity, but where the Hexabiblos conflicts with other sources of Romano-Byzantine law the courts have held it superseded; they are in fact guided by modern works of authority on the Civil Law.

Chapter XXIX

GENERAL CHARACTER OF THE
POST-CLASSICAL LAW

The Corpus Juris of Justinian shows us a system of law differing both in spirit and in detail from that of classical times, but it is no simple task to give an account of the contrast. In the first place, as we have seen, the classical law has itself in large measure to be extracted from the Justinianean sources, and indeed it is only recently that the study of interpolations has shown us how greatly it differed from the law of the Corpus Juris. Secondly, the Corpus Juris itself is not an entirely trustworthy guide to the living law of its own period, because the greater part of it consists of materials taken from the classical sources and adapted more or less successfully to the purposes of the codification. This method necessarily involved the incorporation of some elements which had disappeared from practice, and resulted in an archaistic tendency which was in accordance with the spirit of the age and the taste of an emperor who had set out to revive the glories of the past.[1] Above all, however, the difficulty lies in reconstructing the process by which the changes were effected. The material for the long period which lies between Modestinus and Justinian is by no means plentiful. General history is in many places dark and, when it exists, gives but little information about legal development. There is, of course, a good deal of legislation surviving for which dates can be given, but it is not always preserved in a satisfactory state for our purposes. The constitutions in Justinian's Code have, as we know, been subjected to alteration similar to that suffered by the classical writings in the Digest, and the same is true, though to a much smaller extent, of those preserved in the *Codex Theodosianus*. Juristic writing is scanty; what we have comes chiefly from the West, and must therefore be used with caution for the law of the East. We do not, in all cases, know the dates of what we have, and where we do, as with the barbarian codes, we do not know the previous history of the texts.[2] We have only very meagre accounts of the law schools, whose

---

[1] Cf. Pringsheim, *Die archaistische Tendenz Justinians, St. Bonfante,* I. 549–587; Buckland, "D. XLVII. 2 and the Methods of the Compilers" (*Revue d'histoire du droit,* X (1930), 117–142).

[2] Cf. *supra,* 482, n. 1.

influence was, according to one school of thought, very considerable; and for actual practice there is little beyond what chance has preserved of legal documents among the Egyptian papyri and in isolated inscriptions. There is thus much room for differences of opinion, both as to the nature of the post-classical law and the method of its development, though, as regards the latter, it is not so much the influences at work which are debated, as the relative importance to be attached to those which are generally recognised.

Some characteristics of Justinian's law are of course clear. It is a universal system in which the distinction between *ius civile* and *ius gentium* has become of purely historical and theoretical interest. For the practical meaning of the distinction[1] there is no room in a society where, in effect, every free man is a citizen. In fact, the peculiar institutions of the *ius civile* have ceased to exist. The cumbersome ritual of the scales and copper has disappeared from all departments of the law.[2] *In iure cessio*, which, like it, had been confined to Roman citizens, has gone,[3] and so has the old literal contract.[4] Usucapion, in classical times confined to citizens and not available for provincial land because it could only take effect where Quiritarian ownership was possible, is fused with the analogous institution of *longi temporis praescriptio* which had grown up under the provincial edicts.[5] The distinction between Italic and provincial

[1] *Supra,* 103.

[2] All mention of *mancipatio* is carefully expunged from the Corpus Juris, but there is no record of its abolition apart from the constitutions of Justinian himself which introduced new methods for emancipation and adoption (*infra,* 522). In the *lex Romana Visigothorum* (*Gai. Epit.* I. 6. 3) it is still mentioned as required for emancipation, but the scales and copper have disappeared and *mancipat* is explained as *manu tradit*. In the *ius rerum* its disappearance was no doubt gradual. A constitution of 355 (*C. Th.* 8. 12. 7) requires it for the completion of a gift in certain cases, but it had probably fallen into disuse as far as commercial transactions were concerned before then both in the Eastern and Western provinces, though in Italy itself there are more traces of survival. There indeed it continued to occur even after Justinian's time. But these survivals do not mean that the old ceremony remained in use; this had ceased to be carried out perhaps as early as the late classical period, and mancipation meant only the incorporation of traditional phrases in a document; v. Buckland, 240–241; Collinet, *Ét. historiques,* I. 222–269.

[3] Also by simple disuse. The latest trace is in a constitution of 293 (*Consultatio,* VI. 10).

[4] Pseudo-Asconius, in Cic. *in Verr.* II. I. 23. 60 (Bruns, II. 72), writing in the fourth century, says: *ad nostram memoriam tota haec vetus consuetudo cessavit.*

[5] J. 2. 6. pr.; C. 7. 31. 1. This constitution also abolishes the distinction between *res mancipi* and *nec mancipi*.

land is abolished;[1] any land can be fully owned, though all ownership of land is subject to many restrictions in the public interest unknown to the *dominium ex iure Quiritium* of the classical law.

In the system of intestate succession established by the Novels, agnation, long since undermined by praetorian and imperial legislation, ceases to have any importance whatever. The distinction between civil and praetorian law has almost entirely disappeared. It is true that *hereditas* and *bonorum possessio* still have separate titles in the Digest and in the Code, but this is really the result of using the old materials. In effect there is but one system of inheritance.[2] The difference between praetorian and Quiritarian ownership was finally abolished by Justinian himself. There is less formalism and less rigidity. The only external forms required are such as serve to authenticate documents, including registration, the presence of witnesses, and, in the case of wills, sealing. The old oral formalities, including those of stipulation, have disappeared,[3] and the use of set forms of words is no longer required. Wills can be made in Greek.[4] The order of the dispositions in a will is of no moment,[5] and the distinction between the different forms of words for different types of legacy (as indeed the material differences between the types) has gone.[6] Internally, also, there is no longer any formalism. The general rule, that the intention of the party or parties is to prevail, is insisted upon even at the cost of certainty. One effect of this in the law of wills we have already noticed;[7] another indication is the repeated interpolation of some phrase such as "unless it is otherwise expressly laid down", in texts dealing with the interpretation of contract.[8] It becomes a general rule that a simulated transaction is void; the principles applied are those of the real transaction (if any) which the parties have in mind.[9] Great freedom in defining the effects of a conveyance is allowed; it can even be made subject to a resolutive condition, so that, on the occurrence of a certain event, the property revests *ipso facto* in the conveyor.[10] There is throughout an

[1] J. 2. 1. 40; C. 7. 31. 1.

[2] D. 37. 1. 2: *In omnibus enim vice heredum bonorum possessores habentur;* v. Riccobono, *Mél. Cornil*, II. 277.   [3] *Infra*, 523.

[4] C. 6. 23. 21. 6, of A.D. 439. A constitution of Severus Alexander had probably already allowed this in Egypt; v. Mitteis, *R.P.R.* I. 282.

[5] J. 2. 20. 34.

[6] J. 2. 20. 2; C. 6. 37. 21. Legacies were also fused with *fideicommissa*; J. 2. 20. 3; C. 6. 43. 2.   [7] *Supra*, 494.

[8] E.g. D. 2. 14. 27. 8; 21. 1. 33. pr.

[9] C. 4. 22 (rubric); Partsch, *Z.S.S.* XLII. 227–272.

[10] C. 8. 54. 2 interp.: as shown by comparison with Fr. Vat. 283. For disputed cases v. Buckland, 495 *sqq*.

insistence upon equity as opposed to "strict" law, no longer in the restrained manner of the classical jurists, who conceive of *aequitas* as the principle of justice pervading the whole law, but with an arrogant impatience of legal subtleties.[1] Hence the constant interpolation of such phrases as *benigne tamen dicendum est* followed by a statement reversing the decision given by the classical jurist.[2] These hard cases in fact often make bad law, for the Byzantine lawyer is not always capable of doing anything more than reversing the decision which he finds inequitable; he cannot put a new principle in place of the old.[3]

Closely connected with this reverence for equity is the tendency of legislation to protect those whom it considers weak against those whom it considers strong, even at the expense of general security and credit.[4] Thus the wife is favoured as against the husband, and is, for instance, given a mortgage over all the husband's property to secure her dotal claims, which takes precedence even of mortgages granted by the husband before the marriage.[5] By this enactment Justinian, "the uxorious legislator", as has been said, destroyed the credit of bachelors after having already ruined that of married men.[6]

The ward is protected against the guardian.[7] The debtor is favoured as against the creditor. Not only are there the rules of the *exceptio* and *querela non numeratae pecuniae*, which began to develop at the end of the classical period, but the law of pledge is altered in such a way that the pledgee is forbidden to sell the pledge (unless otherwise agreed) until two years after he has summoned the debtor to pay, or has secured judgment on the debt.[8] If, it being impossible to find a purchaser, the creditor has asked for and received from the emperor a grant of the ownership in the pledge, the debtor can none the less still, during two years, regain his property on paying the debt with interest and expenses.[9] The *beneficium competentiae* given to some debtors is extended to mean that they must

---

[1] E.g. *sed vix est ut id obtineat* in D. 41. 1. 7. 5. Pringsheim, *Z.S.S.* XLII. 643 *sqq.*, thinks that there is a definite distinction between the classical and Byzantine points of view. To the classical lawyer equity was merely a controlling principle, to the Byzantines a separate system to which *ius* must yield. *Contra*, Riccobono, *Mél. Cornil*, II. 253 *sqq.* and 289–300.

[2] E.g. D. 35. 1. 10. pr. Other examples H.-S. s.v. *benignus*; Beseler, III. 41.

[3] E.g. J. 4. 1. 8 compared with Gai. III. 198 and D. 41. 1. 7. 5 with D. 41. 1. 38.

[4] For a magnificent denunciation of this tendency v. Jhering, *Der Kampf ums Recht* (21st ed.), 81 *sqq.*

[5] C. 8. 17. 12. 1.

[6] Girard, 1023.

[7] Also by hypothec; C. 5. 37. 20.

[8] C. 8. 33. 3. 1.

[9] C. 8. 33. 3. 3 B.

not be left destitute by the judgment, whereas in classical law it had meant only that they must not be condemned for more than they have and so need not suffer execution against the person.[1] Tenderness is even shown to bad faith. In classical law, if a man made improvements on land which he possessed in good faith, he could, by means of an *exceptio doli*, refuse to return the land to the owner, unless the owner compensated him for the improvements. In Justinian's time, not only is he given the right to remove the improvements (*ius tollendi*) provided he does not thereby damage the property,[2] but such right is extended even to the possessor in bad faith.[3] The reason for this extension is, no doubt, to be found in the general principle of the Byzantine law that no one should be enriched at the expense of another,[4] a principle of which only the germs existed in classical times. Together with this "humane" attitude of the law, there is also often found an almost pathetic confidence in the power of legislation to do away with evils of an economic character by mere prohibition,[5] and a taste for excessive regulation by statute of matters to which fixed rules can hardly, by their very nature, be applied with success.[6]

Some of the causes of this development lie near the surface. Complete autocracy, combined with increasing difficulty of government due to economic evils, explains, if it does not justify, the frequently futile attempt to forbid by legislation evils which could only have been overcome, if at all, by a far-seeing economic policy. Bureaucratic government explains the attempts to regulate details of life. The introduction of Christianity is no doubt in part, at any rate, responsible for the constant attempt to introduce greater "humanity" into the law and to champion the cause of the weak, and it is, at least in part, the cause of legislation penalising divorce[7] and abolishing the disabilities which attached, under Augustus' legislation, to celibacy. Much, too, can be explained as a "natural" or "organic" development of principles which were already

---

[1] Contrast D. 42. 1. 19. 1 with the *lex gemina*, D. 50. 17. 173. pr., which omits the restriction to donors.

[2] In spite of the rule *superficies solo cedit*.

[3] E.g. D. 6. 1. 37. The interpolation of the *ius tollendi* of the *b.f. possessor* is not universally admitted, but there is no doubt about the *mala fide possessor*; *v.* Pernice, *Labeo*, II. 1. 380 *sqq.*; Beseler, II. 39; IV. 234; Riccobono, "Dal diritto romano classico al diritto moderno" (*Annali del seminario giuridico della R. università di Palermo*, III–IV (1917), 357–527.

[4] Riccobono, *op. cit.* 367.

[5] E.g. Nov. 32.   [6] E.g. Nov. 115. 3 and 4.

[7] Here there seems to be Oriental influence too; Mitteis, *Reichsrecht*, 261.

in existence in classical times. "Equity" was no new thing; many individual cases of "unjustifiable enrichment" were in fact remediable by classical means; formalism, as we have seen,[1] was already giving way, and the agnatic family system had been attacked by praetorian law in classical times.

So much would be very generally agreed, but according to the school of thought which may still be called dominant among modern scholars, the cleavage between the classical law and that of Justinian's day is deeper still, and the causes indicated so far are insufficient to explain it. It is held that an element of the greatest importance in the development of the post-classical law lies in the adoption of principles derived from the native Hellenistic law of the Eastern provinces, which was able, in spite of the *constitutio Antoniniana*, to assert itself successfully against the Roman system. But it is also held that Hellenic influences were felt in another way, and that the law, as it appears in the Corpus Juris, has been profoundly affected by the application of Greek philosophical methods and conceptions in the schools, and the consequent development of generalisations and classifications alien from the practical spirit of the true Roman law.

The survival of native principles in the practice of the Eastern provinces was proved over forty years ago by Mitteis,[2] and these principles did not remain confined to the "popular" law which the imperial authorities refused to recognise even though they could not prevent its application. Diocletian, it is true, seems to have set his face against them, and no small part of the evidence of their survival is provided by rescripts of his reign directed towards the correction of erroneous views based on native institutions and ideas.[3] But the attitude of Constantine was more favourable to Oriental views,[4] and his successors in some cases followed his example. Legislation was often vacillating, and in several cases the final step was only taken by Justinian himself, but there is enough evidence to show that the pressure of popular customs continued to exert itself, and sometimes found its issue in imperial enactments before Justinian.

Oriental influence appears most clearly in the law of the family. For instance, whereas in Roman law the rule was that persons under *patria potestas* were incapable of proprietary rights, the same was not true of the Oriental systems,[5] and an important step towards assimilation between

---

[1] *Supra*, 417–421.   [2] Cf. *supra*, 428.
[3] *V*. especially Taubenschlag, *Das r. R. zur Zeit Diokletians* (Cracow, 1925), 223 *sqq.*
[4] Mitteis, *Reichsrecht*, 548.   [5] Taubenschlag, *op. cit.* 233.

the popular and the official law was taken by Constantine when he enacted that property left by a mother to her children, who were in the *potestas* of their father, should not go, according to the Roman rule, to him, but should be in the separate ownership of the children, the father having only a life-interest and no power of alienation.[1] This rule, as Mitteis has shown, corresponds to a Greek idea which can be traced back as far as the law of Gortyn, that the father cannot deprive the children of property coming from their mother.[2] After Constantine's time the provision was extended so as to include also property received from all maternal ancestors,[3] and Justinian completed the reform by placing all acquisitions by a child in power, unless derived from the father himself, in the same position.[4] The whole conception of *patria potestas* was, in fact, a specifically Roman one, never popular in the East. There are papyri which show that the function of adoption in transferring *potestas* was not understood in Egypt, and Justinian was undoubtedly meeting the wishes of his subjects when he enacted that *adoptio* should no longer normally affect *patria potestas* at all, but should merely give the adopted person rights of succession in the family of the adopter, while he remained under the *potestas* of his natural father.[5] In allowing women in some cases to be appointed tutors of their children or grandchildren, the emperors were also clearly giving way to Eastern practice.[6]

In their treatment of the dowry, Greek and Roman law are quite different. In Roman law it becomes the property of the husband, and on the dissolution of the marriage by the death of the wife he retains it, unless it is a *dos profecticia*, i.e. one provided by her father or other paternal ancestor, and the donor outlives her. In Greek law, on the other hand, the dowry, although subject to the administration of the husband during the marriage, was the property of the wife, and went, if the marriage ended by her death, to her children, if she had any; the husband never took it, nor did the father, if there were children. Legislation of Theodosius II, known to us only through the Syro-Roman law-book,[7] accepted a great part of the Greek rules, and the reform was again completed by Justinian.[8] According to his legislation, the husband

---

[1] C. 6. 60. 1.   [2] *Reichsrecht*, 238.
[3] C. 6. 60. 2 (A.D. 395).   [4] C. 6. 61. 6.
[5] Mitteis, *Grundzüge*, 274–275; Sohm, 530.
[6] C. 5. 35. 2 and 3; Novv. 94 and 118. 5. The administration as opposed to the *tutela* itself might be assigned to women in classical times, but this too was already probably due to Eastern influence; La Pira, *B.I.D.R.* XXXVIII. 53–73.
[7] Mitteis, *Reichsrecht*, 248 *sqq.*   [8] C. 5. 13.

never[1] keeps the dowry on the dissolution of the marriage; if the marriage is dissolved by the death of the husband or by divorce, it goes, as in classical law, to the wife herself; if by the death of the wife, it goes to her heirs, subject only to the rule that *dos profecticia* goes to the father, at any rate if he still had the wife *in potestate* at her death.[2]

The husband's rights are thus reduced in effect to the equivalent of a usufruct lasting for the duration of the marriage, and, as Justinian himself says, although technically he has the ownership, the dotal property "was originally the property of the wife and has remained in fact (*naturaliter*) hers".[3]

Even more definitely Oriental than the post-classical dowry is its counterpart, the *donatio ante nuptias*.[4] Presents made by the bridegroom to the bride were common among the Romans as among other peoples, but in the native law they never attained any particular importance and were for the most part treated like any other gift. The same is true in substance even of post-classical law in the West.[5]

In the Oriental provinces, on the other hand, there was a widespread custom that the bridegroom should give to the bride a substantial gift, the chief purpose of which was to provide for her in case of widowhood, and to serve as a penalty in case of divorce at the instance of the husband,[6] for during the marriage the husband retained control, and indeed it was very common for there to be no actual delivery of the gift at all, but merely the setting aside of certain property to serve the purposes indicated. This institution was not only recognised by the imperial law, but made the subject of a great deal of legislation, which had the effect of making the *donatio* a counterpart on the side of the husband to the dowry on the side of the wife. This legislation itself is the product rather of the Christian idea that man and wife are one flesh and must therefore be treated in the same way,[7] but the recognition of the *donatio* itself is definitely an acceptance of Oriental ideas. Justinian himself describes it as an institution unknown to the ancient lawyers and introduced by later emperors.[8]

---

[1] Apart from special agreement. Possible exception, Corbett, *Roman Law of Marriage* (1930), 202.

[2] Literature, Corbett, *op. cit.* 183.   [3] C. 5. 12. 30. pr.

[4] Renamed *propter nuptias* by Justinian; J. 2. 7. 3.

[5] Mitteis, *Reichsrecht*, 306.   [6] Mitteis, *Reichsrecht*, 301.

[7] Mitteis, *Reichsrecht*, 308, 311.

[8] J. 2. 7. 3. For discussion of the papyrological evidence and the relation of Egyptian practice to Roman law *v.* Scherillo, *Rivista di Storia del diritto Italiano*, II (1929), 457–506; III (1930), 69–95.

In the *ius rerum*, the most interesting example of the influence exercised by Greek conceptions is perhaps to be found in the rules concerning the passing of property on sale. Whereas in the classical Roman law the property in a thing sold did not pass until delivery, but passed then (in *res nec mancipi*) whether the price had been paid or not,[1] the Greek principle was rather that the property passed when the price was paid, irrespective of delivery. This, Pringsheim has shown,[2] was part of a more general idea of "subrogation", i.e. that a thing belongs to the person who has paid for it, so that if *A* has bought a thing with *B*'s money, the thing belongs to *B*. It is not suggested that the principle of subrogation was received as generally applicable in Byzantine law, but there are several instances in which it was applied, the simplest being perhaps that things bought with funds forming part of the dowry are themselves treated as part of the dowry and so in effect the property of the wife.[3] Most striking, however, is the rule of Justinian's law that in the case of sale, even after delivery has been made, the property does not pass unless the price has been paid, security given, or the seller has given the buyer credit. Here the Greek principle has been accepted in part, for though delivery is still necessary, it is not enough without the payment of the price or something which is allowed as an equivalent.[4]

The influence of Greek rules with regard to sale is also seen in the law concerning *arra* or earnest money. In the classical Roman law *arra* served purely evidentiary purposes; but as we have already noticed,[5] in Greek law, where the rule of consensual sale is not so fully developed as at Rome, its object was the much more important one of serving as a forfeit in case the giver (normally the buyer) failed to fulfil his contract, while the recipient, if he failed, had to restore the *arra* and as much

---

[1] This proposition, which is one of the main theses of Pringsheim's *Kauf mit fremdem Geld* (Leipzig, 1916), is much disputed. Pringsheim replies to his critics in *Z.S.S.* L. 333–438. On the parallel question with respect to mancipation cf. *supra*, 147, n. 1.

[2] *Op. cit. passim.*   [3] Pringsheim, *op. cit.* 130 *sqq.*

[4] J. 2. 1. 41. The equivalents allowed are the giving of security by the buyer and the granting of credit by the seller (*fidem emptoris sequi*). To allow the granting of credit as an equivalent appears to take all importance from the rule, for it is possible to see credit whenever the seller makes delivery without exacting immediate payment. But probably *fidem sequi* was intended to mean more than this, and would only be held to have taken place if a document had been drawn up, perhaps one in which the buyer (fictitiously) acknowledged having received the purchase price from the seller by way of loan. This itself would be a recognition of Greek practice; Pringsheim, *op. cit.* 88; *Z.S.S.* L. 388.

[5] *Supra*, 300.

again.[1] The *arra* could thus be said to have a "penitential" function, i.e. either party could withdraw from the bargain, provided he was willing to lose the amount of the *arra*. This penitential function Justinian tried to fuse with the Roman evidentiary function when he enacted what is precisely the common Greek rule that on failure to fulfil the giver forfeits the *arra* and the recipient restores twice the amount.[2]

The texts in which this rule is given are obscure, and that in the Institutes at least in part self-contradictory, so that there is much doubt as to the resulting law. The only point of importance for the present purpose is however clear, namely that there is a definite adoption of a Greek rule.

That the increased importance attached to writing is due to Oriental influence, is generally admitted. It is true that this influence existed already in the classical period, and even before,[3] but that is no reason for overlooking its persistence. We have seen that oral testimony came to be neglected in favour of documentary evidence.[4] The Roman forms of adoption and emancipation were abolished under Justinian and replaced by declarations registered in the archives of a court or a municipality.[5]

Legislation was forced to accept, in some cases, the principle that a transfer of ownership can take place by the execution of a document, without the necessity for actual transfer of possession, the document in such cases being of a "dispositive" character.[6] It was also a further

---

[1] It should be noted that the Greek and the late Roman *arra* is also often a very large fraction of the purchase price, so that a seller who can keep it as well as the thing sold is not likely to have any interest in forcing the buyer to complete the contract.

[2] J. 3. 23. pr.; C. 4. 21. 17. 2. Mitteis, *Grundzüge*, 186, says that Justinian wished to introduce this penitential function but expressed himself "in the worst way conceivable". For literature on *arra* v. Cornil, *Z.S.S.* XLVIII. 52, and Carusi, *St. Bonfante*, IV. 511.

[3] *Supra*, 424–431.

[4] *Supra*, 458.

[5] Adoption, J. 1. 12. 8; C. 8. 47. 11; emancipation, J. 1. 12. 6; C. 8.-48. 6. The legislation dates only from Justinian, but in Eastern practice written documents had been used much earlier; Mitteis, *Grundzüge*, 274–275, *Chrestomathie*, No. 363; Collinet, *Ét. Hist.* I. 51–58. The same development did not take place in the West; Gai. *Epit.* I. 6. 3 (cf. *supra*, 514, n. 2).

[6] For cases of gift at least this cannot be doubted; Buckland, 232, 241, 256; cf. *supra*, 514, n. 2. In C. 8. 53 (*de donationibus*) the requirement of *traditio* has been systematically deleted. In practice physical delivery was not needed in the case of sale either because the simple device of retaining a short usufruct was extended to this case too by the interpolation of the words *vel vendendo* in C. 8. 53. 28 (= C. Th. 8. 12. 9). Hence if the document says that property shall pass to the buyer but that the seller shall have a usufruct for a week, when the week has elapsed the buyer will have the property, free from burdens, although the seller

recognition of the dispositive character of documents, when Justinian laid down that in all cases of sale, where the parties contemplated using a document at all, the contract should not be deemed complete until the document had actually been drawn up and executed in a manner which he laid down.[1] In classical law the parties might, of course, have intended that the document should be dispositive, i.e. that they should not be taken to have consented except by executing it, but it was equally possible that the document should be merely evidence of a consent complete and operative without it.[2]

As regards stipulation, we have seen that in classical times, though writing raised a presumption that the requisite oral form had been completed, presence seems still to have been required.[3] At any rate Justinian says that there was a doubt whether it was necessary to prove the presence of the parties or not.[4] This doubt he settled by providing that if the writing alleged presence of the parties, then a presumption of presence was raised which could only be rebutted by proving that either one party or the other had been absent during the whole day in question from the place (*civitas*) at which the writing was dated.[5] It is noticeable that in the account given of this enactment in the Institutes,[6] the use of such defences is characterised as "wicked" and regarded as a technicality deserving of no sympathy. Justinian clearly therefore shared the popular view that the document ought to suffice. Why he did not confirm it by his legislation, but still allowed the single loophole mentioned in his constitution, is not so clear.[7] Presumably this must be regarded as another instance of his archaistic tendency; he could not bring himself to abolish the last trace of rules depending upon the original oral nature of the contract.[8]

---

is still in possession. On the subject generally *v.* Riccobono, "Traditio ficta", *Z.S.S.* XXXIII. 259–304 (especially 284–295), and XXXIV. 159–255; Collinet, *Ét. Hist.* I. 241–242; Steinacker, *op. cit.* (*supra*, 415, n. 2) 88–105.

[1] J. 3. 23. pr.; C. 4. 21. 17. [2] *Supra*, 427. [3] *Supra*, 429.
[4] C. 8. 37. 14. pr. [5] C. 8. 37. 14. [6] J. 3. 19. 12.
[7] If it was alleged that a slave had made the stipulation on behalf of his master even this loophole was stopped, and it could not be pleaded either that the person in question was not a slave or that he was not the slave of his alleged master.
[8] The whole question of the post-classical stipulation is one of great difficulty. It depends for its solution to some extent on the interpretation of C. 8. 37. 10, a cryptic constitution of Leo's dated 472, which runs as follows: *Omnes stipulationes, etiamsi non sollemnibus vel directis, sed quibuscumque verbis pro consensu contrahentium compositae sint, legibus cognitae suam habeant firmitatem.* On the face of it this constitution need mean no more than that special words and exact correspondence of question and answer were no longer required, but this was in all probability the classical position. (*Contra*, Riccobono, *v. supra*, 429, n. 1.) Buck-

In addition to the written stipulation, the written acknowledgment of debt still continued to exist, subject, as before, to the limitations of the *exceptio non numeratae pecuniae*.[1] In the Institutes, Justinian discusses the matter under the heading *de literarum obligatione*[2] and argues that in his own time too, in spite of the disappearance of the old literal contract,

land (436) suggests that the constitution may merely have restated the existing law, but in that case it seems unlikely that Justinian should have thought it important enough to quote in the Institutes (3. 15. 1), where after speaking of the former necessity for formal words he proceeds: *postea autem Leoniana constitutio lata est, quae sollemnitate verborum sublata sensum et consonantem intellectum ab utraque parte solum desiderat, licet quibuscumque verbis expressus est.* It is thus most commonly held that Leo's constitution made unnecessary the question and answer and even the allegation of question and answer in written documents, and that, so far as purely oral contracts were concerned, nothing was needed but that the parties should meet and express their agreement somehow in speech. The difficulty which this interpretation raises is that if it is accepted there would now logically be no distinction, if the parties had met, between an oral stipulation and an oral pact, and even if the parties had not met, provided they were in the same city (after Justinian's constitution, C. 8. 37. 14), no distinction between a stipulation evidenced in writing and a written pact. Riccobono ("*Stipulatio ed instrumentum*", Z.S.S. xxxv. 214–305; xliii. 262–397; cf. *Mél. Cornil*, ii. 265–267) accepts this position and holds that, as a result of Leo's constitution, stipulation became in effect a consensual contract, and that therefore the law of the Corpus Juris already contains the rule that any agreement is actionable (provided there is *causa*, Z.S.S. xliii. 287 *sqq.*). Logically Riccobono's case is probably unanswerable. The law of the Corpus Juris should have been what he says it was, but the question remains whether we should say that the law was in fact what it logically should have been or what contemporaries thought it was. Riccobono admits ("Punti di vista critici e ricostruttivi a proposito della dissertazione di L. Mitteis", *Annali del sem. giur. di Palermo*, xii (1928), 500–637 at 571) that the distinction between pact and stipulation is still to be found in the Corpus Juris. He says indeed that it was "purely theoretical, or better, a mere historical reminiscence", but its presence and the retention of the distinction between stipulation and the consensual contracts show that the compilers did not make the deduction which they should have made. Nor indeed did later Byzantine writers, who still, for instance, insist that a bare pact to pay interest is not actionable (*v.* Zachariae, *Geschichte des Griechisch-römischen Rechts*, 295). The fact must remain that the compilers did not reach a logical conclusion. When actually faced with the difficulty of distinguishing a pact from a stipulation, they could only take refuge in their favourite solution of all difficulties, the intention of the parties (*v.* D. 2. 14. 7. 12), a peculiarly unfortunate solution in this case, as it is quite inconceivable that two people should make an agreement and lay down specially that it is to have the effect of a pact only, i.e. shall "give rise to an exception, but not an action".

[1] The time for which (*supra*, 430), after having been extended, was reduced to two years by Justinian; J. 3. 21; C. 4. 30. 14.

[2] J. 3. 21.

there is still a "literal obligation", because if a man acknowledges that he owes money which he has not in fact received, he will, after the lapse of two years, have to pay. Justinian is often accused of having here confused a rule of evidence with a rule of substantive law.[1] The ground, it is said, on which the person giving the acknowledgment will have to pay if it comes to an action, is not the writing, but a *mutuum* which will be held conclusively proved by the document. On strict analysis the charge is perhaps justified, but this does not affect the result that in fact abstract force is given (subject to the two years' delay) to a document.

The changes discussed so far found their way into the official Roman law by actual imperial legislation, either of Justinian or of his predecessors, but there were also many changes which were not the product of legislation at all, and could not be, because they were changes of spirit such as no legislator could accomplish. Many can be described generically as involving the triumph of the substantive point of view over the procedural, but there are others which, though no doubt facilitated by this triumph, go further and show a preference for abstract standards, referable to definite and conscious ethical conceptions, over the more empirical rules of the classical period, and a taste for logical arrangement which sometimes degenerates into the multiplication of unreal and practically useless distinctions.

Classifications transcend the boundaries fixed by the division into civil and praetorian law, so that no obstacle now prevents the recognition of obligations having their origin in actions granted by the praetorian edict.[2] Contract similarly becomes a general category embracing agreements made enforceable by praetorian actions as well as those on which civil actions lie, so that it includes not only *depositum* and *commodatum*, which do not figure among contracts in Gaius' Institutes in spite of the *formula in ius*,[3] but also *pignus*, for which the existence of a *formula in ius* is very doubtful.[4] *Emphyteusis*[5] and even *donatio*[6] appear as contracts. Thus, too, the general theory of innominate contracts arises. Classical

---

[1] E.g. Buckland, 461. *Contra*, Collinet, *Ét. Hist.* I. 59–84.

[2] Contrast J. 3. 13. 1: *Omnium autem* OBLIGATIONUM *summa divisio in duo genera diducitur: namque aut civiles sunt aut praetoriae*, with Ulpian, D. 44. 7. 25. 2: *Omnes autem* ACTIONES *aut civiles dicuntur aut honorariae.*

[3] The reason for their absence may, no doubt, be that Gaius is following the arrangement of an earlier work which dated from before the admission of the *formula in ius*.

[4] *Supra*, 297, n. 2.

[5] C. 4. 66. 1; *v.* Bonfante, *Scr. Giur.* III. 141.

[6] C. I. 2. 14. 3; *v.* Pringsheim, *Z.S.S.* XLII. 277.

law had given no action on a formless agreement unless it fell within one of the named categories of consensual contracts. A mere agreement for exchange, for instance, was not actionable, but if one party had performed his part of the agreement and the other failed to hand over the thing promised in exchange, the former could get back what he had given by a *condictio*. There were some cases, however, where this remedy was of no use. If, for instance, the agreement was that *A* should manumit his slave *X* provided *B* manumitted his slave *Y*, and, after *A* had carried out the manumission, *B* refused to manumit *Y*, *A* could not by a *condictio* against *B* undo what he had done. Cases of this sort had to be dealt with by an *actio de dolo* or a special *actio in factum*,[1] neither of which was, any more than the *condictio*, an action for enforcement. In the time of Justinian, however, it is a general principle that wherever there is a reciprocal agreement of this sort, and one party has performed, he can either claim the return of what he has given (where this is possible) or bring an action for fulfilment by the other of his undertaking. The action has a number of names of which the commonest is *actio praescriptis verbis*.[2] On its name and history much has been written,[3] and there is still no agreement, but this much seems fairly clear. A general rule is substituted for the different treatment of individual cases in the classical law, and the category of contract is extended to include all these cases because there is agreement giving rise to an obligation. The word "innominate" does not indeed actually occur in the Corpus Juris, but the distinction between those agreements which are actionable because they fall within one of the named categories, and those which become actionable as a result of the general principle only, is clearly made.[4]

On the other hand, now that consent is insisted upon as the distinguishing feature of contract,[5] it becomes imperative to separate quite clearly from contractual obligations the various types of obligation arising without consent, which had been originally included under the heading of contract,[6] and which the classical law, preoccupied as it was with

---

[1] *V*. e.g. D. 19. 5. 5. 2.

[2] Buckland, 522.

[3] The most exhaustive study is de Francisci's Συνάλλαγμα, *Storia e dottrina dei cosiddetti contratti innominati*, I (Pavia, 1913), II (1916).

[4] D. 2. 14. 7. 2; 19. 5. 2 and 3. In B. 20. 4. 3 (Heimb. II. 379) ὅταν ἀνώνυμον εἴη τὸ συνάλλαγμα is used to translate the longer phrase in D. 19. 5. 3.

[5] Μήτηρ δὲ τῶν συναλλαγμάτων ἡ διάθεσις, "Intention is the mother of contracts", Theoph. *Paraphr.* IV. 19. 8; Stephanus, on B. 14. 1. 5 (Heimb. II. 71), Sch. Ἐντεῦθεν.

[6] *Supra*, 280, n. 4.

procedure, had not greatly troubled to distinguish.[1] Consequently a new category of "quasi-contract" is invented, to include, for example, obligations arising out of *negotiorum gestio* and *tutela*, where there is a relationship analogous to that set up by the contract of *mandatum*, but no agreement between the principal and the agent.[2] The case of "quasi-delict" is parallel. As intention is required for contract, so the mental element of guilt[3] is required for delict, and a place has to be found for some cases of liability from which this is, or may be, absent. The cases included are really all types of delict known already to the classical law, but giving rise to praetorian actions. Now, of course, they are recognised as producing obligations.

In the Corpus Juris itself the *actio praescriptis verbis* is primarily the action for enforcement brought on an "innominate" contract, though it also appears already occasionally in other connections.[4] The Byzantine commentators however extend its use, so that in their hands it becomes a general subsidiary action available in all cases where anything has been given for any special purpose or consideration, and the sphere of contract is thus greatly enlarged.[5] A somewhat similar extension also takes place with respect to delict, by means of the generalisation of the *actio legis Aquiliae*.[6] The statute itself had given an action for direct damage to property only, and the praetor had extended its provisions by granting an *actio in factum* (or *utilis*) where the damage was indirect.[7] There were also some cases, unconnected with the *lex Aquilia*,[8] in which an *actio in factum* was given to a person who had suffered loss by reason of unwarrantable interference with his property, without any injury to the property itself, as, for example, if his slave was freed from chains and thus enabled to escape. In Justinian's Institutes,[9] however, these cases are made to

---

[1] How far the classical lawyers had gone in this direction is much disputed. Riccobono, *St. Bonfante*, I. 123–173, holds that they had already made consent the touchstone and that the Byzantines added nothing to the doctrines already elaborated. But the noun *contractus* is certainly still comparatively rare in the classical period, and the distinction attributed to Gaius in D. 44. 7. 1. pr. between obligations arising *ex contractu*, *ex maleficio* and *ex variis causarum figuris*, even if genuine, is isolated.

[2] Bonfante, *Scr. Giur.* III. 142.   [3] Cf. *infra*, 529–530.

[4] E.g. D. 43. 26. 2. 2 and 19. 2 *eod.* which give it as alternative to the interdict *de precario*.

[5] De Francisci, *op. cit.* II. 12–21.   [6] Rotondi, *Scr. Giur.* II. 444–464.

[7] *Supra*, 286.

[8] Rotondi, *op. cit.* 449.

[9] J. 4. 3. 16. Note however even here the interpolation of *praecipue*; Rotondi, *Scr. Giur.* I. 458.

appear as extensions of the *lex Aquilia*, and the distinction is drawn between the direct action under the statute, the *actio utilis* and the *actio in factum*. If the damage is done *corpore*, i.e. by actual contact, the direct action lies; if there is no contact, the *actio utilis*; if there is no injury to the property itself, the *actio in factum*. But the use of the *actio in factum*, thus conceived as an extension of the *lex Aquilia*, goes much further than the mere inclusion of unwarrantable interference with property; the various other cases in which *actio in factum* is given are all regarded as cases of a single action, based on the principles of the *lex Aquilia*, and indeed the distinction drawn by the Institutes between the *actio utilis* and *actio in factum* is not commonly followed by the Byzantine writers themselves.[1]

The result is something approaching the position in modern French law, according to which any damage culpably inflicted gives rise to an action for compensation,[2] the connection between the general *actio in factum* and the *lex Aquilia* being shown by the application to it of the Aquilian rule that damages are doubled on denial of liability.

Another general change which takes place is a shifting of emphasis from the concrete facts of any legal relationship to the intention (*animus*) of the parties. No doubt the classical jurists had advanced far enough from primitive rigidity to speak a good deal of *animus* and *voluntas*, but when there was any doubt as to the existence of a given relationship, they decided the matter by applying legal canons to the actual facts of the case, not by asking whether the parties had intended that particular relationship. Thus if two people became co-owners of a piece of property intentionally, as for instance by buying it together, they *ipso facto* entered into a contract of *societas*, for they intentionally joined in a common enterprise.[3] If, on the other hand, the co-ownership came about without any intention on their part, there was no *societas*. An interpolated text[4] however shows clearly how different was the Byzantine conception. Here everything is made to depend, not upon the existence of a common enterprise, but on the intention to enter into the contract of *societas*, and even intentional buying together will not result in *societas*, unless the parties had that particular contract in mind.

---

[1] Rotondi, *op. cit.* 445 *sqq.*

[2] Rotondi, *Dalla lex Aquilia all' art.* 1151, *Cod. Civ.* (= French Code art. 1382), *Scr. Giur.* I. 465–578.

[3] D. 10. 3. 2. pr.

[4] D. 17. 2. 31; cf. the contrast between D. 17. 2. 44 and 19. 5. 13; *v.* Beseler, II. 160, IV. 134; Berger, *Teilungsklagen*, 28; 133; Perozzi, *Istituzioni*, II. 300.

Somewhat similarly with *negotiorum gestio*.[1] In the classical law the question whether a person who had incurred expenses which benefited another could claim reimbursement by the *actio negotiorum gestorum* was primarily an objective one. Was the *negotium alienum* or not, i.e. could he be said to have acted on behalf of the person benefited or was it his own affair with which he was concerned? No doubt his intention might play some part in deciding the matter, but there is a very definitely greater emphasis on this subjective *animus* in the Byzantine texts. There the question is, did he do the act with the *animus recipiendi*, i.e. with the definite intention of obtaining reimbursement subsequently from the person benefited? And this *animus* is opposed to the *animus donandi*, the intention of making a gift. Such intention, directed towards a definite legal result, is usually incapable of proof, even if persons not acquainted with the law can be said to have it at all, but proof is more easily obtainable under Byzantine conditions, when the requisite *animus* can be put on record in a document drawn up for the very purpose of making it clear.[2]

Parallel with the stressing of the subjective intention in the formation of contract and other acts in the law, is the development of the subjective element in liability. In the classical law there were a number of cases in which a man was liable for *custodia*, in the sense that he was an insurer against such perils as might be avoided by actually guarding a thing.[3] Of such perils theft is the type, and if consequently a man under such liability lost a thing entrusted to him by theft, he would be responsible to the owner even though no negligence could be proved. The list of persons who were under this type of liability is disputed, but it can be said with some confidence that it included the cleaner and repairer of clothes (stock examples of *conductores operis faciendi* who receive a thing of the locator's to work on) and the borrower (*commodatarius*), as well as innkeepers, stable-keepers and shipmasters who had agreed, however

---

[1] Partsch, *Studien zur N.G.* (1913); Pringsheim, *Z.S.S.* XLII. 310 *sqq.* *Contra*, Riccobono, "Dal diritto romano classico al diritto moderno", *Annali del sem. giur. di Palermo*, III–IV (1917), 165–730, at pp. 244–262. See however now Rabel, *St. Bonfante*, IV. 279–304.

[2] Pringsheim, *Z.S.S.* XLII. 315. For a close parallel to the Roman cases *v.* *Re Rhodes* (1890), 44 *Ch. D.* 94. The general theoretical question whether in any act in the law the intention of the parties must be directed towards the juristic or merely towards the economic (or social) effect involved, cannot be discussed here. See e.g. Windscheid-Kipp, I. 311–312.

[3] For this formulation of the meaning *v.* Seckel, H.-S. s.v. *custodia*, and Siber, *Römisches Recht*, II. 245, where literature (to which should be added Buckland, "Diligens paterfamilias", *St. Bonfante*, II. 87–108) is given.

informally, to keep safe goods belonging to their customers. In the law of Justinian's day, however, though this is still the position of the last class, the liability at any rate of the *commodatarius* has been altered. *Custodia* need not now mean anything more than "care," and the borrower will only be liable if he fails in this; in other words, if he is negligent.[1] In this matter, as generally, the Corpus Juris tends to apply the rule that there should be no liability without fault, a principle which is opposed to the more objective standards of the classical law and has obvious ethical implications. Not infrequently words calling attention to the necessity for such subjective fault are interpolated, and occasionally the principle is made to harmonise with the classical decision by a reference to the possibility that fault may be shown by the choice of unsuitable assistants,[2] or by the very act of entering into a contract in the particular circumstances.[3]

Almost all the examples given here of the effect of Oriental influence and the change of spirit shown by the Byzantine law are the subject of controversy. Even those who agree on the generalities differ widely with respect to particular points. These it is impossible to discuss, but it must be mentioned that the general view described above as dominant is by no means the only one in the field. A different school of thought, of which the leader is Riccobono, minimises the Oriental encroachments, denies entirely the influence of the schools, and holds that the Corpus Juris taken as a whole is scarcely less a distinctively Roman product than is the classical law itself. According to Riccobono,[4] the post-classical law developed organically out of the classical, and resulted naturally from the disappearance of the formulary system. When this had been abolished, the only reason for upholding the distinction between civil and prae-torian law had gone, and with the levelling of the population (as far as

---

[1] The change is shown in some cases by the interpolation of an adjective or phrase qualifying *custodia*. It is said, e.g. D. 13. 6. 5. 5, that a borrower is liable "even for diligent *custodia*". So long as *custodia* meant a definite liability for certain classes of event, there could be no degrees, but if it means subjective care there can be. See Seckel, *loc. cit.*

[2] So-called *culpa in eligendo*; *v.* e.g. D. 19. 2. 11. pr.; 13. 6. 10. 1; 11; 12. pr.; 13. 6. 20. In J. 4. 5. 3 even the absolute liability of *nautae, caupones* and *stabularii* is explained on the ground that they "employ bad men".

[3] E.g. D. 47. 2. 62. 5. So-called *culpa in contrahendo*.

[4] A general statement of his position is given in " Fasi e Fattori dell' evoluzione del diritto romano", *Mél. Cornil*, II. 237–309, together with a list of his works bearing on the subject published up to 1926 (303–309). Since then see especially "Punti di vista critici e ricostruttivi a proposito della dissertazione di L. Mitteis", *Annali del sem. giur. di Palermo*, XII (1928), 500–637.

citizenship was concerned) there remained similarly no basis for the distinction between *ius civile* and *ius gentium*. Nothing consequently stood in the way of the freer, more modern and more equitable elements in the law, which had already been evolved by the Roman jurists themselves, especially in the praetorian system, and had only been held in check by the necessity of accommodating them to the strict system of pleading involved in the formulary system. The development of these elements, assisted by the Christian principles of charity and humanity, accounts for the late law, and was the work, not of teachers, but of practitioners, of the men who had to find some way of adapting the classical rules to new circumstances of procedure. Riccobono does not, of course, deny the presence of innumerable interpolations in the Digest, but he holds that in making them the compilers were merely doing what they had been told to do, that is, bringing the texts into accordance with the results of practice, and that their work was thus mainly mechanical. What appears new is generally only the drawing of consequences from a principle of the *ius gentium* or *ius honorarium*, opposed to the old *ius civile*, which was already *de facto* superseded in classical times.[1]

It is thus, in his view, that the coincidence between pre-Justinianean and Justinian's interpolations is to be explained. Both are due to the registration of practice. The development itself took place mainly in the West, where the Roman tradition was most alive, and there were no schools.[2] A few Oriental institutions such as *donatio propter nuptias* found their way into the law,[3] but nearly all of what is commonly taken to be of Oriental origin is really only the organic development of the Roman law. The rule, for instance, that the dowry is the property of the wife is nothing more than a better formulation of the real position as it had already begun to be at the end of the republic.[4] The alleged change of spirit is similarly an illusion. So far were the Byzantines from developing an independent theory of contract, that it is they especially who use the word in an extended sense so as to include *negotiorum gestio* and *tutela*.[5] The doctrine of obligations *quasi ex contractu* and *quasi ex delicto* owes nothing to the schools of law; it has no value and is the result of hasty adaptation by the compilers of classical texts.[6]

[1] "Punti", 624. [2] "Punti", 572–575.
[3] "Punti", 520–521. Other cases admitted are *arra sponsalicia, tutela* exercised by women and *manumissio in sacrosanctis ecclesiis*. That the extended use of writing was due to Oriental influence is also admitted, but with reservations, *v. Mél. Cornil*, II. 259–261. [4] "Punti", 516.
[5] "Dal diritto romano" (*v. supra*, 529, n. 1), 291, 689 *sqq.*; *St. Bonfante*, I. 166.
[6] "Dal d. r." 314–316.

The theory of subjective *animus* as a Byzantine innovation is also mistaken; it was, on the contrary, the classical lawyers who, in *negotiorum gestio*, insisted that no obligation could arise under that head unless the *gestor* had had the subjective intention of acting in the interest of someone else.[1] The schools had, in fact, no constructive ideas or power; their merit lay only in keeping alive the classical tradition and thus making the compilations possible.[2] In judging the character of the Corpus Juris reference should not be made to the Byzantine writers who comment upon it; since they come after the compilation, their theories cannot be used to explain the origin of the interpolations made in it.[3]

To ascribe systematising conceptions and theories to the Byzantines is a mistake due merely to the preconceived idea that the Romans themselves had no theory. It was on the contrary in the analysis of legal phenomena and their arrangement according to a system that the merits of Roman law lay.[4] There are indeed in Riccobono's view only two periods of Roman law. One is that of the rigid and formal *ius Quiritium*, based on the patriarchal structure of a primitive agricultural community, and comes to an end with the Punic wars. The other, the period in which a universal and flexible system is developed, runs thence to Justinian himself.[5]

There is no doubt of the very great value of Riccobono's work. He has called attention to factors which were in danger of being forgotten in the successes of the search for interpolations. The mistake of identifying all that is post-classical with Byzantinism, and neglecting the Western sources, has often been made.[6] Too little account has been taken of the changes in the law which occurred in the principate itself, and even in that part of it which we call the classical period.[7] It is precisely the great developments of which the classical jurists were the authors that have given them the unique position that they hold in legal history, and much of their work has no doubt been mistakenly ascribed to the Byzantines.[8] But, though all this be conceded, it is still possible to hold that Riccobono's thesis goes too far. The detailed questions on which the decision really depends cannot be argued here, but some general considerations may be urged. Though the abolition of the formulary system rendered possible the fusion of *ius civile* and *ius honorarium*, that

---

[1] "Dal d. r." 247. [2] "Dal d. r." 316.
[3] "Punti", 591. [4] "Punti", 627–628.
[5] "Punti", 600–608. [6] Cf. Levy, Z.S.S. XLIX. 231.
[7] Cf. Buckland, *St. Bonfante*, II. 102.
[8] "The influence of the Eastern schools...is exaggerated, sometimes invented in order to ascribe to someone who cannot be Justinian what is arbitrarily taken from the classical lawyers"; Rabel, Z.S.S. XLVII. 482.

fusion did not follow mechanically without human intervention.[1] Riccobono would have us believe that it was due to the work of practitioners. But they, as he points out, were men of poor intellectual attainments.[2] Under Theodosius the attempt to make a collection of juristic writings failed; a century later, under Justinian, it succeeded. This in itself is sufficient to show that a revival took place and, seeing that Justinian repeats, though in less vehement terms, Theodosius' strictures on the practitioners,[3] the revival is not likely to have been due primarily to them. In the intervening period there were, we know, men of some fame teaching at Beyrout, and it is not therefore a purely gratuitous assumption that they had something to do with the matter. It is true that there is very little direct evidence, but it is not absolutely lacking. The name *actio praescriptis verbis* seems to have been invented in the schools.[4] The *Scholia Sinaitica*, the only fragment of a work produced by the schools which we have, give a general rule with respect to expenses incurred by the husband in connection with the dowry which is certainly not classical, but corresponds to a passage in the Digest.[5] In two cases it is definitely stated by Byzantine writers that the compilers of the Code accepted the view of one of the professors of Beyrout as against that of others.[6] The short time taken over the compilation is another argument which must not be overlooked. Riccobono explains this by saying that the work was mechanical, but even if it was mechanical on the part of the compilers, some of the conceptions with which they operated can only have been the result of a long development.

As Mitteis said, "the new classification of obligations, the considerable changes in the principles concerning the inheritance of and concurrence between rights of action, the remodelling of the conception of liability, the classification of *condictiones*, etc....are ideas which are not produced

---

[1] Cf. Collinet, *Rôle de la doctrine et de la pratique dans le développement du droit romain privé au Bas-empire* (1929), 22. In England the abolition of separate jurisdictions for Law and Equity has not yet produced, and perhaps never will produce, a fusion of the two systems.

[2] "Punti", 549.　　　　　[3] *C. Tanta*, § 17; cf. Collinet, *op. cit.* 28.

[4] Collinet, *op. cit.* 62–65.

[5] § 18 = D. 25. 1. 3. 1; *v.* Peters, *Die oströmischen Digestenkommentare*, 89 *sqq.*; Schulz, *Z.S.S.* xxxiv. 102; Lenel, *Z.S.S.* xxxiv. 379. Riccobono, "Punti", 580 *sqq.*, explains the coincidence by holding, contrary to the general opinion, that the *Sch. Sin.* are subsequent to Justinian's compilations.

[6] Sch. ταύτην τὴν διάταξιν, Heimb. I. 403 and Sch. Θεοδώρου, *sub fin.*, Heimb. I. 704. See Collinet, "Les preuves directes de l'influence de l'enseignement de Beyrouth sur la codification de Justinien" (*Byzantion*, III. 1. 1926), and Levy, *Die römische Kapitalstrafe*, 67–68. Riccobono, "Punti", 548, says that interpretations of statutes "belong to the receptive activity of the schools".

even by the most competent intellects out of nothing, and presuppose the work of generations ".[1] Can we believe that this work was simply that of practitioners? Mitteis did not,[2] and the history of our own law, elaborated by judges whose intellectual capacity has certainly been on the average far higher than that of the post-classical practitioners, contains nothing to encourage us in the view that simplifying classifications can be the result of practice.

Again, it can hardly be right to discount the value of the later Byzantine authors for the solution of the problem, as Riccobono does, simply on the ground that they came after the compilation.[3] Some of the commentators were actually associated with the work and others followed closely after.[4] Their help is thus particularly valuable in understanding the Corpus Juris, because they can show the more modern ideas which in the compilation itself are partly masked by the use of old materials. As Levy's paradox has it, "The most influential codification of all time represented at no time the actual law in force".[5] The Byzantine authors help us to see how it could be applied, and their writings are the best evidence at our disposal for discovering what its compilers intended it to do. In fact, the forces which acted on the development of the law during the period between classical times and the compilation of Justinian must have been of the most various. East and West were subject in part to the same, in part to different influences, and they no doubt influenced each other. Only minute investigation can tell us even a little of the story, but if a few years ago the tendency was to ascribe too much to the Byzantines, there is to-day a danger that the reaction may go too far. A society so sophisticated in its theology cannot have failed to import some similar sophistication into its law, and the host of modern investigations which have gone to show important changes in outlook as well as in detail cannot all be dismissed as illusory. If also Byzantine "subjectivism" is unpopular to-day owing to a reaction from the similar tendency in nineteenth-century jurisprudence, it will perhaps be recognised, when the pendulum swings the other way, that Byzantium contributed much that was of permanent value for the clarification of legal thought.

---

[1] Z.S.S. XXXIV. 413–414. [2] *Loc. cit.*

[3] Cf. *supra*, 532. Riccobono himself in an earlier work ("Il valore delle collezioni giuridiche bizantine per lo studio critico del *corpus iuris civilis*", *Mél. Fitting*, II. 465 *sqq.*) has shown that they continued to use works dating from before the compilation. It seems to follow that there was in fact no break in the tradition, and that consequently we are entitled to use post-compilation literature as evidence of prevalent conceptions.

[4] *Supra*, 508. [5] Z.S.S. XLIX. 240, n. 5.

INDEX

CAMBRIDGE: PRINTED BY WALTER LEWIS, M.A., AT THE UNIVERSITY PRESS